Anonymous

The International critical commentary

On the Holy Scriptures of the Old and New Testaments ..

Anonymous

The International critical commentary
On the Holy Scriptures of the Old and New Testaments ..

ISBN/EAN: 9783337895723

Printed in Europe, USA, Canada, Australia, Japan

Cover: Foto ©Lupo / pixelio.de

More available books at **www.hansebooks.com**

THE INTERNATIONAL CRITICAL COMMENTARY

A

CRITICAL AND EXEGETICAL COMMENTARY

ON

JUDGES

BY

GEORGE FOOT MOORE

PROFESSOR OF HEBREW IN ANDOVER THEOLOGICAL SEMINARY
ANDOVER, MASS.

NEW YORK
CHARLES SCRIBNER'S SONS
1895

Norwood Press
J. S. Cushing & Co. · Berwick & Smith
Norwood Mass. U.S.A.

PREFACE

THE interest and importance of the Book of Judges lie chiefly
in the knowledge which it gives us of the state of society and
religion in Israel in the early centuries of its settlement in Palestine, for which Judges and Samuel are our only sources. In
addition to this, parts of the book are of preëminent historical
value : in particular, ch. 1, which contains by far the oldest and
most trustworthy account of the invasion of Canaan ; and ch. 5,
the Song of Deborah, the only contemporary monument of Israelitish history before the Kingdom. In the following commentary
matters of history, antiquities, and especially the social and religious life of the people in this period, are properly given the
largest place ; not only for their intrinsic interest, but because
the knowledge of these things is indispensable to any right understanding of the history of Israel and of its religion. The work of
the prophets can only be comprehended in its relation to the
national religion of Israel. But before there was a national religion,
there was a common religion of the Israelite tribes which was one
of the most potent forces in the making of the nation. What this
religion was, which they brought with them into Canaan, and what
changes it underwent in contact with Canaanite civilization and
the religions of the land, we learn in no small part from the Book
of Judges ; while here and there, as in the Song of Deborah,
we have glimpses of a remoter past, the adoption of the religion
of Yahweh by the tribes at Horeb, the work of Moses.

To make such a use of the book, it is necessary to distinguish
carefully between the work of the principal author, who wrote in

the 6th century B.C., separated from the times of the judges by
as many centuries as lie between us and the crusades, and the
much older sources from which the stories of the judges themselves are derived.   We must also, as far as possible, define
the age and character of these sources, which are not all of the
same antiquity or historical value.   Nor is it solely on historical
grounds that this is required.   The difficulties which the interpreter finds in the book are in considerable part of a kind for
which exegesis and textual criticism have no solution.   They
have arisen from the changes and additions which the author
made in transcribing his sources, or from the attempt to combine
and harmonize two parallel but slightly different versions of the
same story, and can be cleared up only by ascertaining how this
was done.   Criticism is thus not only obligatory upon the historian, it is an essential part of the work of the exegete.   That the
task is delicate and difficult, and in the nature of the case largely
conjectural, cannot exempt the commentator from trying to
solve these knotty questions.   At the worst, the uncertainties of
criticism are infinitely preferable to the exegetical violence which
is the only alternative.   In the commentary, especially in the
introductions to the several stories, I have discussed the particular problems of criticism with such fulness as they seemed to
demand ; in the Introduction (§ 3–6) the reader will find set
forth the general results to which these investigations lead.

The Hebrew text of Judges, with the exception of part of
ch. 5, is comparatively well preserved ; but in very many places
the ancient versions have a better reading, or a variant which may
not be neglected.   The Greek translations of this book are of
peculiar interest, and perhaps nowhere in the Old Testament can
the difficult problems which this version presents be approached
with more hope of illuminating results.   I trust that the somewhat full registration of the readings of 𝕲 in this commentary

may not be unwelcome to students of the Greek as well as of the Hebrew Bible. An edition of the Hebrew text, with critical apparatus, is in preparation, and will shortly appear in "The Sacred Books of the Old Testament," edited by Professor Paul Haupt.

In the philological notes, I have been mindful of the fact that it is the commentator's duty, not to follow the lexicographer and the grammarian, but to precede them; and have investigated afresh, and as far as possible exhaustively, all questions of etymology, usage, and construction which seemed to require it. If, in many cases, I cannot flatter myself that these investigations have added much light, they have often performed at least the negative service of showing that commonly accepted interpretations are unsound. In the hope that the commentary may be used to some extent by students, for whose reading the Book of Judges is peculiarly well suited, some notes of a more elementary character on the forms of words and on grammatical points have been added.

In conformity with the general plan of the series, all matters of textual criticism and Hebrew philology, together with more detailed and technical discussions of points of criticism, antiquities, and topography, have been kept apart from the body of the commentary, and will be found in smaller type at the end of the paragraphs. It is one of the evils of this arrangement that the grounds of an interpretation must often be sought in another place from the interpretation itself, while in other instances some repetition is unavoidable. It is believed, however, that the separation will prove convenient to many who may use the commentary; and I have endeavoured to diminish its disadvantages by cross-references and full indexes.

I have tried to make good use of all that has been done hitherto for the criticism and interpretation of the book. The commentators whom I have chiefly consulted are named in the

Introduction, § 9, the critics at the end of § 6; other works are referred to in the foot-notes of the commentary. It is not improbable that, in this extensive and scattered literature, I may have overlooked some things of importance; I have not intentionally ignored any. Several books of great value have appeared during the printing of this volume, so that I have, to my regret and loss, been able to use them only in the later chapters; among these I may name particularly Benzinger, *Hebräische Archäologie*, 1894; Nowack, *Lehrbuch der Hebräischen Archäologie*, 1894; G. A. Smith, *Historical Geography of the Holy Land*, 1894; and the 12th edition of Gesenius' *Handwörterbuch*, thoroughly revised by Buhl, 1895.

A list of the principal abbreviations employed will be found on p. 474. They conform, by the editors' desire, to those used in the new *Hebrew Lexicon*, in course of publication under the editorship of Professors Brown, Driver, and Briggs. The references in the commentary have been carefully verified, and will, I trust, be found accurate. In the few instances in which I have not been able to consult a book which is cited, the fact is indicated by a (°) affixed to the title. The citations of Scripture in the body of the commentary follow the chapter and verse numeration of the Authorized Version as given in the Queen's Printer's Bible; in the critical notes the verses are those of the Hebrew Bible (Van der Hooght's ed., 1705).

It is a pleasant duty to acknowledge the assistance which I have received in the preparation of this volume from my colleague and friend, Dr. Charles C. Torrey, Instructor in the Semitic Languages in Andover Theological Seminary, who has read nearly all the proofs, and to whom I am indebted for some valuable suggestions and corrections.

G. F. M.

July, 1895.

CONTENTS

———◆———

P. 7 n. ‡. *Sacred Books of the Old Testament*, ed. by P. Haupt, 1894.

P. 42, l. 33. The conjecture is Giesebrecht's, *ZATW.* i. p. 234.

P. 63 f. See Introduction, p. xxvii f.

P. 70 f. On Astarte see now also G. A. Barton, "The Semitic Ištar Cult," *Hebraica*, ix. p. 131-165; x. p. 1-74.

P. 86, l. 21 ff. and n. ¶. Perhaps *aśratum* is not אשרה but שׁחרת; see G. Hoffmann, *Ueber einige Phön. Inschriften*, p. 26 f. In a tablet in the Brit. Museum (No. 33 obv. l. 3) the name is actually written with an ideogram for Ishtar.

P. 100, 102. On Seirah see v. Kasteren, *Mitth. u. Nachrichten d. Deutschen Palaestina-Vereins*, 1895, p. 26-30.

P. 138, l. 25 f. See W. R. Smith, in Smaller Cambridge Bible for Schools, *Judges*, p. 39.

P. 175, 367. C. Niebuhr, *Studien u. Bemerkungen zur Gesch. d. alten Orients*, 1894,⁰ has analyzed Jud. 6-8, 17-21, and parts of ch. 1. See *Theol. Jahresbericht*, xiv. p. 54.

P. 195, l. 5. The note on 7¹ has been accidentally omitted.

P. 206, l. 29 f. and n.⁰. *ZATW.* ii. p. 175.

P. 242, n.⁰. For 14⁶ read p. 329, 340.

P. 243, l. 27. For 13² read p. 316.

P. 297, l. 1 ff. Compare Introduction, § 7.

P. 315, l. 3 from below. For 18¹ read p. 371 f.

P. 380. With Micah's son as his priest, cf. Wellhausen, *Reste arab. Heidentumes*, p. 13.

P. 417, 419. On Belial see Cheyne, *Expositor*, June, 1895, p. 435-439.

P. 426. With 20¹⁰ cf. 7⁸.

INTRODUCTION.

---

§ 1. *Title. Place of the Book in the Canon.*

THE title, JUDGES, or, THE BOOK OF JUDGES, which the book bears in the Jewish and Christian Bibles,* is given to it because it relates the exploits of a succession of Israelite leaders and champions who, in the book itself as well as in other parts of the Old Testament, are called Judges.† The signification of the Hebrew word is, however, much wider than that of the Greek κριτής, the Latin *judex*, or the English 'judge.' The verb *shâphaṭ* is not only *judicare*,‡ but *vindicare*, both in the sense of 'defend, deliver,' and in that of 'avenge, punish.'§ The participle *shôpheṭ* is not only *judex*, but *vindex*, and is not infrequently synonymous with 'deliverer.'∥ Again, as the administration of justice was, in times of peace, the most important function of the chieftain or king, the noun is sometimes equivalent to 'ruler,'¶ and the verb signifies, 'rule, govern.' In this sense it is most natural to take it in the lists of Minor Judges, where we read, for example of Tola: He judged Israel twenty-three years. . . . And after him arose Jair, the Gileadite, and judged Israel twenty-two years.** It is clear that the writer regarded these judges as a succession of

---

* See note at the end of this §.

† Jud. 2¹⁶· ¹⁷· ¹⁸, 2 S. 7⁷ (corrected by 1 Chr. 17⁶) 7¹¹ (= 1 Chr. 17¹⁰) 2 K. 23²² Ruth 1¹ Ecclus. 46¹¹; cf. Fl. Jos., *antt.* vi. 5, 4 § 85.

‡ The only place in Jud. where it has this sense is 4⁴· ⁵; but this is perhaps not the original meaning of v.⁴.

§ See below, p. 88, 89, and in addition to the authors cited there, Köhler, *Biblische Geschichte*, ii. 1. p. 24.

∥ Jud. 2¹⁶ 3⁹· ¹⁰ 10¹· ² Neh. 9²⁷ Is. 19²⁰; Bachmann, *Richter*, p. 31 n.

¶ Am. 2³ (cf. 1¹⁵) Hos. 7⁷ Mi. 5¹ Ps. 2¹⁰ &c. So also in Phoenician; see note at the end of this §.

** Jud. 10²· ³ cf. 12⁷· ⁸· ¹¹· ¹⁴ 15²⁰ 1 S. 4¹⁸ 7¹⁵ cf. 8²⁰.

xi

chiefs, who arose in different parts of the land, ruling with an authority which was personal and not hereditary.* The same conception is probably to be recognized in 2¹⁷, the Israelites would not obey their judges. The word 'judge' is not used of Ehud, Barak, or Gideon, and seems not to have been found in the oldest of the author's sources.† The title, Book of Judges, was in all probability meant by those who prefixed it to the book to correspond to that of the Book of Kings; the judges were the succession of rulers and defenders of Israel before the hereditary monarchy, as the kings were afterwards. ‡

In the Hebrew Bible the Book of Judges stands in the first division of the Prophets, the Prophetic Histories (Jos., Jud., Sam., Kings),§ which narrate continuously the history of Israel from the invasion of Canaan to the fall of Jerusalem (586 B.C.). In the Greek Bible, Ruth is appended to it, sometimes under one title (κριταί), sometimes under its own name ; and in manuscripts, the Pentateuch, together with Joshua, Judges, and Ruth, frequently forms a codex (Octateuch). ‖ In the history of Israel before the exile, Judges covers the time from the close of the period of conquest and occupation with the death of Joshua to the beginning of the struggle with the Philistines in the days of Eli.¶ A better division, from our point of view, would have been the establishment of the kingdom of Saul, and there is some evidence that, in one at least of the older histories which our author had before him, Eli and Samuel were reckoned among the judges ;** but as Samuel is the central figure in the story of the founding of the

---

* Others of them besides Jephthah (11⁵⁻¹¹) and Gideon may have obtained this power by successful leadership in war.

† Cf. 3¹⁶ 6¹⁴ &c. (deliver).

‡ Whether this title was first given to the canonical Judges, or to one of its predecessors, is not certain. — In the sense indicated above the word Judge is understood by Fl. Jos. (στρατηγοί, ἄρχοντες, μόναρχοι, αὐτοκράτορες ἡγεμόνες, — Ba.), Stud., Reuss (Heldenbuch), al. Book of the Deliverers of Israel, Ephr. Syr., Bachmann, Köhler, al. Of judges in the common sense, it is taken by Ew. (GVI. ii. p. 509), Hitz., Cass., al.

§ נביאים ראשונים.

‖ This fact is not without importance in the history of the text.

¶ Jud. 1¹-2⁵, which describes the invasion and settlement, overlaps the Book of Joshua; see below, p. 7-10.

** See 1 S. 4¹⁸ 7¹⁵, and below, § 4, p. xxiii.

kingdom, it was not unnatural to begin a new book with his birth. The character of the two works shows conclusively that Judges was not composed by the author of Samuel; the peculiar religious interpretation of the history which is impressed so strongly on Judges is almost entirely lacking in Samuel.[*]

The Title. — שׁפטים, Baba buthra 14[b]; Σαφατειμ, Orig.; *Sophtim*, Jerome. Κριται, Melito, Orig., titles in 𝕲[AB al.]; ἡ τῶν κριτῶν βίβλος, τῶν κριτῶν, Greek Ff. generally. Philo (*de confus. lingg.* c. 26, i. p. 424 ed. Mangey), ἡ τῶν κριμάτων ἀναγραφομένη βίβλος; cf. Βασιλειῶν, *Regnorum*, for Kings. *Liber Judicum, Judicum,* in the Latin Church. In Syriac, *Sephar dayyânê* (*dabnai Israil*), Book of Judges (𝕾[PLOII]); another, and perhaps older title is, *Pârûgê dabnai Israil*, The Deliverers of the Israelites (𝕾[A]); cf. Ephrem, i. p. 308. The book was also known by its Hebrew title, *Shâphṭe* or *Shâpheṭê* (𝕾[PLH], BO. iii. 1. p. 5, 62, 71, &c.), which was early corrupted to *Shabhṭê*, as if from שׁבט, *tribe*;[†] so in 𝕾[A], see Ephrem, *l. s. c.* — *Sufetes,* qui summus Poenis est magistratus (Liv., xxviii. 37); quod velut consulare imperium apud eos erat (*ib.* xxx. 7, of Carthage; cf. xxxiv. 61). In Latin inscriptions from Africa we learn of the *sufetes* of a number of cities (*CIL.* viii. No. 7, 765, 10525); sometimes two are named (*ib.* No. 797, 5306). שׁפט occurs frequently in inscriptions,[‡] but it is in most cases uncertain whether ordinary judges or chief magistrates are meant. In Spain and Sardinia (Cagliari), the governors and petty kings were in the Middle Ages called *judices* (Ducange, *s.v.*),[§] in which we may be disposed to see a survival from the times of the Phoenician rule. The *sufetes* of Carthage and the Punic colonies were a regular magistracy, and belong to a much more highly organized political society than the *shôphetim* of the O.T. We might rather compare the δικασταί who held the supreme power at Tyre for brief periods during an interregnum in the 6th cent. B.C. (Fl. Jos., *c. Ap.* i. 21 § 157).[‖]

§ 2. *Contents.*

The Book of Judges consists of three parts: 1^1-2^5, 2^6-16^{31}, 17-21.[¶]

---

[*] On the cognate pragmatism of parts of 1 S. 1-12, see below, p. xxxiv n.

[†] The same confusion of שׁבט, שׁפט, occurs in various places in the O.T., *e.g.* 2 S. 7[?] ℳ, Dt. 1[16] 𝕲.

[‡] See Bloch, *Phoenicisches Glossar,* s.v.

[§] Cf. also *judex* = praeses provinciae, *CIL.* viii. No. 949.

[‖] On the Assyrian *shiptu shapitu,* see Jensen, Z.A. v. 278-280.

[¶] So most recent scholars; Kue., Schrad., We., Sta., Be., Reuss, Bu., Dr., Co., Kö., Kitt., al. For other opinions, especially about the division of 1^1-3^6, see Ba., p. 77-80.

Chapters 2⁶-16³¹ constitute the body of the work, to which
alone the title, Book of Judges, in strictness applies. Ch. 17-21

is an appendix, relating two important events of the period preceding the establishment of the kingdom.* As we find in these chapters no trace of the distinctive historical theories, or the strongly marked style, of the author of 2^6–16^{81}, we may confidently infer that these two stories were not appended to his book by himself, but by some later hand.† Ch. 1, as interpreted by 2^{1-5}, forms a fitting introduction to the present book, showing how the old inhabitants were left in possession of the chief cities of Canaan. Their religion became a snare to the invaders; and thus the culpable failure to extirpate people and gods together was the prime cause of all the evils that befell Israel in the following generations. But although, in this light, 1^1–2^5 is a very good beginning for the book, it cannot have been prefixed by the author of 2^6–3^{31}, whose own extended introduction (2^6–3^6) not only takes no notice of 1^1–2^5, but by its connexion with Jos. formally excludes it. ‡ Like the appendix, 17–21, therefore, 1^1–2^5 must have been introduced by a compiler or editor later than the author of 2^6–16^{31}.

§ 3. The History of the Judges, ii. 6–xvi. 31. Character and age. §

In the Introduction (2^6–3^6), the author gives a comprehensive survey of the history of the entire period. The generation which had seen all the great work of Yahweh, in Egypt, in the desert, and in the conquest of Canaan (2^7), remained true to him; but after the death of Joshua and his contemporaries, Israel fell away from Yahweh, the God of their fathers, and worshipped the Baals and Astartes, the gods of the nations about them. Indignant at this unfaithfulness, Yahweh gave them into the power of their enemies, who subjugated and oppressed them. Moved by their distress, Yahweh repeatedly raised up leaders (judges) who de-

---

* The references to the grandsons of Moses (18^{80}) and of Aaron (20^{28}) show that, in the view of the writer at least, these events took place at the beginning of this period, within a generation after the invasion, not at its end.

† See below, § 5, 6.

‡ See below, § 5, 6, and p. 3 ff.

§ For the titles of the principal works on the subject of this and the following sections, see note at the end of § 6.

livered them from their foes.* But they persisted in the worship of other gods, or relapsed into it when the judge was dead; each generation was worse than those before it. Neither punishment nor deliverance wrought any lasting amendment. The history of each of the judges begins with a few sentences telling us how the Israelites offended Yahweh; how he gave them into the power of this or that hostile people for a number of years; and how he at last raised up a deliverer.† The introductions to the stories of Gideon (6¹⁻¹⁰) and Jephthah (10⁶⁻¹⁶) are longer, and the moral is enforced in the words of a prophet, or of Yahweh himself, upbraiding the Israelites for their disobedience and ingratitude. The history of all these successive oppressions and deliverances thus exemplifies and confirms the representation of the whole period which is given in the introduction.‡ Temporibus . . . judicum, sicut se habebant et peccata populi et misericordia Dei, alternaverunt prospera et adversa bellorum. §

It is clear that in all this the author's purpose is not merely to interpret the history, and explain upon religious principles why such evils befell Israel in the days of the judges, but to impress upon his readers the lesson that unfaithfulness to Yahweh is always punished; that whenever Israel falls away from him, he withdraws his protection and leaves it defenceless before its foes. By historical examples he would warn his contemporaries against a like apostasy. His motive and aim are thus not historical, but religious.‖ In a different, but not less effective way, he inculcates the same truth which all the prophets preached; Yahweh is Israel's God, and the religion of Israel is to keep itself to him alone.¶

The author's motive, the lesson he enforces, and the way in which he makes the history teach it, are almost the only data at our command to ascertain the age in which he lived. Indefinite

* Cf. 3⁹·¹⁵ 4³ᵗ· 5⁷ 10¹⁰ᵗᵗ·; of the repentance of the people we read only in 10¹ᴹ·.
† See 3¹²⁻¹⁵ 3⁷⁻¹¹ 4¹ᶠᶠ· 13¹; cf. p. 62 f.
‡ For the evidence that the introductions to the stories of the judges are by the same author as 2ᵇ⁻3ᵉ, see esp. Kuenen, *HCO²*. i. p. 340 f.
§ Aug., *de civ. Dei*, xvi. 43; cf. xviii. 13.
‖ It is inaccurate to speak of his "philosophy of history"; nothing is further from his mind than a philosophical analysis of the causes of events.
¶ See Reuss, *GAT.* § 275; Kitt., *GdH.* i. a. p. 6 f.

as such criteria may seem, they are, when the character of the work is sufficiently marked, among the most conclusive; and in this case they enable us to determine, beyond reasonable doubt, the period and circle in which the book was written.

That the history of Israel is a divine discipline, righteous, wise, and good, is the great idea of the prophets. In old Israel, as among other nations, defeat in battle, foreign invasion and conquest, were indeed ascribed to the anger of the national god, whom his people, or members of it, had in some way offended. But that Yahweh's anger as well as his favour is moral, and that therefore his dealing with his people is to be understood upon moral premises, was first distinctly taught by the prophets of the 8th century. This principle was naturally applied by them in the first place to the present and the immediate future. But the evils of the present have their roots in the past; and Hosea, looking back over the history of Israel from the time of the settlement in Canaan, sees in it one long, dark chapter of defection from Yahweh, of heathenish worship and heathenish wickedness. It is Hosea, also, who represents unfaithfulness to Yahweh as the one great sin from which all others spring, and who, with a figure drawn from his own unhappy home, brands this unfaithfulness with the name 'prostitution,' by which later writers so often characterize it.[*]

The prophets of the end of the 7th and the beginning of the 6th century judge Judah in the same way in which Hosea, in the last years of the Northern Kingdom, had judged Israel. In the long reign of Manasseh, foreign gods and foreign cults were introduced in Judah on a scale never before witnessed; the principle of exclusiveness which was native in the religion of Yahweh, and which the prophets had proclaimed with ever increasing absoluteness, was recklessly trampled under foot. This was, as Jeremiah constantly declared, the unpardonable sin which nothing short of the destruction of the nation could expiate.[†] Ezekiel represents the exile as the punishment of the sins of Israel in its whole past: in Egypt, in the wilderness, in Canaan, it had always been a

---

* Jud. 2[17] 8[27. 33]; see below, p. 72. — With the following cf. Stade, *GVI.* ii. p. 15 ff.

† See *e.g.* Jer. 15; cf. also 2 K. 22[13-20].

rebellious people, ever falling away from Yahweh into heathenism and idolatry.[*]

The signal fulfilment of the prophets' predictions in the fall of Judah, the destruction of Jerusalem, and the deportation of its inhabitants, set the seal of God's truth not only on their religious teaching, but upon their judgement of the past of Israel. In the light of this judgement, disciples of the prophets wrote the history of the two kingdoms, using and adapting the old records to illustrate and enforce the great lessons which prophecy had taught. The same ruling ideas, the same practical motives, permeate the Book of Deuteronomy, especially the opening and closing chapters,[†] and are indeed so prominent in it that the historical pragmatism of which we have been speaking is frequently, and not inappropriately, called Deuteronomic, and the writers whose work it characterizes, the Deuteronomic school.

To this school the author of Jud. 2^6–16^{31} manifestly belongs. What others had done for the history of the Kingdom, he does for the centuries between the invasion and the days of Samuel.[‡] From the very first generation after the settlement in Canaan, Israel had left Yahweh, to run after other gods and prostitute itself to them; and in this course it persisted through the whole period, in spite of all warnings and chastisements. The part of the book which we are now considering can, therefore, hardly have been written before the beginning of the 6th century.[§]

Other considerations might incline us to put it some decades later. It is antecedently probable that the new school of historians applied themselves first to the history of the Kingdom, where the prophets had gone before them, and in which the moral was more impressive because nearer at hand. From that they would naturally go back to the earlier period. The same inference may perhaps be drawn from the fact that the judgement of Israel's past in our book is more severe than in the Kings. In the latter, the sin of the people is in no small part the worship on the high places, a heathenish form of worship, forbidden by the law, but

---

[*] See esp. Ez. 16 20 23.   [†] Ch. 1–11 27–33; see e.g. 4^{13-40} 28 2_3^{10-23}.

[‡] There is no sufficient ground for identifying him with any one of the Deuteronomic writers in Dt. or Jos., or with the Deut. author of Kings.

[§] Schrader, We., Kue., Sta., Bu., Dr., Co., Kitt., al.

still a worship of Yahweh. In Judges the apostasy is complete; the people abandons Yahweh for the Baals and Astartes.*

The conclusions to which an examination of the contents of the book leads are confirmed by the evidence of its vocabulary and style, in which the affinity to the literature of the end of the 7th century is unmistakable. In the commentary these parallels are noted, and they need not be repeated here.†

§ 4. *The Sources of Judges ii. 6–xvi. 31.*

The characteristics which have been discussed in the last section appear chiefly in the introduction (2^6–3^6) and at the beginning of the histories of the several judges. The stories themselves, with the exception of that of Othniel (3^{7-11}), show few traces of the author's distinctive conceptions or expressions. ‡ Some of them — for instance, Samson's adventures among the Philistines — have little or no relation to the purpose of the book; others relate of the judges things which must have been offensive to the author, such as Gideon's setting up the *ephod* and the sacrifice of Jephthah's daughter; in all, the religious ideas, the language, and style, are entirely unlike his own.§ It is plain therefore, that the author of Jud. 2^6–16^{31} did not write these stories himself, but took them from older sources.

These sources cannot have been oral tradition, or unwritten popular legends, ‖ for, apart from the difficulty of supposing that oral tradition had transmitted to so late a time such lifelike and truthful pictures of a state of society that had passed away cen-

---

* See Stade, *GVI.* ii. p. 21. It is to be observed, however, that in the theory of the Deuteronomic writers, the local cults on the high places were not prohibited till after the building of the temple.

† See especially on 2^6–3^6 3^{7-11} and the introductions to the several stories; cf. also Kue., *HCO².* i. p. 339; Bu., *Richt. u. Sam.*, p. 91 f., 128; Kö., *Einl.*, p. 254.

‡ Kitt. thinks it very probable that the author of 3^{7-11} also wrote 6^{25-32} 7^{2-8} 8^{27}; but these passages appear to me to be derived from one of the chief sources of the book.

§ Compare the story of Ehud (3^{12-30}) with that of Othniel (3^{7-11}). The latter shows us, better than anything else, what these histories would be like if the author had written them himself. We may also compare the chapters of ancient history with which the author of Chronicles supplements Kings, — all, of course, in his own peculiar manner. ‖ Stäbelin, al.

turies before, in reducing oral tradition to writing, the author
would inevitably have left the impress of his own style upon the
stories far more deeply than is the case; the Deuteronomic
peculiarities we have noted above would not be confined to the
beginning and end of the tales. The greater or less unevenness
of which we are always aware in passing from the introduction
to the story which follows, is clearly the joint by which an older
written source is united to the Deuteronomic preface.

If the author employed written sources, our next inquiry is,
whether he made his choice among single tales or different collections of tales, or whether he took them all from some one older
book. This question cannot be answered with entire certainty;
it is quite conceivable that the cycle of stories about Samson, for
instance, may have existed separately; but it is demonstrable, I
think, that the author had before him an older work in which the
exploits of a considerable number of the Israelite heroes were
narrated;[*] and if this is true, it may very well be that this collection was his only source. It is easier to understand how a
story like that of Samson should have been included in the Deuteronomic Book of Judges, if the author found it in the earlier
work on which he based his own, than to imagine that he introduced it for himself from some other source.

A more minute examination of the introduction to the book
(2^6–3^6), and of the setting of the several stories, especially those
of Gideon (6^{1-10}) and Jephthah (10^{6-16}), brings out the fact that
these parts of the work are not entirely homogeneous. The
numerous repetitions and duplications, and the differences in point
of view and phraseology, which, though slight, are unmistakable,
show that more than one writer has had a hand in the composition.[†] Of this fact, which is recognized by most recent
critics, two explanations may be given. One is, that the author or
editor of the present Book of Judges, in incorporating 2^6–16^{31} in
his own work, dwelt upon and emphasized the moral lessons of the
history which his predecessor had enforced; the lack of unity and

---

[*] See next §.
[†] See the commentary on the passages indicated, and esp. p. 63 f., 175 f., 181 f., 275 f.

consistency which the critics have observed would thus be due to interpolation.* The alternative hypothesis is, that the author of 2^6–16^{31} used as the basis of his work an older collection of tales of the Israelite heroes, in which the varying fortunes of Israel in those troublous times were already made to point the moral that unfaithfulness to Yahweh was the prime cause of all the evils that befell the people, — a pre-Deuteronomic Book of the Histories of the Judges.†

The considerations which incline the balance of probability to the second of these hypotheses are the following: (*a*) The elements which are admitted by all not to belong to the principal Deuteronomic stratum in the book do not seem to be superimposed upon it, but embedded in it; and they are more intimately united with their context than the additions by which later editors often try to heighten the effect of their text are wont to be. (*b*) If the author or editor of the present Book of Judges made all these additions in 2^6–16^{31}, we should expect to find his mark upon ch. 17, 18, 19–21 also, which certainly invited a moral comment and application quite as much as some of the stories in the body of the work; but no trace of such an improvement is to be discovered in those chapters. (*c*) The language of the parts of the book in question is distinguished from that of the Deuteronomic writers and editors generally by a more marked affinity to one of the older sources of the Hexateuch (E). ‡ (*d*) Some of the tales, *e.g.* that of Gideon (ch. 6–8), are composite; two somewhat different versions of the story have been united by a third hand, which does not appear to be that of the author of the book, but of an earlier redactor. It is not a remote conjecture that this redactor is also the author of the non-Deuteronomic element in the introduction (2^6–3^6) and other parts of the book. (*e*) The Deuteronomic Book of Judges did not include ch. 17, 18, 19–21; the closing formula, 15^{20}, may perhaps be taken as evidence that it did not contain ch. 16; § 8^{33-35} is an editorial substitute for ch. 9, which has obviously not passed through the hands of the Deuteronomic author.* But ch. 17, 18, and the primary version of the story in ch. 19–21 are akin to the older narratives in 2^6-16^{31}; ch. 16, the death of Samson, is unquestionably from the same source as ch. 13–15; ch. 9, itself composite, is too closely connected with ch. 6–8 to be of different origin. The simplest hypothesis is, that these chapters were contained in the earlier collection, but were omitted by the Deuteronomic author from his book, as unsuitable to his purpose.†

The older book seems to have contained the histories of Ehud, Deborah and Barak, Gideon, Abimelech, Jephthah, and Samson; ‡ not improbably also the story of Micah's idols and the migration of the Danites, and the original form of that of the Levite and his concubine. In what order these stories stood, we cannot make out. Chapters 17, 18, and 19–21, if included in the book, would have their natural place near its beginning; they certainly cannot have stood where they now do, in the midst of the history of the "days of the Philistines," between Samson and Eli. Chapter 10^{6-16}, a formal and extended introduction resembling 2^{6-21}, can hardly have been designed to occupy its present position. §

It is a question of more importance whether the pre-Deuteronomic Judges (to use this name for brevity) ‖ contained other histories not included in the canonical Book of Judges.

The death of Samson (16^{31}) is not the end of a period or a turning point in the history, such as an author would naturally choose for the end of a book; nor is it at all probable that a writer who begins with an introduction of some length, setting forth in advance the moral of the history, would bring his work to so abrupt a conclusion without a word of retrospective comment. It has long been noticed that in 1 Sam. the account of the death of Eli (4^{18}) is followed by the words, " Now he had judged Israel

---

* Bu.; see below, p. 234, 238.

† For a different hypothesis see below, p. xxxvi f.

‡ There is, at least, no apparent reason to ascribe any of these stories to an independent source.

§ See further, below, p. xxiii f. For conjectures about its original position, see p. 276.

‖ Meaning by it the collection which preceded the Deuteronomic Book of Judges, 2^6-16^{31}.

forty years"; precisely the same formula as in Jud. 16[31], cf. 12[7] 10[2,3] 12[9,11,14].* Of Samuel also we read that "he judged Israel as long as he lived" (1 S. 7[15]); and that the words were not originally meant in a justiciary sense, as might seem from v.[16,17], which describe his judicial circuit,† is manifest from the preceding verses, which tell how he delivered Israel from the Philistines by the great victory at Mizpah, concluding in the same way as the accounts of the deliverances wrought by the judges before him: "And the Philistines were subdued, and did not again come into the territory of Israel; ‡ and the hand of Yahweh was against the Philistines as long as Samuel lived" (7[13]). § Samuel was thus, in this narrative, the judge who delivered Israel from the Philistines.‖ In 1 S. 12 also, Samuel is represented, not merely as a prophet or as a justice, but as one who for many years had borne rule over Israel. This speech of Samuel, which contains a retrospect of the period of the judges (v.[7-11]), and solemn words of warning for the future under the newly established kingdom, is precisely the conclusion which we desire for the Book of the Histories of the Judges, corresponding admirably to the parting discourse of Joshua (Jos. 24) at the close of the period of the conquest.¶ There is, therefore, great probability in the opinion of Graf and others that the pre-Deuteronomic Judges included the times of Eli and Samuel, and ended with 1 S. 12.** If this be true, Jud. 10[6-16] †† may originally have been the introduction to the period of Philistine oppression in the same work. ‡‡ These wars were, in fact, and in the historical traditions of Israel, the beginning of a new epoch; and the author may have recognized their importance

---

* Kuenen (*HCO*[2]. i. p. 353) and Wildeboer (*Letterkunde*, p. 274) regard 1 S. 4[1b,2b] as a gloss, on what seem to me insufficient grounds.

† On these verses see below, p. 113.   ‡ Cf. Jud. 3[30] 8[28] 11[33].

§ Cf. Jud. 2[18].

‖ Some critics connect this with Jud. 13[5], where the Angel foretells that Samson shall *begin* to deliver Israel; see p. 317.

¶ Cf. also 2 K. 17[7-23] (Schrad., Kue.); Wildeboer is, however, certainly mistaken in supposing that Jud. 2[6]-3[6] is dependent upon 2 K. 17 (*Letterkunde*, p. 273).

** Graf, *Gesch. Bücher*, p. 97 f.; so Bu. Kue., Wildeboer, al., think that this was true of the Deuteronomic Judges.

†† Excluding Deuteronomic additions.

‡‡ Bu.; see below, p. 276.

by a more extended introduction than those which he prefixed to the other "oppressions."

The pragmatism of this work was similar to that of the Deuteronomic Judges; in it also, as may be seen in the non-Deuteronomic parts of 2^6–3^6, and 10^{6-16}, in 6^{7-10} and in 1 S. 12, the history is interpreted and judged from the prophetic point of view; that the people forsook Yahweh and worshipped the gods of Canaan is here also the *fons et origo malorum;* in it the conflicts of particular tribes and groups of tribes with their neighbours had already become oppressions and deliverances of all Israel, the heroes of these local struggles, the judges of Israel.[*] But, close as the resemblance is, the distinctive Deuteronomic note is absent; the standpoint is that of Hosea and the prophetic historians who wrote in his spirit, rather than that of Jeremiah and the Deuteronomic school.

The age of this older Book of Judges is fixed within these limits; it may with considerable confidence be ascribed to the 7th century, perhaps to the times of Manasseh.

The hand of the author of the older Judges, like that of the Deuteronomic writer, is recognized in the introduction and the setting of the tales rather than in the tales themselves. The question from what sources the latter are derived is only pushed back one step by the discovery of a pre-Deuteronomic collection. The existence of composite narratives, like the histories of Gideon (ch. 6–8), and Deborah and Barak (ch. 4), shows that there must have been more than one such source. The more or less strongly marked diversity in language and style between the several stories also points to diversity of origin. That these sources were old and good collections of the national traditions, the character of the stories sufficiently attests. On closer inspection, one of them appears to be more ancient and of greater historical worth than the rest. In some instances, as for example in that of Samson (ch. 13–16), the author seems to have known but one version of the story, which he has given entire from one of

---

[*] The chronology of this book was different from that of its successor; see § 7. The use of *shōphet,* and some other words and phrases of common occurrence such as הכניע, נכנע, 'subdue, be subdued,' probably also come from it.

his sources; in other cases, as in that of Gideon-Jerubbaal, he united as best he could two somewhat discrepant accounts; in still other cases it is difficult to decide whether the lack of unity and directness in the narrative is to be ascribed to the attempt to combine different versions, or to editorial amplification, or to subsequent interpolations and glosses.

These phenomena are so much like those with which we are familiar in parts of the Hexateuch where the Yahwistic and Elohistic narratives (J and E) have been united by a later writer (Rje) into one composite history, that we can hardly fail to ask the question whether the similarity is not really identity; that is, whether the pre-Deuteronomic Judges was not a part of the great prophetic history which critics designate by the symbol JE, and its sources J and E. That this is the case was affirmed by Schrader, who attempted to separate the two chief sources from each other and from the Deuteronomic elements.[*] More recently Böhme[†] and Stade[‡] have demonstrated the affinity of parts of the book to J and E respectively; while Budde has taken up the problem which Schrader first attacked, and with great acuteness has worked out an analysis of the entire book.[§] On the other hand, Kuenen maintains a sceptical attitude toward all attempts to identify the sources of Judges with J and E in the Hexateuch,[‖] and Kittel combats the hypothesis, arguing that such resemblances as exist are less decisive than the countervailing differences.[¶]

Budde's hypothesis is not intrinsically improbable. There is the best reason to believe that neither J nor E ended with the conquest of Canaan, but that both brought the history down to a much later time, if not to their own day. The parting speech of Joshua, Jos. 24 (substantially E), looks not only backward but forward; it is the end of a book, not of the historical work of which it formed a part; and Jud. 2^{6-10} (Jos. 24^{28-31}), from the same hand, is unmistakably the transition to the subsequent history.

---

[*] De Wette, *Einl*[8]., p. 327–332. For earlier critics who have entertained this opinion, see Wildeboer, *Letterkunde*, p. 168 f.

[†] *ZATW*. v. 1885, p. 251–274.   [‡] *ZATW*. i. p. 339–343.

[§] *Richt. u. Sam.*, 1890. Bu.'s results are accepted by Co., *Einl.*, § 16.

[‖] *HCO*[2]. i. p. 355 f.

[¶] *Stud. u. Krit.*, 1892, p. 44 ff.; *GdH.* i. a. p. 15–18. So also Kö., *Einl.*, p. 252–254, Wildeboer, al.

Jud. 1, J's account of the conquest and settlement of Canaan, is certainly not the end of his work ; $2^{1a.5b}$ here also lead over to the following period.* It is antecedently more probable that these books furnished the author of Judges with his material than that they altogether disappear at the beginning of this period, their place being taken by two unrelated sources having a certain resemblance to J and E respectively.† It must be acknowledged that the resemblances are less marked than might be expected, and are accompanied by noticeable differences. But it should be observed, first, that the ultimate sources, the popular traditions from which the tales of the judges are drawn, naturally had a different origin and character from the legends of the patriarchs in Genesis or the narratives of the Mosaic age ; and, second, that the symbols J and E represent, not individual authors, but a succession of writers, the historiography of a certain period and school.‡ The differences upon which Kittel and König have laid stress are, it appears to me, critically of less significance than the admitted resemblances. Moreover, the problem of the sources in Judges cannot be separated from the same question in Samuel, and in the latter the indicia point to J and E more clearly, perhaps, than in Judges.§

For these reasons I have used the symbols J and E in the commentary, to distinguish the two chief sources from which the narratives appear to be derived, though I am fully aware that the question of their identity is by no means beyond controversy. Those of my readers who are not convinced of this identity may regard the letters J and E as equivalent to X and Y, two otherwise unknown sources, of which X (J) is almost everywhere manifestly the older and historically the more valuable. The author who united them and composed the pre-Deuteronomic Book of Judges was probably one of that school of prophetic historians

---

* Cf. also J's part in $2^{23}-3^6$.

† It is methodologically an unreasonable demand that it should first be proved that J and E included the history of the times of the judges, before we endeavour to identify them in the Book of Judges. What other proof can we have than that we can trace them in its narratives?

‡ In E, for example, there is a well-defined secondary stratum (E_2).

§ We have seen reason to believe that a considerable part of 1 Sam. was contained in the pre-Deuteronomic Judges.

who are commonly represented by the signature Rje.[*] His hand may be most distinctly recognized in $2^{3.}-3^{6}$, where the conflicting representations of J and E are worked into one another with free additions by the redactor in a way with which we are familiar in JE in the Hexateuch.

The age of the two chief sources in Judges $2^{6}-16^{31}$ cannot be very definitely fixed. There are, in this part of the book, no allusions to historical events of later times which might serve us as a clew.[†] Almost the only criterion which we possess is their relation to the religious development. In those parts of the book which are attributed to J, the standpoint of the narrator is that of the old national religion of Israel; there is no trace of prophetic influence, and we can have no hesitation in ascribing this source to a time before the great prophetic movement of the 8th century. Other indications point to a considerably higher antiquity. The stories are manifestly drawn from a living tradition, not from antiquarian lore; they reproduce the state of society and religion in the early days of the settlement in Palestine with a convincing reality which is of nature, not of art, and exhibit a knowledge of the conditions of the time which can hardly have been possessed by an author of the 8th century, after the changes which two centuries of the kingdom and of rapidly advancing civilization had wrought. On such grounds we should be inclined to assign this source to the first half of the 9th century, a date which is entirely compatible with our identification of it with J.

The second main source from which the tales of the Judges are derived (E) appears, wherever direct comparison is possible, as in the histories of Gideon and Abimelech, to be younger than J. It is, however, not all of the same age. The older stratum does not differ very greatly from J, and is also, in all probability, preprophetic; the later stratum is strongly tinged with prophetic ideas, and in its judgement of the religious offences of the people prepares the way for the pragmatism of the Jehovistic (JE) and Deuteronomic History of the Judges. So closely, indeed, does

---

[*] This symbol is, however, not very satisfactory, since the method of these writers was much more that of the historian who largely excepts his sources, than of the redactor who merely combines and harmonizes them.

[†] On $18^{30. 31}$ see below, § 5. p. xxx f.

this element (E₂) approach the standpoint of the latter authors that it is difficult, if not impossible, to decide whether certain passages or verses should be attributed to the one or the other.* Fortunately, the similarity which makes the analysis uncertain makes it also of less importance. The author of the later element in E (E₂) may have lived toward the end of the 8th century or in the first half of the 7th.†

The Triumphal Ode, ch. 5, is much older than the corresponding prose narrative, or than any other of the stories in the book.‡ Whether it was included in J, or in E, or in both of them, cannot be certainly determined. The closing formula, 5³¹ᵇ, may have been added or transposed by an editor. The Ode was in all probability preserved in one of the collections of old Hebrew poetry, such as the Book of Jashar, or the Book of the Wars of Yahweh ;§ but, like other poems from those collections, may early have been incorporated into the prose histories.

The brief notices of the so-called Minor Judges (10¹⁻³ 12⁸⁻¹⁵) begin and close with formulas which, while they have a certain likeness to those which introduce and conclude the stories of the other judges, have also a distinctive difference. ‖ Of each of the five we read that he "judged Israel" so many years, but of the oppressions and deliverances which in the rest of the book alternate with such regularity nothing is said ; of their exploits there is no record ; indeed, beyond the places where they were buried and perhaps the number of their posterity, nothing whatever is narrated of them. Most, if not all, the names of these "judges" appear to be those of clans rather than individuals ; and the years of their rule seem to be independent of the chronological scheme of the book and to disturb its symmetry. It has been conjectured that the names were introduced by an editor to make up the number of twelve judges ;¶ and Wellhausen has strengthened this hypothesis by the observation that the sum of the years of the

---

* It is not impossible, for example, that in the introduction (2⁶-3⁶) a part of what, with Budde, I have ascribed to E, is in reality the work of Rje.

† It is worthy of notice that the "commandments of Yahweh" are mentioned only in 2¹⁷ 3⁴ ; "the covenant of Yahweh," only in 2¹· ²⁰ (Kö., *Einl.*, p. 257).

‡ See p. 127-132.   § Compare 5¹ with Ex. 15¹.

‖ See p. 270 f.   ¶ Nöldeke and many recent scholars.

Minor Judges is almost exactly that of the interregna in the general chronology of the period.[*] The mention of these judges should then be compared with similar antiquarian and genealogical notices in Chronicles. On the other hand, Kuenen, remarking that the characteristic formulas of the Minor Judges stand also at the close of the story of Jephthah (12^7, cf. also 15^{20} 1 S. 4^{18} 7^{15}), and rejecting, partly on this ground, Wellhausen's combination of the numbers, is of the opinion that these five judges were included not only in the Deuteronomic Judges, but in its predecessor, and are thus ultimately derived from one of the sources of the latter work.[†] A third hypothesis is that the Minor Judges stood in the pre-Deuteronomic book, were omitted by the Deuteronomic author, like the story of Abimelech and perhaps ch. 17–21, and restored by the editor of the present Book of Judges. Beyond such conjectures we can hardly go.

§ 5. *The Sources of Judges xvii.–xxi. and of i.–ii. 5.*

The two stories with which our Book of Judges ends, that of Micah's idols and the migration of the Danites (ch. 17, 18), and that of the assault on the Levite and his concubine at Gibeah, with its disastrous consequences to the tribe of Benjamin (ch. 19–21), were not included in the Deuteronomic Judges. They relate, not the deliverance of Israel from the foes that oppressed it, by the hand of divinely commissioned champions, but the fortunes of two tribes, one of which was compelled to leave its earliest seats to find a new home in the remote north, while the second was almost exterminated by the righteous indignation of the other Israelites. If the Deuteronomic author had employed these stories, as perhaps he might have done, to illustrate the moral and religious corruption of the times, the natural place for them in

---

* See below, § 7. This theory is adopted by Budde, who thinks that the shorter formulas in which the names of the Minor Judges are set are patterned after those of the Deuteronomic author (*Richt. u. Sam.*, p. 93 f.); cf. also Cornill, *Einl².*, p. 97 ff.

† *HCO².* i. p. 351 f.; cf. p. 342, 354. A similar view is maintained by Kittel, *GdH.* i. 2. p. 10 ff., except that, in conformity with his general theory, which recognizes no pre-Deuteronomic editor, he supposes that the smaller Book of Judges (ri.) was one of the immediate sources of D.

his book would have been immediately after the introduction ; a place which chronological considerations also indicated. There is no evidence, however, in the introductions to these stories, of any intention to use them in this way. The familiar formulas of D are absent, nor is their place taken by others which might be attributed to the same hand. In the narratives themselves there is no trace of a Deuteronomic redaction.

Whether these stories were contained in the older work which the Deuteronomic author used as the basis of his own, we cannot be so sure. There is certainly no mark of the editor's hand upon them, and it is conceivable that they were preserved independently in one of the sources of that collection. This would account both for the resemblance of the stories to those in 2^8–16^{31} and for the absence of all traces either of Rje or of D in them.[*] But in ch. 17, 18, two narratives appear to have been combined in much the same way as in ch. 6–8, and we should be inclined to attribute this fusion to the same redactor (Rje).[†] It is quite possible that, as this author's work was considerably more extensive than the Deuteronomic Judges, he may have found place in it for these chapters.

That the two versions of the story of Micah and the Danites (ch. 17, 18) are derived from J and E is a natural conjecture. Budde has noted several words and phrases in one of them which seem to point to E. The whole impression which this strand of the narrative makes would incline me rather to ascribe it to J ; decisive evidence is lacking. However that may be, there can be no doubt that the primary version of the story is among the oldest in the book, as it is in many ways one of the most instructive. The second version is apparently younger, but, if I interpret it correctly, there seems to be no reason why it may not come from E.[‡] In 18^{30-31} are two references to historical events : the depopulation of the land (v.^{30}), and the cessation of the temple at Shiloh (v.^{31}). By the former we are probably to understand the depor-

---

[*] That J, at least, survived separately till a late date is probably to be inferred from the preservation of ch. 1.

[†] Many critics, however, think that the appearance of duplication is due to interpolations, rather than to the union of two sources ; see p. 366-369. Ch. 19 is also perhaps composite.   [‡] See p. 370.

tation of the inhabitants of northern Galilee in 734 ; the date of
the latter is unknown. The older narrative in ch. 17, 18, to which
18³¹ seems to belong, can scarcely be brought down to as late a
time as the reign of Tiglathpileser ; the words may have been
added by an editor.[*]

The problem which is presented to criticism by the narrative
of the outrage at Gibeah and the sanguinary vengeance which
almost annihilated the tribe of Benjamin is of a different kind from
any other in the Book of Judges. At first sight, the narrative
seems to be not only entirely unhistorical, but without even a legendary ground — one huge theocratic fiction of very late origin.[†]
Closer examination, however, shows that this is a mistake. The
basis of the narrative, which can be discovered not only in ch. 19
and 21¹⁵ᶠ, but in ch. 20, is a very old story, having an obvious
affinity to the primary stratum in ch. 17, 18, and in tone and language resembling the most ancient parts of the Hexateuch and
the Books of Samuel. This is overlaid, especially in ch. 20, 21¹⁻¹⁴,
by a stratum akin to the latest additions to the priestly history in
the Hexateuch and to the Chronicles. This post-exilic rifacimento
is clearly dependent upon the former version ; the only question is,
whether it once existed separately and was united with the old
story by a third hand,[‡] or whether it was from the beginning
merely a kind of *midrash* upon the original text, in part exaggerating it, in part substituting an account of the events in accordance
with the author's theocratic conception of the ancient history.[§]
The latter appears to me the more probable hypothesis ; but the
other is certainly possible.[||] The primitive story is hardly inferior
in age to any in the book, and may be derived from J. The
secondary version bears, in conception and expression, all the
marks of the extreme decadence of Hebrew literature, and is a
product of the 4th century B.C. more probably than of the
5th. If it was interpolated by its author in the earlier narrative,
as we find it, it may be the work of the editor who appended
chapters 17–21 to the Deuteronomic Judges ; on the alternative
hypothesis, the same editor may have combined the two versions ;
but other explanations are also conceivable.

---

[*] See p. 399–401.   [†] We.   [‡] Bu., Co.
[§] Kue., Kitt., Wildeboer.   [||] See p. 405, 407 f.

The Book of Ruth relates things which happened "in the days when the judges ruled"; in the Greek Bible it immediately follows Judges, and in many early enumerations and catalogues is counted as a part of Judges.[*] Some recent scholars have thought that this was the original place of the book: it was, like ch. 17, 18, and 19–21, an appendix to the Book of Judges proper, ch. 1–16.[†] Ruth is, however, in subject, language, and style, unlike any of the stories in Jud. 1–16, or in 17–21; it is a product of a much later age, and belongs to a wholly different species of literature. As the events narrated in it are supposed to have taken place some half century before the establishment of the kingdom, its natural place in the series of historical books was between Judges and Samuel; or, as falling in the days of the judges, it might be appended to the former book; but this connexion was probably never universal, and may, indeed, have been peculiar to the Greek Bible.

Chapter 1^1–2^5 contains an account of the invasion of Western Palestine by the Israelite tribes, and their settlements, particularly enumerating the cities that they did not succeed in conquering, most of which long remained in the possession of the native Canaanite population.[‡] This account, which in historical value far surpasses any other source that we possess for this period, is manifestly extracted from an older work, and Schrader, Meyer, and others rightly recognize in it J.'s history of the conquest.[§] The narrative has been considerably abridged by the editor who prefixed it to the pre-Deuteronomic Book of Judges,[‖] for the purpose, as we see from his own words in 2^{1b-5a}, of showing how Israel sinned in making terms with the people of the land and leaving them to be a constant snare and peril; it has also suffered to some extent from derangement and interpolation, whether by the editor's own hand or that of scribes. Fortunately, the motive of the

---

[*] So probably by Fl. Jos., *contra Apion.*, c. 8; and expressly by many Christian Fathers.

[†] So Stähelin, Auberlen, al.; see esp. Bertheau, p. 290 ff.; cf. also Schrader in De Wette, *Einl*⁸. p. 395 f.   [‡] See p. 3 ff.

[§] See below, p. 6 f.

[‖] It is more probable that 2^{1b-5a} is by an editor of the school of Rje than that it is from the hand of the post-exilic redactor.

recension gives us confidence that he left intact those features of his original which are of chief interest and importance for us, proving that in the invasion the tribes acted singly, or as they were allied by older ties or common interest; and that Israelite supremacy in Canaan was not achieved by one irresistible wave of conquest, but only after an obstinate struggle lasting for generations.   Fragments of the same source, some of which are a welcome supplement to the narrative in Judges 1, are preserved in the Book of Joshua.[*]

On the Minor Judges, see above, p. xxviii f.

§ 6. *The Composition of the Book of Judges.*

If the results of the critical analysis outlined in § 4 and 5 are substantially correct, the genesis of the book may be conceived in some such way as the following : [†]

Early in the 9th century, the traditions of the invasion and settlement of Western Palestine, of the subsequent conflicts in various parts of the land with the native population or with new invaders, and of the heroic deeds of Israel's leaders and champions in these struggles, were collected and fixed in writing, probably as part of a historical work which included the patriarchal age, the migration from Egypt, and the history of Israel under the kingdom down to the author's own time (J).

Perhaps a century later, another book of similar character and scope was written, containing in part the same stories, but in a form adhering less closely to historical reality (E).   A second recension of this work (E_2) bears very distinctly the impress of the prophetic movement of the 8th century, and specifically of Hosea's teaching, and may be assigned to the end of the 8th or the beginning of the 7th century.   The author's religious

---

[*] See p. 5 f.

[†] It must be borne in mind that any hypothesis we may frame is much simpler than the literary history of which it attempts to give account.   J, E, JE, D, R, &c. represent, not individual authors whose share in the work can be exactly assigned by the analysis, but stages of the process, in which more than one — perhaps many — successive hands participated, every transcription being to some extent a recension.

interpretation and judgement of the history in the spirit of prophecy is the beginning of the treatment so generally adopted by later writers; history with a moral soon becoming history for the moral.

As in the Hexateuch and in Samuel, J and E (E₂) were the chief sources of the great prophetic historical work, JE. Where the author of this work found in his sources variants of the same story, he combined them, sometimes interweaving them so closely as to make the strands almost inextricable, sometimes doing little more than transcribe paragraphs of J and E alternately; adapting his method to the material before him. In many cases he found it necessary, in order to bring his sources into harmony or to preserve the connexion, to insert something of his own; in some places he added with a freer hand. The Book of Judges in JE * seems to have begun with the death of Joshua, and to have closed with the great discourse of Samuel, 1 S. 12, a division which certainly existed in E. It probably contained all the stories in our Judges except that of Othniel; and in view of the character of the succeeding redactions, Rje may, with greater justice than D, be regarded as the true author of the book. JE is a work of the 7th century, but antedates the reforms of Josiah (621 B.C.) and the dominant influence of Jeremiah and the Deuteronomy.

Early in the 6th century, an author belonging to the Deuteronomic school took this work as the basis of his own. As the traces of his hand do not extend to 1 S. 1–12 † nor to Jud. 1¹–2⁵ 17–21, we infer that D's book included only Jud. 2⁶–16³¹ (or perhaps 15²⁰). Eli and Samuel not unnaturally presented themselves to his mind in the character of priest and prophet rather than of judges; and, if historical considerations weighed with him, he may very well have thought that the life of Samuel, from which that of Eli is inseparable, belonged to the history of the founding of the kingdom, rather than to the preceding period. Besides Jud. 17–21, it is certain that D excluded the story of Abimelech, which did not readily lend itself to his moral purpose; 8³³⁻³⁵ is his brief substitute for the omitted narrative. He may also have

---

* It is not of course implied that its author gave it this title.

† The Deuteronomic elements in 1 S. 1–12 have not the distinctive signature of D in Judges.

omitted the Minor Judges,[*] possibly also ch. 16, the tragic end
of Samson ; this would account for the premature closing formula,
15^{20}.[†] On the other hand, he added the deliverance of Israel from
Cushan-rishathaim by Othniel (3^{7-11}), as a typical exemplification
of the theory set forth in the introduction (2^6-3^6), and perhaps
with the additional motive of giving a judge to Judah, which in the
older book was almost the only tribe that furnished none. The
system of chronology is Deuteronomic, as appears from its relation
to the system of the Books of Kings, but whether in its present
form it is the work of D is less certain ; see § 7.

Upon the general introduction, 2^6-3^6, as well as upon the introductions to the stories of the several judges, D impressed the unmistakable Deuteronomic stamp. In his judgement of the history
he had been anticipated by E_2 and JE, but his more rigorous
pragmatism and his distinctive style can in most cases be distinguished with sufficient certainty from the work of his predecessors.
In 2^6-3^6, especially in 2^{6-19}, the Deuteronomic element is very
closely combined with the older text. Budde, whose opinion I
have followed in the commentary,[‡] thinks that D did not, in this
somewhat awkward way, intrude his own point of view into the
introduction of JE, but substituted a new introduction for JE's ;
the two were united, to their mutual detriment, by the final, post-
exilic redactor. The other hypothesis has, however, the advantage of simplicity, and the considerations which weigh against it
are perhaps overestimated. [§]

The Deuteronomic Judges did not supplant the older work
upon which it was founded ; JE's history was in existence long
after the exile. In the 5th or 4th century B.C., an editor united
the two books, and produced the present Book of Judges. In
doing so, he naturally included those parts of JE which D had
omitted, Jud. 1^1-2^5 9 17 18 19-21 ; possibly also the Minor
Judges, 10^{1-5} 12^{8-15}.[‖] The secondary version of the war with
Benjamin in ch. 19-21 is perhaps his work ; and in other parts of
the book traces of his hand may be discerned in minor glosses ;
some of these may, however, be of still later date.

---

[*] This depends in part upon the decision of the difficult questions of the chronology; see § 7.   † Budde.   ‡ P. 63 f.
§ See Kuenen, HCO^2. i. p. 339 f.   ‖ See above.   [•]

On the critical problems discussed in §§ 3-6, see in general Studer, *Richter*, 1835, p. 425 ff.; Schrader in DeWette, *Einleitung*[8], 1869, p. 327-333; Wellhausen in Bleek, *Einl.*[4], 1878, p. 181-203 = *Composition d. Hexateuchs, u. s. w.*, 1889, p. 213-238, cf. 353-357; v. Doorninck, *Bijdrage tot de tekstkritiek van Richteren* i.-xvi., 1879, p. 123-128; Bertheau, *Richter und Ruth*[2], 1883; Kuenen, *Historisch-critisch Ondersoek*, i. p. 338-367 (1887); Budde, *Richter und Samuel*, 1890, p. 1-166; Driver, *Literature of the Old Testament*, 1891, p. 151-162; Kittel, " Die pentateuchischen Urkunden in den Büchern Richter und Samuel," *Stud. u. Krit.*, 1892, p. 44 ff.; *Gesch. der Hebräer*, i. 2. 1892, p. 1-22; Kalkoff, *Zur Quellenkritik des Richterbuchs*, 1893 (Gymnas. Progr.)°.

The theory of the origin of the Book of Judges set forth in the preceding paragraphs is in all essential features that of Budde, whose thorough investigation of the critical problems of the book has been of the greatest value to me throughout. The reader of the commentary will, I trust, discover that I have not accepted Budde's results without a careful re-examination of the whole question; and in many particulars I have been led to form a different opinion. Of other hypotheses concerning the composition of the book, it will be sufficient to mention those of Kuenen and Kittel. The former thinks that Jud. 2[6]-16[31] is a part of a Deuteronomic Book of Judges the end of which is contained in 1 S. 7-12. This book contained all the stories that are now found in the chapters named,* with the solitary exception of 3[31] (Shamgar). The introduction, 2[6]-3[6], is, as a whole, the work of the Deuteronomic writer,† who is the author of the religious pragmatism of the book. He used as the basis of his work a pre-Deuteronomic Book of Judges, in which Othniel as well as Shamgar was not included, while Abimelech was reckoned as one of the twelve judges, whose number was completed by Samuel, or, more probably, by some name which we cannot now recover. This older book was quite different in character from the Deuteronomic work; it knew nothing of a regular alternation of apostasy, punishment, and deliverance; it was a series of portraits of the leaders and heroes of Israel in the period before the establishment of the kingdom; but the unity of Israel was already erroneously antedated, and its deliverance from the hand of its foes represented as Yahweh's answer to its prayer. The author drew a large part of his material from older writings, some of them of Ephraimite origin, which were among the earliest products of Israelite historiography; but the book itself can hardly have been compiled before the first half of the 7th century. Jud. 1[1]-2[5] preserves fragments of a very ancient account of the conquest of Canaan by the Israelite tribes; ch. 17, 18, is also a very old story, which has been considerably interpolated; in ch. 19-21 the old narrative has been thoroughly worked over in the spirit of post-exilic Judaism. These chapters were united with 2[6]-16[31] by the last

---

* Including the Minor Judges.

† It has suffered somewhat from interpolations; and in 3[1-3] the author has incorporated an older fragment which is not altogether in harmony with his own view.

redactor.[*] Kittel differs from almost all recent critics in denying the existence of a pre-Deuteronomic Book of Judges. The author of the Deuteronomic Judges (" Ri ") collected the stories in 2^6–16^{31}, combined parallel narratives (as in ch. 6–8), and embraced them all in his rigorous pragmatism and his schematic chronology. The traces of a different conception and style, which have been taken as evidence that this author worked upon the basis of an older book, are rather to be ascribed to the redactor of the present Book of Judges (R), who introduced a considerable number of glosses and some longer additions to the text of " Ri." [†] This last redactor, who also joined 1^1–2^5 17–21 to 2^6–16^{31}, himself belonged to the Deuteronomic school; but his style, formed on older models, is a degree nearer to that of E in the Hexateuch than that of " Ri." Kittel's theory thus gives us, instead of JE and D, a double Deuteronomic redaction which we might represent by D and Rd. The sources of the tales are not J and E, but unknown ancient collections.

§ 7. *Chronology of the Book of Judges.*

The chronology of the Book of Judges presents a very difficult problem, on which a great deal of learning and ingenuity has been expended, without, as yet, leading to any generally accepted solution. The data contained in the book itself are these :

			YEARS
1.	3^8.	The Israelites subject to Cushan-rishathaim	8
2.	3^{11}.	Peace under Othniel	[‡] 40
3.	3^{14}.	Subject to Eglon, King of Moab	18
4.	3^{30}.	Peace after the death of Eglon (Ehud)	80
5.	4^3.	Oppressed by the Canaanite king, Jabin	20
6.	5^{31}.	Peace after the victory of Barak	40
7.	6^1.	Ravaged by the Midianites and their allies	7
8.	8^{28}.	Peace in the days of Gideon	40
9.	9^{22}.	Dominion of Abimelech	3
10.	10^2.	Rule of Tola	[§] 23
11.	10^3.	Rule of Jair	22
12.	10^8.	The Israelites in Gilead oppressed by the Ammonites	18
13.	12^7.	Rule of Jephthah	[‖] 6
14.	12^9.	Rule of Ibzan	[¶] 7

[*] Kuenen's view is substantially maintained by Wildeboer, *Letterkunde*, p. 165 ff., 26, ff.

[†] Jud. $1^{1a. 4a. 8f.}$ $2^{1b-5a. 13. 17. 20-22}$ $3^{4-6. 31}$. 6^{7-10} 10^{9-16}.

[‡] ⊕ALM ℓ 50.

[§] A few Greek cursives, 22. Fl. Jos., *antt.* v. 7, 5, omits Tola altogether.

[‖] ⊕BPV and several cursives, 60.

[¶] See Euseb., *Chron.* ed. Schoene, ii. p. 52, 53; Jerome, ed. Vallarsi, viii. 288

YEARS

15. 12[11]. Rule of Elon 10
16. 12[14]. Rule of Abdon *8
17. 13[1]. Domination of the Philistines 40
18. 15[20] (16[31]). Rule of Samson 20

The first thing that will be noticed in this table is the frequency with which the numbers *forty* (No. 2. 6. 8. 17), *eighty* (No. 4), and *twenty* (No. 5. 18) recur in it.[†] Each of the greater judges, except Jephthah, secures his country from the attacks of its foes for forty, or twice forty, or half of forty, years. This phenomenon becomes still more striking when we observe that it is not confined to the Book of Judges, but runs through the chronology of the whole period: The wandering in the wilderness lasted forty years; Eli judged Israel forty years (1 S. 4[18]); [‡] David reigned forty years (1 K. 2[11]); Solomon forty (1 K. 11[42]). In 1 K. 6[1], finally, we read, that from the exodus until Solomon began to build the temple, in the fourth year of his reign, was four hundred and eighty years.[§] It is obvious that we have here to do with a systematic chronology, in which a generation is reckoned at forty years, and the period made to consist of twelve generations. [‖]

When we compare the numbers given in Judges with the total

---

* Fl. Jos., *antt.* v. 7, 15, names Abdon, but does not give the years of his rule.

† Compare also No. 15 (ten), and observe how No. 3. 10. 11. 12 balance on either side of twenty.

‡ Ꝺ 20: ᴧΣΘ, Fl. Jos. 40.

§ Ꝺ 440 (Θ[L]. ᴧΣ 480), for some reason reckoning eleven generations instead of twelve. See Preuss, *Die Zeitrechnung der Septuaginta*, 1859, p. 74 ff.

‖ So Hecataeus of Miletus attempted to construct a chronology of Greek antiquity on the basis of the genealogies, reckoning forty years to a generation; see E. Meyer, *Forschungen*, i. p. 169 ff.; Gd.A. ii. p. 8 f. The second great period of Hebrew history, from Solomon to the return from Babylon, is also four hundred and eighty years; see Wellhausen, *Prol*[8]., p. 283 ff.; Stade, *GVI.* i. p. 89 ff. In conformity with this theory, 1 Chr. 6[a ff.] gives in the first period the names of twelve high priests; in the second, according to the corrected text (see Ꝺ), from the first high priest who officiated in the new temple to Jehozadak, who was carried away to Babylon, eleven. The four hundred and ninety years which Daniel computes for the last period, to the coming of the kingdom of the saints, is of almost exactly the same length, though calculated on a different basis (seventy weeks of seven years). On the frequency of 40 in chronologies &c., see Bredow's *Dissertatio de Georgii Syncelli Chronographia*, prefixed to the Bonn ed. of Syncellus, ii. p. 53 ff.

in 1 K. 6[1], however, a large discrepancy appears. The sum of
the years of the oppressions and of the judges is four hundred and
ten years. To this must be added the forty years in the wilderness; the days of Joshua, from the invasion of Canaan until he
and all his generation passed away (Jud. 2[7-10]), for which no numbers are given (x); the forty (or twenty) years of Eli (1 S. 4[1x]); the
years in which Samuel judged Israel (1 S. 7[15],) (y), and the reign
of Saul (1 S. 13[1],) (z), for neither of which have we any data; the
forty years of David (1 K. 2[11]); and four years of Solomon [*]
before the building of the temple was begun: that is, $40 + x$
$+ 410 + 40 + y + z + 40 + 4 = 534 + x + y + z$. In this sum
$x + y + z$ (Joshua, Samuel, Saul) must represent a considerable
number of years; [†] but even neglecting them, the total greatly
exceeds the 480 of Kings. Various hypotheses have been proposed to bring them into harmony. One way by which this can
be accomplished is to suppose that the oppressions and deliverances related in the Book of Judges were not successive, but in
part synchronous. They were, in fact, without exception, local
struggles; and it is not only conceivable, but highly probable, that
while one part of the land was enjoying security under its judge,
other tribes were groaning under the foreign yoke. [‡] Thus Herzfeld supposes that for one hundred and seventeen years, from the
victory of Othniel over the Aramaeans to the beginning of the Midianite forays, the history runs parallel; the subjection of the
southern tribes by the Moabites, their deliverance by Ehud, and
the long peace which followed, falling in the same period with the
oppression of the north by the Canaanites, the war of liberation
under Deborah and Barak, and the forty years' security which their

---

[*] According to the Hebrew way of reckoning.

[†] Josephus gives Joshua 25; Samuel 12; Samuel and Saul contemporaneously
18; Saul after the death of Samuel 22. The Christian chronologists do not differ
very widely; Eusebius gives Joshua 27; Samuel and Saul jointly 40. We should
hardly say that these estimates are excessive. For the whole period Josephus
reckons 592 years (*antt.* viii. 3. 1 § 61; x. 8, 5 § 147) or 612 (*antt.* xx. 10, 1 § 230;
c. Ap. ii. 2 § 19), or in still different ways; see P. Brinch, *Examen chronologiae
Flav. Josephi,* c. 4; Herzfeld, *Chronologia judicum,* p. 12 f.

[‡] On the considerations which may be urged in favour of the hypothesis of
synchronisms, see Walther, in *Zusätze zur Allg. Welthist.,* 1747, ii. p. 400 ff. (cited
by Bachmann).

victory gained.* This synchronism, which is not suggested by a syllable in the text of Judges, is only made out by a series of arbitrary assumptions, such as that nineteen years elapsed between the victory of Othniel and the Moabite invasion. With much greater show of probability, others suppose that the subjugation of the Israelites in Gilead by the Ammonites coincided with the oppression of their brethren in Canaan by the Philistines. Such an hypothesis not only offers no intrinsic difficulty, but seems to be commended by Jud. 10⁶⁻⁸, where we read that, as a punishment for their fresh defection, Yahweh sold the Israelites into the power of the Philistines and the Ammonites. In the following chapters, the author narrates, first, the Ammonite oppression, the deliverance of Gilead by Jephthah, and the rule of his successors, Ibzan, Elon, Abdon (ch. 11. 12); and then (13¹) takes up the story of the long struggle with the Philistines which is so inseparably connected with the beginnings of the kingdom in Israel. The forty years of Philistine oppression, with which the forty years of Eli coincide, thus cover also the eighteen years of Ammonite rule east of the Jordan, the six of Jephthah, seven of Ibzan, ten of Elon (41), while the eight years of Abdon would fall in the time of Samuel. In this form the hypothesis was proposed by Sebastian Schmid; † and, often in combination with other synchronisms, has been accepted by many commentators and chronologists. ‡ In this way the length of the period is greatly reduced, but the exact equation with the four hundred and eighty years of 1 K. 6¹ is obtained only by attributing to the unknown quantities, x, y, and z, in the other member entirely arbitrary values. The most serious objection to the synchronistic hypothesis in any form is, that the chronology of the book is, on the face of it, continuous;

---

* That the twenty years of Canaanite oppression and the forty years of peace which followed fell in the eighty years of peace which the south enjoyed after the death of Eglon, is a hypothesis propounded by older chronologists (Beza, Marsham). Others think that the forty years' peace under Gideon in Central Palestine coincided with the forty years of Barak in the North; &c. On these and other theories see Ba., p. 64 f.

† *Appendix chronologica ad librum Judicum*, 1684.

‡ Vitringa, Carpzov, Marsham, Walther; Ke., Ew., Hgstbg., al.; most recently, with different modifications and more or less artificial subsidiary hypotheses, Bachmann and Köhler.

if the author had intended us to understand that the Ammonite and the Philistine oppressions were contemporaneous, he would have given a much more distinct intimation of his meaning than 10^{e}, and have given it in its proper place in 13^{1}.*

Nöldeke has tried to solve the problem in another way.† He observes that the sum of the rule of the Minor Judges, including Jephthah, is seventy-six years, to which if we add the four years of Solomon before the building of the temple, we obtain another eighty; a coincidence which can hardly be accidental, and which, if designed, shows that the Minor Judges were included in the chronological system of the book. The total of the years ascribed to the judges and kings in the Books of Judges and Samuel, down to the fourth year of Solomon, is three hundred and eighty.‡ To this must be added the forty years of Moses, the years of Joshua (x), Samuel (y), and Saul (z). For Samuel he reckons (from 1 S. 7^{2}) twenty years. We have thus: $40 + 380 + 20 = 440 + x + z$. In this system of forties we should naturally give to the unknown quantities (Joshua, Saul) twenty years each, or unequal numbers together making forty, obtaining thus exactly the four hundred and eighty of 1 K. 6. The years of foreign domination and of usurpers are, as usual in Oriental chronologies, not counted;§ the beginning of each judge's rule being reckoned, not from the victory which brought him into power, but from the death of his predecessor.∥

In principle, this appears to me the most probable hypothesis. I should be inclined, however, to divide the numbers somewhat differently. For Eli, instead of the forty years of 𝔐, I should

---

* Compare the formal synchronisms in the Books of Kings.

† "Die Chronologie der Richterzeit," *Untersuchungen zur Kritik d. A. T's,* 1869, p. 173 ff.

‡ Othniel 40, Ehud 80, Barak 40, Gideon 40, Minor Judges 76 + 4 of Solomon = 80, Samson 20, Eli 40, David 40 = 380.

§ Nöldeke makes the sum of these years 94; viz. Cushan 8, Eglon 18, Jabin 20, Midianites 7, Abimelech 3, Ammonites 18, Philistines 20 (deducting the twenty in the days of Samson, Jud. 15^{20}).

∥ This is the method of Jewish and early Christian chronologers; see Euseb., *Chron.* ed. Schoene, ii. p. 35: post mortem Jesu subjectos tenuerunt Hebraeos aliengenae annis 8, qui junguntur Gothonielis temporibus, secundum Judaeorum traditiones; and so in every following case. So also *Seder Olam,* c. 12, and the Jewish commentators; see Meyer, *Seder Olam,* p. 383 ff.

adopt the reading of ⑤, *twenty*. The forty years of Philistine rule coincide with the time of Samson (20) and Eli (20) ; Samuel liberated Israel from their yoke (1 S. 7). Abimelech is not counted in the succession of rulers, as Nöldeke and most recent chronologists rightly assume ; * but it does not appear to have been noted that the same is true of Saul. For the Judaean author of this chronology his rule was illegitimate ; David was the immediate successor of Samuel.† This inference is confirmed by 1 S. 13¹, where a later hand has attempted to supply the lack of a statement about the length of Saul's reign with the usual formula borrowed from the Books of Kings, ‡ but seems to have left the numbers blank.

We have, then, the following scheme : Moses 40 years, Joshua x, Othniel 40, Ehud 80, Barak 40, Gideon 40, the Minor Judges with Jephthah 76, Samson 20, Eli 20, Samuel y, David 40, Solomon $4 = 400 + x + y = 480$. We may then suppose that the author gave Joshua and Samuel forty years each, an hypothesis which in each case has some slight external support. Joshua lived, like his ancestor Joseph, to the age of 110 years, which, as in Joseph's life, § may most naturally be divided into $30 + 40 + 40$. To Samuel, of whose life and work he had such a full account, the deliverer and judge, the maker and unmaker of kings, it is antecedently improbable that the author reckoned only half a generation ; especially as Samuel was an old man when he died.

If 1 K. 6¹ is the summation of the numbers in Judges and Samuel, and from the same hand, it would follow that the systematic chronology in Judges was not introduced by the Deuteronomic author, but by a later editor, who may have substituted his own cyclic numbers for older ones.‖ But the author of Judges may, himself, conceivably have constructed his chronology on a basis of forty years to the generation. In either case, the length of the oppressions, and of the rule of the Minor Judges (with

---

* Probably Jud. 9 was not contained in the Deuteronomic Judges ; but in any case he was regarded as a usurper.

† Observe that Samuel ruled Israel as long as he lived, 1 S. 7¹⁵.

‡ Not the formula of Judges or Samuel.

§ Gen. 41⁴⁶ ; cf. Gutschmid in Nöldeke, p. 192 f.

‖ The 76 years of the Minor Judges plus the 4 of Solomon would be the most conclusive evidence of this.

Jephthah), which are at least not primarily cyclic, probably represent an earlier stage in the history of tradition; the latter may be derived from E.

On the Chronology of Judges see S. Schmid, *Comm. in Jud.*, 1684, p. 1569–1603; Des Vignoles, *Chronologie de l'histoire sainte*, 1738; ° Herzfeld, *Chronologia judicum et primorum regum Hebraeorum*, 1836; Rösch, "Das Datum des Tempelbaus," *Stud. u. Krit.*, 1863, p. 712–742; Nöldeke, *Untersuchungen zur Kritik des Alten Testaments*, 1869, p. 173–198; Wellhausen in Bleek, *Einleitung*[4], p. 184 f. = *Composition des Hexateuchs*, p. 216 f. (cf. p. 356); *Prolegomena*[3], p. 237 f.; Reuss, *Gesch. des Alten Testaments*, § 277; Budde, *Richter u. Samuel*, p. 135 ff.; Köhler, *Biblische Geschichte*, ii. 1. p. 35–51; Kittel, *Gesch. der Hebräer*, i. 2. p. 9–14; of the commentaries, especially Bachmann (p. 53–74), and Bertheau (p. xi.–xvii.). — Wellhausen notes that the years of the Minor Judges (70) almost exactly correspond to the duration of the interregna (71), and infers that the Minor Judges were introduced by an editor who did not reckon the interregna separately, but included them, contrary to the intention of the author of the chronology, in the rule of the following judges; cf. *Prol*[3]., p. 237 f.; Budde; Cornill, *Einl*[2]. p. 98 f.; and against Wellhn., Kuenen, *HCO*[2]. i. p. 342, Kittel, *GdH.* i. 2. p. 11–13; Wellhn. himself (*Comp.*, p. 356) confesses that he has no longer much faith in such attempts to solve the enigma.

§ 8. *Hebrew Text and Ancient Versions.*

The text of Judges has been transmitted to us in a much purer state than that of the Books of Samuel; indeed, it is better preserved than any other of the historical books; but it is not entirely free from the errors which are incident to transcription. The variants of Hebrew manuscripts seldom enable us to correct these errors. Setting aside the great mass of purely heterographic variations, there are few that materially affect the sense; and of these, very few which are intrinsically superior to the Massoretic text. The critic cannot entirely disregard them, however; especially when the support of the Targum or other of the versions shows that the reading is old.*

---

* For the Massoretic text (𝔐) I have generally followed Baer, *Libri Josuae et Judicum*, 1891. The admirable edition of the Bible by J. H. Michaelis (1720) has also been constantly before me, and I have derived much help from Norzi's critical commentary, *Minchath Shai*, in the Mantua Bible of 1742. For the readings of Hebrew manuscripts and early editions I have relied on J. B. De Rossi, *Variae lectiones Veteris Testamenti*, vol. ii., 1785, which embodies all that is useful

Much more important aid in the restoration of the text is given by the ancient versions. First among these in critical value as well as in age are the Greek versions. I say versions; for Lagarde has demonstrated in the most conclusive way, by printing them face to face through five chapters, that we have two Greek translations of Judges.* It would probably be going too far to affirm that they are independent; the author of the younger of them may have known and used the older; but it is certain that his work is not a recension or revision of his predecessor's, but a new translation. One of these versions is represented by the great majority of manuscripts, including the uncials, Sarravianus (ˢ),† Alexandrinus (ᴬ),‡ Coislinianus (ᴾ),§ Basiliano-Vaticanus (ᵛ),‖ and many cursives. The latter form several well-defined groups, some of which may properly be designated as recensions. One of these (ᴸ) is represented in Judges by codd. 19, 108, 118 (Holmes and Parsons),¶ the Complutensian Polyglot, and Lagarde's *Librorum V. T. canonicorum pars prior*, 1883; and is thought by many scholars to exhibit the recension of Lucian. The second (ᴹ) is a group whose most constant members are codd. 54,

in Kennicott's collations. For the Massora, besides Jacob ben Chayim's edition in the Venice Rabbinical Bible, I have chiefly consulted Frensdorff's edition of the *Ochla we-Ochla*, 1864, and his *Massoretisches Wörterbuch*, 1876: Ginsburg's huge work will be of little use until the volume of apparatus appears.

* *Septuaginta Studien*, 1892. p. 1–72. I had reached the same conclusion in a paper read at the meeting of the *Society of Biblical Literature* in May, 1890, before I learned, through a letter from Prof. Lagarde, that he was preparing this edition.

† In Holmes and Parsons' apparatus, IV and V. Hexaplar manuscript of the 4th or 5th century (Tischendorf) in Leyden, St. Petersburg, and Paris. Published by Tischendorf, *Monumenta sacra inedita*, iii.; the Paris leaves by Lagarde, *Semitica*, ii. Of Judges it contains: 9⁴ˢ–10⁶ 15⁸–18¹⁶ 19²⁵–21¹².

‡ Holmes and Parsons, III. Of the 5th century, in London. Edited by Grabe and successors, 1707–1720, 4 vols. Type facsimile by Baber, 1812–1828, 3 vols. Photographic reproduction published by the Trustees of the British Museum, 1881–1883.

§ Holmes and Parsons, X. Hexaplar; of the 7th century (Holmes). The collation in H.P. is to be controlled by that of Griesbach, in Eichhorn's *Repertorium*, ii. p. 194 ff.

‖ Holmes and Parsons, XI. Of the 9th century (Holmes), in Rome. In Judges it lacks 14¹⁷–18¹. For this MS., H.P. has been my sole dependence. No significance is to be attached, therefore, to the absence of ᵛ from an array in which it might be expected.

¶ Of these, 108 (Vaticanus 330) only is complete in Judges; the others have more or less extensive lacunæ. For this group I have cited Lagarde's edition.

59, 75, 82, which are frequently joined by others. A Leipzig palimpsest (uncial) published by Tischendorf also belongs to this group.* This hitherto inedited recension exhibits the text of Theodoret.† A third group (°) consists of the Venice manuscripts 120 and 121, with the Aldine edition, which is derived from them.‡ Most of the translations made from the Greek follow this version; so the Old Latin (l),§ the Hexaplar Syriac of Paul of Tella (s),‖ the Ethiopic (t),¶ and the Armenian.**

The Hexaplar codices (^{sp al.}) and the Hexaplar Syriac show that this version was the basis of Origen's critical labours. It is, therefore, presumptively the oldest Greek translation of Judges; and in so far as "Septuagint" is equivalent to "the oldest Greek version," the text of ᴬ and its congeners might justly lay claim to that designation.†† It seems to me desirable, however, in the interests of clearness that the name, with all its misleading associations, should be banished from critical use.

The other version is found in the Vatican Codex (ᴮ), Cod. Musei Britannici Add. 20002 (ᵠ),‡‡ and a considerable group of cursives in Holmes and Parsons (ᴺ); viz. 16, 30, 52, 53, 58, 63, 77, 85 (text), 131, 144, 209, 236, 237; the text printed in the

---

* *Monumenta sacra*, i. p. 171-176. It contains of Jud. 11²⁴⁻³⁴ 18²⁻³¹.

† I have projected an edition of it, of which an announcement will be made in due time.

‡ I have not compared the Aldina for myself, but have relied on Holmes and Parsons, compared with the collation in the London Polyglot, vol. vi.

§ The scanty fragments of the Old Latin were collected by Sabatier, and reprinted, with a few gleanings, by Fritzsche, *Liber Judicum secundum LXX interpretes*, 1867. More considerable additions are gathered by Vercellone in his apparatus to the Vulgate (ii., 1864).

‖ This version was made in the year 616-617 A.D., in Egypt, from a Hexaplar codex; see Gwynne, in Smith's *Dict. of Christ. Biography*, iv. p. 266 ff. Judges was published from a MS. in the British Museum, with a reconstruction of the Greek text, by T. Skat Rördam (*Libri Judicum et Ruth*, 1861); and by Lagarde (*Bibliotheca syriaca*, 1892).

¶ Dillmann, *Octateuchus aethiopicus*, 1853. Contains a collation with the Roman text of 𝔊.

** I am unable to use the Armenian version: see Lagarde, *Genesis graece*, p. 18; *Septuaginta Studien*, p. 8 f.

†† Grabe, *Epistola ad Millium*, 1705.

‡‡ Known to me only from Lagarde's collation of Jud. 1-5. On the surmise that a codex in St. Petersburg, which is probably part of the same manuscript, contains the text of Theodotion, see Lagarde, *Septuaginta Studien*, p. 11.

Catena Nicephori represents this family. Grabe, in 1705, proved that this version was of Egyptian origin; [*] a conclusion which is brilliantly confirmed by the fact, that of all the secondary versions only the Sahidic (k) is based upon it.[†] As the quotations in the Alexandrian Fathers from the 2d to the 4th century (Clement, Origen, Didymus) [‡] follow the version represented by $\mathfrak{G}^A$ and its congeners, while Cyrill uses the text which we find in $\mathfrak{G}^{DON}$k,[§] the conjecture is not remote that the latter translation of Judges was made in the 4th century; but much remains to be done before any positive conclusion can be reached.

In this state of the case, I have thought it proper to adduce the evidence of the Greek versions with more fulness than would ordinarily be necessary in a commentary. If the Greek version is to be used at all for the emendation of the Hebrew text, it must be used critically; and to operate, as older commentators did, with "A" and "B," or as some more modern scholars do, with Tischendorf's reprint of the Roman edition and Lagarde's "Lucian," taking the one or the other for "Septuagint" upon the intrinsic probability of readings, is not a critical procedure. [‖]

The Latin version of Jerome is one of the best specimens of his skill as a translator; and is exegetically of the greatest value, because it gives not merely Jerome's own interpretation, but that of his Jewish teachers and helpers. It is of less assistance to the textual critic, because the Hebrew text from which it was made was substantially the Jewish standard text which, having been authoritatively fixed in the 2d century, A.D., has been transmitted to us with great fidelity. For the Latin text itself we have an

---

* In the letter to Mill, cited above. Grabe embarrassed this result by the assumption that the version, or revision, was the work of Hesychius.

† Ciasca, *Sacrorum Bibliorum fragmenta copto-sahidica*, i. 1885. Contains of Judges, 1¹⁰⁻²¹ 1⁷⁷⁻²¹⁸.   ‡ Didymus died 394 or 399.

§ Cyrill became Bp. of Alexandria in 412 A.D.

‖ On the Greek text of Judges, see Grabe, *Epistola ad Millium*, 1705; Ziegler, *Theologische Abhandlungen*, i. 1791, p. 276 ff.; O. F. Fritzsche, *Liber Judicum secundum LXX interpretes*, 1867 (distinguishing three types of text); Schulte, *De restitutione atque indole genuinae versionis graecae in libro Judicum*, 1889; Lagarde, *Septuaginta Studien*, 1892, p. 1–72. For the fragments of Aquila, Symmachus, and Theodotion, Field, *Origenis hexaplorum quae supersunt*, 1875; cf. J. G. Scharfenberg, *Animadversiones quibus fragmenta versionum graecarum V.T. . . . illustrantur emendantur*, ii. 1781, p. 40–85.

excellent apparatus in Vercellone, *Variae lectiones vulgatae latinae Bibliorum editionis*, ii. 1864.

The Syrian Vulgate (Peshitto) also represents in the main the Hebrew Standard text, and is of more importance to the interpreter than to the critic. For the Peshitto, which exhibits a constancy second only to that of the Hebrew, I have compared, in places where its variations seemed to be significant, the *editio princeps* of Gabriel Sionita in the Paris Polyglot ($\mathfrak{S}^P$), from which that in the London Polyglot ($\mathfrak{S}^L$) is derived immediately, and that of Lee at one remove; the photolithographic reproduction of the Ambrosian codex ($\mathfrak{S}^A$); the Nestorian text as edited by Justin Perkins at Ooroomiah in 1852 ($\mathfrak{S}^O$); and an old and excellent manuscript of the Historical Books and the Wisdom of the O.T., of Nestorian origin, belonging to the Harvard Semitic Museum, Cambridge, Mass. ($\mathfrak{S}^H$).

The Targum is seldom of much critical value, but often serves us well as a commentary upon the punctuation, and fills an important place in the history of Jewish exegesis. Its text exhibits considerable variation. I have compared, in critical places, the edition by Felix Pratensis in the first of Bomberg's Great Bibles, 1518 ($\mathfrak{T}^{ven.\,1}$), that by Jacob ben Chayim in the second of those Bibles, 1525 ($\mathfrak{T}^{ven.\,2}$); * Buxtorf's rifacimento of the latter in his Great Bible, 1618–20,† reproduced in the London Polyglot; the Antwerp Polyglot; and Lagarde's edition of the Targum from the great Codex Reuchlinianus at Carlsruhe, *Prophetae chaldaice*, 1872 ($\mathfrak{T}^{reuch.}$) I also collated, in 1888, Codex. Brit. Mus. Orient., 2210, a manuscript from Southern Arabia with supralinear punctuation, dated A.D. 1469 ($\mathfrak{T}^m$). ‡

The only systematic attempt to employ the versions for the emendation of the Hebrew text of Judges is made by A. v. Doorninck, *Bijdrage tot de tekstkritiek van Richteren* i.-xvi., 1879.

§ 9. *Interpreters of the Book of Judges.*

Of the Fathers, the nine homilies of Origen on this book, which are preserved in Rufinus's Latin translation (Orig., *Opp.* ed. Dela-

---

* Known to me only in the edition of 1547.

† The punctuation and orthography are Buxtorf's; nor did he refrain from more serious emendations.   ‡ See Merx, *Chrestomathia Targumica*, Proleg. p. xvi.

rue, ii. p. 458–478) have very little exegetical merit. Theodoret
in his *Quaestiones* (*Opp.* ed. Schulze, i. p. 321–345) discusses
with some fulness a number of the more obscure or difficult passages in Judges with candour and skill. His extensive quotations
are of importance for the history of the Greek text. The commentary of Procopius of Gaza (Migne, *Patrologia graeca*, lxxxvii.
1041–1080), though fragmentary and largely allegorical, is not
devoid of worth. The Catena Nicephori (Leipzig, 1773) draws
chiefly from Josephus, Theodoret, and Procopius, but quotes also
a considerable number of anonymous Greek expositions. Augustine wrote *Quaestiones* on Judges, as on the other books of the
Heptateuch (Migne, *Patrologia latina*, xxxiv. 791–824) ; so did
Isidore of Seville (*ib.* lxxxiii. 379–390). We have also a commentary on Judges by Ephrem Syrus (*Opp.* i. p. 308–330).

The patristic exegesis had only the versions to work upon ; the
history of the interpretation of the Hebrew text begins with the
Jewish commentators of the Middle Ages.* Of these, R. Solomon Isaaki, commonly called "Rashi" (1040–1105 A.D.), in many
ways deserves the foremost place which the judgement of Jewish
scholars generally accords him. He has two of the greatest and
rarest gifts of the commentator, the instinct to discern precisely
the point at which explanation is necessary, and the art of giving
or indicating the needed help in the fewest words. He had an
almost unequalled knowledge not only of the Bible, but of the
whole vast body of Jewish tradition. His interpretation adheres
more closely to the exegetical tradition than that of his successors,
and very often agrees with Jerome's, that is, Jerome's Jewish
teachers. R. David Kimchi (ca. 1160–1235) gave much more
prominence to the grammatical and lexical side of the commentator's task, in which he excelled ; he is a judicious interpreter and
a lucid expositor. Of much less note is R. Levi ben Gerson
("Ralbag," died ca. 1370), whose commentary is printed with
Rashi and Kimchi in the Rabbinical Bibles of Venice and Basel.
Besides these are to be named, Abarbanel (1437–1508), whose
very diffuse commentary is in Judges largely dependent on Levi
ben Gerson ; † and Solomon ben Melech, *Michlol Yophi* (Amster-

---

* Of course, the ancient versions themselves embodied an interpretation of the
original text.   † I have used the ed. of Leipzig, 1686.

dam, 1684), a convenient exegetical hand-book, chiefly abridged
from Kimchi.

Through the *Postillae perpetuae* of Nicolaus a Lyra (ca. 1270–
1340) the Jewish exegesis, and what was even more important, a
sounder exegetical method, passed over into the Church. Later
Catholic commentators of note are Arias Montanus, *De varia
Republica*, 1592 ; Serarius, 1609 ; Jac. Bonfrerius, 1631 ; Corne-
lius a Lapide, 1642 ; Th. Malvenda, 1650.*

Among the early Protestant commentators, Sebastian Münster
(1489–1552) follows the Jewish interpreters, particularly Kimchi,
very closely. Drusius's (1550–1616) learning had a wider range ;
besides the rabbinical commentaries he made good use of the
ancient Greek versions and the Fathers, and deserves the praise
which R. Simon gives him as the most learned and judicious of
the interpreters whose works are collected in the *Critici Sacri*.
The fragmentary annotations of. Grotius often contain interesting illustrations and parallels from Greek and Roman writers. Of
all the older commentaries by far the best, and one of the most
valuable commentaries on Judges, is that of Sebastian Schmid
(1684). The author brings together into his 1642 solid quarto
pages all that had been done before him for the interpretation of
the book. His own exegetical judgement is clear and sound. In
excursus at the end of each chapter (*Quaestiones*), the difficulties
of every kind are discussed with great thoroughness. The commentary of Clericus (1708), a work of a more modern type, is
also deservedly held in high esteem. The marginal annotations
in J. H. Michaelis's edition of the Hebrew Bible (1720) are
excellent ; nor must the notes to J. D. Michaelis's German translation (1774) be passed over. Rosenmüller's *Scholia* on Judges
(1835) contain very little that is new.

The modern period of interpretation begins with G. L. Studer's
admirable commentary,† in which the problems that the book presents to criticism and critical exegesis were first clearly recognized,
and a long step taken toward their solution. Bertheau's commentary in the " Kurzgefasstes exegetisches Handbuch " (1845) is a
work of less originality, but, especially in the second edition (1883),

---

* Of these I have read only a Lyra and a Lapide. Serarius I know through
Schmid. † *Das Buch der Richter*, 1835 ; second (title) edition, 1842.

fills a useful place.   Reuss has given, in French (1877) and German (1892), brilliant translations of Judges, with introductions, and brief but excellent notes.   Keil (1863 ;* 2 ed. 1874) has the stamp of the manufactured article ; Cassel (in Lange, 1865 ; † 2 ed. 1887) is full of curious learning and ingeniously perverse exegesis.   By far the fullest recent commentary on Judges is that of J. Bachmann (1868), which was unfortunately never carried beyond the fifth chapter.   The author's standpoint is that of Hengstenberg, and he is a stanch opponent of modern criticism of every shade and school ; but in range and accuracy of scholarship, and exhaustive thoroughness of treatment, his volume stands without a rival.   Other modern commentaries which require no special note are those of Hervey in the " Speaker's Commentary " (1872) and in the " Pulpit Commentary " (1881) ; and Jamieson, in Jamieson, Fausset, and Brown's " Critical and Experimental Commentary."   A. R. Fausset's *Critical and Expository Commentary on Judges* (1885) is " expository " in the homiletic sense, and "critical" in no sense at all.   The German translation of Judges in Kautzsch's *Das Alte Testament*, 1894 (by Kittel), embodies in a sober and conservative spirit the results of modern critical scholarship.

---

* English translation, Edinburgh, 1868.
† English translation, New York, 1872.

A COMMENTARY ON THE BOOK OF JUDGES.

A COMMENTARY ON THE BOOK OF JUDGES.

I. 1–II. 5. The conquests and settlements of the Israelite tribes in Canaan.

LITERATURE. — E. Meyer, "Kritik der Berichte über die Eroberung Palaes-
tinas," *ZATW*. i. 1881, p. 117–146; cf. Stade, *ibid.*, p. 146–150.

K. Budde, "Richter und Josua," *ZATW*. vii. 1887, p. 93–166 = *Die Bücher
Richter und Samuel*, 1890, p. 1–89. Other writers on the composition of
the Book of Judges, see Introduction, § 6, end.

At the opening of the narrative, we have to suppose the Israelite
tribes encamped in the plain of Jericho (1^{16} 2^{1}), and about to
invade the hill-country. They inquire of the oracle what tribe
shall first attack the Canaanites. Agreeably to its response, Judah
together with Simeon begins the invasion ($v.^{1-3}$). They defeat
and capture Adoni-bezek, and, advancing southward, take Hebron,
Debir, and Hormah, making themselves masters of the mountains,
but are unable to conquer the coast plain ($v.^{4-21}$). The tribe of
Joseph invades the central highlands, and takes Bethel ($v.^{22-26}$),
but has to leave many strong towns, especially along the Great
Plain, in the hands of the Canaanites ($v.^{27-29}$). In the north, no
conquests are recorded; the Israelites settle in the midst of the
native population ($v.^{30-33}$). In the west, Dan is crowded back
into the mountains ($v.^{34-36}$). The Angel of Yahweh removes from
Gilgal to "Bochim." * He reproves Israel for making terms with
the people of the land and sparing their places of worship, and
foretells the consequences of this disobedience.

The words of the Angel show how ch. 1 is to be regarded in
its present connexion. The failure of the invaders to conquer

---

* Perhaps originally Bethel, 𝕲; see comm. on 2^{1}.

the whole land at once is not due to the strength of its walled
towns, or the superiority of their inhabitants in the art and
enginery of war, but to Israel's slackness in carrying out the root
and branch policy enjoined in Ex. 34$^{11-16}$ 23^{31b-33} Dt. 7$^{1-5}$ &c. As
a punishment, Yahweh leaves the Canaanites whom they have
guiltily spared to be the cause of all the ills denounced in those
passages. Their religion is the snare into which Israel is ever
afresh falling. The repeated apostasies and ensuing judgements
which are the subject of the Book of Judges have their origin in
the primal act of disobedience, that Israel did not exterminate the
inhabitants of the land. From this point of view, ch. 1, with
its long list of cities remaining in the hands of the Canaanites,
including many of the most important places in Central and
Northern Palestine, forms a fitting introduction to the present
Book of Judges.

It had, however, no place in the original plan of the book, but
has been introduced by a later editor. For, *a*, the Introduction
gives, in the proper place (3$^{1-6}$), an enumeration of the native
races remaining in Canaan, or on its borders, which makes no
reference to ch. 1 and is not entirely consonant with it. *b*,
Jud. 2$^{6-10}$ is the immediate continuation, in sense and structure,
of Jos. 24^7.* The intrusion of Jud. 1^{1b}-2^5 between two consecutive sentences of the narrative led later, perhaps in connexion
with the division into books, to the creation of a new close for
Jos. 24, v.$^{28-31}$ being restored from Jud. 2$^{6-9}$,† while v.^{32,33} are fragmentary notices from another source which came in appropriately
at the end of the history of that generation.

The whole character of Jud. 1^1-2^5 gives evidence that it was
not composed for the place, but is an extract from an older
history of the Israelite occupation of Canaan. It has not, however, been preserved just as it was in the original source. The
editor, to whom its value lay, not in what it told of the conquests

---

* The translations of Jud. 2^6 in AV. and RV., which conceal this fact, are
grammatically false.

† A careful comparison of the two passages will show clearly, I think, that this
is their true relation, and not, as is still commonly assumed, that Jud. 2$^{6-10}$ was
borrowed by the Deuteronomic author of Judges from Jos. 24$^{28-31}$. Comp. the
somewhat similar case, Ezra 1^{1-3a} = 2 Chr. 36^{22f}.

of Israel, but in the evidence it gave of the incompleteness of the conquest, that is, of the unfaithfulness of Israel, has apparently abridged and adapted it to his purpose; and the trace of still later hands is probably to be recognized in certain additions and changes.

On the critical restoration of the chapter, see Wellhausen, *Einleitung*[4], p. 181-183 = *Composition d. Hexat.*, p. 213-215; E. Meyer, *ZATW*. i. p. 135 ff.; Budde, *ZATW*. vii. p. 94 ff. = *Richter u. Samuel*, p. 2 ff. (cf. 84–89); Kuenen, *Historisch-critisch Onderzoek*, i. p. 356-358; Kittel, *Geschichte der Hebräer*, i. 1. p. 239-245.

Ch. 1^{1a} is an editorial title corresponding to Jos. 1^1; v.^{4}, superfluous and disturbing by the side of v.$^{6-7}$, is probably secondary; v.^{8}, an interpolation induced by v.^{7b}, directly contradicting v.^{21} Jos. 15^{63} cf. Jud. 19^{10-12} 2 S. 5^{6-8}; v.^{9} makes the impression of a general summary by a later hand; v.$^{10.20}$ are severed parts of the original, which may be restored by the help of Jos. 15^{13-14}; v.^{18} flatly contradicts v.^{19}, and is, like v.^{8}, in conflict with the facts; v.^{21} = Jos. 15^{63}, with the change of the original *Judah* to *Benjamin*, in conformity with later representations of the partition of the land; v.$^{19. 21}$, or perhaps $^{21. 19}$, originally stood after v.^{7}. The story of the conquests of Joseph is disproportionately meagre, and has very likely been abridged by the editor; Budde, with considerable probability, conjectures that Jos. 17^{14-18} Nu. $32^{39. 41. 42}$ Jos. 13^{13} originally stood in this connexion. The account of the settlement of the northern tribes may be similarly curtailed. With v.$^{34f.}$ Jos. 19^{47} may once have been joined. In 2^{1-5}, only v.$^{1a. 5b}$, "The Angel of Yahweh went up from Gilgal to *Bethel*, ... and they sacrificed there to Yahweh," can belong to the older narrative; v.$^{1b-5a}$ are in the characteristic manner of the redaction of Judges. On all this, see more fully below in the commentary.

Although thus by no means intact, the passage presents, after the manifest interpolations have been removed, a sufficiently orderly and intelligible connexion. Recent criticism has thus set aside the hypothesis of compilation (Stud.; cf. Preiss, *ZWTh.* 1892, p. 496), and must qualify the strong terms in which the confusion and fragmentariness of the chapter has often been spoken of, *e.g.* by Kuenen.

Fragments of this narrative are also preserved in different places in the Book of Joshua: Jos. 15^{13-19} = Jud. $1^{10-15. 20}$; Jos. 15^{63} = Jud. 1^{21}; Jos. 16^{10} = Jud. 1^{29}; Jos. 17^{11-13} = Jud. $1^{27f.}$. As these passages, which in Judges stand in good connexion, are in Joshua broken up and scattered, fitting so loosely in the context that it would frequently gain by their removal, and strikingly at variance with the prevailing tenor of the book, the explanation which first suggests itself is that they have been inserted in Joshua directly from Judges by a relatively late hand.[*] Against this must be set, however, the fact, properly emphasized by Budde, that in more than one of these parallels, Jos. has preserved the original text, while in Jud. it has been intentionally altered ; see especially v.[10. 20. 19. 21]. This is better explained by supposing that the extracts in Joshua were made, not from Jud. 1, but from the history from which the latter chapter was taken.[†] The hypothesis is confirmed by the fact that, as Dillmann [‡] and Budde [§] have shown, there are other passages in Joshua, to which there is no parallel in Jud. 1, which are almost certainly derived from the same source, viz. Jos. 13[13] (cf. Jud. 1[27. 29. 31]) 19[47] &, and especially 17[14-18].[‖]

This source was not improbably J's history of the conquest.[¶] The author of the Book of Joshua uses J pretty freely in the beginning of his history of the invasion down to the taking of Ai and the treaty with the Gibeonites (8. 9) ; but in the following chapters, which narrate the great victories of Joshua (10–12), and the division of the land (13 ff.), he abandons this source, assumably because its account of the gradual and imperfect subjugation of Canaan by the tribes severally was irreconcilable with his own unhistorical representation of the complete conquest of the land by Joshua at the head of all Israel, the extermination of all its inhabitants, and partition of the conquered territory. Jud. 1[1]–2[5], with the cognate fragments in Jos. 13 ff., accords very well with the undoubted excerpts from J in Jos. 1–9 ; the whole tenor and style of the narrative resembles that of J in the Pentateuch ; as

---

[*] So Hävernick, Bl., Be., Mey., Kue., *HCO²*, Reuss, *al.* — On the relation between these passages in Jos. and Jud., there are other special investigations by Welte, 1842; Keil, *Z. Luth. Th.* 1846, p. 1 ff. The hypothesis that Jud. 1 is a compilation from the Book of Jos. (Stähelin, *Krit. Untersuchungen*, p. 102 ff.; Preiss, *ZWTh.* 1892, p. 496) is sufficiently refuted by the facts stated above in the text. Further, Jud. 1 contains other matter of the same sort (*e.g.* v.[22-27]) which has no parallel in Jos. That this also once stood in Jos., and was omitted, perhaps by R[d], an alternative proposed by Di. (*NDJ.* p. 442), is not probable.

[†] So Ke., Orelli, Kue., *HKO¹.*, Bu., Matthes, Kitt., Kö.   [‡] *NDJ.* p. 442.

[§] *Richter und Samuel*, p. 25 ff. Cf. also Wellh.-Bleek⁴, p. 182 = *Composition d. Hex.*, p. 214.

[‖] This meets the argument of Kue. (*HCO².* i. p. 358) that it is improbable that the editor of Jos. should have independently excerpted from his source exclusively matters which are found in Jud. 1.

[¶] Schrader-De Wette, *Einleitung⁸*, p. 327. Mey., Di., Stä., Bu., Kitt., Co.

particular indications may be noted the precedence of Judah, the name Canaanites, the resort to the oracle, the Angel of Yahweh. The only positive argument of considerable weight on the other side is the meagreness of the relation in Jud. 1, the almost statistical character of much of it, in contrast to the free and vivid narration of J.[*] If, however, as there is independent reason for believing, the editor of Jud. 1 has greatly abridged the older history, this loses much of its force.

The age of the original of Jud. 1 cannot be certainly determined from anything in the chapter itself. It is inferred from v.[21] (the Benjamites live with the Jebusites in Jerusalem " unto this day ") that it was written before the conquest of Zion by David, 2 S. 5 ;[†] but 2 S. 24[16ff.] shows that the Jebusites were not expelled by David ; cf. also 1 K. 9[20f.].[‡] On the other hand, v.[28. 33] describe a state of things which can hardly have existed before the reign of David or Solomon ; v.[29] (cf. 𝔊 and Jos. 16[10]) is probably to be read in the light of 1 K. 9[16], which would bring us down at least to the time of Solomon. There are no historical references in the chapter which conflict with our ascription of it to J.

Whether this be its origin or not, Jud. 1 is, beyond dispute, one of the most precious monuments of early Hebrew history. It contains an account of the invasion and settlement of Western Palestine entirely different from that given in the Book of Joshua, and of vastly greater historical value. In Joshua, the united armies of Israel, under the command of Joshua, in two campaigns (10. 11) conquer all Palestine from the Lebanon to the southern desert, and ruthlessly exterminate its entire population. The land is partitioned among the tribes (13 ff.), who have only to enter and take possession of the territory allotted to them. In Jud. 1, on the contrary, the tribes invade the land singly, or as they are united by common interest ; they fight for their own hand with varying success, or settle peaceably among the older population.

---

[*] König, *Einleitung*, p. 252 f. König exaggerates, however, when he speaks of Jud. 1 as an "ungeschmückte, wortarme Zusammenstellung von Thatsachen." Against the ascription of the chapter to J, see also Be., p. xviii., and Kue., *HCO*². i. p. 357.   [†] Ba., Ke., Cass., Kö., with Jewish (Ki.) and older Christian scholars.

[‡] Budde ("Critical Notes on the Hebrew Text of Samuel") understands 2 S. 5[8] itself as forbidding the slaughter of the Jebusites.

The larger cities with few exceptions, the fertile valleys, and the seaboard plain remain in the hands of the Canaanites. For long, the Israelites were really masters only in the mountains of Central and Southern Canaan, and the two strongest tribes, Joseph and Judah, were completely separated from each other by a line of Canaanite strongholds having Jerusalem as its salient.[*] On the other side, the Great Plain and the fortified cities along its southern margin separated Joseph from the tribes which settled farther north.

Which of these two conflicting representations of the Israelite invasion is the truer, cannot be for a moment in question. All that we know of the history of Israel in Canaan in the succeeding centuries confirms the representation of Jud. that the subjugation of the land by the tribes was gradual and partial; that not only were the Canaanites not extirpated, but that many cities and whole regions remained in their possession; that the conquest of these was first achieved by the kings David and Solomon. On the other hand, the whole political and religious history of these centuries would be unintelligible if we were to imagine it as beginning with such a conquest of Canaan as is narrated in the Book of Joshua. The song of Deborah alone is sufficient to prove this representation altogether false.

From the place in which it stands, and the fact that several of the most important things related in it, such as the taking of Hebron, are also narrated in Jos. in connexion with the conquests of Joshua, Jud. 1 has sometimes been explained as, in the main, a recapitulation of events which happened in the lifetime of Joshua. So Thdt., *quaest.*, 7 (cf. 1), Ki., Abarb., Cler., Schm., Ziegler, Hgstb., Böhl. But, as has been observed above, the parallel passages in Joshua are not an organic part of that book, with whose entire conception of the character of the conquest they but ill accord, and therefore their position does not prove that the events they relate occurred at the time to which they are ascribed by their present context. Others, following the title, v.[1a], put the events related in Jud. 1 "after the death of Joshua."[†] So among

---

[*] The cities named in Jud. 1[35], and those of the Gibeonite confederation, Jos. 9[17]; see Stade, *Z.A.T.W.* i. p. 147; Budde, *Richter und Samuel*, p. 17.

[†] The parallels in Jos. are then explained as anticipatory; that is, the author of that book, in narrating the conquests of Israel, for the sake of completeness, introduced, out of their chronological order, certain things which were not accomplished till a later time; Aug., *quaest.*, 3 (but cf. 6), *Glossa ord.*, Ra; RLbG., Brenz, Ba., *al.* Others, while putting the greater part of the chapter after the death of

modern scholars, Ke., Ba., Be., Cass. This title of the canonical editor (see comm.) is, however, of no authority. In point of fact, the situation presupposed in Jud. 1 and the invasion there described, is, in its character and results, inconceivable if the land in all its length and breadth had already been conquered and its inhabitants exterminated by Joshua. We require, at least, some reference to the revolution by which all the results of Joshua's wars were lost; we must know who sowed the land with dragon's teeth, that in the place of the population which Joshua destroyed, — man, woman, and child, — another generation better able to defend its own sprang up in a night. In default of this, the commentators and historians who treat Jud. 1 as a continuation of the history of the conquest after the death of Joshua are constrained to reduce to the uttermost the extent and importance of Joshua's victories. These victories, it is said, broke the power of the Canaanite confederacies in the north and south, so that they no longer presented a formidable front in the field, but by no means resulted in the subjugation of all Canaan. The fortified towns defied the invaders, or were speedily recovered by them. All over the land, as soon as the first wave of conquest passed, the Canaanites raised their heads again. The reduction of the strongholds, and the occupation of the territory allotted to each, was left to the tribes severally. In this task, some were more persistent and successful than others; some soon came to terms with the people of the land. It is this phase of the struggle that is described in Jud. 1. The harmony thus established between Jos. and Jud. is only attained by substituting for the story of the conquest in Jos. 10–12 a rationalistic version which is as irreconcilable with the text of Jos. as Jud. 1 itself. Of such fruitless victories as left all the work to be done over, of strongholds unsubdued, or Canaanites left to garrison them, the Book of Joshua knows nothing. The register of Joshua's conquests, the cities which he gave to the tribes of Israel for a possession (ch. 12), contains not only the names of the cities which in Jud. 1 are taken by the several tribes (Hebron, Debir, Bethel), but of the far more numerous cities which, as we know both from Jud. 1 and the later history, remained Canaanite for generations, — Jerusalem, Gezer, Taanach, Megiddo, etc.

Jud. 1 can therefore only be understood as a history of the first conquests and settlements of the Israelite tribes in Western Palestine, a counterpart to the Book of Joshua, whose representation it contravenes at all essential points. So Stud., We., Mey., Sta., *GVI.* I. p. 66 l.; Kue., Bu., Kitt., Dr., Co.

In spite of the fundamental contradiction, there are striking agreements between the story of the conquest in Jos. and Jud. 1. The struggle begins in the south (Adoni-zedek, king of Jerusalem, and Adoni-bezek, who dies at Jerusalem); the settlement of Judah and its affined clans is followed by that of Joseph (Jos. 14⁴⁻¹⁵ 15¹⁻¹². ¹³⁻¹⁹ 16¹ff. 17¹⁴⁻¹⁴); the other tribes are provided for

---

Joshua, have referred certain of the events narrated in it to the last years of his life; so Chytraeus (v.⁸⁻¹⁶), Eichh. (v.¹⁰⁻¹⁵), Schnurrer (v.¹⁰⁸⁻³¹); or without attempting to discriminate, v. Lengerke, Wahl.

later, and their standing is different from that of the great southern and central tribes (Jos. 18¹ᶠᶠ·). Jos. 11 is unquestionably related to Jud. 4 (Jabin of Hazor), as Jos. 10 is to Jud. 1⁵⁻⁷. The account of the conquest in Joshua is the product of successive theological reconstructions of the history. Its basis seems to have been a relation closely akin to the original of Jud. 1, if not identical with it; but this historical basis is completely transformed by the ascription of the doings of the several tribes to all Israel, and of the events of succeeding generations to the first period of the invasion, and by the substitution of the theological ideal of a conquest by the people of Yahweh for the sober reality.

I. 1ᵃ· Title. — *After the death of Joshua*] cf. Jos. 1¹. From the hand of the canonical editor to divide the books of Jos. and Jud.* The death of Joshua marked the close of the period of conquest, as that of Moses (Dt. 34⁵ᶜ·) the end of the Exodus and wandering. The division is therefore a natural one, and the title stands in a suitable place after Jos. 24²⁹·³⁰.† What immediately follows, however (1¹ᵇ–2⁵), does not relate things which took place after the death of Joshua, but is an account of the invasion of Canaan and its results, running parallel to Jos., but giving a wholly different representation; see above, p. 7–9.

I. 1ᵇ-8. The Israelites inquire of the oracle what tribe shall first attack the Canaanites. Judah is designated, and, making common cause with Simeon, invades the land. They defeat and capture Adoni-bezek.

The original connexion of 1¹ᵇ is lost. It must have been preceded at least by an account of the passage of the Jordan and the taking of Jericho, the remains of which are probably still to be recognized in the composite narrative in Jos.; perhaps also by a preliminary division of the land to be conquered (v.³). Whether we should also include an account of the operations against Ai (Jos. 8) and the oldest version of the ruse of the Gibeonites (Jos. 9) is more doubtful.‡

---

* See Doorn. p. 17, and esp. Paine, *Bibliotheca Sacra*, 1891, p. 652 ff. A somewhat similar suggestion is made by Ziegler, *Theol. Abhandlungen*, i. (1791), p. 282.

† This ending of Jos. 24 is, however, itself probably restored by the editor from Jud. 2ᵃ⁻¹⁰; see above, p. 4. The natural place for the title in the original context would be before Jud. 2¹¹.

‡ See on these questions, Mey., *ZATW*. i. p. 136; Bu., *Richter und Samuel*, p. 50 ff.; Kitt., *GdH*. i. 1. p. 245 ff.

1. *The Israelites inquired of Yahweh*] consulted the oracle of Y.; cf. 18⁵. The phrase does not occur in the Hexateuch, in which the only reference to the consultation of the oracle (Nu. 27²¹ P.) is differently expressed. It is used not only of the oracle of Yahweh, but of a 'stock' (Hos. 4¹²); teraphim (Ez. 21²⁶); manes (1 Chr. 10¹³). It is natural here to think of the priestly oracle (18⁵ 1 S. 22¹⁰·¹³·¹⁵), by the ephod (1 S. 23⁹ 30⁷), or urim and thummim (1 S. 14⁴¹ ⅁). As in the Pentateuch the latter is in the hands of the High Priest only, Jewish and many Christian interpreters have inferred that the response on this occasion was given by Phineas, son of Eleazar,* but it is unsafe to ascribe this intention to the author, who more probably has in mind the oracle at Gilgal (2¹), long one of the most frequented holy places. The Israelites are, of course, the tribes which settled west of the Jordan.† The story supposes them encamped together in the plain near Jericho (1¹⁶) and Gilgal (2¹), from which point they separate, Judah and Simeon to invade the south, Joseph to occupy the central highlands.

That the tribes, which before the death of Joshua had taken possession of their partially subjugated allotments, now held a council at Shiloh (Procop., a Lap., Ba.) to plan measures against the Canaanites who were left in their several territories; that from the council they returned home and opened a series of campaigns in different parts of the land, Judah making the first attack (Ba.), is a figment without the slightest warrant in the text.

Their question is not, Who shall lead us in a joint expedition?‡ or, What tribe shall have the hegemony?§ but, What tribe shall first invade its own region?‖ as the response and the following narrative clearly show, and as, indeed, the language requires. — *The Canaanites*] collective name for the inhabitants of the land; see on 3³. Those who find in Jud. 1 a continuation of the history in Jos. are compelled to explain the words of the Canaanites who remained unsubdued in the territory of the several tribes,¶ an

---

* Fl. Jos., *antt.* v. 2, 1 § 120; cf. Jud. 20ᵗᶠ. The death of Eleazar is recorded in Jos. 24³³ (cf. ⅁) in close connexion with that of Joshua.

† That they were accompanied and aided in the conquest of the land by the contingent of the tribes east of the Jordan is the representation of E and D.

‡ ⅁LS, Aug., other Ff.   § Fl. Jos., Euseb., Ephr. Syr., Schm., Ew.

‖ Rabb., a Lyra, Masius, Drus., C'er., most moderns.

¶ Procop., Rabb., Brenz, and many.

interpretation which is neither warranted by the text here, nor consonant with the representation of Jos. (cf. 11[16-20]).* — **2.** The oracle designates Judah. In Jos. also the first victories of Israel are gained in the south (ch. 10), and Judah is the first of the tribes west of the Jordan to receive its allotment (ch. 14. 15). It has been suggested above that the author of Joshua had before him an account of the invasion of Canaan strongly resembling Jud. 1. Whether this precedence of Judah, like the part assigned to Judah in J's story of Joseph and his brethren, is to be attributed to the Judahite origin of the narrative, or whether it may preserve a reminiscence of the fact that Judah was the first of the tribes to establish itself in Canaan, cannot well be decided.† —**3.** *Judah said to Simeon his brother*] utique tribus ad tribum (Aug). Simeon was the "brother" of Judah, not only as all the tribes of Israel were brethren, but in the closer kindred of the Leah tribes (Gen. 29[32-33]). The seats of Simeon were in the south of Judah; its towns (Jos. 19[1-9]) were all within the limits of Judah, and in Jos. 15[26-32, 42] are included in the list of the latter tribe (cf. also 1 Chr. 4[28-33]). On Simeon see further below, on v.[17]. Judah proposes that they unite their forces for the invasion, first of the territory of Judah, and then of the more southern district which fell to Simeon. The words imply that the invasion had not yet begun; the two tribes are encamped, with the others, at a point outside of the territory which they subsequently occupied, at Gilgal,‡ as we are to infer not only from 2[1] but probably also from Jos. 14-16; see below. — *Into my allotted territory*] The tribes go up, not to conquer for themselves a lot,§ but each to conquer its own lot. It is clearly presupposed that there was an understanding among them before the beginning of the invasion in what quarter each was to seek its fortune, a preliminary division

---

* See above, the last note, and p. 8 f.

† It is thought by some scholars that Judah entered the land, not from the east, as is assumed in the passage before us, in agreement with all the other sources, but from the south (Graf, *Simeon*, p. 15 f., Kuen., Land, Tiele, Doorn.; cf. Bud., *Richter u. Samuel*, p. 41). I am inclined to think that this is true of Caleb, but not of Judah; see below on v.[10. 20].

‡ Not at Shechem (Be.), or at Shiloh (Ba.); the conquest of this region by Joseph falls, according to the representation of our chapter, after the invasion of the South by Judah.   § Wellhausen.

of the land to be conquered.* It is probable that in its original connexion, v.¹ᵇ was preceded by an account of this partition, and possible that traces of this account may be found in Jos. 14⁶ᶠᶠ· 15¹ᶠᶠ· (Judah) and 16¹ᶠ· (Joseph). It is noteworthy that in Jos. 14–16 these tribes only have their territory assigned to them at Gilgal. In what manner the author of Jud. 1 conceived this division to have been made, we cannot certainly make out ; the reference to the oracle (v.¹ᶜ) and the term " allotment " suggest the sacred lot ; cf. Jos. 18⁶⁻¹⁰. Whether such a partition of the land actually took place is a question for historical criticism ; † the language of these verses leaves no doubt that the author so represented it.

1. שאל באלהים, שאל ביהוה] 18⁵ 20¹⁸·²³·²⁷; freq. (11 t.) in Sam. The ב is originally local; cf. דרש ב, דרש אל, &c. —עלה אל] *march up to, against.* The hostile sense, oftener expressed by על, is sufficiently indicated in the context; cf. עלה ב, *invade* (a region, country), v.³ Nu. 13²¹ Is. 7⁶. —לנו] expressing the common interest; cf. Dt. 30¹²·¹³. We should more likely say, who *of us.* —בתחלה] lit. *at the beginning.* התחלה (inf. n. of החל, *begin*) is not used of order in place or rank but of inception in time; cf. 10¹⁸ מי האיש אשר יחל להלחם בבני עמון, who will first attack the Ammonites.‡ —2. נתתי את הארץ ביד] *I deliver . . . into his power,* give up to him, v.⁴ 2¹⁴ 3¹⁰ 4⁷ and often, especially in the introductions to the stories of the judges, Ex. 23³¹ Jos. 21⁴². &c. The pf. represents the future as, in the thought and purpose of the speaker, already an accomplished fact, an unalterable certainty; Dr.⁸ § 13, Ges.²⁶ § 106, 3 *a.* —3. בגורלי] *in sortem meam* (Aug., 𝔏ᵛᵍ), not *in sorte mea* (𝔏codd. plur. edd., Ba.). גורל is *allotment,* allotted portion of territory, Jos. 17¹⁴·¹⁷, eventually, like κλῆρος, *portion, estate.* —עלה . . . . ונלחמה . . . . והלכתי] *go up with me . . . and let us fight . . . and I will go with thee.* Bidding and promise, cf. v.²⁴. When the bidding or asking clause is felt to be logically dependent, such sentences pass over into the class of conditionals, If you go with me, I will go with you (Paul, *Principien der Sprachgeschichte²,* p. 124).

4. The verse is superfluous ; except the ten thousand slain — a round number for which we need hardly seek an historical source — it tells us nothing which we do not read in the context. By the side of v.⁵⁻⁷ it occasions serious difficulty. As an anticipative

---

* But that Jud. 1 presupposes the great cadaster, Jos. 15–21, and would be unintelligible without it (Be.), cannot be admitted. For the necessary knowledge of the seats and bounds of the tribes, the author's contemporaries did not need to consult the domesday book.

† See Kitt., *GdH.* i. 1. p. 246 f.; Bu., *Richt. u. Sam.,* p. 41 f.

‡ On Jud. 20¹⁸, see note there.

general statement of the result of the campaign which is related
in detail in v.⁵⁻⁷,* it is very clumsy; nor are the interpretations
more satisfactory which refer v.⁴ and ⁵ to successive moments in
the invasion, whether, with Bertheau, we suppose that after a first
·defeat near Bezek, in which he lost 10,000 men, Adoni-bezek
threw himself into the town, where he was again attacked and put
to flight; or, with Cassel, that in the first battle Adoni-bezek was
not engaged.   In either case, we should expect the narrator to
explain in some way the relation between the two defeats of the
same people at the same place.   Probably the redactor, having
abridged his source by omitting the beginning of the story of
Adoni-bezek, filled its place with these general phrases borrowed
from the context.

E. Meyer (*ZATW.* i. p. 135) regards v.⁴ (except הברם and perh. the
number 10,000) as derived from J, and rejects v.⁵ as repetition; he finds
other grounds for suspicion in v.⁷ᵇ compared with v.²¹, and in the use of
אלהים, v.⁷ᵃ, though he does not deny that the story of Adoni-bezek may have
an historical basis.   Kue. doubts the whole of v.⁴⁻⁷ on historical grounds;
Matthes ascribes v.⁶,⁷ to the last hand (canonical editor).   See against Mey.
and Kue., Bu., *Richt. u. Sam.*, p. 3 f.   Kitt. (*GdH.* i. 1. p. 241) thinks that in
v.⁴ the words, *And Y. gave the Canaanites into their power,* may be genuine,
which is certainly not impossible.

Judah alone is named (cf. v.⁸·⁹·¹⁰ — prob. all secondary). —
Their·hand . . . they smote] the men of Judah; the common
distributive plural with a collective noun.   On the Canaanites and
Perizzites, and on Bezek, see on v.⁵. — *Ten thousand men*] 3²⁹
(they slew of Moab ten thousand men) 4⁶ 7³ 20³⁴ 2 K. 14⁷ &c.;
a common round number. — 5. *They came upon Adoni-bezek at
Bezek*] if v. 4 (Judah went up) is from the hand of an editor, the
plural probably referred originally to the allies, Judah and Simeon,
v.³.   There is good reason to suspect that the beginning of the
story of Adoni-bezek, which would have told us who he was, and
perhaps something of the circumstances under which the allies
encountered him, has been omitted by the editor. — *Bezek*] the
name occurs in the O.T. only in 1 S. 11⁸, where Saul musters at
Bezek the force he has raised for the relief of Jabesh Gilead.   The
Bezek of 1 S. 11 is, without doubt, the modern Khirbet Ibzîq, 14

---

* Aburb., Schm., Ke., Bu.

Engl. miles SSW. of Beisān, and a somewhat less distance from
the mouth of Wady Yābis, of which it lies directly west. Many
scholars identify the place in our text with this Bezek.* The
situation, however, does not meet the requirements of the narrative at all. At the beginning of the story, Judah and Simeon set
out from the neighbourhood of Gilgal to invade the region in which
they were afterward settled ; its end (v. 7) brings us to Jerusalem,
and we should naturally infer that the battle took place at no
great distance from that city.† Ibzīq lies wholly outside of this
sphere of action, and in an opposite direction. Others have
therefore supposed that there was another, hitherto unidentified,
Bezek in Judah, ‡ and if the text be sound, this seems necessary. §
Budde thinks that the name Bezek was introduced by an editor,
who derived it merely from the name of the king Adoni-bezek ;
but after the words "they came upon A.," an indication of the
scene of the encounter is certainly expected,‖ and this gap would
not be filled by the words "king of Jerusalem," which Budde conceives originally to have stood in this place. A more serious difficulty is the name Adoni-bezek. This is generally explained, Lord
of Bezek ; but such a formation is altogether anomalous. No compound names of persons in Hebrew are made in this way from the
name of a town, nor — if we should evade this objection by taking
the words appellatively ¶ — is *adōn* used like *melek* of the sover-
eign of a city or country. In names compounded with *adōn*, the
second part is uniformly the name of a god,** Adoni-zedek (Adōnī-
Ṣedeq), Adoniram (Adōnī-Ram), Adonijah (Adōnī-Yahu).†† If

---

* Euseb., Ki., Ew., Hitz., Di., Stud., Be., Ke., MV., SS., al.

† This is confirmed by Jos. 10, according to which the Israelites, coming up
from Gilgal, encounter the enemy at Gibeon.

‡ Cler., Rosenm., v. Raum., Ba., Grove, al.

§ Sandys (1610) notes a Bezek 2 m. from Bethzur (Reland, p. 663), which does
not seem to have been heard of by more recent travellers. Conder would identify
Bezek with Bezkah, 6 m. SE. of Lydda (*SWP. Memoirs*, iii. p. 36). Schotanus
suggested Bozkath (בצקת), Jos. 15³⁹. Cass. takes the noun appellatively, the 'stony
desert' W. of the Dead Sea, without support in Heb. or intrinsic probability.

‖ The words ἐν τῇ Βεζεκ are lacking, however, in 𝕲⁵⁶. ⁸⁹. ¹⁰⁸. τ, perhaps by accident.

¶ So 𝕾.   ** The same is true of compounds of *melek*.

†† Similarly in Phœn.: אדנאנכר, אדנגרבל, אדנשמש. The one apparent exception
in the O.T., Adonikam, Ezr. 2¹³, is differently formed, and, moreover, probably
corrupt; Neh. 10¹⁷ gives him the name Adonijah. See Renan, *Hist. d'Israel*, i.
p. 241; Bu., *Richt. u. Sam.*, p. 64.

the name Adoni-bezek is sound, Bezek must be an otherwise
unknown god, whose name, we might then suppose, the town also
bore. The question is further complicated by Jos. 10, where, in
an account which, notwithstanding its radical divergences, is parallel to Jud. 1¹⁻⁷, and based on the same or a closely similar
source, the head of the Canaanite confederacy which first makes
front against the Israelite invaders is Adoni-zedek, king of Jerusalem. The latter is a normal formation which has a striking parallel in Melchi-zedek (Malki-Ṣedeq),* king of Jerusalem (Gen. 14).
It seems probable, therefore, that in the place of the problematical
Adoni-bezek, king (v.⁷) of some nameless city,† the original of
Jud. 1 (J) had Adoni-zedek, king of Jerusalem. ‡

Bezek (בזק)] Euseb. (*O.S².* 237₅₂) notes two neighbouring villages of the name,
17 R. m. from Neapolis, on the road to Scythopolis (Beth-shean). This is the
Khirbet Ibziq of the Engl. Survey (*Great Map*, sh. 12; *Memoirs*, ii. p. 231,
237), 14 E. m. from Nābulus, with which Eshtori Parchi (A.D. 1322; ed. Venet.
fol. 66ᵃ) had already identified it. — *Adoni-bezek*] Jerome (*O.S².* 31₈ cf. 231₇)
interprets *dominus fulminis*, or *dominus meus fulgurans*. The former might
seem to be a possible Hebrew name; cf. Barak (ch. 4. 5); Βοανεργες (Mar. 3¹⁷);
Scipiades, belli fulmina, &c. But אדני is not used like בעל of the possessor of
a quality or attribute, and בזק *fulmen* rests solely on the probably corrupt text
of Ez. 1¹⁴. The identity of Adoni-bezek, Jud. 1, and Adoni-zedek, Jos. 10,
which was discussed by older Catholic commentators (see *e.g.* a Lapide), is
accepted by many recent critics. § Against the hypothesis adopted above in
the text, Bu. and We. contend that the original form of the name was Adoni-
bezek, as in Jud.; Adoni-zedek in Jos. being an intentional differentiation
in some way connected with Melchi-zedek, Gen. 14. In support of this view
the fact is adduced that in Jos. the MSS. of 𝔊, with singular unanimity,
exhibit Αδωνιβεζεκ (cf. also *O.S².* 265₁₉; 132₄ 231₇); unintentional conformation of 𝔊 in Jos. to Jud. is less probable, it is argued, than differentiation
in 𝔐 for harmonistic reasons, which also led to the omission in Jud. of the
title, king of Jerusalem. But since Adoni-zedek is regularly formed and
supported by analogy, while Adoni-bezek is quite anomalous, it seems more

---

* צדק, Συδυκ (Philo Bybl.), is the name of a Canaanite deity; cf. אדריצדק (name
of a king) on coins (Bloch, *Phoen. Glossar*, p. 55). Cf. צדרא, צדריקב, in S. Arabia
(Praetorius, in *ZDMG.* xxvi. p. 426).

† It is to be particularly observed that he is not called king of Bezek. On the
other hand, the end of his history, v.⁷, shows that he was in some way connected
with Jerusalem.

‡ The last words would naturally stand, not here (Bu.), but at the first introduction of his name, now omitted.

§ The opposite opinion is defended by Kitt., *GdH.* i. 1. p. 277 f.

probable that if there was any intentional change it was in the latter, not in the former.* The motive for such a change need not have been purely harmonistic; this may be one of the not infrequent perversions of proper names by a contemptuous and silly wit, such as perhaps turned חרם מלך 2⁹ into ה׳ מ׳ Jos. 24³¹.† A third variation of this name is exhibited by Fl. Jos., *antt.* v. 2, 2 § 121 (on Jud. 1), Steph. Byz., Procop. Gaz. (on Jud. 1), 𝔊ᴵᴷ·¹⁵⁴ in Jos. 10¹, viz., Ἀδωνιζεβεκ (Ζεβεκ, Ζεβέκη). Whether this is a corruption in Greek, or represents an (intermediate?) variation in Heb., can hardly be determined.

The Canaanites and the Perizzites] the Perizzites coupled with the Canaanites, v.⁴ Gen. 13⁷ 34³⁰ (J), and frequently in the catalogue of the peoples of Palestine, the "seven nations" of Dt. 7¹.‡ We know nothing more about them. "The land of the Perizzites and the Rephaim (giants)," Jos. 17¹⁵,§ is probably a gloss or a corruption, and it is extremely precarious to infer from this collocation, taken with the absence of the name in Gen. 10, that the Perizzites belonged to a still older population which the Canaanites had supplanted and reduced to villeinage.‖ It may rather be questioned whether they were in reality a 'people' (tribe, clan) at all, or only a class of the Canaanite population, the inhabitants of peasant villages, as the name suggests.

הפרזי [פרזי Dt. 3⁵ 1 S. 6¹⁸ are the inhabitants of unwalled villages, פרזות Ez. 38¹¹; cf. MH., *Meg.* 19ᵃ. It is possible that these Canaanite peasants were later imagined to have been a distinct people, and that the pronunciation פרזי is an artificial discrimination from the appellative use. 𝔊 apparently knew nothing of this distinction; for it has Φερεζαῖοι in Dt. and Sam. also, where the later Greek translators render ἀτείχιστοι.

6. *They cut off his thumbs and great toes*] the mutilation doubly disabled him for fighting, and probably also disqualified him for reigning. Clericus quotes from Aelian, *var. hist.*, ii. 9, the story that the Athenians voted to cut off the right thumb of every Aeginetan they captured, ἵνα δόρυ μὲν βαστάζειν μὴ δύνωνται, κώπην δὲ ἐλαύ-

---

* That in Jos. the corruption has infected 𝔊, but not 𝔐, is of no great significance; cf. the variations of 𝔊 in Jud. 2⁹ Jos. 24³⁰ cited below.

† Such wit would be capable of giving a contemptuous twist to בזק.

‡ On these lists, see below, on 3⁶.

§ Wanting in 𝔊.

‖ Dillm., *BL.* iv. p. 46a, cf. *NDJ.* p. 540; Kautzsch, *HWB.*¹ ii. p. 1193.

c

ναν δύνωνται.* Hannibal, according to Valer. Max., ix. 2, ext. 2, mutilated prisoners of war, prima pedum parte succisa. After the surrender of Uxellodunum, Caesar cut off the hands of all who had borne arms (*bell. gall.*, viii. 44). — 7. *Seventy kings, &c.*] This sounds more like a savage boast than the note of contrition, though he recognizes a retribution in his fate. The obvious exaggeration is no reason for questioning the genuineness of the verse,† nor for the conjecture that the number has been raised from *seven*, ‡ nor for supplying in thought, "at different times." § The table was a small, low stand, around which those who partook of the meal sat on the ground, or which was placed before them as they sat upon chairs or couches.‖ We are not, therefore, to imagine the kings actually under the table, but as gathering up from the ground, like dogs (Matt. 15²⁷, *Odyss.* xvii. 309), the fragments which fell as their master ate ; and we may perhaps best represent this if we think of him as sitting, like Saul (1 S. 20²⁵), upon a divan by the wall with the table before him.¶ — *They brought him to Jerusalem, and he died there*] the common, and indubitably the most natural interpretation of these words, viz. that the Israelites, as they now marched to attack Jerusalem (v. 8), carried their captive with them, is beset by great difficulty. The author of this story of the conquest tells us plainly that the invaders were unable to dislodge the Jebusites from Jerusalem (Jos. 15⁶³ Jud. 1²¹) ; — v.⁸, which says the opposite, is for that reason by another and a later hand. To relieve this difficulty, several recent scholars ⁕⁕ give the verb in v.⁷ᵇ an indefinite subject, men brought him, he was brought, *sc.* by his own people, to

---

* The story is repeated or referred to by Xen., *hist. gr.*, ii. 1, 31 ; Plut., *vit. Lys.*, 9 ; Cic., *de off.*, iii. 11 ; Valer. Max., ix. 2, ext. 8. Whether it is true, or only a Peloponnesian slander (K. O. Müller), it shows that such atrocities were not inconceivable even in Greek warfare. Examples among the Persians, Quint. Curt., iii. 20, v. 17 ; Diod. Sic., xvii 69 ; Arabs, Ew., *GVI.* ii. p. 494 n.

† Kue.   ‡ Kitt.   § Ba.

‖ Seemingly the oldest custom among the Egyptians and the Homeric Greeks also ; cf. Erman, *Aegypten u. aeg. Leben*, p. 262 f. ; Buchholz, *Homerische Realien*, ii. 2, p. 161 ff. ; Baumeister, *Denkmäler*, p. 1817 f. ; Lane, *Modern Egyptians⁶*, p. 142 ff. ; Thomson, *Land and Book²*, iii. p. 75 f. ; Benzinger, *Hebr. Archäologie*, p. 113. 123. Reclining at meals was a new foreign fashion in Israel in the 8th century ; see Am. 3¹² 6⁴.   ¶ See the cut in Thomson, *l.c.*, p. 76.

⁕⁕ Cass., Reuss, Bu., Kitt.

Jerusalem ; * a notice which becomes at once more intelligible and more significant if, as has been supposed, he was king of Jerusalem, and that city was not attempted by Judah at this time.

6. וְיָֽרֵן] Pi. *cut off, praecidere:* 2 S. 4¹² (hands and feet); cf. Qal Dt. 25¹². — בהנות ידיו ורגליו] pl. only here and v.⁷; sg. בֹּהֶן Ex. 29²¹ &c. The plural in 𝔐 is formed as from a sg. בֹהֶן which 𝔊ᵘᵐ has throughout in place of 𝔐ᵘᵈ בהן. Arab. has by the side of اِبْهَام the vulgar forms بِهَام and بَاهِم. The noun is prob. fem., like other names of members of the body (Ges.²⁵ § 122. 3 *c*; Stade, § 310 *c*); Gesen. made it masc. through misconstruction of v.⁷; in Arab. it has both genders, the fem. prevailing. — The annexion of two genitives to one noun occurs in Heb. only when the genitives naturally go together, or form a standing phrase, as in חית שבים וארץ Jer. 33²⁶; ארץ זנה חרב ורעב, Dt. 11⁹ Jer. 11⁶ &c.; see also Nu. 20⁸ Is. 22⁶; a striking example is Jud. 7²⁵ ראש ערב וואב. In Arabic the constr. is more freely used. 𝔊ᴬᴮᴺ has here καὶ τὰ ἄκρα τῶν ποδῶν αὐτοῦ, and it is possible that their Heb. conformed to the common construction, Ex. 29²⁰: 𝔊ᴸᴹ s ε support 𝔐. —7. שׁבעים מלכים בהנות ידיהם ורגליהם מקצצים] the ptcp. is to be taken with מלכים (circumstantial); בהנות is adv. accus. of determination (Stud., Be., Ges.²⁵ § 121. 2, n. 1; see Wright, *Arab. Gram.*, ii. § 44 *e*; Howell, *Arab. Gram.*, i. § 83 ff.); cf. 2 S. 15³² Neh. 4¹². For a different construction of these cases see Ew., § 288 *b* (De Sacy, *Gram. Arabe*, ii. § 320 f.; Fleischer, *Kl. Schriften*, i. p. 644). — היו מלקטים] Dr.³ § 135. 5; Ges.²⁵ § 116. 5 n., 2. — שֻׁלְחָן] in older texts only of the king's table (1 S. 20²⁹ and freq.). To be connected not with Heb. שׁדה (= سلم) 'send' (not 'spread out,' MV.), but with Aram. Syr. שְׁלַח (= سلم) 'strip off' (skin of an animal, clothing, &c.); אשׁלח שְׁלַח (MH. שָׁלַח) سَلَم 'skin, hide.' Like the Arab. سُفْرَة (from سفر 'sweep off, strip off'), it was originally a round mat of leather with a drawing-string in the edge, such as is still in use among the Bedawin, which, spread out on the ground, served for a table, drawn up, as a receptacle for food; and was subsequently applied to the wooden or metal tray set upon a stand, which in town life superseded this primitive arrangement. See Lane, *Arab.-Engl. Lex.*, p. 1371 B; Niebuhr, *Arabien*, 1772, p. 52; Doughty, *Arabia Deserta*, 1888, i. p. 148. Whether the name שׁלחן was given it in Heb. because it was originally of leather (Levy, *NHWb.* iv. p. 560), or because it was removed, stripped off, after using, can hardly be decided. The form of the noun is anomalous; Lagarde (*Bildung d. Nomina*, p. 204 f.) rightly regards it as of foreign type, and (with דְּרְבָּן, דְּרְבָּן, דָּרְבָן) borrowed from an Aramaic dialect. Barth (*Nominalbildung*, p. xxix n) explains the ā (instead of the normal ō) as the result

---

* Ges.²⁵ § 144. 3 *b*.; Green, § 245, 2.

of dissimilation, to avoid the sequence of rounded vowels *u* (*o*) *ō*. This is not satisfactory, because: 1, such dissimilation would more probably have affected the first vowel (giving *Jilḫōn*), as in the examples Barth himself has collected in the text; 2, the object of the dissimilation is not attained by substituting *ṭ* (*â = o*) for) (*ō*). םלׁש] *requite*; of divine retribution for evil deeds, Dt. 7¹⁹ Jer. 25¹⁴ &c. — אחרים] in the intercourse between men of different tribes, worshippers of different gods, the common name is naturally used; it is no reason for doubting the genuineness of the verse (Mey.).

8. Of the capture and destruction of Jerusalem as here narrated, there is no trace in the history. Even the Book of Joshua, which relates at large the overthrow of its king Adoni-zedek and the destruction of all the other cities of his confederacy, is significantly silent about Jerusalem (Jos. 10; cf. 12). In Jud. 19¹¹ᶜ it is a city of the Jebusites, "where there are no Israelites," and where, therefore, a belated wayfarer hesitates to seek hospitality. The taking of Jerusalem, with its stronghold Zion, is, in fact, one of the great achievements of David (2 S. 5⁶⁻⁹),* the memory of which is perpetuated in the name City of David. But we are not left to inferences; the author of the history from which Jud. 1 is derived tells us explicitly that the invaders did not — could not — gain possession of Jerusalem. We are fortunate enough to have this statement in two places which it is instructive to place side by side.

Jos. 15⁶³ The Jebusites inhabiting Jerusalem, *the Judahites could not* dispossess; and the Jebusites dwelt with *the Judahites* in Jerusalem, to this day.	Jud. 1²¹ The Jebusites inhabiting Jerusalem, *the Benjamites did not* dispossess; and the Jebusites dwelt with *the Benjamites* in Jerusalem, to this day.

These passages are identical even to the inverted order of the sentence; the only differences are indicated by the italic type. In this variation it can hardly be doubted that Jos. has preserved the original; the editor of Jud. has, as in other places in the chapter, changed *could not* to *did not* in conformity to his theory of the responsibility for this failure, and substituted *Benjamin* for *Judah* in harmony with the partition which allotted Jerusalem to the former tribe (Jos. 15⁸ 18¹⁶· ²⁸). For the converse changes (Stud., Be.), no reason can be assigned. The verse probably stood in the original immediately after v.⁷, or perhaps v.⁷· ¹⁹· ²¹.

---

* 1 S. 17⁵⁴, implying that Jerusalem was already a great holy place of Yahweh, is a gross anachronism.

That this statement, in its original form as it stands in Jos., proceeds from J there is no reason to doubt; it exactly corresponds in substance and form to Jud. 1[20f.]. It follows that v.[8], which flatly contradicts v.[21], cannot be genuine; it was probably inserted by an editor, who perhaps interpreted v.[7], as most commentators have done, to mean that Judah carried Adoni-bezek to Jerusalem, and supplied an express statement of what seemed to him to be necessarily inferred from v.[7b]. Whether this be its origin or not, the verse has no historical value.[*]

To harmonize v.[8] with v.[21] (Jos. 15[63]) and with the known facts, two principal hypotheses have been proposed: 1. They took and destroyed the lower city, but were unable to conquer the citadel (Fl. Jos., antt. v. 2, 2 § 124, cf. Procop. on v.[21]). Later the lower city was rebuilt, and inhabited by Judahites and Benjamites as well as Jebusites; but the latter, holding the castle, were the real masters of the city till the time of David (Cler., Schm., a Lapid., Abarb.). 2. Judah took the city and burned it as related in v.[8], but, as they did not occupy it, the Jebusites soon rebuilt and fortified it so strongly that neither Benjamin, in whose territory it lay, nor Judah, whose border it threatened, was able to reconquer it. After a time, during which it was wholly Jebusite (Jud. 19[11f.]), Judahites and Benjamites settled as metics beside the citizens of the place, and this relation continued till David's time, when, the power passing into Israelite hands, it was reversed (cf. Aug., quaest. 7, Thdt., Ew., Ke., Be., Reuss, Ba.). By the first of these hypotheses v.[8] and v.[21] are made to refer to different things, — the lower city, the citadel; by the second, to different periods, — at the beginning of the invasion, in later times; neither is consistent with the text; if such had been the author's meaning he would have made it plain. — וילחמו וג׳] the verbs cannot be taken as pluperf., *they had fought against J. and taken it, &c.* (Ki., Drus., al.), an interpretation which the syntax of Heb. tenses does not allow. — On Jerusalem and the Jebusites, see on 19[10]. — לפי חרב] see below, on v.[25]. — ואת העיר שלחו באש] 20[48] 2 K. 8[12] Ps. 74[7]; cf. וישלחו אש בביח Hos. 8[14] Am. 1[4.7.10] &c. The older comm. explained the first of these constructions as an hypallage for the second (see esp. Drus.); but such an artificial figure is not natural in prose. 'Cast into the fire' will hardly do, for in all cases in O.T. the obj. is a city or building; 'set on fire' is scarcely a parallel idiom; perhaps the origin of the phrase may be 'send off, get rid of, *by* fire.'

9–15. Judah wages the war in all parts of its territory; the taking of Hebron and Debir; the dowry of Caleb's daughter Achsah. — 9. The verse gives us nothing more than

---

[*] Hitz., GVI. i. p. 102; Stade, GVI. i. p. 161 n.

the familiar names of the three regions into which the territory of Judah was divided by nature, and on account of this general character is suspected.[*] — *The Highlands and the South and the Lowlands*, for the whole land of Judah, resembles Jos. 10[40] (D) 9[1] (Rd) Dt. 1[7] cf. Jer. 17[26] &c. Instead of Lowland (*shephelah*), the author of our history uses Plain (*'emeq*, v.[19.34]). Budde conjectures with considerable probability that the verse was inserted here by the editor in place of v.[19.21], when the latter verses were removed to their present position. Of the three regions named, the Highlands (RV. hill country) are the mountainous backbone of Southern Palestine, attaining its greatest elevation near Hebron ; the South is the steppe region which forms the transition to the true desert ; the Lowland is the coast plain including the Judæan foot-hills.

As the Dead Sea is far below the level of the Mediterranean, while the height of land is much nearer the former than the latter, the mountains of Judah fall off toward the east almost precipitously in three terraces; this is the Wilderness (מדבר) of Judah, a waterless, treeless waste, which only in spring shows a thin film of vegetation. — נגב] from a root not living in Heb., but in Aram. and Syr. meaning 'dry, dry up'; the name, therefore, is probably pre-Israelite. As the Negeb was the southernmost of the natural divisions of Palestine, the name acquired the sense 'south,' just as ים *sea* came to mean 'west.' — השפלה] sc. הארץ, *the low-lying land*. There was a *shephelah* of Israel (Jos. 11[16]), but the name is generally used without further definition for the southern part of the maritime plain, from Joppa to Gaza. It appears to be of Israelite origin.

10. In J the conquest of Hebron is ascribed to Caleb (Jos. 15[14]). In the passage before us Judah gains the victory (v.[10]) and afterwards cedes the city to Caleb (v.[20]). Closer examination of the text shows, however, that this is the work of the editor, and that the older history from which he extracts his material agreed with Jos. 15[14f], and was, in fact, identical with the source of the latter passage. As the story now runs in Jud. 1, Judah first defeats the three giants (v.[10]), and then Caleb drives them out (v.[20]) ; the subject of v.[11] can in its present connexion only be Judah, but the context imperatively requires that it should be Caleb. The text of the older narrative may be reconstructed by the aid of the parallel in Jos. :

Jos. 15[13] And to Caleb the son of Jephunneh he gave a portion in the midst of the Judahites, according to the commandment of Yahweh to Joshua,[*] Kiriath (i.e. the city of) Arba the father of (the) Anak (giants), that is Hebron. [14] And Caleb expelled from it the three sons of Anak, Sheshai, Ahiman, and Talmai, the children of Anak. [15] And he went up thence against the inhabitants of Debir, &c. [16] And Caleb said, &c.

Jud. 1[20] And they gave to Caleb Hebron, as Moses had bidden, and he expelled from it the three sons of Anak. v.[10] [And Judah went against the Canaanites who lived in Hebron — the ancient name of Hebron was Kiriath Arba —; and they smote] Sheshai, Ahiman, and Talmai. [11] And he went thence against the inhabitants of Debir, &c. [12] And Caleb said, &c.

The editor ascribes Caleb's conquest to Judah,[†] and makes it a victory over the Canaanites, where the older narrative spoke only of Anakim. To accomplish this, he removed v.[20] from the beginning of this story to the end of the account of the conquests of Judah and inserted the words enclosed in brackets (Bu., *Richt. u. Sam.*, p. 4 ff.).

Hebron, 22 Rom. miles S. of Jerusalem, [‡] in the highest part of the mountains of Judah, lies in a valley running from NW. to SE. The modern city is built partly in the bottom, partly on the slope of the eastern hill.[§] With the region south of it Hebron belonged to Caleb ; on this clan see note below on v.[15]. — *The name of Hebron in earlier times was Kirjath-arba*] Jos. 14[15], cf. "Kirjath-arba, that is Hebron" Gen. 23[2] 35[27] Jos. 15[54] 20[7], see also 15[13] 21[11]. The original meaning of the name is probably *Tetrapolis;* the peculiar construction of the numeral, which later scribes did not recognize, is evidence of its alien origin, if not of its remote antiquity. Hebron has not been discovered in the lists

---

* See Jos. 14[f–15].

† The next step in this progress was to attribute the conquest of Hebron and the extermination of the giants to Joshua and all Israel, Jos. 10[36f.] 11[21f.].

‡ O.S[2]. 209[99].

§ If it occupies exactly the ancient site, it was one of the very few cities in Palestine which did not stand on a hill. On Hebron see Rob., *BR[2].* i. p. 213 f., ii. p. 72 ff.; Rosen, *ZDMG.* xii. p. 477 ff.; Sepp, *Jerusalem*, i. p. 486–502; Guérin, *Judée*, iii. p. 214–256; Lortet, *Syrie*, p. 317–333; *SWP. Memoirs*, iii. p. 305–309, 333–346; Bäd[3]., p. 139 ff.; Wilson in *DB[2].*, *s.v.*

of places in Palestine conquered by Egyptian kings of the 18th
and 19th dynasties,[*] nor in the Amarna letters, although the authority of the governor of Jerusalem extended to places further
south. In Nu. 13[22] we are told that Hebron was built "seven
years before Zoan in Egypt," by which we should probably understand the restoration of the latter city at the beginning of the 19th
dynasty. — *They smote Sheshai, Ahiman, and Talmai*] Jos. 15[14]
Nu. 13[22]; the three giants (" sons of Anak ") whom Caleb drove
out (v.[20]). The editor has widely separated words which in J
stood in immediate connexion ; "he (*i.e.* Caleb) drove out the
three giants, Sheshai, Ahiman, and Talmai "; cf. Jos. 15[14]. The
names are of distinctively Aramaic type ; Talmai is the name of an
Aramæan king of Geshur, whose daughter was wife of David and
mother of Absalom (2 S. 3[3] 13[37]), and inscriptions recently found
at El-Ola near Teimā mention two kings of Lihhyān named
Talmī ; † Ahiman 1 Chr. 9[17], Sheshai (Shashai) Ezr. 10[40].

10. וישם חברון וג׳] parenthetic nominal sentence; perhaps an archaeological
gloss of the editor. —לפנים] *formerly, previously;* v.[11, 23] 3[3] &c. —קרבת ארבע]
the numeral *four* is recognized by Jerome (*de situ, etc.,* OS[2]. 84[10]) : Arbe,
id est quattuor, eo quod ibi tres patriarchae, Abraham, Isaac et Jacob, sepulti
sunt, et Adam magnus, ut in Jesu libro scriptum est (Jos. 14[15]). ‡ The same
Midrash, *Ber. rab.* § 58 (on Gen. 23[2]). Kirjath-arba is interpreted *Tetrapolis* by Luc. Osiander (1578), Ew., Furrer, Cass., Di., De., al.; with the
anomalous (not Hebrew) construction of the numeral cf. באר שבע *Seven
Wells.* Such a name might be given to a town in which four kindred or
confederate clans were settled in as many separate quarters; § compare the
Phœnician Tripolis — the native name has not been recovered — founded by
Tyre, Sidon, and Aradus. ‖ Later readers, however, took Arba as the name

---

* The identification of " Khibur " in inscriptions of Ramses III. with Hebron
(Sayce, *KP.* n. s. vi. p. 32, 39; *Higher Criticism,* p. 333, cf. 336 f.) is devoid of
all plausibility. Whether the name Hebron has anything to do with the *Habiri* so
often mentioned in the Amarna letters (Sayce, al.) is not yet clear.

† D. H. Müller, *Epigraphische Denkmäler aus Arabien,* p. 5; cited by Sayce,
Higher Criticism, p. 189.

‡ See also *ep.* 108, 11 (*Opp.* ed. Vall., i. 694), where he adds: licet plerique
Caleb quartum putent, cujus ex latere memoria monstratur.

§ It is conceivable that Hebron (? ' confederation') is of similar origin. — It is
worthy of note, though probably only an accidental coincidence, that the modern
city is divided into four quarters (Rosen, *ZDMG.* xii. 1858, p. 487) ; though its
recent growth makes the division less clearly marked than it was a few years ago.

‖ Strabo, xvi. 2, 15, p. 754; Diod. Sic., xvi. 41; Scylax, p. 42.

of a man, the ancestor of the giants of Hebron. So 𝔐 in Jos. 15¹³ 21¹¹ קרית, ‏14¹⁵ קרית ארבע האדם הגדול בענקים, ארבע אבי ענק, "the city of Arba, the greatest man among the Anakim." In all these places 𝔊 has preserved the original reading, πόλις A. μητρόπολις Ἐνακ (τῶν Ἐνακ, τῶν Ἐνακιμ), i.e. קרית ארבע אם הענק.* A later editor or scribe, who did not catch the sense, and took ארבע for a *masc.* pr. n., altered אם to אבי; האדם הגדול is another miscorrection. A kindred misapprehension of בני הענק (giants; see on v.²¹) made ענק also, in spite of the article, a man's name, and so provided the giants of Hebron with a genealogy reaching back two generations: Arba — Anak — Sheshai, Ahiman, Talmai (Ges., Stud., al.) — אחימן] so, as the noun type demands, Bomb¹., Mich.; the receptus אֲחִימָן is due to popular etymology, אחי כָן, *frater meus quis?* (Philo, Jerome, al.); cf. Nu. 13²², and Norzi *in loc.*

11-15. Jos. 15¹⁵⁻¹⁹. — **11.** *He went thence*] in the present context the subject must be Judah, but v.¹² and Jos. 15¹³ show that it was originally Caleb; see on v.¹⁰. — *Debir*] evidently a place of some importance in the Negeb (v.¹⁵), or on the edge of the hill country, to which it is also reckoned (Jos. 11²¹ 15⁴⁹). It is probably ed-Doheriyeh, or Dâhariyeh,† four or five hours SW. of Hebron. This village, which stands in a conspicuous position on a flat ridge, is the meeting point of the routes from Gaza, Beersheba, and other places south and east, and is counted the end of the desert journey for travellers coming from those quarters, the frontier settlement of Syria. The situation relatively to the places named in Jos. 15⁴⁸⁻⁵⁰ is also suitable; note that Debir is named in immediate connexion with Anab (Jos. 11²¹ 15⁵⁰), which lies very near Dâhariyeh.‡ — *Kirjath-sepher*] the name is commonly explained from the Hebrew *sepher* 'writing, book'; so 𝔐, 𝔊 πόλις γραμμάτων, 𝔏 *civitas litterarum*, 𝔗 קרית ארכי *i.e.* Archive-town.

---

* Suggested by Schleusner, *Thes. s.v.* μητρόπολις. For אם in this sense cf. 2 S. 20¹⁹ and Phoen. coins, ללאדכא אם בכנן, Gesen., *Mon. Phoen.*, p. 270 f., tab. 35; Schroeder, *Phönis. Sprache*, p. 275 and pl. 18, 5; יצר אם צדנם, Gesen., *Mon. Phoen.*, p. 262 f., tab. 34; Schroeder, *op. cit.*, p. 275, pl. 18, 2.

† In the former way (الظهريّة) it is written and explained by Eli Smith; the second (الظاهريّة, Guérin, *SWP. Name Lists*) is more probably right.

‡ See Rob., *BR².* i. p. 209, 211; Wilson, *Lands of the Bible* (1847), i. p. 349 ff.; Palmer, *Desert of the Exodus*, p. 394 f.; Trumbull, *Kadesh Barnea*, p. 102 ff.; *SWP. Memoirs*, iii. p. 402. The identification was proposed by Knobel (on Jos. 15¹³, ¹⁹; 1861). Conder, in apparent ignorance of his predecessor, speaks of it as one of the most valuable identifications due to the survey (*Tent Work*, 1879, ii. p. 93).

So tempting a name could not fail to give rise to a multitude of speculations ; the town was so called because it was the depository of the earliest records of post-diluvian history (Masius), or of the public archives of the Canaanites or Anakim (Neubauer), or as the seat of a famous library (Arias Montanus), "like those of the great cities of Babylonia and Assyria" (Sayce).* Some recent critics, like the writer last named, are inclined to draw large inferences about the civilization of Canaan from this library,† whose existence, it must be remembered, depends solely on a possible Hebrew etymology of a proper name not of Hebrew origin.

וילך משם] Jos. 15¹⁵ וַיַּעַל, 𝔊ᴮᴺᴼ | Jud. καὶ ἀνέβησαν. Hollenberg (ZATW. i. p. 101 f.), Bu., Kitt. restore ויעל here; וילך 𝔐 𝔊ᴬᴸᴹ s was occasioned by וילך v.¹⁰. Rosen (ZDMG. xi. 1857, p. 50 ff.) would find the name Debir in Debîrwān or Idbīrwān, a high and abrupt hill an hour and a quarter W. of Hebron, and the springs of v.¹⁵ in 'Ain Nunkur,' two miles or more WSW. of the city; so Ew. (earlier), Roed., v. Raum., Cass. The site is, however, much too near Hebron; Achsah could not complain in going thither that she was being sent off into the Negeb country (v.¹⁶). Van de Velde suggested Khirbet ed-Dilbeh, two hours SW. of Hebron in a valley abounding with springs; but this again does not fit the story; Achsah begs for the springs just because they do not abound about Debir. Ewald (GVI. ii. p. 403) thought of el-Burģ (Rob., BR². ii. 216 f.), a mile or more W. of ed-Dāhariyeh. See further on v.¹⁶. The etymology of Debir is altogether obscure.‡ As appellative, דביר is in Heb. the adytum of the temple (1 K. 6⁵·¹⁹ 8⁶), commonly explained as the rear, i.e. western part of the building. Sayce, reverting to Jerome's oraculum, place where the god speaks to his priests, infers that Debir was famous for its oracle as well as its library, — the two being probably closely connected (Higher Criticism, p. 55). — קרית ספר] 𝔊ᴮᴺ k (Καριασσω-φαρ) 𝔖 a § pronounce סֹפֵר, Scribe-town. There are two names in the O.T. with which this is naturally compared, ספר (𝔐 acc. סְפָרָה 𝔏 Sephar 𝔊 Σωφηρα) in Southern Arabia (Gen. 10³⁰) and ספרוים Sepharvaim (2 K. 17²⁴ &c.), commonly, but falsely, identified with the Babylonian Sippar (Abu Habba). ‖ In both of these also Jerome discovers the Heb. sepher, 'book' (OS². 10₂₁ 47₁₇). An etymological myth of the same kind which modern critics spin out of the

---

* Others have imagined that it was so named because alphabetic writing was there invented (Hitz., Kneucker) ; or because it was famous for the preparation of writing materials — skins or papyrus — (Schm.) ; or as the seat of the oldest university (a Lyra, Serar., a Lap., al.).   † Sayce, Higher Criticism, &c., p. 54 ff.

‡ דבר as the name of a city occurs in Sabaean inscriptions (MV.).

§ 𝔖ᴼ, however. ܣܦܪ. Comp. the Egyptian name below.

‖ See Fr. Delitzsch in Calwer Bibellexikon², p. 827.

name Kirjath-sepher seems early to have attached itself to that of Sippar (Σιπφαρα, Ptol., v. 18, 7), where Berossus tells us that the records of the antediluvian world were buried by Xisuthrus, the Babylonian Noah, and preserved from the waters of the flood (Müller, *fr. hist. gr.*, ii. p. 501, Euseb., *chron.*, ed. Schoene, i. p. 21, 22). The etymology is adopted by Bochart (Sippara = ספרא), and recently by Ménant, who interprets "la ville des livres" (*Babylone et la Chaldée*, 1875, p. 96). See, against this derivation, Fr. Delitzsch, *Paradies*, p. 210, Sayce, *Hibbert Lect.*, p. 168 n. — To connect ספר in קרית ספר with Aram. and MH. ספר, 'border, frontier,' as I formerly suggested (*PAOS*. Oct. 1890, p. lxx.), gives a suitable sense, Frontier-town, but the phonetic difficulties now seem to me decisive against this explanation. Another name of Debir-Kirjath-sepher, acc. to Jos. 15⁴⁹, was קרית סנה; see comm. on Jos. *l.c.* — Kirjath-sepher is recognized by W. M. Müller (*Asien u. Europa*, p. 174), in Baʿti tu-pa-ḫra (determinative "Writing"), *i.e.* "House of the Scribe" (ספר, as in 𝕲ᴮ 𝕾), in Papyrus Anastasi I.

12. *Whoever smites Kirjath-sepher, &c.*] cf. 1 S. 17²⁵; from the sequel it appears that the captured city also fell to the victor. — **13.** *Othniel the son of Kenaz, the younger brother of Caleb*] 3⁹ Jos. 15¹⁷. The last words may grammatically be referred either to Kenaz or to Othniel, and interpreters have always been divided upon the question whether Othniel was Caleb's nephew [*] or his brother.[†] The words *who was younger than he* favour the latter construction. The age of Kenaz is irrelevant; the notice is pertinent only as indicating that the disparity in age between uncle and niece was not as great as might be thought, or (in 3⁹) as explaining how Othniel so long outlived Caleb. [‡] — **14.** *When she came*] We are perhaps to imagine that she had been sent for from a place of safety, such as Hebron, where she had been left during the campaign against Debir. The order of the narrative is not against this; the fulfilment of Caleb's promise is properly related in v.¹²ᵇ; an important incident connected with the marriage is added in v.¹⁴ᶜ. Others, with a less natural interpretation of the verb, explain, as she was going from her father's house, where the marriage had taken place, to her husband's new home, escorted

---

[*] 𝔅ᴮᴺ υἱὸς Κενεζ ἀδελφοῦ Χαλεβ; so Calv., Schm., Cler., Pfeiffer, J H Mich., Ew., Ba., Reuss.

[†] 𝔅ᴬ ᵃˡ. 𝕷 filius Cenez frater Caleb; so Orig., Thdt., Procop., *Temurah* 16ᵇ. Ra., Ki., Abarb., and most moderns, Ke., Cass., Be., Di., Bu., Kitt., al.

[‡] It seems to me not improbable that the words, which are not found in Jos., were first introduced in 3⁹, and thence at second hand into 1¹⁴.

on the way by her father. — *She instigated him to ask of her father a piece of land*] as Achsah herself makes the request, we should rather expect, *he instigated her to ask, &c.** If we adhere to the canon, *proclivi scriptioni praestat ardua,* the best explanation is doubtless, she persuaded him that they should ask;[†] it was her suggestion, and the execution of the plan naturally devolved upon her, but it was with his full knowledge and consent. We hardly see, however, why the author should take the pains to tell us that. — *She slipped off her ass*] 1 S. 25[21] Gen. 24[64] 2 K. 5[21]; a mark of reverence, here and in 1 S. 25[23] the posture of a respectful suppliant.[‡] —*What is it?*] What wouldest thou? (RV.) is somewhat too definite. — **15.** *Give me a present*] lit. *a* (real, tangible) *blessing;* Gen. 33[11] 1 S. 25[27] 30[26] 2 K. 5[15] &c. —*Thou hast put me in the Negeb region.*][§] Others, *thou hast given me the Negeb region,*[‖] which is grammatically hard to justify, and yields an inferior sense. The district of Debir to which Achsah was going had not been given to her, but belonged to Othniel by conquest. On the Negeb see on v.[9]; as the root is not in use in Biblical Hebrew, it is inadmissible to render it here appellatively, *a dry land;*[¶] nor is it necessary to emphasize the contrast in this way, the scarcity of water in the Negeb was well enough known. —*Give me Gullath-maim*] the words, usually translated *springs* or *wells of water,* are, like the following Gullath-illith and Gullath-taḥtith ("the upper springs and the nether springs," RV.), a proper name of alien origin and — so far as the first element is concerned — of uncertain meaning. If Debir is rightly identified above (on v.[12]), the waters so named are doubtless those of Seil ed-Dilbeh, about two-fifths of the way from Hebron to ed-Dhâriyeh. This is one of the best watered valleys in southern Palestine, counting no less than fourteen springs and having even at the end of the dry season a running stream three or four miles long. The springs are in three groups: the first, six in number, at the head of the valley; the

---

* 𝔊𝕷 cf. 𝔖, Doorn., Bu.   † Abarb., Schm., Ba.
‡ Illustrations from the modern East, Niebuhr, *Arabien,* p. 44, 50, *Reisebeschreibung,* i. p. 139, 239 f.; Seetzen, *Reisen,* iii. p. 190 (Ba.).
§ 𝔊𝔖𝕿, RV., Stud., Ke., Be., Cass., Reuss, al.
‖ 𝕷, AV., Ra., Ki., Schm., Cler., Ba., al.
¶ 𝕷 *terram arentem,* Ke., Cass., cf. Stud.

second, five springs, of which Ain ed-Dilbeh is the largest, a mile
or more further down along the road from Hebron, in an open
valley; the third, smaller springs near the lower end of the Seil.[*]
The first two of these groups may very well be the Gullath-illith
and Gullath-taḥtith of our verse. The possession of these springs
must always have been a matter of great importance; and the
story before us — which is not an irrelevant scrap of family history — is told to explain or establish the claim of Achsah, a branch
of the Kenizzite clan Othniel of Debir, to waters which by their
situation seemed naturally to belong to the older line, the Calebites of Hebron.

12. אבר] without explicit antecedent; Ges.[26] § 138, 2. — וילבדה] pf. consec.
after אשר יכה; Dr.[3] § 115 (p. 130 f.). — ונתתי] apodosis of a virtual conditional
sentence; cf. Gen. 44[9] Ex. 21[13], Ges.[26] § 112. 5, *a*, δ; Friedrich, *Die hebr.
Conditionalsätze*, p. 66. — **13.** עתניאל בן קנו אחי כלב] examples of apposition
to the genitive, 1 S. 14[3] 2 S. 13[3]; to the governing noun, 1 S. 9[1b]. 1 S. 26[5]
1 K. 16[7] Is. 37[2] &c. — **14.** בבואה] cannot be, at the moment of departure
from her father's house (Drus., Ba., cf. 𝕲[Bal.] Jos. ἐν τῷ ἐκπορεύεσθαι, 𝕲[M] Jud.
id.), and would hardly be used if the meaning were, as they were on the way
to her husband's house (𝕷 Jos., cum pergerent simul; Jud., quam pergentem
in itinere monuit vir suus, &c.). — ותסיתהו] *she instigated him:* the verb usually
in a bad sense, 1 K. 21[25] 2 K. 18[32] 2 S. 24[1] 1 S. 26[19]. The difficulty occasioned
by the gender of the verb and its suffix is evaded by all the versions (exc. 𝕿)
in different ways, but a comparison of their variations in Jos. and Jud. is not
favourable to the supposition that they read ויסיתה, *he instigated her* (Doorn.,
Bu.); nor is it explained how this easy and natural reading was supplanted
in both Jos. and Jud. by the much more difficult ותסיתהו of 𝕸. Many commentators harmonize, She urged him to ask for the field, but, finding him
unwilling, undertook the business herself (Ki., I.Osiander, Cler., Be., Ke.,
Cass.). — השדה] *the field;* Jos. 15[18] better שדה *a field* (𝕲[HMNal.] Jud. ἀγρόν);
the article probably dittography of the preceding ה (Stud., Doorn., Hollenb.).
— ותצנח] צנח only here (= Jos. 15[18]) and 4[21] (see note there). It is not
found in MH., and, indeed, a root צנח appears only in Eth. ('await, wait for,
lie in wait'), after which J. D. Mich. interprets here, When she reached the
end of her journey she waited upon her ass, *i.e.* did not dismount. It is safer
to be guided by the context, illustrated by the passages cited above; so 𝕿𝕾,
Rabb. and most. 𝕲 ἐβόησεν or ἀνεβόησεν (Jos.), ἐγόγγυζεν [καὶ ἔκραξεν](Jud.),
𝕷 *suspiravit*, probably do not represent a different text, but are attempts at
the unknown word guided by the analogy of צוח (Is. 42[11] MH.) or אנה; the
same interpretation in the Haggada, *Temurah* 16[a]. — **15.** הבה לי] Jos. 15[19]

---

substitutes the more common הנה under the influence of the following ויחן. — [כי ארץ הנגב נחתני] the suff. cannot be indirect obj. (for לי) or second obj.; for if such a construction of this very common verb had been possible in Heb. we should have had other examples of it in the O.T. or MH. In the sense, *thou hast put me into the Negeb region*, we might desiderate the prep., אל ארץ הנגב (cf. 2 S. 11[16]), or בארץ הנ׳; but the acc. of place is perhaps sufficient, especially if we may suppose that the original text had ארצה הנגב (Gen. 20[1]),[*] which would exclude all ambiguity; the loss of ה local before the article (haplography) is not infrequent. —[גלה כים] is a proper name like מְשׂרפות ים (משרפת) Jos. 11[8] 13[6]; so rightly 𝔊 Jos. 15[19] Γωλαθμαιμ, Euseb., *OS².* 245[34] cf. 127[27], Schm. This appears more clearly in גלת תחתית, גלת עלית, 𝔐 *gullōth* (pl.); the discord of number thus needlessly created has led in Jos. to mis-correction of the adjj. (גלת עַלִיות, תַחְתִיות); the older and correct tradition in 𝔊 Jos. 15[19] τὴν Γωλαθ τὴν ἄνω καὶ τὴν Γωλαθ τὴν κάτω, 'A Jud. 1[15] τὴν Γολλαθ κ.τ.ἑ. Golath (or Gullath) is a fem. sg. with the old ending *at* which is preserved in many Canaanite names of places, e.g. Zephath v.[17], Baalath 1 Ki. 9[18], Sarephath 17[9] (Bö. i. p. 413). That the name is of Canaanite (not Israelite) origin is manifest from the adjj. עלית, תחתית, for which we have in Hebrew only העליונה, התחתונה; e.g. הברכה העליונה Is. 7[3]. It is idle, therefore, to seek for it a meaning and etymology in Hebrew; גלה, 1 K. 7[41. 42] Zech. 4[2. 3] gives no light. The word was unknown to the ancient translators; 𝔊 renders (in Jud.) λύτρωσιν ὕδατος, associating it with נאלה; 𝔏𝔖𝔗 merely guess from the context, 'watering-place, well-watered spot'; the common interpretation, 'springs' (Ra., Ki., al. mu.) has no other origin.[†]

On Caleb and the kindred clans see Nöldeke, *Die Amalekiter*, 1864, p. 20; *Untersuchungen zur Kritik des A. T.*, 1869, p. 176–179; Graf, *Der Stamm Simeon*, 1866, p. 16–18; Kuenen, *Godsdienst van Israël*, i. p. 139 ff., 177 ff., *Religion of Israel*, i. p. 135 ff., 176 ff.; esp. Wellhausen, *De gentibus et familiis Judaeis, etc.*, 1870; *Composition des Hexateuchs*, p. 337 f.

Caleb and Othniel are branches of the Bene Kenaz, an Edomite tribe (Gen. 36[11. 15. 42]), closely related to Jerachmeel.[‡] These clans, separating from the main stock of their people, found new homes, Jerachmeel in the eastern Negeb, Caleb in the hill country north of it as far as Hebron. The latter, the more settled branch of the Kenizzites, eventually coalesced with their northern neighbours of Judah, and came to be reckoned one of the chief clans of that tribe (cf. Nu. 13[6] 34[19] 1 Chr. 2[9. 18ff. 42ff.]).[§] In David's time, however, Caleb was still distinct from Judah (1 S. 30[14]), and Jos. 15[13] cl. 14[6ff.]

---

[*] In the Hexat. ארץ הנגב is characteristic of E; Di., *NDJ.* p. 618.

[†] M. A. Levy (*Phöniz. Stud.*, i. p. 26) thought that the words לגלת הבם were to be read in a Punic inscription (Num. 8, Ges., *Mon. Phoen.*, tab. 47), but the decipherment is probably false.

[‡] Compare also the names in the genealogies of Caleb and Jerachmeel, 1 Chr. 2. 4, with the Edomite genealogies, 1 Chr. 1; We., *De gentibus*, p. 38 f.

[§] The Chronicles hardly know any other Judahites.

explains how Caleb came to be settled in the midst of Judah. The Calebites, as has been intimated, probably made their way into their new seats from the south; their old homes lay near the passes from that quarter, and a reminiscence of the fact seems to be preserved in the story of the spies, in which — in its original form — Caleb alone maintains the possibility of a successful invasion from that side, and receives Hebron as the reward of his faith (Nu. 13 Jos. 14⁶ᶠ).* From the emphasis of the exception it is to be inferred that Caleb alone, not Judah, entered from this direction.

16. A branch of the Kenites accompany Judah to the vicinity of Arad; then, going on to the south, join their kinsmen (Amalek). — The text has suffered badly, and the restoration is at more than one point doubtful; the general sense, however, is sufficiently certain. The Hebrew has, *and the sons of . . . Kenite,*† *Moses' father-in-law, went up,* &c. The apparent lacuna is filled in ⑤ by supplying the name, Jethro (Ex. 3¹), or, better, Hobab (Nu. 10²⁹ Jud. 4¹¹), and inserting the article, the Kenite. E. Meyer would substitute the clan name, as in all other cases in the chapter, reading, *Kain,*‡ *the brother-in-law of Moses, went up,* &c. In view of 4¹¹ it seems to me preferable to restore, *and Hobab the Kenite, Moses' father-in-law, went up;* see critical note. — *From the Palm City*] 3¹³. Jericho, the Palm City, Dt. 34³ 2 Chr. 28¹⁵. The situation of Jericho suits 3¹³ and the verse before us. The Palm City is named, not as the old home of the Kenites,§ which Hobab had long before left to cast in his lot with Israel,‖ but as the point from which he set out with Judah on this campaign. The narrative represents the invaders as coming down from the north (Jerusalem, Hebron, Debir, Arad, Zephath); and v.¹⁻⁴ cl. v.²² suppose that Judah and Joseph set out from the same place, probably the Jordan valley near Gilgal (2¹; see also on 1²²). Jericho is, therefore, entirely suitable here, and there is no reason to look for another palm city in the south. — *To the wilderness of Judah which is in the Negeb of Arad*] belonging to, or in the neighbourhood of, that city. So, rather than *in the south of Arad,*¶ Hebrew usage seems to require us to translate; cf. 1 S. 27¹⁰ 30¹⁴.

---

* We., *Comp.*, p. 337 f.
† RV., "The children of the Kenite," tacitly emends by supplying the article.
‡ Jud. 4¹¹.   § Bertheau.
‖ Nu. 10²⁹ (J) with its original sequel.   ¶ English version and most scholars.

Arad (Nu. 21¹ 33⁴⁰ Jos. 12¹⁴') is generally identified with Tell Arad, a round detached hill about 16 Eng. miles S. of Hebron.* The language of the text appears self-contradictory; the Wilderness of Judah, the barren steeps in which the mountains break down to the Dead Sea,† and the Negeb are distinct regions (see above on v.⁹), and it hardly seems possible that a part of the Wilderness could be described as lying in the Negeb of Arad. The suspicion is strengthened by the variation of 𝔊, which has *at the pass* (descent) *of Arad* (cf. Jos. 10¹¹). It is very doubtful, however, whether this represents the original reading of 𝔐, as Doorninck and Budde assume. —*And he went and dwelt with the Amalekites*] leaving Judah, he continued southward into the desert and made his home with the nomadic Amalekites. So one of the principal recensions of 𝔊; 𝔐 has *with the people*, which would also be possible if we might, with a slight emendation, read *his people; i.e.*, the main body of the Kenites. The sense would be substantially the same, for the Kenites were neighbours and kinsmen of the Amalekites (1 S. 15⁶); see below.

ובני קיני חתן משה] when the gentile adj. is used of an individual, as is supposed by RV. here, the article is indispensable; it can only be dropped where the gent. adj. has become by appropriation a personal name, or where it is personified and takes the place of the eponymic ancestor, as in Gen. 36²² (החרי), &c.‡ The only grammatical translation of the text as it stands is *the sons of Keni* (n. pr.); so the Midrash, *Mechilta*, Jithro 1, fol. 65ᵃ Weiss, &c. 𝔊 supplies the missing name; 𝔊ᴮᴺ Ιοθορ = יתרו Ex. 3¹; ᴸᴹ ﬡ t Ιωβαβ, ▲ k Ιωαβ = חבב Jud. 4¹¹ Nu. 10²⁹. Stud. and Mey. infer that neither name stood in the Heb. copies before these translators; but *Jethro* may be the substitution of the more frequent name of Moses' father-in-law for the unfamiliar *Hobab* (cf. Ιοθορ for Ραγουηλ Ex. 2¹⁸ in many codd.). In view of the sg. verbs in v.ᵇ § it is probable that the original reading was *Hobab the Kenite*, rather than *the sons of Hobab* (see Bu., *Richt. u. Sam.*, p. 9 n., 86). Mey.'s attractive conj. ויהן חתן משה קיה is approved by Kue. (*HCO²*. i. p. 367) and Bu.

---

* On Tell Arad see Schubert, *Reise*, ii. p. 457 f.; Rob., *BR²*, ii. p. 101, 201; Van de Velde, *Narrative*, ii. p. 83 f.; Palmer, *Desert of the Exodus*, p. 402; Guérin *Judée*, iii. p. 182 f.; *SWP. Memoirs*, iii. p. 403, 415.

† Especially, it would seem, in the northern part; En-gedi is the most southern in the list of towns in this region, Jos. 15⁶¹ᶜ.

‡ The apparent exceptions are all, for one reason or another, suspicious; see Roorda, *Gram. Hebr.*, § 472 *fin.*

§ The plur. in the first verb, ויל, is natural conformation to the new subj. בני קיני.

(p. 9, but see p. 86); but 4¹¹ obstinately stands in the way. Even if the words בני חבב חתן משה there are a gloss (Mey., Bu.), or the whole verse a late interpolation (Matthes, Kue.), the knowledge that Moses' father-in-law was a Kenite, of which there is no other intimation in the O.T., must have been derived from 1¹⁶.—חתן] = *the girl's father*, 19⁴, חתנה wife's mother, Dt. 27²³ cl. Lev. 20¹⁴; cf. Ex. 18^{1. 2} Jethro, Moses' father-in-law. So here ᵺ, *Mechilta*, Ra., Ki., al. Many scholars render חתן when used of Hobab (Jud. 4¹¹ 1¹⁶; some also Nu. 10²⁹, where, however, a different construction is possible), *brother-in-law* (Thdt., Luth., Cler., Be., Ba., Ke., Cass., Reuss, Bu., Kitt., AV., RV., al. mu.). Others more indefinitely, *relative* (ᵺ *cognatus*), relative by marriage (*affinis*, Schm.). It is not impossible that חתן, like Ar. خَتَن, may have been used in the wider sense of a man's wife's near kinsmen, such as her father, or brother (Abulw., Ibn Ezra); but there is no certain instance in the O.T. of any other meaning than *father-in-law*, with which also the participial form better accords (cf. Stade, *ZATW*. vi. p. 143 n.). The passages in the Pent. which refer to Moses' marriage are conflicting and baffle analysis; cf. Ex. 2¹⁶⁻²²; 3¹ 4¹⁸ 18^{1ff.}; Nu. 10²⁹ Jud. 4¹¹ (1¹⁶). According to E his wife was a daughter of Jethro, a Midianite : J seems to have represented him as marrying the daughter of Hobab ben Reuel,* a Kenite, but the redaction has introduced great confusion. —עיר התמרים] on the palms of Jericho see Theophrast., *hist. plant.*, ii. 6, 8; Strabo, xvi. p. 763; Fl. Jos., *b. j.* iv. 8, 3; i. 6, 6; Plin., *n. h.*, v. 70; xiii. 44, &c.; Arab authors (Muqaddasi, Yāqūt) in Le Strange, *Palestine under the Moslems*, p. 396 f. They have now entirely disappeared. Of Jericho the name Palm City is here understood by *Sifre* on Num. 10^{29. 33}, § 78, 81 (fol. 20ᵃ 21ᵇ ed. Friedm.), Ra., Thdt., Procop., and most commentators. Cler. suggested the φοινικών described by Diod. Sic., iii. 42, Strabo, xvi. p. 776, on the Arabian shore of the Red Sea (cf. Ptol., vi. 7, 3); see Bochart, *Phaleg*, ii. c. 22 (i. p. 118 ed. Villemandy). Others have thought of Tamar, Ez. 47¹⁹ 48²⁸ (ᵺ Jericho) perhaps also 1 K. 9¹⁸, at the SE. limit of the Holy Land; probably Θαμαρω, Ptol., v. 16 8, Θαμαρα, Euseb., *OS.*² 210₈₄, on the road from Jerusalem to Aila, which Rob. (*BR.*² ii. p. 202) would locate at Kurnub.—ערד] seems to be named in the Egypt. king Shishak's (Shoshenq) lists of conquests in Palestine; see W. M. Müller, *Asien und Europa*, u. s. w., p. 168. The Onomastica put it down at 20 R. m. from Hebron, 4 m. from Malatha, which corresponds sufficiently closely with the situation of Tell Arad. From Nu. 21¹, where the Israelites on their first advance from the south suffer a repulse at the hands of the king of Arad, we should rather look for Arad in the southern Negeb, near the border of the desert; but it is unsafe to lay great stress upon this.† Mey. (*ZATW*. i. p. 132, 137 n.) regards ערד in Jud. 1¹⁶ as a misplaced marginal correction of ערד, v.¹⁷, and accordingly restores ערד in v.¹⁷ (in conformity with Nu. 21¹⁻³) and cancels it in v.¹⁶; see *contra*, Bu., *Richt. u. Sam.*, p. 10 f.

---

* Reuel is an Edomite clan; Gen. 36^{4. 10}.   † See below, on v.¹⁷.

D

— בנגב עָרַד [בירכר יהודה אשר ידרח בנגב עָרַד *on the south of A*. would be not בנגב עָרַד, but סננב עָרַד ויֵרַד; cf. מקרם לנן עֶרן Gen. 3[24], בצמון ידֵי Jos. 8[11], כים לֵי Jos. 8[9], &c. The various recensions of 𝕾 all have ἐπὶ καταβάσεως Αραδ = בכורד עָרַד; in other respects they differ considerably. Doorn. and Bu., following 𝕾[AL] ς ε εἰς τὴν ἐρημον Ἰούδα τὴν οὖσαν ἐν τῷ νότῳ ἐπὶ καταβάσεως Αραδ, and rejecting ἐν τῷ νότῳ as false doublet (in Heb. בנגב, בכורד) to ἐπὶ καταβάσεως, restore מרכר יהורה אשר בכורד עָרַד. But Ἰούδα does not belong to the original text of 𝕾; it is lacking in 𝕾[MO], asterisked in ς, and stands in 𝕾[B] in a different place; presumably it was not in the Hebrew from which they translated. I propose a different solution; viz., that בכורד (ἐπὶ καταβάσεως) is an old error for בכירכר, as in Jos. 8[24]; אשר בנגב is a gloss to עָרַד from Nu. 21[1] introduced into the text in the wrong place; יהורה a natural complement to בכירכר * thus left without a genitive. It may be added in confirmation that, if Arad be rightly identified with Tell Arad, there is no steep pass (מורד) in the neighbourhood of it (see Guérin, *Judée*, iii. p. 182). — [וילך וישב את הָעָם] μετὰ τοῦ λαοῦ Αμαληκ 𝕾[N] k.† τοῦ λαοῦ is doublet, corrected after 𝕸 ;הָעָם the translator read את עֲמֵלק (Hollenberg, *ZATW*. i. p. 102; Mey., Kue.), or, in view of הָעָם in 𝕸, better, את הָעֲמֵלֵי (Bu., *Richt. u. Sam.*, p. 9 f., Kitt., Dr., *TBS*. p. 93). As this is not suggested by the context and cannot well have arisen by accident, while it admirably agrees with the facts (1 S. 15[6] &c.), it may be confidently adopted. Otherwise we might emend את עֲמֵו. We reconstruct accordingly, וחכ רקיני חהן כשה צלה בעיר התמרים את בני יהורה כירכר עָרַד וילך וישב את הקינלקי.

On the Kenites see Andr. Murray, *Comm. de Kinaeis*, Hamburg, 1718[0]; Nöldeke, *Die Amalekiter*, p. 19 ff.; Wellhausen, *De gentibus, etc.*, p. 30 ff.; Kuenen, *Godsdienst*, i. p. 179 ff. = *Religion of Israel*, i. p. 179 ff.; Stade, " Das Kainszeichen," *ZATW*. xiv. p. 250 ff. The Kenites are frequently associated with the Amalekites (1 S. 15[6] Nu. 24[20-22]; cf. also Gen. 36[10. 12]), and were in all probability a branch of that people.‡ But while Amalek was hostile and treacherous (Dt. 25[17f.] Ex. 17[8-16]), the Kenites were friendly to Israel, and according to J allied by marriage to Moses. The original sequel of Nu. 10[29-32] (J) no doubt narrated that Hobab, yielding to Moses' importunity, accompanied Israel in its further migration. In the invasion Hobab consorted with Judah (Jud. 1[16]) and followed that tribe into the south, § but, true to his Bedawin instincts, soon roamed beyond the border into the pastures of his kinsmen of Amalek. The old relations between the Kenites and Judah were maintained, however, in the time of David (1 S. 27[10] cf. 30[20]). Later

---

* In 𝕾[B] to בנגב.

† 𝕾[B], which belongs to this family, has here, as in a good many other places, been revised.

‡ The Kenites belong to the same group with the Kennizzites (Gen. 36, cf. 15[19]). The common opinion that they were closely related to the Midianites is at variance with all that we know about the two peoples, and rests only on the harmony which editors and commentators have forced upon the divergent traditions of J and E. The connexion of the Rechabites (Jer. 35) with the Kenites (1 Chr. 2[55]) is also very doubtful. § Note the towns קין Jos. 15[57], רִינה 15[22].

the feeling of the Israelites was less friendly (Nu. 24⁷ᶠᶠ·). In Jud. 4 we find a sept of the Kenites, Heber, pitching their tents far in the North; see comm. on 4¹¹.

17. Judah helps Simeon to destroy Zephath-Hormah. — According to the agreement (v.³), the allies next invade the territory of Simeon in the south of Judah. — *Zephath*] the name only here; see below on Hormah. — *They devoted it*] to destruction, razing the town and exterminating its inhabitants, to the glory of Yahweh; cf. 21¹¹ Nu. 31 Dt. 2³⁴ 3⁶, &c., Jos. 8²⁴ᶠᶠ· 10³⁷ᶠᶠ· 11¹¹ᶠᶠ·, &c., esp. 1 S. 15ᵐ·. According to Dt. 7² 20¹⁶ᶠᶠ· the wars with the Canaanites were always to be such holy wars of extermination. Similarly the Moabite king Mesha records in his inscription how at the bidding of Kemosh he took Nebo from Israel and put to death the whole population, "men and boys, wives and maidens, and slave girls; for to Ashtar-Kemosh I devoted it" (l. 16 f.); and again of Ataroth, "I killed all the people of the city, a fine sight(?) for Kemosh and Moab!" (l. 11 f.); cf. also 2 K. 8¹².* — *So the city came to be called Hormah*] because it had been visited with the *herem;* "Devoted City." The same explanation of the name Nu. 21³. The etymology is scarcely historical; Hormah more probably signified "inviolable, sacred"; cf. Hermon. Hormah was a city of southern Judah (1 S. 30³⁰)† towards the frontier of Edom (Jos. 15³⁰ cl. v.²¹), ‡ occupied by Simeonites (Jos. 19⁴ 1 Chr. 4³⁰). In the catalogues it regularly precedes Ziklag; cf. also Nu. 14⁴⁵ Dt. 1⁴⁴. The data are insufficient to fix the locality, and no trace of the name has been discovered. According to our verse the native name of the place was Zephath, which Robinson would connect with the pass Naqb es-Safā, SE. of Kurnub, § while Rowlands and many recent writers would identify with Sebāta or Sebaita, two and a half hours S. of Khalaseh. ‖ It is, however, highly

---

* On the *herem* see Ew., *Alterthümer*, p. 101 ff., = *Antiquities*, p. 75 ff.; Merx, *BL*, Ri., *HWB*, Rüetschi, *PRE*², s. v. "Bann"; W. R. Smith, *Religion of Semites*, Lect. iv. and esp. Add. note, p. 427-435; Stade, *GVI*. i. p. 490 f.

† Named, as here, immediately after the Kenites of the Negeb.

‡ Jos. 15 represents Idumaea as contiguous to Judaea along its whole southern frontier, as it was in fact after the exile.   § *BR*². ii. p. 181.

‖ Rowlands in Williams, *Holy City*², i. p. 464; Tuch, *ZDMG*. i. p. 185; Wilton, *The Negeb*, p. 198-206; Palmer, *Desert of the Exodus*, p. 371 ff. The place had been previously visited by Seetzen, *Reisen*, iii. p. 44.

improbable that the old Canaanite name Zephath should have survived to our time, while Hormah, the name by which alone the
place is known in the O.T. history, has entirely perished.

17. ויחרימו אותה] the Hiph. is denom. fr. חֵרֶם. The primary meaning of
the latter is not very remote from קָדֵשׁ; both denote inviolability, and, in a
religious sense, withdrawal from common use or contact. But in the further
development of this idea in Heb. they go in opposite directions: קדשׁ applies
to things which God appropriates to himself because he chooses them for his
pleasure or service; חרם to things which he prohibits to men because he hates
them with peculiar hatred. Both are inviolable: the first are holy, and it is
sacrilege to pervert them to profane uses; the second are also sacrosanct, and
whatever touches them contracts the same character and is doomed to the
same fate. They thus represent opposite sides of the common idea of *taboo*
(on which see Fraser, *Enc. Brit*[9]. xxiii. p. 15 ff.). The root קדשׁ is found
only in the North Semitic languages; חרם in them all, cf. Ar. حرام ,
حريم ; Nabat. חרם, 'inviolable,' Euting 2ₐ and p. 28; Palmyr., de Vogüé,
35; Himyar., Halévy, 50, 176₂, &c.* — ויירא את שם העיר חרמה] the use of the
3 sg. m. with inherent indef. subj. (miscalled 'impersonal') is not infrequent
in this verb; 2 S. 2[16] Gen. 11[9] 16[14] 19[22], Ges.[26] § 144, 3 a. — From Nu. 21[1-3]
it would appear that the older native name of Hormah was Arad, and that,
with the neighbouring Canaanite cities, it was destroyed by Israel during their
earlier wanderings in revenge for hostile acts of its king; whence its name
Hormah. Critics who do not, like Cass., Ba., assume that the city was twice
destroyed and renamed, explain Nu. 21[3] as narrating by anticipation the
destruction of the place by Judah and Simeon, Jud. 1[17] (Stud., Kn., Ew., Be.,
We., Mey., Di.). On this hypothesis it must be assumed, further, that
Zephath and Arad (both equivalent to Hormah) designate the same place,
which creates a fresh difficulty.† A more probable solution is, that the words
מלך ערד in Nu. 21[1] are an interpolation; ‡ they disturb the structure of the
verse and make serious difficulty with v.[3]. If the words are omitted, בקום (v. 3)
is the *region* in which the destroyed cities stood, which also better suits
Nu. 14[15] Dt. 1[44] (from Seir to Hormah). It is then not necessary to connect
Nu. 21[1-3] with Jud. 1[17] in any way; they contain two explanations of the
name Hormah. — The identifications proposed by Rob. and Rowlands are
founded upon Nu. 21[1-3], both assuming that the attack on the Canaanites
proceeded from Kadesh; eṣ-Ṣafā is a pass leading into the mountains from
'Ain el-Weibeh (Robinson's Kadesh); Sebaita lies north of 'Ain Qudes
(Rowlands' Kadesh); neither is anywhere near Tell Arad. — On Simeon,

---

* Nöldeke in Euting, *l. c.*
† Mey. removes this by writing ערד for ערד in Jud. 1[17]; see above on v.[16].
‡ The name may have come, by association with Hormah, from Jos. 12[14].

see Dor:, *Die Israeliten zu Mekka*, 1864; Graf, *Der Stamm Simeon*, 1866; Wellhausen, *Comp.*[2], Nachträge, p. 353-355; Stade, *GVI*. i. p. 152 ff.

18, 19. The Coast Plain. — The two verses flatly contradict each other; v.[18] tells us that Judah captured the three principal cities of the plain, Gaza in the south, Ashkelon in the middle, and Ekron in the north, with their territory. That is in effect the whole region occupied in latter times by the Philistine confederacy; v.[19] says that Judah, with the help of Yahweh, got possession of the mountainous interior, but was unable to conquer the lowlands, where the formidable war-chariots of the natives could operate. This agrees with 3[3] Jos. 13[3], where Philistia, like Phoenicia and Coele-Syria, · is represented as being a part of Canaan which Israel did not conquer.* The hypothesis that Judah took these cities in the first onset, but was unable to maintain its hold on the plain,† does not relieve the difficulty in our verses; a writer who meant that must have expressed himself quite otherwise in v.[19]. The phraseology of v.[18] is also strikingly different from that of the rest of the chapter. Nothing remains but to pronounce v.[18] an editorial addition of the same stamp as v.[8] and of equally unhistorical character.‡ — **19.** *Yahweh was with Judah*] v.[22]. *The Highlands*] see above, on v. 9. The position of the verse suggests the question whether the Judaean Negeb is tacitly included, so that Highlands as a *designatio a potiori* has here a wider extension; § or whether the Negeb, occupied by Caleb, Othniel, Kain, and Simeon, is distinguished from the possessions of Judah proper. ‖ Meyer, however, with good reason, restores v.[19. 21] to their natural place after v.[7].¶ — *They were unable to expel, &c.*] see critical note. — *The Plain*] is here as in v.[34], the coast plain west of Judah, in which the cities named in v.[18] stood.** Others †† take the word (*'emeq*) collectively for the wide valleys in the mountains of Judah, such as the Emeq Rephaim near Jerusalem

---

* Jos. 15[45-47] (R: Di.) includes the Philistine cities in the list of towns belonging to Judah, in conformity with v.[12] which makes the (ideal) boundary of the tribe the Mediterranean Sea.

† Ki. and Abarb. on 3[3]; a Lyra, Schm. (*qu.* 14), Ew., Be., Ke., Ba.

‡ Mey., Bu., Kitt., Renan, *Hist.*, i. p. 246; cf. Stud.

§ Bertheau.   ‖ Bachmann.   ¶ So also Bu., Kitt.

** Fl. Jos., *antt.* v. 2, 4, Thdt., *qu.* 6, Stud., Ke., Be., and most.   †† Ba.

(2 S. 5[14]), Emeq ha-Elah (1 S. 17[2]), &c.; but these would be untenable, even with chariots, after Judah had taken the hill cities.
—*Iron chariots*] 4[3] Jos. 17[16. 18]. * Probably of wood, strengthened
or studded with iron ; * *currus falcati* (𝔏) seems to be an archaeological anachronism. Chariots were, as the Egyptian monuments
prove, a strong arm in the military establishment of the Palestinian and Hittite kingdoms, whence they were introduced into
Egypt.

18. ‏וילכד יהודה‏] 𝕲 l 𝕤 𝕽 harmonizing, οὐκ ἐκληρονόμησεν,† which Ziegler
(cf. Cler.) and Doorn. accept, explaining ‏וילכד‏ 𝔐 as transcriptional error for
‏וירא לכד‏. But if v.[19] had originally been prefaced by such a statement, it
would probably have been differently introduced (*e.g.* ‏כי יהוה היה את יהודה וג׳‏);
observe also ‏לכד‏ (v.[8. 12. 13]), and esp. ‏נבורה‏ (as 1 S. 7[14] and often) instead of
‏בנותיה‏, elsewhere throughout the chapter.‡ Bu. (*Richt. u. Sam.*, p. 6 n.)
supposes that v.[18], except the first two words, was originally a gloss to ‏הנקב‏
v.[19]; the contradictory beginnings of the verse in 𝔐 and 𝕲 proceed from two
different scribes who independently introduced the gloss into the text. The
statements of Fl. Jos., *antt.* v. 2, 4 § 128 and v. 3, 1 § 177, are manifestly derived from our text, but agree neither with it nor with each other.—On the
cities named in v.[18] see *DB*[2]; on Gaza also below on 16[1], on Ashkelon, on
14[19].—**19.** ‏לא להוריש‏] that this mode of expression is abstractly possible
must perhaps be admitted, though there is no complete parallel; cf. Am. 6[10],
Dr.[3] § 202, 2; Ges.[26] § 114 n. 2. But in the context the impersonal, *it was
impossible to expel*, is less suitable than *he* (Judah) *was unable to expel*.
Jos. 15[63] 17[12] make it most probable that the author wrote ‏לא יכל להוריש‏; cf.
also 𝕲𝕷𝕿:§ the verb ‏יכל‏ was cancelled by R or a scribe on dogmatic
grounds. 𝕿 relieves the difficulty by premising "after they had sinned" (cf.
2[1. 10ff.]); an anonymous commentator in Cat. Niceph. writes, οὐκ ἠδυνήθησαν,
οὐκ ἐπὶ ἀδυναμία εἴρηται, ἀλλ' ἐπὶ ῥαθυμία.∥—‏הוריש‏ cannot be always translated by the same English word, but is to be rendered according to the
context, 'conquer, occupy, expel,' &c.—‏נכס‏] is etymologically a deep depres-

---

* See the description of Egyptian war-chariots in Wilkinson, *Ancient Egyptians*[2], i. p. 222 ff.; Erman, *Aegypten*, u. s. w., p. 649 ff., 720 f.; W. M. Müller,
Asien u. Europa, p. 301 (Syrian), 329 (Hittite).

† See further, Lagarde, *Septuaginta Studien*, i. p. 20, 22.

‡ The rendering of ‏לכד‏ by ἐκληρονόμησεν points to a different hand from the
translator of the rest of the chapter (cf. v.[12. 13]), and perhaps justifies the inference
that v.[18] (which from its contents cannot have been inserted by the editor of
Jud. 1) was interpolated after the Greek version was made.

§ These versions could, however, scarcely render otherwise, and 𝔏 and 𝕾, at
least, probably had our text; 𝕾 translates, *did not destroy*.

∥ Similarly R. Moses es-Sheikh supplies ‏יכל‏ ‏לא רצה להוריש‏.

sion; in usage the name is not given to a narrow valley or ravine, but to a
broader and more open valley or low plain, such as the Plain of Jezreel,
Jos. 17[16] &c. That it belongs to the definition of an 'emeq to lie between or
be shut in by hills (Rob., *Phys. Geog.*, 70), so that the coast plain could not
be so called (Ba., Graf. on Jer. 47[b]), is not warranted. See further, *M.
Shebiith*, ix. 2, esp. *Tos. Shebiith*, vii. 10 f. — For the last words of the verse
𝕲 has ὅτι Ῥηχαβ διεστείλατο αὐτοῖς, prob. by corruption of (ה)ברוב to הרביב;
cf. Jos. 17[14.18] where ἵππος ἐπίλεκτος may have a similar origin (cf. We., *De
gentibus, etc.*, p. 31, *TBS.* p. 18).

20. Caleb expels the giants of Hebron. See above on v.[10]. —
As Moses had bidden] Nu. 14[24] Dt. 1[36] cf. Jos. 14[12ff.] 15[13ff.]. — *The
three giants*] Sheshai, Ahiman, and Talmai. v.[10]. The inhabitants
of Hebron are called Canaanites (v.[10]) and Amorites (Jos. 10[5] E),*
— both general names for the native population of Palestine.
The legends of the conquest made Hebron one of the chief seats
of a giant race, the remnants of the autochthones who everywhere
preceded the historical peoples; † Nu. 13[23] (J) Jos. 15[13] 14[15]
11[21f.]. "Sons of Anak" (AV., RV.) gives the erroneous impression that Anak is the name of the father of these giants, — an
error which was shared by early Jewish scribes and translators.

בני הענק] is a phrase like בני החיל 'warriors,' and signifies 'men of great
stature,' lit. 'of (long) neck'; cf. Jerome, *de situ, etc.* (*OS²*. 112₇), Enacim,
quos gigantes et potentes intellegere debemus; Schultens, *Iob*, p. 383. The
article categorically prohibits taking ענק as a proper noun. The genealogy
Arba (*i.e. Four*), the father of Anak (*Long-neck*), the father of Sheshai, &c.
(Jos. 15[13] 21[11]) is the result of a series of blunders; see on v.[10].

21. Jerusalem. — See above on v.[8] and cf. Jos. 15[63]. The author doubtless wrote *Judah* (Jos. 15[63]), which was changed by a
later hand to *Benjamin* in accordance with Jos. 18[28] cf. v.[16] 15[x].
The probable order of the narrative in J was v.[7. 19. 21], or v.[7. 21. 19]. ‡
Did not expel] Jos. 15[63], *could not expel;* doubtless the original
reading of J, which has been changed as in v.[19], for similar reason. § — *The Jebusites dwelt with the Benjamites*] Jos. 15[63] *with the
Judahites.*

---

* The Hittites at Hebron, Gen. 23 (P), are subject of controversy. There is
no reason to suppose that the name is used with greater ethnographical exactness
than Canaanite in J or Amorite in E.

† See Dt. 2[10-12. 21f.] ᴮ.   ‡ Mey., Bu., Kitt.   § Budde.

22-29. Joseph invades Mt. Ephraim and takes Bethel. Cities which Manasseh and Ephraim did not conquer. — The oldest history of the conquest represented the invasion of Central Palestine as independent of that of the south and subsequent to it, a representation which also underlies the narrative in Jos. What is here related of Joseph is apparently an abridged but otherwise unaltered extract from the older history (J), corresponding to the account of the conquests of Judah. — *The house of Joseph also went up*] as Judah had done ; the sentence is the formal counterpart of v.¹. *House of Joseph* v.³⁵ Jos. 17¹⁷ (J) 2 S. 19²¹ 1 K. 11²⁸ Am. 5⁶, &c. Here it tacitly includes Benjamin, as well as Ephraim and Manasseh ; cf. 2. S. 19⁴¹, where the Benjamite Shimei says, " I am come to-day, the first of all the house of Joseph." * — *And Yahweh was with them*] as he was with Judah (v.¹⁹). Budde's conjecture, *and Joshua with them,*† is extremely ingenious, but equally hazardous ; see critical note. In connexion with this conjecture Budde surmises that in the original context of J a short account of the operations against Ai (Jos. 8) preceded v.²³. — **23.** *Reconnoitred at Bethel*] caused an examination to be made in order to find out the best way to surprise or attack the town. — *The ancient name of B. was Luz*] Gen. 28¹⁹ 35⁶ 48³ Jos. 18¹³ (all P or R). In Jos. 16² the two seem to be distinguished (" from Bethel to Luz "), and it has been inferred from the passages in Gen. also that the Israelite sanctuary, Bethel, was at a little distance from the old Canaanite city, Luz ; ‡ the conclusion is, however, in both cases precarious. In JE (Gen. 28) the origin of the name Bethel is connected with the vision which Jacob had there in his flight from the wrath of Esau, and the sacred stone (βαίτυλος) which he set up on the spot (v.²²) ; in P (Gen. 35⁹⁻¹⁵) with a theophany on the same spot as he returned from Paddan Aram. In the times of the kingdom it was the most famous holy place in Central Palestine, 1 K. 12²⁸ᶠᶠ· 13 2 K. 10²⁹ 17²⁸ Am. 7¹⁰· ¹³ 3¹⁴ 4⁴ 5⁵ Hos. 10⁵ Jer. 48¹³, &c. It is the modern Beitîn, about twelve miles north of Jerusalem on the way to Nâbulus (She-

---

* On Benjamin, see Stade, *GVI.* i. p. 160 f.

† *Richt. u. Sam.*, p. 58 f.; accepted by Kitt., *GdH.* i. 1. 243.

‡ So a Lap., Ges. (*Thes.* p. 194), Ew. (*GVI.* i. 435 f.), Di. on Gen. 28¹⁹, Guérin, al. mu.

chem).* — **24**. *The men on the watch*] the Israelite scouts or pickets; cf. 1 S. 19[11] 2 S. 11[16]. — *Show us the way to enter the city*] not *the entrance into the city, i.e.,* the gate (AV., RV.), which they could see for themselves; but the most advantageous point for an assault or surprise.† — *They put the city to the sword*] v.[15. 16] 18[27] Gen. 34[26] 1 S. 15[8], &c. The phrase is used constantly in describing the wars of extermination waged, or to be waged, against the Canaanites, and against the Amalekites; cf. also Jud. 20[37. 48] 21[10] 1 S. 22[19] 2 S. 15[14] 2 K. 10[25].‡ — *Let the man and all his family go*] cf. Jos. 2[12ff.] 6[22. 25] (Rahab); *family* is to be understood in the larger sense, not merely of his household, but of his kindred. — **26**. The man migrated to the north beyond the Israelite settlements, and founded a new Luz. The author thus accounts for the existence in his time of a town bearing that name in Coele-Syria or the Lebanon. — *The land of the Hittites*] is tacitly contrasted with the land of Israel; § see further on 3[3]. Beyond this we have no clue to the site of the northern Luz; the appellative meaning of the word in Arabic (*lauz* 'almond') makes identification with any of the numerous modern places of like-sounding name more than usually precarious.

22. בְנֵי יוֹסֵף] 𝔐codd. (ca. 15 Kenn. and De Rossi) 𝔊 (as generally in Jos. and Jud.) בני יוסף of υἱοὶ Ἰωσήφ, which Kitt. adopts. But as בני יוסף is in the Octateuch by far the commoner phrase, the variant has no significance, especially after the plural verb, where the correction of the *constructio ad sensum* (Ges.[26] § 145, 2; Roorda, § 595) to grammatical concord is very natural. — The name Joseph has recently been recognized in the name *Y-śa-p-'a-ra, i.e.,* Joseph-el, ‖ in the catalogue of the Syrian conquests of Thothmes III. in the 16th cent. B.C.; though for the present the discovery creates new and perplexing problems rather than solves any. See E. Meyer, *ZATW.* vi. p. 1 ff.; Groff, *Rev. Égyptologique,* iv. p. 95 ff.°; Sayce, *Higher Criticism, &c.,* p. 337–339; most recently, W. M. Müller, *Asien u. Europa,* p. 162 ff., who regards them as names of places (not of tribes) in Central Palestine. See below on Asher, v.[31], p. 52. — וַיְרֻעַ עֲמָם] 𝔊ALM,¶ Euseb., καὶ Ἰούδας μετ' αὐτῶν. Bu. (*Richt.*

* On Beitîn see Rob., *BR².* i. p. 447 ff.; Guérin, *Judée,* iii. p. 14–27; *SWP. Memoirs,* ii. p. 295 f., 305; Bäd³., p. 215.

† Vatabl., Cler., Schm., Stud., Ke., Ba., Kitt.; less probably, a secret entrance, Abarb., Be.' ‡ On the usage see Be., on 1[8], p. 15 f.

§ Outside of Canaan, Ki., Schm., Cler., al.

‖ Cf. *Y-'-ḳ-b-'-rạ, i.e.,* Jacob-el in the same list.

¶ The secondary versions fail us; 𝔖 k are lacking; ℭ omits by omoeoteleut. from Βαιθήλ v.[22]—Βαιθήλ v.[23]; 𝔏 is supported by 𝔊BN'.

u. Sam., p. 58 f.) conj. that the author wrote וירושע; as Joshua seemed impossible in this context, the name was altered to יהודה (𝕲), but this, too, conflicted with the foregoing narrative and was changed to יהוה. But instead of these clumsy alterations the simple and only natural remedy was to drop the words altogether.* The origin of the variant in 𝕲 is much more probably to be explained by the accidental corruption of יהוה to יהודה in the copy from which the translation was made. In the story of the taking of Bethel as narrated in v.²³⁻²⁶ there is no reference to a leader such as Joshua, and hardly room for such a one. — 23. In Jos. 16² יהוה is perh. merely a gloss to בית־אל, "from Bethel-Luz" (Di. *in loc.*); † it is hardly likely that in defining a long boundary by four or five points two places would be named which are so near to each other as to be ordinarily identified. The inference from Gen. 28¹⁹ (Jacob did not pass the night *in* the Canaanite town) is only really cogent upon the assumption of the strictly historical character of the narrative. In the partition of the land Bethel is allotted to Benjamin (Jos. 18²² cf. Neh. 11³¹), but the course of the boundary (Jos. 18¹³ cf. 16¹ᶠ·) seems to leave it in the territory of Ephraim; see comm. on Jos. 18. The Onomastica (*OS²*. 209₁₅ 230₉ 83₂₀ 100₈) locate Bethel on the left of the Roman road from Jerusalem to Neapolis (Shechem), 12 R. m. from the former; so also the Bordeaux Pilgrim (Reland, p. 416; *Palestine Pilgrims' Text Soc.*, p. 19). Later Christian travellers looked for it much farther north (reff. in Rob., i. p. 449 n.); but the true site was still pointed out to Jewish pilgrims (Carmoly, *Itinéraires*, p. 130, 249; Eshtori Parchi, fol. 68ᵃ ed. Venet.). It was identified with Beitîn by the missionary Nicolayson in 1836, and by Rob., *BR²*. i. 447 ff.; the soundness of the identification is defended (against Thenius) by Graf in an exhaustive discussion, *Stud. u. Krit.*, 1854, p. 851–858. — ויתירו [חור (c. c. acc.) 'explore, reconnoitre,' Nu. 13. 14, *passim*. The Hiph. is better taken as 'direct causative' (Kö. i. p. 205 f.) 'institute an exploration, reconnaisance,' rather than 'send out scouts' (הריב), 'have scouts reconnoitre' (Ra., Ki. after 𝕿, Stud., Rö., Ba.), or as equivalent to Qal (Tanch., R. Jes., Schm. (dub.), MV., al.); in the former case על would perhaps be expected (Be.), in the latter the acc. The text is perhaps at fault; 𝕲 παρενέβαλον 𝕷 *cum obsiderent* suggest ויחנו ב 9⁶⁰; Sta. (*SS. s.v.*) proposes ויצורו, which would be construed with על rather than ב. 𝕲𝕷 may, however, be merely attempts at the sense; the former led Fl. Jos. to imagine a long siege of Bethel (*antt.* v. 2, 6 § 130 f.). — [בית יוסף οἶκος Ἰσραηλ 𝕲ᴬⱽᴸᴼ υἱοὶ Ἰσραηλ⁵⁴·⁷⁵; 𝕲ᴮᴺ vacat. The subject is superfluous, and the variants perhaps indicate that it is not original in 𝕵. — 24. [השכרים צבר in a hostile sense, 'have a place in observation,' almost equivalent to 'invest'; 2 S. 11¹⁶ 1 S. 19¹¹ Job 13²⁷ Ps. 56⁷ 71¹⁰. — [איש יוצא 𝕲ᴮᴺ καὶ ἰδοὺ ἀνὴρ ἐξεπορεύετο = איש יצא והנה, Doorn. — [הראנו ... וקשינו] construction as in

---

* All the more, that the story of Ai, to which they are supposed to have formed the introduction, has been dropped.

† 𝕲ᴮ kr have Λουζα not here but after Βαιθηλ v.¹, but this may be accidental; 𝕲ᴺ supports 𝕵.

v.⁹; see note there. — 25. חרב לפי] lit. 'according to a sword's mouth,' *i.e.* as
fiercely as a sword is wont to devour, unsparingly; so De., Di. (on Gen. 34²⁶),
Ba., al. Perhaps, however, פה had in this phrase lost its literal meaning,
'mouth,' as it usually does in לפי, so that it only conveyed the notion, 'according to, in the manner or measure of.' The prep. should not be taken instru-
mentally, *with the edge of the sword*, which would, besides, require the article;
see Giesebrecht, *Präposit. Lamed*, p. 95, 98 f. — וחתים ארץ] the ambiguity of
Greek transcription sometimes confuses חתים Hittites with כתים Cyprians, both
of which may be represented by Χεττιειμ; * cf. Fl. Jos. *antt.* i. 6, 1 § 128, ix. 4,
5 § 77. Misled by this confusion Euseb. (*OS²*. 302₆₉) writes, Χεττιειμ· γῆ
Χεττιειμ ἡ Κύπρος, ἔνθα πόλιν ἔκτισεν Λουζα; † cf. Procop. on Jud. 1²⁶ al.
Some modern scholars also have connected כתים with חתם; so Stud. on
Jud. 1²⁶, Ges., *Mon. Phoen.*, p. 152 f., cf. p. 122, *Thes.* p. 726; Movers,
Phönisier, ii. 2. p. 203 ff.; Fürst, *HVB²*. p. 453. But the inscriptions of
Citium which Ges. cited in support of this identity prove to have been mis-
copied or misread; see E. Meyer, *ZDMG.* xxxi. p. 719 f. — In the Talmud
(*Sotah*, 46ᵇ) Luz is a place famous for its blue dyes (cf. also *Sanhedr.* 12ᵃ),
which points, perhaps, to a site not very remote from the Phoen. coast. See
Neubauer, *Géog. du Talmud*, p. 156. — Proposed identifications of Luz in
our verse are Luweizeh (Rob., *BR².* iii. p. 389), four or five miles from Tell
el-Qâdî (Dan), ‡ and Kâmid el Lauz (Rob., *l.c.* p. 425) § on the western
side of the Bika' above Ḥaṣbeiyā, once a place of considerable importance
(Abu-l Fidā, *Tab. Syr.* ed. Koehler, p. 93; Le Strange, *Palestine under the
Moslems*, p. 347, cf. p. 39).

27. Cf. Jos. 17¹¹⁻¹³. As on the south Joseph was separated from
Judah by a line of Canaanite towns, ∥ so on the north it was confined to the mountains and cut off from the fertile plain and the
tribes which struggled for a foothold beyond it in Galilee by a
chain of fortified cities guarding all the passes. At the eastern
end of this cordon was Beth-shean, on the main road to Damascus; at the western extremity, Megiddo, on the road up from the
coast, commanding thus the great commercial and military road
between Egypt and the east. — *Beth-shean*] Jos. 17¹⁶ a stronghold
of the Canaanites, whose iron chariots deterred the tribe of Joseph
from the attempt to extend their border in that direction. It
was in possession of the Philistines at the end of Saul's life (1 S.

---

* כתים = Χεττιειμ Jer. 2¹⁰ Ez. 27⁶; cf. Nu. 24²⁴ 𝔊ᴹ 1 Chr. 1⁷ 𝔊ᴸ 1 Macc. 1¹.
† But cf. *OS².* 275₂₉.
‡ Conder (*SWP. Memoirs*, i. p. 96) has revived this suggestion.
§ Perhaps the Kumidi of the Amarna tablets; a principality of S. Phoenicia.
∥ See above, p. 8; and below on v. 9.

31^{10} 2 S. 21^{12}), having perhaps recently been wrested ; / (.
from the Canaanites; but was conquered by Israel, prob.b.;
under David, and was subject to Solomon (1 K. 4^{12}; see also on
v.^{28}). It is the modern *Beisān*, situated at the point where the
narrow eastern extension of the Great Plain begins to fall off
rapidly to the Jordan valley, and by its position completely commanding this pass.* — *And its dependencies*] lit. 'daughters, daughter towns'; places to which Beth-shean stood in the relation of a
μητρόπολις;† Nu. $21^{25. 32}$ 32^{42} Jos. 15^{45} Jer. 49^2 Ez. 16^{46}, &c. —
Taanach] in the O.T. generally coupled with Megiddo (5^{19} 1 K.
4^{12} Jos. 17^{11} 12^{21}); now Ta'annuk on the edge of the Great Plain
about six miles NW. of Genin, and about four SE. of Leggūn
(Megiddo).‡ — *Dor*] Jos. 11^2 12^{23} 17^{11} 1 K. 4^{11} 1 Chr. 7^{29} cf. Jud.
1^{31} 𝕲; on the sea coast south of Carmel, nine Roman miles N.
of Caesarea.§ Its ruins lie near the modern village of Ṭanṭūra. ||
The name of Dor in this place interrupts the orderly progress of
the enumeration of the cities along the margin of the Great Plain
from East to West; we should expect it to stand in the last place
as it does in 1 Chr. 7^{29}, which appears to be derived from Jud. 1^{27},
and are tempted to conjecture that it has been accidentally transposed. — *Ibleam*] Jos. 17^{11} (not in 𝕲) 1 Chr. 6^{55} (Eng. vers. 6^{70})
cf. 𝕲. From 2 K. 9^{27} it appears to have been near En-gannim,
the modern Genin, and the name has probably survived in (Wady
and Bir) Bel'ameh, half an hour S. of Genin.¶ Others, with less
probability, would identify Ibleam with Gelameh, a little village on
a knoll three miles and a half S. by W. from Zer'in (Jezreel) on the
road to Genin.** — *Megiddo*] see the passages cited above under
Taanach; also 1 K. 9^{15} 2 K. 9^{27} 23^{29}. The whole plain is called

* Descriptions of the site in Seetzen (who visited it in 1806), *Reisen*, ii. p. 161 ff.;
Rob., *BR²*. iii. p. 326 ff.; Van de Velde, *Narrative*, ii. p. 356 ff.; Guérin, *Samarie*,
i. p. 284-298; *SWP. Memoirs*, ii. p. 83, 101-114 (with plans).

† See above on v.^{10}, note.

‡ See Schubert, *Reise*, iii. p. 164; Rob., *BR²*. ii. p. 316, iii. p. 117; Guérin,
Samarie, ii. p. 226 ff.; *SWP. Memoirs*, ii. p. 68.

§ Δωρα 1 Macc. 15^{11}; Fl. Jos., *c. Ap.*, ii. 10 § 116; *OS²*. 283₃.

|| Guérin, *Samarie*, ii. p. 305-315; *SWP. Memoirs*, ii. p. 3. 7 ff.; *Bäd³*., p. 238.

¶ Ke., Di. (*NDJ*. p. 545); *SWP. Memoirs*, ii. 47 f., 51 f.; Bäd³., p. 228. See
also Schultz, *ZMDG*. iii. p. 49; Guérin, *Samarie*, i. p. 339 ff.

** Knob., Cass., Grove, Wilson (*DB².*).

from it the Plain of Megiddo (Zech. 12[11] 2 Chr. 35[22]), as the Kishon is called the River of Megiddo (Jud. 5[19]). Megiddo was evidently a place of capital strategic importance, and is named in both Egyptian and Assyrian inscriptions. In later times the name completely disappears; neither Josephus nor Eusebius and Jerome are acquainted with it. Robinson [*] established, to a high degree of probability, that Megiddo occupied the site of the Legio of the Onomastica, the modern Leggūn, at the point where the main road from the coast, having crossed the range of hills which extending to the SE. connects Carmel with Samaria, emerges into the Great Plain. Its position must always have made it the key to the western end of the plain as Beth-shean was to its eastern end.[†] — *The Canaanites resolved to remain in that region*] stubbornly maintained their hold upon it. — **28.** *When Israel became strong enough*] the subjugation of these cities appears to have been the work of David; their power had doubtless been greatly weakened by the struggle with the Philistines, who, at the beginning of Saul's reign, or shortly after, had probably conquered the rest of them as we know they did Beth-shean. They were all subject to Solomon, 1 K. 4[1ff.]. — *They impressed the Canaanites in the working gangs*] employed on public works (1 K. 9[20]). From the earliest times to the days of the Suez canal, the corvée has been in the East the means by which great public works have been executed. According to their traditions, the Israelites had been set to such labour in Egypt; Solomon employed it on a large scale in his buildings and fortifications, and, in spite of 1 K. 9[22], it bore heavily not only upon aliens but on Israelites (1 K. 5[13ff.] 12[4. 10. 18]). Megiddo and Gezer (v.[3]) were fortified by him by impressed labour, doubtless largely of their own Canaanite inhabitants (1 K. 9[15]). — *But by no means expelled them*] the population of these cities continued to be largely Canaanite; Beth-shean, in particular, was, even to the latest times, more foreign than Israelite.

27. *Beth-shean*] Βαιθσαν, ἥ ἐστιν Σκυθῶν πόλις Θ, 2 Macc. 12[29] Judith 3[10]; Σκυθόπολις, Fl. Jos., *antt.* xii. 8, 5 § 348, &c.; Euseb. *OS*[2]. 237[55]. According

---

[*] *BR*[2]. ii. p. 328 ff., iii. p. 116 ff.

[†] See Van de Velde, *Narrative*, i. p. 350 ff.; Guérin, *Samarie*, ii. p. 232 ff.; Bäd[3]. p. 229 f.

to Georgius Syncellus (*chronog.*, i. p. 405 ed. Bonn.)* it had this name from
a body of Scythians who were left behind in the reflux of the great Scythian
invasion (Hdt., i. 105 f.); cf. Aug., *qu.* 8. It is not improbable that this is
merely a learned combination. Other ancient references to the place, see
Reland, *Palaestina*, p. 992 ff.; Schürer, *Gesch. d. jüd. Volkes*, u. s. w., ii.
p. 97 ff.; Jewish authors, Neubauer, *Géog. du Talmud*, p. 174 f., Zunz in
Asher's *Benjamin of Tudela*, ii. p. 425, cf. p. 400 f.; Arab geographers, Le
Strange, *Palestine under the Moslems*, p. 410 f. The name is not to be read
in the Egyptian inscriptions as many have done; Müller, *Asien u. Europa*,
p. 193.— *Taanach*] is found in the lists of Palestinian cities subdued by
Thothmes III. (16th cent. B.C.) and Shishak (10th cent.), in the former in
immediate juxtaposition to Ibleam; see W. M. Müller, *Asien u. Europa*,
p. 170, 195. Euseb. (*OS².* 262₄₃) locates it 3 R. m. from Legio; Eshtori
Parchi (fol. 67ᵇ ed. Venet.) found it, with unchanged name, 1 hr. S. of
Megiddo (Leggūn). — *Dor*] Reland, p. 738 ff. (where, with other ancient
notices, an extract from the larger work of Steph. Byz.); Schürer, *GjV.* ii.
p. 77–79. According to the Papyrus Golinischeff, the maritime town *D-i̯rạ*
(Dor) was, in the time of Ḥri-ḥor (before 1050 B.C.), in the hands of the
Takara, one of the tribes which invaded Canaan with the *Purusati* (Philistines); see W. M. Müller, *Asien u. Europa*, p. 388. The irregular order
of the present enumeration, which springs to and fro — Taanach, Dor, Ibleam, Megiddo — may have given rise to the conj. En-dor, which in Jos.
17¹¹ 𝔐 stands as a doublet to Dor and in 𝔖 has displaced it; but En-dor does
not belong in this company at all. The name is properly written not ראד,†
as here, but ראר Jos. 17¹¹ 1 K. 4¹¹, כין ראר Ps. 83¹¹, חבר ראר Jos. 21²²; see
Massora on Jos. 17¹¹ and Norzi. That this is the original form of the name
appears from the Assyrian text cited by Schrader, *KAT².* p. 168, and is put
beyond question by the inscription of Eshmunazar (*CIS.*, Pars i., i. no. 3,
l. 19).— *Ibleam*] in 2 K. 9²⁷ we should not translate *to the garden house*
(*EV.*), but to Beth-haggan (Sta., Klo.), *i.e.* En-gannim Jos. 19²¹ Γιναή Fl. Jos.
antt. xx. 6, 1 § 118, on the edge of the Great Plain, the border town between
Samaria and Galilee (*b. j.* iii. 3, 4), now Genin (Rob., *BR².* ii. p. 315 f.;
Guérin, *Samarie*, i. p. 327–332; *SWP. Memoirs*, ii. p. 44). "The pass (ascent) of Gur, which is near Ibleam," must have been in the edge of the hills.
The situation of Bel'ameh suits all these indications.‡ Gelameh (Rob., *BR².*
ii. p. 319; Guérin, *Samarie*, i. p. 326 f.; *SWP. Memoirs*, ii. p. 84), in the
open plain an hour N. of Genin, suits neither in name nor in situation; it can
never have been a place of great strength, and there is no pass in the neighbourhood. Eshtori Parchi (fol. 67ᵇ) and Conder (*SWP. Memoirs*, ii. p. 98)
identify Ibleam with *Yebla*, NW. of Beisān. — *Megiddo*] Egyptian references,

---

* Cf. Pliny, *n. h.*, v. 74, Scythopolim, antea Nysam, a Libero Patre sepulta nutrice
ibi Scythis reductis.

† Numerous codd. (De Rossi) have ראר.

‡ Bel'ameh may also be the Βελαμων of Judith, 8³ (Βελμεν 4⁴ 7³ codd., ℥ Belma).

Müller, *op. cit.* p. 195 f.; Amarna tablets, Sayce, *Acad.* Feb. 7, 1891, p. 138;
Assyrian, Schrader, *KAT²*. p. 168 = *COT*. i. p. 156. The identification with
Leggūn is due to Eshtori Parchi (1322; fol. 67ᵇ, Zunz, in Asher's *Benj. of
Tudela*, ii. p. 433); in modern times it seems to have been first suggested
in an anonymous review of Raumer's *Palaestina* in the *Münch. gelehrt.
Anzeigen*, Dec. 1836, p. 920 (Rob.). Legio (Λεγεων) is freq. mentioned in the
Onomastica; as the intersection of several roads it is used as the base from
which the distance of a number of places is reckoned; under the name
Leggūn it is often named in the Arab geographers (Le Strange, *Palestine*, &c.,
p. 492 f.). Tell el-Muteсellim (Thomson, *Land and Book²*, ii. p. 214; Guérin, *Samarie*, ii. p. 237) may have been the citadel of Megiddo, as Tell
el-Ḥiṣn was of Beth-shean. Conder (*PEF. Statements*, 1877, p. 13 ff.,
cf. 190–192; *SWP. Memoirs*, ii. p. 90 ff.) would put Megiddo at Khurbet
el-Muġedda', in the valley 3 m. SW. of Beth-shean; the situation is impossible. Others (so Spruner-Sieglin, *Atlas*) identify it with el-Muġeidil, an
hour and a quarter SW. of Nazareth. — להוריש ... ולא יכלו] Jos. 17¹² ולא יכלו;
see above, on v.¹⁹. — ויואל הכנעני וג׳] not *began* (𝕭, as usually), nor *consented*,
agreed (Ba., Cass., after older scholars). The verb means 'make up one's
mind, resolve, decide,' either of one's own motion, Gen. 18²⁷ Dt. 1⁶ 1 S. 12²²
&c., or at the instance or request of another, Jud. 19⁶ 17¹¹ 2 K. 6³ and often.
But we are not warranted in putting so much into it as, 'they had to submit
to reside in that (limited) region on conditions fixed by the Israelites,' of
which villeinage (v.²⁸) was the ultimate, if not the immediate, import (Ba.);
cf. Ex. 2²¹ Jud. 17¹¹, further v.³⁵ cf. Jos. 19⁴⁷. — 28. וישם את הכנעני למס] Jos. 17¹³
וירש. The etymology of מס is obscure; possibly it is a loan-word. It is a
body of men impressed to labour on public works, frequently defined מס עבד,
working gang. Ex. 1¹¹ the Egyptians set over the Israelites שרי מסים, *i.e.*, not
επιστάται τῶν ἔργων (𝕭), but *gang-foremen*. The word can be used of a
whole population which is subject to the corvée; fig. (Prov. 12²⁴') of an
individual who is reduced to this status. It nowhere in the O.T. has the
meaning 'tribute, tributary,' which the exegetical tradition attaches to it. A
distinction between מס and מס עבד, such as Ba. tries to establish, does not
exist. — והוריש לא הורישם] *did not drive them out at all*. The absol. object.,
Ges.²⁸ § 113, 3 a; Ew. § 312 a. — For a comparison of the parallel passage,
Jos. 17¹¹⁻¹³, and discussion of its relation to Jud., see Be., p. 37 f.; Di., *NDJ*.
p. 544 ff.; esp. Bu., *Richt. u. Sam.*, p. 13 ff.; Kitt., *GdH*. i. 1. p. 244.

29. **Jos. 16¹⁰.** Ephraim did not conquer Gezer, which formed
a Canaanite enclave in the territory of that tribe. — *Gezer*] on the
SW. border of Ephraim (Jos. 16³). In David's time still indepen-
dent(1 S. 27⁸ 2 S. 5²⁵ 1 Chr. 20⁴),* it was conquered in the following

---

* In Jos. 13² also we should probably read רוזרי for הנשורי; We., *TBS.* p. 139;
Dr., *TBS.*, p. 163; Mey., *ZATW.* i. p. 126 n.; cf. also Ew., *GVI.* ii. 467. On the
other side, Di., *ad loc.*

reign by the Pharaoh and given to his daughter, Solomon's queen ; Solomon rebuilt it as a frontier fortress against the Philistines (1 K. 9[15-17]). It is the modern Tell Gezer, discovered in 1870 by Clermont Ganneau, between 'Amwās-Nicopolis and 'Aqir-Ekron. — *The Canaanites dwelt in the midst of them at Gezer*] Jos. 16[10], "The C. dwelt in the midst of Ephraim unto this day, and were subjected to compulsory labour," which is not a free expansion of Jud.,[*] but represents the original reading of J (cf. v.[28. 30. 33. 35]) ; the text in Jud. has been abbreviated.[†] The words "unto this day" do not necessarily imply a time prior to the destruction of the city by the Egyptians (1 K. 9[16]) ;[‡] the extermination of the Canaanite population need not be taken so literally.

Gezer] is named in the lists of Thothmes III. (Müller, *Asien u. Europa*, p. 160), and in Amarna tablets (Sayce, *Acad.*, Feb. 1891, p. 138). According to 1 K. 9[16] (cf. 1 S. 27[8]; 2 S. 5[25] is indecisive, 1 Chr. 20[4] can hardly prove the contrary) it was in Solomon's time a Canaanite (not Philistine) city, though it may earlier have been subject to the Philistines. Gezer (Γάζαρα, Γάζηρα) was an important place in the Maccabaean wars; 1 Macc. 4[15] 7[45] 9[52] (Fl. Jos., *antt*. xiii. 1, 3 § 15) 13[53] 14[84] (Fl. Jos., *b. j.* i. 2, 2) 15[28. 33] (Fl. Jos., *antt*. xiii. 9, 2 § 261). Euseb. (*OS*[2]. 244[14]) puts it 4 R. m. N. of Nicopolis. The Arab geographers mention Tell Gezer as a fortress in the Province Filastin (Le Strange, *Palest. under the Moslems*, p. 543). For Ganneau's discovery of the place, see *PEF. Statements*, 1873, p. 78 f.; 1874, p. 276 ff.; 1875, p. 74 ff. A boundary stone was found with the inscription גזר תחם; *Acad. des Inscript.*, *Comptes rendus*, 1874, p. 106 ff., 201, 213 f., 273 ff.; see also *SWP. Memoirs*, ii. 428–439 (with plan).

30-33. The northern tribes settle among the older population; the principal cities remain in the possession of the Canaanites. —

The entrance of these tribes into western Palestine was independent of the invasion of Judah (v.[1ff.]) and Joseph (v.[22ff.]), and if the author's representation — which also underlies Jos. 18[1ff.] — be correct, later in time. Its results were also much less considerable ; even in the mountains of Galilee they did not gain the mastery as their brethren had done in the mountains of Ephraim and Judah. The newcomers were fain to settle among the Canaanites where they could find place ; the mass of the population in

---

[*] Be., cf. Ew., *GVI*. ii. p. 464.

[†] Bu., *Richt. u. Sam.*, p. 15; Kitt., *GdH*. i. 1. p. 244.

[‡] Bleek, *Einl*[6]. p. 151 f., Ba., al.

this "heathen district" (Galilee of the Gentiles) was probably for many centuries not Israelite.

The tribes of Zebulun, Asher, and Naphtali are named. The omission of Issachar is not easily accounted for, since the Song of Deborah (ch. 5) shows that in early times it was a prominent tribe and had much to suffer from the Canaanites (cf. also Gen. 49¹⁴). It is hardly likely that it is included under Joseph,* more probably it has been omitted, through accident or design, in the abridgment of the chapter.

30. *Zebulun*] settled in the western part of Lower Galilee, in the hills north of the Great Plain; see Jos. 19¹⁰⁻¹⁶. — *Kitron and Nahalol*] Nahalol appears among the cities of Zebulon, Jos. 19¹⁵ 21³⁵; Kitron only here. Neither has been identified. — *Were subjected to compulsory labour*] see on v.²⁹ and note on v.²⁸. — **31.** *Asher*] north of Zebulun and west of Naphtali, in the mountainous country behind the Phoenician coast. — *Acco*] only here in the Hebrew Old Testament.† It was renamed Ptolemais (Act. 21⁷), probably in honour of Ptolemy II., but the new name did not supplant the old one. It is the St. Jean d'Acre of the crusaders the modern ʿAkkā, on the coast north of the headland of Carmel. ‡ — *Sidon*] the famous Phoenician city, the modern Ṣaidā. §

Ahlab, Achzib, Helbah, Aphik, Rehob] of these places only Achzib can be identified with any confidence. It is the Ecdippa of the Greek and Roman geographers, on the coast nine Roman miles north of Ptolemais, ‖ the modern ez-Zib, between ʿAkkā and Tyre.¶ Of the others, a highly probable emendation of Jos. 19⁵⁹

---

* We., *Comp.*, p. 215; cf. Mey., *ZATW*. i. p. 142 f.; against this view, Bu., *Richt. u. Sam.*, p. 44 ff.

† נהלל is to be restored (for נהלל) in Jos. 19³⁰ with 𝕲ᴺ cf. M (Reland, Hollenb.), and according to a widely accepted conj. of Reland, in Mi. 1¹⁰ (for נהלל); see Ryssel, *Micha*, p. 23 ff.

‡ On Acco see Fl. Jos., *b. j.* ii. 10, 1 f.; Reland, p. 534 ff.; Rob., *BR²*. iii. p. 89 ff.; Guérin, *Galilée*, i. p. 502-525; Lortet, *Syrie*, p. 159-168; *SWP. Memoirs*, i. p. 160 ff.; Schürer, *GjV*. ii. p. 79 ff.; Neubauer, *Géog. du Talmud*, p. 231 f.; Le Strange, *Palestine under the Moslems*, p. 328-334.

§ On Sidon, Reland, p. 1010 ff.; Pietschmann, *Phönizier*, p. 53 ff.; Rob., *BR²*. ii. p. 476-485; Ritter², xvii. p. 380 ff.; Renan, *Mission de Phénicie*, p. 361 ff.; Guérin, *Galilée*, ii. p. 485-506; Lortet, *Syrie*, p. 91-116; Bäd³. p. 279-283.

‖ Jerome, *OS²*. 95₁₄.   ¶ Ritter, xvi. p. 811 f.; Guérin, *Galilée*, ii. 164 f.

E

would restore Ahlab, or Helbah, which is perhaps a variant of the same name, before Achzib ; it was probably on the coast between Achzib and Sarepta. Aphik and Rehob are found together in the catalogue of cities of Asher, Jos. 19³⁰ ; they were apparently further inland. — **32.** *The Asherites settled among the inhabitants of the land*] the words clearly express the difference between the situation in this part of the land and that south of the Great Plain. In the latter region the conquest was incomplete, but the Israelites were, at least in the mountains, the predominant element in the population ; in the north there was no conquest at all, and Asher and Naphtali settled among the native inhabitants as best they could. — *For they did not drive them out*] we may with confidence assume that the author of the older history wrote, as elsewhere, *could not.* — **33.** *Naphtali*] settled in the eastern half of Upper Galilee, having Zebulon and Issachar on the south and Asher on the west. — *Beth-shemesh*] Jos. 19³⁸ ; not identified. — *Beth-anath*] coupled with Beth-shemesh (Jos. *l. c.*) in the list of fortified cities in Naphtali, is perhaps the modern village 'Ainītha, six miles WNW. from Qades (Kedesh of Naphtali).* The name shows that it was an old seat of the worship of the goddess Anath,† as Beth-shemesh of the worship of the Sun. — *They settled, &c.*] see above on v.³². — *Became subject to impressment*] v.³⁰ ; see on v.²⁸ ²⁹. — Beth-shemesh and Beth-anath were not the only cities in Naphtali which maintained their independence ; in 4³ᶠᶠ· a Canaanite king of Hazor has subjugated all the northern tribes. From the predominance of the alien element in this region it was called the Foreign District (*Gelīl ha-goyīm*, Galilee of the Gentiles, Is. 8²³ = AV. 9¹), or shortly, the District (*Gelīl*, Galilee ; 1 K. 9¹¹ 2 K. 15²⁹). It was subject to Solomon, who fortified Hazor (1 K. 9¹⁵), and ceded twenty towns in it (the Cabul) to Hiram, king of Tyre (1 K. 9¹¹⁻¹³).

30. We may safely disregard the combinations נהלל = כהלל (*Jer. Megillah*, i. 1) = Ma'lūl, 3½ m. W. of Nazareth (Schwarz), or 'Ain Māḥil (Conder) ; as well as the identification — by an etymological Midrash — of Kitron with

---

* So Van de Velde, *Narrative,* i. p. 170 ; Guérin, *Galilée,* ii. p. 374 ; Mühlau, in Ri. *HWB.; SWP. Memoirs,* i. p. 200.

† Cf. Beth-anoth in Judah, Anathoth in Benjamin ; E. Meyer, *ZDMG.* xxxi. (1877) p. 718. See below on 3³¹.

Sepphoris (*Meg.* 6ᵃ). The tradition of the names is not such as to inspire unqualified confidence. In Jos. 19¹⁶ we find הבית ונהלל (6ᴮ Καταναθ), in 21³⁴ ירהה is prob. another variant of the same name; *Jer. Meg.* i. 1 identifies יסר with וסניה (see Neubauer, *Geog. du Talm.*, p. 189). — For נהלל here 6ᴮ has Δωμανα, *i.e.* רמנה Jos. 21³⁵. — וברין] see Frensdorff, *Mass. Wörterb.*, p. 281 f. —31. אחלב] The same place is no doubt meant in Jos. 19²⁹, where the emendation מחלב אכזיבה (?) (בחילבה, בְּאחלב) for the unintelligible מהבל א (Stud., Hollenb.; cf. 6ᴮ ἀπὸ Λεβ,⁵⁴ ἀπὸ Αλεβ) seems imperative. The order of enumeration (restoring עכו v.³⁰) is from N. to S. An inscription of Sennacherib,* which recites his successes in Phoenicia, names in order, Sidon, *Bit-Zi-it-ti* (בית זיה), Sarepta, *Mahalliba, Utu-u,*† Achzib, Acco. Fr. Delitzsch (*Paradies*, p. 283 f.) and Schrader (*KAT²*. p. 173) compared *Mahalliba* with Ahlab, Helbah, and W. M. Müller (*Asien u. Europa*, p. 194, n.) conj. that בחלב was the original name in the O.T. also. This does not commend itself; but it is altogether probable that Ahlab, Helbah, and Mahalliba are variations of the same name, ‡ the meaning remaining the same. If this be so, we may venture to conjecture that it was the old name of the *Promontorium album* of Pliny, the modern Rās el-Abyad, midway between Tyre and Achzib; cf. Plin., *n. h.*, v. 75, Ptolemais, quae quondam Acce ... Ecdippa, promunturium Album, Tyros. — Many identify Ahlab with the Gush Ḥalab of the Talmuds, the Γισχαλα of Josephus (*b. j.*, ii. 20, 6; iv. 2, 1 ff.; *vit.*, 10, &c.), now el-Gish, NW. of Safed; but this, although in the Talmud ascribed to Asher (*Menachoth*, 85ᵇ, cf. *Sifre*, Dt. § 355, fol. 148ᵃ ed. Friedm.), is much too far inland for our context, and, indeed, for the boundaries of Asher.§ Still more remote is חרב (Aleppo), or הלבה, prob. Ḥisn Ḥalbā (Le Strange, p. 352) in the district of Tripoli (Eshtori Parchi, fol. 60ᵃ ed. Venet., Asher, *Benj. of Tudela*, ii. 415). — אכזיב] in the Talmud גזיב, N. of Acco; *Tos. Ohaloth*, xviii. 13, and often (Neubauer, p. 231-233); 'Εκδιππα, Ptol., v. 15, 5; cf. Fl. Jos., *antt.* v. 1, 22 § 85, *b. j.* i. 13, 4; *Ecdippa*, Plin., *n. h.*, v. 75. The identification with ez-Zib is as old as Maundrell (1697). — אפיק] not 'Αφακα in the Lebanon, N. of Beirut, at the sources of the Adonis (Nahr Ibrahim), famous for its worship of the Syrian Aphrodite, the modern Afqā (older scholars in Reland, p. 572, Ges. *Thes.*, Rosenm., v. Raum., Ba., Ke., Cass., al.), which is much too far north for the present context and that of Jos. 19³⁰. ‖ The name is not uncommon. — רהב] also a common name.

---

* Taylor Cylinder, col. ii. l. 38-40; Schrader. *KAT²*. p. 288.

† Query = הפק Jos. 19²⁰ ? The name *Usû* also in Egyptian inscriptions, Müller, *Asien u. Europa*, p. 194.   ‡ Cf. Ahmed and Mohammed.

§ On Gush Ḥalab see Neubauer, *Geog. du Talmud*, p. 230 f.; el-Gish, Rob., *BR²*. ii. p. 445 f.; Guérin, *Galilée*, ii. p. 94-100; *SWP. Memoirs*, i. p. 198, 224-226. It is freq. mentioned by Arab. Geographers (Le Strange, p. 463). Eshtori Parchi observes that Gush Ḥalab is almost a day's journey from Acco; he can explain its belonging to Asher only by the fact that the boundaries of the tribes overlapped (fol. 67ᵃ).

‖ Aphaka in the Lebanon is probably intended in Jos. 13⁴; see J. D. Mich., *Suppl.*, p. 114; cf. Budde, *Urgeschichte*, p. 350.

The Rehob of our text (and Jos. 19⁹⁷) cannot be the same as Beth-rehob near Dan (Jud 18²⁸). It is very likely Rehob in Asher that is meant in the Egyptian lists cited by Müller, *Asien u. Europa*, p. 153; see his note there. It seems probable from the order in Jos. 19²⁹, ³⁰, and from the fact that in other catalogues of the towns on the Phoenician seaboard the names nowhere occur, that Aphik and Rehob were not on the coast, but in the interior. The omission of Tyre from this list is significant. — The name Asher appears in the Egyptian inscriptions of Seti and Ramses II.* among the peoples with whom those kings waged war in northwestern Palestine, in the same region where the Israelite tribe Asher is located by the O.T.; see W. M. Müller, *Asien u. Europa*, p. 236 ff.† Like the names Joseph-el and Jacob-el (above, p. 41), this fact opens large questions about the settlement of the Israelites in Palestine, upon which we cannot enter here. — בית ענת] occurs among the conquests of Seti and Ramses II. (Müller, *op. cit.*, p. 195, 220), with divine determinative, as was observed by De Rougé in 1852 (*Mém. de l'Acad. des Inscr.*, xx. 2, 1861, p. 181). There is another Ainâta on the eastern slope of the Lebanon not far from the Bisherreh cedars (Burton, *Unexplored Syria*, ii. 138 f.; Thomson, *Land and Book*¹, Lebanon, &c., p. 272, 313; Bäd³. p. 350). For other attempts to identify Beth-anath, in accordance with the indications of Euseb., *OS²*. 236₄₅ cl. 224₇₀, see Ba.

34, 35. Dan is forced back into the mountains. — The verses differ strikingly from the rest of the chapter in the use of the name Amorite instead of Canaanite. In the Hexateuch the former is characteristic of E (and D), the latter of J.‡ Verse³⁶, which shares this peculiarity, is clearly fragmentary and misplaced. For these reasons, which he fortifies by other peculiarities of expression in the verse, Meyer separates v.³⁴⁻³⁶ as the work of another hand. § Budde has shown, however, ‖ that, whatever explanation we may give of the substitution of Amorites for Canaanites, v.³⁴ᶠ· are probably derived from the same source and context as the rest of the chapter. — *Dan*] first tried to get a foothold on the southwest of Ephraim. The language of the text perhaps implies that in the beginning they pushed further toward the Lowlands, but were soon checked and pressed back by the

---

* Before the date now generally accepted for the Exodus, therefore.

† M. Jastrow, Jr., in *JBL*. xi. p. 120, points out that the *Ḥabiri* and *Milkil* (*mare Milkil*) of the Amarna tablets correspond to two of the clans of Asher, Heber and Malchiel (Nu. 26⁴⁵).

‡ We., *Comp.*, p. 341; Mey., *ZATW.* i. p. 121 ff.; Bu., *Urgeschichte*, p. 345 f.

§ *ZATW.* i. p. 126, 135; so also Stade, *GVI.* i. p. 138 n.

‖ *Richt. u. Sam.*, p. 15 ff.; see also Kitt., *GdH.* i. 1. p. 244, and note below.

natives, who crowded them into a small district about Zorah and
Eshtaol, where we find them in Jud. 13-16. The main body of
the tribe, finding these limits too narrow, migrated to the head-
waters of the Jordan, where they established themselves about
Laish, renamed Dan (Jud. 18 f. Jos. 19⁴ᶠᶠ). —*The Amorites*] in E
and D comprehensive name for the pre-Israelite peoples of Palestine. The author (J) from whom this notice is derived probably
wrote *Canaanites*,* as throughout the chapter. —The contrast
between the mountains and the plain, as in v.¹⁹ cf. also Jos. 17¹⁶.
The broad valleys which extend inland, like that of Aijalon (Jos.
10¹²) † are doubtless included, but not exclusively meant. —35.
Cf. v.⁵⁷ —*Har-heres*] only here. Generally, and with great probability, regarded as the same with Beth-shemesh (1 K. 4⁹ 2 Chr.
28¹⁸),‡ or Ir-Shemesh (Jos. 19⁴¹), which stand in immediate connexion with Aijalon and Shaalbim, and then to be identified with
the modern 'Ain Shems, on the south side of Wady Ṣurār, opposite
Ṣur'ah (Zorah).§ —*Aijalon*] Jos. 19⁴² 10¹², on the Philistine border
(1 S. 14³¹); subject to Solomon (1 K. 4⁹); fortified by Rehoboam
(2 Chr. 11¹⁰); according to the same authority, conquered by
the Philistines under Ahaz (2 Chr. 28¹⁸). Conclusively identified
by Robinson with the modern Yālō,‖ about two miles E. of
'Amwās (Nicopolis), on the southern side of the valley. Aijalon
commanded the descent to the plain by W. Selmān, as Beth-
shemesh did that by W. Ṣurār (Sorek); cf. 1 S. 6⁹. —*Shaalbim*]
1 K. 4⁹ Jos. 19⁴². Knobel, Conder, and others would find it at
Selbit, on the north side of the valley, two miles N. of 'Amwās,
and about three miles NW. of Yālō. The site is not unsuitable,
but the similarity of the names is extremely slight, and all other
data are wanting. — *The hand of the house of Joseph rested heav-*

---

* Hardly *Philistines*, as Bu. (p. 18 n.) is tempted to conjecture, — a reading
which editors or scribes would be much less likely to change. Nor does the name
Amorites include the Philistines, as Mey. erroneously gathers from 1 S. 7¹⁴
(*ZATW.* i. 123). The date of the Philistine invasion is uncertain; but their
occupation of the lowland may have crowded the Canaanites back upon Dan.

† Merg ibn 'Omeir; Rob., *BR².* iii. p. 144; *Phys. Geog.*, p. 113.

‡ So Cler., Hiller (*Onom. sacra,* 1706, p. 560).

§ Rob., *BR².* ii. p. 224 f.; Guérin, *Judée,* ii. p. 18-22.

‖ *BR².* ii. p. 253 f., iii. p. 144 f.; see also Guérin, *Judée,* i. p. 290 ff.; *SWP.
Memoirs,* iii. p. 19.

ily upon them] lit. *grew heavy;* cf. 1 S. 5⁶. The language does
not strictly refer to conquest. The places seem to have come
under Israelite dominion before the division of the kingdom; they
are all included in one of Solomon's prefectures (1 K. 4⁹). Beth-
shemesh was Israelite still earlier (1 S. 6).

34. As v.³⁶, in any case, is not the original sequel of v.³⁴ᶠ·, it is unsafe to
infer much from their present juxtaposition. Moreover, in v.³⁶ the text is
corrupt precisely in the critical words; for *Amorites* we must read *Edomites*
(Hollenb., Bu., Kitt.). The form of v.³⁴ᶠ· corresponds as closely to the rest
of the chapter as the different situation admits, and the coincidences in
phraseology become more significant against the other differences; observe
נמס in contrast to הר v.⁶⁴ (v.¹⁹), ויואל לשבת v.³⁵ (v.²⁷ Jos. 17¹²), בית יוסף v.³⁵
(v.²². ²³), ויהיו לבס v.³⁵ (v.³⁰. ³³ Jos. 16¹⁰); cf. v.³⁵ᵇ with v.²⁸ᵃ, v.³⁴ᵇ with v.¹⁹ᵇ
(Bu., *Richt. u. Sam.*, p. 16). The contents of the verse fully agree with what
we know of the fortunes of Dan. There remains only the name Amorite,
which can hardly be allowed to outweigh these evidences of unity of origin.
The change may have been made by an editor; or the corruption in v.³⁶ may
have worked back into the preceding verses, with which that was thought to
be closely connected. —וילחצו] יחץ lit. 'squeeze, crowd,' Nu. 22²⁵, trop. Am.
6¹⁴ Jud. 10¹²; freq. in ptcp. לוחצים, 'oppressors,' Jud. 2¹⁸ 6⁹ &c. 1 S. 10¹⁸. —
כי לא נהגו] better ולא נהגום Jos. 19¹⁷ 𝕲, Bu., Kitt. —**35.** חרס [הר חרס, 'the
sun,' Job 9⁷; cf. תמנת חרס Jud. 2⁹, כירביליה התרס 8¹³, עיר התרס Is. 19¹⁸ (Heliopolis in Egypt = בית שמש Jer. 43¹³).* Beth-shemesh, a border town of the
Israelites (1 S. 6⁹· ¹²ᶠᶠ·), on the boundary of Judah (Jos. 15¹⁰), to which tribe
it is reckoned to belong (Jos. 21¹⁶); cf. *OS².* 237⁵⁹. —*Aijalon*] Jerome (*OS².*
89₂₈), correcting on Jewish authority an error of Euseb., puts it 2 R. m. from
Nicopolis on the way to Jerusalem; cf. *ep.* 108, 8 (*Opp.* ed. Vallarsi, i. 690).
—*Shaalbim*] The name Selbiṭ (سلبيط) cannot represent שעלבים; see the
thorough investigations of Kampffmeyer in *ZDPV.* xv. xvi. 𝕲 translates
ἀλώπεκες, from which it may be inferred that Hebrew had a noun שעלב
corresponding to ثَعلب, as well as שועל, ثَعَل, ثُعالة. Aq. Symm. Theod.
Σαλαβειν, which, corrupted to Θαλαβειν, has found its way as a doublet
into 𝕲ᴮ. The other variations of 𝕲 in this verse are particularly interesting.
—והכבד יד] 𝕲 adds ἐπὶ τὸν 'Αμορραῖον. Cf. ותכבד ירו 3¹⁰ 6². —Doorn.
(p. 11 f.) regards 33ᵇ 35ᵇ as patriotic interpolations (cf. 𝕲 v.³⁰. ³¹); the
Israelites cannot have thus subjected the more numerous and stronger native
population. These notices, however, describe the situation at a later time,
after the consolidation of the Israelite power in Canaan.

36. The Edomite frontier. — The verse has no connexion with
the preceding. The Pass of Akrabbim was on the southern or

---

* See on 2⁹. The text of Jud. 14¹⁸ (ההרסה) is corrupt.

southeastern frontier of Judah, toward Edom (Nu. 34[2]. Jos. 15[1-4]) ;
Sela, an Edomite stronghold (2 K. 14[7]) which lay still further
east. The Hebrew text has *the boundary of the Amorites*, which
could only be understood of the old southern boundary of their
land, which thus became the limit of the Israelite conquests. This
would, however, be a singularly roundabout way of making a plain
statement. It is therefore in the highest degree probable that,
following certain recensions of ⑮, we should restore, *the boundary
of the Edomites was, &c.*[*] This description of the southern
boundary has no connexion with the seats of Dan in the West ;
it would stand appropriately after v.[16] (the Kenites) or v.[17] (Simeon), but from the form of v.[36] it may be doubted whether this
was its original place. I am inclined to conjecture that the
source from which the material of Jud. 1 was derived contained
a brief description of the frontier between Israel and its neighbours on different sides, of which only this fragment has been preserved. —*The Edomites*] the nearest kinsmen of the Israelites and
their neighbours on the SE. —*The Akrabbim Pass*] Scorpion Pass.
Doubtless one of the principal passes leading up from the Arabah ;
probably the Naqb eṣ-Ṣafā, by which the main road from Petra to
Hebron ascends.[†] — *To Sela and beyond*] Hebrew text and versions, *from Sela*, which gives us two points of departure remote
from each other and no further limit. Sela (The Cliff) is commonly identified with the later capital of the Nabataeans, Petra ;
but this identification, in itself dubious, [‡] is here impossible. The
boundary between Judah and Edom can never have run from
Naqb eṣ-Ṣafā to Wady Mūsā. We require a point near the southern end of the Dead Sea, which equally well suits 2 K. 14[7] Is. 16[1].
The emendation is easy and seems necessary. It is doubtful
whether the end of the verse is complete.

⑮[BN] exactly represent 𝔐, with which 𝕷𝕮𝕾 also agree; but ⑮[ALM] 𝕮 𝕤 (sub
obel.) have τὸ ὅριον τοῦ ᾿Αμορραίου ὁ ᾿Ιδουμαῖος. ᾿Ιδουμαῖος prob. represents

---

[*] Budde, *Richt. u. Sam.*, p. 18 f.; Kitt.,*GdH.* i. 1. p. 243. Hollenberg (*ZATW.*
I. p. 102–104), in closer agreement with ⑮, proposed " the border of the Amorites
were the Edomites," &c.

[†] Knob., Grove (*DB*1.), Ri. (*HWB.* s. v.), Di. (*NDJ.* p. 209), Be., al. Descriptions of the Naqb eṣ-Ṣafā, Rob., *BR*2. ii. 180 f.; Schubert, *Reise*, ii. p. 443, 447 ff.

[‡] See Buhl, *Gesch. der Edomiter*, p. 34 f.

a sound correction in Hebrew. — בהסלע] 𝕲ᴬᴹ ε ἐπὶ τῆς πέτρας, probably correction of אדד. A terminus ad quem is indispensable; כ in בהסלע may easily have originated in dittography. We should accordingly restore the text as follows : ונבוד האדסי מסעלה עקרבים הסלע וסעלה.

On the Edomites, see K Buhl, *Geschichte der Edomiter*, 1893. The name occurs in a passage of the Papyrus Anastasi, where permission is asked for Bedawin of 'A-du-ma (Edom) to pass the frontier fortress at T*-ku (Succoth) to pasture their flocks in the fields of the Pharaoh; Müller, *Asien u. Europa*, p. 135. In the Assyrian inscriptions frequently; Schrader, *KAT²*. p. 149 f. — מעלה עקרבים] ὅριον τοῦτο τῆς Ἰδουμαίας (Lat., *Judaeae*) ἀνατολικόν, Procop.; cf. also 1 Macc. 5⁸. Rob. (*BR²*. ii. p. 120) proposed the line of cliffs, fifty to a hundred and fifty feet high, which cross the Ghor in an irregular curve from NW. to SE., seven or eight miles S. of the Dead Sea, the point at which the Arabah breaks down to the lower level of the Ghor. But apart from the fact that this is no *pass*, it falls with Rob.'s false identification of Kadesh ('Ain el-Weibeh). The description of the boundary (Nu. 34ᵃ⁻ Jos. 15¹⁻⁴) requires a pass on a line between the southern end of the Dead Sea and Kadesh ('Ain Qudeis). The conditions are best fulfilled by Naqb eṣ-Ṣafā; Naqb ibn Mār (Wilson, *DB²*. s. v.) is also possible. W. az-Zuweireh (De Saulcy) is much too far north. — רסיל] is understood as the name of the Edomite capital, Petra, by Procop., Vatab., Cler., Rosenm., Ew. (*GVI*. i. p. 338); Stud., Be., Cass., Oett., al. The equivalence of the names is seductive, but the identification has no more substantial basis. The passages in which Sela occurs (Jud. 1³⁶ 2 K. 14⁷ Is. 16¹)* all seem to point to a cliff near the southern end of the Dead Sea; we may perhaps conjecture that it was the modern eṣ-Ṣāfieh, a bare and dazzlingly white sandstone promontory a thousand feet high.†

II. 1–5. The Angel of Yahweh goes up from Gilgal; he upbraids the Israelites for sparing the people of the land, and foretells the consequences. Origin of the name Bochim. — That 2¹⁻⁵ is to be joined to 1 is now generally recognized; 2¹ᵃ·⁵ᵇ is the fitting close of the account of the conquest and settlement in ch. 1; 2¹ᵇ⁻⁵ᵃ connects ch. 1 with the Book of Judges (2⁶ᶠ·), and explains to us in what sense and with what intention ch. 1 was prefixed. — Verse ¹ᵃ is the counterpart of Jos. 18¹ (P).‡ Israel being now firmly established in Canaan, the religious centre is transferred from the plains of Jericho, where they first gained a

* Is. 42¹¹ is too indefinite to be taken into account.

† Buhl, *op. cit.*, p. 20.

‡ We., *Comp.*, p. 215; Mey., Kue., Sta., Bu. — In P, 18¹ must originally have stood before 14¹⁻⁵ (We., Di.).

foothold in Western Palestine, to a sanctuary in the heart of the land.   This change is signalized by the removal of the Angel of Yahweh,* his presence manifested in oracle and theophany, from Gilgal to the new holy place, which, upon his appearance there, is consecrated by sacrifice (v.⁵ᵇ).   The transfer of the religious centre to Bethel marks the end of the period of invasion, as the preceding period of migration ended with the encampment at Gilgal (Jos. 5¹⁰⁻¹²).   What stands between (v.¹ᵇ⁻⁵ᵃ) is in substance and form strikingly different from ch. 1, and bears the stamp of the school of Hebrew historiography which, for lack of a more suitable general name, we call Deuteronomic.†   It does not exactly agree with 2¹¹ᶠ, however, still less with 2⁶³ 3¹⁻³, and on external grounds also cannot be ascribed to the author of that Introduction to the Book of Judges.   It doubtless comes from the hand of the editor who introduced ch. 1 in this place.‡

1. *The Messenger of Yahweh*] not a prophet,§ but, as always in Jud., Yahweh himself as he appears to men in human form or otherwise sensibly manifests his presence ; cf. Ex. 3² 32³⁴ 23²⁰ᶠ Nu. 20¹⁶ Jos. 5¹³⁻¹⁵ ; see comm. on 6¹¹.   The appearance of the *mal'ak* (theophany) at Bethel is the sign that Yahweh will henceforth there receive the worship of his people and make himself known to them (Ex. 20²⁴). ‖ — *From Gilgal*] Jos. 4¹⁹ᵇ·²⁰ 5¹⁰ 2 S. 19¹⁵·⁴⁰.   Between the fords of the Jordan and Jericho, where the Israelites first encamped after crossing the river, and where, according to Jos. 9⁶ 10⁶ᶠ·¹⁵·⁴³ 14⁶, they long maintained a standing camp.¶   The name, which occurs elsewhere in Palestine, seems to be derived from ancient stone circles (cromlechs) ; ** cf. Jos. 4²⁰.   Gilgal was, in the eighth century, a frequented sanctuary ; Amos (4⁴· 5⁵) and Hosea (4¹⁵ 9¹⁵ 12¹¹) name it with Bethel and

---

* Cf. Ex. 23²⁰.   † We., Mey., Sta., Kue., Bu., Kitt., Dr.

‡ Bu., *Richt. u. Sam.*, p. 20.

§ 𝔈 (𝔊𝔖 vid.) Rabb., Drus., Stud.; specifically, Phineas, *Midr. Tanch.*, 𝔈ᴶᵉʳ. RLbG., Cass. — An angel, Thdt., Aug., a Lap.; in human form, Ephrem.

‖ Examples of the establishment of an altar at the scene of a theophany, Gen. 12⁷ᶠ· 26²⁴· 35¹ᶠ·; or of the appearance of the Messenger of Yahweh, Jud. 6²⁴ 13¹³⁻²⁰ 2 S. 24¹⁵ᶠ.—See further, W. R. Smith, *Religion of Semites*, Pt. i. p. 108 f.

¶ Representation of E ?   It is probable, though not certain, that the same place is meant in 1 S. 7¹⁶ 10⁸ 11¹⁴ᶠ. &c.

** The etymology proposed in Jos. 5⁹ is more ingenious than plausible.

Beersheba as one of the chief seats of Yahweh worship. Modern explorers have found traces of the ancient name in Tell Ĝelĝūl and Birket Ĝilĝulīyeh. — *To Bethel* (?)] the Hebrew text, which is confirmed by all the versions, *to Bochim, i.e.*, to the place subsequently so named from the weeping there on this occasion (v.⁵ᵃ).* In v.¹ we expect, however, the older name of the place, and a name of greater note. This is perhaps preserved in the conflate text of 𝔊, which beside ἐπὶ τὸν κλαυθμῶνα (Bochim) has *and to Bethel and to the house of Israel*.† Bochim ("Weepers") may then be connected with Allon Bacuth ("Weeping Tree") below Bethel (Gen. 35⁸; see on v.⁵). Since, according to Jos. 18¹ 19⁵¹, the tabernacle was at Shiloh, others think that Bochim must have been near that sanctuary. ‡ The original sequel of v.¹ᵃ was ⁵ᵇ, "and they sacrificed there to Yahweh"; see below, *ad loc.* — 1ᵇ. *I brought you up from Egypt*] so the context and the following tenses require; 𝔐 *I will bring you up*. The false tense suggests that some words have fallen out at the beginning of the sentence, and various attempts have been made, beginning with the ancient versions, to fill the lacuna. The most satisfactory of these is, *I visited you and brought you up, &c.*; but it is not impossible that this improves on the author. — *The land which I sware to your fathers*] this reference to the oath made to the forefathers is very common in Dt. (1⁸ 𝔊 1³⁵ 6¹⁰·¹ᵃ·²³ 7¹³ 8¹ 11⁹·²¹ 19⁸ 26³·¹⁵ 28¹¹ 30²¹ 31²⁰·²¹·²³, &c.) and in editorial additions to other books of the Pentateuch (Rje. Rd.; cf. Gen. 50²⁴ Ex. 13⁵·¹¹ 32¹³ 33¹ Nu. 14¹⁶·²³ 32¹¹); § the promise, Gen. 17⁷ (J) 13¹⁵ 15¹⁸ 26³ 28¹³ᵃ; also 17⁸ 35¹² (P). — *I will never annul my agreement with you*] in the light of v.², not the covenant with the forefathers just spoken of, but that of Ex. 34¹⁰ᶠᶠ, to which the reference in the following is unmistakable. — 2. *You shall make no terms*] Ex. 34¹²; the command that accompanied his promise and constitutes the obligation of the other part. — *Pull down their altars*] Ex. 34¹³, "pull down their altars and shatter their stone pillars (*maṣṣebahs*) and hew down their wooden posts" (*asherahs*) — the sacred sym-

---

* The use of the name in v.¹ is explained as an anticipation; Rabb., Aug., Drus., Cler., Stud.

† The emendation *Bethel* is adopted by We., *Comp.*, p. 215; Mey., Kue., Bu., Kitt.

‡ Cass., Ba., al.　　　　　　　§ Di. on Dt. 1⁸.

bols which stood beside the altars; cf. Dt. 7^5 12^3; further Ex. 23^{24} Nu. 33^{52}. Jos. $23^{12f.}$.—*You have not heeded my injunction*] cf. Ex. $23^{11f.}$. The words contain the author's judgment on the failure to exterminate the Canaanites, ch. 1.—*What have you done ?*] 8^1 Gen. 3^{13}; What is this you have done? not, Why have you done this?*—**3.** *And I also said*] many understand this as a declaration of present purpose, setting it over against *I said*, v.[1]: I said I will not break my word with you, I will drive out these nations (Ex. $34^{10f.}$); but you have disobeyed my command to make no terms with them; therefore I have now also said, I will not drive them out.† But if this antithesis had been designed, v.[3] would hardly begin as it does, *and I also said*, but rather, *therefore I say*, or, *so I now say*. It is preferable, therefore, to regard v.[3] as referring to a previous warning such as Jos. 23^{13} Nu. 33^{55},‡ from which the peculiar expression in v.[3b] is perhaps derived. That this threat was now to be carried out, did not need, after v.[2b], to be expressly declared.—*They will be thorns in your sides* (?)] so the text is usually filled out from Nu. 33^{55}, cf. Jos. 23^{13} (a *scourge* [?] on your flanks). The text, which can be literally translated only, *they will be sides to you*, may be explained as an unintelligent abridgment of one of these passages. Others would translate, in parallelism with the next clause, *they will be traps for you*; § cf. Jos. 23^{13b}.—*And their gods will be a snare to you*] Ex. 34^{12} 23^{33} Dt. 7^{16}. Not an occasion of sin only, but a cause of sudden and unexpected ruin; cf. Is. $8^{14.15}$, Yahweh is "a springe and a snare to the inhabitants of Jerusalem." Augustine, however, goes too deep when he infers from the verse, "nonnulla etiam de ira Dei venire peccata." ‖—**4.** *The people broke out into loud weeping*] 21^2 1 S. 11^4, &c.—**5.** *They gave the place the name Bochim*] *i.e.*, Weepers. The subject may be indefinite,—*so the place got the name B.* (𝔊[Aal.]). A place Bochim is not otherwise known. It is perhaps a far-fetched etymological

---

* 𝕷.𝕾, Lth., Cler., Schm., AV., RV. al. mu.

† So 𝕷, Thdt., Ra., Schm., Trem.—Jun., Cler., Stud., Ba., Reuss, Kitt.—Application of the principle, "Frangenti fidem fides frangatur eidem," Schm.

‡ Abarb., Ke.

§ Abulw., Cler. (*retia*), Lth., Fr. Delitzsch.

‖ See Schm., *qu.* 2.

explanation of a name Beka'im (2 S. 5²³) ; * cf. also the valley
of Baca (Ps. 84⁷), and Allon Bacuth (Gen. 35⁸). — *They sacrificed there to Yahweh*] original sequel of v.¹ᵃ. It is not improbable that the older history related the building of the altar at
Bethel, and perhaps other things, which have been supplanted by
v.¹ᵇ⁻⁵ᵃ ; but there seems to be no reason to regard the context as
so fragmentary that the original connexion and intention cannot
be made out.†

Older scholars regarded 2¹⁻⁵ as a fragment having no connexion with either
what precedes or what follows (Ziegler, *Theol. Abhandl.*, i. 1791, p. 295); or,
misled by the similarity in tone between 2¹ᵇ⁻⁵ᵃ and 2⁶–3⁶, as a piece taken
from some other context and set here as a prelude, or text, to the following
(Stud.). Another point which was much discussed by earlier commentators
is whether the events here related occurred before or after the death of
Joshua; see Cler., Schm., *qu.* 3, Stud. — 1. *Gilgal*] according to Fl. Jos., *antt.*
v. 1, 4 § 20, in the plain E. of Jericho, 10 stadia from that city and 50 from
the Jordan; Euseb. (*OS².* 243₉₄ cf. 233₆₅) describes it as a deserted site 2 R.
m. E. of Jericho, still holy to the people of the neighbourhood; cf. Jerome, *ep.*
108, 12 (*Opp.* i. 696, ed. Vall.). A Gilgal, with a church in which the twelve
stones set up by Joshua were shown, was visited by pilgrims down to the 7th or
8th cent. ‡ Zschokke in 1865 found a mound covered with large stones which
the Arabs called Tell Gelgûl (*Beiträge zur Topographie der westl. Jordansau,*
p. 28); cf. Guérin, *Samarie,* i. p. 117 ff., who discovered the mosaic floor of
a church. Conder identifies Gilgal with Birket Gilguliyeh (*Gt. Map,* sh. 18
Ps), nearer to Erihā (Jericho); see *PEF. Statements,* 1874, p. 36–38; *SWP.
Memoirs,* iii. p. 173, 191.—אל רבכים] v. 5 בכים; the art. is perhaps an additional ground of suspicion. 𝕾, with substantial unanimity, ἐπὶ τὸν κλαυθμῶνα
καὶ ἐπὶ Βαιθὴλ καὶ ἐπὶ τὸν οἶκον Ἰσραήλ. § The first words (cf. the pl. Κλαυθμῶ-
νες, v.⁵) may reasonably be suspected of being a later conformation to 𝔐 (We.);
Bu. (*Richt. u. Sam.,* p. 21) regards the rest of 𝕾 as genuine, and restores
ויעל מלאך יהוה מנלגל אל בית אל ואל בית ישראל, or בית יוסף; so also Kitt. I
suspect that בית ישראל is merely an accidental doublet of בית אל. ‖ A critical
significance has sometimes been attached to the space (פס-א) in the middle
of the verse, as indicating a lacuna or break in the text; but it is more

---

* Appellatively a kind of tree. 𝕾 etymologizes in the same way in 2 S. 5²³ and
Ps. 84⁷, translating κλαυθμών as here. The place cannot be the same as in 2 S.;
the latter is in the vicinity of Jerusalem. Hitz. (*Ps.* 84⁷; *GVI.* i. p. 107) identifies
the valley of Baca with the Bochim (Bekaim) of our text.

† Kuenen.   ‡ See *DB².* s. v.

§ In 𝕾 the crit. signs are confused; but doubtless meant to athetize all after
κλαυθμῶνα.

‖ Ziegler expresses a similar suspicion, but thinks of a Greek corruption.

probably connected with an older or discrepant division of the verses.* —
אֶזְרָה] the versions have supplied various beginnings for the sentence which
do not meet the difficulty. Stud. and Be. would insert אעברהי (I proposed to
bring you up, &c.; cf. Ra.); Böttch. (*Neue exeget. Krit. Aehrenlese*, p. 74)
conjectured אֶעֱלֶה (future), פֹּה פִּקְרְהִי אֶהְכֶם וָאֹמַר אֶעֱלֶה וג׳ cf. Ex. 3^10. Gen.
50^24, which Doorn. improves upon by reading וָאֹמַר for יֹאמֶר אֶעֱלֶה. This
gives us an unimpeachable text. The speech of the angel is, however, a cento
of quotations and reminiscences, and it is at least possible that the author here
copied Ex. 3^17a without correcting the tense. Attempts to explain אֶעֱלֶה grammatically (Roorda, § 367; Dr.§ 27 γ; Ges.§ 107 1 *a*; Ba., al.) are forced, and
do not account for the following וָאָבִיא. — לֹא אָפֵר בְּרִיתִי] *make of no effect,*
annul, 1 K. 15^19; in religious sense common in Jer. Ez. Dt. and later. — 2.
Ⓖ presents a longer text, probably amplified from the parallels in Ex. and Dt.
Doorn. and Bu. (*ThLZ.* 1884, 211), on the contrary, think that 𝔐 has been
abridged. The "singular antithesis," *make no terms . . . but pull down their*
altars, at which Doorn. stumbles, stands just so in Ex. 34^12. 13. — לֹא הִכְרְתוּ בְרִית]
the phrase כרת בכית (usually with עָם or אֵת, here with לְ, as in 1 S. 11^1, 'prescribe
terms to') apparently originated in the rite described in Jer. 34^18ff., cf. Gen. 15^10.
See the parallels collected by Bochart, *Hierozoicon*, l. ii. c. 33 (i. p. 332 ff. ed.
Rosenm.), Di. in *BL.* s. v., "Bund"; and on the probable significance of the
rite, W. R. Smith, *Religion of Semites*, Pt. i. p. 461 f.; further, Valeton, in
ZATW. xii. 225 ff. On the etymology and signification of בריח see on
2^20. — נתץ [סוֹבְחוֹתֵיהֶם תְּתֹּצוּן] 'pull down, pull to pieces,' Ex. 34^13 Dt. 7^5 12^3
Jud. 6^28. 30. 31 2 K. 23^12; of houses (Is. 22^10), tower (Jud. 8^9. 17), cities
(Jer. 4^26), &c. The altars were probably built of stones, Ex. 20^25 1 Macc.
4^44f.. The form of the verb, with preservation of *o* and ending *ūn*, also
Ex. 34^13, Bö. § 930. — וְאֵת מַצֵּבֹתָם כַּה] Ges.^23 § 136, n. 2. — 3. נגרש [לֹא אֲגָרֵשׁ
Ex. 23^28. 29. 30. 31 33^3 34^11 Jos. 24^12. 18 Jud. 6^9; frequent in E (Bu., *Richt. u.*
Sam., p. 159). — וְהָיוּ לָכֶם לְצִדִּים] cf. Nu. 33^55 לְצִנִּינִים בְּצִדֵּיכֶם, Jos. 23^13 לְשֹׁטֵט
בְּצִדֵּיכֶם וְלִצְנִנִים בְּעֵינֵיכֶם. In view of the apparent reference to this threat, it is
probably best to correct Jud. to conform to Nu. Whether hasty abridgment
or transcriptional accident has produced the present text is uncertain. The
ancient versions seem to have read or guessed לְצָרִים or לְצֹרְרִים, cf. אהכם וצררו
Nu. 33^55; so Ⓖ εἰς συνοχὰς | *in angustias, in pressura*, 𝕷 *hostes*, ℭ לְבַעֲקִין.
Stud., Be., Doorn. would emend accordingly; but the reading of these verss.
has the marks of a bad (though natural and old) conjecture; the idea thus
conveyed is too self-evident to suit the emphatic context; moreover, צר is
never found in a similar connexion. 'Abulw., connecting צדים with צור ' hunt,'
interpreted ' snares, traps,' and this explanation has been recently revived by
Fr. Delitzsch, *Hebr. Lang.*, p. 29 f., *Prolegomena*, p. 75 f., comparing Assyrian

---

* The former opinion was maintained by Morinus and many older scholars (see
Ges., *Lehrgebäude*, p. 124); the theory has lately been revived by Graetz and
controverted by Sidon; see *Theol. Jahresbericht.* iv. p. 18; Graetz' rejoinder,
Monatsschrift. f. G. u. W. d. Judenthums, 1887, p. 193–200.

נוקְשִׁים 'trap, springe.' Another comparatively simple solution would be to pronounce יָצוּרִים (cf. צָדָה Ex. 21[18], esp. 1 S. 24[12]), 'huntsmen, trappers.' — עיָּו] the form of this n. pr. loci (act. ptcp.) strengthens the suspicion that the pronunciation has been deflected in favour of the etymology.

II. 6–XVI. 31. THE HISTORY OF ISRAEL IN CANAAN IN THE DAYS OF THE JUDGES.

II. 6–III. 6. Introduction; the religious pragmatism of the history.

After the great assembly and solemn covenant at Shechem (Jos. 24[1-27]), Joshua sends the people away to occupy the lands which have been allotted to them (2[6]). Israel continues faithful to Yahweh as long as Joshua and the survivors of his generation live, but after they have passed away, and a new generation comes up who have not seen the great deliverances and victories of their God, the heathenizing of Israel begins (v.[7-10]). The people neglect Yahweh for the worship of the Baals and Astartes, the gods of Canaan (v.[11-13]). Yahweh visits his anger upon them by the hand of their foes and they are brought into great straits (v.[14]). Anon, moved by their groans under foreign tyranny, he raises up champions who deliver them; but they do not even then abandon the worship of other gods, and the death of the judge is always a signal for a worse relapse into heathenism (v.[16-19]). In indignation at this incurable unfaithfulness, Yahweh vows that he will not complete the expulsion of the peoples of the land, but will leave them to tempt Israel. The Israelites intermarry with their neighbours and adopt their religion (2[20]–3[6]).

This general introduction contains an interpretation and judgement of the history of the whole period, which is represented as "an almost rhythmical alternation of idolatry and subjugation, return to Yahweh and liberation" [*] The motives out of which it is constructed reappear in the particular introduction to the story of each of the Judges. A typical example is 3[12-13]: The Israelites again did what displeased Yahweh, and Yahweh gave Eglon, king of Moab, power over Israel. . . . And the Israelites served

---

[*] Vatke, *Biblische Theologie*, 1835, p. 181.

Eglon, king of Moab, eighteen years.   And the Israelites cried
unto Yahweh, and he raised them up a deliverer, Ehud ben Gera,
the Benjamite, &c.   Compare $3^{7\cdot11}$ (Othniel), $4^{1\cdot3}$ (Deborah), 13^1
(Samson).   In $6^{1\cdot4.\ 7\cdot10}$ (Gideon) and $10^{6\cdot16}$ (Jephthah) the theme
is developed at greater length, the latter passage being closely
parallel to 2^6–3^6.   It is clear from the prominence given to the
pragmatism that the author's aim was moral and religious rather
than purely historical ; the lesson of the history is for him the
chief thing in the history.*   He has, however, contented himself
with emphasizing the lesson in this way, and has hardly touched
the stories themselves.   See further on $3^{7ff.}$

The introduction, 2^6–3^6, is not homogeneous.   Ch. $2^{6\cdot10}$ is the
transition from the history of the conquest under Joshua to that
of the Judges, and is found, with slight variations, in Jos. $24^{28\cdot31}$
also.†   In v.$^{11\cdot23}$ two very similar accounts have been intimately
combined ; while in 2^{23} $3^{1\cdot6}$ fragments of an independent narrative
(J) also enter into the composition.

On the analysis of 2^6–3^6 see Bertheau², p. viii. f., xix. f., 55 ff., esp. 61 f.;
Budde, *Richt. u. Sam.*, p. 92–94, 155 ff.; E. Meyer, *ZATW*. i. p. 144 f;
Kuenen, *HCO²*. i. p. 338 ff.; Kittel, *Stud. u. Krit.*, 1892, p. 51 ff., *GdH*. i. 2.
p. 5 f.   Although Kuenen, after setting aside v.$^{13.\ 17}$ as interpolations, finds no
ground for challenging the unity of $2^{11\cdot23}$, which he ascribes as a whole to the
Deuteronomic author, the composite character of the passage is recognized by
most recent critics.   It is evident in the duplication of almost every clause;
cf. v.^{12} with v.^{18}; v.^{14a} (he gave them into the power of spoilers) with v.^{14b}
(he sold them into the power of their enemies); v.$^{16f.}$ with v.$^{18f.}$.   The character of these doublets points to composition (Bu.), rather than to editorial
expansion or interpolation.   We can separate two parallel accounts, each
of which is almost completely preserved; the two are, however, in thought
and phrase so much alike, and the style of the redactor so similar to that of
both, that the analysis is difficult and doubtful.   To one of them (E) may be
assigned $2^{6.\ 8\cdot10.\ 13.\ 14a.\ 16.\ 17.\ 20.\ 21}$.   This is the principal narrative and is intact,
lacking only perhaps some such words as, "And the Israelites cried unto
Yahweh" (cf. 3^{15}), before 2^{16}.   To the other belong $2^{7.\ 12.\ 14b.\ 15.\ 18.\ 19}$, in which
the nexus between v.^{7} and v.^{12} is wanting, having been supplanted by the words

---

* The book is, as Reuss says, "die naturliche, und nur in andrer Form vorge-
tragene P r e d i g t eines Propheten, der um sich her das fremde Wesen und Ver-
derben in erschreckender Weise überhand nehmen sah" (*Gesch. d. Alten Test.*,
§ 275.)

† On the relation between Jos. and Jud. see below on 2^6.

of E. Verse[11] is an addition by the last editor (R).* The second of the s exhibits throughout the peculiarities of conception and expression which we find in the Deuteronomic strata of the Hexateuch and the Deuteronomic writers in the Book of Kings, as well as in the introductions to the stories of the several Judges, and may be confidently ascribed to the same school. For brevity, and without attempting to define its relation to the cognate parts of Dt. and Jos., this element in the book will henceforth be designated by the signature D (Deuteronomic author of Judges). With general agreement between the introductions of E and D, there are slight differences of representation which should not be overlooked. In E the sin of Israel is the worship of the Baals and Astartes, the gods of Palestine (2^{18}); in D the adoption of the religion of the surrounding nations (v.^{13} cf. 10^6). In E they are delivered into the hand of plunderers (שׁסים v.^{14a}); in D sold into the power of the enemies who surround them (v.$^{14b. 15}$), with which compare 3^{12} (Moab), 6 ff. (Midian), $10^{6ff.}$ (Ammon), 13 ff. (Philistines). In E they do not obey their judges but persist in apostasy (v.^{17}), in consequence of which Yahweh resolves not to drive out any more of the nations which Joshua left unsubdued (v. $^{20. 21}$); in D a reform under each of the judges is followed at his death by a worse relapse (v.$^{18. 19}$). In 2^{23}-3^6 fragments of a third source are found;† ch. 2^{23a} 3^2 give an altogether different explanation of the incompleteness of the conquest from 2^{21} $3^{1a. 4}$, and are ascribed by Mey. and Bu. (cf. Kitt.) to the author of ch. 1 (J).‡ The list of nations, 3^3, is thought by these scholars to be derived from the same source, but this seems to me less probable; 2^{23a} 3^2 appear to me to refer backward to ch. 1, and neither to require nor admit after them a list like 3^3. This list, which corresponds to Jos. $13^{2ff.}$ rather than to Jud. 1, together with 3^{1a}, I am inclined to attribute to E, whose narrative would then run: $2^{20. 21}$ $3^{1a a-3. 4}$; $3^{4. 6}$ bear the stamp of Rje rather than E, and may have as their basis a text of J; 2^{23} $3^{1a β}$ are redactional, though perhaps not by the same hand.

II. 6–10. The Israelites settle on the lands allotted them. Joshua and his contemporaries pass away. The new generation.

—6. = Jos. 24^{28}. — *Joshua dismissed the people, &c.*] the conclu-

---

* Be.'s analysis is : A $2^{11a. 13. 14-19}$; B $2^{11b. 12. 20-23}$ 3^{1-6}. A belongs to the framework of the book, and is interpolated by its author in the older introduction (B). Bu. materially improves upon this : A (= Deut. author) $2^{11. 13. 14-16. 18. 19}$; B (= E) $2^{13. 20-22a}$ $3^{5. 6}$; A and B were united by a later editor (R) who added v.^{17}.

† First recognized by Meyer, *ZATW*. i. p. 145.

‡ Mey.'s analysis (*ZATW*. i. p. 145) is : J 2^{23a} $3^{1b. 2. 3}$; E 2^{23} (= 3^4) 2^{2b} $3^{1a. 5. 6.}$ (continuation of Jos. $24^{19ff. 27}$). Bu. (*Richt. u. Sam.*, p. 159 f.) ascribes to E 2^{22a} $3^{5. 6}$; 3^4 is introduced by R to recover connexion. The original, doubtless very brief, form of 2^{23}-3^9 (in substance J), can hardly be recovered. Kitt. regards 2^{23} 3^{1-3} (prob. J) as the only old part of this passage; E is not represented. Kue. also thinks 3^{1-3} an extract from an older source; 2^{23} 3^4 form the setting given it by the author of Judges.

sion of the account of the great assembly at Shechem and the parting exhortations of Joshua (Jos. 24$^{1-28}$; substantially E). It was followed by the death and burial of Joshua (v.^{29} Jos. 24$^{29f.}$), to which E's description of the subsequent apostasy of Israel and its consequences (v.$^{10.13.14a.16f.20f.}$) immediately attached itself. The insertion of Jud. 1^{1b}–2^{5}, and the division of the books, left the story in Jos. without a suitable close, and accordingly Jud. 2$^{6.8.9}$ were restored in their original connexion in Jos. (24$^{28-31}$), carrying over with them Jud. 2^{7} (= Jos. 24^{31}), an addition of D.* — 7. = Jos. 24^{31} (𝔊 24^{29}). The verse is not by the same hand as v.^{10}, to which it is parallel; v.^{10} is the sequel of v.^{9} in E, v.^{7}, in expression and representation Deuteronomic, is its counterpart in D. — *The elders who survived Joshua*] the *sheikhs*, the head men of the clans and families, who were the natural guardians of Israelitish custom, law, and religion.† It is not used with primary reference to age, ‡ though the elders here meant were doubtless the coevals of Joshua. — *Who survived Joshua*] lit. *prolonged days after J;* a very common phrase in Dt. (*e.g.* 4^{40} 5^{33} 11^{9} 17^{20} 22^{7} 30^{18} 32^{47}) and Deuteronomic passages in other books (*e.g.* 1 K. 3^{14}; cf. also Ex. 20^{12}); otherwise infrequent (Is. 53^{10} Prov. 28^{16} Eccl. 8^{13}). — *Who had seen all the great work of Yahweh*] v.^{10} Jos. 24^{31} *had known, experienced.* The "great work of Yahweh" is not to be limited to the conquest of Canaan, but comprehends his whole great deliverance, the exodus, the wandering, and the invasion, of all of which Joshua's generation had been witnesses; cf. Dt. 11$^{2-7}$, where Moses recalls to the Israelites, as they are about to cross the Jordan, how their eyes had seen "all the great work of Yahweh which he wrought" (v.^{7}), specifying the Egyptian plagues, the deliverance of Israel and destruction of the Egyptians at the Red Sea, &c. (v.$^{2-4}$ cf. 7$^{18.19}$). The author of Jud. 2^{7}, like the author of Dt. 11$^{2-7}$ 5$^{2f.}$ 7$^{18f.}$, represents the exodus and the conquest as falling within the lifetime of a single generation. In the memory of these signal manifestations of Yahweh's power and grace, that generation remained faithful to him even after their great leader passed away; cf. v.^{10}. — 8. = Jos. 24^{29}. The beginning of the verse in Jos., *and after these things, i.e.,* after Joshua

---

* Cf. Stud., Hävernick, *Einl.*, ii. i. p. 79.   † Be.   ‡ Ba.

·had delivered his farewell address and the people had entered upon the possession of their allotments, may be part of the original text, but is not indispensable. — *The servant of Yahweh*] of Joshua, perhaps the addition of an editor;[*] Dt. 34[5] Jos. 1[1] and often of Moses, see Dillmann on Dt. *l. c.* — *A hundred and ten years old*] the age of his ancestor Joseph, Gen. 50[22. 26] (E). — **9.** = Jos. 24[30]. — *They buried him within the bounds of his estate*] on the lands which were allotted to him (Jos. 19[49]) ; not " on the boundary," &c. — *Timnath-ḥeres*] Jos. 24[30] 19[50] *Timnath-serah*, probably a metathesis to get rid of a name of heathenish sound ; see note. Timnath is the modern Tibneh, NW. of Gifnā (Gophna) on the road to the coast. On the northern side of the hill which lies over against the town to the south are remarkable tombs, in one of which Guérin would recognize the burial place of Joshua.[†] Samaritan, Jewish, and Moslem tradition in the Middle Ages fixed on a site nearer Nābulus (Shechem), at Kefr Ḥārith or at 'Awerteh.[‡] — *The Highlands of Ephraim*] see on 3[27]. — *North of Mt. Gaash*] cf. " the Wadies of Gaash," 2 S. 23[30] = 1 Chr. 11[32] ; there is no other clue by which to fix the location. — **10.** *All that generation*] the contemporaries of Joshua ; see above on v.[7]. — *Were gathered to their fathers*] 2 K. 22[20] ; compare the equivalent expressions, be gathered to his people, go to his fathers, sleep with his fathers. The original reference is to the family sepulchre, in which, as in a common abode, the members of the family dwell together, and perpetuate in that shadowy existence the relations of the former life. By a natural extension the phrases are applied also to the nether world, in which, by their clans, and tribes, and nations, all the dead dwell. In later times they are only a euphemistic circumlocution for death. § — *Another generation*] Joel. 1[3] ; the defection began with the next

---

[*] 3 in Jud. 1[1] also.

[†] On Tibneh see Eli Smith in *Bibliotheca Sacra*, 1843, p. 483 ff.; De Saulcy, *Voyage en Terre Sainte*, ii. p. 238 ff., Guérin, *Samarie*, ii. p. 89-104 ; *PEF. Statements*, 1873, p. 145, 1878, p. 22 f.; *SWP. Memoirs*, ii. p. 299 f., 374-378.

[‡] Kefr Ḥārith, about 9 m. SW. of Nābulus, is accepted by Conder (*SWP. Memoirs*, ii. p. 284 f.; *PEF. Statements*, 1878, p. 22 f.) and G. A. Smith, *Hist. Geogr. of the Holy Land*, 1894, p. 351, n. 3.

§ See Böttcher, *De inferis*, p. 54 ff.; Schwally, *Leben nach dem Tode*, p. 54 ff.; Moore, in *Andover Review*, ii. 1884, p. 433 ff. 516-518 (literature).

generation after the invasion. —*Who did not know Yahweh and
the work which he wrought for Israel*] see on v.⁷ Jos. 24¹¹.   Not
would not acknowledge Yahweh (Ex. 5² 1 S. 2¹²), but, did not, by
personal experience, know him as Deliverer, Leader, Conqueror
(cf. Dt. 11²⁴ 13², &c.) ; they had not shared those wonderful ex-
periences which had been to their fathers the proof of Yahweh's
power and his jealous love for Israel, and made it inconceivable
that they should turn from him to other gods ; cf. Ex. 1⁸.*

6. This seems more probable than the alternative hypothesis, that, after
the insertion of Jud. 1¹–2⁵, the close of Jos. 24 was repeated in Jud. 2⁶ff. to
resume connexion.   That the text in Jos. appears in some points more original (ויהי אחרי הדברים האיה v.²⁹ ; the position of v.³¹ = Jud. 2⁷ †) is not conclusive. — That the events narrated in 2⁶⁻¹⁰ cannot be posterior in time to
v.¹⁻⁵ was recognized by older commentators, who tried to get over the difficulty
by exegetical artifices.   Schm. connects : Caeterum quomodo, quae Angelus
Jehovae praedixit, impleta fuerint, ex his sequentibus apparebit : *Postquam
dimisit Josua*, etc.   The structure of the following verses is suspended ; the
apodosis begins in v.¹¹, Tum vero fecerunt filii Israelis malum, etc.   Similarly
Ba. : What is narrated in v.⁶⁻¹⁰ᵃ is to be regarded as virtually in the pluperfect ; v.¹⁰ᵇ· ¹¹ connects with and continues v.⁵.   Cf. also Ra., Ki., Abarb. — **9.**
הבנת חרס] probably Portion (sacred territory) of the Sun ; cf. Har-ḥeres (1³⁵ ;
see note there), Beth-shemesh, &c.   In Jos. (24⁵⁾ 19⁶⁰) המנה סרח, and so
ⳑⳠ here.   This is not the true name of the place (Stud., Ges. *Thes.*, ‡ Be., al.),
for which הבנת הרס Jud. 2⁹ is transcriptional error ; neither are חרס and סרח
from the same root by metathesis, like כשב, כבש (Ki., Abarb., Schm.), or from
different roots of the same meaning (Ba.) ; but ה׳ הרס is the original, and ה׳
סרח is prob. not accidental error but intentional mutilation of a name which
savoured of idolatry (Juynboll, *Chron. Samar.*, p. 295). §   There are numerous
examples of similar procedure ; cf. esp. Is. 19¹⁸, where for the same reason
חרס has been altered to הרס, or, in a few manuscripts, to חרם.   The latter
reading is found in some codd. and ed. Soncino in Jud. 2⁹.   Possibly θαμνασα-
χαρ 𝕲 Jos. 24³⁰ (21⁴⁰ Jud. 2⁹ᶜᵒᵈᵈ·) represents another transposition.   Cf. also
Baba bathra 122ᵃ·ᵇ, Ra. on Jos. 24³⁰ Jud. 2⁹. — At the beginning of our era
Thamna was the chief town of a toparchy which lay to the NE. of Lydda
(Diospolis) in the old territory of Ephraim (Fl. Jos., *b. j.* iii. 3, 5 ; Plin.,
n. h., v. 70 ; Euseb., *OS²*. 219₈₄ cf. 260₃ 239₈₃ 211₉₁ ‖).   Here in the 4th cent.

---

* Noting the similarities of phraseology.

† In 𝕲 this verse stands in Jos. in the same position as in Jud., immediately
after v.²⁸ = Jud. 2⁶.

‡ Etymologizing, without warrant in usage, *portio abundans v. redundans.*

§ Hävernick (*Einl.* ii. 1. p. 79) considered ה׳ חרם the old Canaanite, סרח ת׳ the
Israelite name.   ‖ See also Schürer, *GjV.* ii. p. 138 f.

the tomb of Joshua (ἐπίσημον . . . μνῆμα) was shown (*OS²*. 261₁₁ 246₁₁; Jerome, *ep.* 108, 13). It was identified with the modern Tibneh by Eli Smith in 1843 (*Bibl. Sacr.*, p. 483 f.). Guérin, in 1863, was convinced that he had discovered the tomb of Joshua in the most western of the rock tombs over against the town. Many niches for lamps in the forechamber prove that it was once a frequented shrine; and it is not improbable that it is the same that was shown to Christian pilgrims as the sepulchre of Joshua in the 4th century. For confirmation, the Abbé Richard in 1870 found in and before the tomb flint knives, which he combined with Jos. 24³⁾ 21⁴⁾ **6**. — There are a number of other places bearing the name Timnath: one in the hill country of Judah (Jos. 15⁵⁷, prob. also Gen. 38¹²ᶠᶠ·); another the scene of Samson's exploits (Jud. 14. 15; Jos. 15¹⁹ 19⁴⁴). The name Tibneh is also found east of the Jordan in 'Aǧlûn (Tristram, *Land of Israel*, p. 458 ff.). *— 10. יִרְאֶה־אִישׁ] יִרְ in this sense freq. in Dt., *e.g.* 11² 9² 11²⁸ 13³· ⁷· ¹⁴ 28²³· ³⁵· ⁶⁴; cf. Jer. 9¹⁶, &c. (Di., *NDJ.* p. 588).

11-19. The defection of Israel; neither punishment nor deliverance works amendment. — A summary of the whole history. — 11-13. The defection.

Verse ¹¹ is not the original sequel of v.¹⁰ (E), which is rather to be found in v.¹³, neither is it in place before v.¹² (D), which it anticipates; probably, therefore, inserted by the editor (R), employing motives of both E and D. — *The Israelites did what displeased Yahweh*] lit. *that which was evil in his eyes*. Standing formula in the introduction to the stories of the several judges (3⁷· ¹² 4¹ 6¹ 10⁶ 13¹; cf. Dt. 4²⁵ 9¹⁸ 17² 31²⁹), and especially in the judgements passed on the character of the kings of Israel and Judah (1 K. 15²⁶· ³⁴ 16²⁵· ³⁰ 22⁵² 2 K. 3², &c.); seldom in Samuel (1 S. 15¹⁹ 2 S. 12⁹ cf. 1 S. 12²⁰), which was never subjected to thorough Deuteronomic redaction. The *evil* is generally, though not always, an offence against religion, the worship of other gods, or of idols of Yahweh; see the examples above.— *Served the Baals*] the gods of the Canaanites among whom they lived (3⁵ᶠ·), then, in general, fell into heathenism; see further on v.¹³. — **12.** The verse shows in every clause its filiation with the Deuteronomic literature. — *Forsook Yahweh*] 10⁶· ¹⁰· ¹³, and often throughout the O.T. — *God of their fathers*] only here in Jud.; frequent in Dt. (1¹¹· ²¹ 4¹ 6³ 12¹ 26⁷ 27³ 29²⁵ cf. Ex. 3¹⁵· ¹⁶ 4⁵ Jos. 18¹·). — *Who brought them out of the land of Egypt*] the great de-

---

* The genitive, very likely in these cases also originally the name of a god, has been dropped.

liverance gave him a right to their allegiance. It stands thus as
the first of the Ten Words (Ex. 20² Dt. 5⁶), the ground of
obligation and motive of obedience. Unfaithfulness has the baseness of ingratitude (Dt. 8¹¹ᶜ· 13¹⁰, &c.). — *Followed other gods*]
2¹⁹ Dt. 8¹⁹ 11²⁸ 13² 28¹⁴ Jer. 7⁶ 11¹⁰ 13¹⁰, and freq. — *Of the gods of
the surrounding nations*] Dt. 6¹⁴ 13⁷ᶠ·. — *Exasperated Yahweh*] the
verb nowhere else in Jud.; Dt. 4²³ 9¹⁸ 31²⁹ 32¹⁶; freq. in Deuteronomic strata of Kings and in Jer. It connotes defiant provocation:
superbe peccaverunt, nec curaverunt, si maxime Deus indignaretur
(Schm.). — **13, 14.** Verse ¹³ is a doublet to v.¹².* As v.¹² clearly
belongs to D, v.¹³ may be ascribed to E and connected immediately with v.¹⁰. — *Forsook Yahweh*] see on v.¹²ᵃ; cf. also in E, Jos.
24³ᴵ Dt. 31¹ᵃᶠ·. — *And sacrificed to Baal and Astarte*] on the text
see critical note. The Baals and Astartes, *i.e.* the heathen gods
and goddesses, are coupled in the same way in Jud. 10⁶ 1 S. 7⁴
12¹⁰; † cf. Baals and Asheras, Jud. 3⁷. Baal signifies 'proprietor,
possessor' of something, and requires a complement, expressed or
implied, thus: Baal-Ṣor, the Lord of Tyre; Baal-Sidon, Baal-Leba-
non, Baal-Hermon, also Baal-Shamen, the Lord of the Heavens; ‡
or Baal-zebub, Baal-berith, &c. It is not a proper name; the name
of the Baal of Tyre, *e.g.*, was Melqart; in Israel the Baal (Proprietor) was Yahweh (Hos. 2¹⁶, Heb. 2¹⁸). § There were thus innu-
merable Baals, some of them having proper names of their own,
others distinguished only by the place where they were worshipped, or by some attribute. In any religious community the
god to which it belonged would ordinarily be spoken of merely as
the Baal, the Lord, further definition being unnecessary; but there
was among the Canaanites and Phoenicians no one god named
Baal. In the Old Testament the plural is sometimes used of this
multitude of local deities; sometimes, as here, the singular, for
the whole genus false god in contrast to Yahweh. ‖ — *Astarte*]

---

* An elaborate exegetical explanation of this doublet in Abarb.

† Both probably E (e).

‡ That Baal was a solar diety is, however, an inveterate error. It is not certain
even that Baal-ḥamman was such; see E. Meyer, in Roscher, i. 2870.

§ Cf. also names such as Eshbaal (son of Saul), Baaljada (son of David =
Eljada), and even Baaljah, *i.e.* Yahweh is Baal.

‖ Cf. Hos. 13¹ Jer. 2⁸, esp. 11¹³ Zeph. 1⁴. See Sta., *ZATW.* vi. p. 303 f.

Phoen. 'Ashtart; Heb. 'Ashtoreth.* One of the most widely
worshipped of the Semitic divinities; in Babylonia and Assyria
as Ishtar, in southern Arabia as 'Athtar, in Syria as 'Athar. From
1 K. 11^{5, 33} 2 K. 23^{13} it might appear that the worship of Astarte
was specifically Phoenician, but this would be an erroneous inference; it was evidently common through all Palestine, east and
west of the Jordan. She had a temple among the Philistines
(1 S. 31^{10}), gave her name to a city in Bashan, Ashtaroth-
karnaim (Dt. 1^4 Gen. 14^5), and appears in the Moabite stele of
King Mesha ('Ashtar-Kemosh, l. 17). Numerous inscriptions
from Phoenicia and its colonies attest the wide diffusion and importance of her cult, which was early introduced into Egypt also.
As the principal female deity of the Canaanites, the name of
Astarte is used in the O.T. in conjunction with Baal as a quasi-
appellative for goddess, for which the Hebrew language possesses
no proper word.†

11. הבעלים] the plural here and in עשתרות v.^{13} does not refer to the many
images of the gods (Aug., *quaest.* 16, Ki., Ges., Stud., al.), nor to the manifold
local forms of one god (Renan, comparing the many Virgins of Catholic
lands, ‡ Baethgen, al.); but to different gods. — 13. ויעבדו לבעל ולעשתרות]
the incongruity of number is most probably to be removed by reading לעשתרת
sg., though the plural is supported by 𝕸 and verss. It would make no
difference in the sense if we made both plur. The construction of the verb
presents a more serious difficulty; עבד ל for עבד with accus. is unexampled; §
in Jer. 44^8 יעבד (> 𝕲𝕾) is doublet or gloss to להקטר. This corruption suggests
the correction for our verse; I conjecture that the author wrote ויקטרו *burnt
sacrifices* (Jer. 7^9 11^{13, 17} and often, Hos. 11^2, &c.), which was altered, by
accidental conformation to v.^{11}, or intentionally, for emphasis, to ויעבדו. On
BAAL see Baudissin, *PRE*^2. ii. p. 27-38, where the older literature is pretty
fully given (p. 37 f.); Pietschmann, *Gesch. d. Phönizier*, p. 183 f.; Baethgen,
Beiträge zur Semit. Religionsgeschichte, p. 17 ff.; W. R. Smith, *Religion of
Semites*, Pt. i. p. 92 ff., and art. "Baal" in *New Dict. of the Bible;* E. Meyer,
art. "Ba'al" in Roscher, *Lexikon der Griechischen und Römischen Mythologie*,
i. 2867-2880. On ASTARTE, Baudissin, *PRE*^2. i. p. 719-725 (older lit., p.

---

* With malicious substitution of the vowels of *bosheth*.
† Similarly in Assyrian (in the plural), *ilâni u-ishtarâti*, gods and goddesses;
Schrader, *KAT*^2. p. 180; Tiele, *Babylonisch-Assyr. Geschichte*, p. 538. In the treaty
of Ramses II. with the Hittites we read of the "'Astart of the Hittite country," just
as of the Sutḫ of Ḫeta; W. M. Müller, *Asien u. Europa*, p. 330.
‡ As Aug. had the many Junos.
§ In 1 S. 4^9 the meaning, 'be subject to,' is different.

725); Pietschmann, *op. cit.*; Baethgen, *Beiträge*, p. 31 ff.; Barton, "Ashtoreth and her Influence in the O.T.," *JBL.* x. p. 73 ff.; E. Meyer, art. "Astarte," in Roscher, i. 645-655. A satisfactory etymology and explanation of the name עשתרת has not yet been given; see Lexx. The fem. ending seems to be distinctly Canaanite (Phoenician, Hittite).

14, 15. The punishment. — **14.** The two halves of the verse are obviously doublets; v.ᵃ is probably the continuation of v.¹³(E), v.ᵇ its counterpart in D. — *Yahweh was incensed against Israel*] v.²⁰ 3⁸ 10⁷ cf. 6¹⁰; a common phrase. — *He gave them into the power of pillagers*] a somewhat unusual word; v.¹⁶ 1 S. 14⁴⁸ 2 K. 17²⁰ Is. 10¹³; see note. — *He sold them into the power of the enemies who surrounded them*] parallel to the preceding (v.ᵃ), in different terms; 3⁸ 4² 10⁷ cf. 4⁹ Dt. 32³⁰ 1 S. 12⁹ Ez. 30¹² Is. 50¹; for the last clause see 8³⁴. The punishment is inflicted by the hand of the same surrounding nations for whose religion they had forsaken their own (v.¹²). The words may have originally followed immediately after v.¹², "they exasperated Yahweh." — *They were no more able to stand before their enemies*] Jos. 7¹² cf. Lev. 26³⁷ᶠ· Nu. 14⁴²⁻⁴⁵. — **15.** *In every campaign*] lit. *wherever they went out* (to war); see note. Others, in every undertaking, in omni negotio, propter quod exiverunt.ᵃ — *The hand of Yahweh, &c.*] Dt. 2¹⁵. — *As Yahweh had threatened*] the reference is not to any single passage expressly containing this threat,† but to the whole tenor of such chapters as Dt. 28 (cf. esp. v.²⁵·³⁰⁻³⁴·⁴⁸ᶠᶠ·) and Lev. 26 (esp. v.¹⁷·³⁶⁻³⁹); cf. Is. 30¹⁷. — *And they were in great straits*] Gen. 32⁷ 2 S. 13².

16–19. Not even the judges whom Yahweh from time to time raises up to deliver them are able to reclaim them from their evil ways. — Verses ¹⁶·¹⁷ and v.¹⁸·¹⁹ are entirely parallel; v.¹⁶ with its sequel v.¹⁷ is by the same hand as v.¹⁴ᵃ (E); v.¹⁸·¹⁹ correspond in D and connect with v.¹⁴ᵇ. — **16.** *Judges*] the judges of this book are the champions and leaders of Israel in its conflicts with its enemies and oppressors. The name is synonymous with *deliverer* (v.¹⁶·¹⁸ 3⁹·¹⁵·³¹); see note on 3¹⁰. — *Delivered them from those that pillaged them*] v.¹⁴ᵃ. It is possible that some such words as "And the Israelites cried unto Yahweh" (3¹⁵) have been dis-

---

ᵃ Schm.; similarly Ba.   † Certainly not Jos. 23¹⁸ Jud. 2¹⁻³ (Schm., Ba.).

placed by v.[14b. 15].—17. Continues the preceding.[*] Even their
deliverers had no influence over them. — *They apostatized to
other gods*] lit. *went whoring after other gods*, 8[27. 33] (Gideon's
ephod) Ex. 34[15. 16] Dt. 31[16] cf. Lev. 17[7] 20[5. 6]. They deserted
Yahweh, their own god, and gave themselves up, body and soul,
to other gods. The figure suggests both the sin of unfaithfulness
and the shame of prostitution. It is very common in the literature of the 7th century, and probably originated with Hosea,
whose own bitter experience with his adulterous wife became for
him the type of the relations of Yahweh and Israel (Hos. 1-3
cf. 9[1], &c.).[†] — *They soon turned aside, &c.*] Ex. 32[8] Dt. 9[12. 16] 11[16]
31[29].—Their fathers, the generation of Joshua (v.[10. 22] cf. v.[7]),
walked in obedience to God's commands; their descendants did
not follow their example. — 18. Parallel to v.[16] (see above); observe *enemies*, as in v.[14b], in contrast to *pillagers*, v.[14a. 16].—*Yahweh
was with the judge*] cf. Jos. 1[5]. — *For Yahweh was moved to pity
by their groaning*] motive of the deliverance, v.[8]. Not *repented*,
i.e. changed his mind and gave up his purpose to punish them.
— *Tyrants and oppressors*] the words are synonymous; see note.
—19. Counterpart of v.[17], with a slight difference of representation; in v.[17] they pay no heed to the efforts of the judges to restrain them from their apostasy; [‡] in v.[19] it is implied that their
propensity to heathenism was held in check during the life of the
judge only to break out the more violently at his death. — *At the
death of the judge they would relapse*] the tenses express what
happened over and over again with the regularity of law. This is
the conception of the history which dominates the Deuteronomic
setting of the stories of the judges; see 4[1] 8[33], &c. — *Worse than
their fathers*] Jer. 7[26] 16[12]. Not the godly fathers of v.[10. 17. 22],
but the generations which preceded them, and had sinned in the
same way under former judges; each was worse than the last. —
In running after other gods] they went to still greater lengths in
the evil way on which their ancestors had entered (v.[12]). — *They
did not drop any of their practices or of their obstinacy*] lit. *stub-*

---

[*] Bu., Kue., regard v.[17] as a late interpolation; see note below.

[†] See Smend, *Alttestamentliche Religionsgeschichte*, p. 188 ff.

[‡] As Israel in later times gave no heed to the warnings and expostulations of
the prophets.

born way; viz., those of their predecessors. The collocation "practices and way" (or ways) is frequent in Jer., *e.g.* 4[18] 7[1,3] 18[11].

14. כיד שׂסים ויֶשׁסו אורם] the punctuation distinguishes, without difference of meaning, כסה v.[16] 1 S. 14[48] 23[1] 2 K. 17[20] &c. from כבם 1 S. 17[53] Is. 13[16]; cf. כסה and בסם, רבה and רבם. Syn. of בזו Is. 17[14] 42[22] Jer. 30[16], 'plunder, pillage.' The word seems to have been borrowed by the Egyptians as a designation for the nomadic robber-tribes of the desert south of Palestine (*Ja-su, Ja-sa,* pron. *šōs*); see W. M. Müller, *Asien u. Europa,* p. 131 f. — **15.** בכל אשׁר יצאו] *quocumque egrederentur;* i.e., quamcumque expeditionem aggrederentur (Cler.); so rightly Ki., cf. Jos. 17.9 2 K. 18[7]. יצא, 'march out to war,' make a foray (11[8]), campaign (2 S. 11[1] Am. 5[8] Dt. 28[7] and often); see Lex. — **16.** וֹיִישׁיעֵום] sc. the judges: 𝔊 καὶ ἔσωσεν αὐτοὺς Κύριος. — **17.** Bu. (*Richt. u. Sam.,* p. 92) and Kue. regard v.[17] as an interpolation, interrupting the connexion between v.[16] and v.[18], introducing a new motive, disobedience to the judges, and in expression varying from the Deut. pattern. If the analysis proposed above be sound, v.[17] is the sequel of v.[16], while v.[18] connects immediately with v.[16]. The last two clauses of v.[17] hang somewhat awkwardly, and may, if any one chooses, be ascribed to R; there is no reason for attributing the whole verse to him. — סרו מהר] the inf. abs. in adverbial accusative, cf. v.[28] Ex. 32[8] Dt. 7[4] &c., Ew. § 280 c. — **18.** וכי הקים י׳ . . . . . . והיה] pf. . . . . pf. consec.; recurring event in past time, Job 1[5] Jud. 6[3] Gen. 38[9] (אם); 8[1] Hos. 11[1]. — מן [בנאהקם] of the origin of his emotion, its cause. — נחם [להצירם וחקיהם] 1[34] 4[8] 6[9] 10[12] Ex. 3[9] 1 S. 10[18] 2 K. 13[4.23] Am. 6[14] &c. נחם Joel 2[31]; common in Aram.; in 𝔗𝔊 the usual equivalent of Heb. נחם. — **19.** וֹשָׁבוּ והשחיתו] impf. frequentative; Hiphil of conduct, *behave badly.* — ללכת וג׳ . . . [ללכת וגהשתרחות להם] the first gerundial inf. (see on v.[22]) specifies the particular in which they behaved worse than their fathers; the following inff. (ולעבדם וג׳) are a species of explicative apposition to ללכת, showing wherein the following of other gods consisted (Schm. well, *serviendo illis, et incurvando se illis*), not the motive of the Israelites (*to serve them*). — לא [מעלליהם מן הפילו ממעלליהם] of partitive object; cf. 1 S. 3[19] Est. 6[10]. Others render, did not desist from their practices, &c., giving the Hiph. an internally transitive force for which there seems to be no example or necessity. מעללים in bad sense, Is. 3[8] Jer. 11[18] &c.

20, 21. The penalty of Israel's persistent defection; Yahweh will not drive out any more of the nations which remained unconquered at the death of Joshua. — Cf. v.[21]. The verses are with much probability ascribed by Budde to E; * but in conformity with our analysis of the preceding we should connect them with v.[16c], rather than with v.[13] as he does. — **20.** *Inasmuch*

---

* *Richt. u. Sam.,* p. 158 f.

as this people have transgressed the injunction I laid upon their fathers] Jos. 7¹¹ (E). RV. lit., *my covenant which I commanded their fathers.* The verbs (transgress, enjoin) show that *berith*, rendered in our versions with mechanical uniformity *covenant*, is not here conceived of as a mutual compact or agreement, but as an ordinance of Yahweh, a rule prescribed by him. In general, in the older literature,[*] *berith*, in its religious use, is a formal act by which the relations between Yahweh and his people are regulated, or the relation thus regulated. Its author is God alone ; man's part is only to accept it. In speaking of it, according to circumstances, the thought may rest chiefly, or even exclusively, on one or the other of its two sides ; on the solemn promise and pledge of his favour which Yahweh has freely given, or on the character and conduct which he requires, which are in effect the terms of friendly intercourse with him and the enjoyment of his blessings. In the former case it becomes, as in v.², almost equivalent to *promise ;* in the latter, to *commandment, injunction,* as here, so that it may stand in parallelism to *law (torah),* as in Hos. 8¹.[†] The commandment given to the fathers was, that they should worship Yahweh alone ; cf. Ex. 34¹²⁻¹⁶ 23²⁴ᶠ. ³²ᶠ. — **21.** *I, on my part, will not drive out, &c.*] ; by their violation of his injunction they have forfeited the promise that accompanied it and was virtually conditional upon their fidelity (Ex. 34¹¹ 23²³. ²⁷⁻³¹). — *A single man of the nations that Joshua left when he died*] cf. Jos. 23¹². Jud. 2²⁴ 10¹³.

20. גוי הזה] גוי seldom of Israel ; Ex. 19⁶ 33¹³ Jos. 3¹⁷ 4¹ Zeph. 2⁹ (parallel to עם, which is the usual word) Is. 1⁴. Possibly the word is chosen for this reason ; הז itself sometimes has a tone of alienation like *iste ;* cf. Is. 6⁹ 8¹². — ברית] apparently only in Hebrew. The older etymological theory is well represented by Simonis : [‡] foedus ... sic dicitur a *dissectione* animalium, in pangendis foederibus usitata ; similarly J. D. Mich., Ges. *Thes.,* and many ; most recently König, *Hauptprobleme der altisraelit. Religionsgeschichte,* p. 85 = *Religious Hist. of Israel,* p. 152. Others suppose a development like that in *decidere, decisio ; scheiden, entscheiden,* &c. ; so E. Meier, *Wurzelwb.,* 1845,

---

[*] J E and D in the Hexateuch, and the cognate strata in the historical books.

[†] See J. J. P. Valeton, Jr., "Das Wort ברית in den jehovistischen und deuteronomistischen Stücken des Hexateuchs," *ZATW.* xii. p. 224-260 ; cf. *ib.* p. 1-22 (in the Priestly Law) ; Smend, *Alttest. Religionsgeschichte,* p. 294 ff.

[‡] Cf. Castell, *Lex. Heptaglott.,* s. v.

p. 514, MV., al. The assumed primary meaning, however (כרה ' cut '), is factitious. Fr. Delitzsch, *Hebrew and Assyrian*, compares Assyr. *baru*, ' decide.'
See Brown, *Hebrew Lexicon*, s. v. — In O.T. usage the notion of agreement is
manifestly prior to that of either command or promise, and probably this
reflects the older history of the word. For the free nomadic Semite, all right
which did not exist by nature in the bond of blood originated in compact;
We., *Proleg.*,² p. 443 f., Engl. transl. p. 418 f.; H. Schultz, *Alttest. Theol.*,⁴
401 ff. = *Old Test. Theol.*, ii. p. 2 ff. — כָּבַר בְּרִית] Dt. 17² Jos. 7¹¹ 23¹⁶ 2 K. 18¹²;
cf. רָקַע v.¹ Dt. 31¹⁶·²⁰, כָּנָה Dt. 4²³, עָזַב Dt. 29²⁴, מָאַס 2 K. 17¹⁵ (Valeton, *ZATW.*
xii. p. 235). — צִוָּה] with בְּרִית Jos. 7¹¹ 23¹⁶ 1 K. 11¹¹. — 21. אֲשֶׁר עָזַב יְהוֹשֻׁעַ]
unusual use of עָזַב; cf. 2 S. 15¹⁶. — וַיָּמֹת] which Joshua left *and died*. 𝕲 has
instead, καὶ ἀφῆκεν (subj. Yahweh) = וַיַּנַּח, as principal verb of the next sentence; perhaps neither is original.

22–III. 6. — Motives of Yahweh in leaving these nations; enumeration of them; consequences to Israel. — 22. Cf. 3⁴.

Verse ²ᵇ has a distinctly Deuteronomic colour; v.²ᵃ is ascribed
by Budde, not without some hesitation, to E.[*] But the connexion with v.²¹, as the history of interpretation shows, is loose and
ambiguous; and the motive for leaving the nations, to try Israel,
is not easily reconciled with v.²⁰ᶠ, where they are left as a punishment for Israel's confirmed unfaithfulness. It seems more probable, therefore, that v.²² is altogether by a different hand from v.²⁰ᶠ,
presumably that of an editor. — *In order to prove Israel by them*]
cf. 3¹ᵃ·⁴. Assuming the unity of the context, interpreters have
been divided in opinion whether the clause is a continuation of
the words of Yahweh in v.²¹, *that by them I may prove Israel*,[†] or
the writer's explanation of God's purpose, *that he might prove
Israel.*[‡] The latter is the more probable construction, and if the
verse be the addition of an editor the only natural one. The
object of the trial is to know whether Israel, thus exposed to close
and constant contact with heathenism, will remain faithful to its
own religion. [§] — *Keep the way of Yahweh*] observe the institutions
and ordinances of his religion, Gen. 18¹⁹ Dt. 5³³ Jer. 5⁴·⁵; often
in plural, *ways of Y.*, Dt. 10¹² 11²² &c., which was probably the
original reading here (see note). Compare the equivalent terms
of 3⁴. The phrase expresses more nearly than any other in the

[*] *Richt. u. Sam.*, p. 159.   [†] 𝕷, Lth., Schm., RV., al.   [‡] Aug., Stud., Ba., al.
[§] On the theological questions which this temptation or probation suggests, see
Aug., *qu.* 17; Greg. Magn., *Dial.*, iii. c. 14 *fin.*; a Lapide, *in loc.*; Schm., *qu.* 12.

O.T. what we call *religion*, from the external point of view, as
the fear of Yahweh does the inner side of religion; compare the
use of ὁδός, Acts 18²⁵·²⁶ 9² &c. — *As their fathers did*] 2⁷.

22. רֹלִכֶּן נטה] Dt. 8²·¹⁶, cf. לִנְסׂת Jud. 3¹·⁴. At this distance from the
principal verb, the writer would probably have expressed *ut experiar* by the
personal construction רֹלִכֶּן אֲנֹסָּה, avoiding all ambiguity. — [דרך יהוה ללכת בם
for בם 𝕲𝕳𝕾 give a sing.; Houbig. and Doorn. emend בה. More probably,
however, the author wrote דרכי יהוה (masc. plur.), from which the present text
arose by accident. The plur. בם in 𝕸 is explained of the many commandments, statutes, and ordinances which constitute the *way of Y.* — ללכת] gerundial, v.¹⁷·¹⁹ 1 S. 12¹⁷ 14³¹ 2 S. 3¹⁰ Jer. 44⁷·⁸; Ges.²⁶ § 114, n. 4; Dr.³ § 205.

23. Verse ²³ᵃ, with 3², clearly belongs to a different circle of ideas
from 2²⁰ᶠ· or 2¹² 3¹. In 2²³ᵃ 3² Yahweh does not drive out the people of Canaan at once, in order that the succeeding generations of
Israelites also may have experience of war. This explanation accords well with J's point of view, and to that writer the verses are
with considerable probability ascribed by E. Meyer.* Verse ²³ᵇ
may perhaps be an editorial addition, connecting the statement of
v.²³ᵃ with the time before Joshua's death (v.²¹); it is possible, however, that the editor has only substituted the name *Joshua* for an
original *Israel.* — *Yahweh left these nations*] the reference is obviously to nations of which the writer had already spoken, not to the
list below in 3³. If our analysis be substantially correct, we shall
most naturally think of ch. 1, in the fuller form in which it once
existed, in which, as appears from v.³⁴, not only the cities within
their own borders which Israel did not conquer were named, but
the boundaries of the surrounding nations. — *Not expelling them
at once*] cf. Ex. 23²⁹ᶠ· Dt. 7²²ᶠ·, which differ materially, however, in
conception and expression. The reason for the gradual expulsion
is given in 3². — *Did not give them into the power of Joshua*] the
commentators have found it very hard to explain how this could
be a punishment for the defection of Israel after the death of
Joshua, as in the present connexion it must be; quas nimirum
non dederat in manum Josuae,† is what the connexion imperatively requires, but this cannot be extorted from the Hebrew text.
— **III. 1.** Verse ¹ᵃ is the introduction to the catalogue v.³; v.¹ᵇ is

---

a doublet to v.²ᵇ. — *To try Israel by them*] it was a disciplinary judgement; cf. Dt. 8². ¹⁶. This sense would be possible in the assumed context of E (2²⁰. ²¹ 3¹ᵃ. ³); perhaps, however, the words were added by the redactor; cf. 2²² 3⁴. — *Namely all those who had no experience of all the wars of Canaan*] the generation following the invasion; corresponding to those who knew not Yahweh and the great things he did for Israel (2¹⁰ cf. 2⁷). The words are difficult and inappropriate in their present connexion; they may be either an editorial addition derived from v.²ᵇ, or, more probably, a gloss to v.²ᵇ intruded into the text in the wrong place.*
— **2.** The original sequel of 2²¹ .† The text is clearly corrupt; the restoration is somewhat uncertain. The most conservative course is to follow 𝕲; *merely for the sake of the successive generations of Israelites, to familiarize them with war.* A bolder reconstruction would be, *merely in order that the Israelites might have experience of war.* The sense is not materially different. 𝕃 well, ut postea discerent filii eorum certare cum hostibus, et habere consuetudinem praeliandi. The incompleteness of the conquest is not attributed to the sinful slackness of Israel (2¹⁻⁵), nor is it designed as a trial of Israel's fidelity to its religion (2²² 3¹), nor a punishment for its persistent infidelity (2²⁰ᶠ.); it is a wise appointment of Yahweh, that his people, from generation to generation, may have occasion to cultivate the virtues which only war develops, and learn by experience the superiority of their god to those of the heathen. — *Only those who had not known them before*] the generation of the invasion had had this training and experience; it is their descendants who are meant in v.ᵃ. The half verse is superfluous and may be secondary; v.¹ᵇ is a doublet to it.

23. לְבִלְתִּי הֹרִישָׁם] the proper negative of the inf. (8¹); here in gerundial use (see on v.²² above), as in Jos. 23⁶ לְבִלְתִּי סוּר וגֿ, *not turning.* — **III. 1.** אִיבֵּר רֵנִיחַ יהוה] 𝕲ᴬⱽᴸᴹ s᾽Ιησοῦς; conformation to 2²¹. — לְנַסּוֹת בָּם אֶת יִשְׂרָאֵל] Σ. ἀσκῆσαι ... καὶ διδάξαι τοῦ πολέμου τὴν τέχνην (Thdt., qu. 8). — **2.** לְמַעַן דַּעַת דֹּרוֹת בְּנֵי יִשְׂרָאֵל] the subject of the inf. cannot be Yahweh as in v.⁴, *that he might know the generations* (Schrör., Be., Ke., Reuss), expressing the motive of

---

* Stud.

† That 3² is not consonant with its present context is observed by Ziegler, who regards it as an interpolation.

putting them to the trial (v.¹); for then we can make nothing of the rest
of the sentence.* As the text stands it must be rendered, *in order that the
generations of the Israelites might know* (𝔖𝔗, Ra., Ki., Cler., Schm., Stud.,
Ba., Cass., and most). But then the inf. has no object, or rather another
verb is interposed, ללמדם מלחמה, — *to teach them — war*.† The whole sentence, though intelligible, is overloaded and clumsy. 𝔊 omits the first inf.,
לדעת, which relieves the worst of the difficulty. ‡ It is more satisfactory,
though bolder, to treat דרות as corrupt doublet of דעת, and ללמדם as a gloss to
the latter, or substitute for it; with the structure cf. Jos. 4²⁴, למען דעת כל עמי
הארץ וגו׳. Cler. compares Livy, xxxix. 1. — אשר לפנים לא ידעום] the pl. masc.
suff. referring to מלחמה is intolerable; the writer or scribe very likely had in
mind the מלחמות כנען of v.¹ᵇ; the discord in gender is not so unusual. The
half verse is not improbably an editorial restriction like v.¹ᵇ; observe the over
emphatic use of רק as well as the false concord just noted. — רק] restrictive
particle, with nouns (1 S. 1¹⁸ Am. 3²), verbs (Jud. 14¹⁶), and particles
(2 K. 21⁸). It does not always limit the next following word, but often
stands at the beginning of the sentence, limiting the emphatic word in it,
which has not, however, as in Arab. after اِنَّمَا, a fixed position in the
sentence.

3, 4. The peoples which Yahweh left within the bounds of Palestine to try the faith and obedience of Israel.

— The intro-
duction to these verses seems to be 3¹ᵃ, *these are the nations which
Yahweh left.* The verses accord better with the representation of
E (or D) than of J, to which source v.³ is attributed by Meyer
and Budde; see above, p. 64. With the catalogue compare Jos.
13²⁻⁶. — *The five tyrants of the Philistines*] Jos. 13³ 1 S. 6¹⁶⁻¹⁸. The
five are Gaza, Ashkelon, Ashdod, Gath, Ekron. The word rendered *tyrant (seren)* is used only of the Philistines, and is evidently the native name. That these cities were not conquered
by Israel agrees with the statement in 1²² and contradicts 1¹⁸; see
there. — *And all the Canaanites*] in J, as we have observed in
ch. 1 above, *Canaanite* is the comprehensive name for the populations west of the Jordan which the Israelites in part subjected and
among whom they settled. § It is hardly possible to reconcile *all*

---

* The verb in the relative sentence must, as Ba. urges, have the same subj. as
the inf.; *to teach them war* is another end, not easily harmonized with getting
knowledge of Israel.

† Ew. (*GVI.* ii. p. 382) would pronounce ללמד (Qal), *that they might learn.*

‡ For לבלתי with a noun, see Gen. 18²¹ Dt. 3²⁶ 2 K. 8¹⁹ Is. 45⁴ &c.

§ E. Meyer, *ZATW.* i. p. 121 ff.; iii. p. 306–309; Budde, *Urgeschichte*, p. 345 ff.

the Canaanites here with the usage of J ;[*] in the context, as Schmid has justly observed, the words cannot refer to the unsubjugated Canaanites in Israelite territory (ch. 1), but to a compact population on its borders.[†]   In E (and consequently in D), however, the name Canaanite seems to be employed in a more restricted sense for the inhabitants of the lowlands of western, and especially southwestern Palestine ;[‡] Nu. 13[29] (E) Dt. 1[7] (cf. 11[30]) Jos. 5[1] ; further, Jos. 13[3.4] 2 S. 24[7] Zeph. 2[5]. This corresponds, as far as I can judge, with the use of the name in Egyptian sources, and would be altogether suitable in the text before us, as well as in Jos. 13[3], "the Philistines, and the Avvim in the south — all the territory of the Canaanites." For this reason also it is better to ascribe the verse to E. [§] — *The Sidonians*] Jos. 13[4]. Here, as often, the collective name for the Phoenicians. [‖] Sidon, the ancient metropolis, gave its name to the entire people, and the denomination persisted after the political and commercial hegemony had long passed to Tyre ; see 10[6] 18[7] 1 K. 5[6] (Heb. 5[20]). — *The Hittites inhabiting Mount Lebanon*] conjectural emendation ; 𝕳 and the versions have *Hivvites*, by a transcriptional error which occurs in 𝕳 in Jos. 11[3] also.   The Hivvites were a petty people of Central Palestine (Gen. 34[2] cf. [30] 36[1] Jos. 9[7]) ;[¶] the seats of the Hittites, on the contrary, were in Coele Syria and the Lebanon (1 K. 10[29] 2 K. 7[6]; cf. Jud. 1[26] 2 S. 24[6] 𝕲),[**] where the Egyptian inscriptions also place them.   The emendation is therefore necessary. — *From Mt. Baal Hermon as far as the Gateway of Hamath*] Jos. 13[5] defines their southern boundary somewhat more precisely as "Baal-gad at the foot of Mt. Hermon." Baal-gad, according to Jos. 11[17] (cf. 12[7]) the northern limit of Israelite

---

[*] That it is left to the reader to understand, "all those, namely, who were mentioned above in ch. 1" (Bu.), is much too loose writing to impute to the author.

[†] Schm., p. 297 ; so also Ba.

[‡] Also, apparently, of the lower Jordan valley and its southern extension, the 'Arabah. See Masius on Jos. 13[4].

[§] It is, of course, possible that the words "and all the C." are interpolated ; the difference of form gives some ground for the suspicion.

[‖] So also in Homer, *Od.* iv. 84, &c.

[¶] Compare also the catalogue of the "seven nations," in which the normal order is, Perizzites, Hivvites, Jebusites ; Ex. 33[2] &c. (13 times).

[**] See, however, Klostermann on the last passage.

conquest under Joshua, was in the valley of the Lebanon, the
Biqā', and must therefore have been on the western side of Mt.
Hermon, perhaps at the modern Ḥāṣbeiyā.*— *Hamath*] frequently
mentioned in Egyptian and Assyrian inscriptions as well as in the
O.T., is the modern Ḥamā, a city of 60,000 inhabitants, on the
Orontes (el 'Āṣi),† — *The Gateway of Hamath*, often named as
the northern limit of Palestine (Am. 6^{14} 2 K. 14^{28} 1 K. 8^{65} Ez. 47^{20}
48^1 Nu. 34^8 cf. 13^{21}), is probably the plain Ḥöms, some 30 miles
south of Ḥamā, at the intersection of four passes, and of main
roads from the coast, the Syrian desert, and north and south
through Coele Syria.

The verse implies that the boundaries of Palestine are the
desert on the south, and the northern end of the Lebanon range
on the north, and from the Antilebanon and the Jordan valley to
the sea. ‡ The whole of this territory Israel regarded as included
in the gift of Yahweh. Its actual possessions, however, were of
much more modest dimensions. The entire seaboard, the Philistine lowlands and the plain of Sharon, as well as the Phoenician
coast north of Carmel and the whole region of the Lebanon §
remained in the hands of its old inhabitants or were conquered by
other invaders like the Philistines. This difference between the
ideal and the actual boundaries of the land of Israel is frequently
noted.

On the Philistines see *New Bible Dictionary* (A. & C. Black), s. v.,
where the older literature will be found; Hitzig, *Urgeschichte u. Mythologie
der Philistäer*, 1845; Stark, *Gaza und die philistäische Küste*, 1852; Pietschmann, *Phönizier*, p. 261 ff.; Schwally, "Die Rasse der Philister," *ZWTh.*
xxxiv. p. 103–108; W. M. Müller, *Asien u. Europa*, p. 387 ff. — The Philistines,
so far as our present knowledge goes, did not make their appearance in Palestine until the age of Ramses III. Shortly before the time of Saul they
subjugated not only Judah (Jud. 15^{11}) and Joseph (1 S. 4), but the Canaanites
in the Great Plain (1 S. 31^{10}), and it is natural to surmise that these successes
were gained in the first impetus of the invasion. Under David Israel freed
itself from them, and they were thenceforward confined to the southern part

---

* Kneucker, *BL.* i. p. 331; Ba., Di., *NDJ.* p. 499 f.; Bäd². p. 297.

† On Hamath see Pococke, *Description of the East*, ii. 1. p. 143 f.; Burckhardt,
Travels in Syria and the Holy Land, 1822, p. 145 ff.; Rob., *BR².* iii. p. 551; Bäd².
p. 398 f.; Arab geographers, Le Strange, p. 357–360.

‡ Cf. 1 K. 8^{65} 2 K. 14^{25} Am. 6^{14}.

§ The northernmost settlement of Israel was at Dan.

of the seaboard plain with its five cities. — *The Canaanites*] in Egyptian texts Canaan (*Ka-n-'-ng*) appears to be a district of southwestern Palestine not very remote from Egypt.[*] In the Amarna correspondence the land *Ki-na-aḥ-ḥi* is mentioned a number of times, in connexions which point to the vicinity of the Phoenician cities (Acco, *Berl.* 8; Tyre, *Lond.* 30).[†] The Phoenicians called themselves Canaanites, their land Canaan.[‡] Before the advent of the Philistines the plain south of Carmel was no doubt occupied by the same race as the coast north of it, and Canaanites seem, at least in Southern Palestine, to have occupied also the hill country back from the coast.[§] The current etymological explanation of the name, 'Lowland, Lowlanders' (Rosenmüller, *Bibl. Alterthumsk.*, 1826, ii. 1. p. 75 f., Ges., al. mu.), in contrast either to Aram, or to the Amorites ('Highlanders'), is false both in language and fact; see my note, *PAOS.* 1890, p. lxvii-lxx. The texts cited above for the more restricted use of the name Canaanite in E and D are too summarily disposed of by Mey. and Bu., who, because they conflict with the representation of J, regard them all as late and erroneous theory. But the theory itself has its origin in the usage of E. — *The Sidonians*] in Gen. 10^16 Sidon (Phoenicia) is the oldest son, *i.e.* the most important people, of Canaan; but Bu. is perhaps right in his contention that in the O.T. the name Canaanites is never specifically employed for the Phoenicians.[||] See further, Smend, *HWB*[1]. s. v. "Sidon"; Pietschmann, *Phönizier*, p. 106 f. — On the Hittites, see the literature, *DB*[2]. s. v. (i. p. 1379); and add Jensen, review of Peiser, *ZA.* vii. 357-366; also "Grundlagen für eine Entzifferung," u.s.w., *ZDMG.* xlviii. p. 235 ff. — In Jos. 11^3 the departure from the usual order of the catalogue suggests that Hivvites and Hittites have accidentally exchanged places, and this suspicion is confirmed by 𝔊^HM al. k. We. (*TBS.* p. 218) emends accordingly, *the Hittites at the foot of Hermon.* The same correction is made in Jud. 3^3 by Mey. (*ZATW.* i. p. 126) and Bu.; the objections of Di. (*NDJ.* p. 497) are of no great force. The Hittite empire in Syria, with which the Egyptian kings of the 19th dynasty waged long and obstinate war for the possession of the land of Amor (Northern Palestine, Coele Syria), had disappeared before the advent of the Israelite tribes in Palestine. The Hittites of

---

[*] E. Meyer, *ZATW.* iii. p. 308 f.; Wiedemann in Budde, *Urgeschichte,* p. 346 n.; Pietschmann, *Phönizier,* p. 97; Müller, *Asien u. Europa,* p. 205 ff. Müller thinks that it does not include Phoenicia, for which a special name (*Ḏa-hi*) exists; but the inference is perhaps unwarranted.

[†] Communication from Prof. D. G. Lyon; see also Halévy, *REJ.* xx. p. 204 ff.; Delattre, *PSBA.* 1891, p. 234.

[‡] Canaan (כנע) on a coin of Laodicea, above, p. 25 n.; Xνα = כנע, Hecataeus [? Abder.], Müller, *fr. hist. gr.,* i. p. 17; Choeroboscus, Bekker, *anecd. gr.,* iii. p. 1181; Euseb., *praep. ev.,* i. 10 § 26; Steph. Byz., *s. v.* With this shorter form Kinaḥḥi in the Amarna tablets must be connected.

[§] This must be inferred from the usage of J.

[||] *Urgeschichte,* p. 348 ff., against Ha., Di., *BL,* art. "Kenaan"; Kautzsch, *HWB.,* art. "Canaaniter," al.

G

the Lebanon in the O.T. are, so far as we can judge, Semites, of the Palestinian, rather than the Aramaean, branch of the race. Heth is a son of Canaan
(Gen. 10^b), and the inclusion of their country in the ideal limits of the
promised land shows that it was regarded as part of Canaan. — *Baal Hermon*]
i.e. the Baal of Mt. Hermon; cf. Baal Lebanon in Phoen. inscription. Many
scholars identify Baal-gad, Baal-hermon, with the modern Bāniās (Paneas,
Caesarea Philippi), on the southern end of Mt. Hermon; so Schwarz, Ges.
Thes.; Rob., *BR²*. iii. p. 409 f.; v. Raum., Sepp, Ke., Be., MV., SS., al. The
only positive argument for this view is derived from 1 Chr. 5^23; but this late,
and in 𝔐 corrupt, verse cannot stand against the explicit statement that Baal-
gad was in the Biq'ah, with which the site of Bāniās cannot be reconciled.
Still less can Baal-gad be Ba'albek (Heliopolis),* which by no stretch of
imagination could be said to be at the foot of Hermon. On Hermon as a
sacred mountain see Euseb., *OS²*. 217₈₇; Jerome, *ib.* 90₁₉; Hilary on Ps. 132;
DB². i. p. 1340. — *Hamath*] the name is found in Egyptian and Assyrian
inscriptions; under the Seleucidae it was renamed Epiphaneia (Ptol., v. 15, 16;
Plin., *n. h.*, v. 23 § 82; *OS²*. 257₁₈; Jerome, on Ez. 47^16); but the old name
remained in local use (Fl. Jos., *antt.* i. 6, 2 § 138). — חמת לבוא קֵי] this use of
the inf. is almost confined to this phrase, Am. 6^14 Jos. 13^5 &c.; besides,
1 Chr. 5^9 Ez. 47^16 (on wh. see Co.). It is therefore not strange that 𝔊 should
take it as n. pr. On the situation see Post in *DB¹*. (Amer. ed.) ii. p. 987 f.;
cf. Rob., *BR²*. iii. 568 f.; Van de Velde, *Narr.*, ii. 469–471; Ba.; on the
routes also E. Meyer, *GdA.* i. p. 222 f.

4. *They served to try Israel by*] cf. 2^22 3^1b. Continuation of v.^3
by the same hand (E). The conception is a frequent one in E
(Gen. 22^1 Ex. 20^20) as well as D. — *To know, &c.*] Theodoret
(*qu.* 8) will not allow that God tries men for the sake of knowing
what is in them; it is only to let them develop and reveal their
true character; similarly Aug. (*qu.* 17, 3): non ut sciret Deus
omnium cognitor, etiam futurorum, sed ut scirent ipsi, et sua con-
scientia vel gloriarentur, vel convincerentur. The author's theology was not so profound.

**5, 6. The Israelites dwell among the natives of the land,
intermarry with them, and worship their gods.** — Meyer and
Budde, in accordance with their analysis of the foregoing, ascribe
these verses to E; but they contain nothing characteristic of E;
the catalogue of nations suggests rather Rje (cf. Ex. 34^11) or a
Deuteronomic hand (cf. Dt. 7^1-4 Jos. 23^12). It seems to me more
probable that the verses are substantially from J, amplified by an

---

* Iken, J. D. Mich., Ritter.

editor, as the cognate passage in Ex. 34 has been. Such a notice might very well close J's account of the settlement in Canaan; his narrative was not devoid of religious judgement, though it was not so dogmatic as in E and D. — *The Canaanites, &c.*] to the six peoples here recited the complete catalogue of the "seven nations" of Palestine (Dt. 7[1]) adds the Girgashites (Jos. 3[10] 24[11]); but usually only these six are named (Ex. 3[8, 17] 23[23] 33[2] 34[11] Dt. 20[17] &c.). On the Canaanites, see on 3[3]; Hittites, 3[3]; Perizzites, 1[3]; Hivvites, 3[3] and note below; Jebusites, 19[10ff.]. — *The Amorites*] in E and D the comprehensive name for the peoples whom Israel conquered and succeeded on both sides of the Jordan.[a] In Egyptian texts the land of Amar, or Amor, is Northern Palestine, with the region of the Lebanon in whole or in part.[†] It is at least a noteworthy coincidence that in the historical tradition of the northern tribes we find the name Amorites, in that of the southern tribes (J), Canaanites. [‡] That the Amorites were of a different race from the Canaanites, there is no conclusive proof. — **6.** The Israelites intermarried with the native inhabitants; cf. Ex. 34[16] Dt. 7[3ff.] Jos. 23[12]. — *And worshipped their gods*] the connubium in itself involved the recognition of one another's religion, and was naturally followed by participation in the cultus; cf. 1 K. 11[1.4.11] &c. Religious exclusiveness in the ancient world was possible only upon terms of complete non-intercourse.

5. The Nations of Palestine. On the lists see *Ochla we-Ochla*, No. 274. The catalogue seems to be nowhere original either in J or E, but to be filled in by Rje or Rd.; see Mey., *ZATW.* i. p. 124 f.; Bu., *Urgesch.*, p. 344 ff.; Di., *NDJ.* p. 272. § Here it is to be suspected that only the first name, *the Canaanites*, is original; observe the ensuing asyndeton. — רְחֵי] like פרוי (1[6]), is supposed by many to have been originally descriptive of a mode of life, people who lived in חרי, Bedawin encampments; cf. חיה יאיר Nu. 32[41], and

---

[a] Steinthal, *Zeitschr. f. Völkerpsychologie*, xii. p. 267; We., *Comp. d. Hexat.*, p. 135, 341 f.; Mey., *ZATW.* i. 121 ff.; Bu., *Urgeschichte*, p. 344 ff.

[†] See E. Meyer, *ZATW.* iii. p. 306 ff.; Müller, *Asien u. Europa*, p. 213 ff., who restricts the term to the Lebanon region. Cf. also the use of the name in Amarna correspondence (letters of Aziru), and of *mât amurri* in Assyrian inscriptions; Delattre, *PSBA.* 1891. p. 215-234.

[‡] Cf. also Amos. Müller (*op. cit.* p. 231) is unreasonably skeptical about the existence of Amorites in Central Palestine, or even in Galilee.

[§] Bacon (*JBL.* x. p. 115 n.) asserts that this list is never interpolated in E; but query.

Arab. ‏جَـ‎.* So Ges. *Thes.* (*paganus*), Fürst, MV., Di. on Gen. 10[17], Sayce,
al.; cf. Ew., *GVI.* i. p. 341 = *HI.* i. p. 237. But the Hivvites of Shechem
and Gibeon (Gen. 34 Jos. 9) were surely not Bedawin; nor is it probable that
a descriptive name of the sort would have clung to them in spite of their
change of life. Perhaps the older interpreters in the Onomastica were more
nearly right in connecting it with ‏חיה‎ † (θηριώδεις, ὥσπερ ὄφεις); it is conceivable that it is an animal name, the Snake clan. — *Amorites*] the etymological
interpretation, 'Highlanders' (Simonis, and many), is purely fictitious, like the
corresponding explanation of Canaanite (above, on 3[5]); though in E and D
the Amorites are represented as the inhabitants of the mountainous interior of
Western Palestine, the land conquered by Israel (Nu. 13[29] Dt. 1[7]). The Amorites are represented in Gen. 10[16] as a Canaanite people, like the Phoenicians
and Hittites. Sayce has attempted to prove that they belonged ethnologically
to a distinct race; ‡ in language, religion, and civilisation, however, they are
not in any way distinguished in the O.T. from the other peoples of Palestine.

III. 7–11. Othniel delivers Israel from Cushan-rishathaim.
—The Israelites displease Yahweh by neglecting him for the
worship of the gods of Canaan (v.[7]). In anger he gives them
up to Cushan-rishathaim, king of Syria on the Euphrates, to
whom they are subject eight years (v.[8]). At last, moved by
their cries, he raises up a deliverer in the person of Othniel ben
Kenaz, who goes to war with Cushan, and by God's help prevails
over him (v.[9. 10]). The land enjoys security for forty years, until
the death of Othniel (v.[11]).

The pragmatic introductory and closing formulas in which each
of the stories of the judges is set, § are here, where they are
employed for the first time, appropriately expanded to their complete typical form. This amplitude of the setting, however, only
makes more conspicuous its emptiness. ‖ It contains nothing but
the names of Othniel and Cushan, the former of which is derived
from 1[13], the other is an enigma; no single detail of the struggle
is recorded, — it is evident that the author knew none. Nor does

---

* On the original meaning of ‏جَـ‎ (tent) see De Goeje in W. R. Smith, *Religion of Semites*, Pt. i. p. 256 n.

† A connexion of ‏חוי‎ with ‏חַוָּה‎ (Eve) may also be suspected; Cass., We., *Comp.*,
p. 343.

‡ See his article, "The White Race of Ancient Palestine," *Expositor*, July, 1888,
p. 48–57; *Races of the O.T.*, 1891. p. 112 ff. 　　§ See Introduction, § 3.

‖ The lack of substance in the story was felt by Fl. Jos., who fills in incidents
apparently suggested by events of the Maccabaean struggle (*antt.* v. 3, 2 § 179–184).

the bare fact pass unchallenged. The subjugation of Canaan at
this time by an enemy from so remote a quarter is highly improbable,* if not beyond the bounds of possibility; its liberation by
Othniel, a Kenizzite clan in the extreme south, scarcely less
improbable. It can hardly be regarded as evidence of inordinate
skepticism that many recent scholars have doubted whether this
typical oppression and deliverance has any basis of fact, or even
of tradition, and have surmised that the author filled the blanks in
his scheme with the first chance names at hand.† That of Othniel
would naturally suggest itself, and had the advantage of giving a
judge to Judah ; whence that of Cushan came it is idle to guess.

The method by which Sayce (*Higher Criticism*, p. 297 ff.) procures the
"verdict of the monuments" against the critics on this point is eminently
characteristic. We are told that the people of Mitanni (according to Sayce
the native name of Aram-naharaim) were among the foes — "Libyans,
Sicilians, Sardinians, Greeks, Cypriots, Hittites, and Philistines" — who combined against Egypt in the reign of Ramses III. (p. 298); and from the fact
that the King of Mitanni does not figure at Medinet Habu among the conquered foe, Sayce concludes that he probably remained behind in Syria or
Palestine (p. 300); the eight years that Cushan oppressed Israel would
exactly correspond with the eight years between the beginning of the Libyan
attack on Egypt and the campaign of the Pharaoh in Syria (303 f.). Prof.
Sayce gives no references. The land of Mitanni (Miten) is mentioned, so
far as I can ascertain, but twice in the inscriptions of Ramses III., ‡ and that,
not in any connexion with the incursion of the northern barbarians, but in
those catalogues of remote and strange countries which were compiled in
order that the Pharaoh might seem as great a conqueror as Thothmes III.,
from whose inscriptions many of the names are derived.§ That "we know
from the Egyptian records that Mitanni or Aram-naharaim took part in the
invasion of Egypt" is an assertion for which Prof. Sayce owes it to us to
produce the evidence. Without this proof, the whole combination is as base-
less as it is ingenious. ‖

---

* It involves, it must be remembered, not only the conquest of the Israelite
tribes, but of the Canaanites, with their strong cities (ch. 1).

† We., *Comp.*, p. 219; Bu., *Richt. u. Sam.*, p. 94 f.; Sta., *GVI*. i. p. 69.

‡ See Sayce himself, p. 300.

§ On the character of these lists, v. E. Meyer, *Gesch. Aegypt.*, p. 319; Müller,
Asien u. Europa, p. 284, who affirms that the name of Miten never occurs in a historical text after the 18th dynasty.

‖ Kitt., who does not admit that Othniel is an unhistorical figure, imagines that
the story is a dim reminiscence of the wars of Ramses III. and Tiglath Pileser I.
in Palestine (*GdH.* i. 2. p. 70).

7. See on 2[11]. — *Forgot Yahweh, &c.*] Dt. 6[13] 8[11. 14. 19] 32[18] 1 S. 12[9] Hos. 2[15] Jer. 3[21] &c. ; cf. also Jud. 8[34]. — *Served the Baals*] see on 2[13]. — *And asherahs*] in by far the greater number of instances in the O.T. the *asherah* is a wooden post or mast, which stood at the place of worship ; see on 6[25ff]. In this verse, how- ever, as in 1 K. 18[19] 2 K. 23[4],* it is evidently intended for the name of a divinity ; and as in these passages Asherah stands by the side of Baal precisely as Astarte does elsewhere (2[13] 10[6] 1 S. 7[4] 12[10]), it was a natural inference that Asherah was only another name (title or epithet) of Astarte.† The wooden *asherah* was then supposed to be the symbol or image of this goddess. Others distinguish Asherah from Astarte in different ways. ‡ On the other hand, the existence of a goddess Asherah is denied by some conservative scholars, § and by many recent critics ; ‖ the passages which seem to prove the contrary are to be explained either as metonymy (the name of the symbol being put for that of the goddess), or as the confusion by late writers of the symbol *ashe- rah* with the goddess Astarte. So far as the O.T. is concerned these scholars are right ; it gives no sufficient evidence that a goddess Asherah was worshipped by Canaanites or Israelites. The name, Ebed-asherah,¶ in letters found at el-Amarna, may signify no more than that the *asherah* post itself was esteemed divine, a fetish, or a cultus-god, as no one doubts that it was in O.T. times. See on the whole question, my article, " Asherah " in the new Bible Dictionary.

In 1 K. 18[19] the 400 prophets of Asherah are interpolated (We., Sta., Klo.); 2 K. 21[7] האיברה פסל, פסל is gloss, in the same sense in which 2 Chr. 33[7] substitutes פסל; 1 K. 15[13] = 2 Chr. 15[16] לאשרה מפלצת is not, " a horrible thing (traditionally, Priapus, phallus) *to* Asherah," but, *as an asherah ;* 2 K. 23[7] לאשרה בתים is obscure and prob. corrupt; if the traditional *vestments* be right,

---

* Cf. also 2 K. 21[7] 1 K. 15[13].

† This is doubtless the cause of the frequent confusion in the versions ; see also Thdt., *qu.* 55 *in 4 Reg.* The identification is accepted by Selden, Spencer, Ges., Vatke, Stud., Be., Renan, Schrader, al. mu.; more doubtfully Baudissin.

‡ *E.g.*, Movers, *Phönizier*, i. p. 560 ff.; Sayce, *Cont. Rev.*, xliv. p. 391 f.; *Higher Criticism*, p. 80 f.

§ Hgstbg., Ba., Baethgen.

‖ We., Sta., G. Hoffmann, W. R. Smith, Bu., al.

¶ *Abad-Aš-ra-tum*, &c., sometimes written with the divine determinative ; Schrader, *Z.A.* iii. p. 363 f.

it would not prove the existence of a goddess or an idol, but only that the sacred post was draped. 2 K. 23⁴ remains, the only passage beside our text in which there can be no doubt that a divinity is meant; but even here it may only be one of the common cases in which part of the apparatus of worship has become an object of worship — a cultus god. That later writers took the *asherahs* for heathen deities, or idols, is perhaps to be inferred from the appearance of a new fem. plur. אשרות, 2 Chr. 19² 33³ Jud. 3⁷¹; in Old Hebrew the name of the class is אשרים, from which the nom. unitatis is formed in the usual way, אשרה, which owes its fem. gender, not to its being or representing a female divinity, but to grammatical formation.

8. Cf. 2¹⁴. — *Cushan-rishathaim*] the second name suggested to Hebrew ears *rish'ah*, wickedness, and the traditional pronunciation probably intends "Cushan (? the Nubian) of double-dyed villainy"; * compare similar displays of wit in the names of the kings Bera and Birsha Gen. 14²,† Tabal Is. 7⁶ &c. — *Aram-naharaim*] Gen. 24¹⁰ Dt. 23⁴ Ps. 60 (title)'. RV. *Mesopotamia*, ‡ that is, the whole immense region between the Euphrates and the Tigris, from the mountains of Armenia and the continuation of the Taurus in the north to the latitude of Babylon, or even to the Persian Gulf. § The Aram-naharaim of the O.T. probably did not extend farther east than the Chabōras (Ḫābūr); ‖ it may, like the Egyptian Naharin, have included also a more or less extensive tract west of the Euphrates.¶ — **9.** *The Israelites cried to Yahweh*] standing formula; v.¹⁵ 4³ 6⁶·⁷ 10¹⁰ 1 S. 12⁸·¹⁰ cf. Ex. 2²³ 14¹⁰ Jos. 24⁷. — *Yahweh raised up a deliverer, &c.*] v.¹⁸. *Deliverer* is synonymous with *judge;* cf. 2¹⁴·¹⁸. — *Othniel, &c.*] see on 1¹³. — **10.** *The spirit of Yahweh came upon him*] καὶ ἐγένετο ἐπ' αὐτόν 𝔊, not *fuitque in eo* 𝔏. Cf. 11²⁹ Nu. 24² 1 S. 19²⁰·²³ and, with expressions which give more prominence to the suddenness or violence of the seizure, Jud. 6³⁴ 13²⁵ 14⁶·¹⁹ 15¹⁴ 1 S. 11⁶ 16¹³. To the energy of the spirit of God is attributed whatever seems to transcend the limits of man's own sagacity or strength; the heroic valour of the judges, the wisdom of the ruler (Nu. 11¹⁶ᶠ· 1 S. 16¹³), the genius

---

* *Sanhedr.*, 105ᵃ; *Yalqut;* Ki., Abarb. *in loc.*

† 𝔗ᵐ· ¹·; *Beresh. rab.* § 42 (ed. Sulzb., f. 37ᵃ).

‡ So 𝔊 in all other places and many codd. here, 𝔏, Vat., Schm., Cler., Ba., Be., Ke., al. mu.   § Strabo, xvi. p. 746; Ptol., v. 18, 1; Plin., *n. h.*, v. 66.

‖ Kiepert, Nöld., Di., Mey.

¶ See E. Meyer, *Gesch. Aeg.*, p. 227; W. M. Müller, *Asien u. Europa*, p. 249 ff.

of the artist (Ex. 31³ 36¹), the inspiration of the poet (2 S. 23¹),
the divine frenzy of the *Nebiim* (1 S. 10¹⁰), the revelations of the
prophet (Ez. 3²⁴ &c.), extraordinary feats of any kind (Jud. 14⁶
cf. 1 K. 18⁴⁶); see in general, Is. 11² 28⁶.   In many of its manifestations, especially in older times, it was thought of as a physical
force (Jud. 14⁶ 15¹⁴ 1 K. 18¹²·⁴⁶ 2 K. 2¹⁰ &c.).   Extraordinary evil
as well as good is caused by it; for example, Saul's madness
(1 S. 16¹⁴ 19⁹), false prophecy (1 K. 22²³).* — *He vindicated
Israel*] RV. and most, *judged Israel;* but the verb means not so
much 'pronounce a judgement' as 'establish a right,' and in the
present context it is parallel to *deliver* v.⁹, as in 2¹⁶·¹⁸ 10¹·²; cf.
" He . . . that vindicates his country from a tyrant " (Massinger).
Others, *became judge*, began to exercise the office of judge; †
without warrant in usage.   The following clauses explain how he
vindicated Israel. — *He went to war*] 2¹⁵ cf. 1 S. 8²⁰. — *He got the
upper hand of Cushan*] prevailed over him, 6² Ps. 89¹³ cf. Jud. 1³⁵.
The language imports that he not only liberated Israel, but subjugated the oppressor; cf. 6². — 11. *The land enjoyed security forty
years*] it was exempt from further attacks for a whole generation.   This formula of the editor also v.³⁰ 5³¹ 8²⁸ cf. Jos. 11²³ 14¹⁵.
The forty years run from the victory of Othniel to his death;
cf. 2¹⁸, " Yahweh was with the judge and delivered them from their
enemies as long as the judge lived."   On the chronology, see
Introduction, § 7.   Othniel's death was the end of the period
of security, the beginning of a new period of apostasy and disaster; cf. 2¹⁹.

— 8. כושן רשעתים] Cushan is the name of a Bedawin tribe connected with
Midian (Hab. 3⁷), perhaps a subtribe of that people (Nu. 12¹; Moses'
Midianite wife is a *Cushite, i.e.* of Cushan).   An incursion of these Bedawin,
and their defeat and expulsion by the Kenizzites of Debir (Othniel), is conceivable enough; and if the names are taken from any historical connexion,
we might conjecture that it was from some such story.   כושן is related to כוש
as רושן to רוש, קינן to קין, כנען to כנע Xνα, יתרן to יתר &c.; observe the frequency
of clan names in *an* in the Midianite genealogy, Gen. 25², in comparison with
the Ishmaelites, 25¹³ᶠᶠ.   The pronunciation כושן prob. intends a *st. cons.*, after

---

* Maimonides, *More Nebochim*, Pt. ii. c. 45; Oehler, *Alttest. Theol.*, § 65; Schultz,
*Alttest. Theol.*⁴ p. 586 f. = *Old Test. Theol.*, ii. p. 202 f.; König, *Offenbarungsbegriff
d. A. T.*, i. p. 171 ff.; Smend, *Alttest. Religionsgeschichte*, p. 460 ff.
† Lth., Schm., Cler., Rosenm.

the analogy of Aram-naharaim, to which also the dual רִשְׁעָיֵם is probably conformed. —ארם נהרים] apparently "Aram of two rivers"; the ancients thought of the Euphrates and Tigris, many moderns of the Euphrates and Chabōras, or Belias * (Beliḥ); others of the Euphrates and Orontes,† or Euphrates and Chrysorrhoas (Baradā). ‡ It may fairly be questioned, however, whether the pronunciation which makes the noun dual is not factitious. As a geographical term נהרים probably corresponds to the Egyptian *Naharin* § (there is no trace of a dual form), which lay on both sides of the upper Euphrates; see Meyer and Müller cited above, p. 87 n. The name would then signify merely " River-Syria." The only cities in Aram-naharaim which are named in the O.T. are Ḥarran (Gen. 24¹⁰) and Pethor (Dt. 23⁵ cf. Nu. 22⁵); the latter was on the west side of the Euphrates (Schrader, *KAT*². p. 156).

— **10.** וישפט את ישראל] an exhaustive examination of the usage of the verb שפט by Prof. H. Ferguson is to be found in *JBL.* viii. p. 130–136; see also Bachmann, p. 25 ff. That שָׁפַט often means 'give judgement,' מִשְׁפָּט 'judicial decision,' needs no illustration; cf. only 1 K. 3²⁸. But it is often 'do justice, or get justice done,' 'give one his rights or his dues.' It is thus equivalent on the one hand to ' defend, deliver,' on the other to ' condemn, punish.' 1 K. 8³² illustrates both; cf. the Latin *vindicare* in both senses. See Is. 1¹⁷ (‖ ריב) Jer. 5²⁸ Ps. 10¹⁸ 72⁴ 26¹ (vindicate me, O Yahweh). It is parallel to חלץ Ps. 43¹; הצדיק, הציל, פלט, 82³⁴; הושיע 72⁴. In Judges it is synonymous with the last-mentioned verb, 2¹⁶·¹⁸ 3⁹ᶠ· 10¹ᶠ· &c.; cf. Neh. 9²⁷, where מושיע stands for שופט; and so well established is this signification that שפט is construed, like other verbs of delivering, rescuing, with מן or מיד, 1 S. 24¹⁶ 2 S. 18¹⁹·³¹. This is probably the sense in 1 S. 8²⁰; the Israelites demand a king, "that our king may vindicate (judge) us, and march out at our head and fight our battles " (𝕿, Drus., al.), closely parallel to the present passage.

III. 12–30. Ehud kills Eglon, king of Moab, and liberates Israel.

— The Israelites again offend Yahweh, who enables the king of Moab to defeat them, occupy Jericho, and hold Israel in subjection for eighteen years (v.¹²⁻¹⁴). From this tyranny they are delivered by Ehud ben Gera, a left-handed Benjamite, who by a ruse secures from Eglon a private audience (v.¹⁵⁻²⁰), assassinates him (v.²¹ᶠ·), escapes (v.²²⁻²⁶), and at the head of his tribesmen from Mt. Ephraim cuts off the Moabites west of the Jordan (v.²⁷⁻²⁹). The land enjoys a long period of security (v.³⁰).

The author of the Book of Judges has furnished this story with

---

* Βίληχα, Βάλισσος.   † Howorth, *Acad.*, Jan. 17, 1891, p. 65.

‡ Halévy, *Mélanges d'épigraph.*, p. 81.

§ In the Amarna correspondence *Naḥrima*, with Canaanite, instead of Aramaic, plural ending.

the usual pragmatic setting, employing in both the introduction
(v.$^{12\text{-}15}$) and conclusion (v.$^{24\text{-}30}$) material derived from the older
narrative.　As in other cases, he converts the story of a local
struggle into a chapter of the religious and political history of all
Israel.　The unity and integrity of the story itself (v.$^{15b\text{-}27}$) has
until recently been unquestioned ; only the beginning has been
supplanted by the phrases of D, and the sequel of v.^{27} is not
completely preserved in v.$^{24\text{-}29}$.　Winckler, however, has lately
endeavoured to prove that the narrative is composite, and to separate it into its elements, J and E.[*]　Neither his analysis nor his
exegesis is likely to be accepted, but he has shown that the story
is not as homogeneous as has been generally believed.　Verse ^{20},
in particular, is not the sequel to v.^{19}, but a variant parallel to it ;
and in the following verses to the end traces of duplication may
be discovered (see esp. v.$^{26ff.}$).

It is natural to suppose that the memory of Ehud's exploit was
kept alive among his tribesmen of Benjamin ; his story retold on
holidays at Gilgal.　It has the quality of the best Hebrew folk-
stories, and is beyond doubt one of the oldest in the book.　From
what source it was extracted by the author of Judges, it is difficult
to decide with confidence.　Stade ascribes it to E,[†] chiefly on the
ground of resemblances between 3^{15} and $10^{10.\,13}$; but the expressions in 3^{15} are probably from the hand of D (cf. 3^9).　Schrader,
on the contrary, attributes it to J,[‡] and as between the two the
impression which the whole tenor of the narrative makes is favourable to the latter hypothesis. [§]

The events related are in nowise improbable.　It would indeed
be strange if the success of the Israelites in establishing themselves
west of the Jordan had not tempted others to follow their example.
The Moabites, whose territory, except in the times of the greatest
expansion of Israelite power east of the Jordan, extended to the

---

[*] *Alttestamentl. Untersuchungen*, 1892, p. 55-59.　Winckler's analysis is : J.
3^{14}. 15aβ, b. 17. 18. 19aβ, b. 20b.3. 21. 22. 24aa, b. 25aa. 26bβ. 27aa. 28a. 28ba. 29 ;　E. 15b.... 16.... 19aa.
20.... 21. 24aβ, b. 25aβ, b. 26a, ba. 27. 28bβ. 29.

[†] *ZATW*. i. p. 343.

[‡] De Wette, *Einl.*[8], p. 327.

[§] So also Bu., *Richt. u. Sam.*, p. 100.　Bu. notes that הרברה v.^{26} is found besides only in J (Gen. 19^{16} 43^{10} Ex. 12^{33}) ; this is perhaps true also of the Hiph.
החיל v.^{25} (Gen. 8^{10} J),　Winckler also attributes the principal narrative to J.

northern end of the Dead Sea or beyond, may very well have
brought under their power the plain of Jericho and the adjacent
parts of Mt. Ephraim (Benjamin). The well-designed and boldly
executed ruse by which the tyrant is slain, and in the ensuing
confusion his retainers cut off, has altogether the note of reality.
Nöldeke,[*] while recognizing this, thinks that the name of the
deliverer cannot be historical: Gera is a son (Gen. 46[21]) or
grandson (1 Chr. 8[3]) of Benjamin, i.e. a Benjamite clan, Ehud
himself a great-grandson (1 Chr. 7[10] cf. 8[6]); the concurrence of
the names of two clans of the same tribe is conclusive. There
is no difficulty, however, in supposing that a clan of Benjamin in
later times bore the name of the hero Ehud; or even that, without
this, the name was introduced into the genealogies of the chronicler directly from our text.[†]

**12-14. The Israelites again offend Yahweh; with his sup-
port Eglon attacks them and occupies Jericho; they are subject
to Moab eighteen years.** — The usual introduction; only the
name of Eglon and his conquest of Jericho, the Palm City, are
derived from the old story; the rest is made up of the set formulas of D. — **12[a].** 4[1] 10[6] 13[1] cf. 3[7] 6[1] 2[11] (comm. there). — *Yahweh enabled Eglon to prevail over Israel*] it was Yahweh who, to
punish the sin of his people, gave him this power; cf. Ez. 30[24]
Jer. 27[6-8] 43[10f.] Is. 45[1ff.]. Somewhat similarly Mesha, king of Moab,
in his inscription: "Omri was king of Israel; and he oppressed
Moab a long time, because Chemosh was angry with his land." —
13. Eglon allied to himself the Ammonites and Amalekites; very
likely an exaggeration of D.[‡] The Ammonites were the neighbours of Moab on the NE. and their nearest kindred. The
Israelite settlements in Gilead interposed between them and the
Jordan.[§] Moab and Ammon appear as allies against Israel in
2 Chr. 20[1] also. The Amalekites were Bedawin, chiefly of the
southern desert, against whom the Israelites cherished an impla-
cable hatred; see on 1[16] and especially on 6[3]. — *He went and beat
Israel and occupied the Palm City*] of the war itself we learn

---

[*] *Untersuchungen zur Kritik des A. T.*, p. 179 f.; so also Sta., *ZATW.* i. p. 343,
GVI². i. p. 68.   [†] So also Budde, *Richt. u. Sam.*, p. 100.
[‡] Budde, *Richt. u. Sam.*, p. 99.   [§] See further on 11[4].

nothing from these general phrases, and are tempted to surmise that the author of Judges has here curtailed the story. The Palm City is Jericho; see on 1[16]. The mention of Jericho here has been found difficult. According to Jos. 6[21-25] Joshua totally destroyed the city and laid the site under a ban; 1 K. 16[34] records the rebuilding of the city in the reign of Ahab and the fulfillment of Joshua's curse. In the intervening centuries the place is named only here and in 2 S. 10[5]. These passages are commonly harmonized with 1 K. 16[34] by the supposition that down to the time of Ahab Jericho had been an unwalled town, and that Hiel drew upon himself the curse by attempting to fortify it;[*] but the passage before us would rather lead us to infer that Jericho was a strong place, the possession of which secured Eglon's hold on his conquests west of the Jordan; and it is not very probable that David left this important position, one of the two great eastern gateways of his kingdom (cf. 2 S. 10[6]), unfortified. — 14, 15[a]. cf. v.[8b-9].

12. ‏עגלון‏] as the name of a man only in this chapter. As a topographical name it occurs repeatedly east of the Jordan in the modern form 'Aglūn; cf. Eglon in Judah (Jos. 10[3, 34]), modern 'Aglān. Roman names such as Juvencus, Vitellius, Vitulus have been compared; see Ba. — *Moab*] the land of Moab lay east of the Dead Sea, stretching eastward to the confines of the desert. On the southwest it bordered on Edom; on the northeast it had the Ammonites for neighbours; and on the north, Israelite tribes, Reuben and Gad, the former of which early disappears (see on Jud. 5[16]). — ‏כל כי עשו וג‏] in this use ‏כי‏ is much less frequent than ‏אשר‏; the instances are Dt. 31[17] Jer. 4[28] Mal. 2[14] Ps. 139[14]. Cf. ‏אשר יען‏ and ‏יען כי אשר‏, ‏ערב כי‏ and ‏ערב כי‏, and see Ew., § 336 c; Roorda, § 506. — 13. ‏וייריש‏] the plur. refers to the allies, but the change of subject is harsh; 𝕭𝕷 give a sing.

15–18. Ehud, chosen to convey the tribute to Eglon, secretly arms himself; he presents the tribute and dismisses the bearers.

15[a,b]. *Ehud ben Gera*] the author passes over to the older narrative which he incorporates. Gera is a Benjamite clan (Gen. 46[21] 2 S. 16[5] &c. — Shimei ben Gera — 1 Chr. 8[3, 5, 7]); that Ehud is also a clan name is less certain, and if true would not prove the name of our hero unhistorical.[†] The deliverer comes from the tribe on whose soil the Moabite invaders had planted themselves.

---

[*] Ew., *GVI.* iii. p. 490, Ke., Ba., Be., Di., al.   [†] See above, p. 91.

— *A left-handed man*] the literal and original meaning seems to
have been, a man with his right hand drawn up, contracted by
accident or disease ; but in usage it has come to signify no more
than one who has not the natural use of his right hand, *left-
handed*. He took advantage of this defect, in consequence of
which his movements excited no suspicion until he struck the
fatal blow ; see on v.$^{16. 21.}$. — *The Israelites sent by him tribute*]
lit. *a present;* 2 S. 8$^{2.6}$ 1 K. 5^1 (EV. 4^{21}) 2 K. 17$^{3.4}$ Hos. 10^6 Ps.
72^{10} &c.[*] — On the question whether Eglon's residence was at
Jericho or east of the Jordan, see on v.^{28}. — **16.** Ehud provided
himself with a weapon peculiarly suited to his purpose. — *A two-
edged dirk a* gomed *long*] the name of the measure does not occur
elsewhere in the O.T. ; it appears to correspond to the Greek
πυγμή, the distance from the elbow to the knuckles of the
clenched fist, about thirteen or thirteen and a half inches. The
old translators and most modern commentators think of a shorter
dagger, a span long ; but the description of Eglon's corpulence
(v.^{17}) is pertinent only in relation to the fact that a long dirk was
buried, hilt and all, in his belly.[†] — *He hung it under his clothes
on his right thigh*] the opposite side from that on which the sword
was usually worn, so that if the guards of the king felt for concealed weapons it would not be likely to be discovered ; while at
the same time, if it was more than a mere stiletto, it was in
the most convenient place for a left-handed man to draw. —
17. *Now Eglon was a very fat man*] a circumstance of importance in the sequel of the story is parenthetically introduced by
anticipation at the first meeting of Ehud and Eglon, instead of in
v.^{20} or ^{22}. — **18.** Comparing small things with great, we may illustrate this presentation of tribute by the famous reliefs on the
black obelisk of Salmanassar, depicting the payment of tribute
by Jehu, with their long procession of Israelites bearing the treas-
ures of their land to present to the king.[‡] — *He dismissed the*

---

[*] So in other languages ; *e.g.* δῶρα, Diod. Sic., i. 58 ; cf. Hdt., iii. 89, &c.
[†] Stud.
[‡] Layard, *Monuments of Nineveh*, 1849, fol. Ser. 1. no. 53 ; *Nineveh*, 1849 (8vo),
p. 347 ; cf. also the payment of tribute to Sennacherib at Lachish ; Egyptian scenes,
Lepsius, *Denkmäler*, Abth. iii. pl. 115-118 ; E. Meyer, *Gesch. d. alt. Aegyptens*, p. 242,
244.

people who carried the tribute] the payment was, of course, made
in kind, so that a considerable number of porters would be necessary, but in the East under such circumstances it is customary to
employ a much larger number than is necessary; the size of the
retinue is a mark of honour.   From the following verse * (cf. v.*)
we must infer that Ehud accompanied them part way on their
return, and when he had seen them safe beyond the reach of
subsequent pursuit, returned alone to the king's residence.

15. 20¹⁶', אַטֵּר [אִישׁ אַטֵּר יַד יְמִינוֹ, 𝕲𝕷 *ambidextrous:* 𝕲𝕾 more correctly,
drawn up, drawn out of shape.   The vb. אטר (cognate with אצר) Ps. 69¹⁶',
'contract, close'; Ar. أطَرَ, 'bend into a hoop.'   The adj. אָטֵר, of the
regular type for defects and deformities, would accordingly mean, maimed by
having the hand bent double, drawn shut, so distorted as to be useless
(Abulw., Ki. *Lex.*, Ra., Tanch., al.).   In 20¹⁶, however, the writer cannot
mean that the 700 Benjamite slingers, this *corps d'élite*, were all maimed or
deformed,† and in MH. the meaning *left-handed* is well established; cf. *Shabb.*,
103ᵃ, *Menach.*, 37ᵃ mid., *Bechor.*, 45ᵇ (see Ra. on the last two passages),
Tos. Bechor., v. 8 (ed. Zuckerm., p. 540₈).   So Fl. Jos. here, τῶν χειρῶν τὴν
ἀριστερὰν ἀμείνων κἄν' ἐκείνης τὴν ἄτασαν ἰσχὺν ἔχων; Abarb., Stud., Ke.,
Be., Ba., Cass. — 16. פִּיּוֹת שְׁנֵי] plur. of פֶּה, Ki., Ol., Sta.   It was δίστομον
ξίφος, Eurip., *Hel.* 983, cf. Ecclus. 21⁸ Hebr. 4¹² Apoc. 1¹⁶, *gladius anceps*,
Prud., *Cathem.*, vi. 85; a two-edged dirk, not as Jerome glosses in his translation, "habens in medio capulum," a double-ended dagger, which is incompatible with v.²² — גֹּמֶד אָרְכָּה] the Jewish interpreters explain *gomed* as a cubit,
more exactly, a short cubit, cubit minus the fingers; see Ra. *in loc.*, Rashbam
on *Baba bathra*, 100ᵃ, *Aruch*, s. v. גמר²; cf. *Jer. Yoma*, iv. 4 (41ᶜ). ‡   So it is
translated here by 𝕾 a.   It would thus correspond exactly to the Greek πυγμή
(Poll., ii. 147, 158).   See my note in *JBL.* xii. p. 104.

19-22. Ehud contrives a private interview with the king and kills him. — 19. Ehud returns alone. — *From the sculptured stones near Gilgal*] probably rude stone images; § the translation *quarries* ‖ is an unnecessary and unwarranted departure from the well-known meaning of the word; *graven images* ¶ perhaps too

---

* If it be the original sequel of v. 18.
† This holds even if the words are a gloss, as Bu. conjectures.
‡ See also Weiss on *Mechilta*, fol. 59ᵃ; Jastrow, *Dictionary*, s. v.
§ 𝕲𝕷, Lth., Schm., Stud., al.
‖ 𝕲𝕾, Jewish and many Christian commentators, AV., RV.
¶ AVᵐᵍ. RVᵐᵍ., and elsewhere uniformly in the text.

specifically suggests statues. Gilgal itself probably had its name from an old stone circle (cromlech),* whose stones, according to a popular tradition, were set up by Joshua to commemorate the passage of the Jordan (Jos. 4²⁰); and it has frequently been surmised that the sculptured stones or images of our text are in some way connected with the stones erected by Joshua.† Others, gathering from v.¹⁹·²⁰ that when a man had passed this point he was safe on Israelite soil, suppose that they were boundary stones (images) set up by Eglon. ‡ — *I have a private communication for thee*] a natural pretext, and all the more likely to be admitted without suspicion because Ehud had just brought the tribute of his tribesmen; cf. v.²⁰. — *He commanded, Silence !*] the command is addressed not to Ehud,§ but to the attendants,‖ who are to leave him in privacy. — 20. The verse seems to be parallel to v.¹⁹, rather than a sequel to it. In v.¹⁹ Ehud appears before the king in his public audience room and announces that he has a secret communication to make to him; the king has the room cleared, leaving Ehud alone with him. In v.²⁰ Ehud goes in to him as he is sitting in his roof-chamber alone and announces that he has a divine communication for him. The difficulty was early felt, and various exegetical expedients have been proposed to relieve it. The favourite explanation is that the words of Ehud in v.¹⁹, "I have a private communication to make to thee, O King," were not spoken by him in person in the public audience, but were conveyed to the king by an attendant; upon receiving this message Eglon dismissed his court and received Ehud alone in his private apartments.¶ Another hypothesis is, that after hearing the words of Ehud, spoken in public, Eglon dismissed the bystanders and retired to his private roof-chamber, whither Ehud was presently conducted.** Either of these suppositions is easy

---

* See on 2¹.

† Fr. Junius, Ew., Knob., Vaihinger, Stud., al., with very various — and equally groundless — hypotheses about the nature of the connexion.

‡ RLbG. (alt.), a Lap., Schm., Hgstbg., Ke., Ba., Cass.

§ ⲐBN, Ki., Abarb., Schm., a Lap., Cass., Doorn. al.

‖ ⲂⲀⲖⲁ‧ⲖⲤⲦ, Fl. Jos., Ra., RLbG., Stud., Ke., Be., Ba., al.

¶ Lth., Stud., Ke., Be., Ba.; cf. RLbG., Schm.

** To take the verb in v. 20 as pluperf., *Now Ehud had entered, &c.* (Doorn.), only aggravates the difficulty.

enough in matter of fact; but neither of them is exegetically plausible. If the author had meant the first, he would have given Ehud's words in a different form;[*] if the second, he would not have left it to the imagination of the reader. — *Where he was sitting in his cool upper story alone*] not in the public divan. The *upper story* ('*aliyah*, still called in Arabic by the same name) is an additional, ordinarily third, story raised above the flat roof of the house at one corner, or upon a tower-like annex to the building. It generally contains but a single apartment, of larger or smaller dimensions, through which latticed windows on all sides give free circulation of air, making it the most comfortable part of the house. — *I have a divine communication for thee*] cf. v.[20]. The words naturally suggest a communication from the God of Israel which had come to Ehud, whether by dream,[†] oracle, or otherwise, and which it concerned Eglon to hear.[‡] Others suppose that Ehud meant by the intentionally ambiguous phrase, I have God's business with you, a divine commission to execute upon you.[§] It does not appear that the author had this ingenious equivocation in mind; or that he would have thought it worth while to protect, by so slender a pretext, Ehud's reputation for veracity. He tells of it as a clever and successful ruse, with no more reflexion on its morality than on that of the assassination itself. — *He arose from his chair*] presumably as a sign of reverence for the oracle.[‖] The movement, which Ehud may have reckoned upon, gave him an opportunity to get within striking

---

[*] I have a private communication *for the king*.

[†] Fl. Jos.

[‡] They are so understood by 𝕿𝕾, Ra., and most interpreters, ancient and modern. It is not necessary, however, to suppose that Ehud assumed the character of a prophet (Cler., al.).

[§] Schm., Stud., Be., Ba.; Schm. even imagines that Eglon so understood the words. Cf. Aug., *qu.* 20: Potest non esse mendacium, quandoquidem verbi nomine solet etiam factum appellare Scriptura, et re vera ita erat. On the whole question see further Schm., *qu.* 7. 8; Ba., p. 234 f.

[‖] *Sanhedr.*, 60[a]. Rabb., Cler., Stud., Ke., al. According to the Midrash the marriage of Ruth (the daughter or granddaughter of Eglon) was the reward of this piety; *Ruth rab.* on 1[4] (fol. 29[d], ed. Sulzb.), *Yalqut*. Other explanations, such as, he arose in joy at the announcement (Fl. Jos.), or in alarm at Ehud's menacing words and gestures (Be.), to call his guards, or to defend himself or fly (Schm.), are in varying degrees improbable. Schnurrer suggested that he wished to draw nearer to Ehud for greater secrecy; cf. perhaps 𝕲.

distance without exciting suspicion, which he could hardly have done if Eglon had remained seated, and for this reason it is related. — 21. Ehud, still without arousing suspicion, reaches with his left hand for his dirk (v.[10]), quickly draws, and plunges it into the king's belly. — 22. The force of the blow was such that, in spite of the length of the weapon, the hilt followed the blade in ; the dirk was doubtless without either guard or cross-piece. — Ehud left the knife sticking in the wound. — *And the fat closed after the blade*] the fat which covered the intestines ; cf. v.[17]. It is not necessary to infer from the preceding clause that the whole hilt, pommel and all, disappeared ; so that there is no conflict between the two statements.* The last words of the verse are very difficult, and almost certainly corrupt. The most probable interpretation is, *and the dirt came out*] the feces ; not from the wound,† but through the anus, the usual consequence of such a wound in the abdomen. ‡ This somewhat drastic touch is altogether in the vein of the narrator ; cf. v.[16. 17. 24b]. The emendation of the Hebrew text which it necessitates is not difficult. The translation preferred in RV., *and it* (*sc.* the sword) *came out behind,*§ gives a mere guess at the meaning of the word, and is grammatically unsound. The rendering of RV[mg.], *he* (Ehud) *went out into the antechamber,*‖ is only possible if, with Winckler, we ascribe the words to a different author from the first clause of v.[23]. For other hypotheses see note.

19. ורוא בכ] the nominal sentence emphasizing the contrast; he dismissed the bearers, but *himself* turned back, &c. — כר־ים] plur. to the sg. פֶסֶל; images of gods Dt. 7[25] 12[3] Is. 21[9] cf. Hos. 11[2] Mi. 1[7], in human or animal forms Dt. 4[16-18] cf. v.[23. 25]. So here 𝕲[ABL.] 𝔰 (= Θ) γλυπτῶν, 𝕲[M] Thdt. εἰδώλων,¶ 𝕷. — וייאמר רָם] an exclamation like *Hush! Hist!* Am. 6[10] &c. — 20. ורוא יָבֵב] circumstantial; Dr³. § 160 — בעֲרִיַת הִמְּקֵרָה] cf. v.[24], *cool upper-story*. So in sense 𝕲𝕷, while 𝕿 thinks of the upper story of a summer palace (Am. 3[15]). Such 'aliyahs are frequently mentioned in the O.T.; in private

---

* Though it would be possible to ascribe them to two different sources.

† Vatabl., cf. RLbG.

‡ So 𝕷, statimque per secreta naturae alvi stercora proruperunt, 𝕿, *Beresh. rab.*, § 99, Rabb., Lth., AV., al.

§ So, with various modifications, Schm. (*aversa pars corporis*), Cler. (*postica pars corporis, supra clunes*), Tr.-Jun., Rosenm., Simonis (*podex*), Ges. *Thes.* (*interstitium pedum*), Maurer (*stercoreus*), &c.　　　　‖ 𝕲.

¶ 𝕲[GN] ἀνδρῶν ; ? transcriptional error for ἀνδριάντων.

II

houses (guest chambers) 1 K. 17¹⁹. ²³ 2 K. 4¹⁰. ¹¹, as well as in palaces, 2 K. 1² (latticed windows), Jer. 22¹³. ¹⁴ (spacious). A similar structure was sometimes erected over a city gate, 2 S. 19¹ (EV. 18³³), or at an angle of the city wall (?) (Neh. 3³¹. ³³); often in Talm. Cf. ὑπερῷον Acts 1¹⁸ 9³⁷. ³⁹ 20⁸. In the modern East, see Shaw, *Travels*, 214-216 (N. Africa); Niebuhr, *Reisen*, i. pl. 68 (Ṣan'ā'), Thomson, *Land and Book²*, ii. p. 634, 636 (fig.). — [אשר לו לבדו lit. is rightly connected by most scholars with the verb, *sitting . . . alone;* not *in his private* 'aliyah (Vatabl.). — [רבר אלהים] not *aliquid admirandum et stupendum* (Brenz); phrases like חתת אלהים (Gen. 35⁵) describe the terror as caused by a god (panic). — אלהים is naturally used in speaking to a foreigner: but in the mouth of Ehud means Yahweh, and would be so understood. — כסא] *chair.*. Chairs were found in private houses (2 K. 4¹⁰), but are more frequently mentioned as the seat of persons of rank, for instance, of Eli (1 S. 1⁹ 4¹⁸), the queen mother (1 K. 2¹⁹), esp. the king (1 K. 1⁴⁶ כסא הכלוכה &c.). The latter stood so high as to require a foot stool (הרם), or was raised on a platform and approached by steps (1 K. 10¹⁹). See representations of Egyptian chairs and thrones, Wilkinson, *Ancient Egyptians*, ed. Birch, i. p. 408 ff.; cf. also Buchholz, *Homerische Realien*, ii. 2. § 85; Baumeister, *Denkmäler*, p. 1650 ff. — 21. [ויהקעה בבמנו] the vb. 4²¹ (driving a peg) 2 S. 18¹⁴ &c. — 22. [ויבא ונ'] 𝕲 reads as a causative, and Bu. would emend ויבא, *he* (Ehud) *caused the hilt to enter*, which is less natural than 𝔐 — [הנצב] *hilt, haft*, Arab. niṣāb. — [להב] *blade;* lit. *flame.* — [ויצא הפרישנה] the subject cannot be *the sword*, for חרב is fem.; it might grammatically be *the blade*, להב, but it is hardly in accordance with the natural logic of speech to go back to this noun. Moreover, the meanings attributed to פרשדן by those who construe thus are fictitious, the product of most improbable etymological combinations, that with Ar. فرشل 'straddle' being not the least absurd. In the present context the subject cannot be Ehud, whose exit is regularly related in the next following words; no author is negligent enough to write, *and he went out to the* parshedon, *and Ehud went out to the* misderon.* If we make Ehud the subject, we must either assume that one of these two clauses is a gloss to the other (Ew., Bö., al.), or that they came from two different sources and have been most awkwardly juxtaposed by the compiler (Winckler). Against the former alternative it may properly be urged that the supposed explanation is as obscure as the word to be explained. It is barely possible, however, that פרשדן is a Greek gloss (? προστῷον), or the corruption of such a gloss. The translations προστάδα, παραστάδα ('A) τὰ πρόθυρα (Σ) are guesses following hints in the sound of the word. In this obscurity it is perhaps best, with Jewish exegetical tradition, to find in פרשדנה the subject of the vb., and then to emend with Nö.,† Bu., הפרש Ex. 29¹⁴ &c., the *feces* (in the stomach and bowels — not excrement); פרשדנה may have arisen by accidental conformation to מסררונה v.²³ᵃ.

---

* So Kl. rightly says.　　　† *Untersuchungen*, p. 180 n.

23-26. Ehud's escape. — **23.** *Ehud went out to the . . .*]
Heb. *misderōn;* from the context, the name of the part of the
building to which Ehud passed from the *'aliyah*, and through
which he made his exit from the house. The meaning of the
word is, however, unknown, and in our ignorance of the construction and arrangement of the house, it is of little use to guess.
The various renderings proposed — guard-room, vestibule, portico,
arcade, gallery, balustrade, staircase, &c. — show the inadequacy
of etymology to determine the meaning of a technical word. —
And closed the doors of the upper story upon him] *sc.* on Eglon,
shutting him up in the chamber. The plural, *doors*, of the two
leaves of a double door (1 K. 6³¹f. ³⁴ cf. Jud. 16³ 1 S. 21¹³).* The
last words of the verse, *and locked them*, are, as the false tense
proves, the addition of a scribe, who, observing that the doors
were locked (v.²⁴. ²⁵), missed an explicit statement here that Ehud
locked them. — **24.** *So he went out*] he emphatic ; in English we
should subordinate the clause, *after he went out, &c.* — Eglon's
servants came, and found the door of the upper story bolted.
From the connexion of the clauses, as well as from what follows,
it is naturally to be inferred that they saw Ehud pass out by the
usual way ; they would not have sought to intrude unsummoned
upon a private interview, and in v.ᵇ they evidently believe their
master to be alone. — *It must be that he is relieving himself in the
cabinet of the cool chamber*] the sense of decency in such matters is very highly developed among Orientals, as it was in general
in the civilized peoples of antiquity. — **25.** *They waited till they
saw that they were mistaken*] lit. *to the point of confusion* (2 K. 2¹⁷
8¹¹) ; an idiomatic expression suggestive of confounded hopes or
expectations, perplexity, perturbation. Then, as he did not open
the door, they took the key and opened it. In the locks still
in common use in the East the bolt is shot by hand, or by means
of a thong. A number of pin-tumblers then drop into corresponding holes in the bolt and lock it. The key, which is used
for unlocking only, is a flat piece of wood in one end of which
are set pins corresponding in number and position to the tumblers
of the lock and in length to the depth of the bolt.† It is

---

* So θύραι in Hom.

† Sometimes the key is a bent piece of metal; but the principle is the same.

slipped lengthwise under the bolt, which is undercut for the purpose, until its pins entering lift the tumblers clear and allow the bolt to be pushed back.[*] The references in the O.T. make it altogether probable that the locks of the ancient Hebrews were of this pattern. — Having opened, they found their master lying dead; cf. the very similar scene, Judith 14[16f.]. — **26.** The two halves of the verse have the appearance of doublets;[†] the first clause of v.[b] cannot be construed in continuation of v.[a], and as a circumstantial clause depending from the preceding — he escaped . . . *he having passed over,* [‡] — is unusually awkward. The structure is exactly parallel to v.[a], and the significant verb, *he escaped,* is found in both halves. — *While they were delaying*] v.[24f.]. — *He passed the sculptured stones*] the way in which these are mentioned here and in v.[19] is thought to indicate that this was the last Moabite outpost, beyond which he was in no danger of being stopped or overtaken by the enemy;[§] but in our ignorance of the topography this is a somewhat uncertain inference; the words may be meant only to describe the road Ehud took. In v.[26] we might even translate, *he crossed* (sc. the Jordan) *to,* or *near, the sculptured stones;* [‖] see below. — *To Seirah*] otherwise unknown. If v.[27] is the original sequel of v.[26b], it must have been a place on the edge of the highlands of Ephraim.

It is commonly assumed, though without any distinct intimation in the text, that the scene of Ehud's exploit was Jericho, v.[13],[¶] where Eglon resided, either permanently, or, as is more probable, at the time for the collection of the yearly tribute. But it is difficult, if not impossible, to reconcile this with v.[18f. 26b], since Gilgal is not on the way from Jericho to Mt. Ephraim, but in exactly the opposite direction, toward the fords of the Jordan leading to the land of Moab.[**] All becomes natural, however, if we assume that

---

[*] Russell, *Aleppo*[2], 1794, i. p. 21 f.; Lane, *Modern Egyptians*[5], p. 19 f.; Thomson, *Land and Book*[2], iii. p. 413; cf. Wilkinson, *Anct. Egyptians,* ed. Birch, i. p. 353 f.

[†] Winckler. [‡] Driver[2], § 160 (p. 199); cf. 4[1].

[§] RLbG., Schm., al.; see on v.[19]. [‖] Bu.

[¶] Fl. Jos., Ba., Cass., and most.

[**] We cannot evade this difficulty by supposing that a different Gilgal is meant, (Masius, Ke., Ba., Ph. Wolff, in Ri. *HWB*[1]. p. 518); in this connexion with Moab and Jericho, Gilgal in the Jordan valley would necessarily be understood. If the author had intended another, he must have added some definition.

the residence of Eglon was east of the Jordan, in the land of
Moab, which is on other accounts also the more probable hypothesis.* The name of the place need not have been mentioned;
or it may have been subsequently omitted.†

23. הבכסדרונה] the versions seem all, in one way or another, to connect
the word with MH. (Aram. Syr.) סדר ' row, rank '; 𝕲 ἐξῆλθεν τοὺς διατεταγμέ-
νους, 𝕮 ראנסירא (ἔξεδρα), 𝕾 ܐܣܛܘܢܐ (ἐνστός); similarly Abulw., Ra.,
Ki., RLbG., Drus., Cler., and most moderns. — בעדו] *upon him* (Eglon), not
after himself (*i.e.* אחריו Gen. 19⁶); Gen. 7¹⁶ 2 K. 4⁴. — ונעל] the tense admits of
no grammatical explanation, cf. 7¹⁸ 16¹⁸ 2 S. 13¹⁸. Other instances Drᵌ. § 133;
Roorda, § 536. — **24.** והוא יצא] the nom. sent. describing the circumstances
or conditions under which the following action took place; see on the whole
subject, Drᵌ. § 156 ff. — אך] אך הסיך הוא את רגליו restrictive; the only explanation of the closed door is, &c. Ew. § 354 *a*; Lex. *s. v.* The phrase *cover one's
feet* (1 S. 24⁴) is a euphemism from the posture assumed in evacuating the
bowels, the long garments forming a tent-like covering over the lower extremities (RLbG.); so 𝕲𝕷𝕿𝕾 (vid.), Ra., Ki. (*Comm.*), Drus., Cler., Schm., Ke.,
Cass., al.‡ Not *urinate* (𝕲ᴮ, Ki. *Lex.* and *Comm.* on 1 S. 24⁴, Mi. Yophi); v.
M. Yoma, iii. 2; Bochart, *Hierozoicon*, ed. Rosenm., i. p. 777 ff. The root is
סכך; Ki. *Comm.*, Bö., Ol., Kö. i. p. 354. — חדר המקרה] cstr. of חדר, Ol. § 134 *d*;
Sta. § 191 *c*. Probably a cabinet or closet in the מקרה (𝕲ᴬⱽᴸᴹᴼ ᵴ ᵗ ἐν τῷ
ἀποχωρήσει τοῦ κοιτῶνος, 𝕾, RLbG., Schm., Rosenm., Cass., al.). That in
this sense we should necessarily have חי עלית הס׳ (Ba.) is too strong an assertion. — **25.** ויחילו עד בוש] the Hiph. in this sense only Gen. 8¹⁰ (J). § In עד
בוש (2 K. 2¹⁷ 8¹¹) בוש is inf. (Drus.), not pf. (Ki.); cf. עד רבה 2 Chr. 24¹⁰.
From the way in which it is used it seems that the original significance of the
vb. was no longer very distinctly felt, and that the phrase had become equivalent to *a long while* (Fl. Jos. πολὺν χρόνον); cf. עד מאד *very*. It is unnecessary
to assume two roots (Castell, Stud., Fürst). — מפתח] nom. instrum., Is. 22²²
1 Chr. 9²⁷. — נפל ארצה מת] *fallen to the ground, dead.* The ptcp. of the
intrans. vb. is nearly equivalent to an adjective, *prostrate on the ground;*
cf. 4²² 19²⁷ 1 S. 5³ ⁴ 31⁶. See Schultens, *Origines*, p. 144 (comparison of
Hebr. with Gr. and Lat. idioms of vb. 'fall'). — **26.** עד התמהמהם] for עד with
inf. cf. Ez. 33²² Jon. 4². The original meaning of עד, 'duration,' distinctly
appears in these phrases; cf. 2 K. 9²², Ew. § 217 *e*. The verb 19⁸ 2 S. 15²⁸;
in Hexat. Gen. 19¹⁶ 43¹⁰ Ex. 12³⁹ (all J). — והוא עבר את הפסילים] "not the
mere addition of a fresh fact like ויעבר, but the justification of the preceding
נמלט," — *he having passed;* Drᵌ. p. 199. If the text is not composite, this is

<hr>

* So Ra., Schm., Stud., F. W. Schultz. According to Winckler, J laid the scene
in Moab; E in Jericho.   † Bu.
‡ Cf. *Berachoth*, 62ᵇ; Fl. Jos., *b. j.* ii. 8, 9; Burckhardt, *Travels*, &c., p. 445, 518 f.
§ If the text be sound.

the only possible construction. The accus. is commonly interpreted, *he passed the images;* cf. 1 S. 14²³.* Bu. proposes, *he crossed* (the Jordan) *near the images*, comparing Gen. 32²², which is, however, usually explained like the preceding example. A third possibility is, *he passed over to the images*, cf. 11²⁹ and note there. Winckler's conj. ‏נבד אה הפ‎, *he sacrificed to the images*, is a particularly unhappy conceit. — ‏השעירהה‎] n. pr., acc. of limit of motion after ‏נביס‎ (Gen. 19¹⁷ Is. 37³⁸). The article is evidence only that the meaning of the name was kept in mind, not that it should be translated as appellative (Ra., *thicket, bush*). ‏שעיד‎ Jos. 15¹⁰ on the boundary of Judah is much too far away. Winckler would seek Seirah east of the Jordan.

27–29. Ehud raises the Israelites; they seize the fords and cut off all the Moabites on that side of the Jordan. — The narrative is not free from derangement and repetition, which are generally attributed to the interference of the editor, but may arise from the combination of two accounts. — **27.** *When he came*] in the context, we must suppose, to Seirah, though we should in that case expect the particle *thither*. Some recensions of 𝔊 have, *to the land of Israel*, which may be only an addition of the translator, but shows that the incompleteness of v.²⁷ᵃ was felt, and is entirely suitable to the context. — *Sounded the alarm*] lit. *blew the* war *horn;* a summons to arms, 6³⁴ 1 S. 13³. — *The Highlands of Ephraim*] 2⁹ 4⁵ 7²⁴ Jos. 17¹⁵ 1 K. 4⁸ &c.; the mountainous interior of Central Palestine, from the Great Plain south to the neighbourhood of Jerusalem; see note. The Israelites from the neighbouring parts of this region rose at Ehud's call and hastened down, under his lead, to the plain of Jericho. — **28.** The first half verse comes rather late after v.²⁷ᵇ; the second, *they followed him down*, is parallel to v.²⁷ᵇ. This interruption of the natural progress of the story is commonly ascribed to the editor who added v.²⁸ᵃ; † it is possible, however, that v.²⁸ is the original sequel of v.²⁶, and v.²⁹ of v.²⁷, which would give us two complete and parallel accounts. — *Follow me down*] 𝔐 erroneously, *pursue me.* — *They seized the fords of the Jordan against the Moabites*] thus cutting off the retreat of those who were on the Israelite side of the river; cf. 7²⁴ 12⁵. ‡ The fords here meant are the lowest

---

* That this requires ‏נבד ב‎ (Winckler) is a rash assertion.

† Bu.

‡ Fl. Jos., Ra., RLbG., Schm.; not in order to prevent help from coming from the Moabite side (Ki.). Cler. combines the two explanations.

fords of the Jordan, near Gilgal (Jos. 2⁷ 2 S. 19¹⁵).* Others interpret, *the fords leading to Moab, the Moabite fords;* but this is not
distinctive, for all the lower fords of the Jordan led to Moab, and
12⁵, where the construction is the same, cannot well be explained
in this way. — **29**. The verse, as a whole, is ascribed by Budde to
the author of the Deuteronomic book of Judges; but see above
on v.²⁶. — *Ten thousand men*] see on 1⁴. — *All stout and valiant
men*] there were no others among them; † not, *every stout and
valiant man,* ‡ as though they let others go, in conflict with the
following, *not one escaped.* The Moabites are represented as an
army of occupation, rather than as settlers.

27. ויהי בבואו] 𝔊ᴮᴾᴺᴼ ᵃˡ· ‡ + εἰς γῆν Ισραηλ, a natural addition if the residence of Eglon was supposed to be east of the Jordan (cf. Ra.). It is conceivable, on the other hand, that the words were dropped from 𝕴, as conflicting
with the supposition that the scene of Ehud's deed was Jericho. If Seirah had
been meant, the author would probably have written בבואו שמה; if Mt. Ephraim,
the sentence would have been differently arranged. — ויתקע בשופר] the horn
(κερατίνη, *buccina* §) as a signal calling men to arms, Jud. 6³⁴ 1 S. 13³ 2 S. 20¹;
warning of approach of the enemy, Am. 3⁶ Ez. 33⁶ Jer. 4⁵ 6¹ &c.; in battle,
Am. 2²; sounding the recall, 2 S. 2²⁸ 18¹⁶ 20²². On the form and fabrication
of the *shôphar,* and its religious uses, see C. Adler, *P.A.O.S.,* Oct. 1889, p. clxxi.;
The Shophar — its Use and Origin, 1894 (Rep. of U. S. Natl. Museum for
1892, p. 437-450). — *The Highlands of Ephraim*] the mountains which form
the backbone of Central and Southern Palestine extend from the Great Plain
southward, gradually increasing in elevation to the vicinity of Hebron, south
of which they fall off, the hills terminating about Tell 'Arad and Beersheba. ‖
The northern half of this region is the mountain country of Ephraim, occupied
by West Manasseh, Ephraim, and Benjamin; the southern, the mountain
country of Judah. There is no natural boundary between the two; the limit
shifted with the southward expansion of Joseph. At the time of our story the
territory of Joseph was separated from Judah by a Canaanite belt of which Jerusalem was the central stronghold; see above, p. 8. — **28.** רדפו אחרי] read רדו
𝔊 and v.ᵇ; 2 K. 5²¹ (Ba.) is not parallel to this use of רדף. — לבואב] equivalent to a *dativus incommodi;* cf. 𝕿 כל מואב, Ba., Reuss. Not *vada Jordanis
quae transmittunt in Moab* 𝕷, Schm., Cler., Be., al. (אל כ); or periphrasis for
a second genitive, τὰς διαβάσεις τοῦ Ἰορδάνου τῆς Μωαβ 𝔊𝕾, the Moabite
fords of the Jordan. — **29.** שָׁמֵן] כל שמן וכל איש חיל] originally 'fat,' then

---

* *SWP. Memoirs,* iii. p. 170. There are now two fords, one at the pilgrims'
bathing place (Maḥâdet Ḥâgleh); the other, at present overgrown, a mile or more
south of it. The former must always have been the main crossing.

† AV.   ‡ RV.   § Jerome on Hos. 5⁴.
‖ Robinson, *Phys. Geog.,* p. 32-36.

'robust, vigorous.' Others interpret, 'rich, great' (Ki. *°*, RLbG., Cler., al.), a familiar metaphor, but an inapposite sense in this place.

30. *Moab was subdued*] 8²⁸ 11³³ (cf. 4²³) 1 S. 7¹³, in the closing formulas with which the stories of the several judges are brought to a conclusion. In the present instance the results of Ehud's deed seem to be exaggerated. The story itself tells only of the assassination of the king and the slaughter of the Moabites west of the Jordan, clearing the land of Israel of these intruders ; of a subjugation of Moab it gives no hint. — *The land enjoyed security eighty years*] two generations ; cf. v.¹¹ above, and see Introduction, § 7.

רי ויכנע מואב] *Moab was subdued :* 8²⁸ 11²³ 1 S. 7¹³ 1 Chr. 20⁴ 2 Chr. 13¹⁸ Ps. 106⁴²; the Niph. is passive to Hiph. (2 S. 8¹ = 1 Chr. 18¹). Not to be confounded with the trop. sense, 'be subdued in spirit, submit' to the judgements or reproof of God (Lev. 26⁴¹ 1 K. 22¹⁹ &c.). The phrase belongs apparently to the "pre-Deuteronomic" Book of Judges; see We., *Comp.*, p. 219; controverted by Kitt., *Stud. u. Krit.*, 1892, p. 50.

On the moral aspects of Ehud's deed — on which the narrator in Jud. 3 certainly wasted no reflections — and on the difficulties which the story made for the older biblical apologetics, see Schmid, *quaestiones* 7-10: Num Ehud Egloni mentitus est? Num Eglonem Ehud decepit? Licuitne Ehudi Eglonem tyrannum occidere? Quomodo cum impulsu et instinctu divino conciliandum est, quod Ehud adeo solicite ad caedem Eglonis se praeparavit, tempus atque alia circumspexit atque observavit?— In more modern fashion, Bachmann, p. 231 ff.

III. 31. Shamgar kills six hundred Philistines with an ox-goad. — Shamgar is often reckoned as the first of the six "Minor Judges." * The verse which tells his brief story exhibits, however, none of the distinctive formulas of the list 10¹⁻⁵ 12⁸⁻¹⁵ ; † and, what is more conclusive, Shamgar is not embraced with them in the final chronological scheme of the book ; neither the period in which he wrought deliverance for Israel nor its duration is given. ‡ Chapter 4¹ (D) ignores Shamgar, connecting immedi-

---

* See Introduction, § 7.   † See on 10¹.
‡ The Jewish explanation is that he died in the first year of his office; Fl. Jos., Juchasin, Abarb., a Lap., al.

ately with 3³⁰ ("when Ehud was dead"). It is to be inferred from these facts that the story of Shamgar's exploit was inserted here by a hand not only later than the Deuteronomic author of 3³⁰ 4¹, but than the editor who introduced the "Minor Judges" and made them a place in the chronology.*

After him came Shamgar ben Anath] Shamgar is named in Jud. 5⁶, where, with Jael, he represents the hour of Israel's deepest humiliation under the hand of its foes, just before the appearance of Deborah, and there is no reason to doubt that he is a historical figure. The story of the slaughter of the six hundred Philistines reminds us of Samson, but, in its form, still more of the exploits of David's heroes, 2 S. 21¹⁶⁻²² 23⁸ᶠ,† and is very likely extracted from the same or a similar source. The name Shamgar is foreign; perhaps Hittite. Anath is a goddess of whose worship there are many evidences in Palestine in names of places which were seats of her cult, ‡ and whose name appears on Egyptian monuments from the 18th dynasty. — *He smote the Philistines*] all the evidence we have goes to show that the Philistines did not seriously trouble the central tribes until shortly before the time of Saul; see above on 3³ (p. 80). The Song of Deborah celebrates the victorious issue of the struggle of the central and northern tribes against the Canaanites, who in the days of Shamgar (5⁶) had brought Israel to such straits. It knows nothing of a contemporaneous oppression by the Philistines. As a champion of Israel against the Philistines, therefore, Shamgar appears too early. § — *With an ox-goad*] ‖ the Syrian ploughman's goad is a formidable weapon, sometimes eight feet long, armed at one end with a spike, at the other with a chisel-shaped blade for cleaning the plough; and on occasion would make a very good substitute for a spear. But the six hundred men have always taxed the credulity of the commentators, who have had recourse to various rationalizing subterfuges. Clericus, for example, explains that Shamgar did not kill

---

* See Ewald, *GVI.* ii. p. 514 (cf. 449) = *HI.* ii. p. 317; Nö., *Untersuch.*, p. 180; cf. also We., *Comp.*, p. 217 f.; Bu., *Richt. u. Sam.*, p. 166 (meant to replace Abimelech, the latest addition to the book).   † We., *Comp.*, p. 218 n.

‡ Beth-anath in Galilee, Jud. 1³³; Beth-anoth in Judah, Jos. 15⁵⁹; Anathoth near Jerusalem; the modern *'Aināta* on the Lebanon (see above, p. 52).   § We.

‖ Bochart adduces in illustration, *Il.* vi. 132-135, and Nonnus, *Dionys.*, xx. 315 ff.; cf. Eustath. on *Il.*, *l.c.*

six hundred men with his own hand, but headed a peasants' revolt in which so many Philistines fell.* —*And he too delivered Israel*] see on 2[16]. The form of the expression of itself would arouse the suspicion that the introduction of Shamgar was an afterthought.†

Whether Shamgar is the original hero of this story may be doubted; Jud. 5[1] certainly suggests no such deliverance. The similarity of the exploit to those of David's *Gibborim* has been often observed (*e.g.* by Schm.). The resemblance to the slaughter of the Philistines at Lehi by Shammah ben Agé (2 S. 23[11f.]) is particularly striking; and the conjecture may not seem too hazardous that the feat of David's comrade has been ascribed, perhaps partly in consequence of the similarity of the names, to the Shamgar of 5[6], of whom nothing was known. Cf. also Jud. 15[14ff.] (Samson at Lehi). With the name Shamgar we may perhaps compare Sangar, king of Gargamiš (then the chief city of the Hittite country) in the days of Ašurnaṣirpal and Salmanassar II. (9th cent. B.C.); ‡ cf. also Samgar-nebo Jer. 39[3]. There was a kingdom Sangara on the upper Tigris; § a river Sangarius in Asia Minor (*Il.* iii. 187, xvi. 719; Strabo, xii. p. 543; Ptol., v. 1, 6). The similarity of the names may be purely accidental; on the other hand it may be evidence of the movements of population in these regions. — *Anath*] is represented in an Egyptian stele in the British Museum, sitting, holding shield and javelin in the right hand, while with the left she brandishes a battle axe;∥ in other places she appears on horseback similarly armed,¶ or sitting upon a lion.** That she was especially worshipped by the Hittites (E. Meyer) is not indisputable. In what relation this goddess stands to the Babylonian *Antu* is not certain; see Schrader, *ZDMG.* xxvii. p. 404, and, against him, E. Meyer, *ib.* xxxi. p. 716 ff. The evidence given by the Amarna tablets of long and profound Babylonian influence in Palestine at an early period makes it probable that they are not independent.†† — The form of the name שמגר בן ענת is unusual; the conjecture that it is abbreviated for בן עכר ענת (Baethgen, p. 141) is inadmissible (Nö., *ZDMG.* xlii. 479); cf. rather בן ריר. — בן הבכר הבכר] the abs. probably כליר, a common form of *nom. instrum.*, Sta. § 272 *a*, cf. Barth, *Nominalbildung*, p. 262. Descriptions in *M. Kelim*, xxv. 2; *Wayyiqra rab.*, § 29; Abulw., quoting R. Sherira; Maundrell (1697) in *Early Travels in Pal.*, ed. Wright, 1848, p. 475 f.; Rob., *BR2.* iii. 62; esp. Schumacher, "Der arab. Pflug," *ZDPV.* xii. p. 160 f.; Post, *PEF. Qu. St.* 1891, p. 112–114.

---

* Similarly a Lyra, al.   † Bertheau.

‡ Tiele, *Babyl.-Assyr. Gesch.*, p. 175, 189 f., 197 f., 200 f.

§ Frequently mentioned in Egyptian inscriptions; W. M. Müller, *Asien u. Europa*, p. 279; Erman, *Aegypten*, p. 682; also in an Amarna letter, *PSBA.*, June 1888, p. 569.   ∥ Wilkinson, *Anct. Egypt.*, ed. Birch, iii. p. 236.

¶ Lepsius, *Denkmäler*, Abth. iii. pl. 138.

** De Vogüé, *Mélanges d'archéol. orient.*, p. 47.

†† On Anath see further, De Vogüé, *Jour. Asiat.*, 1867, p. 125 ff. = *Mélanges d'archéol. orient.*, 41 ff.; Baethgen, *Beiträge*, 52 f.

IV. Deborah and Barak deliver Israel from the Canaanites; the defeat and death of Sisera.

LITERATURE. — G. A. Cooke, *The History and Song of Deborah*, 1892.

The Israelites again offend Yahweh, who gives them into the power of Jabin, the Canaanite king of Hazor, and Sisera, his general, for twenty years (4^{1-3}). Deborah, a prophetess, instigates Barak to take the field against Sisera (v.$^{4-9}$). He raises Zebulun and Naphtali and occupies Mt. Tabor. Sisera, advancing against him through the plain, is attacked and routed, and his army cut to pieces (v.$^{10-16}$). Sisera escapes on foot to the tent of Jael, who conceals him in the tent and kills him while he sleeps (v.$^{17-22}$). Jabin is subdued (v.$^{23f.}$).

The Song of Deborah, ch. 5^{2-31}, is a triumphal ode, celebrating the victory of the Israelites under the lead of Deborah and Barak over Sisera and the kings of Canaan, and the death of Sisera by the hand of Jael. The poem is in places obscure or unintelligible, in consequence chiefly of corruption of the text; but its general tenor is clear. By the vividness of every touch, and especially by the elevation and intensity of feeling which pervades it, it makes the impression of having been written by one who had witnessed the great events which it commemorates.* The prose narrative, 4^{4-22}, also gives an account of a rising of Israelite tribes instigated by Deborah and led by Barak, and of the defeat and death of Sisera. The relation of this narrative to the Song must be our first inquiry.

The chief points of difference between the two are these: 1. In the poem the kings of Canaan assemble to battle (v.^{19}). Sisera is evidently at their head, the greatest king among them (v.^{30}). In his palace the queen-mother, whose ladies-in-waiting are princesses (v.^{29}), sits expecting his return (v.$^{28-30}$).† In the prose narrative, ch. 4, Sisera is only the general of Jabin king of Hazor (v.$^{7.17}$), who in v.$^{2.23.24}$ (D) is even called king of Canaan. 2. In ch. 5 all the tribes around the Great Plain — Ephraim, Benjamin, Machir (Manasseh), Issachar, Zebulun, Naphtali — join in the struggle, while the more remote tribes, Dan, Asher,

---

* See Introduction to ch. 5, below.
† In v.^{30} some find mention of the queen; see comm. there.

and even Reuben and Gilead beyond the Jordan, are bitterly reproached for selfishly standing aloof from the cause of all Israel. It is the uprising of a whole people. In ch. 4, on the other hand, Barak collects a force of ten thousand men out of Zebulun and Naphtali only.* 3. The most striking difference is in the description of Sisera's death. In 4^{21}, as he lies fast asleep on the ground in the tent, Jael with a hammer drives a tent-pin through his temples into the earth. In $5^{25\cdot27}$, on the contrary, as he is standing at the door of the tent drinking milk from a bowl, Jael strikes him a crushing blow on the head, and he sinks dead at her feet.†

Closer examination shows that the account in ch. 4 is not entirely self-consistent. Jabin king of Hazor, or of Canaan, has really nothing to do with the story; he takes no part in the struggle, and only reappears in v.^{17} and the editor's words at the end. Sisera is here, too, the real protagonist; and that in this version of his story also he was originally represented as a king is clear from the fact that he has a residence city of his own, remote from Hazor. The topographical data of the chapter are conflicting, and make it impossible to form a consistent conception of the battle and the flight. The Israelites assemble at Kedesh in Naphtali, as if for an attack upon Hazor; but march, peaceable and unmolested, by the gates of the enemy's capital to Mt. Tabor. Sisera advances against them from Harosheth (v.^{13}), and the battle takes place in the plain at the foot of the mountain. The routed Canaanites flee toward Harosheth, closely followed by the Israelites (v.^{16}). Sisera escapes alone on foot to the encampment of Heber the Kenite near Kedesh (v.^{17} cl.^{11}), many hours distant to the north, with Barak in hot pursuit. His flight took him straight through the territory of the tribes which were in arms, and past the very doors of his master's city. Why did he not take refuge within its walls rather than in the tent of a nomad?

---

* In 5^{16} it seems that both Deborah and Barak belong to Issachar; while in ch. 4 Deborah's home is in the heart of Mt. Ephraim, and Barak's at Kedesh in Naphtali. The text of 5^{15}, however, is too insecure to permit us to lay great stress upon this.

† See in general, We., *Hist. of Israel*, p. 240-242; *Comp.*, p. 220-223; Sta., *GVI².* i. p. 178; Kue., *HCO².* i. p. 345 f.; Bu., *Richt. u. Sam.*, p. 104-106; Co., *Einl².*, p. 93-95; W. R. Smith, *OTJC².*, p. 132; Wildeboer, *Letterkunde des Ouden Verbonds*, p. 35-39.

These inconcinnities probably result, at least in part, from the combination of two narratives ; one an account of a war waged by Zebulun and Naphtali against Jabin of Hazor, the other of the war with Sisera king of Harosheth and his allies which is the subject of the Song of Deborah. The two have been superficially harmonized at the most essential point by making Sisera the general of Jabin. An analysis of the chapter is scarcely possible ; nor can we say what common feature led to the incongruous union.

The analysis is attempted by Bruston, " Les deux Jéhovistes," *Revue de Théol. et Philos.*, 1886, p. 35 f. (quoted by Bu., *Richt. u. Sam.*, p. 70 n.) as follows : to the first Jehovist he ascribes . . . 4⁷ᵇ·³· ³ᵇᵃ· ⁴⁻⁹ (with minor traces of redaction in v.⁷· ⁹) ¹⁰ᵃᵝ· ᵇ· ¹²⁻¹³ᵃ· ¹⁶ 5¹⁻³¹ᵃ; to the second, 4¹· ²ᵃ· ᵇᵃ· ³ᵇᵝ· ³ᵃ [words corresponding to 3ᵃ· ¹³] ¹⁰ᵃᵃ· ¹¹ [defeat of Canaanites at Kedesh] ¹³ᵇ· ¹⁷⁻²⁴ 5³¹ᵇ. — If v.¹⁷ᵇ is not an editorial addition, Heber must belong to the story of Jabin (Bu., Co.), and as Jael unquestionably belongs to that of Sisera, it might be conjectured that in making her Heber's wife the writer who combined the two stories had attempted to harmonize them by an artifice similar to that by which Sisera was made Jabin's general; and it might be further surmised that in the original story Jabin met at the tents of Heber a fate like that which overtook Sisera at the hand of Jael. But all this is mere conjecture.

The war of Zebulun and Naphtali against Jabin, king of Hazor, and his allies is recounted in Jos. 11¹⁻⁹, where it is magnified into the conquest of all the northern Canaanites by Joshua and all Israel, in the same way in which the victory of Judah and Simeon over Adoni-zedek (Adoni-bezek) of Jerusalem (Jud. 1⁴⁻⁷) is elaborated in Jos. 10 into the account of Joshua's conquest of all Southern Canaan. We may surmise that the story of Jabin, of which we have the fragmentary remains in Jud. 4 Jos. 11, came from the same source from which Jud. 1 and the kindred fragments in Jos. were derived (J).* Too little is left of it to make a reconstruction possible ; but it is a not improbable conjecture that in its original connexion this story formed a chapter in the account of the conquest of Northern Canaan, corresponding to the taking of Hebron by Caleb and of Bethel by Joseph, the positive complement of Jud. 1³⁰· ²³. The story of Sisera in ch. 4, after the elimination of the elements derived from that of Jabin, gives us a number of details which are not found in ch. 5 ; viz., the name of

---

* Bu., *Richt. u. Sam.*, p. 66 ff.

Deborah's husband, Lapidoth; her home, between Bethel and
Ramah; * Barak's father's name, Abinoam, and his residence,
Kedesh in Naphtali; † Sisera's city, Harosheth ha-goyim; his
chariotry; the position of the Israelites before the action, at
Tabor. In the description of Sisera's end there is both a close
resemblance and a striking difference between the two versions.
Wellhausen, ‡ W. R. Smith, § and others think that 4^{71} originated
in a prosaic misunderstanding of 5^{28} (see comm. on the vv.). It
would not follow, however, that ch. 4 is merely a bald prose version of ch. 5. ‖ Dependence on the poem, in this and other
particulars, does not exclude the use of other sources of tradition,
from which the details mentioned above may have been derived;
and there is no substantial reason to doubt that the basis of ch. 4
is an old prose story of Sisera, which, though not rivalling the
Song of Deborah in antiquity, is not conspicuously inferior to
the other stories in the book.

It is an interesting question, and one the solution of which,
if it could be reached, would be of considerable importance,
whether the prose narrative was originally prefixed to the Ode as
an introduction, perhaps in such a collection as the *Sepher
ha-yashar*, in the manner familiar to us in the great Arab collections. There are no very decisive considerations on either
side; on the whole, the impression which ch. 4 makes upon me
is unfavourable to this hypothesis. From what source the story of
Sisera in ch. 4 is derived can hardly be determined.¶ It is introduced in the usual way (4^{1-3}); the close is found in $4^{23f.}$; the
chronological note, naturally, in $5^{31f.}$.

**1-3. The Israelites again offend Yahweh; he gives them
into the power of Jabin, king of Canaan, who cruelly oppresses
them for twenty years.** — The regular introduction; the stories of

---

* This trait is, however, probably introduced by a later hand; see on v.⁴.

† Perhaps this, too, is an error.   ‡ *Comp.*, p. 222.

§ *OTJC²*., p. 132; Sta., *GVI²*. i. p. 178 n.

‖ "Eine Reproduction, die die speziellen Züge verwischt und verfälscht;" We.,
Prol²., p. 251. — The converse opinion of Vernes and others, that the poem is
derived from the prose narrative, see below, Introduction to ch. 5.

¶ For E we might point to אשה נביאה v.⁴ (cf. Holzinger, *Einl. in den Hexateuch*,
p. 209 f.), and ויהם יי v.¹⁵ (1 S. 7¹⁰ &c.).

Jabin and Sisera are combined and harmonized by making Sisera
the general of Jabin. — 1. Cf. 2[11] 3[7. 12]. — *Ehud being dead*] post-
poned circumstantial clause, introducing a fact essential to the
understanding of the situation.* The author's theory is that the
judges restrained the people from displeasing Yahweh as long as
they lived ; cf. 3[11] and 2[19] (in contrast to 2[17]). Observe that
Shamgar is ignored ; the verse connects immediately with 3[30], just
as 3[12] does with 3[11]. — 2. *Yahweh sold them*] 2[14]. — *Jabin, the*
king of Canaan, who reigned in Hazor] the tendency to turn the
history of the Israelite tribes into the history of the Israelitish
nation, which is conspicuous in the editing of the book,† shows
itself in the transformation of Jabin king of Hazor (v.[17] Jos. 11[1])
into the king of Canaan (v.[23. 24]) ; here the two are harmonized,
Jabin the king of Canaan, who reigned, i.e., had his capital (Jos.
13[12. 21]), *in Hazor*. — *Hazor*] has not been certainly identified ; it
must be looked for not far from Kedesh.‡ Robinson fixed on
Tell Khureibeh, about an hour south of Kedesh ; § Wilson ‖ and
Guérin ¶ prefer Khirbet Harreh, the ruins of a fortified place
about the same distance SE. of Kedesh, overlooking the Ḥuleh ;
Conder and others would recognize the name in its Arabic equivalent, Ǵebel Ḥaḍireh, three miles SSW. of Kedesh, a little west of
the modern village of Deishūn.** — *His general was Sisera*] in
this way the story of Sisera is harmonized with that of Jabin ;
see above, p. 108 f. Sisera did not reside in his master's capital,
Hazor, but had a city of his own like an independent king.†† —
Harosheth ha-goyim] v.[13. 16]. Now generally identified with
el-Ḥārithīyeh, in the narrows of the Kishon valley at the western
end of the Great Plain ; see on v.[13]. — 3. v.[8], see 3[9]. — *Nine*
hundred iron chariots] v.[13] 1[19] ; by means of them he kept command of the plain ; Jos. 17[16. 18] (J). Thothmes III. counts nine

---

* Dr[s]. § 159; Ges.[26] § 141. 2, n. 2 ; § 156. 1. 2.   † See above, p. 90.
‡ Cf. 2 K. 15[29] Jos. 19[36ff.]. 1 Macc. 11[67] ; Masius on Jos. 11[1].
§ *BR*[2]. iii. p. 364-366.
‖ *Jour. Sacred Lit.*, 1866, p. 245; see *SWP. Memoirs*, I. p. 237 f.
¶ *Galilée*, iii. p. 363 ff.; so also Di.
** See *DB*[2]. s. v.; *SWP. Memoirs*, i. p. 204; Schürer, *GjV.* i. p. 185 n.; Bäd[s].
p. 264.
†† The text cannot mean that *Jabin* lived at Harosheth ('Thdt., Ki., al.; v.
Drus.).

hundred and twenty-four chariots among the spoils of his victory in the battle of Megiddo.[*] — *He oppressed Israel cruelly for twenty years*] half a generation.

2. The name Hazor appears in the list of Thothmes III. (No. 32) and in the Papyrus Anastasi (Müller, *Asien u. Europa*, p. 173); also in the Amarna despatches. It was fortified by Solomon (1 K. 9[16]), as a place of commanding importance in Upper Galilee, and captured by Tiglath Pileser (734 B.C.; 2 K. 15[29]). The most definite clue for the determination of the site is given by 1 Macc. 11[67], cf. Fl. Jos., *antt.* xiii. 5, 6 f. § 154-162; v. 5, 1 § 199. Extensive ruins at Tell Harreh show that it was once a place of considerable size and strength; those at Tell el-Khureibeh are less important; at Gebel Hadireh none have been discovered. The last-named site perhaps best agrees with the indications in 1 Macc. No great stress can be laid on the similarity of the name; for *hadireh* is a common Arabic appellative ('sheepfold, pen'). — The relation of the Jabin of our text to the one in Jos. 11, and the question how Hazor, which was totally destroyed by Joshua, is here again the centre of the Canaanite power in the north, are much discussed by older commentators beginning with Thdt. (*qu.* 10). The common solution is, that Hazor had been rebuilt (Thdt., a Lyra, a Lap., Masius, Schm., Cler., al. mu.), and that the Jabin here named was a successor, and probably descendant, of the Jabin of Jos. 11. The title *king of Canaan* gives a good deal of trouble to the conscientious old commentator Schmid, who justly observes that Canaan was not a political unity, under one king; cf. also Cler. — סיסרא] the form of the name is not Canaanite, and probably not Semitic; we may perhaps compare the numerous Hittite names ending in *-sira* (*Iltasira, Maurasira*, &c., Müller, *Asien u. Europa*, p. 332). It is found also in the list of Nethinim (native temple-slaves) Ezra 2[53] Neh. 7[55]. — נחירה] 8[1] 1 S. 2[16] Ez. 34[4].

4, 5. Deborah. — 4. The verse belongs to the old story of Sisera.

Deborah was the moving spirit in the Israelite rising which overthrew Sisera (5[7. 12. 13] 4[6. 9f. 14]). — *A prophetess*] in the older sense of the word, an inspired woman; cf. Ex. 15[20]. Impelled by the spirit of Yahweh, she roused her countrymen to fight (4[6f.] 5[12]), and in his name promised them victory. We may compare the German Veleda, who instigated and supported Civilis in the attempt to throw off the Roman yoke,[†] and, in

---

[*] Brugsch, *Gesch. Aegyptens*, 1877, p. 303.

[†] Ea virgo nationis Bructerae late imperitabat, vetere apud Germanos more, quo plerasque feminarum fatidicas, et, augescente superstitione, arbitrantur deas. Tuncque Veledae auctoritas adolevit; nam prosperas Germanis res et excidium legionum praedixerat. Tac., *hist.*, iv. 61, cf. *Germ.* 8.

more modern times, Joan of Arc.[*] — *Wife of Lapidoth*] cf. 2 K.
22[14] Ex. 15[20] Lu. 2[36]. The name has given occasion to all manner
of conceits, among which we need only mention that which finds
in Lapidoth ('torches, flashes'[†]) another name of Barak ('lightning').[‡] — *Was judging Israel*] so the verb is interpreted in v.[5];
the latter verse is, however, secondary. In the connexion of the
original narrative (v.[4.6]) we should render, in accordance with the
constant usage of the book, *she delivered Israel*, vindicated it;
see on 3[10]. — **5.** A circumstantial addition by a latter editor, who
took the verb in v.[4] in the sense of 'judge, give judicial decisions,'
describing the way in which she exercised her judicial functions:
she did not, like Samuel (1 S. 7[16f.] §), go on a circuit, but the
Israelites from all quarters resorted to her at her home. — *She
used to sit under the Deborah Palm*] as arbitress, to settle dis-
putes (v.[b] cf. 1 S. 22[6]).[‖] Others, *she dwelt under* it (cf. 2 K.
22[14]);[¶] but it is unlikely that the author represented even the
prophetess-judge as having her house or tent beneath the holy
tree. There was a Tomb of Deborah below Bethel (Gen. 35[8] E),
where, according to the ancestral legend, Deborah the nurse of
Rebekah was buried. The name of the Mourning Tree (Allon-
bacuth) under which it stood was explained of the mourning for
Deborah. This tree is in all probability the same with the
Deborah Palm,[**] the origin of whose name the writer evidently
connects with Deborah, the prophetess and judge. This association of names is probably responsible for the idea that Deborah's
home was in the heart of the mountains of Ephraim. From 5[15]
it would appear that she was of the tribe of Issachar; and both
ch. 4 and 5 naturally lead us to think that her home was in or
near the plain of Jezreel. The conjecture is then not remote that
it was at Daberath ($\Delta\alpha\beta\epsilon\iota\rho\omega\theta$, $\Delta\alpha\beta\alpha\rho\alpha$) Jos. 19[12] 21[28], the modern

---

[*] Paulus, Réville, Cass.   [†] Of lightning, Ex. 20[18].

[‡] The identification is ancient midrash; see *Yalqut*, Ki., RLbG., old Cath.
comm.; recently Hilliger, cf. We., Bu., Cooke.

[§] These verses seem to stand in the same relation to v.[15] in which Jud. 4[6] does
to v.[4].   [‖] So RLbG., Abarb., Cler., Reuss, al.

[¶] Ki., Schm., a Lap., Stud., Ba.; Ke., Be. confusedly combine the two interpretations.

[**] Abarb., Tuch, Ew., De., Di. Ew. plausibly combines it also with the Tabor
Tree of 1 S. 10[3] (*GVI.* iii. p. 31).

1

Debūrīyeh at the western foot of Tabor. The similarity of the names is at least striking.[*] — *Between Ramah and Bethel*] in the same region in which Samuel afterwards judged Israel (1 S. 7[16]). The Benjamite Ramah is meant; the modern er-Rām, two hours north of Jerusalem.[†] On Bethel see on 1[23]. — *The Israelites went up to her for justice*] to have their causes decided in accordance with the common law of Israel.

4. *Deborah*] in Heb. means ' Bee '; cf. the Greek name Μέλισσα.[‡] Animal names of women are not uncommon in the O.T.; Ba. collects the following: Zipporah (little bird), Hoglah (grouse), Huldah (weasel), Eglah (heifer), Rachel (ewe), Jael (wild-goat). — [אשה נביאה] cf. [איש נביא] 6[8], [איש לוי] 19[1] 20[4], [איש כהן] Lev. 21[9], [איכה זונה] Jud. 11[1] 16[1], [אשה פילגש] 19[1], [אשה אלמנה] 2 S. 14[5] &c. (cf. Engl. colloq., ' widow woman '), [נערה בתולה], &c. Apposition of genus and species, Ges.[26] § 131. 2 *a*. The other prophetesses named in the O.T. are Miriam (Ex. 15[20]), Huldah (2 K. 22[14]), Noadiah (Neh. 6[14]); cf. Anna, Luke 2[36]. *Megillah*, 14[a] enumerates seven. — [אשת לפירות] the only natural interpretation is that which takes ר as the name of Deborah's husband (cf. 2 K. 22[14]). Men's names with fem. endings are not uncommon in the O.T.; cf. Naboth, 1 K. 21[1ff]. The translation, *ein Weib von Feuergeist* (Cass.; similarly Ar. Montanus, Fr. Bö., al.) is pure *midrash*; cf. *Megillah*, 14[a], *Yalqut, in loc.*, and the Rabb. commentators. — [היא שׁפְטָה] 𝕸 and apparently all verss., *judicabat;* and this interpretation is presupposed by v.[5]. If, however, the verb is synonymous with [הושׁיע] as in 2[16.18] 3[9ff.] 10[1f.] (see on 3[10]), which was no doubt the meaning in the original connexion, we require not the ptcp., but the histor. pf., [היא שׁפְטָה וג׳]. — [היא] resuming the subject after the two appositive phrases; cf. Gen. 3[12] Jud. 7[4] &c. — 5. [והיא יושבת] the words admit either interpretation, *sat* or *dwelt;* for the first cf. 6[11] 1 S. 14[2] 1 K. 13[14] 19[4]; for the second, Jud. 4[2] 10[1] 1 K. 5[5] 2 K. 22[14] &c. (Ba.). Doubtless the author meant that her home was in the neighbourhood of the holy tree. — [תחת תמר דבורה] Verss., *under Deborah's palm*, § 𝕸 [תֹּמֶר דבורה] : [תֹּמֶר דבורה] (Jer. 10[5]). The intention of this pronunciation and accentuation ‖ is not manifest. There is no evidence that [תֹּמֶר] is a collective, ' palm grove ' (Bö., i. p. 458 f.). 𝕮 has some other curious information about Deborah; she lived in 'Atarōth of Deborah,[¶] had palm trees at Jericho, gardens at Ramah, &c.; cf. also *Megillah*, 14[b]. — *Ramah*] lay on the road north from Jerusalem beyond Gibeah (19[13]), and is elsewhere named in connexion with Gibeon and Beeroth

---

[*] On Debūrīyeh see *SWP. Memoirs*, i. 363. Cf. Niebuhr, *Reconstellation des Deboraliedes*, p. 11 f.

[†] Rob., *BR*[2]. i. 576; Guérin, *Samarie*, i. p. 199-204; *SWP. Memoirs*, iii. p. 13.

[‡] Freq. title name of priestesses of Demeter, Rhea, Artemis.

[§] The constr. of [תמר] does not occur in the O.T.

[‖] With the disjunctive cf. Gen. 14[18]; Wickes, *Prose Accents*, p. 50 f.

[¶] Modern 'Aṭāra, midway between er-Rām and el-Bireh.

(Jos. 18²⁶), Mizpeh and Geba (1 K. 15⁷¹ᶠ· Is. 10²⁹). See also Fl. Jos., *antt.* viii. 12, 3 § 303; *OS².* 287₁; Jerome, *Comm. in Hos.* 5⁸; *in Sophon.* 1¹ᵇᶠ. It was rightly identified with er-Rām by Brocardus (ca. 1283), *Descriptio,* etc., c. 7; Eshtori Parchi (fol. 68ᵇ), and other mediæval Jewish travellers.—למישכם] on the various senses of this word see Batten, *JBL.* xi. p. 206-210.

6-9. Deborah calls on Barak to take the field against Sisera. — 6. The original sequel of v.¹. — *Barak ben Abinoam*] the name *Barak* (Lightning) occurs in Palmyrene and Sabaean inscriptions, as well as among the Carthaginians (Barcas). — *From Kedesh in Naphtali*] Jos. 19³⁷; "in Galilee, in the Highlands of Naphtali" (20⁷); the modern Qades, west of the Ḥūleh.* This is, as has been remarked above, a natural rendezvous for a rising against Jabin of Hazor, but hardly for a campaign against the Canaanites in the Great Plain; and makes insuperable difficulties in the account of Sisera's flight. — *Doth not Yahweh, the God of Israel, command thee?*] now, by me, his prophet. The question which compels the hearer himself to make the affirmation is more forcible than the affirmation of the speaker; cf. v.¹⁴ 6¹⁴ Jos. 1⁹ 1 S. 10¹ &c. — *Yahweh the God of Israel*] 5³·⁵ 6⁸ 11²¹·²³ 21³ cf. Ex. 5¹ 34²³ Jos. 24²·²³ Is. 17⁶ 21¹⁷, frequent in Jer.† — *March on Mt. Tabor*] Tabor (8¹⁸), now Gebel eṭ-Ṭōr, is at the head of the northern arm of the Great Plain, the southern end of a low range of hills. It is a symmetrical, rounded mountain (λόφος μαστοειδής, Polyb., v. 70), presenting from the south the aspect of a segment of a sphere, from the north that of a truncated cone. The summit is an oblong platform nearly three thousand feet from east to west, and about thirteen hundred in its greatest transverse diameter. Its situation and natural strength made it a most advantageous position for the Israelites in a war with the Canaanites of the Plain.‡ — *Ten thousand men of Naphtali and Zebulun*] that the levy is made from these tribes rather than from those nearer to the plain, and from these only, in contrast with ch. 5, would agree better with the story of Jabin than with that of Sisera. — **7.** *And I will draw out to thee*] Yahweh, by his

---

* Rob., *BR³.* iii. p. 366-369; Guérin, *Galilée,* ii. p. 355-362; *SWP. Memoirs,* i. p. 226-230; Bäd³. p. 264.　　　† Not in Amos or Hosea.

‡ See Burckhardt, *Travels in Syria,* 1822, p. 332-335; Rob., *BR².* ii. p. 351-360; Guérin, *Galilée,* i. p. 143-163; *SWP. Memoirs,* i. p. 388-391.

prophet, promises to lead the enemy on to his ruin; cf. Ex. 14[4]. Sisera's march from Harosheth against the Israelites at Tabor would bring him into the valley of the Kishon (v.[13]), whose streams, swollen perhaps by a sudden flood, turned defeat into disaster (5[21]). On the field of battle, see on 4[13] and 5[21]. — *Jabin's general*] the words, and the corresponding clause, v.[17b], are not an interpolation by D or a still later hand; [*] but were introduced by the older editor who combined the stories of Jabin and Sisera.[†] See above, p. 109. The title here used is given in the history of the Israelite kingdoms to an officer who was at the head of what we should call the national militia. He was charged with the enumeration and enrollment of the men liable to military service (2 S. 24[2]), raised the levies when war broke out, and commanded them in the absence of the king (*e.g.* 2 S. 11). The same system doubtless existed in the neighbouring states, for example, in Aram-zobah (2 S. 10[16]), Aram (2 K. 5[1]), [‡] &c. — *His chariot corps and his troops*] the common mass of footmen in distinction from the chariot corps, which was composed of men of rank and wealth who were trained in arms. — **8.** Barak accepts the commission only on condition that Deborah accompany him into the field. The presence of the prophetess will not only ensure to him divine guidance (v.[14]), but give confidence to him and his followers. — **9.** Deborah answers that she will, of course, go with him; but forewarns him that the chief glory of the victory will not fall to him, but to a woman. — *Howbeit thou wilt not gain the glory in the expedition on which thou art going*] the rendering of our version, *the journey . . . shall not be for thine honour*, suggests, if it does not distinctly express, a sense quite foreign to the text; Deborah was not dissuading him from going. — *Into the power of a woman*] not Deborah, as numerous scholars understand, § influenced partly by an erroneous interpretation of this verse, partly by ch. 5, in which the fame of Deborah does indeed eclipse that of Barak; but Jael, ‖ as is quite clear in the sequel of the story,

---

* Be., Di.   † Kue., Bu., *Richt. u. Sam.*, p. 67, 107.

‡ Cf. also Gen. 21[22, 32] 26[26] (Philistines of Gerar). See Sta., *GVI.* i. p. 276.

§ Jerome (*ep.* 65, 1), Ki., Abendana, Cler., Hitz., Reuss.

‖ Orig., Ambros., Ephrem, Tanch., Schm., Ba., Be., Ke. Unsatisfactory fusion or confusion of the two interpretations, Fl. Jos., *antt.* v. 5, 3 § 203 cl. § 209; RLbG., Abarb., Cass., Oettli.

4[m]. The words of Deborah are generally understood to be a reproof of Barak's lack of faith and courage. Instead of accepting with alacrity the divine mandate, he insisted that she, a woman, should take the field with him; as a penalty, the glory which he should have gained by the death of Sisera is taken from him and given to a woman.[*] This interpretation is not, however, required by the text or suggested by the context, in which there is no sign of disapproval. That Sisera did not fall on the field, but was killed in his flight by Jael, was a well-established feature of the story; it is natural that the author should make the prophetess foretell this at the outset, and unnecessary to construe the prediction as even an implicit condemnation. It is not at all clear that the writer regarded Barak's urgent desire to have the prophetess with him as blameworthy. — *She went with Barak to Kedesh*] where he mustered his clans. As the story now stands, she accompanied him from the vicinity of Bethel to Kedesh in Naphtali, a journey of four or five days. There is no great intrinsic improbability in this; but it is very likely, on other grounds, that in the original form of the narrative the homes of the two leaders were not so far apart.

6. *Kedesh of Naphtali* †] also called Kedesh of Galilee, to distinguish it from other places of the same name (Kadesh or Kedesh, *i.e.* Holy Place). Kadesh on the Orontes has already been mentioned (see on 3[8]). 1 Chr. 6[57] (EV. 6[72]), in a list of Levitical cities, names a Kedesh in Issachar, in conjunction with Daberath (Deburiyeh); and We. (*Comp.*, p. 221) and others have conjectured that in the redaction of our story this has been confused with the more famous place of the name in Naphtali; but the corresponding list in Jos. 21[28] (cf. 19[21]) gives the name *Kishion*. There is a Tell Abu Qudeis on the southern side of the Great Plain, midway between Ta'annuk and Leggun, about a mile north of the road between them, which is perhaps the Kedesh of Issachar, and a Khirbet Qadish near the southern end of the Sea of Galilee, in the territory of Naphtali. — ‏הלא בא‎] Jos. 1[9] Ru. 2[9]. For this use of ‏הלא‎ introducing in the form of a question a statement which commands assent, cf. Dt. 11[3'] 1 S. 20[5f] Mi. 3[1], Ges.[25] § 150. 2, n. 1. The verss. freq. render it by ἰδού, *ecce*, &c. The pf. refers not to an injunction given by Moses (Dt. 20[17]; Ra., after *Mechilta*), or to an earlier communication from Deborah (Ki.), but

---

[*] Fl. Jos., Jerome, Ki., Schm., Stud., Ba., Be., Ke., al.

† On Kedesh in Naphtali see further 2 K. 15[29] 1 Macc. 11[63-74], Fl. Jos., *b.j.* iv. 2, 3; cf. ii. 18, 1; *antt.* xiii. 5, 6 § 154; *O.S*[2]. 271[20]. See Eli Smith, *Bibl. Sacra*, 1843, p. 11; 1849. p. 374-376.

to the command which follows; cf. 6¹⁴ (Abarb., Cler.). —ולמשכח ולך] 5¹⁴ 20⁵⁷; transitively, v.⁷ In describing military operations the vb. seems to be nearly equivalent to פשט (see on 20⁵⁷) and to be construed in a similar way; cf. פשט ב (Chr. — in the older books אל or על), נלחם ב &c.; cf. de Dieu on Jer. 5⁸; Stud. on Jud. 4⁶; Ges. *Thes.* s. v. —7. ומשכתי] transitively, *draw;* with acc. pers. Ps. 28³ Job 40²⁵. —המונו] 'mass, multitude'; equivalent to עם v.¹³, the common soldiers; Ez. 31² 32²⁰. —9. כי אפם] limiting a preceding statement or correcting an erroneous inference which might be drawn from it; cf. Am. 9⁸ Nu. 13²⁸ Dt. 15⁴ 1 S. 1⁵ 6. It may here be merely a check to extravagant expectations; it is not necessary to supply in thought, "in consequence of my going" (Ki., al.). —לא תהיה תפארתך] lit. *thy glory* — that which is naturally anticipated from success in such an enterprise — *will not come,* be achieved (Schm., Ba.). The interpretation, *the fame will not be thine (victoria non reputabitur tibi* 𝕷; Lth., Stud., Reuss, Kitt., al. mu.), is too free, and accentuates too strongly the antithesis between this and the following clause.

10-16. The battle; rout of the Canaanites. —10.

In accordance with Deborah's direction (v.⁶), Barak assembled the tribes of Zebulun and Naphtali at Kedesh. — *There went up at his back ten thousand men*] of these tribes. Lit. *at his feet;* cf. 8⁵ Ex. 11⁸ 1 K. 20¹⁰ &c. — *And Deborah went with him*] to Mt. Tabor (v.¹²). The words probably belong to the old story of Sisera; see on v.⁹. —11. The narrator pauses here, before going on to describe the battle, to say what was necessary about the scene of Sisera's death; where Heber's tent was pitched, and how these Kenite nomads came to be so far in the north, in order that the story might not be interrupted in its midcourse by these explanations. The verse is therefore in a suitable place,[*] and not superfluous by the side of v.¹⁷; there is no reason for regarding it as an addition of the last editor.[†] It seems, however, to have come from the story of Jabin; see below. The words, *the sons of Hobab, Moses' father-in-law,* may be a gloss borrowed from 1¹⁶ or the source of ch. 1; but *the Kenite* is original here. [‡] — *Heber the Kenite had separated from Kain*] from the body of his tribe, which roamed in the region south of Judah; see on 1¹⁶. [§] Heber occurs also as

---

[*] See Schm., Cler., Be., Bu.

[†] Matthes, *Th. T.* xv. p. 609. Kue., *HCO²,* i. p. 367.

[‡] See Bu., *Richt. u. Sam.,* p. 68, against Mey., *ZATW.* i. p. 137 n. 3.

[§] On the wandering branches of Arab clans (*ṭawāif*), see W. R. Smith, *Kinship and Marriage,* p. 37.

the name of a clan of Asher (Gen. 46[17] Nu. 26[45]), as well as in Judah (1 Chr. 4[18]).* — *And pitched his tent as far as the Tree of Basaanim, which was by Kedesh*] cf. Gen. 13[18]. This was the northern limit of his wanderings, and the site of his encampment at the time of our story. The place is named in Jos. 19[33] on the boundary of Naphtali, but in a connexion which does not enable us to determine its situation.† Heber the Kenite appears, therefore, to belong originally to the story of Jabin; see below on v.[17] and 5[24]. — **12 f.** Sisera, being informed of Barak's movements, assembles his forces, including nine hundred iron chariots (v.[3, 7] 1[19]), and marches from Harosheth to the Kishon. — *Harosheth ha-goyim*] commonly explained, "the Harosheth of the (foreign) nations"; cf. *Gelil ha-goyim*, Is. 8[23] 9[1]; possibly in distinction from a neighbouring Israelite Harosheth. ‡ The place is mentioned only in this chapter (v.[2, 13, 16]). It must be sought, not in the vicinity of Hazor, § or elsewhere in Upper Galilee,‖ but in or near the Plain, where alone the chariots would be an effective arm; cf. Jos. 17[16-18] Jud. 1[19]. Thomson ¶ identified it with the modern Tell Harothieh (Hārithīyeh), in the narrows of the Kishon valley commanding the entrance to the Great Plain from the Plain of Acre. The similarity of the names is more striking than conclusive; but the situation is not unsuitable, though somewhat remote.** — *The Kishon valley*] v.[7] 5[21] 1 K. 18[40] Ps. 83[9]. The Kishon, after the Jordan the most considerable stream in the land of Israel, drains the Great Plain, flowing in the main parallel to the range

---

* M. Jastrow, Jr., suggests that this clan name may be in some way connected with the Ḥabiri of the Amarna correspondence; see *JBL.* xi. p. 120. Müller (*Asien u. Europa*, p. 174) thinks that the name *Kenite* here (cf. 5[24]) has nothing to do with the nomadic Kenites of the South, but is derived from a town *K'in*, which according to the Egyptian inscriptions lay in the Great Plain (cf. p. 153).

† Conder (*Tent Work*, ii. p. 132) suggests Khirbet Bessūm, on the plateau west of the Sea of Galilee, not far from Qadish (Kedesh); see below on v. 22, p. 125 f. Cf. G. A. Smith, *Hist. Geography*, p. 305 f.

‡ Ba.; more probably *goyim* originally a particular tribe or people (Duhm).

§ Cler.　　　　　‖ Van de Velde, Kiepert, Kneucker, al.

¶ *Land and Book*, 1863, ii. p. 143 f.; 2 ed. ii. p. 215 ff.

** The conjecture has been accepted, with more or less confidence, by most recent writers; Be., Ba., Conder, Socin, G. A. Smith, al. It is only possible, however, if the story of Sisera be separated from that of Jabin; if the chapter is treated as a unit, Harosheth must be sought, as Van de Velde and others rightly argue, in Upper Galilee.

of Carmel, and emptying into the sea at Ḥaifā. Its most remote
southern affluents come from the neighbourhood of Genin; the
northern branch rises near el-Mezra'ah, west of Mt. Tabor.[*] It is
the latter that is meant here. — **14.** Deborah gives the signal for
the attack, and the assurance of victory.[†] Budde, comparing 3^{28}
(Jos. $10^{8.23}$ 8^{18a}), suspects that 14^4 is an addition of D, which in
turn has become the occasion of secondary additions in 𝔊 in v.[*]
The verse is, however, in entire accord with the relations between
the prophetess and the chieftain in v.[6f], and in form corresponds
closely to v.[6] — *Hath not Yahweh gone out before thee?*] the
question, as in v.[6], a more forcible assertion. *Gone out;* to battle,
as often, see note on 2^{15} (p. 73). Yahweh is a mighty warrior (Ex.
15^3 Ps. 24^8); his name is Yahweh of hosts, the god of the embattled
ranks of Israel (1 S. 17^{45}); in the sacred chest (ark) he accompanies them to the field (1 S. 4); he marches out for them, or
with them, to battle (Hab. 3^{13} Zech. 14^3 cf. Ps. 44^9); or comes
storming from his ancient seats in tempestuous fury, discomfiting
the foe and delivering his people (5^{4f}; see comm. there). —
Barak, with his ten thousand men, rushed down to the plain, by
his sudden onset apparently surprising Sisera upon ground unfavourable to the manœuvring of his chariots, which thus became a
source of disorder and disaster. During Vespasian's campaign in
Galilee (A.D. 67) the Jews, who had fortified the summit of
Tabor, attempted to surprise the Roman cavalry in the plain
under Placidus, but through his ruse the enterprise miscarried.[‡] —
15. *Yahweh routed Sisera*] struck the foe with panic, threw them
into confusion and flight; Ex. 14^{24} Jos. 10^{10} 1 S. 7^{10}.[§] Josephus
supposes that their discomfiture was caused by a great storm (cf.
5^{20f}). — *All the army*] v.[16] Ex. 14^{24} &c.; cf. other expressions v.[7.13];
the mass of footmen in distinction from the chariot corps. — *At
the point of the sword*] see note on 1^{25}. The phrase appears incongruous with the verb and superfluous in the context; it has

---

[*] Rob., *BR*[2]. ii. p. 363-366; *SWP. Memoirs*, i. p. 265 ff.

[†] On women in battle among the Arabs see Doughty, *Arabia Deserta*, I. p. 61;
cf. ʿAyesha at the Battle of the Camel, Muir, *Caliphate*, p. 361 ff., &c.

[‡] Fl. Jos., *b. j.* iv. 1, 8.

[§] Chytraeus quotes Pindar (*Nem.* ix. 63), ἐν γὰρ δαιμονίοισι φόβοις φεύγουσι καὶ
παῖδες θεῶν.

perhaps been introduced here accidentally or unadvisedly from v.¹⁶. — *Sisera dismounted from his war-chariot*] being hard pressed by his pursuers and unable to extricate his chariot from the rout, perhaps entangled in the morasses of the Kishon or cut off by its streams (see on 5²¹), he abandoned it, and escaped from the field on foot, alone. — **16.** The routed Canaanites, horse and foot, fled toward Harosheth ; Barak, pursuing them to the very gates of the city, made an utter end of them. — *There was not as much as one left*] Ex. 14²⁸ ; not a single fugitive lived to reach safety within the walls. It is not intimated that the city itself was taken ; it may safely be inferred that it was not.

10. וירד] is not Hiph. (Ki., Schm.), but Qal; the subj. is not Barak (𝕴, Lth., al.), but "ten thousand men" (𝕲𝕷𝕾). The sg. with plur. numeral subj. is unusual ; Ex. 32²⁸ Jud. 7³ 12⁶ 1 S. 4¹⁰ 2 S. 24¹⁵ are not precisely similar. See Roorda, ii. p. 361 f. — ברגליו] following at his heels; 8⁵ Ex. 11⁸ 1 S. 25²⁷ 2 S. 15¹⁷·¹⁸ &c.; equivalent to אחריו v.¹⁴. — עשרת אלפי איש] regularly we should have אלפים as in v.⁶; the other instances of this anomaly, according to the Massora, are Ex. 32²⁸ Job 1³ (twice), cf. אלפי רבבה Gen. 24⁶⁰. It is perhaps only accidental; an abbreviation not properly resolved. — **11.** נפרד Gen. 13⁹·¹¹·¹⁴ cf. 10⁵·³². — בצעניב אלון] Baer אלון, as also in 12¹¹·¹². In בצענים, ב is not the preposition (𝕲ᴸ Jos. 19³³, OS². 294₆₂, 𝕷 Jos. Jud., 𝕾, Mas., Drus., Schm., Cler., AV., RV., and most moderns), *in Sa'anim ;* for in that case אילן would require the article, as in האשל ברכה 1 S. 22⁶ 31¹³; cf. also Jud. 6¹¹ האלה אשר בעפרה, 9⁶ Gen. 35⁴ Jos. 24²⁶ &c. We must, therefore, take בצענים (ב radical) as genitive; cf. v.⁶ Gen. 12⁶ 13¹⁸ 14⁶ 35ˣ Dt. 11³⁰ 1 S. 10⁹ and esp. Jud. 9³⁷ אלון מעוננים. In Jos. 19³³ the name is written בצעננים, to which the Qᵉrē in Jud. 4¹¹ conforms. It is more probable, however, that the true form of the name is preserved in the text of Jud. (Kethib); cf. כנענים; and on nouns with n suffix in general, Barth, *Nominalbildung*, p. 343 f.; Suyūṭi, *Muzhir*, ii. p. 136. — אילון] the punctuation discriminates איל, אילה, אלון from אילה, אלין; but in unpointed texts these could not be distinguished, nor can we put much confidence in the constancy of the traditional pronunciation in face of the bewildering inconsistency of the versions. Celsus (*Hierobotanicon*, i. p. 34 ff.) thought that the Massorites consistently distinguish 'terebinth' (אילה, אלה, אלון, א־) from 'oak' (אלון), and this theory has been generally accepted, though with no agreement in the distribution of the names; see J. D. Michaelis, *Supplementa*, p. 72 ff.; Rosenmüller, *Bibl. Alterthumsk.*, iv. p. 229 ff.; Ges. *Thes.* p. 50 f.* There is no real foundation for the discrimination; the words signify in Aramaic 'tree' simply; in Hebrew usually, if not exclusively, 'holy tree,' as the place, and primitively the object of worship,

---

* Against the whole theory, Lowth on Is. 1²⁹.

without regard to the species. The Deborah Tree (אַלּוֹן Gen. 35⁸) is a palm (Jud. 4⁵), &c. See We., *Prolegomena²*, p. 248 n. = *History of Israel*, p. 238; Sta., *GVI.* i. 455. On holy trees in Palestine, Baudissin, *Studien zur semit. Religionsgeschichte*, ii. 143 ff., esp. 223 ff. — [אשר את קדש] 3¹⁹ 1 K. 9², cf. ם; 2 S. 24¹⁶. — 12. [וייעדו] indef. subj., Ges.²⁸ § 144. 3 *b*. — [עלה] c. acc., Is. 7¹. — 13. [ויזעק] v.¹⁰; call out and assemble by the war cry; cf. the passive (Ni.) 6³⁴ᶠ 18²²ᶠ 1 S. 14²⁰ &c. — [עם] soldiery, 9³⁴·³⁷ and often; here equivalent to הכון v.⁷., כחנה v.¹⁶. — *Harosheth*] at Sheikh Abrēk the Galilean foot-hills project in a sort of bastion towards Carmel, forming a narrow pass through which the Kishon flows, the hills here rising some 350 feet above the bed of the stream.[*] About a mile and a half northwest of Sheikh Abrēk, in the narrowest part of the pass, el-Ḥārithiyeh lies on the side of the hill, which above it is covered with a fine oak forest. The Kishon at this point flows close to the rocky base of Carmel, on the opposite side of the pass, and here the main road must always have crossed the river. A stronghold at Ḥārithiyeh would thus command the entrance to the Great Plain from the Plain of Acre, and the commercial highways which led through it. The situation of el-Ḥāri-thiyeh is not incompatible with the conditions of the narrative in ch. 4, or with ch. 5; but the arguments by which Thomson supported the identification are far from decisive, and the similarity of the names may easily be accidental. — 14. [קום] *Up!* Summons to action; 5¹² 7⁹ 8²⁰·²¹ Ex. 32¹ 1 K. 21⁷ and often. — [זה היום אשר וו] the pronominal complement of the relative particle אשר is omitted, as commonly after antecedents denoting time or during which; Dr., *TBS.* p. 149 n.; Ew. § 331 *c* 3. — [יצא לפניך] on the verb see note on t¹⁶. The phrase is used of the leader, general, king, at the head of his forces, יצא 1 S. 8²⁰ &c.; of Yahweh as the leader of Israel in war, 2 S. 5²⁴ cf. Dt. 9⁸ (קבר ירני) &c. — 15. [ויהם יהוה את סיסרא] הם (subject always God) 'inspire with panic terrors,' drive men beside themselves, so that they accomplish their own ruin. See, besides the examples cited in the text, Ex. 23²⁷ 2 S. 22¹⁵ Ps. 144⁶. The object is generally the enemy in war; see, however, Dt. 2¹⁵. — *Before Barak*] Jos. 10¹⁰ cf. 1 S. 7¹¹. — [לפי חרב] the words cannot be joined to ויהם in any sense which the usage of the phrase warrants; they are either miswritten for the following לפני ברק or borrowed from v.¹⁶. — [הרכבה] *chariot, wagon*, 5²⁸ 2 K. 5²¹·²⁶ 9²⁷ &c. (רכב is usually collective, 'chariot-corps'). The name, with the thing, passed from the people of Palestine to the Egyptians (*marakabuti*, Müller, p. 301; above p. 38 n.). — 16. [ויפל... לפי חרב] Jos. 8²⁴. — [לא נשאר עד אחד] stronger than *not one* (לא נשאר אחד Ex. 8²⁷ 10¹⁹); cf. Ex. 9⁷ 2 S. 17²². The prepositional phrase is the logical subject of the verb, Ew. § 305 *a*.

17-22. The death of Sisera. — 17.

Sisera escapes on foot to the tent of Jael. From v.¹⁷ᵃ, especially when taken with v.²², it is obvious that the narrator represented the tent of Jael as not

---

[*] *SWP. Memoirs*, i. p. 263.

very remote from the battle field.   Verse [17b], on the other hand,
taken with v.[11], carries us to the vicinity of Hazor and Kedesh (in
Naphtali, v.[6]), forty or fifty miles away.   The most probable solution of the difficulty appears to be the supposition that Heber the
Kenite originally belonged to the story of Jabin; Jael, to that of
Sisera.   In that case v.[17aa] is derived from the latter source, v.[17b]
from the former.   The words, *the wife of the Heber of Kenite*,
are possibly from the same source as v.[17b], and the conjecture may
be hazarded that in the story of Jabin the wife of Heber played a
part similar to that of Jael in the story of Sisera; see above,
p. 109.*   The alternative is to regard v.[11] and v.[17b] as editorial
additions; but we should then still have to ask whence the editor
had the names and why he introduced them here; moreover, the
editor (R) calls Jabin *king of Canaan*, not *king of Hazor*. —
*There were friendly relations between Jabin king of Hazor and
Heber the Kenite*] the nomads had not been victims of the oppression from which the Israelite peasants had suffered, and had
not taken part in the rising of Naphtali.   In the present connexion the words explain why Sisera fled to the tent of Jael. —
18. Jael came out to meet him, as she saw him approaching. —
Walk in, my lord; walk in to my tent; have no fear] cf. Gen.
19[1f]. Unlike v.[17b], the natural inference from these words is, not
that Sisera directed his steps to these tents to seek refuge in
them, but that he came upon them in his flight and was induced
by Jael to turn aside and conceal himself there.   The illustrations which the commentators have collected of the ceremonies
with which a fugitive now claims protection at an Arab tent are in
either case irrelevant.† — *She covered him up with the rug*] or
perhaps, *tent curtain.*   The exact meaning of the word is unknown; the renderings proposed can only claim to be suitable to
the context. — **19.** *Give me a little drink of water*] Gen. 24[43]
(J). — *She opened the milk-skin*] the lamb or goat skin in which

---

* In 5[24] the words "the wife of Heber the Kenite" are regarded by many
critics, on formal grounds, as a gloss.   The same explanation would have to be
given of the words "the wife of Heber" in 4[21].

† Wetzstein, *Reisebericht,* p. 148; Quatremère, "Les asiles chez les Arabes,"
Mem. de l'Acad. des Inscriptions, xv. 2, 1842, p. 307-348.   If Heber and Jael origi-
nally belonged to different stories, we may dismiss another mooted question; viz.,
Why did Sisera seek refuge in the tent of Jael rather than in that of Heber?

milk was kept, and poured him a drink into a bowl (cf. 5²⁵).*
Her hospitality exceeded his modest request (cf. 5²⁵). His confidence was naturally confirmed by this token of friendliness. —
And covered him] again. We miss the adverb in Hebrew as
much as in English. — **20.** He bids her stand at the door of the
tent to put the pursuit off the track, if it should come that way.
Then, overcome by weariness, he gives himself up to the sense of
security and falls asleep. It is quite needless to ascribe to the
draught an intoxicating or stupefying quality.† — **21.** When he
was sound asleep, Jael took one of the pins with which the tent
ropes are fastened to the ground (Is. 33²⁰), and a hammer, and
stealthily crept to his side where he lay in the inner part of the
tent.   The tent pin was not of metal ‡ — the bronze pins of the
tabernacle belong to the luxury of that structure — but, as still in
the tents of the Bedawin, of wood. §   The hammer was probably
the mallet with which the tent pins were driven. Among the
Bedawin pitching the tent is woman's business, and so no doubt it
was in ancient times ; the mallet and pin were accustomed implements, and ready at hand. ‖ — *And drove the pin into his temple so
that it went down into the ground*] transfixing his head. — *He
being sound asleep and exhausted*] circumstantial clause, explaining how it was possible for her to kill him in this way ; see note.
It was certainly an unusual way, and more ingenious than sure ; a
blow of the mallet upon the temple was a much simpler and safer
plan than to try to drive the blunt wooden pin through his head.
Wellhausen ingeniously conjectures that this description of Sisera's death originated in a prosaic misunderstanding of the poetic
parallelism in 5²⁶.¶   This is not improbable, though the obscurity
of the terms in 5²⁶ forbids too confident assertion ; but we should
not be warranted in inferring that the author of ch. 4 is also the
author of this misunderstanding.** — **22.** *Lo, there was Barak*] he
came up at that instant ; the particle calls attention to the striking

---

* See Doughty, *Arabia Deserta*, i. 221, 382, 430, &c.
† Fl. Jos., Rabb., a Lyra, Drus., a Lap., al.   ‡ Fl. Jos., RLbG., Cler., Ba.
§ Orig., Aug., R. Moses esh-Sheikh; see Shaw, *Travels*, 1757. p. 221 ; Burck-
hardt, *Bedouins and Wahâbys*, i. p. 39.   ‖ Doughty, *Arabia Deserta*, i. 221, &c.
¶ *Comp.*, p. 222 ; W. R. Smith, *OTJC²*. p. 132.
** We., Sta.; *contra*, Kue., Bu., Co., Cooke. See above, p. 110.

coincidence ; cf. Gen. 29⁶ Jud. 11³⁴ 1 S. 9¹⁴. In the narrative as
it now runs, Sisera flees from the field in a northerly direction to
the vicinity of Kedesh in Naphtali ; Barak first follows the rout
of the Canaanites to Harosheth at the western extremity of the
Great Plain,* then strikes off to pursue Sisera fifty or sixty miles
through Galilee, and comes up just as Jael has killed him ; which
is obviously impossible. The hypothesis that Barak did not
accompany the main pursuit westward to Harosheth, but followed
Sisera in his flight in the opposite direction, does violence to v.¹⁶.†
See note below.

17. יָעֵל] on animal names see on v. 4, and 7²⁵. — **18.** סירָה] twice oxytone,
as frequently before a following א (including יהוה); ‡ see Ew. § 228 *b*; Ol.
§ 228 *c*; Kö. i. p. 443. — וַתְּכַסֵּהוּ בַּשְּׂמִיכָה] 𝕲ᴬᴸᴹᴼ | **s** ἐν τῇ δέρρει, which in most
cases stands for Heb. הַיְרִיעָה; cf. Hesych., and Schleusner, *s. v.* We should
then perhaps think of one of the goat's-hair curtains which are used to divide
the tent. § The exegetical tradition in general, however, is for a rug or wrap
of coarse stuff, such as is used to sleep in, and worn as a mantle in cold and
stormy weather (𝕲ᴮᴺ𝕾𝕿); or a thick coverlet with long nap (R. Hai Gaon,
Ra., Ki.). The Syr. ܣܡܝܟܐ compared by Ges., Ba., Be., al. acquires the sense
triclinium, pulvinar from the custom of reclining at meals, leaning on the
elbow, and has nothing to do with the word in our text. — נאוד] only here;
elsewhere in O.T. נאד (pronounced *nōd*), MH. ניר. — **20.** עֲמֹד] the masc. imv.
in direct address to a woman is anomalous. The use of the undefined predicate (3 sm.) when it precedes its subject (Ges.²⁵ § 145, 7) is not analogous;
and the examples of irregularity in the use of the imv. alleged by Ba. (Mi. 1¹³
Nah. 3¹⁵ Is. 32¹¹), al., do not lessen the difficulty here. We require the fem.,
עִמְדִי (Ol. § 234 *b*). — וְאָמְרַתְּ . . . וְשָׁאֲלֵךְ וְאָמַר אִישׁ אִם יָבֹא וְהָיָה] normal structure
and sequence of tenses in continued hypothesis; Dr.³ § 121, p. 130, § 136. I. *a.*
— אָיִן] *No!* Ges.²⁵ p. 465. — וַהֲצִנָהּ] intrans., as in 1¹⁴ (𝕲ᴮᴺᴹ **s**); others,
transitively, *defixit, infixit* (𝕲ᴬᴾⱽᴸⱽ𝕷𝕾𝕿). — וְהוּא נִרְדָּם וַיָּעַף] the words are
pronounced and connected in two ways : וְהוּא נִרְדָּם וַיָּעַף וַיָּמֹת, *he had fallen
into a deep sleep and was exhausted,* and וְהוּא נִרְדָּם וַיָּעַף וַיָּמֹת,‖ *he being fast asleep
— so he swooned and died.* The first makes the circumstantial clause consist
of two verbs, which stand in a most unnatural order; the second gives a
highly superfluous analysis of the act of dying, especially as the swoon could

---

* Supposing it to be rightly identified with Ḥarithiyeh.
† G. A. Smith, *Hist. Geog.,* p. 396 n., adopting Conder's view that Kedesh was
near the southern end of the Sea of Galilee.
‡ Once before ר, 3 times before ך.
§ Or as a kind of fly or awning. On the Arab tent see Burckhardt, *Bedouins
and Wahábys,* i. p. 37 ff.; Doughty, *Arabia Deserta,* i. 224 ff.
‖ Wickes, *Prose Accents,* p. 140; cf. Norzi.

form no distinguishable physical moment in the passage from deep sleep to
instant death. I prefer therefore to pronounce וְהוּא נִרְדָּם וַיָּעַף, *he being sound
asleep and completely exhausted* (יָעֵף adj.); וַיָּעַף **馬** is to be connected with עיף
(med. ◌). — **22.** If, with Conder and Smith, we look for Kedesh and Heber's
encampment by the Sea of Galilee at Qadish and Bessūm, the identification of
Harosheth with el-Ḥarithiyeh will have to be given up, not only as incompatible with v.¹⁶, but as altogether too remote from the scene of action. Tell
Abū Qudeis (? Kedesh of Issachar; cf. above, p. 117), between Ta'annuk
and Leggūn, lies in the direction of Ḥarithiyeh, and (again assuming that H.
is Harosheth) would suit v.¹⁷ᵃ·¹⁶ᶠᶠ· well enough; but it cannot be the Kedesh
of v.¹⁷ᵇ cf. ¹¹ (Heber the friend of Jabin of Hazor). On the whole, therefore,
we do not gain much by trying to substitute another place of the name for
Kedesh in Naphtali.

23, 24. The subjugation of Jabin. — The regular close of the
story ; cf. 3³⁰. — **23.** *God subdued Jabin*] in the story itself we
have uniformly *Yahweh;* the use of *Elohim* here falls in well
with the hypothesis that the subjugation of the oppressors, which
is a standing feature in the close of the stories of the judges,
belonged originally to the pragmatism of E ; *i.e.* is pre-
Deuteronomic. The variations of the versions here, however,
make it somewhat doubtful whether *Yahweh* or *Elohim* was the
original reading. For the verb in active construction cf. Dt. 9³
Neh. 9²⁴ 1 Chr. 17¹⁰. — *King of Canaan*] v.²·²⁴ (D) ; in the story
itself he is called *king of Hazor* (v.¹⁷ ; see on v.²). — **24.** *The
hand of Israel bore harder and harder on Jabin*] cf. 3¹⁰ (D).
The relation in v.³ᵇ was completely reversed. — *Till they finally
destroyed Jabin king of Canaan altogether*]. — The chronological
note corresponding to 3¹¹·³⁰ &c. stands naturally at the end of
ch. 5.

—**23.** וַיַּכְנַע אֱלֹהִים] 𝔊ᴮᴳᴺ ὁ θεὸς, ᴬᴸ·ᴹ ϛ κύριος ὁ θεὸς, ᴼ κύριος, 𝕷 Deus, 𝕾
רי, בריא.—**24.** הָרֵךְ וְקָשֶׁה . . . וְהֹלֵךְ] double absolute object, the second being
an adjective; 1 S. 14¹⁹ 2 S. 18²⁵. See Stud., p. 489; Ges.²⁵ § 113. 3 n. 2.

The morality of Jael's deed, even more than that of Ehud, has
been the subject of great searchings of heart among the apologists
who have felt it necessary to judge it by the standard of absolute
ethics, and to justify it in that forum. That the inspired prophetess should extol Jael for what, in all the circumstances, bears the
appearance of a treacherous murder (5²⁴ cf. ²⁴·³¹), is, of course,
the greatest difficulty of all. We need not follow these inter-

preters into the morasses of casuistry into which an unhistorical idea of religion and revelation leads them. To justify the deed by the standards of Christian morality, it is necessary to lower those standards to the level of the deed. See Abarb., a Lap., Schm. (*qu.* 16), and esp. Bachmann, p. 288–297, where additional literature will be found.

V. The Triumphal Ode.

LITERATURE.* — C. F. Schnurrer (1775), in *Dissertationes philologico-criticae,* 1790, p. 36–96; cf. J. B. Köhler in Eichhorn's *Repertorium,* vi. 1780, p. 163–172, xii. 1783, p. 235–241; Herder, *Briefe das Studium der Theologie betreffend,* 1780, *Geist der hebr. Poesie,* 1783 (*Werke,* ed. Suphan, x. p. 77 ff.; xii. p. 172 ff.); K. W. Justi, *National-Gesänge der Hebräer,* ii. 1816, p. 210–312; G. H. Hollmann, *Commentarius philologico-criticus in Carmen Deborae,* 1818; R. D. C. Robbins, "The Song of Deborah," *Bibl. Sacra,* 1855, p. 597–642; J. W. Donaldson, *Jashar,* 1854, p. 237 ff., 261 ff.; E. Meier, *Übersetzung und Erklärung des Debora-Liedes,* 1859°; † G. Hilliger, *Das Deborah-Lied übersetzt und erklärt,* 1867; G. Bickell, *Carmina V. Ti. metrice,* 1882; *Dichtungen der Hebräer,* 1882; A. Müller, *Das Lied der Deborah,* 1887 ("Königsberger Studien," i. p. 1–21); M. Vernes, "Le cantique de Débora," *REJ.* xxiv. 1892, p. 52–67, 225–255; G. A. Cooke, *The History and Song of Deborah,* 1892; C. Niebuhr, *Versuch einer Reconstellation des Deboraliedes,* 1894.

The Song of Deborah is an epinikian ode celebrating the victory of the Israelites over the Canaanites near Taanach. After an opening strain of praise to Yahweh for the great deliverance (v.[2-5]) the poet describes the state of things which preceded and provoked the war (v.[6-8]). Verse[12], with its invocation of Deborah and Barak, leads over to the Israelite rising; the tribes which took part in the glorious struggle receive their meed of praise (v.[14, 15a, 18]), while reproaches and taunts are heaped upon those which held aloof (v.[15b-17]). Then follows the battle itself and the rout of the foe (v.[19-22]), and the death of the flying king by the hand of Jael (v.[24-27]). The anxiety of Sisera's mother as his return is delayed, the expectation of triumph and spoil, which is raised

---

* The older literature, to the beginning of this century, in Justi, *National-Gesänge der Hebräer,* ii. 1816, p. 217–225; see also Bachmann, *Richter,* p. 298–301; Reuss, *Gesch. d. A.T.,* § 101. Only the most important titles are given above.

† See also his *Gesch. der poet. National-Literatur der Hebräer,* 1856, p. 79 ff.

again only to be more cruelly disappointed, form the tragic climax of the poem (v.[28-30]), which ends with the strain:

"So perish all thine enemies, O Yahweh!"

The movement of the poem is throughout straightforward and natural. It sets before us, first, the situation before the revolt; second, the rising of the tribes; third, the victory and its sequel, the death of Sisera. Notwithstanding many obscurities in particulars, especially in v.[13-15], the main tenor of the narrative from v.[12] on is sufficiently clear. The same is true of v.[2-7], but in the intervening verses ([8-11]) the difficulties are so accumulated that it is hardly possible to be sure even of the general sense and connexion of the passage. Verse[9] seems to resume the theme of v.[2], and the distinctly marked new beginning in v.[12] shows at least that v.[10, 11] must be joined to the preceding. We have then, as the natural divisions, *a.* v.[2-11], *b.* v.[12-18], *c.* v.[19-31]. The connexion between *b.* and *c.* is, from the nature of the matter, closer than between *a.* and *b.*, but this is not a sufficient reason for dividing the poem into two, a Hymn of Thanksgiving (v.[2-11]); and the Triumphal Ode (v.[12-31]).* On the contrary, v.[2-11] form the natural and indispensable introduction to the Ode.

The obscurity of the middle of the ode was remarked by Lowth.† It is of quite a different nature from the difficulties which we encounter in the opening verses and in the latter half of the chapter. These are due to our defective knowledge of its very ancient poetical language, and affect particular words or phrases without preventing our understanding the general meaning of the passage. In v.[8-15], on the other hand, while clauses here and there are plain enough, the whole is unintelligible; as is superabundantly proved by the translations which are given by the commentators. We cannot lay this obscurity to the charge of the author, who in the other parts of the poem writes clearly and directly, but must infer that by some accident of transmission

---

* Ewald, *Dichter d. A. B[2].*, i. p. 186 ff. Ewald supposes that the Ode was composed for a different occasion from the Hymn; viz., for the triumphal procession "perhaps on the evening of the same day."

† *De sacra poesi Hebraeorum*, p. 274: "Media, ut verum fateamur, obsederunt haud exiguae obscuritates, multum officientes Carminis pulchritudini, nec facile dissipandae, nisi uberior historiae lux accederet."

these verses have suffered peculiarly. It would seem that, in a manuscript through which our text is descended, this place had become in good part illegible. The scribe who copied it made out as much as he could, but was not always successful in recovering the vanished letters. The obscurity of the text thus established would naturally become a fresh source of corruption. This corruption is in the main older than the Greek translators, who in the worst places read substantially as we do and therefore give us little help toward a restoration of the text.*

Critics have been almost unanimous in attributing the Ode to a contemporary, and a participant in the glorious struggle which it celebrates. So, to make but a single quotation, Kuenen writes, " Form and contents alike prove that it is rightly ascribed by all competent judges to a contemporary." † This consensus has recently been challenged by Seinecke ‡ and especially by Maurice Vernes, § but neither the methods nor the conclusions of these critics have commended themselves to other scholars.

Seinecke, whose work in general is marred by a perverse fondness for paradoxes, gathers from v.[31] that the ode was not written to celebrate the victory over Sisera at all; but, like Ex. 15, to encourage the author's contemporaries by reminding them of the great deeds of Yahweh in long by-gone days, when the enemies of Israel were so fearfully punished that not one of them was left. The idea of Yahweh's coming from Edom (v.[4]) is inconceivable in ancient times, it is parallel to Is. 63 and refers to a future parousia; the colossal exaggeration of v.[20], " They fought from heaven, the stars in their courses fought against Sisera," corresponds to the notions of later times, and is to be compared with Jos. 10[12-14]; v.6 (Jael a judge) and v.[14] (" Ephraim, whose root is in Amalek," cf. 12[16]) contain mistakes which a contemporary

* Probably few scholars would now agree with Ewald (*Dichter*, i. p. 178 n.) and E. Meier (*National-Literatur der Hebräer*, p. 89) that the text of the poem has been transmitted to us substantially intact — not to mention the more extravagant notions of its impeccability entertained, *e.g.* by Bachmann (p. 517 ff.). August Müller (*Das Lied der Deborah*, 1887, i. ff.) has proved, on the contrary, that the corruption is extensive and deep-seated. Whether it also is beyond all remedy, is a question about which opinions will differ; see, on the other side, Budde, *Richt. u. Sam.*, p. 102-104.

† *HCO³*. i. p. 346; so also Vatke; We., *Comp.*, p. 222 f.; Reuss, *G.A.T.* § 101; Sta., *GVI*. i. p. 178. Sporadic doubts of older scholars (De Wette in 1817, — afterwards retracted, — Hartmann, Rödiger; see Ba., p. 510) were without influence.

‡ *Gesch. d. Volkes Israel*, i. 1876, p. 243-245.

§ *RHR*. vii. 1883, p. 332-338, and often subsequently; see below.

K

could not make. The language exhibits Aramaisms and other marks of late date, especially the relative ʃ; the style is artificial; v.[10], for example, is "a frigid conceit of post-exilic times," reminding us of the beginning of Ps. 1. Finally, the names of Barak, Lapidoth, and perhaps Deborah have an unhistorical ring. "We are forced to conclude, therefore, that the story of the conflict of Barak and Jael against Jabin and Sisera is a bit of old Hebrew mythology, in which the cleansing and purifying powers of nature, thunder, lightning, and flame, are arrayed against the mist and clouds." [*] Vernes [†] contests the common opinion that the poem, compared with the prose narrative (ch. 4), has preserved a number of historical details and bears the fresh impress of the events. On the contrary, though the prose story is late and exhibits numerous inconsistencies, it is drawn from older sources, and is infinitely superior to the poem. In the former, only two tribes take part in the struggle; in the latter this is exaggerated to a national movement, all Israel is oppressed, almost all Israel unites against the foe. Vague and inaccurate phrases such as "new gods" (v.[8]), "the kings of Canaan" (v.[19]), "the times of Jael" (v.[6]), point to a date remote from the events. Moreover, besides ch. 4, the author has made use of other writings which are themselves late. The names of Taanach and Megiddo (v.[19]) are taken from Jud. 1[27] or Jos. 12[21], that of Meroz [‡] perhaps from the same passage in Jos.; the representation of Dan as settled on the seaboard (v.[17]) can only come from the unhistorical partition of Palestine in Jos. The poem must, therefore, be later than the latest stratum of Jos. "If the prose narrative is not older than the 5th cent. B.C., the song put into the mouth of the prophetess-judge may without hesitation be dated a century or a century and a half later." M. Vernes' final estimate shall be given in his own words: "Nous disons donc du chant du Débora que c'est une œuvre éminemment artificielle, dont quelques tirades éloquentes ou brillantes ne peuvent pas dissimuler le vide." In his later articles in the *Revue des études juives*, M. Vernes reiterates this criticism at length, in connexion with an exposition of the chapter, and adds an elaborate argument from the language of the poem, which, so far from being archaic, is paralleled throughout by that of the *K'etubim*, and often only there; so that the linguistic evidence also brings the Song of Deborah into the company of the latest books of the O.T. [§] It is impossible here to examine this argument in detail; so far as it seems worth while, we shall take notice of his observa-

---

[*] A mythical interpretation was earlier given to the poem by Steinthal ("Die Sage von Simson," *Zeitschrift für Völkerpsychologie, u.s.w.*, ii. 1862, p. 164), who finds in Deborah and Jael the beneficent rain-clouds, in Barak the lightning. This explanation was adopted also by Goldziher (*Der Mythos bei den Hebräern*, 1876, p. 162 = *Mythology among the Hebrews*, 1877, p. 256).

[†] *RHR*. vii. 1883, p. 332-338; *Précis d'histoire Juive*, 1889, p. 110 n.; *RHR*. xix. 1889, p. 65 f. = *Essais bibliques*, 1891, p. 163-165; finally, *RÉJ*. xxiv. 1892, p. 52-67, 225-255.   [‡] Probably Meron, Jos. 12[28] cf. 12[19].

[§] See the summary, *l.c.*, xxiv. p. 249 f.

tions on the usage in the critical notes below. Here it can only be said in
general that, so far as M. Vernes accurately states the facts, they do not justify
his conclusions.   But philological ἀκρίβεια is not M. Vernes' strong point,
and his statements are frequently most deceptive half-truths. For example,
"*garaph* (v.²¹) s'explique par l'araméen," suggests that נרף in this sense is a
distinctively Aramaic word, whereas the use of the word in the Song has
much closer parallels in Arabic.

The representations of the Song agree entirely with the historical situation, so far as we are able from our very scanty materials
to reconstruct it. We detect in it none of the anachronisms by
which a later writer so easily betrays his own age ; * nor does the
atmospheric perspective of the narrative indicate that the writer
stood at a distance from the events which he relates.   It exhibits
neither the vagueness which is the first result of the blurring of
details in tradition, nor the artificial circumstantiality which marks
the subsequent attempt to recover them.†   The impression of
reality which we receive from the Ode is hardly to be paralleled
in another poem in the Old Testament ; and a comparison with
others, especially with the Song of Moses (Ex. 15), the subject of
which has the greatest resemblance to the Song of Deborah,
strengthens this impression. ‡   These considerations have of
course no weight with those to whom the poem is "an eminently
artificial work," the rhetoric of which is sometimes ingenious and
eloquent, sometimes strained and affected. § Against such æsthetic
judgements there is no arguing.

The priority of the Ode to the prose narrative in ch. 4, and its
superiority in point of historical truth, appear from the compari-

----

* As when, for example, in the "Song of Moses" (Ex. 15) Israel is already
established in Canaan (v.¹³ff.), and — unless v.¹⁷ᵇ· be rejected as an interpolation
— the temple in Jerusalem already built.

† The indefiniteness of which Vernes complains is chiefly obscurity arising from
corruption of the text or context. He appears never to suspect the Massoretic text
nor the translation which he finds in the popular commentaries.

‡ The inference from the impression of reality to the contemporary origin or the
historical truth of a narrative is not stringent. It is the pre-eminent gift of the poet
to *create* this impression even when his story conflicts with our knowledge ; — think
of Homer, Dante, Shakespeare. But the objective character of the art which is
capable of producing such an illusion is not easily exemplified among Semitic
poets. It is a simpler and more probable explanation in the present case, that the
poem was made by one under the immediate inspiration of the events, than that it
is a supreme work of the creative imagination.   § Vernes.

son instituted above in the Introduction to ch. 4 (p. 107 f.).   It is especially clear in the accounts of Sisera's death, 4[18-22] 5[24-27].   See further the commentary on the last named verses.

In the opinion of the great majority of scholars, Deborah herself is the author of the Ode.[*]   It is attributed to her in the title (v.[1]), which, however, since we do not know how ancient this superscription is, and since in other cases the titles are frequently in error,[†] cannot by itself be regarded as decisive.   Here the title seems to be distinctly confirmed by v.[7], " until I, Deborah, arose ; till I arose, a matron in Israel."   Unfortunately, this evidence is not as conclusive as it seems ; ᵹ and 𝕃[‡] have the verbs in the third person, "until Deborah arose," and even in 𝔥 the form of the verbs is ambiguous, and may equally well be rendered, " until thou didst arise, Deborah." [§]   The latter interpretation accords with v.[12], "Awake, awake, Deborah ; awake, awake, deliver a song," which the parallel half verse, " Arise, arise, Barak," &c., forbids us to take as the self-invocation of the poet.   In v.[15], again, Deborah is spoken of in the third person.   The natural and almost necessary inference from these verses is that Deborah herself is not the author of the Ode. [||]   The other indications of her authorship which commentators have found in the words of the song are indecisive ; in some of them the text is insecure, in others the interpretation.   Much has sometimes been made of the so-called psychological evidence ; the recital of Jael's deed (v.[24-27]) and the description of the scene in Sisera's palace (v.[28-30]), it is said, could only have been written by a woman.[¶]   This is a matter which hardly admits of argument, but it is certainly a false note when Bertheau finds in the reference to Sisera's mother a touch of woman's sympathy.[**]

The historical value of the Song of Deborah can hardly be exaggerated.   It is the oldest extant monument of Hebrew literature, and the only contemporaneous monument of Hebrew history

---

* So, e.g., Ew., Dichter d. A.B., i. p. 186 f.; Hitz., GVI. i. 112; Renan, Hist. du peuple d'Israël, i. p. 316.

† E.g., in the ascription of many of the Psalms to David, and in attributing Ex. 15 to Moses.   ‡ Both without variation.   § See below, in loc.

|| We., Geschichte, 1878, p. 252; Reuss, Graetz, Kue., A. Müller, Kitt., Cooke, al.   ¶ Herder, Réville, Ba., Be., Cass., al.

** See also Ba.; and, for a contrast, Herder (Briefe, u.s.w., Brief 7, end).

before the foundation of the kingdom. When we compare the
situation of the tribes, as it appears in the poem, with the fragmentary traditions of the invasion and settlement in ch. 1, we see
that Israel had in the meantime established itself more securely
in the land. The Highlands of Ephraim seem to be completely in
the possession of Joseph, and we may infer from the part taken
in the struggle by Issachar, Zebulun, and Naphtali, that the latter
tribes, too, had gained a firmer footing in Galilee, while Issachar
had probably already planted itself on both sides of the narrow
valley which at the eastern end of the Plain separates the hills on
the north and south. The Canaanites, however, were still masters
of the Plain; their fortified cities commanded the passes which
entered, and the roads which traversed it; their formidable
chariotry kept the Highland footmen on either hand in awe
(cf. Jos. 17[16-18]). With increasing numbers and strength, it was
inevitable that the Israelites should turn their eyes to the fertile
fields and rich traffic of the Plain. After a period probably of
peaceful expansion, the Canaanite city-kings, alarmed perhaps at
the steady encroachments of Israel, took the aggressive. They
blockaded the main roads and cut off communication; from their
cities they sent out bands and harried the country, so that the
unwalled villages were deserted.[*]

Incited by Deborah, most of the Israelite tribes concertedly
took up arms to put an end to this intolerable state of things.
From the south of the Plain came the three branches of Joseph,
Ephraim, Benjamin and Machir; from the north Zebulun, Issachar
and Naphtali. Each tribe and clan was led by its own chiefs,
who are repeatedly mentioned with especial honour. The united
forces were commanded by Barak, a chief of Issachar, or perhaps
of Naphtali.[†] The Israelites east of the Jordan, Reuben and
Gilead (Gad), were also summoned by Deborah's emissaries, but
either did not respond at all or dallied irresolute till the time for
action was over; nor did the more remote northern tribes, Dan
and Asher, join in the rising. In the Ode these tribes are bitterly
reproached for their selfish indifference to the cause of Israel, and

---

[*] If this is the meaning of v.[7a]. It does not appear from the poem that ne and
was so completely overrun and subdued as it was by the Philistines in the days of
Saul.   [†] See v.[18].

their conduct is contrasted with the alacrity with which Zebulun and Naphtali braved the dangers of the field. When Israel is arrayed in arms against Canaan, every tribe and clan is bound to come to the support of Yahweh among the valiant warriors.*

We see from this that the Israelite tribes, although separated and to some extent broken up in the invasion and settlement of Palestine and the transition from nomadic to agricultural life with all its profound changes, felt themselves to be one people. This consciousness must have come down from a time when the tribes were more closely united than they were in the first centuries of their settlement in Canaan. But it does not spring solely from the fact that they were, or believed themselves to be, of one race, or from the memory of the days in which they had wandered and fought side by side; it has a deeper root in their religion. Israel is the people of Yahweh (v.$^{11, 13}$); its enemies are his enemies (v.^{31}); its victories, his victories (v.^{11}).† To him the enthusiasm with which chiefs and people offered themselves for the holy war is gratefully ascribed (v.$^{2\ 9}$);† the oracle pronounces his curse on the villagers of Meroz for not coming bravely to his aid. The whole Ode is a triumphal Te Deum to Yahweh, Israel's God.

Yahweh was not a god of Canaan, whose worship Israel, in settling in the land and learning to till the soil, had adopted from the natives, but the god of the invaders, by whose help they conquered Canaan. His seats were in the distant south, whence he comes to succour his people and discomfit their foes, "going forth to war from Seir, marching from the region of Edom." Thither, long after the time of Deborah, Elijah journeyed through the desert to the old holy mountain, where he found Yahweh (1 Ki. 19). It is the old and constant tradition, that at this holy mountain Israel solemnly adopted the religion of Yahweh. This coincides with the implications of the poem noted above, and explains, as hardly anything else could, the strength of the religious feeling and the consciousness of religious unity which express themselves in the Ode. The indirect confirmation which is thus given to the tradition that connects the beginnings of the religion of Israel, the great work of Moses, with the holy mountain (Horeb, Sinai) is of no slight weight.

The battle was fought near Taanach and Megiddo (v.^{19}), on the southern side of the Plain. The Canaanite city-kings of these

---

* For this reason it is very significant that Judah is not named at all. It is difficult to avoid the inference that the poet did not count it among the tribes of Israel. It was originally a small tribe, which grew into importance by union with clans of different stock (Caleb, &c.), and it was separated from Joseph by a Canaanite belt (see above, p. 8); but these things hardly account for its absence from the song. Simeon and Levi are also wanting; Reuben is the only one of the older, southern group of Leah-tribes that is named.

† So, at least, these verses are generally understood.

and neighbouring cities, relying on their chariots and their superiority in arms, gave battle in the open field. Their leader, Sisera, was doubtless the king of one of these cities; and the glimpse of his court and harem which is given us in v.$^{28-30}$ shows that he was a powerful and opulent prince. The Israelites were able to raise forty thousand men.* They were peasants from the hills, and were armed only with peasants' weapons; a regular military equipment was hardly to be found among them (v.^{8}). The Canaanites were routed; the treacherous Kishon, perhaps swollen by a sudden flood, with its marshes and holes, completed their ruin. Sisera, in his flight, passed by the village of Meroz (?), whose Israelite inhabitants suffered him to escape.† At the door of Jael's tent he halts to beg a drink of water; she gives him a great bowl of milk, and, as he buries his face in it in his thirst and haste, fells him with a blow that crushes in his skull.

The results of the war are unknown to us. It is hardly probable that Israel took from the Canaanites any of their strong cities, but the power and prestige of the Canaanites and their terrible chariots received a severe blow.‡ The union of Yahweh's people at the call of Deborah in a holy war must have done much to strengthen the feeling of oneness in race and religion, and their success have deepened their faith in Yahweh of armies, the god of the embattled ranks of Israel. Thus the victory in the plain of Megiddo foreshadowed and prepared the way for the kingdom of Saul and David.

The Song of Deborah is unsurpassed in Hebrew literature in all the great qualities of poetry, and holds a high place among Triumphal Odes in the literature of the world. It is a work of genius, and therefore a work of that highest art which is not studied and artificial, but spontaneous and inevitable. It shows a development and command of the resources of the language for ends of poetical expression which prove that poetry had long been cultivated among the Hebrews. Few fragments of this earlier

---

* This is a round number, and naturally not below the mark. Whether the total fighting strength of Israel is meant, or that of the tribes engaged, is a question which can hardly be answered.

† This seems to be the point of the contrast with the blessing of Jael.

‡ Such as the English yeomen at Agincourt dealt to the prestige of chivalry.

poetry have come down to us ; probably few survived to the centuries with which our Hebrew literature begins, but we cannot doubt that the nomadic forefathers of Israel took the same keen delight in lyric poetry which is so strongly marked a trait of the Arabs.*

The form of the Ode has received much attention from students of Hebrew poetry, and many attempts have been made to reduce it to metre and divide it into regular strophes.† Some of these schemes are very ingenious ; but those of them which adhere more closely to the Massoretic text are so irregular that the terms metre and strophe seem to be misapplied, while those which achieve greater regularity do so by more or less violent operations upon the text. They help us very little to a better understanding of the poem, and can only with great caution be used as a canon for the emendation of its obscure and corrupt places. All that can safely be said is that the principal pauses in the poem are after v.[11] and v.[23], and that the prevailing rhythm of the poem has four beats to the line.

1. *And Deborah sang, and Barak*] cf. Ex. 15[1]. The title was probably prefixed by the editor who incorporated the poem in his Book of Judges, and expresses his opinion that the Ode was composed by Deborah, and sung in celebration of the victory. The grammatical construction makes it not impossible that the words *and Barak* are an addition by a later hand, suggested by the apostrophe in v.[12b]. ‡ — *On that day*] the day of victory ; there is no reason to think that the writer meant the words in the looser sense, *at that time* (cf. Jer. 7[21] 34[13] &c.), nor can they be understood of

---

* It is an erroneous inference, however, that there must have been an extensive poetical *literature* before Deborah. Early poetry was not preserved in books, but in the breasts of men. It is quite possible that the Song of Deborah itself was thus perpetuated for generations ; though we do not need to invoke the aid of this hypothesis to explain the state of the text, and cannot admit it as a warrant for a radical reconstruction of the poem, such as is attempted by Niebuhr.

† See Fr. Köster, *Stud. u. Krit.*, 1831, p. 72 ff.; Ewald, *Dichter des A. B.*, i. 1. p. 178 ff.; E. Meier, *Poet. National-Literatur der Hebräer*, p. 79 ff.; J. Ley, *Grundzüge des Rhythmus*, u.s.w., p. 214 ff.; Bertheau; G. Bickell, *Carmina V. T. metrice*, p. 195 ff.; C. A. Briggs, *Pres. Review*, vi. 1885, p. 501 ff.; A. Müller, *Königsberger Studien*, i. p. 10 ff.; &c. On other schemes, see Ba., p. 521 ff.

‡ Be., al. For various conjectures about the part that Barak had in the Song, beginning with Ephrem, see Ba.

a subsequent celebration of the triumph or commemoration of the victory. But, as we have seen above (p. 132), Deborah was probably not the author of the poem, and it certainly bears none of the marks of improvisation. Nor is there any evidence in the Song itself that it was sung by Deborah, alone or with Barak.[*]

2, 3. Exordium.[†] — The poet announces his theme. — **2.** The meaning of the two essential words in the first half-verse is obscure. Most recent interpreters adopt the rendering of some of the Greek translators : *For the leading of the leaders in Israel, for the volunteering of the people, praise ye Yahweh.*[‡] The poet, according to this interpretation, calls upon his hearers to praise God that chieftains were found to head the rising of the clans, and that the people nobly responded to their call. This gives a good parallelism between the two members, and the whole corresponds in sense to v.[9] (the marshals of Israel, the volunteers among the people). The meaning ascribed to the words *biphĕrōa' pĕra'ōth*, however, rests only on very insecure etymological conjecture, and is exposed to grave, if not insuperable, grammatical difficulties. The translation of the second clause shares the uncertainty which attaches to the parallel first clause, though all the words are familiar; cf. 2 Chr. 17[16] Ps. 110[3]. — *Bless ye Yahweh*] render him grateful homage, magnify him. — **3.** The rulers of the nations are summoned to hearken to the praises of Yahweh. The poet would make the world a witness of Yahweh's mighty acts and compel it to own his greatness; cf. Dt. 32[1.3]. — *Hear, ye kings ; give ear, ye potentates*] the two verbs are often coupled in poetical parallelism ; cf. Gen. 4[23] Ex. 15[26] Nu. 23[18] &c. ; the two nouns also occur together, Ps. 2[2] Hab. 1[10]. The words are addressed to the rulers of the nations of the world, so far as they were within the horizon of the poet's contemporaries ; they shall learn the great might of Yahweh and his jealousy for his people Israel. — *I, to Yahweh I*

---

[*] The attempts to distribute the parts of the Song between the two singers, with or without the addition of a Chorus, are very artificial. See, *e.g.* Fr. Böttcher, *Die ältesten Bühnendichtungen*, u.s.w., 1850; Donaldson, *Jashar*, p. 237 ff. Older schemes may be seen in Ba.

[†] A translation of the Ode will be found below, p. 171 ff.

[‡] So Schnurrer (1775), Herder[1], Hollm., Ges., and with minor modifications, most commentators in this century.

will sing] *for my part; not I, even I, will sing unto the Lord*
(EV.), which is doubly unjust to the emphasis of the line.
Observe the repetition of the pronoun, which has a weight in
Hebrew that we cannot give it in translation. The note of tri-
umph rings in this exaltation of the subject. Most interpreters
find in this dominant *I* the self-consciousness of Deborah, heroine
and poet, but for reasons already set forth this is improbable.
Wellhausen thinks that the *I* of this verse, as of Ex. 15, is Israel.*

1. ותשר דבורה וברק] Deborah has the leading part; Barak is in an altogether secondary position; cf. Nu. 12¹ Ex. 15¹. RLbG. and Abarb. (cf.
Ephr.) think that by this construction the writer meant to imply that Barak
had no part in the composition of the Ode, of which Deborah alone was the
author.   ותשר, from שיר *med. i;* Kö., i. p. 510 f. — 2. [בפרע פרעות וג׳ 𝕲ᴬᴸᴹᴼ
Θ l s ε *ἐν τῷ ἄρξασθαι ἀρχηγοὺς ἐν Ισραηλ,* cf. 𝕲 Dt. 32⁴². The intention of
the translators is no doubt correctly expressed by Procop., *δηλοῖ ἡ ῥῆσις· ἐν
τῷ ἄρχοντας ἐν τῷ Ισραηλ ἀναφαίνεσθαι, καὶ τὸν λαὸν αὐτοῖς ὑπείκειν ἑκόντα.*

פרע is compared with Arab. فَرْع 'eminent man' (lit. 'top' *cacumen*), and
the fem. is explained as the so-called intensive fem. (Wright, *Arab. Gram.*,
i. p. 157), used esp. in names of callings, titles of respect, and the like;
e.g. nassābat, 'consummate genealogist,' *'allāmat,* 'perfect scholar,' &c.; in
Heb., perhaps, הֹרָךְ, סֹפֶרֶת, &c. (Ges.²⁵ § 122, 4 *b*); or as one of the words
which are fem. in tropical significations (Bö. § 645 cf. 630). 𝕲ᴮᴬᴺ *ἀπεκα-
λύφθη ἀποκάλυμμα ἐν* I. (Σ, more clearly, *ἐν τῷ ἀνακαλύψασθαι κεφαλὰς*) connect
the words with פֶּרַע Nu. 5¹⁸ Lev. 13⁴⁵, פֶּרֶע 'head of long hair' Nu. 6⁵ Ez. 44²⁰.
Cass. and Vernes, also, interpret of the wild streaming locks of the warriors
who have consecrated themselves to the holy war.† 𝔖 and 𝔗 (combined with
other interpretations) give the root the sense which it ordinarily has in Syr.,
Aram., and MH. (but not in BH.), *for the retribution, the avenging,* of Israel's
wrongs; similarly Ki., Abarb., Schm., Köhler, Herder², al. Some modern
scholars, starting from the assumed primary meaning 'loose,' render the verb,
'set free, liberate'; so Lth. (*das Israel wider frey ist worden*), Cler., J. D.
Mich., Justi, Stud. Neither of these interpretations is justified by usage, and
neither makes a passable parallel to v.ᵇ. — בדרך] nowhere else takes ב in the
sense 'for, on account of'; we should expect עַל (Dt. 8¹⁰). This difficulty
exists equally for all the interpretations recorded above. The more natural
rendering of the prep. is *with;* and we might perhaps translate, *with long
streaming locks in Israel, with free gifts of the people, praise ye Yahweh,*
thinking of vows and offerings of gratitude for the victory achieved; or we

---

* *Comp.,* p. 223; see on the other side, Be., *ad loc.*
† The second clause is then rendered in a corresponding way of the taking of a
warrior's vow.

might give ב with inf. its temporal sense. — 3. שמעו ... האזינו] cf. also Dt. 32¹
Is. 1². ¹⁰ 32⁹; with a third synonym, הקשיב, Hos. 5¹ Is. 28²³ — רוזנים] a word of
the higher style, parallel to מלכים Ps. 2² Hab. 1¹⁰ Pr. 8¹⁵ 31⁴, to שפטי ארץ
Is. 40²³. — אנכי ליהוה ונ׳] the accents rightly set off the first pronoun; cf.
Ps. 76⁴, Dr. § 198, Obs. 2. — אזמר] *make melody, music, canere vel voce vel
fidibus* (Cic., *divinat.*, ii. 59, 122; cf. זמרא רמותא, זמרא רבנא, זמרא, *Gittin*, 7ᵃ);
often coupled with שיר (Ps. 21¹⁴ &c.). The root is prob. onomatopoetic; see
Hupfeld, *Zeitschr. f. d. Kunde d. Morgenlandes*, iii. p. 394 ff., iv. p. 139 ff.,
Psalmen², i. p. 38 f.

4, 5. The awful coming of Yahweh.

— After the exordium
(v.³ᶜ·) the poet hurries us *in medias res* and describes the coming
of Yahweh from his ancient seats in the South to succour his
people. The cause of his coming is exposed in the following
verses (v.⁶ᶠᶠ·). This is the only natural explanation of v.⁴ᶜ; the
mention of Sinai in v.⁵, which seems to require a different interpretation, is a gloss. With the description of Yahweh's advent
compare Dt. 33² Hab. 3³ᶠᶠ· Ps. 68⁷ᶠᶠ·, also 2 S. 22⁸ᶠᶠ· (Ps. 18⁷ᶠᶠ·) Mi. 1²⁻⁴
Ps. 97²⁻⁵; cf. *Il.* xiii. 17-19. — 4. *Yahweh, when thou wentest
forth from Seir, when thou marchedst from the region of Edom*]
the words do not refer to the descent of Yahweh upon Mt. Sinai
(Ex. 19¹⁶ᶠᶠ·) or Horeb (Dt. 4¹⁰⁻¹² 5²ᶠᶠ·) at the institution of the
religion of Israel.[*] The imagery bears a certain resemblance to
the passages last cited, though only in features common to all
such manifestations; but the sublime phenomena which attended
the giving of the law have no obvious connexion with the subject .
of the poem, nor is any suggested by the author. If a contrast
had been intended between the great deeds of God for Israel in
former days and the recent humiliation,[†] or a comparison of his
intervention in the destruction of Sisera with the prodigies at
Sinai,[‡] it must have been intimated in some way. After the
announcement of the theme in v.³ᶜ· we expect praises of Yahweh
for the great deliverance he has just wrought, not an irrelevant
historical reminiscence. Finally, Yahweh did not come to Sinai
from Seir, from the plateau of Edom (v.⁴ᵃ), to give the law; and
no plausible or even possible explanation of these words has
been proposed by the commentators who interpret v.⁴ᶜ· of the

---

[*] ᭐, Ra., a Lyra, Schnurrer, Rosenm., Ke., Be., Hilliger, Ba., Robertson, Cooke,
al. mu.   [†] Schnur., Ew., Be., Vernes, al.   [‡] Rosenm.

theophany at Sinai.   Others, comparing Dt. 33² Hab. 3³ᶠᶠ., refer
the verses to earlier wars, such as those against Sihon and Og, in
which Yahweh led his people to victory,* or to the whole progress
through the desert to Canaan with Yahweh at their head.† But
this again is not in the text, and the same objections from the
context which were urged against the former interpretation are
valid against this. ‡

Text and context constrain us, therefore, to interpret the verses
of the coming of Yahweh to the help of his people in the war
with Sisera.§   The ancient seats of Yahweh were not in Canaan,
but in the South, at Sinai (J, Ex. 19¹¹·¹⁸·²⁰, P *passim*) or Horeb
(E, Ex. 3¹ 18⁵ 33⁶ Nu. 10³³ &c., D *passim*) ; the latter is the tradition of the northern tribes (1 K. 19⁸), and is probably to be
assumed here.   Horeb was in the land of Midian, *i.e.* in Arabia,
east of the eastern prong of the Red Sea, the gulf of 'Aqabah,‖
among mountains which form the southern continuation of the
range east of the 'Arabah.   From Horeb, Yahweh would come
into Canaan from Seir, from the plateau of Edom, as in our verse.
Cf. especially Dt. 33² Hab. 3³. — *When thou wentest forth*] to
battle ; see on 2¹³ 4¹⁴. — *Marchedst*] the two verbs are similarly
coupled in Hab. 3¹²·¹³ Ps. 68⁸; cf. the corresponding noun
2 S. 5²⁴. — *Seir*] is the home of Esau, the land which was given
him by Yahweh, as Canaan was given to Jacob (Jos. 24⁴ Dt. 2⁵ cf.
Gen. 32⁸ 33¹⁴).   It is the mountain range east of the 'Arabah,
from the southern end of the Dead Sea to the Gulf of 'Aqabah,
now called in its northern part el-Gibāl, in the southern esh-
Sherāh.¶ — *The region of Edom*] identical with Seir ; see Gen.
32³ and cf. also 36⁸. — *The earth quaked, the heavens dripped*]

* Ibn Ezra (on Dt. 33 Ps. 68), RLbG., cf. Ki.

† Ephr., Procop. (including the deliverance from Egypt), Cler., Lette, Justi, Ew.,
Cass., Vernes.

‡ See Schm., p. 463 f., whose statement of the matter can hardly be bettered,
though he is finally constrained by the mention of Sinai to adopt an interpretation
which he has himself shown to be untenable.

§ Köhler (1780), Hollmann, Stud., Reuss, We., Sta., W. R. Smith, al.

‖ Aelaniticus sinus.   Horeb was a distance of eleven days' journey, by the Mt.
Seir road, from Kadesh Barnea (Dt. 1²).   These are really the only clues that we
possess.

¶ See Buhl, *Geschichte der Edomiter*, p. 2 ff.; cf. Müller, *Asien u. Europa*,
p. 135 f.

cf. 2 S. 22⁰⁰· (= Ps. 18⁷ᶠ·) Mi. 1ᴺ· Ps. 97¹⁻⁵ 144ᴺ·. For *dripped*, which might have been taken up accidentally from the next hemistich, several recensions of 𝕲 have, *were in commotion;* Budde conjectures that this represents the original reading, *the heavens swayed.* — *The clouds dripped water,* 5. *the mountains streamed*] in the derivative passage, Ps. 68⁸, these lines are lacking. The second verb is generally translated *trembled* (cf. Is. 64¹), but *streamed* is a more natural rendering of the Hebrew word and gives a better parallel, especially if we adopt the reading of 𝕲 in the previous member. — *Before Yahweh (that is, Sinai), before Yahweh, the God of Israel*] the words *that is, Sinai* are a gloss to *the mountains* in the preceding clause ;* originally, as its form shows, a marginal note, made by some one to whom the language of v.ᴺ· suggested Ex. 19. Subsequently it intruded into the text in the wrong place. The rhythm of the passage also gains by the removal of the words.

4. נצעדך] with dagesh, distinguishing the inf. from the noun (Pr. 4¹²); Ew. § 255 *d*; Ol. § 160 *b*. The primary meaning seems to be, 'walk with great steps, stride, stalk'; of the stately march of a religious pomp, 2 S. 6¹⁸ cf. 2 S. 22³⁷ Pr. 4¹² Job 18⁷, also Jer. 10⁵ Pr. 7⁸. — שדה אדום] Gen. 32⁴, parallel to שדה ; ארץ שעיר is used of Moab (Gen. 36³⁵ Nu. 21²⁰ &c.), Aram (Hos. 12¹³), Ephraim (Obad. 1¹⁹ cf. Jud. 20⁶), Philistines (1 S. 6¹ 27⁷· ¹¹), Amalekites (Gen. 14⁷). It is not specifically the plateau in distinction from the mountains, but is simply *the region of Edom.* — גם שמים נטפו] the particle is not climacteric, but cumulative; each clause adds a trait to the completeness of the description. נטף is 'drop, drip,' in distinction from 'pour, flow,' in a continuous stream; usually with acc. as in the next clause. 𝕲ᴾⱽᴸⁿᴼ ş ἐταράχθη A ἐξεστάθη ᴹ ἐξέστη.† I *turbatum est* (Verecundus), *i.e.* נבהו (Bu., *Richt. u. Sam.*, p. 104). נזלו is not 'melt away,' as commonly affirmed, but 'move in waves, be violently agitated,' like the Arab. ـاع (Abulw., Vollers, SS.). —

5. הרים נזלו] in Is. 63¹⁹ (accidentally repeated 64²) the vb. is pronounced נזלו, by which the Ni. of זלל is prob. intended (cf. נזלו Is. 34⁴); O 𝕿𝕾 interpret *shake*. So here 𝕲 ἐσαλεύθησαν I *commoti sunt* (Verecundus) 𝕿𝕾, followed by most recent comm. and lexx. (Ges., MV., SS., BDB., Hollm., E. Meier, Stud., Ke., Be., Ba., Bi., al.). The pronunciation of 𝕳 is then explained as due to false analogy to the 3 sg. pf. of the normal verb. The parallelism, however, esp. if we read נבהו in v.⁴, is better satisfied if we derive the word from נזל 'stream.' In the first two members we see the earth quaking, the heavens

---

swaying; * in the last two, the clouds dropping rain, the torrents streaming down the sides of the mountains. For the vb. cf. Job 36²⁸ Is. 45⁸ Jer. 9¹⁷ and the poet. use of נוֹזְלִים 'streams' Ex. 15⁸ Ps. 78¹⁶ &c. The suppression of the acc., which is expressed in the preceding clause, occasions no difficulty. So 𝕃 *montes fluxerunt.†* — זה סיני] Ps. 68⁹. Commonly taken deictically, *yon Sinai, Sinai there;* others, *Sinai, I say.* The first would only be natural if Sinai were in sight, and for neither is there sufficient grammatical warrant. Examples superficially similar are collected in the grammars, *e.g.* Green, § 252, 2 *a*; Ges.²⁶ § 126, 5 n. 2, § 136 n. 3, and esp. Driver in BDB. *Lex.*, s. v. זה; but they need to be carefully sifted. In some the pron. is pred.; in a good many others (esp. in the Pss.) we may recognize the influence of Aramaic syntax; Ex. 32¹ (זה משה) 1 K. 14¹⁴ (see Klost.) Is. 23¹³ (see Duhm) are glosses, in which זה is used just as we use "*i.e.*" The suspicion that in Jud. 5⁶ also the words are a gloss receives some confirmation from the variations of the Greek versions; see my edition of the Hebrew text in *The Sacred Books of the Old Testament,* &c. Σ alone renders quite grammatically τουτέστι τὸ Σινα; cf. also Ps. 68⁹.

6–8. The state of things before the war.

— Travel on the highways was stopped, and travellers were constrained to take roundabout byways; the country was harried by armed bands of Canaanites, so that the Israelite peasants were compelled to abandon their villages. This is not a mere instance and illustration of the insecurity of the land under Canaanite misrule; it is the grievance which was the cause of war. — **6.** *In the days of Shamgar ben Anath, in the days of Jael*] the period immediately preceding the appearance of Deborah as leader and deliverer (v.⁷ᵇ). The asyndeton would imply that Shamgar and Jael were contemporaries. The latter can be no other than the heroine celebrated in v.²⁴ᶠᶠ; ‡ not an otherwise unknown judge of the same name, § in which case the author must have distinguished them in some way, *e.g.* by adding the name of his father. The difficulty, however, which this hypothesis is created to relieve is a real one. It is singular that the name of this Bedawi woman should be coupled with that of Shamgar. And how can the period before the rise of Deborah be called *the days of Jael,* when the deed which made her famous was only the last act in

---

* To the ancients the firmament was as solid as the earth.

† Rabb., Schm., Cler., Ew., al.

‡ Fl., Rabb., Schm., Cler., Rosenm., Ke., Ba., and most.

§ Teller (1766), Köhler, Hollmann, Ges., Stud., Be., Oettli; a female judge, Green (1753), Justi. Ew. conjectures that Jair (10²) is meant.

the deliverance which Deborah had already achieved? The best
that can be said is, that, although Shamgar and Jael, both of
whom in different ways wrought deliverance for their people, were
living, they did nothing to free Israel from the tyranny of the
Canaanites until Deborah appeared. But it must be confessed
that this is not very natural; and it would perhaps be better to
regard *in the days of Jael* as a gloss.* If this be so, the question
will arise whether Shamgar was originally an Israelite hero at all.
In the comm. on 3[31] it has been shown that as a deliverer of Israel
he belongs to the latest redaction, and that the slaughter of the
Philistines is premature. If 5[6] is interpreted independently of
this unhistorical exploit, it would be quite as natural to see in him
the oppressor of Israel as its champion.[†] The name is strangely
foreign and heathenish.[‡] The obvious objection to this interpretation is, that Shamgar plays no part in the struggle; the chief of
the enemy is Sisera.[§] — *Caravans ceased, and those who travelled
the roads went by roundabout paths*] the first words are usually
interpreted, as in 𝕳, *the highways were disused;* cf. Is. 33[8]. It
is doubtful, however, whether the verb will bear this meaning, and
the parallelism is impaired. Commerce between different parts
of the land was cut off, and those who were compelled to journey by themselves took circuitous and unfrequented bypaths. —
7. The first half-verse evidently continues the description of the
wrongs which Israel suffered in the days of Shamgar. The meaning of the words, however, is uncertain. The noun (*pĕrazōn*)
occurs again in v.[11], but no rendering which suits one of these
places seems to be possible in the other. In v.[7] we might perhaps give it the sense, *village population,* or better, by a slight
emendation, read, *hamlets ceased;* the peasants deserted their
villages for the protection of the walled towns. This is appropriate enough in the context, and may be right.[∥] If so, the word

* Geddes, Bi., Cooke.   † Cf. " in the days of the Philistines," 15[20].

‡ See above, p. 106. It would be the solitary instance in the O.T. in which an
Israelite bears openly the name of a heathen god (Baethgen, *Beiträge*, p. 140 f.).

§ We should have to supplement the hypothesis by another, that Shamgar had
died before the war and been succeeded by Sisera. The names are alike in being
neither Canaanite nor Hebrew.

∥ It is so interpreted by 𝕰𝕾, Abulw., Ra., Ki., Schm., Cler., Köhl., Ke., Cass.,
Ba., Bu., al. Cf. 𝕲𝖴𝖔𝖕 * 1 (Aug., al.)

in v.[11] must be given up, a step which, in the unintelligible and indubitably corrupt text there, we need not hesitate to take. The rendering *mighty men,** or *counsel, leadership, rule, judges,*† is recommended by the fact that it would be possible in v.[11] also; but has no support in usage or etymology, and in v.[7] is less appropriate to the context and parallelism.

The repetition of the verb *ceased* without a subject may be accidental, or a subject synonymous with *pĕrazōn* may have fallen out of the text.‡ — *Till thou didst arise, Deborah*] the verbs may be either the first person or the second person feminine with the old ending; v.[12] (cf. v.[15]) makes it probable that the latter is intended.§ Budde thinks v.[7b] a gloss; see note. — *A matron in Israel*] the phrase occurs in the Old Testament only in 2 S. 20[19], a city and a mother in Israel (𝔊 correctly, μητρόπολις),‖ from which Niebuhr infers that Deborah also was not a woman, but a town, Daberath-Debūriyeh.¶

חדל [חדלו ארחות 'leave off'; intrans., 'stop, cease' Ex. 9[34] Dt. 15[11] &c.; that it may also mean 'lie idle' is not established by 1 S. 2[5] Job 14[6]. It is on all accounts preferable to pronounce the noun אֹרְחוֹת, 'companies of wayfarers'; the same correction of the punctuation is demanded in Job 6[18. 19] (caravans). —נְתִיבוֹת] נתיבה [הלכי נתיבות is a poet. synonym of דרך, cf. Jer. 18[15]. —Ps. 125[5] cf. עֲקַלְקַלּוֹת Is. 27[1]; in MH. both words are used tropically of tortuous conduct. ארחות[2] is erroneously repeated from the preceding line, to the detriment of both the poetical expression and the rhythm.** —7. חדלו פרזון [נישראל] v.[11]. פְּרָזוֹת Ez. 38[11] Zech. 2[8] are unwalled hamlets, הַפְּרָזִי 1 S. 6[18] Dt. 3[5] the peasant population of such hamlets; cf. also Esth. 9[19] and MH. פרוז. It is barely possible that the abstract פרזון might mean 'peasantry,' and be construed as collective with a plural verb; but as in this collective use we find elsewhere הַפְּרָזִי, it would be preferable to emend here פְרָזוֹה, which is actually found in a few codd.; so Stud. —עַד שַׁקַּמְתִּי דְבוֹרָה] the rel. שׁ with this pointing twice in the verse, also Cant. 1[7]; cf. Jud. 6[17] 7[12] 8[26], Ges.[26] § 36; SS., *s. v.* The rel. שׁ is frequent in late BH. (Cant., Eccl., &c.), and in MH. supplants אשר altogether; but it is unsafe to infer that it was of late origin, and hence that the half-verse is a gloss (Bu.), or the whole poem of late date (Seinecke, Vernes).†† We have equally little ground for pronouncing ד א

---

* 𝕷 *fortes;* similarly 𝔊𝔅𝔊𝔐N 𝔩 (Verecundus); cf. Hab. 3[14].
† Teller, Schnurrer, Ges., Hollmann, Be., Reuss, Vernes.
‡ Bu.
§ See above, p. 132.
‖ See above, p. 25 and n.
¶ *Reconstellation,* p. 11.
** Briggs.
†† Observe נאשר, v.[27].

peculiarity of a northern dialect (Nachtigall, Bö., al.).* The relatives אשר and ש are probably of different origin, and may have existed side by side in all periods of the language. For יִקּם 𝕲 | 𝔱 𝔏 have the third person, *until Deborah arose;* 𝔚 would then be a later change to the first person, dictated by the theory that Deborah was the author of the Ode (v.¹).† It is simpler to take the form יִקּם as 2 s.f. with the old ending i (Ges.²⁵ § 44. 2 n. 4); Rödiger (1839), Bö., Graetz, We., A. Müller, Reuss, Kitt.

8. Continues the portrayal of the situation in Israel at the outbreak of the war, as is evident from the second half-verse. ‡ — *A shield was not to be seen, nor a spear, among forty thousand men*] the hyperbole is not to be pressed; nor does the language imply that the Israelites had been disarmed, as, according to a late and exaggerated story (1 S. 13¹⁹⁻²²), they were by the Philistines in the days of Saul. But, compared with the well-equipped soldiers of the Canaanite kings, they were a motley concourse, armed with such rude weapons as each man could lay his hands on, or hurriedly fashion from the implements of his peaceful calling.§ Verse⁸ is unintelligible. The English version, following 𝕿 and Jewish commentators, ‖ connects the verse with the following, and understands it to refer to Israel's sin in worshipping strange gods and its consequence, a hostile invasion: "They chose new gods; then was war in the gates." ¶ This translation of the last hemistich is impossible; that of the first, for grammatical reasons, very improbable. Moreover, if the poet had meant to speak of the apostasy of Israel as the cause of the evils that had befallen it, the natural place to do so was before v.⁶, where the description of those evils begins. But that he construed the history of his times as the author of the introduction to the Book of Judges does (2⁶ᶠ·) is nowhere intimated in the Ode, and is in itself most improbable. Other attempts to extract a meaning from the

* Neubauer and Sayce thought that they found the letters ‏בע‎ on a stone weight, prob. of the 8th cent. B.C., which was found on the site of Samaria; but the reading is disputed. See *Acad.*, Aug. 2, 1890, p. 94; *Athenaeum*, Aug. 2, 1890, p. 164. The controversy in the *Academy*, 1894, is reprinted in *PEF. Qu. St.*, July, 1894, p. 220-231; 284-287.   † See We., *Comp.*, p. 223 n., cf. p. 356; Bi.

‡ E. Meier would put v.⁸ after v.⁹; cf. A. Müller, Cooke.

§ Such seems, at least, to be the meaning; the mutilated context warns us against too confident an interpretation.   ‖ Ra., Ki., Tanch., RLbG., Abarb.

¶ Cf. Dt. 32¹⁷ Jud. 2¹¹⁻¹⁶. So Drus., Cler., Schm., Schnurrer, Hollm., Stud., Ba., Cass., Reuss, Oettli, al. mu. The first clause is rendered in the same way by 𝕲.

L

clauses are not more successful. Jerome translates : Nova bella elegit Dominus,* et portas hostium ipse subvertit ; clypeus et hasta si apparuerint in quadraginta millibus Israel. Ewald and others, "They chose new judges (*elohim*)," † namely, Deborah and Barak. In the last hemistich 𝔖 and some recensions of 𝔊 find "barley bread" (cf. 7¹³). ‡ See critical note.

9–11. The text of these verses has suffered so badly that there is no reasonable hope that any art or skill by the critic will ever be able to restore it. The ancient versions found the text in substantially the same state in which it has been transmitted to us, and had no tradition to guide them in interpreting it. The disjointed words and phrases to which we can attach a probable sense do not afford a sufficient basis for conjecture ; the con- nexion is impenetrably obscure. We are here, as more than once in the following verses, in very much the same case as the epi- graphist who has before him a badly defaced or mutilated inscrip- tion, the difficulty of deciphering which, he has reason to suspect, is increased by partial and unskilful attempts at restoration. What can, with more or less confidence, be made out is this : § ⁹ My heart (goes out) to the rulers (?) of Israel — those who offer themselves freely among the people — bless ye Yahweh — ¹⁰ men that ride reddish asses — that sit on . . . — and that walk on the road . . . — ¹¹ from (?) a sound of . . . between watering-places — there they rehearse the righteous acts of Yahweh — the right- eous acts of . . . in Israel — then went down to the gates the people of Yahweh. ‖

Verse⁹ seems to repeat the motive of v.², but unfortunately the one is as obscure as the other ; v.¹⁰ is generally explained as calling

---

* 𝔖, *God chose a new thing*, Ephrem, Lth., al.; generally understood of the deliv- erance of Israel by a woman. Cf. also RLbG., alt.

† Meier, Be., Briggs, al.; cf. Ex. 21⁸ 22⁷·⁸ (Ew.).

‡ It is obviously impossible, as it would be unprofitable, in the obscure and cor- rupt places of this poem, to discuss or even record all the guesses of commen- tators. I shall pass over in silence such as seem to me to have no claim to serious consideration. The curious reader may consult Bachmann.

§ I abstain from any interpretative punctuation.

‖ Cf. A. Müller, p. 16 f. Perhaps it may not be superfluous to give a warning against the inference that because so many words can be recognized, therefore so much of the text is sound.

upon the persons there described, perhaps representing different classes of society or men of different pursuits, to join in singing Yahweh's praises for the security which they now enjoy, in contrast to v.⁶⁷ᵃ. The archers (??) among the watering-places are also supposed to have something to do with celebrating Yahweh's righteous acts. The first part of the poem would thus end, as it began, with a summons to laud and magnify Yahweh's great name. Verse ¹¹ᵇ is, upon this supposition, entirely unsuitable after v.¹¹ᵃ and before v.¹²; it has been conjectured that it is accidentally misplaced from v.¹³ᵃ.* This interpretation of v.⁹⁻¹¹ makes the verses interrupt and delay the swift movement of the poem in a way that is quite unlike the author.† After the appearance of Deborah (v.⁷ᵇ), we expect to hear of the preparations for the war, and this is confirmed by v.¹¹ᵇ, — *then marched down to the gates the people of Yahweh;* cf. also v.⁸ᵇ. With v.¹² the war itself begins.

8. ‏יבחר אלהים חדשים‎] against the interpretations which make *God* subject, it is decisive that throughout the poem the name ‏יהוה‎ is used; ‏חדשים‎ *new things* (‏חדשׁות‎ Is. 48⁶) or *new men* is in this collocation fatally ambiguous. The same objection holds against *It* (Israel) *chooses* (or, *when it chooses*) ‡ *new gods;* an author who meant to be understood would hardly write thus. Moreover, the idea is foreign to the poem, and is introduced in an inappropriate place. Perhaps a scribe may have tried to restore the partly illegible words of his copy by the help of Dt. 32¹⁷; cf. Jud. 10¹⁴. *New judges* ascribes to ‏אלהים‎ a fictitious sense and adds a new element of ambiguity. — ‏אז לחם‎ ‏שׁערים‎] § it is difficult to imagine what is intended by this anomalous pronunciation; see Ges. *Thes.*, and Ba. After ‏אז‎ we expect a finite verb, as in v.¹¹·¹³·¹⁹ (‏אז נלחמו וג׳‎) ²², and ‏שׁערים‎ is apparently accus.; but ‏לחם‎ (Ps. 35¹ 56²·³) would be very suspicious here, and *then he assaulted the gates* would hardly admit any interpretation but that of Jerome. 𝕲ᴬᴾⱽᴸᴹᴼ Ι ς ϵ 𝔖 ὡς ἄρτον κρίθινον, *i.e.* ‏לחם שׁערים‎ 7¹³ (cf. Thdt., Ephr., Aug.), which is certainly the most natural pronunciation of the consonants. For a conjecture based on this, see Bu., *Richt. u. Sam.*, p. 103; cf. also Kautzsch, *Textkrit. Erläut.*, u. s. w., in his translation of the O.T., p. 6. — ‏אם‎ [‏כנן אם יראה‎] ‏אם‎ of the oath, or, perh. better, interrogative, demanding for its answer an emphatic *No!* (Dr³. § 39 β). On 𝕲ᴬ ᵃˡ· σκέτη πεπλθων κ.τ.ℓ. see Ew., *GGA.* 1867, p. 635 f.; We., *TBS.* p. 8; Field, *Hexapla*, ad loc. The meaning is not that no one dared to

---

* Bu.

† This difficulty would not be so serious, if, with Ew. we made of v.⁹⁻¹¹ an independent poem; see above, p. 128.   ‡ 𝕲 *They chose.*

§ Many codd. ‏לְחֶם‎, ‏יָחֶם‎ (De Rossi); against the Massora, *Ochla we-Ochla*, No. 373.

raise a hand against the oppression (Schm., Stud., al.). — The number, 40,000, is in notable contrast to the standing 600,000 of the post-exilic history of the Exodus (Hollm., Stud., We.). — **9.** רבי לחוקקי ישראל] 𝔖, Schm., Ew., al. supply אמר *says;* better, simply, *belongs to, goes out to,* in gratitude and affection (𝔏 *diligit,* Ra., Ki., Cler., most moderns). חוקק (Is. 10[1]) seems to be the same as מחקק v.[14] (see there) Dt. 33[21]; the form is best explained as ptcp. Qal. — המתנדבים בעם וגי] closely resembles v.[2], and is equally obscure; the ptcp. is hardly appositive to הוחקים (Stud.), but its counterpart in loose construction (Schm., Schnur.). — **10.** I see no way to do anything with שיחו, on which, unfortunately, the understanding of the whole verse depends. It is commonly translated, *tell forth, proclaim, laud* (𝔊𝔏, most comm.; cf. Ps. 105[2] 145[5]); others render *consider, meditate, muse* (Cler., Schm., Schnur., Herd., Ba., al.), which the usage would rather admit, but which is even less suitable in the context. — אתנות צחרות] on the colour (gray, or tawny, inclining to red) see A. Müller, p. 4–6. On riding asses, see on 10[4]. — ישבי על מדין] the noun is unknown. The older interpreters, by an impossible etymology, explain it, *judgement,* or *place of judgement;* most moderns derive it from מד (plur. מדים 3[16]),[*] with Aramaic plural ending. As the sense *garments* is obviously unsuitable, it is assumed that the word had the wider sense, *cloths;* hence either, *saddle-cloths, housings,* or (rich) *carpets* (so the most). The phrases are supposed by many to designate different social classes, with great diversity of opinion as to what classes or how many; others, laying the emphasis on the verbs, imagine the call to be addressed to every Israelite, whatever he may be about; cf. Dt. 6[7] Ps. 139[8] Is. 37[25] Ps. 1[1] &c. (so Stud., Reuss, al.). — **11.** מקול מחצצים בין משאבים] מחצצים † is formally possible as denom. Piel from חץ 'arrow,' 'men that shoot arrows' (Ki., RLbG., Kuypers, Lette, Ges., al. mu.); others, 'cast lots with arrows' (Schultens), for the division of the booty (Schnur., al.); while others still derive it directly from חצץ, to which they give the meaning 'divide' *sc.* the spoil (חלק; Hollm., Stud., Ba.). ‡ But the difficulty lies not more in this word than in the preposition בן and the noun משאבים (lit. '‚ places where water is drawn'). There is no clue to the meaning of the line. — שם יתנו] the obscurity of the preceding prevents our seeing to what place שם refers, or what is the subject of the verb. תנה 11[40] is frequently compared with Arab. ثَنَى iv., 'eulogize' (or 'defame'). But as equivalent of Heb. תנה the word is not conceivable in old Hebrew. — צדקות יהוה] seemingly manifestations of his justice in defending and delivering his people; cf. 1 S. 12[7] Mi. 6[5] &c. — צדקה פרזונו בישראל] see on v.[7]. In the context פרזונו must be gen. subj.; *country people* (Ba.) will not do here; *rulership, rule* (Be.) or *leadership, leaders* (Stud., Reuss, al.) are unsupported, and do not

---

* Hiller, Schnur., Ges., al. plur.

† Every conceivable Heb. etymology of this word was discussed by Jewish scholars in the Middle Ages; see Tanch., quoted in Ges. *Thes.* p. 511.

‡ Bu. conjectures קול מצחקים, *Hark, how joyful they are!*

suit v.⁷. — וני ירדו אז] many commentators, taking ישׂרי as jussive conⁿ 1³⁰.
the imv. שׁירי, feel constrained to make a jussive also of ירדו, either eme.ⁱₒₙ
ירדי (Schnur.) or forcing this sense upon the pf. (Hollm., al.). The £.ₙ
(metonomy for cities; cf. 𝔊) are thought by some to be those of the Israelite.
to which they now return in peace and security, cf. v.⁸ (so, with various
modifications, Stud., Ke., Ba., al.); others, with greater probability, interpret
of the gates of the enemy's cities, against which Israel now marched (ℒ, Ew.,
Be., Reuss, al.).

**12–22. Israel marches into battle; defeat and flight of the
Canaanites.** — The second part of the Ode. After an opening
apostrophe to Deborah and Barak, we see the tribes march down
to the fray and hear the reproachful questions which the absence
of others evokes. Then we are in the midst of the combat; the
heavens themselves fight against Sisera, the torrents of Kishon
sweep his proud host to ruin. The text of v.¹²⁻¹⁵ is so corrupt that
we can hardly read more than the names of the tribes; but their
general purport is manifest. From v.¹⁶ the text is better preserved. — **12.** *Rouse thee, rouse thee, Deborah; rouse thee, rouse
thee, strike up the song*] interpreters who assume that in these
words Deborah calls upon herself to sing the Ode of Victory find
it hard to explain why this invocation stands thus in the middle
of the Ode, instead of beginning it.[*] The explanation of Studer
and others, that this is the real beginning of the Ode, to which
v.² ¹¹ is merely a proœmium, hardly relieves the difficulty; we
should have to go a step farther, and with Ewald, regard v.²⁻¹¹ as
a distinct poem. The complete parallel between the call to
Deborah in v.¹²ᵃ and that to Barak in v.¹²ᵇ makes it improbable,
however, that in the former Deborah addresses herself; and we
have seen other reasons for believing that the heroine is not the
author of the Ode. In view of the following context, verse¹²ᵇ is
best understood as a summons to Barak, not to participate in the
celebration of the triumph, but to attack the enemy; and, accordingly, v.¹²ᵃ, which cannot be separated from v.¹²ᵇ and referred to
in earlier time,[†] is to be explained, not as a call to Deborah to
sing a song of victory, but to strike up the song of battle.[‡] The

---

[*] On this difficulty see, *e.g.* Schnur., who would supply, *I said*. Niebuhr in his
Reconstellation actually puts v.¹² in the place of v.².   [†] Stud., Ba., al.

[‡] Schnur., Köhl., We., Reuss, cf. Bi., Cass. (Reminiscenz an das Schlachtlied
selbst).

raise a is then in a suitable place. The poet sees the people of
is in weh marching to attack the foe (v.[11b]) and breaks in with an
Ey postrophe to the two leaders; to Deborah, to fire the hearts of
ner countrymen by song; to Barak, to make prisoners the proud
foemen.[*]   The obscurity of the preceding verses, however, makes
it impossible to say with confidence that this is the transition
intended by the poet. — *Up, Barak; lead captive thy captive
train, son of Abinoam*] a bold prolepsis; but not an unnatural
one for a poet after the event.   With an equally admissible pronunciation of the Hebrew word we might translate, *lead captive
thy captors*, and surmise that Barak, like Gideon (8^{18-21}), had his
own wrongs to avenge as well as those of his people, a touch of
personal interest which we should welcome.[†]

13-15ᵃ. The tribes are in motion against the enemy. — The
verses are so mutilated that we can make out little more than the
bare names of the tribes. — **13.** The second member may be
read, *The people of Yahweh marched down for him*[‡] *as heroes*
(cf. v.[23]); something of the same kind seems to have stood in the
preceding line, of which there remains, *then marched down . . .
nobles.*   In view of the parallel it might be conjectured that the
name *Israel* was originally found in this line. — **14.** In the first
two lines nothing is certain but the names, Ephraim and Benjamin.   "From Ephraim their root (is) in Amalek — after thee
Benjamin among thy peoples"[§] — is nonsense which must give
the most courageous translator pause. — *From Machir marched
down truncheon-bearers, and from Zebulun those who carry the
muster-master's staff*] Machir is here Manasseh, of which tribe it
was the principal branch.[‖]   In later times the seats of Machir
were in Gilead; but there is good ground for the opinion that the
conquest of this region was made, not in the first invasion of the
lands east of the Jordan by Israel, but subsequently, by a reflux

---

* This is preferable to the explanation which makes the words a shout of the
Israelite host as they go into battle (Stud. alt., al.).

† We., Sta., Bu., Kitt.   ‡ 𝔊ᴮ ᵃˡ.; ℜ *for me.*

§ That is, after thee came Benjamin, &c. (Schnur., Köhl., Hollm., Stud., al.), or,
after thee, O Benjamin! (Schm., alt., Ew., Mei., Ba.)

‖ Machir the first-born son of Manasseh (Jos. 17[1]); or his only son (Gen. 50[23]
Num. 26[29ff.]).   See Kue., *Th. T.* xi. 483 ff.

movement from Western Palestine.* On Zebulun, see on 1[30]. The *muster-master* (lit. *writer*) in the later military organization (2 K. 25[19]) was an officer who had charge of the enumeration and enrolment of the troops; a kind of adjutant general.† In our text it is probably the chieftains themselves who muster the quotas of their own clans; the poet evidently seeks changing expressions for the often recurring idea, chiefs. — **15ᵃ**. Issachar, which is not named at all in ch. 1, ‡ is here mentioned with special honour as the tribe of Deborah, and apparently of Barak also. Unfortunately the text is here again in such disorder that the latter point at least is extremely doubtful. The first line may perhaps be made to read, *And the princes of Issachar* were *with Deborah*, or, were *the people of Deborah;* the rest defies translation. The second line connects Barak also in some way with Issachar; but, in accordance with the uniform structure of the preceding verses, we should rather expect the name of another tribe; and, on the other hand, the omission of Naphtali from this list is strange, especially in view of v.[18]. In the third line the words, *into the plain . . . at his feet,* suffice to show that the verse, like those before it, describes the tribes pouring down from their hills into the plain to give battle to the Canaanites. The original seats of Issachar seem to have been south of Naphtali and southeast of Zebulun, probably in the hills between the two valleys which descend from the eastern end of the Great Plain to the Jordan (Wady el-Bîreh, Nahr Gâlûd); it may comparatively early have occupied a part of the range of Gilboa, south of the latter valley. Toward the northwest it reached to the foot of Tabor, where it met both Zebulun and Naphtali. § The territory occupied by Issachar was one in which it was peculiarly difficult to maintain its independence, and in Gen. 49[14] the tribe is taunted for the ignoble spirit in which it preferred peace to freedom. ‖

12. צורי] the accent is shifted for rhythmical variety, the first two being *milra'*, the last two *mil'el;* cf. Is. 51[9], Ges.[26] § 72 Anm. 3; Bö. § 1134; Ba.,

---

* Smend, *HWB*[1]. p. 936; Sta., *GVI.* i. p. 149; Bu., *Richt. u. Sam.*, p. 34 ff.

† JDMich., Schnur., Ba., al. Cf. also 1 Macc. 5[42]. ‡ See above, p. 49.

§ All this is merely conjectural; the tribe is not named in Jud. 1, and the boundaries and towns assigned to it in Jos. 19[17-23] represent a much later time.

‖ See Sta., *GVI.* i. p. 170 f.

p. 367. — The alliteration רברי ... רבורה is very likely designed; * with רבר שָׁבְיֶךָ שְׁבִי cf. 2 S. 22¹ Dt. 31³⁰. — שְׁבִי [ושבה שָׁבְיֶךָ collective; cf. Ps. 68¹⁹ (Yahweh); so 𝕲𝕷𝕿 and most comm. It is possible to pronounce שָׁבְיֶךָ *thy captors*, cf. Is. 14²; so 𝕾 a, Lth., JDMich., We., Sta., Bu. — 13. ירד *bis*] the context requires in both instances the perf. יָרַד (𝕲ᴮᴳᴺ𝕾𝕿, JDMich., Schnur., Stud., Ew., Be., and most recent scholars); cf. יָרְדוּ v.¹¹ ¹⁴. 𝕸 יְרַד undoubtedly intends an apocop. impf. Pi. from רדה (Ra., Ki.; cf. Stud.; Ges.²⁶ § 69, 1 *c*). — שָׂרִיד [שריד לאריריס is the *survivor* of a battle or calamity, often parallel to פלט; collectively Is. 1⁹. There is nothing in the usage of the word to warrant the rendering *a little band* (Köhl., Stud., Cass., Reuss, and most) †; nor can ראיריס, in view of the parallel בנכורים (cf. v.²³), ‡ refer to the enemy (𝕿, Rabb., JDMich., Schnur., Herd., Stud., al.). — 𝕸 (cf. 𝕷𝕿) joins עָם to the first member of the verse, § to carry out its misinterpretation of ירד; it is rightly connected with the following (עם יהוה) by 𝕲ᴮᴳᴺ, λαὸς Κυρίου κατέβη αὐτῷ ἐν τοῖς κραταιοῖς, ‖ in which αὐτῷ (ירי) is also to be preferred to 𝕸 ירי. ¶ In the light of the parallelism, it may be conjectured that the unintelligible שריד ל in v.ˢ is a corruption of ויבראל. — In בנכורים the כ is perhaps *in the character of*, as (Ges.²⁶ § 119, 3 *b*. 1), rather than *among*; certainly not *against*. — 14. כָּנִי [מְנִי אפריס twice in this verse (cf. כובול v.ᵇ) Is. 46³ Mi. 7¹² Pss. Job. — [שרשם בעמלק is commonly translated, *their root is in Amalek* (or, *whose root*, &c.), and explained, they are firmly established in that part of the territory of Ephraim called the Amalekites' Mountain, that is, in the region of Pirathon (12¹⁵, see comm. *ad loc.*); ** so Hiller (1707), Schnur., Köhl., Hollm., and almost all comm. in the present century. But, apart from the enigmatical form of the expression, the author cannot mean that only those clans of Ephraim which were settled in that district came to the war (Ew., Be.); and that that region was the centre and stronghold of the tribe is neither in accord with the evidence of history nor relevant in this context. The words stand in the place where we should have the predicate of the sentence; it is equally awkward to have to borrow a verb from ירד v.¹³ (Schnur., Stud.) or from ירדו v.¹⁴ᶜ (Ba.). שרשם is probably the corruption of a verb, and for בעמלק we may conjecture that the original reading was בעמק, which is given by 𝕲ᴬᴵᴾᴸᴹᴼ Θ l s ε; cf. v.¹⁵ ובעמק שלח וג (see there). — [אתריך בנישין בעמשיך

---

* See on the whole subject, Casanowicz, " Paronomasia in the O.T.," *JBL* xii. 1893, p. 105 ff.; also separately, Boston, 1894.

† A remnant, that is, in comparison with the enemy; a little band of Israelites who have escaped from former defeats. Ba. quotes Verg., reliquiae Danaum atque immitis Achillei.

‡ *Remnant of the nobles* (Hollm., Ew., Mei., Be., al.) is difficult to justify grammatically.   § So among modern interpreters, Hollm., Ew., Ke., Be., Ba.

‖ Some Heb. codd. connect in the same way (De Rossi); so W. Green, JDMich., Schnur., Köhl., Mei., Donalds., Bi., Cass., Reuss, Briggs, al. mu.

¶ Köhl.

** The older commentators explained the words of wars against Amalek; so 𝕿, Rabb., Ephr., a Lyra, Cler., al.

the same Greek texts give us אחיך, which may with reason be preferred (*thy brother Benjamin*); but עמיך is suspicious on account not only of the Aramaic form of the plural (cf. Neh. 9²⁸·³⁴), but even more of the plural itself; *among thy kinsmen* (*populares*) is less natural here than *in thy ranks*, בגדך. It would be rash, however, to emend in this desperate context. — כְּהֹחֲקֵֽק] בהחה Nu. 21¹⁸ syn. of מִשְׁעֶנֶת, Gen. 49¹⁰ parallel to שֵׁבֶט, is a *staff*, carried by men of rank and authority; here it is the man who carries such a staff as the emblem of his authority (see the parallel clause); cf. Is. 33²² (∥ מלך) מחֹקֵק Ps. 60⁹ Dt. 33²¹ (?). The interpretation, *law-giver, law-giver's staff*, is merely an etymological deduction, and is not sustained by usage. — בְּעֵֽמֶק בְּשֵׁבֶט סֹפֵר] בְּ סֹפֵר cf. 1 K. 22³⁴, the usual construction in Arab.; we might also render, those who march *with the* שֵׁבֶט, &c.; cf. on 4⁶. With סֹפֵר in this use cf. שׁוֹטֵר (from a root of similar meaning; often coupled with שׁׁטֵר), cf. 2 Chr. 26¹¹. In 2 K. 25¹⁹ שַׂר הַצָּבָא, וְסֹפֵר שַׂר הַצָּבָא הַמַּכְבִּיא אֶת עַם הָאָרֶץ may reasonably be suspected of being a gloss; in Jer. 52²⁵ the words have been rendered grammatically correct by dropping the article before סֹפֵר. Klost. takes סֹפֵר (or סֹפֶן) as n. pr. Bu. conjecturally joins סֹפֵר in Jud. 5¹⁴ to the following verse: וְשָׂרַי. — 15ᵃ. שָׂרַי בְיִשָּׂשֹכָר עִם דְּבוֹרָה; cf. W. Green (1753), שָׂרַי בְּרִים וגֹ' שָׂרַי בְּיִשָּׂשֹכָר עִם דְּבוֹרָה] *my princes* is obviously impossible; the correction שָׂרֵי (constr. before preposition), *princes in Issachar* (Schnur., Stud., Be., al.),* though grammatically admissible, is otherwise not much better; שָׂרֵי יִשָׂשכָר *the princes of Issachar* gives a satisfactory sense, but we cannot be confident that this restores the original text. For עִם we might also read עַם (Bu.). — וְיִשָׂשכָר כֵּן בָּרָק] Stud. conjectures that instead of this second *Issachar*, which neither 𝔊 nor 𝔏 seem to have read, the original reading was *Naphtali*; cf. 4⁹ 5¹⁸. The insertion of כ before the first member of the comparison removes the grammatical harshness; but it is difficult to imagine a worse anticlimax than, *and as was Issachar so was Barak*. — בָּעֵמֶק שֻׁלַּח בְּרַגְלָיו] the passive is certainly wrong (Müller); the unintelligibility of the preceding clause forbids us to say more than this. Perhaps the same verb which in v.¹⁴ has been corrupted to בעמק originally stood here also.

15ᵇ–18. The encomium of the tribes which under their gallant chieftains marched down to the fray (v.¹³⁻¹⁵ᵃ) is followed by reproaches of those who were missing from the ranks of Israel; their conduct is contrasted with the shining example of Zebulun and Naphtali (v.¹⁸). Natural as the transition is, the text can scarcely be intact; a stichos corresponding to v.¹³ seems to be lacking.† — **15ᵇ.** Modern interpreters nearly all translate, *By the*

---

* Other explanations of the form give us grammatical anomalies; see Ba. It will probably not occur to any one to fortify the hypothesis of a plural absolute in ־ by the plurals of this form in the Senjerli inscriptions (see D. H. Müller, *WZKM.* vii. 1893, p. 119 f.).   † A. Müller.

watercourses of Reuben (RV.) ; cf. Job 20[17].[*] The old versions all, in one sense or another, render, *divisions*,[†] which is probably to be preferred ; the fractions of the tribe were divided in counsel, and squandered in dissensions the time for deeds. — *Great discussions*] lit. *investigations of mind;* to find out one another's feeling and purpose. The text is to be corrected by v.[16b],[‡] where in the repetition of the line the important word has been better preserved. For the meaning, cf. 1 S. 20[12]. — (16) The reproaches cast upon the recreant tribes are couched in the form of taunting questions. — *Why satest thou between the . . . ?*] the last word, which occurs besides in Gen. 49[14] in a similar figure for base inertness (cf. also Ps. 68[13]), is translated by most recent interpreters, *folds*, enclosures surrounded by a paling or hedge for the protection of the flocks.[§] The rendering, *ash-heaps*, or heaps of refuse, by the villages or encampments of the tribe, adheres more closely to the concrete meaning of the cognate Hebrew words, which is here our only clue. In the next clause the translation of Jerome, after some of the Greek versions, is generally adopted, *ut audias sibilos gregum;* which recent scholars rightly interpret, not of the bleating of the flocks,[‖] but of the piping of shepherds among their flocks;[¶] better, perhaps, of the calls of the shepherds to their flocks. The rest of the verse is repeated by mistake from the end of v.[15].[**] The seats of Reuben were east of the Dead Sea in northern Moab (Num. 32[3f.]), where its relation to the native population was probably not unlike that of Asher and Naphtali among the Canaanites in Galilee (1[31f. 33]). Like Simeon, it seems never to have settled down to agriculture. In ancient times, according to the patriarchal legend, one of the leading tribes of Israel, the first of the Leah group, it early in the historical period dwindled into insignificance. In the Moabite inscription of Mesha it is not mentioned ; Gad has taken

---

[*] JDMich., Schnur., Herd., Köhl., Hollm., Ew., Be., Ba., al.

[†] So also Schm., Stud., Fürst, Delitzsch (on Job 20[17]), MV., al. (*districts*).

[‡] Houbig., Köhl.; cf. the ancient versions.

[§] Pagninus, Lth., AV., Ludolf, Teller, Köhl., Ges., Hollm., Ew., al. mu.

[‖] S., Lth., Bochart, Schm., Cler., Schnur., Herd., al.

[¶] Ges., Hollm., Stud., Ew., Be., Ba., al. mu.; the *pastoria sibila*, Ovid, *Met.*, xiii. 785.

[**] Teller, Reuss, A. Müller, Cooke. Bi. conj. that a line (v.[16c]) has been lost.

its place ; and in Dt. 33⁶ the prayer for Reuben is, May Reuben
live and not die. The fate of the tribe was ascribed to an ancestral curse, Gen. 49ᵂ·, the cause and meaning of which are not
clear.* — 17. *Gilead remained on the other side of the Jordan*]
Gilead is the region east of the Jordan, north and south of the
Jabbok (Nahr ez-Zerqā), with shifting limits in either direction.†
The name is sometimes used for the whole of the Israelite possessions east of the Jordan, of which it was indeed the chief part.
It was occupied by the tribe of Gad, which is doubtless meant in
our verse.‡ The disposition of Reuben and Gad to pursue their
own interests and let their brethren on the other side of the Jordan fight their own battles is reflected in Nu. 32¹ᶠ·.

The more distant northern tribes also stood apart and were not
represented in the ranks of Israelite warriors. — *And Dan, why
does he live neighbour to the ships ?*] the words are difficult ; but
there seems no sufficient reason for suspecting the text, § which is
supported by the parallel line about Asher. This parallel also
shows that the northern settlements of Dan (18⁷ᶠᶠ·) are meant, ‖
not the earlier seats of the tribe in the southwest (1³⁴ᶠ· ; see
there).¶ In neither place did Dan actually come down to the
seaboard.** The words would be quite inexplicable if we had to
translate, *why did he remain in the ships* (RV.). The rendering
adopted above, which gives the meaning of the verb more exactly,
removes the difficulty, if we may interpret, Why does he live as
a dependent, under the protection of the Phoenician sea-farers ?††
This was probably the situation of the Danites, as it had been of
the inhabitants of Laish before them (18⁷· ²⁸). The only objection
to this explanation is, that *ships* is a somewhat remote metonymy
for a seagoing people ; compare, however, 'ship coast' for sea
coast, Gen. 49¹³. — *Asher abode toward the coast of the Great
Sea*] cf. Gen. 49¹³, of Zebulun. — *And remains by its landings*]

---

* See Sta., *GVI.* i. p. 151 f.   † See on 11⁶.
‡ Cf. Ps. 60⁷. 𝔖 here reads *Gad*. The conquests of Manasseh in northern
Gilead are probably later than the time of Deborah ; see above, on v.¹⁴.
§ Bu., *Richt. u. Sam.*, p. 16 n.; cf. Kitt., *GdH.* i. 2. p. 65 n.
‖ Procop., Ki., Cler., Stud., Cass.   ¶ Köhl., Hollm., Be., Ba., al.
** Even in Jos. 19⁴⁶ Joppa lies outside his border (Ki., Stud.).
†† Cf. 𝔊 εἰς τί παροικεῖ πλοίοις ; it is not necessary to suppose that Danites served
on Phoenician ships (Stud., al.).

the last word is found only here ; 𝔏 *in portubus morabatur.* The
parallel line, the meaning of the root, and the use of derivatives
of the corresponding root in Arabic make the general sense sufficiently certain.   Asher occupied the mountainous inland, behind
the Phoenician coast, and it is not impossible that Asherites may
have settled in the Phoenician towns, as they did among the
Canaanites in the interior.   There is no reason to imagine that
they had established themselves on the seaboard in any other
way ; and in view of what is said of Dan it is hardly necessary to
press the language even as far as this.   See further on $1^{31f.}$. —
18. In strong contrast to the unpatriotic or cowardly conduct of
the eastern and northern tribes stands the conspicuous gallantry
of Zebulun and Naphtali.* — *Zebulun is a band that recklessly
exposed itself to death*] lit. *that contemned its life to death.*† —
And Naphtali, upon the heights of the open field] Naphtali displayed equal valour.   The last words cannot refer to the home of
Naphtali among the hills of Galilee,‡ but to the field on which
the two tribes won this renown. §   The expression seems, however, inappropriate to the scene of the battle against Sisera, in
the plain on the banks of the Kishon ($v.^{19. 21}$).   Many commentators think that Mt. Tabor ($4^{6. 12. 14}$) is meant ; ‖ but Tabor is not
mentioned in the Ode, which locates the field of battle, not at the
foot of the mountain (4^{14}), but on the other side of the plain
near Taanach.   The word used for *heights* does not necessarily
denote a great elevation, but is rather a relative term (cf. Prov. 8^2
$9^{3. 14}$) ; and may perhaps be employed here of the mounds and
hillocks in the plain, which, however inconsiderable, were positions
of advantage in the battle, especially as rallying points for the
hard-pressed Canaanites before the rout became complete.
These elevations, where the enemy fought with the ferocity of

---

* According to ch. 4 these two tribes furnished the whole army of Barak.

† For parallels from Arabic sources illustrating the use of the verb, see Schultens, *Animadversiones,* p. 66; Lette, Schnur., *ad loc.* Cf. *e.g., Hamasa,* ed. Freytag,
p. 47.

‡ Schm., Cler., Schnur.; the mountain tribes in contrast to the servile low-
landers, Stud., Ew.

§ Köhl., Hollm., al.

‖ Ra., RLbG., Abarb., and many; where the assembled tribes were filled with
heroic valour (Ba.).

desperation, Zebulun and Naphtali with reckless hardihood stormed and carried. So, at least, we can imagine it; a certain interpretation is hardly to be given. There is something tempting in 𝕷's *in regione Merome*; the words would then refer to former exhibitions of impetuous bravery by these tribes, perhaps against Jabin; but the text of 𝔘 is supported by 𝔊, and 𝕷 probably does not represent a different reading, but an ungrammatical translation.

16b. [כמלגות ראובן] in Job 20¹⁷ פלנות is explained in the parallel line נחלי רבש וחמאה. פלנים, usually in the phrase פרני ביב, are primarily canals and ditches distributing water for irrigation; cf. Prov. 21¹ Ps. 46⁴ and the vb. Job 38²⁵, also Arab. *falaǧ*.* We can hardly imagine, however, that Reuben was at this time so far advanced in agriculture; v.¹⁶ shows that it was chiefly a pastoral tribe. For this reason it seems better to understand the word here of the divisions of the tribe; cf. פלנות, כמאגות, 2 Chr. 35³·¹², and cognate words in Aram. and Syr.† — חקקי [חרקי יב] Is. 10¹¹ 'decrees, edicts'; the form is scarcely to be derived from הק (Ol., p. 628; Ges.²⁵, p. 261), but from a parallel form *hēq*; cf. יב cstr. pl. חרבי Jer. 6⁴. But no meaning that can legitimately be given to חק is suitable here. ‡ The true reading is preserved in the misplaced repetition of this line, v.¹⁶ᵇ; חקרי לב; see there. — **16.** [כין הבישפתים] Gen. 49¹⁴ cf. אכ הבכנון בין שפהים Ps. 68¹⁴. The ancient versions for the most part render *between the territories, boundaries*,§ or *between the ranks* of the two armies (Σ); ‖ 𝔊ᴮᵁᴺ in Jud. ἀνὰ μέσον τῆς διγομίας, cf. Gr. Venet. Gen. 49¹⁴ ἀνὰ τὰ ἡμιφόρτια; so Ki. on Gen. *l.c.* and *Lex.* s.v.; Schm. The interpretation *enclosure* is found in Abulw. *Lex.* s.v., Ki. on Jud. 5¹⁶ (*sheep-pens*), Abarb., Pagninus, Ludolf (*Lex. Aethiop.*, 1661, p. 66; 1699, p. 76), Teller, and NWSchroeder, and is adopted by most modern commentators.¶ The etymological arguments by which this explanation is supported may be seen in Ges. *Thes.* p. 1471 f. (Roed.); they are, as Stud. justly remarks, far-fetched and very dubious. We should perhaps rather compare אֲשָׁפ̇ת (also MH.), שפ 2 K. 4³⁸ Ez. 24³, and Ar. ‏ثفى‎, &c. (Schultens); the stones on which the pot is supported over the fire, fireplace.** — [שרקות עדריב] cf. Is. 5²⁶ 7¹⁸ Zech. 10⁸ (‖ הבץ); the verb is not used in the O.T. or MH. of playing on a

---

* JDMich., *Supplementa*, p. 2013 (Irrigation ditches); Schnur.

. † Cf. 𝕷 *divisio contra se Ruben*. Of divided mind, perfidy, Ra.; aloof on the other side of Jordan, Ki.; &c.

‡ The contrast between great resolves at first and great vacillation afterwards (Schnur., Stud., Ew., Be.) does not lie in the words, and if intended must have been in some way indicated.   § So Stud.

‖ So Ra., Ba.; Reuben tried to be neutral in the struggle.

¶ *Canales unde pecora bibunt* (cf. Arab. *safita*; JDMich., Schnur.) is phonetically impossible.   ** Cf. Lette, and W. R. Smith, *Religion of Semites*, p. 357.

pipe. — לב [חִקְרֵי לב is obj. gen. (cf. Jer. 17[10] Prov. 25[3] &c.), and the phrase can hardly mean self-questionings, hesitating between *pro* and *contra*.* Jewish interpreters understand the words of the questionings which the absence of Reuben causes among the other Israelites. — 17. וירן לבה ינור אניות [נור c. c. acc. Is. 33[14] Ps. 5[6] 120[6]; not, *why does he fear the ships* (Schm., JDMich.; recently, Niebuhr). Bu. (*Richt. u. Sam.*, p. 16 n.) conj. ונאהיו; cf. Cooke. — ולחוף ימים] the plur. Gen. 49[18] Dt. 33[19] (of Zebulun) &c. — [סּפרציו only here; the suff. prob. refers to חוף. Cf. Arab. فُرْضَة, place where boats or ships are drawn up, or where they lie to unload. The translation *bays, harbours*, is scarcely warranted.

19-22. The battle; rout of the Canaanites. — *The kings came, they fought*] observe the effect of the asyndeton. — *The kings of Canaan*] united against Israel under the lead of Sisera. — *At Taanach, on the waters of Megiddo*] on Taanach and Megiddo see on 1[27] (p. 44 ff.).† The waters of Megiddo are the Kishon and its branches in the neighbourhood of that city. The field of battle was therefore on the southern side of the Great Plain, not, as in ch. 4, at the foot of Mt. Tabor at the head of its northern arm. Taanach is separated from Tabor by the greatest breadth of the plain, about fifteen miles. — *They made no gain of money*] it was a most unprofitable campaign for them ; a sarcastic meiosis. The gains of war were in the ancient world one of the principal causes of war ; cf. Ex. 15[9]. — **20.** *From heaven fought the stars*] this division ‡ preserves the rhythmical balance of the distich, which is needlessly destroyed by the massoretic punctuation. The words are a poetical description of the intervention of Yahweh to discomfit the enemy and give victory to Israel ; the powers of heaven themselves were arrayed against Sisera § and the victory was not won by the prowess of Israel alone. ‖ It is not necessary to suppose that the poet represented the stars as animated beings, the host of Yahweh,¶ which in some unseen way

---

* Schultens, *Animadvers.*, p. 100, notes that in Arabic other verbs of inquiring, investigating, are tropically used of altercation.

† On Megiddo see also G. A. Smith, *Hist. Geography*, p. 386 ff., and Conder, *Crit. Review of Theol. and Phil. Lit.*, iv. 1894. p. 290 f. The attempt to find the name Megiddo in Nahr Muqatta' (Smith) ought to be given up once for all.

‡ Procop., Cler., Trendelenburg, Köhl[2]., Herd., Mei., Bi., Briggs, A. Müller, al.

§ Procop., Ew., Be., Ba., al.   ‖ RLbG.

¶ Hollm.; cf. Ges., *Jesaia*, ii. p. 329.

gave aid to Israel ;* or that the figurative language is to be interpreted of a furious storm which threw the Canaanites into confusion.† See on v.²¹. — *From their paths they fought with Sisera*] lit. *highways;* their established and unchanging track through the sky. The preposition is not to be explained, *leaving* their paths, ‡ to descend and take part in the battle, but *manentes in ordine et cursu suo adversus Sisaram pugnaverunt* (₤) ; we should avoid the ambiguity by translating, *in* their paths. — **21.** *The stream of Kishon swept them away*] not merely the bodies of the slain,§ but the living. The Kishon is not in this part of its course a permanent stream, much less at ordinary times a dangerous torrent.‖ The battle must have been fought in the winter or spring, more probably the latter ; and it is possible that a heavy spring shower suddenly swelled the stream, though it is not necessary to infer this from either v.²⁰ or v.²¹.¶ — The next words are obscure ; one of the Greek translations** and the Targum interpret, stream of the ancients, stream where great deeds were done in ancient times ; †† but even if this presented no formal difficulties, it is a strange title to give to the river ; ancient mountains (Dt. 33¹⁵) is not parallel. Another interpretation, suggested by Abulwalid is, stream of encounters, ‡‡ where the two armies met ; or stream of champions. §§ The former lacks analogy in Hebrew ; the latter is a distinctively Arabic turn of the word. — The next line

---

* Stud. Many older commentators thought that the angels were meant; so Ephrem, Schm., Cler., al. mu.

† Fl. Jos., *antt.* v. 5, 4 § 205 f., gives a highly embellished description of this storm ; see also Schnur., Hollm., Ke., Reuss. Cf. the Midrash, *Pesachim*, 118ᵇ. Cass. thinks of a night attack.   ‡ Ew., Be., al.   § ₤.

‖ On the Kishon, and the hydrography of the Great Plain in general, see Rob., *BR²*. ii. p. 363 ff.; *SWP. Memoirs*, i. p. 265-267 ; ii. p. 39. See also Shaw, *Travels*, 1757, p. 274 f.; and Ba., *ad loc.*

¶ It is said that in the battle of Mt. Tabor, Apr. 16, 1799, a number of Arabs were drowned in the stream coming from Debūriyeh, which then inundated a part of the plain (Burckhardt, *Syria*, p. 339). Napoleon himself speaks only of the drowning of great numbers in the Jordan, which the rains had swollen making the ford dangerous (Bertrand, *Campagnes d'Égypte et de Syrie*, ii. p. 88).

** ϬBGN. The other recensions of Θ, with ₤₷, take the word as a proper noun ; so Cler.

†† Or, *ancient stream*, Ba.; cf. RLbG., Abarb.

‡‡ Trem.-Jun., Piscat., Lette (alt.), Schnur., Köhl., Hollm., Briggs, al.

§§ Brave stream, Ew.; der alte Siegesbach, Reuss.

is quite unintelligible ; *conculca anima mea robustos,*[*] or, *concul-cabit fortiter,* is simple bathos, and, aside from that, most inappropriate as the conclusion of v.[20. 21], which tell how heaven and earth conspired to destroy Sisera. Probably what originally stood here formed the end (predicate) of the second stichos of v.[21], the repetition of the words *stream of Kishon* being a gloss to the subject.[†] The line would in that case correspond in sense to the preceding. — 22. The verse describes, not the charge of the Canaanite chariot corps, but its precipitate flight. We hear in the Hebrew words the wild rush of the frantic steeds. — *Then the horses' hoofs pounded*] sc. the earth ; [‡] but see critical note. — *With the gallop galloping of his steeds*] cf. the description of the charge in Nah. 3[2f.] : "The swish of the whip, and the thunder of wheels, horses galloping, chariots bounding, horsemen mounting, a flash of swords, a gleam of lances," &c.

19. בצע כסף] many interpreters render, *a piece, bit, of silver* (Tanch., Schnur., Köhl., Hollm., Ew., Be., Reuss, al.); but there is no reason to prefer this supposed etymological explanation to the sense which alone is supported by Hebrew usage. — 20. כן שמים נלחמו] the erroneous division of the lines in 𝔐 has led some commentators to construe נלחמו impersonally (Lth., Schnur.), or to supply אלהים as subject (Schm.). — ממסלותם] on the form of the suff. see Bö. § 887; cf. Is. 59[7]. — עם סיסרא קם] נלחם עם 1 S. 13[5] 17[23] 1 K. 12[21] and freq. — 21. נרף] נרף MH. 'shovel, scoop, scrape' up, or out (Levy, *NHWb.* i. p. 364); in 𝔖 equivalent of Heb. יבב (*e.g.* Is. 8[6]); cf. Arab. *ǵarafa*, used of a torrent; *ǵuruf* or *ǵurf*, a bluff scooped out and undermined by a torrent; *ǵuráf*, a torrent that sweeps everything away, &c. (Lette, Hollm.). — נחל קדומים] 𝔊[BGN] χειμάρρους ἀρχαίων, those who were in old times, predecessors. § Some modern scholars regard it as an abstract noun denoting 'antiquity,' connected with קדם as נזורים with נזר, זקונים with זקן, קדומים with קדם, &c. (see Dietrich, *Abhandl. zur hebr. Gram.*, p. 35 f. ; Barth, *Nominalbildung*, p. 85); so Ba. If we were to go to the Arabic dictionary for the word, it would be the simplest thing to connect it with قَلدوم (*T.A.* ix. p. 19 end), one who is always in the front of the fray, a bold, daring man; comparing for the form, Lagarde, *Bildung der Nomina*, p. 59 f. The words נחל קישון at the end of the line are omitted by Bi. as "repetitio prorsus inutilis." — תדרכי] cannot legitimately be turned into a past tense (Ki., RLbG.,

---

[*] 𝔏, Ra., JDMich., Stud., Ba.

[†] An alternative hypothesis is that a line has been lost ; see A. Müller.

[‡] Schnur., Hollm., Reuss, al.

[§] For other variations see my edition of the Hebrew text.

Schnur., Köhl., Hollm, al.); it is now generally rendered as a jussive (Stud.), but the second pers. of the jussive is rare, except after אל, and no reason is apparent why the imperative should not have been used here as usual. — עז] is construed by many, especially older scholars, as direct object (*robur* metonymy for *robustos*); by others as accus. of manner (Herd., Ew., Hitz., Be., Cass., Reuss, al.). In accordance with the suggestion made above (p. 160), we might conjecture something like עז נפשׁי דרך הרומים נחל (trample under foot, cf. Is. 63³); but we can have no confidence in any such restoration. — **22.** אז הלמו וג׳] the vb. v.²⁶ Is. 16⁸ Ps. 74⁶ &c., 'give a heavy blow, pound.' The construction generally adopted by modern interpreters labours under two difficulties; the suppression of the object (the earth), and the preposition מן in the next line. The old versions all took the verb as passive, or at least neuter, as do also Ki., RLbG., Abulw., Tanch., Schm., Cler.; and it must be admitted that the construction is much simplified by the rendering, *then the heels of the horses were battered by the gallop galloping of his steeds.* It would then be preferable to pronounce הֻלְמוּ (Pual). — כדהרות דהרות אבּיריו] the repetition probably imitative of the sound of galloping hoofs, as well as intensive in sense; cf. the exx. in Ew. § 313 *a*.. Observe the suspended *stat. constr.* in the first word. The root only Nah. 3² סוס דֹהֵר; not in MH. Etymological connexion with דור (JDMich., *Supplem.*; Ges. *Thes.*, al.) is very improbable; more likely the word is onomatopoetic. — אבּיריו] *his steeds;* Jer. 8¹⁶ 47⁸ 50¹¹. The suff. refers loosely to the enemy. Others translate, *under the wild driving of their mighty men* (Hollm., Stud., Be., Ba., Reuss, al.); but this gives a less perfect parallelism and assumes that דהר could be used not only of the horse, as in Nah., but of the charioteer. The only reason for this somewhat forced interpretation vanishes if we make הלמו passive.

23-31. Death of Sisera. — The third division of the Ode consists of two parts ; the flight and death of Sisera (v.²³⁻²⁷), and the scene in his palace, where his mother and her women await his return (v.²⁸⁻³⁰). — **23.** The curse is obviously a foil to the following blessing (v.²⁴) ; the conduct of the people of Meroz is contrasted with that of Jael. From this fact, as well as from the position of the verse, we may probably infer that the enemy in his flight passed this Israelite village, whose inhabitants, instead of cutting him off, like cowards allowed him to escape.* — *Curse Meroz*] the place is unknown, and we have no clue to its situation. Assuming that it must have been a town of considerable note, some scholars have surmised that the name Meroz is miswritten, by accident or design, for Merom (Jos. 11⁵),† or Meron (Jos. 12²⁰

---

* Hollm., Stud., Ew., Don., Be., Ke., Ba., Reuss, Müller, al.
† Pagninus, Cler., Fr. Bö., Fürst.

M

cf. 11[1] ⑤),* or Meroth (Fl. Jos., *b.j.* ii. 20, 6) ;† but the premise is insecure, and the places suggested are all too far from the field of battle. It is more probable that Meroz was a mere hamlet which lay in the line of Sisera's flight. The various identifications that have been proposed by modern travellers may safely be dismissed.‡ — *The Messenger of Yahweh*] not the human messenger who bears the word of Yahweh, his prophet, § but God himself as he reveals himself to men, cf. on 2[1] 6[11]; we should think here more naturally of the Yahweh who goes before his people into battle (4[14] cf. 5[4f.]), and with the use of *Messenger* compare Ex. 23[20. 23] and Jos. 5[13-15].‖ But it must be conceded that the phrase has here some difficulty. — *Because they came not to the help of Yahweh*] the position of the verse, in the midst of the description of the Canaanites' wild flight, shows that the words refer, not like v.[16b-17] to their failure to join the rising of the tribes, but to their failure to help destroy the vanquished foe ; cf. 7[24] 8[5-9. 16-17]. — *To the help of Yahweh as brave men*] cf. v.[13b] Ps. 55[19] &c. Or, *among the brave ;*¶ not, *against the valiant foe.*** — **24.** In contrast with the cowardice or perfidy of the men of Meroz, the fearless devotion of Jael appears doubly glorious. — *Blessed above women shall Jael be*] the Hebrew superlative ; the most blessed of them all. — *Above Bedawin women shall she be blessed*] lit. *women in the tent, tenting women ;* cf. 8[11] Gen. 4[20] Jer. 35[7], Arabic *'ahlu-lwabar,* the people of the hair-cloth tents, Bedawin.†† The words, *the wife of Heber the Kenite,* are a gloss derived from 4[17], which entirely destroys the balance of the verse.‡‡ — **25.** The poet sets us before the door of Jael's tent, where Sisera has paused a moment in his flight to beg a drink of water. —*Water he asked, milk she gave*] the pronouns are very effective ; no need to name the actors in this tragedy. — *In a bowl fit for lords she handed him sour milk*] a large milk bowl ; cf. 6[38]. The milk is artificially soured by being shaken for a few moments

---

* Kruse, Ew., Don., Vernes.   † Justi, Krochmal, Boettger.

‡ See Ba., p. 452.

§ Deborah (4[4]) Köhl., Cass.; Barak ⑤ (but the word is apparently a gloss), Ra.

‖ Stud.; cf. Ke.   ¶ So most.

** Justi, Stud., Cass., Niebuhr.   †† Schnur., Stud., al.

‡‡ Bi., A. Müller, Bu., Oettli. Professed metricians like Ley may find it sufficient to call the unhappy verse a "decameter (catalectic?)"!

in the skin kept for the purpose, in which the portion adhering to the inner surface of the skin from former occasions serves as the ferment to sour the new milk. It is a most grateful and refreshing drink, the best the Bedawin have to give.* —26. As he was hastily draining the bowl, Jael seized some heavy object that lay close at hand and felled him to the earth with a blow. — *She reaches her hand to the pin*] the word ordinarily means a pin or peg, frequently, as in 4^{21}, a tent pin; or an implement shaped like a peg (Dt. 23^{13} Jud. 16^{14}). — The words in the next line which name or describe the weapon are very obscure. They are generally translated, *workmen's hammer*,† comparing 4^{21}; but it is extremely doubtful whether the Hebrew will bear this sense, and the expression is certainly a strange one. The following verbs make it clear that it was a heavy, blunt implement which crushed Sisera's skull; a mallet or hammer would be entirely suitable in the context, but no light is thrown on the difficult words. It is a question of more importance, whether in the two lines two different weapons are meant, a pin and a mallet (?), as in 4^{21}; or whether, as in the poetical parallelism is intrinsically not less probable, one weapon under two names or descriptive epithets. In answering this question we cannot be governed by the prose story (4^{21}), which is later than the Ode, and may have followed a different tradition or even have originated in a misunderstanding of 5^{26}.‡ The verbs in v.^{26} speak of pounding, smashing, rather than piercing; and v.^{27} seems to be decisive. It describes the collapse of a man who, standing, receives a mortal blow on the head; not the writhing death agony of one who is pinned to the ground; see comm. there. Wellhausen thinks that the *pin* is the handle of the mallet; A. Müller and others doubt this. The uncertainty as to the precise nature of the implement renders it doubtful what is meant by the *pin;* but the main point is not affected by this doubt. Jael used one weapon, not two. § — *And strikes Sisera a blow, destroys his head*] puts it out of existence. The second verb not elsewhere in O.T. — *Smashes and*

---

* Doughty, *Arabia Deserta*, i. p. 263, cf. ii. 304; so Schnur., al. The opinion that the milk was intoxicating, see above, p. 125.

† Ki.; smiths' hammer, Ew., al. after ₤; see crit. note.

‡ See above, p. 110. § See against this view, Be. and Reuss.

demolishes his temple] lit. *makes it vanish*. The two lines are symmetrical ; the first verb in each describes the act, the second the result. In view of this symmetry we might be tempted to conjecture that the name Sisera is a later addition ; *she smote, destroyed his head*, &c. — **27.** *At her very feet he sank down, fell, lay still*] observe the effect of the asyndeton in the swift succession of verbs. The interpreters who, in harmony with 4[27], assume that Sisera was lying asleep, are compelled to do great violence to these words. Bachmann candidly says that in accordance with the usage of the three verbs elsewhere, singly or in conjunction, they would be understood as they are translated above, he went down on his knees, fell prostrate, and lay there dead ; [*] but he feels constrained, in defiance of usage, to render instead, he writhed, fell (*i.e.* died), lay there dead.[†]   Others, to explain his fall, imagine that Sisera was lying on a raised bed ! [‡] — The words, *at her very feet he sank down, fell*, are accidentally repeated. [§] — *On the spot where he sank down, there he fell, killed*] lit. *a victim of violence*.

23. אורו כרוז] the 2 pl. is addressed to the people. For Meroz 𝕲 ΑΜΟ aL Μαζωρ; otherwise the tradition of the name is constant. — ארור ארו] the inf. abs. gives a strong emphasis, curse with all your might. ארר means, not 'revile, utter curses,' but 'blast with an efficacious curse.' Many have inferred that the indignant Israelites destroyed the town (Be., Cass., Reuss; cf. 𝕿). — לעזרת יהוה בגבורים] it is perhaps better to pronounce בגבורים, in the character, quality, of heroes; cf. 11[16], Ges.[26] p. 366. — **24.** תברך כנשים] opp. of ארר Gen. 12[3] &c., is also not a benevolent wish, but an effective invocation. The imperf. is stronger than the usual ptcp. ברוכה.   As the verb with its pers. subj. is necessarily definite, כ has not merely comparative force (more blessed than other women), but superlative (the most blessed). — **25.** בספל אדירים] ספל 𝕲ΒΝ, not infrequent in MH., a bowl or basin, here probably of wood.[‖] Beside MH., the word סיפלא is found in Palestinian Aramaic, both Jewish (𝕿 Nu. 15[7]) and Christian (*Evang. Hierosol.*, John 13[5] = κυτηρ); in Assyr. *saplu* (Schrader, *KAT*[2] p. 208[18]). On Arab. *sifl* see Fleischer, *Kleinere Schriften*, ii. p. 556 f.; Fränkel, *Aram. Lehnwörter im Arab.*, p. 67. M. Vernes, "*céphel*, coupe, appartient au chaldéen et au syriaque," makes the reader rub his eyes. אדירים (v.[18] Nah. 3[19] Jer. 14[3] &c.), 'mighty men.' With the notion of extraordinary strength that of extraordinary stature is naturally

---

[*] See also Stud.   [†] Similarly many others ; see crit. note.
[‡] Hollm., Rosenm., al.; against this very absurd theory see Stud.
[§] Reuss, A. Müller, Bu.   [‖] See Burckhardt, *Bedouins and Wahábys*, i. p. 46.

connected, as *e.g.* in the case of Saul; and as a bowl for giants would be of corresponding proportions, we should probably be not far from the mind of the author if we rendered, *in a huge bowl;* cf. אל הררי, אל ארוי, &c. The genitive is, however, not a mere circumscription of the adjective.—[חמאה] parallel to חלב Dt. 32¹⁴ Is. 7²². It is not butter (versions and many), nor cream (Stud., Ba., Be., Cass., al. mu.), neither of which is in accordance with the usage of the word or the habits of Bedawin, but soured milk, the meat and drink of the nomads (Schnur.). See Burckhardt, *Bedouins and Wahâbys,* i. p. 239 f.; Doughty, *Arabia Deserta,* i. p. 263, 325, 382.—**26.** ידה ליתר [השליחנה] ידה is parallel to ימינה, as in Is. 48¹³ Ps. 21⁹ 26¹⁰ &c. (Ba., We.); not in distinction from it, her *left* hand (𝕲𝕷, J. Kimchi, RLbG., Cler., Köhl., Hollm., Be., Ke., Oettli, al. mu.). השלחנה is pointed as 3 pl. fem.* How the punctuators construed this it is difficult to imagine; fortunately it is also unnecessary. Most recent grammarians pronounce as 3 s. f. with suff. תשלחנה (De Dieu, Cler., Schnur., Be., Ol., Sta., Ges.²⁵, Kö., Bi., al.), taking ידה as a *casus pendens; her hand — to the pin she reaches it.* The versions show no trace of this ending or suff. —[להלמות עמלים] the ancient translators found these words perplexing: 𝕲ᴬᴹᴼ s (cf.ᴸ) exhibit εἰς ἀποτομὰς κατακόπων, apparently meaning, "for the decapitation of exhausted men"; cf. 𝕿 למיתבר רשיעין ואנסין; 𝕲ᴾⱽ ᵃˡ. (O ᵃˡ. as doublet) l τοῦ εἰς τέλος (לכליב) ἀχρειῶσαι. The commonly received translation is that of Aquila, εἰς σφῦραν κοπιώντων (𝕲ᴮᵁᴺ), 𝕷 ad *fabrorum malleos,* 𝕾 𝕳 *to the carpenter's hammer;* that the weapon must be a hammer or mallet seemed certain from 4²¹ (הַמַּקֶּבֶת). But although a derivative of הלם might, for all we know, be the name of a mallet, the form הלמות does not tolerate such an explanation. The afformative *ût* is, to say the least, very rare in Old Hebrew, and is specifically the ending of secondary abstract nouns,† much like *tas* in Latin, and never makes *nomina instrumenti.* Probably the punctuation intends a secondary development of the infinitive after the Aramaic fashion, as 𝕿𝕲ᴾⱽ ᵃˡ. understand it; ‡ but this is quite impossible. We do not gain much by pronouncing הלמות (𝕷), for, assuming that הלמה might mean 'mallet,' how many hammers are we to suppose that Jael used on her guest's head? Finally, עמלים does not mean *artisans* (smiths, carpenters), but men who are worn out, or wear themselves out, with toil and hardships; 'hammer of hard-working (or weary) men' § is a singular metonymy for a heavy hammer!—[ומחקה ראשו] the verb, only here in O.T., is freq. in MH. in the sense, 'scrape off, efface, erase'; in Arab. *maḥaqa* is 'destroy utterly,' so that no trace of the thing remains, 'annihilate.' Most interpreters, assuming that the word must be synonymous with the preceding הלמה, translate, *smote, shattered,* or the like, frequently supporting the rendering by hazardous etymologies; but the context does not require us to depart from the sense

---

· * Other explanations may be found in the older grammars; cf. Ges. *Lgb.,* p. 800; Bö. § 929 δ. The reading of 𝕸 is defended by Hollm., Stud., Ba.

† See Barth, *Nominalbildung,* p. 413 f.　　　‡ So Ra.; עמלים means Sisera.

§ Cf. Ki., RLbG., JDMich., Herd., Stud., Ke., al.

which MH. and Arab. suggest and which the parallel clause confirms. — מחצה
וחלפה רקתו] it seems preferable, with many codd., to omit the conjunction
before the first verb. מחץ 'smash, shatter' by a heavy blow, as with a club or
mace, Ps. 110⁶ 68²² (the head) Dt. 33¹¹ (loins) Ps. 18³⁹. The second verb,
חלמה, is usually translated *pierced, transfixed*, sc. with the pin (Versions, Ra.,
Ki., Cler., Schm., Hollm., Ew., and almost all recent scholars). Job 20²⁴ is
alleged in support of this rendering; but the cases are not at all parallel. The
image of the swift arrow pursuing and overtaking the fleeing man is easily
connected with the ordinary usage of חלף; that the shaft pierced his vitals is
implied by the following rather than said in חלכרו־. In Jud. 5²⁶ there is no
such connexion; it is impossible to associate making a hole in a man's head
with any sense in which we know the verb חלף in O.T. or the cognate
languages. Here again the meaning *transfix* has been invented to suit the
situation described in 4²¹. If 5²⁶ had been interpreted for itself, no one
would ever have thought of such a rendering. I take חלפה to correspond to
מחצה in the foregoing line, 'cause to pass away, vanish'; cf. the intrans. use
Is. 2¹⁶; trans. Is. 24⁵ (|| הסר, סכר).—27. בין רגליה] the preposition need not
be taken literally; * it is more emphatic than אל or על. Schnur. and others
compare the Arab. idiom, بين يديه, in his presence, &c.; but it may be
doubted whether the expressions are really parallel.—כרע נפל שכב] the first
two verbs together Ps. 20⁹ cf. Is. 10⁴; כרע and שכב Nu. 24⁹. כרע is prop. 'bend
the knees,' kneel, or crouch, squat on the heels; cf. Jud. 7⁵·⁶ 1 S. 4¹⁹ 2 K. 1¹³
&c.; said of a mortally wounded man whose knees fail under him 2 K. 9²⁴.
That it could be used of the spasmodic drawing up the legs, as of a man who
while lying received a death wound,† is not inconceivable; it is the sequence
נפל כרע which makes this impossible. נפל is indeed not infrequently used (esp.
in the ptcp.) of one who is prostrate on the ground (3²⁵ 19²⁷ 1 S. 31⁸ &c.),
but only of one who has fallen (A. Müller).—שדוד] a victim of violence.
The vb. of persons Jer. 5⁶ Ps. 17⁹, cf. Pual (of nations) Jer. 4¹³ &c.

28–30. In Sisera's palace.

28–30. In Sisera's palace. — With the vision of the king lying
dead at the feet of his slayer still before our eyes, the poet
transports us to Sisera's palace, where the queen-mother is
anxiously watching for her son's return. The presentiment of
evil which she herself stifles; the sanguine confidence of the
ladies of her court, who see in imagination the division of the
booty, an Israelite maiden or two for each man, and abundance

---

* Stud., Reuss, al., *e.g.* imagine that she held his head between her knees while
she drove the pin into his temple; cf. Donaldson. The Haggada (*Jebam.*, 103ᵃ)
gives the words an obscene sense.

† Cler., Ba., al. mu.; Schm., incurvavit se, quasi se de terra erecturus; sed
erectus aliquousque, rursus concidit et jacuit. Similarly Schnur., Cass., Oettli, al.

of the richly dyed and embroidered stuffs which they themselves
prize so highly — all this is depicted with inimitable skill. Their
light-hearted anticipations form a striking contrast to the ill-sup-
pressed forebodings of the mother's heart, and the whole scene pro-
duces on the reader, who knows the ghastly reality, an incomparable
effect. Lowth * justly says that there is nothing in literature more
perfect in its kind than these verses. It is only modern senti-
mentality that can discover in this passage the note of a woman's
pity for the mother of the fallen king. It is the pitilessness of
triumph ; we need not say, the exultation of gratified revenge.†
— **28.** *Through the window she peered*] the effect of the transition is heightened by this postponement of the explicit subject
to the second clause ; the reader must himself feel who this
anxious woman is (cf. v.²⁰). The verb rendered *peer* is used of
one who, leaning forward, looks down on something below him ;
cf. 2 S. 6¹⁶ Nu. 23²⁸ &c. The meaning of the next verb (EV.
cried) ‡ is doubtful ; the root is not found elsewhere in the O.T.
In Aramaic it means, sound the trumpet, raise a clamour, in war
or jubilee ; in one instance in MH. it seems to be used of the
clamorous cry of the mourning women ; § but neither of these
senses is appropriate here, ‖ and for the sake of the parallelism,
especially in these interlocked lines, we desiderate a synonym of
the preceding *peer*, as 𝔊ᴬᵃˡ. 𝔗 render ; see crit. note. — *Through
the lattice-window*] the translation is conventional ; we know the
word, which occurs here and in Prov. 7⁶, only as a synonym for
window. — *Why does his chariot corps fail to come ? Why tarry
the hoof-beats of his chariots ?*] the first sign of the return of the
warriors would be the distant sound of horses feet ; cf. v.²². —
29. *The sagest of her princesses answer*] there is a fine irony in
the allusion to the wisdom of these ladies, whose prognostications
were so wide of the truth. The next line is very variously interpreted. Many recent commentators make it parenthetic, *but*

---

* *De sacra poesi Hebraeorum*, p. 118-120 ; cf. also Herder, *Briefe, das Studium
der Theologie betreffend*, 7ter Brief. † See Herder.

‡ Cler. (*exclamavit*), Hollm., Be., Ke., Reuss, al.; others interpret more definitely; *ululavit* (𝕃), *heulet* (Lth.), similarly RLbG., Ew., al. mu.

§ If the text be sound ; see crit. note.

‖ In the first it is taken by Schultens, Lette, al. (joyous anticipation of victory).

she (*sc.* the mother) *kept repeating her words to herself,*[*] constantly reverting to her foreboding questionings. I prefer, with older scholars, to translate, *Yea, she herself replies to herself;*[†] she tries to silence her presentiment by the same kind of answer which her sage companions give her. — **30.** *No doubt they are finding, dividing booty*] lit. *are they not;* the tenses depict the scene. Cf. Is. 9[3]. — *A wench or a couple of them for each man*] a coarse word seems to be intentionally employed. Women captives were the slaves of the captors; cf. Dt. 21[10-14]. In the remainder of the verse some awkward repetitions mar both the rhythm and the sense. It is clear only that richly dyed and embroidered stuffs are meant, in the distribution of which the women of Sisera's harem had a keen interest.[‡] Reuss, by omitting the intrusive words, restores the verses:[§] *Booty of dyed stuffs for Sisera; A piece of embroidered work or two for the neck of the booty.*[|] The last words cannot be right; it is absurd to imagine that the victors used these rich stuffs to deck out for the triumphal procession the beasts they had taken;[¶] and if the meaning were that they adorned with them the shoulders of their fair captives,[**] these would hardly be called simply *the booty,* nor would this word be used in one line for the dyed stuffs themselves, and in the next for the prisoners who are arrayed in them.[††] The parallelism would lead us to expect here a designation of the person or persons for whom these costly prizes were destined, corresponding to the words, *for Sisera,* in the first half of the verse. Ewald very ingeniously conjectured, *for the neck of the queen,*[‡‡] changing but one letter of the text. Reuss, supposing the queen mother to be speaking, emends, *for my shoulders.* In the general disorder of the text in this verse, it is impossible to

---

* Lth., Ew., Be., Ke., Oettli.

† Ra., Cler., Schm., JDMich., Köhl., Stud., Cass. Others, she replied to the one of the ladies who spoke (Hollm.); or took back her words of doubt (Schnur., Justi).

‡ Lowth quotes *Aen.* xi. 782, Femineo praedae et spoliorum ardebat amore.

§ So A. Müller. Bickell reconstructs differently; see crit. note.

| Reuss, *for my neck;* see below.

¶ JHMich., Schnur., Rosenm., al.; cf. 1 S. 15[19].

** Schm. (alt.), Justi, Röd., Ba., Cass., Ke.

†† Embroidered ornaments for the neck of the dyed garments; Schm., Cler.

‡‡ Be., Oettli, Renan, Kautzsch.

feel much confidence in any restoration. — **31.** With consummate
art the poet breaks off, leaving to the imagination of the reader,
who knows all, the terrible revelation of the truth. — *So shall
perish all thine enemies, Yahweh*] cf. Ps. 68²·³ 92⁹. The one
word *so* brings it all before our eyes again ; how proudly they
marched out under the admiring eyes of their ladies ; how gaily
they rode into the fray ; the repulse, the defeat, the panic ; the
wild flight — *sauve qui peut;* the king's death by a woman's
hand, disgrace worse than death ; the anguish and dismay of those
who loved him. *So* perish all thine enemies ! — *But his friends* •
shall be as when the sun rises in his might] splendid, invincible ;
vanquishing, annihilating the darkness of the night, the mists of
dawn. No more fitting or impressive figure could be conceived ;
cf. Ps. 19ˢ. — *And the land enjoyed security for forty years*] the
chronological note of the editor of the book ; cf. 3¹¹.

28. [כער החלון] Gen. 26⁸ Jos. 2¹⁵ 1 S. 19¹² Joel 2⁹. — [ותיבב] יבב is in all the
Targums the usual equivalent of Heb. הריע, the noun יבבא of הרועה; † but in
the places where הריע means 'cry out in terror or anguish' (Is. 15⁴ Mi. 4⁹) it is
not rendered by יבב, nor is such a sense demonstrable in Syriac. Under these
circumstances it is unsafe to base an interpretation on *Jerus. Jebamoth*, xv. 5
(fol. 15ᵈ; ed. Sitomir fol. 78ᵃ) קול הסוכנת ביבבתו בין הבתים; *Tos. Jebam.*,
xiv. 7 (ed. Zuckerm. p. 259₁₃), reads הזכרתו. 𝕲ᴬᴸ 𝖘 (sub aster.) ‡ have here
κατεμάνθανεν (elsewhere used for verbs of seeing, gazing), 𝕿 בריא § 'looked
attentively'; which might lead to the conjecture that they read ותבט. More
probably they were guided only by the context. Menahem and Ra. seek an
etymological connexion with בבה 'pupil of the eye.' The tense of ותיבב
conforms to the regular sequence of tenses in prose; but has no parallel in
the Ode (cf. Ex. 15), and makes a most prosaic impression. ‖ — [אשנב] we
know the word only as a synonym of חלון. The rendering *lattice* comes from
𝕲ᴬᴸᴹᴼ ᵃˡ. Θ ‖ 𝖘 διὰ τῆς δικτυωτῆς. The etymology which has done duty since
Lette (Roed. in Ges. *Thes.*, MV., al.), connecting the word with Arab.
šaniba ' it (the day) was cool,' is phonetically impossible.¶ Other interpreters
think of a narrow window, loop-hole in the wall; so 𝕲ᴮᴼᴺ ἐκτὸς τοῦ τοξικοῦ.

• 𝕃𝕾 *thy* friends.

† Not quite as constantly in the prophets proper as in other books.

‡ This reading has been displaced in many other codd. by a doublet. 𝕲ᴮᴼᴺ vac.

§ So edd. Venet.¹·³ and codd. Br. Mus.; בריא (Buxt., al.) is mispointed. Ki.
cites ואוריקו as the reading of 𝕰; the sense would be the same.

‖ Cf. Dr⁴. § 132 n.

¶ It is almost a pity these etymologists did not think of the modern Arabic
meaning of *šanab*, ' moustaches.'

—סרוּג [מרוּג סרוּג is stronger than לָ֫מָּה, 'why in the world'. בשׁשׁ cf. Ex. 32[1],
disappoint the expectation of his coming, fail to come (cf. note on 3[25]); here
parallel to אחר 'put off, delay'. — אֶחֱרוּ] on the form of the Pi. see Ges.[26] p. 170
n. 3; Kö. i. p. 397. — פְּעָמֵי מַרְכְּבוֹתָיו] Bi. makes the prosaic observation, *currus
non facit gressus*, and cancels פֹּעֲמֵי! — 29. [חַכְמוֹת שָׂרוֹתֶיהָ תַּעֲנֶנָּה] ● with the
superlative cf. Dt. 33[19] Is. 19[11] &c., Ges.[26] § 133, 3 n. 1. The verb is pronounced as 3 s. f. with suff. 3. s. f. But this discord of number is intolerable;
we should pronounce תַּעֲנֶינָה 3 pl. f., and suppose that the object pronoun was
omitted, being easily supplied from לה in the next line. An alternative would
be to pronounce the noun חָכְמוֹת,† *the wisdom of her princesses answers her.*
The abstract noun may be followed by the singular verb as in Prov. 9[1], and
we should be able to retain the suff. in תַּעֲנֶנָּה. On the whole, however, the
former construction is probably the safer one here. — [אַף הִיא תָּשִׁיב אֲמָרֶיהָ לָהּ]
הָשִׁיב אֲמָרִים 'answer', like הֵשִׁיב דָּבָר; cf. Prov. 22[21] לְהָשִׁיב אֲמָרִים לְשֹׁלְחֶךָ. The
suffix is unusual, but not against the logic of speech; ‡ on the contrary, it
seems altogether suitable to the emphasis on the reflexiveness of the action;
she returns her answer to herself. It is unnecessary, with Bi., to substitute for
the last pronoun לְנַפְשָׁהּ. This is the only interpretation of the words that
preserves the parallelism, which is rudely disturbed by making them a parenthetic circumstantial clause; and it is also much more like the poet to
make the anxious mother catch at the straw of hope that shall so cruelly
disappoint, rather than with too true foresight reject the reasonable answer
of her ladies. — 30. [הֲלֹא יִמְצְאוּ] the question carries the affirmation into the
mind of the hearer; cf. 4[8. 14] &c. Note the force of the tense, they are ever
finding fresh booty. — רַחַם רַחֲמָתַיִם cf. 15[16] Is. 17[6] Am. 1[3ff.] and similar collocations of consecutive numbers to indicate that the numeral is to be taken
loosely. Here it gives the effect of a certain lordly disregard, a wench or
two, what matter, more or less? רחם, only here in Heb., is used by Mesha of
Moab (l. 17) in recounting the captives he had taken from Israel. § It is
probable that this is a tropical use of the word רחם 'womb'; cf. the contemptuous *cunnus* for woman in Latin. ‖ — [לְרֹאשׁ גֶּבֶר] *per capita*. In this
sense גֻּלְגֹּלֶת is common in later Heb. (P and Chr.); גֶּבֶר (Mesha l. 16) is
rare in old Heb. prose except in the distributive phrase לִגְבָרִים (Jos. 7[14. 17. 18]
I S. 10[21] 𝕲); cf. Ex. 10[11] 12[37] (?) Dt. 22[6] &c. — שְׁלַל צְבָעִים] *booty of dyes,*
for dyed stuffs; cf. MH. בִּגְדֵי צְבוֹנִים *Jer. K'thub.*, vii. 7 (fol. 31[c], ed. Sitomir
fol. 41[a]). Bi. omits לְסִיסְרָא שְׁלַל צְבָעִים; Reuss and Müller om. שְׁלַל צְבָעִים and

---

● Norzi prefers תַּעֲנֶנָּה as the reading of old and correct codd.; so ed. Venet.
1547 al. The Massora (*Ochla we-Ochla*, No. 369) treats it as a plur.; cf. *Dikduke*
§ 55; Kö. i. p. 547, 559 f. As sg. it is rendered by 𝕷 *sapientior ceteris uxori-
bus;* cf. Ki., *each one.*

† The same change is rightly made by Hitz., De., al. in Prov. 14[1], cf. 9[1].

‡ Ba.

§ Of the versions only 𝕷 has come near the true sense; the words are rightly
interpreted by Ra., Ki., Lth., Schm., Cler., al. ‖ Hor., *Sat.* i. 3,107.

רקם two words further on. — רִקְמָה] Ez. 16¹³ Ps. 45¹⁵ &c.; embroidery, in which patterns were worked with a needle in various colours.* The name, which apparently signifies 'variegated,' may also include stuffs woven in patterns of different colours.† How such things were prized is to be seen from 2 S. 1²⁴, where also spoils of war are perhaps meant. The dual רקמתים does not mean 'embroidered on both sides,' but 'a couple of pieces of embroidery,' precisely as in רחבתים above. — לצוארי שלל] Ew. conj. שֵׁגָל, *queen* (Ps. 45¹⁰ Neh. 2⁶). The pl. צואר is not conclusive against this (A. Müller); cf. Gen. 27¹⁶ 46²⁰ 45¹⁴ &c. W. Green suggested לצוארי שׁלָל, for the neck of him that takes the spoil, sc. Sisera; cf. S, RLbG., Buxt., Tremell., Hollm., al. Teller, Don., conj. לצוארי; Reuss, Briggs, al. לצוארי שלל, for my neck, as a spoil; E. Meier יצוארי שלל (De Sacy יצוארו), cf. 𝕲ᴬᴮ ᵃˡ.; 𝕷 *ad ornanda colla.* Bu. reconstructs שלל צבע צבעים לסיסרא שלל רקמה רקמתים לצוארי.—31. E. Meier regarded this verse as a later addition to the Ode, on account of its contents and because it has no place in the system of strophes, *i.e.* of Meier's strophes. Winter also (*ZATW.* ix. 1889, p. 223 ff.) strongly doubts its genuineness. To him the idea expressed in אהביו is a stumbling block. — Observe the paronomasia in אהביו and אויביך.

Translation of the Ode.‡

2. While   .   .   .   in Israel,
   While the people offer freely, bless ye Yahweh.

3. Hear, ye kings; give ear, ye rulers:
   I, to Yahweh I will sing,
   Will hymn to Yahweh, Israel's God.

4. Yahweh, when thou wentest forth from Seir,
   Marchedst from the region of Edom,
   The earth quaked, the heavens swayed (?);
   The clouds dripped water,

5. The mountains streamed before Yahweh,
   Before Yahweh, the God of Israel.

6. In the days of Shamgar ben Anath, caravans ceased,
   And wayfarers travelled by roundabout paths.

7. Hamlets (?) ceased in Israel,
      .   .   .   .   ceased,
   Till thou didst arise, Deborah,
   Till thou didst arise, a matron in Israel.

---

* *Joma*, 72ᵇ, sub fin.; Ki. *Comm.;* Schroeder, *de vestitu mulierum*, p. 221 f.; Braun, *de vestitu sacerdotum*, ed. za., p. 301 ff.

† Ki. *Lex.* s.v. Many scholars think that woven stuffs are exclusively meant; see Hartmann, *Hebräerin*, i. p. 401 ff.; iii. p. 138 ff.

‡ This translation is ancillary to the preceding interpretation, and is as literal as possible. No attempt has been made to produce a literary version of the poem, or to imitate its rhythm.

8.　.　　.　　.　　.　　.　　.　　.　　.　　.　　.
　　.　　.　　.　　.　　.　　.　　.　　.　　.　　.
　　Shield was not to be seen, nor spear,
　　Among forty thousand in Israel.
9.　My heart turns to the marshals (?) in Israel,
　　Those who freely offer among the people, bless ye Yahweh.
10.　.　　.　　.　　.　　.　　.　　.　　.　　.　　.
　　.　　.　　.　　.　　.　　.　　.　　.　　.　　.
11.　.　　.　　.　　.　　.　　.　　.　　.　　.　　.
　　.　　.　　.　　.　　.　　.　　.　　.　　.　　.

　　Then marched down to the gates the people of Yahweh.　　.

12.　Rouse thee, rouse thee, Deborah, strike up the song;
　　Up, Barak, and take thy captives, son of Abinoam.
13.　.　　.　　.　　.　　.　　.　　.　　.　　.　　.
　　The people of Yahweh marched down for him as heroes.
14.　.　　.　Ephraim　　.　　.　　.
　　.　　.　　.　Benjamin　　.　　.　　　　　.
　　From Machir marched down truncheon-bearers,
　　And from Zebulun those who lead with the muster-master's staff.
15.　And .　　.　　.　Issachar with Deborah;
　　And .　　.　　.　Barak　　.　　.　　.

　　.　　.　　.　　.　　.　　.　　.　　.　　.
　　Among the divisions of Reuben were great discussions.
16.　Why didst thou sit still among the dung-heaps,
　　Listening to the calling of the flocks?
17.　Gilead remained beyond the Jordan;
　　And Dan, why does he seek the protection of the ships?
　　Asher sat still on the shore of the Great Sea,
　　And remained by its landing-places.
18.　Zebulun is a tribe that recklessly exposed itself to death,
　　And Naphtali, on the heights of the open field.
19.　The kings came, they fought;
　　Then fought the kings of Canaan,
　　At Taanach, by the waters of Megiddo;
　　Gain of silver they did not make!
20.　From heaven fought the stars,
　　From their paths they fought with Sisera.
21.　The stream of Kishon swept them away,
　　The stream of　　.　　.　　.
22.　Then were battered the heels of the horses,
　　From the gallop galloping of his steeds.

23.　Curse ye Meroz, saith the Messenger of Yahweh,
　　Curse ye bitterly its inhabitants,

Because they came not to the help of Yahweh,
To the help of Yahweh, like brave men.

24. Blessed above all women shall Jael be,
Above all nomad women shall she be blessed.

25. Water he asked, milk she gave;
In a bowl for lords she brought him sour milk.

26. Her hand to the pin she reaches,
And her right hand to the   .   .
And hammers, destroys his head,
Smashes and demolishes his temple.

27. At her very feet he sank down, fell at full length, lay still;
On the spot where he sank down, there he fell, killed.

28. Through the window peered   .   .   .
The mother of Sisera through the lattice:
Why does his chariotry fail to come?
Why tarry the footfalls of his chariots?

29. The sagest of her princesses reply,
Yea, she answers her own question:

30. No doubt they are finding, dividing booty;
A wench or two for each man,
Booty of dyed stuffs for Sisera,
A piece of embroidery or two for the neck of .   .   .

31. So shall perish all thine enemies, Yahweh!
But his friends shall be as when the sun rises in his power.

VI.–VIII. Gideon delivers Israel from the Midianites. — The Israelites again offend Yahweh, who allows the Midianites to harry them for seven years. At every harvest time the Bedawin hordes come down upon them and strip the land bare (6^{1-6}). The cause of this punishment is explained by a prophet ($v.^{7-10}$). The Messenger of Yahweh appears to Gideon and summons him to free Israel from the incursions of Midian ($v.^{11-24}$). At the bidding of Yahweh, Gideon destroys the altar of the Baal of the place and cuts down and burns the sacred post (*asherah*) ; he is saved from the vengeance of his towns-folk by the shrewd speech of his father ($v.^{25-32}$). The Midianites again invade the land, and encamp in the Plain of Jezreel. Gideon raises his clansmen of Abiezer, also the rest of Manasseh, Asher, Zebulun, and Naphtali; he is assured by a miracle that Yahweh will save Israel by his hand ($v.^{33-40}$). At the command of Yahweh his force is reduced to ten thousand, and then, by a singular test, to three hundred men

(7^{1-8}). Encouraged by an ominous dream which he heard a Midianite telling to his tent-mate (v.$^{9-14}$), he furnishes his three hundred men with torches, earthen jars, and horns, and surrounds and alarms the camp of Midian, which breaks up in wild flight (v.$^{15-22}$). While he follows them up, the Ephraimites head them off in the valley of the Jordan and slay the two chiefs (v.$^{23-25}$). Having appeased the jealousy of the Ephraimites (8^{1-3}), he pursues the Midianites across the Jordan. The people of Succoth and Penuel refuse him food and are threatened with dire vengeance (v.$^{4-9}$). He surprises the foe where they thought themselves secure and captures the two kings (v.$^{10-12}$). Returning in triumph, he visits exemplary punishment on Succoth and Penuel (v.$^{13-17}$), and puts to death his prisoners to avenge his slain kinsmen (v.$^{18-21}$). He refuses the kingdom which his grateful countrymen offer him (v.^{22}), but takes the golden ornaments they have stripped from the slain and from their camels to make an idol (*ephod*), which he sets up at Ophrah (v.$^{24-27}$). The Midianites are quelled and dare not lift their heads again; the land is secure for forty years (v.^{28}). The story closes with a brief notice of Gideon's family (v.$^{29-32}$) and of the relapse of Israel after his death (v.$^{33-35}$), which forms the connexion with the story of Abimelech, ch. 9.

Studer (1835) called attention to the fact that $8^{4f.}$ is not the sequel of the foregoing narrative. In $7^{24f.}$ the Midianites are intercepted in their flight by the Ephraimites, and the two chiefs, Oreb and Zeeb, killed. When Gideon, who is in pursuit of them, comes up, the Ephraimites inveigh violently against him because they were not summoned at the beginning, and are only appeased by his flattering comparison of their achievement with his own: Is not the gleaning of Ephraim better than the vintage of Abiezer? God has given into your hands the two chiefs of Midian; what have I been able to do to compare with you? The quarrel itself, and especially Gideon's reply, show that the pursuit was over; vintage and gleaning were both complete. In 8^{4-21}, on the contrary, we find Gideon and his three hundred men following the retreating marauders across the Jordan, with such uncertain prospect of success that the townsmen of Succoth and Penuel scoffingly refuse to furnish the food he needs for his hungry men.

He pushes on, surprises the camp of the Bedawin, and makes prisoners the two kings of Midian, Zebah and Zalmunna. Nothing can be clearer than that 8^{4-21} is not from the same source as 8^{1-3} with its premises in the preceding narrative. Closer examination shows that ch. 6, 7 are not of one piece throughout; $6^{25ff.}$, e.g., is not the continuation of 6^{11-24}; the second sign, 6^{36-40}, is strange after the miracle 6^{21}; compare also 6^{34} with 6^{35} 7^{2-8}, and on the other hand 6^{34} with $7^{23f.}$ 8^{1}.* The question thus arises whether those parts of ch. 6^{1}-8^{3} which obviously do not belong to the principal narrative are additions made to the old story by the author of the Book of Judges or later editors; † or whether two stories have been united by a redactor. ‡ In the latter case we have further to inquire whether the antecedents of 8^{4-21} are to be found in either of these sources, or whether we have to recognize in $8^{4ff.}$ the end of a third story, whose beginning has been entirely supplanted. § Finally, it is to be asked whether any one, or all, of the sources of these chapters can be identified with the old books of Israelite history which are used in the composition of the Hexateuch. ‖ These questions are as yet far from a definitive solution; the attempt which is made below can claim only the character and value of a critical experiment.

On the critical problems of ch. 6-8, see Studer, p. 212-215; Wellhausen, *Comp.*, p. 223-228; *Prol*., p. 250 ff.; Bertheau, p. xxii. f., 129 ff.; Stade, *GVI.* i. p. 181-192; Böhme, *ZATW.* v. p. 251 ff.; Kuenen, *HCO*. i. p. 343 f., 346 ff.; Budde, *Richt. u. Sam.*, p. 107-125; Cornill, *Einl*., p. 95 f.; Kittel, *Stud. u. Krit.*, 1892, p. 55-60; *GdH.* i. 2. p. 71-74; Winckler, *Altorientalische Forschungen*, p. 42 ff. — In regard to the main narrative in 6^{1}-8^{3}, the differences among the critics named above are not very great. Wellhausen leaves to it 6^{1-21}. ¶ $3ff.$ $7^{1.9-23}$ 8^{1-3}, and the original account of the making of the ephod in $8^{22ff.}$. Stade defines it somewhat more precisely, assigning to it the basis of Rd's introduction in 6^{1-6}, $6^{11-24a.}$ $33f.$ $7^{1.9-25}$ 8^{1-3}.** Kitt.: $6^{2-6a.}$ $11-24.$ $33f.$ $36-40$ $7^{1.9-11.}$ $13-25$ $8^{1-3.}$ $4-27a$.†† The remainder of the chapters consists, according to all these critics, of additions by different hands and of different dates; 8^{4-21} is

---

* See We., *Comp.*, p. 223-226; Sta., *GVI.* i. p. 181 ff.

† We., Sta., Kue., Kitt.

‡ Be., Bu., Co.　　§ So all the critics cited.　　‖ Böhme, Bu., Co.

¶ Of course excepting the traces of the editor's hand in the introduction.

** 7^{23} is not all from one hand; v.^{25b} a harmonistic addition.

†† Except the last words of 6^{9} (the Amalekites and Bene Qedem); 7^{13-22} has been retouched.

from a second source, from which ch. 9 also is derived.[*] Bu., whose analysis is adopted by Cornill, finds in ch. 6^1–8^3 two sources united by a redactor; viz., J $6^{2b-6a.}$ $^{11-24}$ † $7^{1.}$ $^{9-11.}$ $^{13.*}$ $^{14.*}$ $^{15-22.*}$ $^{23-25}$ $8^{1-3.}$ ^{29}; E $6^{7-10.}$ $^{25-32.}$ $^{36-40}$. To the first editor (Rje) he ascribes extensive additions in 6^{2-6}, interpolations in $6^{11-x.}$, 6^{35} $7^{2-8.}$ ^{12}, the introduction of the horns in 7^{15-22}, perhaps the latter part of 8^{27}; to Rd the characteristic phrases in $6^{1.}$ ^{2a} 8^{28}, perhaps the end of 8^{27}. Ch. 8^{4-21} is the end of an independent story, which is not, however, an irreconcilably divergent account of the events narrated in 6^1–8^3, but relates to an entirely different occurrence. Bu. rightly declares against the exaggerated contrast drawn by previous critics between 8^{4-21} and 6^1–8^3, which makes the latter historically worthless. ‡ It is assumed by all these critics, beginning with Wellhausen, that the antecedents of the story 8^{4-21} cannot be found in 6^1–8^3. The postulates of the former are, it is said, of a wholly different kind. Instead of following a divine call to deliver Israel, Gideon has, like Barak (5^{12}), a personal wrong to avenge; the Midianites in a foray have killed his brothers ($8^{18f.}$). To avenge their blood he raises his kinsmen of Abiezer, pursues the Bedawin across the Jordan, overtakes and surprises them on the border of the desert, and makes them pay the penalty. The motive, the actors, the scene of the action, are different. But, on the other hand, the resemblances between the two stories are not less striking; the Abiezrites (6^{34}), the three hundred men (7^8), the two chiefs or kings of Midian whose names sound so suspiciously alike, are the real actors in both. The pursuit across the Jordan and surprise in their own desert does not exclude a previous night alarm and flight like that narrated in $7^{15ff.}$. § That Gideon had a wrong of his own to avenge, is not incompatible with the representation that he was called of God to deliver Israel from the scourge; the sharp severing of natural and religious motives is more in the manner of the modern critic than of the ancient story-teller. On the other hand, especially if 6^1–8^3 are regarded as composite (Bu., Co.), it is very inconvenient to have 8^{4-21} left over; such a remainder may not unfairly be deemed a failure of the solution. The attempt may therefore be made to discover the beginnings of the narrative 8^{4-21} in the preceding chapters. ‖ They are, of course, not to be found in that strand of the story which ends with 7^{24}–8^3, with which 8^{29} appears to connect immediately. The account of the night attack on the camp of Midian, 7^{15-22}, is composite; the horns are not introduced by the redactor (from Jericho; Bu.), but belong to a different version of the story.¶ In one account the panic is caused by the shattering of earthen jars, the sudden flashing out of hundreds of torches, the war-cry, For Yahweh and Gideon! The Midianites flee in

---

[*] On the latter point Kitt. expresses himself guardedly; cf. also Kue.
† After the removal of some editorial interpolations; see below.
‡ Cf. also Kitt., *GdH.* i. 2. p. 73 n.   § Cf. 8^5; Kue.
‖ Compare Winckler, who regards 6^1–8^3 as composite (JE); 8^{4-22} as a homogeneous extract from J added by a later hand. As in 3^{12-30} (Ehud), I am unable to follow his analysis.   ¶ Be.; see below on 7^{16}.

wild disorder (v.²¹). In the other the camp is alarmed by horns on every
side sounding the attack; the Midianites, in the darkness thinking that the
Israelites are upon them, lay wildly about them and kill one another (v.²²).*
The antecedents of these two accounts are easily discoverable in 7¹⁻¹⁵; 7²⁻⁸
belongs to the trumpet version of the story; Gideon's reconnoissance, 7⁹⁻¹⁴, to
the other. In ch. 6, Budde's analysis may in the main be followed. Accordingly we have: J, part of the older material incorporated in 6²⁻⁶, 6¹¹⁻²⁴·⁸⁴
7¹·⁹⁻¹¹·¹³⁻¹⁵,† the version of the stratagem in v.¹⁶⁻²⁰ in which the jars and
torches appear, v.²¹, part of v.²²ᵇ describing the direction of the flight, 8⁴⁻²¹,
v.²⁴⁻²⁷ᵃ substantially, v.³⁰ᶠ·: for E, 6²⁻⁶ in part, 6⁷⁻¹⁰·²⁸·³²·³³, [the call of
Gideon to deliver Israel], v.³⁶⁻⁴⁰, v.³⁵ᵃ (Manasseh), 7²⁻⁶, that version of v.¹⁶⁻²⁰
in which the horns play the chief part, v.²²ᵃ·²²ᵇ (in part), v.²³(?) ²⁴ᶠ·8¹⁻³·²⁹.
In ascribing this part of the story to E, I do not affirm that it is all by one
hand; 6⁷⁻¹⁰, e.g., seems to be one of those secondary pieces which we so often
find in E contexts, both in the Hexateuch and the Books of Samuel. The
editorial additions in ch. 6–8 (9) are not very extensive or important.

1–6. The Israelites offend Yahweh; he allows the Midian-ites to overrun and plunder them for seven years.

— In this
introduction the familiar phrases of D appear in v.¹·⁶ᵇ; his hand
is also probably to be recognized in certain notes of exaggeration
in v.²⁻⁵. The substance of v.²⁻⁶ᵃ must be derived from the old
story which runs through the following chapters. The verses are,
however, much overloaded, and it is probable that more than one
source has been put under contribution.

1. Introductory formulas of the editor; see on 2¹¹·¹⁴. — *Midian*]
the most important of a group of tribes in N.W. Arabia which the
Israelite historians reckoned to their own race (Abraham), though
not of the full blood (the concubine Keturah, Gen. 25¹⁻⁶ J), and a
step farther removed than the Ishmaelites. The land of Midian,
i.e. the district occupied by the settled part of the tribe, was in
the northern Ḥigāz, east of the Gulf of 'Aqabah, where a town
of the name lay. The nomad branches of the tribe wandered
northward along the margin of the desert, making forays into
the pastures and cultivated tracts of Edom, Moab, ‡ and Gilead,
and even pouring across the Jordan into Western Palestine. § —

---

* See also Winckler, p. 50 f.
† Disregarding minor traces of the editor's hand.   ‡ Cf. Gen. 36⁸⁵.
§ On the wanderings or migrations of modern Arab tribes to the north, see
Doughty, *Arabia Deserta*, i. 271 f.; especially the wide range of the 'Anezy, *ib.*
p. 330 ff.

Seven years] on the chronology see Introduction § 7. — 2. *The power of Midian prevailed over Israel*] 3^{10} cf. 3^{13}; words of the editor who transforms the annual forays of the Bedawin into a subjugation and seven years' oppression.* To the same hand belongs v.⁴ᵇ, and, in part at least, the amplification of v.³⁻⁵. — *For safety from Midian they made the . . . which are in the hills, and the caves, and the fastnesses*] cf. 1. Sam. 13^6. The word which is omitted in the translation must in the context mean a place of concealment or security; its precise signification is unknown. The meaning *ravines, gorges*, ascribed to it in the lexicons rests solely on an absurd etymology. The author thus accounts for the abandoned hill-forts and rock dwellings scattered over the land, which perhaps were really the work of a more primitive population. Many remains of this sort are still found east of the Jordan. — **3–5.** The yearly inroads of the Bedawin robbed the Israelitish peasants of the fruit of their toil and greatly impoverished them.† The verses are not a unit, as appears not only from the awkward surplusage, but from the false sequence of tenses. This redundancy is not altogether due to editorial amplification; both the sources from which the following chapters are derived must have had such an introduction, and probably both have been drawn upon here. — **3.** The disorder of the text is sufficiently shown by a literal translation : Whenever Israel had sown, Midian used to come up, and Amalek and the Bene Qedem, and (they) used to come up against it (Israel). **4.** And they encamped against them (Israel) and destroyed, &c. The confusion of tenses, which in English is only awkward, is in Hebrew ungrammatical. The Amalekites are Bedawin whom we generally meet in the deserts south of Palestine ; the Bene Qedem, as their name imports, come from the east, the great Syrian desert. The introduction of the names here is very likely an exaggeration of the editor ; cf. on 3^{13}. It is possible, however, that the exaggeration already existed in E ; cf. v.³³ 7^{12}. Of the rest, we may surmise that the frequentative tenses come from one source (?E), the narrative aorists from the other. Following this clue it is possible

---

* See Introduction § 6, and above on 3^{12-30} (p. 90).

† Similar incursions of tribes east of the Delta into Egypt, Burckhardt, *Syria*, p. 558 f.

to construct out of the verses two tolerably complete parallel accounts; but the combination can be made in more than one way, and we cannot feel any confidence that our analysis thus recovers the sources. Cf. also 7^{12}. — *As far as the vicinity of Gaza*] in the extreme south-west. — *And they would not leave any thing to live on in Israel*] frequentative tenses, as in v.^{3a}. — *And sheep and ox and ass*] Jos. 6^{21} 1 S. 22^{19}; *sc.* they would not leave. The words may be a gloss to the preceding *subsistence*. — 5. The duplication of clauses and confusion of tenses continues. — Locusts afford an effective figure for the swarming, hungry hordes of invaders; Quid enim locustis innumerabilius et fortius, quibus humana industria resistere non potest.[*] — 6. *Israel was greatly reduced by reason of Midian*] cf. 2 S. 3^1. — The second half of the verse is editorial; cf. on 3^9. Observe Bene Israel (as in v.^{1}) in contrast to Israel v.^{3}.

1. The name Midian appears in the towns Μοδίαια or Μοδούνα, Ptol., vi. 7, 2, and Μαδιάμα (further inland) vi. 7, 27; cf. Euseb., *OS*[2]. 276$_{53}$.[†] According to the Arab geographers, it lay five days south of Ailah on the eastern side of the Red Sea.[‡] In the Hexateuch, E brings Moses before the Exodus into intimate relations with Jethro, the priest of Midian (Ex. 2$^{16f.}$. 18$^{1ff.}$). The Mountain of God (Horeb) [§] was in the land of Midian (Ex. 3^1); thither Moses led the people from Egypt. Though it is not expressly stated, the narrative of E hardly leaves room for doubt that the Midianites worshipped Yahweh at Horeb before Moses; and the name יהוה, till then unknown to the Israelites and having no natural etymology in their language, is perhaps of Midianite origin. Close relations between Israel and Midian are also indicated by the recurrence of Midianite clan names in Judah, Reuben, and East Manasseh.[‖] The Midianites appear as caravan traders (Gen. 37$^{28.36}$ Is. 60^6); nomads dwelling in tents (Hab. 3^7). The latest stratum of the narrative of the Exodus (P) brings Israel into conflict with the Midianites in the plains of Moab shortly before the crossing of the

[*] Jerome, on Joel 1^6.

[†] See also 1 K. 11^{18}.

[‡] Le Strange, *Palestine under the Moslems*, p. 497 f. On modern Midian, see Burton, *Gold Mines of Midian*, 1878; *Land of Midian*, 1879.

[§] In P Sinai. According to Yāqūt, Tūr Sinā is the name, 'in the language of the Nabataeans,' of a mountain near Madyan, which is an extension of the range above Ailah. See Le Strange, *l.c.* p. 73.

[‖] Nöldeke, *BL.* iv. p. 218. Epha, Gen. 25^4, is in 1 Chr. 1^{46} a concubine of Caleb; 2^{47} a son of Jahdai (in Judaean clan list); Epher, 1 Chr. 4^{17} (Judah) 5^{24} (East Manasseh); Hanoch, Gen. 46^9 (Reuben).

Jordan (Nu. 25⁶⁻¹⁸ 31 Jos. 13²¹). Nu. 25⁶⁻¹⁸ is a substitute for the fragmentary story of the offence at Baal Peor, Nu. 25¹⁻⁵ (JE); and, with its sequel
ch. 31, has no historical worth; the introduction of the sheikhs of Midian in
Nu. 22⁴·⁷ is probably harmonistic. To judge from the echoes in the later
literature, the defeat of the Midianites narrated in Jud. ch. 6–8 must have
been most disastrous. "The day of Midian" is for Isaiah (9³, cf. 10²⁶; also
Ps. 83¹⁰·¹²) synonymous with a signal and irretrievable catastrophe. It has
often been surmised, though without any very good grounds, that the defeat
inflicted upon them by Hadad of Edom (Gen. 36³⁵) fell about the same time.
After the time of the Judges the Midianites scarcely reappear in the history. See further, Nöldeke, *BL.* iv. p. 217 f.; *Die Amalekiter*, u. s. w., 1864,
p. 7 ff. — **2.** מפני מדין] best taken literally, *from before*, as with verbs meaning
'withdraw, flee, conceal,' and the like; cf. v.¹¹ᵇ 9²¹ 11³ &c. — בנהרות] 𝔊ᴬᴺ
τρυμαλιδι, 𝔊ᴾⱽᴸᴼᴹ 𝔗 𝔰 μάνδραι, Orig. *septa*, pens, kraals, cf. 1 S. 13⁶. The
etymological explanation of Jewish comm., subterranean chambers or caves
with a small opening for light (נהר),* is not more improbable than that
adopted from Schultens (Job, p. 49) † by Ges. and many modern scholars,
which connects it with Arab. *manhar* (on which see Lane, p. 2858ᶜ); see Stud.
RLbG., 'beacons,' perhaps towers for fire signals from hill-top to hill-top, to
give warning of the approach of the enemy; cf. Abulw. — ואת המכרות] Bu.
suspects that the words are a gloss to the preceding. — המצדות] 1 S. 23¹⁴·¹⁹ 24¹,
with כירה Ez. 33²⁷; cf. the fortress Μασάδα Fl. Jos., *antt.* xiv. 11, 7 § 296; *b.j.*
vii. 8, 3 ff. On Amalek see Nöldeke, *Die Amalekiter*, 1864; Bertheau, *BL.*
s. v. The historical notices of Amalek all locate them in steppes or desert
south of Palestine; see 1 S. 15 (Saul) 1 S. 30 (David), cf. also Nu. 14⁴³·⁴⁵.
In the traditions of the Exodus, Israel was attacked by the Amalekites before
reaching the sacred mountain, probably in traversing the deserts north of the
Sinaitic peninsula (Ex. 17⁸ff. E); cf. Dt. 25¹⁷⁻¹⁹ 1 S. 15². The relentless wars
waged upon them by Saul and David seem to have broken them up; they are
scarcely mentioned in the later history. The oracle of Balaam (Nu. 24²⁰)
foresees their complete disappearance. A fragmentary notice in 1 Chr. 4⁴²f.
tells us that a band of Simeonites exterminated the last remnant of the race in
their refuge in Mt. Seir. — The Bene Qedem (Easterns) are mentioned in
Jer. 49²⁸ (in conjunction with the Kedarenes), and Ez. 25⁴·¹⁰, where they are
evidently inhabitants of the deserts east of Ammon and Moab; cf. also Is. 11¹⁴.
— **4.** ויחנו עליהם] the impf. cons. after the frequentatives is not in itself without
analogy (negligent lapse into simple narration; cf. 12⁵ᶠ·, and see Dr². § 114;
TBS. p. 24), but the vibration between the two constructions in this and the
following verses is hardly to be so explained. — מחיה] *subsistence*, 17¹⁰ (MH.);
cf. *victus* from *vivere*. — יבול] Dt. 32²² 11¹⁷ Lev. 26⁴·²⁰ Ez. 34²⁷. — **5.** ואהליהם
יבאו] Qerē ובאו conforming to the preceding יעלו. 𝔊ᴬᴸᴹᴼ 1 𝔰 𝔥 παρέφερον
= יבאו. — לשחתה] Piel Gen. 13¹⁰ 19¹³·²⁹ &c.; cf. Hiph. v.⁴.

---

* Ra., Ki., Abarb.; cf. Wetzstein, *Hauran*, p. 46.
† Cf. Schm.

7-10. Yahweh sends a prophet to upbraid the Israelites for their defection. — When the Israelites in their distress cry to Yahweh, he sends a prophet, who calls to mind the great deeds of their god in saving them from Egypt and giving them the land of Canaan, and recites the fundamental law, which here, as in Ex. 20⁼, has its ground in the great deliverance God has wrought : You shall not adopt the religions of Canaan. This prohibition they have disregarded. Cf. 2^{1b-5a} 10^{11-16} 1 S. 7^{3f.} 10^{17-19} 12^{6-23}.

The speech breaks off abruptly with this introduction. We miss in the words of the prophet the positive accusation and the denunciation of Yahweh's anger, and in the narrative, the result of his reproof, which not only the whole drift and purpose of the speech, but the analogy of similar discourses in Judges and Samuel, leads us to expect ; cf. 2^{1-3} and especially 10^{11-16}. It is not likely that the author left the speech thus without the point which is its reason for being ; more probably the conclusion was dropped by the compiler who subjoined v.^{11ff.} from the parallel narrative. The incompleteness of the speech, as well as the evidence of language and style, which in this case is unusually decisive, shows that v.^{7-10} are not to be ascribed to the compiler,[*] but to an Elohistic hand.[†] — **7.** *On account of Midian*] the Hebrew phrase is not very common and is all but confined to E.[‡] — **8.** *A prophet*] lit. *a prophet-man ;* cf. 4⁴.[§] — *Yahweh the God of Israel*] 4⁶ ; corresponding phrases are, I am Yahweh thy God (Ex. 20²), and, Yahweh our God (Jos. 24^{17}). — *I led you up from Egypt and brought you out of the slave house*] the place where you were slaves. This deliverance is the origin of the peculiar relation between Yahweh and Israel and the ground of its obligation to keep itself to him only. It is therefore constantly recalled as the prime motive to faith in Yahweh and faithfulness to him alone, or to aggravate the guilt of unfaithfulness by exposing its folly and baseness and justify the extreme severity of judgement ;

---

[*] D; so Be., We., Sta., Dr., Kitt.　　[†] Bu., *Richt. u. Sam.*, p. 107 f.

[‡] See Holzinger *Einl. in den Hexateuch*, p. 182 f.

[§] Cf. 1 S. 2^{27}. On these anonymous prophets, who play the chorus to the story, see Sta., *GVI.* i. p. 182 n. The motive here is obvious ; reformation must precede deliverance. According to Jewish authorities (*Seder Olam* c. 20), the prophet of our text was Phineas.

cf. Am. 3[1b] Hos. 13[4] Jud. 2[1] 1 S. 10[18] &c. — **9.** *I rescued you from the power of Egypt*] Ex. 3[8] 18[9. 10], cf. Jud. 8[34] 1 S. 12[10. 11], also Jud. 10[11] (a different verb). — *And from the power of all your oppressors*] 2[18] esp. 1 S. 10[18].[*] — *And expelled them before you and gave you their land*] the pronouns grammatically refer to the oppressors, but the writer is thinking of the populations of Canaan ; † cf. Jos. 24[12f. 18] Ex. 34[11] 23[28]. — **10.** *I am Yahweh your God*] Ex. 20[2]. — *You shall not revere the gods of the Amorites, in whose land you dwell*] with the form of the expression cf. 2 K. 17[35–40], in substance Ex. 20[3] (Dt. 5[7]) Ex. 34[14] Dt. 6[13-15] 12[30c]. On the Amorites, see above on 3[5].

8. הכליתי אהכם מכצרים] common in E, but not characteristic of that work (Di.); see Holzinger, p. 186. — בית עברים] *ergastulum ;* Ex. 13[3. 14] 20[2] Jos. 24[17] Dt. 5[6] 6[12] &c. (E, Rje, D). — **9.** לחזיכם] see on 1[34] 2[18]. — וָאֹמְרָה] Baer, with a few codd. and old edd., as the context requires.‡ The *recepta* is וָאֹמַר; examples of the same anomaly, in some instances explicitly prescribed by the Massora, see Bö. § 973, 2 ; Dr[3]. § 66 n. On the use of the verb see above on 2[3]. — וָאֶתְּנָה] the energetic (cohortative) form in the consec. tense; cf. v.[10] 10[12] 12[8] (*ter*) Dr[3]. § 69, Obs. It is particularly common in the case of אתנ (Nu. 8[19] 1 S. 2[28] 2 S. 12[8] Is. 43[28]), where perhaps compensation has something to do with it.

11-24. The Call of Gideon. — First account.

The Messenger of Yahweh appears to Gideon and summons him to deliver Israel from the Midianites. He protests that the task is beyond his powers, and is assured of the support of Yahweh. Gideon brings food to set before the stranger, at the touch of whose staff fire bursts from the rock and consumes the bread and meat. The visitor vanishes. Gideon recognizes that it was the Messenger of Yahweh and fears for his life. He is reassured, and builds the altar, Yahweh-shalom, which stands in Ophrah.

The passage has no connection with v.[7-10] ; its premises are rather to be found in v.[2-6]. In what follows, v.[25-32] is not the sequel of v.[11-24], but a second account of the call of Gideon and the building of the altar. The closest parallels to v.[11-24] are the

---

* The similarity between Jud. 6[8f.] and 1 S. 10[18] is such as to prove either that they are from the same hand or that one author has copied the other.

† This awkwardness leads Ki. to interpret of Sihon and Og; cf. Schm.

‡ Ew., *Krit. Gram.*, p. 555; cf. Kö., i. p. 190.

appearance of Messenger of Yahweh to the parents of Samson, Jud. 13$^{2\cdot23}$, and the appearance of Yahweh to Abraham at the sacred trees of Mamre, Gen. 18$^{1f.}$ (J). In Jud. 6$^{11\cdot24}$ 13$^{2\cdot23}$ the whole conception and representation, as well as the more external features of language and style, strongly resemble the Yahwistic narratives of the Hexateuch, and the passages are with considerable probability ascribed by Böhme, Budde, and Cornill to the same author.*

The narrative has suffered some changes at the hand of the redactor or later editor, the distinctive note of which is the anticipation of Gideon's recognition of his visitor (v.^{22a}). In the attempt to separate these secondary elements and restore the original context, Böhme undoubtedly goes too far;† Budde's analysis is more conservative, but still perhaps subtracts more than is necessary.‡ Verse ^{17b}, in which Gideon already recognizes the Messenger, but wishes to have the confirmation of a miracle, is clearly not original. Verse ^{20}, in which the flesh and the cakes are disposed on the rock as on an altar and the broth poured out as a libation, is also secondary. Corresponding changes have not improbably been made in v.^{16}, and in v.$^{18\cdot 19}$.

11. *The Messenger of Yahweh*] 2^1 5^{23} 13$^{3ff.}$. The *Mal'ak Yahweh* is a theophany. In all the old accounts of such appearances the *mal'ak* is, first or last, identified with the deity; see Gen. 16$^{7\cdot14}$ 21$^{17\cdot19}$ 22$^{11\cdot14.\ 15\cdot18}$ 31$^{11\cdot13}$ Ex. 3$^{2ff.}$ Jud. *h. l.*, 13$^{3ff.}$; cf. also Gen. 32$^{24\cdot30}$ with Hos. 12^{4f}, Gen. 48$^{15.\ 16}$; further Gen. 18. 19, in which Yahweh appears precisely as elsewhere the *Mal'ak Yahweh*. In the Yahwistic narratives in the Pentateuch, as in Judges ch. 6 and 13, the Messenger of Yahweh appears in human form and converses freely

---

* The resemblance is admitted by Kue. (*HCO*². i. p. 355), who questions the validity of Böhme's inference. Kitt. (*Stud. u. Krit.*, 1892, p. 57 f.) points out countervailing differences; cf. also Kö., *Einl.*, p. 253 f., and on the whole question whether J and E can be traced in Jud., see above, Introduction § 6.

† *ZATW.* v. p. 251 ff. Böhme (p. 259) leaves for the original story only v.^{11} to קמרה (הֲעוֹרִי to ונרקון), הטיב to (conclusion to סרין), v.$^{12.\ 13a.\ 14a}$ ויאמר to ישראל, v.$^{17a.\ 18a}$ אליך to, v.$^{18b.\ 19a}$ to בצוה (19b) v.$^{21\cdot24}$. (The parts about which he is less confident in parenthesis.)

‡ *Richt. u. Sam.*, p. 108 f.; cf. Co., *Einl*². p. 95 f. Budde (p. 109) ascribes to J, v.$^{11\cdot13a.\ 18b}$ from וקרה on, v.^{14a} from ויאמר on, v.$^{15.\ 16}$ (read כי יהוה) v.$^{17a.\ 18a}$ to והוצאתי (the original object has been supplanted), v.$^{18b.\ 19a}$ to בצוה, v.^{19b} to האיה, v.$^{21\cdot24}$.

with men : in E this anthropomorphism is shunned ; the Messenger speaks from heaven, or in a dream, or is revealed in the flames of the burning bush (Ex. 3²).*—*And sat down*] like a wayfarer seeking rest in its shade. — *Under the holy tree that is in Ophrah*] on holy trees see on 4¹¹ (p. 121 f.).† Ophrah, v.²⁴ (cf. 8²⁷) Ophrah of the Abiezrites, the Abiezrite Ophrah, probably to distinguish it from a Benjamite town of the same name (Jos. 18²³ 1 S. 13¹⁷). The site is unknown ; from ch. 9 it may be probably inferred that it was not very far from Shechem.   Fer'atā six miles WSW. of Nābulus has been suggested,‡ but this is more probably Pirathon (12¹⁵).§ — *Which* (tree) *belonged to Joash the Abiezrite*] the holy tree was in the possession of Gideon's family, just as in the other narrative (v.²⁵) the village altar of Baal belonged to Jerubaal's father.   The Abiezrites were a clan of Manasseh (v.¹⁵ Nu. 26³⁰ | Jos. 17²). — *Beating out wheat in the wine-press*] threshing in the ordinary way was not to be risked ; the threshing-floors were especially exposed places.¶   The wine-press, on the contrary, a square or oblong vat excavated in the sloping surface rock, afforded some concealment.**   Hither Gideon had brought a few sheaves of wheat and was whipping them out with a stick on the floor of the press. — **12.** The Messenger shows himself and salutes Gideon. — *Yahweh is with thee*] the answer shows that in Hebrew (in which the copula is not expressed) the sentence is felt to be an assertion,†† rather than a wish. — *Stalwart hero*] in Jud. only 11¹ (Jephthah) ; 1 K. 11²⁸ 2 K. 5¹ &c. ; cf. Jud. 18². — **13.** The salutation sounds to Gideon almost ironical ; the present distress is plain proof that Yahweh is not with them. — *Where are all his wonderful interventions*] Ex. 3²⁰ 34¹⁰ Jos. 3⁵ Mi. 7¹⁵. —

---

* See Kosters, " De Mal'ach Jahwe," *Th. T.* ix. 1875, p. 369-415 ; Schultz, *Alttest. Theol⁴.* p. 600 ff. = *Old Test. Theol.*, ii. p. 218 ff. ; Smend, *Alttest. Religionsgeschichte*, p. 42 ff. Older literature and theories, see Oehler, *Alttest. Theol.* § 59. 60 ; cf. Schm., *quaest.* 3.

† On holy trees and tree worship in general, see the literature in Chantepie de la Saussaye, *Religionsgeschichte*, i. p. 61 ; Tylor, *Primitive Culture³*, ii. p. 214 ff. ; Frazer, *Golden Bough*, 1890, i. p. 56-108.

‡ *SWP. Memoirs*, ii. p. 162.

§ Rob., *BR².* iii. p. 134 ; Guérin, *Samarie*, ii. 179 f.

‖ The name is mutilated, perhaps not by accident ; cf. ⊕.   ¶ See on v.⁸⁷.

** For a description of the wine-press, see Rob., *BR².* iii. p. 137 ; cf. Nonnus, *Dionys.*, xli. 331 ff.   †† Fl. Jos., Aug., al.

Which our fathers recounted to us] phrase parallels, Ps. 44¹ 78³; cf. Ex. 12²⁶ 13⁸·¹⁴. — *But now Yahweh has cast us off and given us into the grasp of Midian*] cf. Jer. 12⁷ 1 S. 12²² 1 K. 8⁵⁷ 2 K. 21¹⁴.*

11. מלאך] is found in Heb. only in a concrete, personal sense, 'messenger'; or, as we might perhaps translate, 'agent,' thus making the relation of the word to מלאכה more obvious. There is no warrant in usage for an explanation of the phrase מלאך יהוה which goes back to an assumed abstract sense, 'the sending of Yahweh' (Vatke, Ew., Reuss, al.). — אשר ליואש] *the tree* . . . which belonged to Joash (₲, Cler., Reuss, Kitt.), not *Ophrah* which belonged to J. (₷ a. Ki., Drus., Schm., Stud., Be., Oettli). — ונרעון בנו חבט וגו] *as Gideon was*, &c.; circumstantial clause. חבט Is. 28²⁷ Ru. 2¹⁷ cf. Dt. 24²⁰. — נת is properly the upper trough, in which the grapes are trodden; יקב (7²⁸) the lower one, in which the must is collected. — להניס] Ex. 9²⁰. — **13.** בי אדני] v.¹⁵ 13⁸; a deprecatory formula, if I may speak without offence, begging your pardon; cf. Gen. 43²⁰ 44¹⁸ Ex. 4¹⁰·¹³ (all J), Nu. 12¹¹ 1 S. 1²⁶ &c. — ויש יהוה] if he really is, as you say. Instead of a conditional sentence with subordinated protasis (אם), we have simple parataxis; cf. 13¹² 2 K. 10¹⁵. So very often in older English; *e.g.* And it please your grace, you did once promise me (Shakespeare). See *New English Dictionary*, i. p. 317ᵇ. — איה] skeptical; 'what has become of'; cf. the ironical use of the particle 9³⁸ Jer. 2²⁸ Dt. 32³⁷ (אי) &c. — נפלאותיו] things extraordinary, surpassing men's power or comprehension (cf. פלאי 13¹⁸); especially of the wonderful interventions of God in the history of his people, and (later) the wonders of his works in nature.† References to Yahweh's wonderful deliverances are frequent in the Psalms, but it does not follow that all references to them are so late. The exx. cited above (Ex. 3²⁰ 34¹⁰ Jos. 3⁵) all occur in Yahwist contexts. In the passage before us the words, if not original (J, cf. the Hiphil 13¹⁹), must be ascribed to Rje, not to Rd, in whom the word seems not to occur. — ועתה נטשנו יהוה] can hardly be separated from the foregoing (Bu.), but stands or falls with it. Cf. Jer. 23³³·³⁹ esp. 12⁷, which Böhme, without sufficient reason, regards as the source of the phrase in our text; see also Is. 2⁶. — נכף כרין] for the more common בכיד, v.¹⁴ 1 S. 4⁸ 2 S. 19¹⁰ &c.

14. *Yahweh turned to him*] ‡ with the following (v.¹⁴⁻¹⁶) cf. Ex. 3¹⁰⁻¹². The Messenger is Yahweh himself; see above on v.¹¹.

---

* From these parallels, chiefly in writings of the age of Jeremiah or later, Böhme infers that v.¹³ᵇ is an editorial enlargement on the original question, v.¹³ᵃ. Budde agrees as to the beginning of v.¹³ᵇ (as far as *from Egypt*), but attributes the rest (*but now*, &c.) to the first narrator, connecting it with v.¹³ᵃ.

† Cf. the verb 2 S. 13² Dt. 17⁸ 30¹¹; of God., Gen. 18¹⁴ Jer. 21⁸ 32¹⁷. ₰.

‡ Böhme, Bu., ascribe the words to an editorial hand, but I see no sufficient reason for this.

𝕲 ὁ ἄγγελος Κυρίου to conform to v.[11].— *Go in this might of thine*] visible in his powerful frame and the vigorous strokes of his staff, which drew from the visitor the admiring address, *stalwart hero*, v.[12]; not, the might which is now given thee.* — *Do not I send thee ?*] † the question as in 4[6]. Since the visitor does not reveal himself in his true character till v.[21], we should expect rather, *doth not Yahweh send thee ?* cf. 4[6]. We may suppose either that Gideon took his visitor for a man of God (cf. 13[6]), or, more probably, that the author lapsed from strict dramatic propriety; see also on v.[16].— **15.** Gideon remonstrates that he is not equal to the task. — *How* (by what means) *should I deliver Israel ? My sept is the poorest in Manasseh, and I the most insignificant man in my family*] cf. 1 S. 9[21]. The protestation is, no more than that of Saul, to be taken too literally. Both the following narratives assume that the hero's family was one of rank and influence in the clan. — **16.** *Yahweh said to him, Surely I will be with thee*] 𝕲[B al], *the Angel of the Lord said to him, the Lord will be with thee.* If it be thought too violent a supposition that the author here, as in v.[14], used the first person in conformity with the knowledge of his readers that the speaker was Yahweh, rather than with Gideon's supposed ignorance of that fact, we may conjecture that the original text was simply, *and he said, Yahweh will be with thee,* ‡ and that in supplying the explicit subject and recasting the sentence to correspond with it, the editor of 𝔚 had Ex. 3[12] in mind. — *As one man*] Nu. 14[15]. --**17.** Gideon asks the stranger to wait till he can set food before him, and prepares him a meal; cf. Gen. 18[3-8] Jud. 13[15-19]. — *If I find favour in thy sight*] Gen. 18[3]; a favourite phrase of the Yahwist in the Pentateuch. § — *Make me a sign that thou art speaking with me*] Gideon recognizes his supernatural visitant, but for assurance desires a sign such as is given in the sequel. The half-verse thus anticipates v.[21f.] in a way that the author of the latter verses cannot have done ; v.[17a] connects immediately with v.[17a], just as Gen. 18[2a] does with v.[3b. 4], and has no ulterior purpose. Verse[17b] is therefore an editorial addition, probably by the same hand which inserted v.[20]

---

* Ki., Be., al. This strength of faith, Thdt.
† Böhme regards this clause also as secondary.   ‡ 𝕲[FV al].; Bu.
§ Di., *NDJ.* p. 625; Holzinger, *Einleitung in den Hexat.*, p. 97 f.

under the impression that the meal Gideon prepared was intended from the first as a sacrifice, contrary to Gen. 18[3-8] and esp. Jud. 13[15f.].[*] That the words are not part of the original narrative, is in some degree confirmed by the unusual relative particle ש.[†] — 18. Originally followed immediately upon v.[17a]; see above. — *My offering*] Gen. 33[10] 43[11] 1 S. 10[27]; a present to the guest. It is not impossible that the word has been substituted for the original expression, in conformity with the theory that Gideon from the beginning intended a religious offering; see note. — 19. *Gideon prepared a kid*] 13[15. 19]; in Gen. 18[7] the rich sheikh Abraham kills a calf. — *An ephah of flour*] The quantity (more than a bushel) is altogether disproportionate, especially in the circumstances; cf. 1 Sam. 1[24], where an ephah of flour is enough to go with a three year old bullock (𝔊 𝔖; 𝔐 *three* bullocks !), Gen. 18[6]. — *The meat he put in a basket and the broth in a pot, and brought it out to him under the tree and presented it*] cf. Gen. 18[8]. Böhme and Budde ascribe the half verse (Bu. excepts, *and brought it out to him under the tree*) to the redaction. It seems improbable, however, that these concrete details, which are not essential to the conception of an offering, or, indeed, consonant with ritual customs, were introduced by an editor.

15. כי ארני] the pronunciation, in distinction from ארני v.[18], means to intimate that Gideon now recognizes his visitor as divine. — אלף [אלפי הדל] is, like משפחה, a branch of a tribe (שבט) larger than the family (בית אב); see 1 S. 10[19-21]. — הצעיר] 1 S. 9[21]; often in the sense *minor natu*, Gen. 25[23] 43[33] 48[14] &c. — 16. כי אהיה עמך] *verbatim* Ex. 3[12]. It has been conjectured above that the author wrote, יהוה יהיה עמך (1 S. 17[37]); cf. 𝔊. — 17. [ועשית לי אות perhaps the sign also was suggested by Ex. 3[12]. The words must be construed as apodosis; cf. Gen. 33[10]. עשה אוה Ex. 4[17. 21] Nu. 14[11. 22] Jos. 24[17] Dt. 11[3]; nowhere in precisely this sense, in which we should expect נתן אות (Jos. 2[12]). — שָׁאתה מדבר עמי [we expect רמדבר (Gen. 45[12]), *that it is thou that speakest;* the article may have been accidentally omitted. The relative ש in Jud. 5[7] 6[17] 7[12] 8[26]; שָׁ only here in O.T., elsewhere before gutturals שֶׁ. — 18. Böhme ascribes v.[18aβ] (and bring out my offering and set it before thee) to an editor; Bu. thinks that the editor has changed the original object of the verb (food; cf. Gen. 18[5] Jud. 13[16]) into a religious offering. But it is not clear that מנחה need be taken in this specific sense; ‡ the verb (הניח) certainly does not suggest such an intention. The noun may possibly have been chosen on

---

account of its ambiguity, as a hint, not a bald anticipation, of the disposition of what Gideon set before the stranger.[*] — ‏והוצאתי‎ . . . . ‏כר נאי‎] see on 16[2]; Dr[3]. § 115 (p. 134). — 19. ‏איפת קמח כצות‎] he prepared it *as unleavened cakes*, made it up into cakes; cf. 1 S. 28[24], Gen. 18[6] Nu. 11[8] (‏עשה‎), Ex. 12[39]. The ephah was according to the smallest computation over a bushel. — ‏הבשר‎] (so Ki., Norzi, Baer) v.[20] Is. 65[4] (Qerē); ζωμός, *jus;* of. Arab. *maraq;* others understand the pot liquor in which the meat had been boiled (Ki.; cf. Schm.). — ‏סל‎] a closely woven shallow basket or tray, Gen. 40[17] &c. — ‏פרור‎] Nu. 11[8] 1 S. 2[14] a cooking vessel, of what kind we have no means of ascertaining. Böhme (*l.c.* p. 254) rejects v.[19a] with v.[20]; the broth was introduced by some one who thought a libation indispensable; the whole representation presumes that a religious offering is intended. So Bu. also. But if the object was to convert Gideon's hospitality into a sacrifice, it would have been done unmistakably. In no ritual that we know was meat presented in a basket (as unleavened cakes were) or a libation made of broth. It is conceivable that such rites existed in this early time; [†] but not that such a description proceeds from a late editor. I find in the words, however, no certain evidence of a sacrificial intention; even ‏ויגש‎ is properly used of bringing food to one, putting it within his reach (Gen. 27[25]).

20, 21. The food which Gideon brings out is converted into an offering. Fire from the rock consumes it; the Messenger vanishes. — **20.** *Messenger of God*, instead of *Messenger of Yahweh*, is striking, and with some other peculiarities of expression arouses the suspicion that the verse is by a different hand. This suspicion is strengthened by the contents of the verse; and Böhme and Budde are probably right in regarding it as a later addition to the story. Verse[21] connects equally well with v.[19]. See further in crit. note. — **21.** The Messenger touches the food with the tip of his walking-stick, at which fire springs up from the rock and consumes it; cf. 1 K. 18[38] 2 Chr. 7[1] 2 Macc. 2[10-13] Lev. 9[24]. — *The Messenger of Yahweh passed from his sight*] this is in conflict with v.[21.22], in which Gideon addresses his visitor and is answered by him as though still present. That the reassuring voice (v.[23]) came back from heaven [‡] is in no way intimated in the text. Probably the words are an addition suggested by 13[20]; [§] the

---

[*] Stud. On the other hand, the word may have been the occasion of the editor's misunderstanding and led to the other changes in the verses.

[†] We., who is inclined to see here a very old custom.

[‡] Ki., RLbG., Schm., and many.

[§] Observe how completely the two stories are fused by Fl. Jos., *antt.* v. 8, 3 § 283 f., and cf. the unconscious conformation in the interpretation of Ki., al.

unsuitable position of the clause is explained by a comparison of 6[22] with 13[22]. — **22.** *Oh, my lord Yahweh !*] cry of consternation or distress ; Jos. 7[7], Jer., Ez. ; cf. Jud. 11[31]. — *Because I have seen the Messenger of Yahweh face to face*] and therefore must die. The belief that such a sight forebodes the death of him whose profane eyes have thus violated the mystery of godhead, Jud. 13[22] Gen. 16[13] 32[30] Ex. 20[19(16)] 33[20] Is. 6[5]. — **23.** Yahweh reassures him. — *Thou art safe*] lit. *it is well with thee;* cf. Gen. 43[23] Jud. 19[20]. — **24.** Gideon builds an altar which in the author's day was still standing in Ophrah, the name of which, *Yahweh-shalom* (Yahweh is well-disposed), perpetuates the words of God in v.[23]. Examples of altars with commemorative names, Gen. 33[20] * 35[7] Ex. 17[15]. That v.[22b-24] are an integral part of the original narrative is rightly maintained by Böhme † and Budde, ‡ against Wellhausen. §

20. מלאך האלהים [as in 4[22] (*q.v.*) the tradition is conflicting; only 𝕲[BN] supports 𝔐; all other versions have *Angel of the Lord.* The text will hardly sustain the inference that the original narrator of 6[1]-8[3] used Elohim and not Yahweh.ǁ האלהים in 𝔐 may be due only to transcriptional accident; so far as appears, both Rje and Rd write מלאך יהוה. Compare the divine names in Nu. 22 Jud. 13.¶ — Other differences, v.[20] סלי, v.[21] צור ; v.[20] the rare demonstrative הלז (1 S. 14[1] 17[20] &c.). — **21.** [משענת] etymologically, something on which a man leans for support, Ex. 21[19] Zech. 8[4], perhaps a walking-stick rather than a staff (שבט, מטה,); cf. 2 K. 18[21] Ez. 29[6ff]. — [ויראך יהוה הרך מעיניך 13[20] וייכל מלאך יהוה בלהב המזבח. The two narratives are throughout so much alike that further assimilation in such details was almost inevitable. Kosters seems to go too far in thinking that 6[18-23] has been worked over throughout in conformity with ch. 13.** — **22.** [כי כל כן] in the Hexateuch chiefly in J. — כניס אל פנים] Gen. 32[31] Ex. 33[11] Dt. 34[10] cf. 5[4]. — **24.** [יהוה שלום] many scholars take the second noun as genitive, (altar of) the Yahweh of Welfare, cf. יהוה צבאות;†† but this is unnecessary (see 1 S. 25[6]) and against analogy; cf. rather יהוה נסי (altar) Ex. 17[15], יהוה צדקנו (prophetic name of Jerusalem) Jer. 33[16]. Other names of a similar sort are יהוה יראה Gen. 22[14], יהוה שמה Ez. 48[35]. — [בעפרה אבי העזרי] cf. גת פרשתים 17[7] בית לחם יהודה, &c., Ew. § 286 c; Roorda,

---

* But the original word here was *stele* (massebah).   † *ZATW.* v. p. 252 f.

‡ *Richt. u. Sam.,* p. 109.   § *Comp.,* p. 226; cf. Sta., *GVI.* i. p. 184.

ǁ We., *Comp.,* p. 226 ("possibly").

¶ See Klostermann, *Neue kirchl. Zeitschrift,* i. p. 712-716, whose caution on this point deserves attention, in spite of exaggeration.   ** *Th. T.* ix. p. 397 f. n.

†† So Lth., Drus., Cler. (alt.), Ges. (supposing an inscription ליהוה שלום; cf. Schm.), Stud., Sta., al.

§ 449. — We. (*Comp.*, p. 226) finds that the altar and sacrifice (?) of v.²²⁻²⁴ come *post festum;* the original altar was the stone itself. Stade (*GVI.* i. p. 183 f.) thinks the verses possibly the close of a lost account of the origin of the holy place at Ophrah. But when the changes made by editorial hands in the preceding verses are recognized, v.²²⁻²⁴ is seen to be the natural and almost indispensable close of the narrative before us in v.¹⁴ff.

25–32. Call of Gideon. — Second account. Yahweh calls Gideon first of all to destroy the altar of Baal which belongs to his father and the sacred post (*asherah*) that stands beside it; to build on a designated spot an altar of Yahweh, and offer upon it a certain bullock as a dedicatory sacrifice. He does so by night. When the sacrilege is discovered and its perpetrator detected, the townspeople demand that he be put to death. His father Joash persuades them to leave it to Baal to avenge the outrage done him, "If he is a god let him take his own part." The oracular words of Joash, who as the custodian of the holy place was naturally the priest of Baal, explain the name Jerubbaal.

These verses are loosely joined to the foregoing by the words, *in that night* (cf. 7⁹), but so far from being the continuation of v.¹¹⁻²⁴, v.²⁵⁻³² belong to a second and altogether different account of the call of Gideon. The writer who narrates in v.²⁴ the building of the altar, Yahweh-shalom, cannot have gone on to relate the building of another altar of Yahweh in v.²⁶ff., nor did the author of the latter verses have before him v.²¹⁻²⁴. In v.¹¹ the holy tree at Ophrah, on the land of Joash, is the sacred spot where Yahweh appears, and there is no intimation that Israel is addicted to heathenish cults, or that its calamities are the punishment of defection; in v.²⁵ff. Joash is the proprietary custodian of the village altar of Baal with its sacred post (*asherah*), and these must be destroyed before Yahweh will deliver his people. The premises of v.²⁵⁻³² are to be found rather in v.⁷⁻¹⁰. The latter verses break off abruptly (see p. 181). We may infer from the analogous passages (2¹ᵇ⁻⁵ᵃ 10¹¹⁻¹⁶ 1 S. 7³ff. 10¹⁷⁻¹⁹ 12⁶ff.) that in the original connexion the prophet went on to upbraid them more specifically for their lapse into heathenism (worship of Baal), and to declare that it was for this that Yahweh had given them over to their foes. As a sequel to this, Gideon is called to begin the reformation by destroying the village altar of Baal and restoring the abandoned

worship of Yahweh. Budde appears to me to be right in seeing
in v.³⁻³, not a free amplification of the story by a later author,[*]
but part of a parallel narrative, which may with considerable
probability be ascribed to E.

25. *That night*] cf. 2 S. 7⁴ 2 K. 19³⁵. In the present connexion, the night after the appearance of the Messenger of
Yahweh to Gideon; originally, if our analysis is correct, the night
after the prophet delivered his reproof (v.⁷⁻¹⁰). — Verse²⁵ᵃ speaks
apparently of two bullocks, and in the sequel we read of the
sacrifice of *the second bullock* (v.²⁶·²⁸); but what is to be done
with the other does not appear. The text is unintelligible, and
no satisfactory emendation has been suggested. Kuenen[†] proposed to restore, with the aid of v.²⁷, *Take ten men of thy servants
and a bullock of seven years*, but it is difficult to imagine how this
could have been so corrupted. See critical note. — *Pull down the
altar of Baal which thy father has, and cut down the sacred post
which is by it*] the altar was the holy place of the town (v.²⁸ᶠ·);
Joash was its custodian by proprietary right, as the family of
Micah would have become of his temple in Mt. Ephraim (17⁵ᶠ·),
or as Gideon's descendants would have been of the image of
Yahweh in Ophrah (8²⁷).[‡] — On Baal see above on 2¹³ (p. 69 f.).
— *The sacred post which is by it*] the sacred post (*asherah*) was
of wood, and, if we may argue from v.²⁶, of considerable size.
Such posts seem to have belonged to every Canaanite place of
worship (Ex. 34¹³, altars, steles, asherahs, Dt. 12³ 1 K. 14²³ 2 K. 17¹⁰
Is. 17⁸), and in old times stood not only beside the altars of the
Baals, but by those of Yahweh (Dt. 16²¹), even in the temple at
Jerusalem (2 K. 21⁷ 23⁶). According to Jewish tradition the
asherah might be a living tree, and many modern scholars infer as
much from Dt. 16²¹; but usually, beyond question, it was a post or
mast. The shape of the *asherah* is not certainly known; but it
is not improbable that *asherahs* are represented by the posts of
varying forms, often with a conical top, which occur so frequently
in sacrificial scenes on Assyrian marbles, and on Assyrian, Phoeni-

[*] We., Sta., Kue., Kitt.; see above, p. 175 f.

[†] In Doorn., p. 70 n.; adopted by Kautzsch.

[‡] On such rights in holy places see We., *Reste arabischen Heidentumes*, p. 128 f.;
cf. Ibn Hishām, ed. Wüstenfeld, p. 54 f.

cian, and Cypriote seals and gems.[*] The origin and meaning
of the *asherah* arc also involved in obscurity. — **26.** Gideon is
directed to build an altar to Yahweh on a different site. — *On the
highest point of this stronghold*] the word which follows is not
intelligible in this context ; either it is a technical term the meaning of which is lost, or, as seems more likely, the text is at fault.
It is to be presumed that, as in the parallel narrative (v.[24]), the
writer has in mind an altar standing in his day, and that the words
describe its site. He is to dedicate the altar by the sacrifice of a
bullock, using for fuel the wood of the sacred post which he has
cut down. The whole burnt offering is the proper dedicatory
sacrifice. — *The second bullock*] v.[28]. The words are grammatically
unimpeachable, but the disorder of v.[25] makes it doubtful whether
they are correct ; not improbably *the second* is interpolated in
both verses, to conform to the (corrupt) text of v.[25].

25. That the text is corrupt should need no demonstration; פר השׁור and
פר היׁני שׁבע שׁנים are meaningless and grammatically impossible collocations
of words. *The second bullock of seven years old* (EV., following 𝕲𝕷𝕾)[†]
would be בן שׁבע ינים. As nothing is said in the sequel about any other
bullock, many interpreters infer that only one is spoken of here, and translate,
Take the bullock which belongs to thy father, *even* the second bullock, &c.;
so Trem.-Jun., Pisc., AV., RV., Ke., al.; the conjunction is explained in the
same way (*et quidem*) by Ew., Stud. (cf. RJes.); it is omitted by 𝕲[ALM].
Ingenious, but improbable explanations of the *second* bullock (second calf of
its dam) are given by Abulw., Tanch. (on 1 S. 15[9]); cf. Ki., Roed. (Ges. *Thes.*
p. 1451), Bö., al. RJes. and Stud. interpret *fatted*; Ew. connects ינ־ with
ינה in the sense, *annosus*. The word is omitted by 𝕲[MNPV] sub ast. **𝕤**; apparently פר השׁור and פר השׁני are doublets, and both corrupt. 𝕲 suggests the
conjecture הפר השׁכֵן (cf. 1 S. 15[9], We., Dr.), but the corruption is probably
deeper. With the *seven years* it seems impossible to do anything at all;
cf. 𝕿, *Temurah*, 28[b], Ra., RJes., al.; Hitzig conjectured that they were
accidentally introduced from 6[1]. — והאשׁרה אישׁר עליו הכרת] not *upon* the altar,
but *beside* it. אשׁרה almost uniformly 𝕲 ἄλσος 𝕷 *lucus* AV. *grove;* RV.
Asherah, explained (Ex. 34[13] mg.), the wooden symbols of a goddess Asherah.
The *asherah* is named in conjunction with high places, altars, steles, carved
stones, images. The verbs which are used in describing the making and
erection and the destruction of an *asherah* show that it was an upright

---

[*] See numbers of them in Lajard, *Culte de Mithra*, 1857; Ohnefalsch-Richter,
Kypros. See further, art. "Asherah" in *New Bible Dictionary* (A. & C. Black);
W. R. Smith, *Religion of the Semites*, p. 171 ff. On the goddess Asherah, see
above on 3[7] (p. 86 f.).   [†] Or, *a* second bullock.

wooden post or mast.* From Dt. 16²¹ it has been inferred that it was
originally a living tree,† for which the post is then supposed to be a conventional substitute; see *e.g.* Di. on Dt. *l.c.* But in this passage we should not
translate, *an asherah of any kind of tree* (RV.), but, *an asherah,—any
wooden object.*‡ For עץ 'pale,' cf. Dt. 21²². As yet the Phoenician inscriptions, in which the word has been found once or twice, throw no light on the
subject. The etymology of the word is also obscure. G. Hoffmann would
connect it with Arab. *athar;* perhaps only the *mark* of a place of worship.
The Assyr. *aṣru, aṣirtu,* pl. *aṣrâti,* also *eṣrêti,* which Fr. Delitzsch and others
interpret 'holy place, sanctuary, temple,'§ have also been compared. See
New Bible Dictionary, s. v. — 26. מעז] perhaps a natural stronghold rather
than a fortification; cf. צור מעז Is. 17¹⁰. The word does not occur elsewhere
in the historical books; cf. מצורה in the story of David. — נכיריכה] מערכה is a
row or rank; in hist. books, of soldiers in line of battle, but hardly, place
where the ranks are formed (*place d'armes*).‖ Jerome interprets of the wood
regularly laid upon the altar, similarly Ke. (MH. usage); Stud., Be¹., of the
courses of stone of which the altar was to be built (cf. the verb, Nu. 23⁴);
Cler., Be²., al., of a rampart or bastion built of courses of masonry. — בעצי
האשרה] עצים *fire wood* Gen. 22⁷·⁹ Is. 30³³ and often.

27-32. Gideon destroys the altar of Baal. He is saved from the wrath of his townsmen by Joash. — 27.

Gideon with ten of
his men carries out the divine command. In this narrative Joash
is supposed to be a man of much importance in the community,
with a numerous household of servants, a representation quite
different from that of v.¹¹⁻²⁴.¶ For fear of his fellow townsmen,
and of his own family, who as the custodians of the holy place
would be most incensed by its destruction, Gideon did his work at
night. — 28. The townspeople awoke in the morning to find the
altar of the Baal pulled to pieces and the sacred post cut down.
The second half-verse is somewhat clumsily phrased and is not
improbably the addition of a scribe, who missed an explicit mention of the fulfilment of the direction in v.²⁶ᵇ. — 29. Upon investigation they ascertain that Gideon is the perpetrator of the
sacrilege. — 30. They demand that Joash surrender his son to
them, that he may expiate his offence by death. To take him by

---

* So Saad. and Abulw. translate.

† Cf. *Sifre* on Dt. 12³ (§ 61); *Abodah zarah,* 45ª·ᵇ; Ra., Ki.,

‡ Cf. *Sifre* § 145; *Tamid,* 28ᵇ. Not impossibly the words כל עץ are a gloss.

§ *Assyr. Handwörterbuch,* p. 148. See against Delitzsch, Jensen, *Kosmologie,*
p. 200.   ‖ Cf. Schm., JHMich.   ¶ Note especially v.¹¹·¹⁵.

force might embroil them with the kindred of Joash and be the
beginning of a blood feud whose end no man could foresee. So
the Qoreish at Mecca tried to persuade Mohammed's uncle,
Abū Ṭālib, to withdraw from him his protection, that they might
kill the pestilent agitator without incurring the vengeance of his
family.* — 31. Joash, who as the proprietary custodian of the
holy place may be supposed to speak also for the god, rebukes
their presumption ; will they intervene to prevent Baal from vin-
dicating himself? — *To all who were arrayed against him*] lit.
stood; others, *who stood near him*, in which sense the words are
superfluous. — *Will you take up Baal's quarrel? Or will you
vindicate him?*] save him from his adversary ; cf. Job 13⁸. — *If
he is a god, let him take his own part*] deorum injuriae dis curae.†
In the thought of the writer, which, however, we must beware of
attributing to Joash, the words have an ironical point ; Baal's
inability to defend himself is a proof that he is no god ; cf.
1 K. 18²¹⁻³⁹. The conditional sentence would naturally follow
immediately upon the question in v.ᵃ : Will *you* take Baal's part?
will *you* defend him? If he is a god, let him take his own part.
This obvious connexion is broken by the sentence which is interposed : *Whoever takes up his* (Baal's) *quarrel shall be put to
death by morning*] in these words, the difficulty of which cannot
be evaded by a different translation, Joash appears to threaten
with death any one who rashly puts himself forward as the
champion of Baal ; he will defend his son by force if need be.‡
This would be in itself a conceivable sequel to his question ; but
a very tame one compared with v.ᵇ, *If he is a god*, &c. ; both
cannot be original. Probably, therefore, the intruding words were
added here by an editor or scribe ; perhaps originally a gloss
intended for a different place or in a different sense. At the end
of the verse the words, *because he pulled down his altar*, seem to
have been repeated from v.²⁵ᵇ with superfluous explicitness. —
32. Explanation of the name Jerubbaal. — *He* (Joash) *gave him
that day the name Jerubbaal*] better, pronouncing the verb as
passive, *He* (Gideon) *was called, he got the name. — That is to*

---

* Ibn Hishām, ed. Wüstenfeld, p. 167-169.

† Tiberius ; Tac., *annal.*, i. 73.   ‡ RLbG., Schm., Cler.

say, *Let Baal contend with him, because he pulled down his
altar*] Jerubbaal is another name of Gideon (7^1 $8^{29.34}$ 9 *passim*);
in the present shape of the narrative the relation between the two
is not clear. For a hypothesis about the use of the names in the
older stories of J and E, see on 7^1. For several centuries after
the occupation of Canaan the word *ba'al* (proprietor) was used
by the Israelites as innocently as *el* (*numen*) or *adōn* (lord), and
men whose loyalty to Yahweh is above suspicion gave baal-names
to their children. Saul had a son Ishbaal; Jonathan, a son
Meribaal; David, a son Baaljada. As in similar compounds of
el and *adōn*, the unnamed deity is no other than Yahweh. So,
doubtless, it was with Jerubbaal. In later times, through the
operation of causes which we cannot develop here, the baals of
Canaan are set over against Yahweh the God of Israel, and the
name baal becomes the very signature of heathenism. The old
proper names compounded with baal then became a stumbling
block, and in our texts are generally mutilated. Jerubbaal
becomes Jerubbesheth (2 S. 11^{21}), as Ishbaal is perverted into
Ishbosheth.* In our text also it is assumed that the Canaanite
Baal (v.$^{25f.}$) is meant, but by an ingenious etymology the name
is made to signify, Adversary of Baal.

27. כעשות ונ׳ . . . כאשר ירא את בית אביו] combination of two common
constructions of ירא, with the acc. of the person feared, and with כי and
the inf., fear to do something; cf. Ex. 34^{30}. — 28. ויהי הפר השני העירה] passive
with direct obj. in acc.; Ges.^{26} § 121, 1; on the frequency of this construction
in late Hebrew, see Giesebrecht, *ZATW*. i. p. 263 f. — הבנוי] Neh. 7^4 Cant. 4^4
Ps. 122^3. — 31. לכל אשר עמד עליו [עמד על in the sense 'stand up against one'
(קום על) is found only in late Hebrew (Ges., Stud.), but we may take עמד in
its usual meaning and still give to the preposition a hostile force. — האחם
הריבון לבעל]† the emphatic pronoun in contrast to the last clause, If he is a
god let him contend for *himself*. Cf. Job 13^8 אם לאל תריבון. — הושיע] *vindicate, avenge*; 1 S. $25^{26.31.33}$. Observe how the old imperfect endings roll out
in the energy of speech. — אשר יריב לו [אשר 𝕲 (with various turns) and 𝕷 (*qui
adversarius est ejus*) take ל ריב in the sense of ריב אל *contend against*, Jud. 21^{22}
Jer. 12^1 Job 33^{18}; but in this connexion the author cannot have employed the
preposition with a force exactly the opposite of that which it has in the preceding and following clauses, especially as he had the choice of three or four

---

* See We., *TBS.* p. 30 f.; Baudissin, *Studien zur semit. Religionsgeschichte*, i.
p. 108 n.; Driver, *TBS.* p. 195 f.

† 𝕲^{B} puts the words into the mouth of Gideon.

usual and unambiguous expressions. — ‫[יומת ער הבקר‬] the Hophal would hardly
be used if the meaning was that Baal would slay him.* ‫ער הבקר‬ *by morning;*
usually the morning of the following day; cf. Jud. 16³ 1 S. 25²² 2 S. 17²² &c.
(Stud.). Others interpret here of the same day, *during the morning* (Schm.,
Cler., JHMich., Be.†). — ‫[יריב לו‬] Job 13⁸; for reflexive force of suff., cf. Gen.
22¹⁶ Ex. 32¹⁸ &c. — 32. ‫[ויהרא לו‬] perhaps better ‫וַיִּרָא. — יְרֻבַּעַל‬] the author
explains the name as if it were made from ‫ירב בְּעֵל‬ *let Baal contend.* Such a
compound would not be strange (cf. ‫יְרִיב‬), and this etymology is accepted
by many modern scholars (‫יָרִיב בַּעַל‬ *Baal contends;* Kue., Dr., Baethgen).
This seems to be excluded, however, by the fact that the impf. of ‫רב‬ is *yarib*
(twice in this verse), and that no trace of an alternative *yarūb* exists. We.
(*TBS.* p. 31), with greater probability, thinks that the name is formed like
‫יִרֻאֵל‬,‡ in meaning equivalent to ‫יְרִיּדֹ‬, 'Yahweh founds.'§

33-35. The Midianites invade the land; Gideon summons his countrymen to resist them.

The hordes of Midian and its allies
cross the Jordan and encamp in the Great Plain. The spirit of
Yahweh fills Gideon; he raises his clan, Abiezer; then his tribe
Manasseh; finally, he calls out the tribes north of the plain,
Asher, Zebulun, and Naphtali. Verse³⁴ belongs to the first narrative (v.¹¹⁻³⁴, J) and may originally have followed immediately upon
v.²⁴; in this narrative the description of the invasion preceded
the appearance of the Messenger of Yahweh to Gideon (v.¹¹ᵇ).
Verse³³ may then be from the hand of E, who, if our surmise be
correct,‖ described at the beginning in general terms the annual
forays of Midian, and might therefore appropriately relate here
particulars of their last invasion. The author of 7²⁻⁸ must have
narrated how Gideon called out at least his own tribe, Manasseh,
and, if we may argue from the numbers, probably others; but this
account would naturally stand after 6³⁶⁻⁴⁰, in which Gideon, who
seems to be at home, seeks the assurance of a sign that he is
truly called of God to deliver Israel. Verse³⁵ may, therefore, be
derived in part from E, but has been attracted from its original
position by the parallel v.³⁴; the number of tribes called out is

---

* In Ez. 18¹⁸ the influence of the common legal formula for the death-penalty
explains the unusual expression; cf. 𝕲A al. L.S.

† Be. misstates the usage; ‫ער בקר‬ is found chiefly in P.

‡ Cf. also ‫ירושלם‬.

§ So also Baudissin, *Studien,* u. s. w., i. p. 108 n.; cf. Sta., *GVI.* i. p. 181 n.

‖ Above, p. 178; the Amalekites and Bene-Qedem are probably added by R, as
in other cases.

probably exaggerated by the redactor. Certainly, in its present form, 6^{36} is in conflict with 7^{23}; but we cannot be confident that the latter verse is original. On the other hand, v.^{36} must have been preceded in E by an account of the calling of Gideon to deliver Israel, which has been omitted by Rje as superfluous after 6^{11-24}.

33. Cf. v.$^{3-5}$ 7^{12}. — *The Plain of Jezreel*] so called from the city Jezreel, the modern Zer'in, on a spur projecting from the Gilboa range. The Valley of Jezreel (Jos. 17^{16} Hos. 1^{5}) is in the vicinity of that city, the eastern end of the great depression which divides the highlands of Central Palestine from Galilee; there is no evidence that the name was in Old Testament times extended to the whole plain.* Until quite recent times such inroads of Bedawin into the Great Plain have been of frequent occurrence.† — **34.** *The spirit of Yahweh took possession of Gideon*] lit. *put him on*, as a garment, clothed itself with him; 1 Chr. 12^{18} 2 Chr. 24^{20}. On the spirit of Yahweh, see comm. on 3^{10}. — *He sounded the war horn*] 3^{27}. — *Abiezer was called out*] v.^{35} $7^{22.23}$ 1 S. 14^{20} and often; cf. the active, $4^{10.13}$. He raised his own clan; and it is not improbable that in J the three hundred men with whom he puts the Bedawin to flight and pursues them over the Jordan were merely these clansmen. — **35.** The critical questions which this verse raises have been discussed above. — *Through all Manasseh*] his own tribe. West Manasseh only can be meant. — *Asher, Zebulun, and Naphtali*] see on 1^{30-33} (p. 49 f.); here, as in ch. 1 and 4, Issachar is passed over. The two halves of the verse are constructed on the same model; ‡ the second is perhaps an exaggerating addition. In 7^{23} Naphtali, Asher, and Manasseh are called out *after* the success of Gideon's stratagem, to pursue the fleeing foe. It is hardly possible that both verses are original. — *They went up to meet them*] may be from E's narrative: He sent messengers through all Manasseh, and they went up to meet the Midianites. — *Went up*, in the military sense; marched against them. In the present connexion the words form an awkward parallel to the end of v.*.

---

* See Furrer, *BL.* iii. p. 302; Bäd.^{3}, p. 229; G. A. Smith, *Hist. Geog.*, p. 385.
† Thomson, *Land and Book*^{3}, ii. 179 f.   ‡ Cf. also 7^{24a}.

33. The plain is called the plain of Megiddo (Zech. 12[11] 2 Chr. 35[22] Esdr. 1[27]); the Great Plain (1 Macc. 12[49], Fl. Jos., *antt.* viii. 2, 3 § 36; *b.j.* iv. 1, 8 § 54); the great plain of Legio (Euseb., *OS*[2]. 246[54]); the great plain of Esdraelon (Judith 1[8]); see also above on 1[5f.] (p. 43 ff.). It is the historical battlefield of Palestine; see esp. G. A. Smith, *Hist. Geography*, p. 391-410. — **34.** ורוח יהוה לבשה וג] the same tropical use in 𝕮 here and 1 Chr. 12[18], 𝔖 here; in Syriac freq. of demoniac possession (*PS.* 1887). — ויזעק] Niph. as pass. to Hiph.; 18[22. 23]; cf. נזעק 7[23. 24].

36–40. The sign of the fleece. — Gideon asks a sign that God will deliver Israel by his hand. A fleece exposed at night on the threshing floor is drenched with dew, while the ground around is dry. In a second test the fleece alone is dry, while the ground is wet with dew. It is scarcely to be supposed that after the wonderful manifestation of the Messenger of Yahweh, v.[21-23], Gideon ventured to require another sign; the premises of v.[36-40] are not to be sought in v.[11-24], but in the missing parallel account of the call of Gideon, in which the summons to be the champion of Israel probably came, not through the Messenger of Yahweh, but, as commonly in E, in a dream or night vision.* A revelation of this kind may well require the attestation of a tangible sign such as Gideon here proposes. This hypothesis is confirmed by the fact that in v.[36-40], in contrast with v.[11-24], we have without exception *Elohim* (v.[40]) and *ha-Elohim* (v.[36. 39]) instead of *Yahweh* and *Mal'ak Yahweh*. We may, therefore, with much probability attribute v.[36-40] to E.

36. *As thou sayest*] v.[37b]; the words now refer to v.[14-16]. — **37.** The hard, bare surface of the threshing floor and its exposure to the wind made it the most suitable place for such an experiment.† — **38.** The test resulted as he had proposed; in the morning he squeezed the fleece and drained out of it dew enough to fill a bowl with water. — **39, 40.** To make sure that this was not due to some natural cause, he proposes to invert the experiment; this time the fleece alone shall be dry, while all the ground is covered with dew. On the following morning he finds it so.

---

* Bu., *Richt. u. Sam.*, p. 110 f.

† On Syrian threshing floors, see Wetzstein, in *Zeitschrift für Ethnologie*, 1873; Rob., *BR*[3]. ii. p. 83; *DB*[2]. i. p. 65 f.

36. אם ישך מושיע] Gen. 24⁴². ⁴⁹ 43¹ 1 S. 23²⁰; corresponding constr. of אין
Ex. 8¹⁷ 1 S. 19¹¹; עור Ex. 9². See Dr⁵. § 137 (a). — **37.** גֹּרֶן] some modern
Arab. dialects *jurn* (Moḥiṭ, p. 243), or *gurān* (Bar Baḥlūl, ed. Duval, 41);
Ethiopic, see Di. *Lex.* (perhaps loan-word). — **38.** וַיָּזַר] generally derived
from זור; Kö. (i. p. 328) would make it from זרר, an (imaginary) softer form
of צרר. There is better ground for thinking that the root is זיר. — רספל] 5²¹.
— **39.** אל יחר אפך] Gen. 44¹⁸ Ex. 32²². — וארגבה אך הפעם on הפעם see on 15⁸
16²⁰. The clause has very likely been borrowed from the intercession of
Abraham, Gen. 18³². It is superfluous before the following, *let me try it only
this time with the fleece,* and the sentence gains much by its removal (Bu.).

VII. 1–8. Gideon's numbers are reduced to three hundred men.

— Gideon, with thirty-two thousand men, encamps near the
enemy, at Ain Harod. At the command of Yahweh, who will
not have the victory attributed to human might and prowess,
Gideon dismisses all who fear the encounter. Of the ten thousand that remain, three hundred are picked out by a singular test ;
these are furnished with the provisions and the horns of the rest,
who are dismissed to their homes. The great numbers presup-
pose the raising of more than one tribe (6³⁵), and, like that verse,
conflict with 7²³ᶠ·, where the tribes are called out after the success
of Gideon's attack, to pursue the fleeing enemy and intercept
their retreat. The aim of the whole story (v.²⁻⁸) seems to be to
enforce the lesson that it is as easy for Yahweh to deliver by few
as by many (1 S. 14⁶), and that to rebuke man's vaingloriousness
he chooses the weak things of the world to put to shame the
strong (1 Cor. 1²⁶⁻²⁷ ; Studer). The verses seem to be from E,
and belong perhaps to a secondary stratum of that work.[*] Verse¹,
on the other hand, seems to be the continuation of 6³⁴, and to be
continued in 7⁹ᶠ·. — **1.** *While the camp of Midian was north of
Gibeath ha-Moreh*] the text has, *north of him, from Gibeath ha-
Moreh, in the plain,* which cannot be right. The cause of the
disorder is perhaps contamination from v.⁸. In our ignorance
of the topography, the restoration is merely conjectural. As 6³³
locates the camp of the Midianites in the Plain of Jezreel, Ain
Harod and Gibeath ha-Moreh have naturally been looked for
there. Stanley would find the former in 'Ain Gālūd, a very
copious spring at the foot of Gilboa, about half an hour east of

---

[*] Bu. ascribes them to Rje; see above, p. 176.

Jezreel (Zer'în).* Gibeath ha-Moreh is then supposed to be the
hill now called Nebī Daḥi, on the northern side of the valley,
above Sōlem (Shunem). The positions would thus be very much
the same which were occupied by Saul and the Philistines before
the battle of Mt. Gilboa (1 S. 28⁴ cf. 29¹). These conjectures rest,
however, on a most insecure foundation. Ch. 6³⁵ is not from the
same source as 7¹, and it is not certain that the author of the
latter (J) laid the scene of action in the Plain of Jezreel. The
name Moreh occurs elsewhere only in the neighbourhood of
Shechem (Gen. 12⁶ Dt. 11³⁰), and, in the absence of any other
clue, it is the least hazardous supposition that the same place is
meant here. The other indications in J agree very well with this
hypothesis. In this narrative Gideon has behind him his clan,
Abiezer, whose seats are about Ophrah, probably not very far
from Shechem.† In his pursuit of the Midianites he crosses
the Jordan not far from Succoth, by the fords ordinarily taken
between Shechem and Gilead (Gen. 33¹⁷. ¹⁸⁻²⁰ ; see below on 8⁵),
as he would do if he had come down by Wady Fār'ah ; the composite verse 7²⁵ shows that the direction of the flight and pursuit
was differently described in the two sources.‡

1. ירבעל הוא גדעון] if *Gideon* had been original here and *Jerubbaal* been
introduced by a subsequent hand (Kitt.), we should have had, *And Gideon,
that is, Jerubbaal.* — עין חרד] cf. the gentile, חרדי 2 S. 23²⁵ (1 Chr. 11³⁷).
Graetz conj. for חרד עין, עין דאר Ps. 83¹¹. — ובחנה כרין היה לו בצפון מגבעת המורה.
בעמק] Bu. emends, after v.⁸⁵, היה לו מתחת מצפון לגבעת המורה ונ'. It seems to
me more probable that combination with v.⁸ is responsible for the disorder of
the text, and I should prefer to restore היה בצפון לגבעת המורה, omitting לו and
בעמק. Another possibility היה לו מצפון בגבעת המורה. — 'Ain Ġālūd was early supposed to be the scene of David's fight with Goliath (*Itin. Hierosol.*).§ Eshtori
Parchi (fol. 67ᵇ) calls this a Moslem blunder. It is more likely that the
similarity of the name was the occasion of the error, than that a mislocation of
the conflict with the Philistines (under the influence of 1 S. 28⁴) gave rise to
the name. 'Ain Ġālūd is often identified with the Tubania of the Talmud
and the crusading historians; Eshtori Parchi rightly distinguishes them, and
'Ain Tuba'ūn is in fact about a mile NE. of 'Ain Ġālūd (*SWP. Memoirs*, ii.

---

* *Sinai and Palestine*, 1856, p. 338. So Furrer, *BL.* iv. p. 239; Be., G. A. Smith,
Hist. Geography, p. 397 f.; al. Descriptions of 'Ain Ġālūd in Rob., *BR².* ii. p. 323 f.;
Guérin, *Samarie*, i. p. 308 f.; *SWP. Memoirs*, ii. p. 79. Cf. also *DB².* i. p. 1288.

† See above, on 6¹¹.   ‡ On Tabor, 8¹⁸, see there.

§ See Rob., *BR².* ii. p. 324; G. A. Smith, *Hist. Geog.*, 397 f. n.

p. 79). Conder (*SWP. Memoirs*, ii. p. 81) would find Ain Harod in 'Ain el-Gemaīn, much nearer Beisân, imagining that a reminiscence of the "two troops" of Israel and Midian survives in the name. Nebi Daḥi is now often called Little Hermon. — נבעה הבורה [cf. אלון בורה Gen. 12⁶, אירוני בורה Dt. 12⁴; cf. אלון מעונים Jud. 9³⁷ (see there).

2–8. Gideon dismisses all but three hundred picked men. —

2. Yahweh will not give the enemy into the power of Gideon's army. — *Lest Israel vaunt itself against me, saying, My own hand wrought deliverance for me*] cf. Is. 10¹³⁻¹⁵ Dt. 8¹¹⁻¹⁸ 9⁴ᶠ, and with the last phrase 1 S. 25²⁶·³¹·³³. — Gideon shall first dismiss all who are lacking in courage. — **3.** Proclaim to the people : *Whoever is fearful and in terror*] cf. Dt. 20⁸; a similar measure with a different motive. The second verb (*ḥârad*) perhaps plays upon the name *Harod*, though it is not intimated that the name is derived from this *terror*.[*] The following words, translated in RV., *and depart[†] from Mt. Gilead*, present great difficulty. The meaning of the verb, which is found only here, is unknown, and the mention of Mt. Gilead (east of the Jordan, 5¹⁷) is quite irreconcilable with the topography of the story. The emendation of Clericus, *Gilboa*, would bring the situation into accord with 6³³; but if Gideon was, as is supposed, encamped on Mt. Gilboa, the direction to return home *from Mt. Gilboa* is entirely superfluous.[‡] Ewald surmises that the words are an old proverbial saying in East Manasseh, in the present context meaning no more than "slink from the field of battle."[§] But the use of such an expression by the writer, without explanation, would simply invite misunderstanding. — Twenty-two thousand men availed themselves of this permission; ten thousand remained with Gideon. — **4.** The numbers are still too great; Yahweh prescribes a new test. — *Take them down to the waters, and let me separate them for thee there*] remove the inferior elements which are not fit for the high enterprise; the figure is taken from the refining of the precious metals by smelting out the baser admixture of the ore; Is. 1²⁵ Mal. 3²·³. What waters are meant, we cannot determine. The common opinion that they are the Nahr Gâlûd, the stream which rises in 'Ain Gâlûd (see

---

[*] Ew., al.   [†] Margin : *go round about*.   [‡] Dathe, Stud.
[§] *GVI.* ii. p. 543; so Sta., *GVI.* i. p. 150; Bu., *Richt. u. Sam.*, p. 112 n.

on v¹), and, fed by other springs, flows past Beisān to the Jordan,
labours under all the uncertainties and difficulties which beset
Stanley's hypothesis. Yahweh will there tell him who shall go
with him and who not. — **5.** Those who throw themselves flat on
the ground, with their faces to the water, and lap it up with their
tongues like dogs, are to be set by themselves, and those who
kneel down to drink (from their hands), by themselves. — **6.** *The
number of those who lapped* with their hands to their mouths
amounted to three hundred men] the words, *with their hands to
their mouths*, are as 𝔊 shows, a gloss, and in this place an erroneous gloss; to lap with the tongue, and to raise water to the
mouth with the hand, are precisely the two different ways of
drinking which are here distinguished. Perhaps the words were
meant to stand at the end of v.⁶, where they would be a correct
explanation; see note. The contradiction at this point between
v.⁵ and v.⁶ has involved the whole interpretation in obscurity.
Clericus imagines the three hundred drinking standing : * intelli-
guntur qui manu aquam hauserant, eamque e manu stantes bibe-
bant, nequaquam inflexis genibus; they were the hardy warriors
who did not yield to their thirst,† or were too eager to be at the
enemy to stop even to drink. Josephus, on the contrary, thinks
that they were the greatest cowards in the army, who in the
presence of the foe were afraid to drink in the usual manner. ‡
The miraculous character of the deliverance is thus heightened.
The interpretations are equally far-fetched; if any significance is
to be attached to the way in which the three hundred drink, we
should find it in the comparison to dogs (v.⁵); they were the
rude, fierce men; compare the name Caleb. § It is doubtful,
however, whether the character of the three hundred is in the
writer's mind at all. — **7.** Yahweh will deliver Israel by means of
the three hundred; all the rest of the people shall go to their
homes. — **8.** Those who are sent home leave their provisions and
their horns with Gideon, who is thus enabled to furnish each of

---

* Cf. Be., Ke., Cass.; against this impossible theory see Stud.
† Or who disregarded convenience; cf. Aug.
‡ *Antt.* v. 6, 3 § 217; Thdt.; cf. Procop.
§ In the number 300 (Greek ϒ) the Fathers saw an allegory of the cross; see
Aug., *quaest.* 37.

his three hundred men with a horn. The verse is clearly written
with reference to v.[16f.], to explain how Gideon came to have so
many horns at his disposal. The repeated change in the subject
of the verbs is harsh and the text is in at least one place at fault.
Perhaps v.* in its present form is the work of a redactor, who is
preparing for v.[16-22]; see note. — *The camp of Midian was below
him in the valley*] corresponds to v.[1], and is E's introduction to
the surprise of the Midianite camp in v.[16-22].

2. מהֵחי . . . רַב] מן comparative with infinitive, Gen. 4[13] 27[1] 29[19] Dt. 28[66]
1 K. 8[64], Roorda, § 485. — [ההפאר עלֵ] Is. 10[15], *glory over*. — [ירי הושיעה לֵי]
1 S. 25[26, 33] cf. Is. 59[16] 63[5] Ps. 44[4] 98[1]; [הושיע לֵ] 10[14]. — 3. [ויזפר מהר הגלעד] in
rendering *depart, set forth quickly*, &c., the versions (GLS) seem to have
been guided only by the context and the preposition; *depart early* (AV.),
sc. in the morning, follows Ra., Ki., RLbG., Drus., al. in connecting the word
with Aram. צפרא 'morning'; *make a circuit* (Abulw., Tanch., Ges., Stud.,
Be., Cass., al.; cf. Ki. *Lex.*), connects it with Heb. צפירה 'fillet'* (*encircling*
the head), cf. Ez. 7[7.10]. Others compare Arab. صفر in the sense 'run quickly,'
or 'spring, bound'; so SS. The context would make the general meaning of
the verb sufficiently clear if the following words מהר הגלעד were intelligible in
this place. JDMich. conj. מַהֵר, *flee quickly to* Mt. Gilead; but this is both
intrinsically improbable and in direct conflict with v.[7.8]. Cler. proposed מהר
הגלבע, from Mt. *Gilboa*, which is adopted by Hitz., Be., Graetz, Ke., Doorn.,
Reuss, al.; but Dathe and Stud. rightly observe that the words are then meaningless. Ewald's old Manassite saying, in which Gilead is used proverbially for
the battlefield, is without the slightest foundation or plausibility. Cass. elabo-
rates a somewhat similar theory. Stud.'s explanation is, that, as the Midianites
in the Plain of Jezreel lay between the men of the northern tribes (6[35]) and
their homes, they are bidden to cross the Jordan, and by a circuit through
Mt. Gilead go around the enemy. But if this was the author's meaning he
could not have expressed himself more obscurely. If a conjecture may be
ventured in this state of the text, I would suggest, ויצרפֵם נרען *Gideon put them
to the test;* for the verb cf. v.[4].† — 5. [כל אשר ילֵק בלשונו מן הםים] the vb. להק
(onomatopoetic) 1 K. 21[19] (*bis*) 22[38]; cf. לחֵך Nu. 22[4] &c.; GBN ἀπὸ τοῦ
ὕδατος, better than ἐκ (GAVLM). — [הצֵיב אותו לבר] of persons, Gen. 33[15] 43[9]
47[2]; cf. of things Jud. 6[37] 8[27]; see note on the latter verse. לבֵר without suffix,
Ex. 26[9] 36[16] Zech. 12[12.13.14]. — וני] [וכל אשר יכרע ונ] the vb. see on 5[27]. At the end
GALMN (cf. s) adds μεταστήσεις αὐτὸν καθ' αὑτόν, PV μεταστήσεις αὐτόν.
The words may have been accidentally omitted in 𝔐; the nature of the

---

* Originally 'braid, plait.'
† Cf. RJes., who regards ויצפר as equivalent to ויצרף by metathesis. Gractz
conj. ויפרץ 'break through.'

attestation makes it less likely that they were added by 𝕲, cf. 𝕷.𝕾.—6. בירב־
אל מירם [similarly 𝕲ᴮᴺⱽᴼ (cf. Fl. Jos., *antt.* v. 6, 3 § 217), probably Θ; see
Grabe, *Ep. ad Millium*, p. 14; Field, *ad loc.* An explanation of לקח which
is in contradiction to בלשונו v.⁵; obviously an erroneous gloss. In its place
𝕲ᴬᴸᴹ | ʠ have the correct gloss ἐν τῇ γλώσσῃ αὐτῶν; conflation of the two
in 𝕲ᴾⱽᴼ ʂ. Perhaps the gloss in 𝕽 was meant for the end of v.⁶, where it
would be right in fact (Doorn.); hardly genuine at the end of v.⁵ (Bu.),
against which the change of number seems conclusive; at the end of v.⁴,
whether the words were genuine or a gloss, we should expect בידו אר מיו.—
8. The change of subject in וייבא is abrupt and awkward; only less so, that
in שלח v.ᵇ; צדה הצם is incorrect. For the latter, the emendation צדה הצם (or
ציר הצם Jos. 9⁴·¹⁴) would suffice to remove the grammatical difficulty; but the
statement that the three hundred took the provisions of the rest of the people
is not obviously relevant. Gideon was not planning a long campaign and had
no need to encumber his three hundred men with the rations of ten thousand.
If the author meant to explain how Gideon's men got the jars of v.¹⁶ᵃ as well
as the horns, he would hardly have said it so indirectly, especially as the
provisions were certainly not transported in earthen jars. If we were sure
that such was his intention, we should without hesitation emend כֵּדֵי הצם, with
which בידם also would better accord. But as in v.¹⁶⁻²² the horns come from
one version of the stratagem, the jars from the other, this emendation or
interpretation would constrain us to regard v.⁸ᵃ as the work of a redactor
displacing the original beginning of the verse, in which the name of Gideon
probably stood. If v.¹⁶⁻²² were homogeneous, v.⁸ᵃ might be restored: וייקח את
צדה הצם מידם, which would remove all formal difficulties.— איש לאהליו] ₁ S. 13⁴
4¹⁰ 2 S. 19⁹, לאהריו Jud. 20⁸; cf. לשקבו ₆.⁷ 9⁵⁵ &c. The phrase is a survival
from the nomadic life; the plur. refers to the group of tents belonging to the
family or clan.

9-15. Gideon, creeping down to the camp by night to reconnoitre, hears a Midianite tell an ominous dream.

— The verses
belong to the first narrative (J), and originally followed immediately on v.¹.— **9.** *That night*] cf. 6²⁵. In the present context, the
night following the dismissal of the greater part of Gideon's force
(v.²⁻⁸); in its original connexion, the night after he encamped by
the spring of Harod (v.¹).— *Up, descend on the camp*] attack the
enemy at once; cf. 4¹⁴.— If he is afraid to attack, he shall go
down with a single attendant and hear the talk of the camp; he
will then hesitate no longer. Gideon does so.— **10.** *Thou and
Phurah, thy page*] lit. *boy;* the armour-bearer or attendant of a
warrior of rank, 9⁵⁴ ₁ S. 14⁶ &c.— **11.** *To the outskirts of the
armed men who were in the encampment*] cf. *to the outskirts of
the camp,* v.¹⁷·¹⁹. The precise meaning of the word translated

armed men is uncertain ; cf. Ex. 13¹⁸ Jos. 1¹⁴ 4¹². It is natural to
imagine that in such a raid a part of the invaders, better armed
and perhaps better disciplined than the rest, lay along the front of
the camp to cover it from attack ; see note. — **12.** The immense
numbers of the invaders ; cf. 6³⁻⁵ 8¹⁰. The verse in its present
form cannot belong to the original narrative ; it has either been
amplified and exaggerated by an editor, or is wholly his work,
combining motives borrowed from 6³⁻⁵. — *Like the sand on the sea
shore*] a common simile for countless numbers ; Jos. 11⁴ 1 S. 13⁵
2 S. 17¹¹. It is probably meant, not of the camels, but of the
enemy themselves ; but it hangs very loosely at the end of the
verse and may be an addition by a still later hand. — **13.** Just
as Gideon came within hearing, a Midianite was telling his comrade a dream. — *A cake of barley bread*] the specific meaning of
the word rendered from the context, *cake* or *loaf*, is not known.
We are probably to imagine a round, flat, hard-baked ash-cake,
trundling through the camp till it strikes the tent and turns it
upside down. The tent is the natural symbol of the nomad ; the
barley cake might very well represent the peasant. As barley is
an inferior grain, many interpreters find in the words a scornful
allusion to the poverty of the Israelite peasantry, who were
reduced to eating what is fit food only for animals. It is doubtful, however, whether this is intended ; there seems to have been
a particular kind of barley ash-cake or griddle-bread (Ez. 4¹²),
and *ṣelûl* may be the specific name for a cake of peculiar shape
or solidity, which was made of barley meal. — *It came to the tent*]
not the tent of the head chief,* but that of the narrator, or, perhaps better, in view of the symbolical character of the dream, to
a tent. The definite article is idiomatically used in Hebrew when
an object is made definite in the imagination of the speaker by
what is done with or to it in the story. — *And struck it*, and it fell,
and turned it upside down, and the tent lay prostrate] the words
printed in Roman letters are redundant ; comparison with 𝔊, and,
in the latter instance, the false tense in 𝔐, show that they are
glosses. — **14.** His comrade interprets the portent. — *This is nothing else than the men of Israel*] the text has, *the sword of Gideon*

---

* Fl. Jos., Be., al.

ben Joash, the man of Israel; but this is a later and erroneous interpretation. The barley bread naturally represents the peasantry as a class, not an individual among them; the Hebrew phrase translated *the men of Israel* is uniformly collective; and it is hardly likely that the first narrator made his Midianites know by name the deliverer whom Yahweh had just called from the flail. The words, *the sword of,* may be original, but more probably they come from v.[20]. — *God has given into his hand Midian and all the camp*] *God,* not *Yahweh,* is proper in the mouth of a foreigner; cf. 3[20]. Amplification by the editor may be suspected here also. *Midian and all the camp* is redundant, and, of the two, the order of the sentence indicates that the latter is original; it also corresponds to the description of the portent (v.[13]). *Midian and* is perhaps from the same hand which over-filled the first half of the verse by the insertion of Gideon's name. — **15.** Gideon accepts the omen, returns to his own camp, and prepares for an immediate attack. — *Prostrated himself*] in homage to the deity who gave the omen. — *Up! for Yahweh has given into your hand the camp of Midian.*

9. רד במחנה [v.[11] cf. 1 S. 26[10] (כמלחמה). — 11. החזקנה ידיך] 2 S. 2[7] Zech. 8[9. 13]. — כֹּ [אל קצה החמשים] (so uniformly; see Norzi and Lonzano on Ex. 13[18]). In Jos. 1[14] 4[12], men in fighting order; syn. חלוצים (Jos. 4[13] Nu. 32[30. 32] Dt. 3[18]). —12. נמליב בכבד] the verb was perhaps suggested by the comparison to locusts, *had lighted* (and lay) in the plain; it is scarcely to be connected with the sense, 'fall upon, attack' (c. ב pers.), Jos. 11[7] &c. (Be., SS., al). — שֶׁעֶר] see on 6[17]; cf. Giesebrecht, *ZATW.* i. p. 280 n. — 13. צליל '] Qerē צליל, perhaps meaning to hint a connexion with צלה, cf. 'A. From the context, a round (disk-shaped) cake or loaf; 𝕲 μαγὶς Σ κολλύρα 'A ἐγκρυφίας 𝕷 *subcinericius panis.* לחם is possibly a gloss on the rare word. The conjecture of G. Hoffmann is ingenious, but improbable: *a clash of fighting about the gates went circling about the camp* (צליל לחם שְׁעָרִים, cf. 5[8]).[*] Barley was a grain of inferior value; if 2 K. 7[1] may be taken as an average estimate, worth about half as much as wheat. It was used for bread, as in the *maṣṣōt* of the Feast of Unleavened Bread, cf. further 2 K. 4[42] Ez. 4[12] John 6[9. 13], also Ru. 2[17] &c.; and as provender for (the king's) horses, 1 K. 5[8] (EV. 4[28]), cf. *Pesach.,* 3[b] *inf.* In early times its use for food was well-nigh universal; then as a cheaper and coarser diet it was chiefly consumed by the poorer classes; finally it became almost exclusively provender for animals. See Plin., *n. h.,* xviii. 72, antiquissimum in cibis hordeum. — 74, panem ex hordeo antiquis usitatum vita

* QPB.

damnavit, quadripedumque fere cibus est. Fl. Jos., *antt.* v. 6, 4 § 219 (on the present passage), μᾶζαν ἐδόκει κριθίνην ὑπ' εὐτελείας ἀνθρώποις ἄβρωτον. There is no reason to think that in old Israel the use of barley bread was as restricted as it became in later, not to say in modern, times. — מההפך בכתה [cf. Gen. 3²⁴, the flaming sword that turned in every direction; it seemed to be everywhere. Others, simply *turning over and over*, or *rolling* like a wheel, which seems less in accordance with the usage of the verb. — [כד האהל many Greek MSS. add, *of Midian*. — [ויפל > 𝕲ᴾⱽᴸᴹᴼ sub aster. **s**. — [ונפל האהל the false tense betrays the gloss; the words are wanting in 𝕲ᴾⱽ ɴ. 71. 74. 121. — **14.** [אין זה כי אם Gen. 47¹⁸ (? J); with verb (pf.) Am. 3⁴ ⁴. זאת, the content of the preceding relation, what passed in the dream; fem. pron. where in Greek or Latin we should have the neuter. — [איש ישראל is grammatically definite, and in usage regularly collective, *the* (body of) *Israelite men* (*die israelitische Mannschaft*), Jud. 7²³ 8²² 9⁵⁵ 20²⁰; so all similar phrases, *e.g.* איש אפרים 7²⁴ 8¹ 12¹, איש בנימין 20⁴¹, איש יהודה 15¹⁰ 1 S. 15⁴ 2 S. 19¹⁷· ⁴²· ⁴³· ⁴⁴ 20⁴ 2 K. 23³ &c. The apparent exceptions are איש יששכר Jud. 10¹, איש בנימין 1 S. 4¹²; * cf. Nu. 25⁸. With the name of Gideon falls also the word חרב; cf. v.²⁰.— **15.** [בספר in this sense only here, though ספר ' recount, relate,' is common; cf. Engl. ' tale ' = ' number ' and ' narrative.' — [ואת שברו *interpretation* (so only here; syn. פתרון and — late — פשר); lit. *the breaking of it,* a trope similar to the ' solution ' of an enigma, &c.

16–22. Gideon's stratagem; panic and flight of the Midianites.

— The narration is redundant and confused. To carry a lighted torch concealed in an earthen jar would give full occupation to both hands; how Gideon's men managed the horns besides does not appear.† Kuenen thinks that the torches and jars may have been added by the editor. ‡ Budde recognizes in them an original and characteristic feature of the story; in his opinion it is rather the horns, "which come from Jericho," that the editor has brought in. The following narrative, however, gives plain evidence, not of editorial amplification, but of the attempt to combine two accounts. This is particularly clear at the beginning and end of the passage (v.¹⁷, v.²¹· ²²). The doubling is such as the mere introduction of the horns would not produce; and further, as Kuenen rightly saw, the blowing of the horns now constitutes the principal strand of the narrative. We have found

---

* See We., Klost., *ad loc.* The exx. in Ew. § 290 *a* 3, to which Dr., *TBS.* p. 38, refers, are inconclusive.

† Studer's explanation is not satisfactory.

‡ *HCO³.* i. p. 347.

above two accounts of the call of Gideon and of the raising of
his countrymen against Midian. In the sequel of the story, not
only 7[23ff.] but 8[4ff.] represents the enemy as in full flight.[*] The
source from which the latter is derived also presumably told how
they were put to flight; and as from 8[11ff.] it does not appear that
they had previously sustained an actual attack, it may be inferred
that they had been alarmed by a stratagem such as is described
in 7[16-22]. These facts seem to commend the hypothesis that the
trumpets are derived from one source, the jars and torches from
the other. The former may with considerable probability be
ascribed to E; the latter will then come from J. If the latter,
as there is some reason to believe,[†] laid the scene of action, not
in the Plain of Jezreel, but in the vicinity of Ophrah, the execution of this original manœuvre is more easily conceivable; the
jars could be fetched by Gideon's clansmen from their homes for
this purpose. The redactor has united the two diverse accounts
as best he could, binding them together with clauses borrowed
from one or the other of his sources. That in which the trumpets
play the leading part, being the more detailed, furnished the warp
of his fabric.

To E may be ascribed: v.[16a, bα] [and said to them] [17b. 18a, bα. 19a, bα. 20aa. 2b]
(from יהוה וישם) [22b] (in part) [23ff.]. J's narrative, which is less completely
preserved, probably ran somewhat as follows: [He gave them, or, they took]
empty jars, and torches in the jars (v.[16bβ]); and he said to them, See from
me what to do, and do likewise (v.[17a]). [They surrounded the camp; Gideon
gave the signal by breaking his jar (? v.[19bβ])]; ‡ and they broke the jars and
grasped the torches (? in their left hands, and in their right their *swords!*)
and cried, For Yahweh and Gideon! (v.[20aβ, b•]). And they stood as they were
around the camp, and all the camp ran away. And they fled (v.[21]) to ...
(v.[24] in part).§

16. *Gideon divided his three hundred men into three bodies*]
the object of this division was to make a simultaneous demonstration from different sides of the encampment; the disposition is
not further detailed. — *And furnished them all with horns, and
empty jars, and torches inside the jars*] the horns probably belong

---

* Note הרר, v.[4.5]; Kue.   † See above, p. 200.   ‡ Recast by Rje.
§ With this attempt at an analysis, cf. Be., p. xxii, and Winckler, *Altorientalische
Forschungen*, p. 50 f.

to one version of the story (E), the jars and torches to the other
(J) ; see above. The horns, and perhaps the jars also, are provided for in v.⁹ᵃ (R) ; see comm. there and note (p. 203 f.). The
jars were used to conceal the light of the torches till the Israelites
had got into position around the camp ;* these were broken with
a startling crash which would sound to the terrified Midianites
like the clash of arms.—**17, 18.** Gideon instructs his men.—
You shall see from me and do likewise] an unusual breviloquence ;
cf. 9⁴⁸. In v.ᵇ the same thing is repeated in common phrase, *and
as I do, so shall you do.* These words are not improbably editorial ; beside the detailed instructions in the following verse they
are superfluous, and v.¹⁸ᵃ would connect much better with the
preceding if they were away : *When I reach the outskirts of the
camp,* 18 *and blow a blast on the horn, . . . then you also shall
blow, &c.*] the Midianites, hearing the charge sounded on different
sides of the camp, would be bewildered by the expectation of a
simultaneous attack from several quarters.—*And say, For Yahweh and Gideon*] introduced by the editor from the other narrative (v.²⁰) ; observe the colourless, *say*, for *shout.*

19. *The beginning of the middle watch*] the night was divided
into three watches ; the first watch, the middle watch, and the
morning watch (1 S. 11¹¹). The division into four watches
(Matt. 14²⁵ Mk. 6⁴⁸) was adopted from the Romans ; see note.—
They had but just posted the guards] Jer. 51¹² cf. 6¹⁷. More
precise note of time ; it was immediately after the turn of the
watch, not far from eleven o'clock. It is not intimated that this
was a relief guard ; the Midianites may not have thought it necessary to keep guard during the evening. In v.¹⁹ᵃ Gideon was able
unobserved to approach near enough to the camp to hear their
talk.†—*And blew the trumpets, and smashed the jars which they
had in their hands*] the juxtaposition of the two clauses corresponds to v.²⁰ ; the second is probably derived in substance from
J (Gideon smashed the jar he held ; cf. v.¹⁶ᵃᵝ) ; but it has been
thoroughly recast by the redactor ; observe the construction, on
which see note.—**20.** *The three companies*] as soon as the signal

---

* See Lane, *Modern Egyptians*⁶, 1860, p. 120.
† These verses, however, are probably not from the same source as v.¹⁹,

P

was given, the other two divisions joined their blasts to those of
Gideon's own command. — *And shattered the jars*] the other
strand of the narrative (J). — *And held on to the torches*] the
text adds, *with their left hands, and with their right, the horns to
blow.* This is obviously harmonistic; it is a question, however,
whether the editor added it all of his own conception, or whether
he only altered an older text. If, for *the horns to blow*, we should
substitute *their swords*, the words might be thought to be an
original part of the narrative.[*] But the swords play no part in
the rout of the Midianites, as the author explicitly tells us (v.^{21}, J);
the words are therefore better attributed wholly to the redactor.
— *And cried, For Yahweh and Gideon!*] this seems to be the
original form of the war cry (cf. v.^{18}).[†] The word *Sword!* is
probably a gloss; cf. v.^{14}. The cause of Israelites against foreign
foes is Yahweh's cause; and he who smites for Gideon, smites for
Yahweh (see introduction to ch. 5; esp. p. 134). It is a historical misapprehension, however, to describe the conflict with
the Canaanites (ch. 4. 5) or Midianites (ch. 6–8) as a religious
war; and especially to compare it with the wars of Islam.[‡]

16. ‏שלשה ראשים‎] technical term for divisions of a military force; esp.
columns or parties formed to execute a concerted attack or stratagem; 9$^{34ff.}$
1 S. 11^{11} 13$^{17f.}$ Job 1^{17}. It is a second accusative after ‏ויחץ‎; cf. 1 S. 11^{11}
(‏וישם‎), Ges.^{26} § 117, 5 *c*. — ‏שופרות‎] see on 3^{27}. — ‏כד‎ [‏כדים ריקים‎ is a vessel used
to draw and carry water, Gen. 24$^{14ff.}$ 1 K. 18^{34} Eccl. 12^{6}; to keep meal in,
1 K. 17$^{12-16}$. So in MH., for honey, oil, barley, dates; see Levy, *NHWb.* ii.
p. 293 f. In all cases where we can form a judgment, a vessel of some size.
‏ריקים‎ 2 K. 4^{3} (‏כלים‎). — ‏לפדים‎] *torches*, not *lamps* (‏נר‎), cf. 15$^{4ff.}$; see the description in *Aruch*, s.v.; Levy, ii. p. 517. Thomson's illustration (*Land and
Book*^{2}, ii. p. 182): "I have often seen the small oil lamps of the natives
carried in a pitcher or earthen vessel at night," is not at all in point. —
17. ‏כמני הראו וכן תעשו‎] learn your part from me by observing what I do. ‏כן‎
refers to the unexpressed object of ‏הראו‎; cf. 9^{48}. — ‏רנה אנכי בא וג׳‎] cf. 9^{49}
Gen. 50^{5} Jos. 2^{18} 2 S. 17^{9} &c. — 18. ‏סביבות כל המחנה‎ [‏סביבות‎ adverbial accusative; cf. ‏סביב ל‎ v.^{21}. Of the instances of the plur. a considerable part are in
passages generally ascribed to E; see Gen. 35^{6} 41^{48} Ex. 7^{24} Nu. 11$^{24.31.32}$ 22^{4}
Jud. 2^{12}. — ‏ליהוה ולגדעון‎ [ ] 𝕲^{VMNO} praem. ῥομφαία; so also 𝕾𝕿 and some codd.
of 𝕳 (De Rossi): conformation to v.^{20}; see note there. — 19. ‏ובאה איש‎]
read ‏ובאה האיש‎; the article accidentally dropped after the final ‏ה‎. — ‏ראש‎
‏האשמרת התיכונה‎ [‏לראש אשמרות‎, Ex. 14^{24} 1 S. 11^{11} ‏אשמרת הבקר‎] cf. Lam. 2^{19}

---

* Bu., Winckler.   † Bu.   ‡ Baethgen, *Beiträge*, p. 206 f.

The *middle watch* implies that the night was divided into three, not four, parts. On this subject see *Berachoth*, 3ᵇ. — אך הָרֵם הֵקִימוּ [אך restrictive; there had been no time for anything more; cf. Gen. 27⁸⁰ אך יָצֹא יָצָא יַעֲקֹב, Jacob had barely gone out; see also Jud. 3²⁴. The words are understood by not a few older interpreters to refer to Gideon and his men: they had barely roused the guards (*i.e.* had reached the furthest outposts of the camp), when they sounded; so 𝕲ᴮ ᵃˡ. 𝕷𝕾, Lth., Cler. (הקים in this sense, Gen. 49⁹ Nu. 24⁹). — נסֹף [ונסֹף הכריס וג' Kal, Jer. 22²⁸ ¹ (>𝕲); Pi. Jer. 48¹² Ps. 2⁹ &c. The inf. absol. continuing a finite tense, 1 S. 2²⁸ Gen. 41⁴³, Roorda, § 385; Ew. § 351 *c*; Ges.²⁶ § 113, 4 *a*. The construction is more common and freer in the later literature. — **20.** בלֹמדים . . . וַיַּחֲזִיקוּ] in the original context probably, *held on to, kept*, as in v.⁸; in the sense of the editor who added the following clause, *grasped*. Notice further the change of construction; in the first clause ב, in the second the acc.; הֵקְרֹע also comes in tardily after all the blowing already done (v.¹⁹·²⁰ᵃ). — חֶרֶב ליהוה ולגדעון] not equivalent to a genitive, *gladius Domini et Gedeonis* (𝕷, Lth., EV., Drus., Cler., Cass., Kitt., al.). חרב is rather an exclamatory sentence of one member (Paul, *Principien*, p. 104), probably psychological predicate (observe the indetermination); cf. Ges.²⁶ § 147, 3.

21. *And they stood where they were*] lit. *each man in his place*; cf. 1 S. 14⁹. They did not rush in, sword in hand, but remained as they were, waving their flaring torches and shouting their war-cry. The rest of the verse presents considerable difficulty, though the meaning is plain enough. The first verb, *all the camp ran*, is not usual in sense 'run away, flee,' and if so interpreted is an unnecessary anticipation of the following, *they fled*. The renderings, *took to their heels*, or *ran together*, are not sustained by usage. Perhaps, by a slight change in the Hebrew, the text should be emended, *all the camp awoke, and they set up a wild cry and fled*. The verb then adds an effective touch to the description of the night alarm. — **22.** *And they blew the three hundred horns*] repeated by R, to give the following description of the panic in the camp the same connexion which it originally had in E (after the first words of v.²⁰). — Imagining that the Israelites had taken the camp by surprise, and in the madness of fear each thinking his comrade a foeman, they turned their swords against each other, and the panic became complete. — *Yahweh set each man's sword against his comrade*] cf. 1 S. 14²⁰ 2 K. 3²³ 2 Chr. 20²³. — The direction of the flight is not made clearer by the multiplication of names in v.²²ᵇ, in which the fusion of two sources

is to be recognized. The sites of the places named are not
certainly known. From v.²⁴ it appears that E represented the
Midianites as turning southward through the Jordan valley, in
which they are intercepted by the Ephraimites. In J, if our surmise about the scene of the action be correct, they would naturally
flee eastward by the main route from Shechem to the other side
of the Jordan, which descends into the great Wady Fār'ah.
From the difference of construction in Hebrew, it is probable
that *Sererah* is not derived from the same source as *Beth-shittah*.

21. ויריצו כל המחנה ויריעו וינוסו] the verbs must all have the same subject; viz.,
the Midianites (6ℓ, AV., Cler., al.). The Kethib וינסו represents an interpretation which made Gideon's men the subject of both the last verbs: they
shouted the war-cry and put (them) to flight (RV.); not, they (Midianites) tried
to save their goods (Jud. 6¹¹; Be.).—For ירץ I would emend ויקץ, *all the
camp awoke;* see above.—ויריעו] *shouted in alarm,* raised a great cry, Mi. 4⁹
Is. 15⁴ cf. Hos.,5ⁿ (ℓ, Ki., Schm., Cler., Be., al.); 6 ἐσήμαναν καὶ ἔφυγον, prob.
sounded the retreat (Ra., Stud., al.).—**22.** ויתקעו שלש מאות השופרות] these
words are hard to construe: *they blew the three hundred horns,* gives undue
prominence to the instruments. *The three hundred horns sounded* (6ᴬᵛᴸᴹᴼ),
is against the usage of the verb. Very likely the editor wrote שלש המאות
ריעו בשופרות, *the three hundred blew their horns* (תקע c. c. acc. as in Jer. 4⁵ &c.);
this construction might easily give rise to misunderstanding, since throughout
the passage the verb is construed with ב.—וכל המחנה] ו accidentally repeated
from בריהו. Such cases are often explained as instances of ו explicative, *et
quidem;* Ew. § 340 *b; BDB.* s.v.—Of the places here named, *Abel-meholah,*
the birthplace of Elisha (1 K. 19¹⁶), was, in the system introduced by Solomon, included in a prefecture which extended from Taanach and Megiddo in
the Great Plain, by Jezreel and Beth-shean, into the Jordan valley. Euseb.
(*OS².* 227₃₅ cf. 97₁₁) suggests a village, Βηθμαελα, 10 m. S. of Scythopolis;
doubtless in the modern Wady Mālih. This name, however, is given by
the warm salt spring in the Wady,* and has nothing to do with Meholah.
There is even less ground for Conder's identification of Abel-meholah with the
neighbouring 'Ain Helweh (Sweet Spring).† *Sererah* is commonly supposed
to be miswritten for Seredah (1 K. 11²⁶),‡ and the latter to be the same as
Sarthan (1 K. 4¹² 7⁴⁶), with which it seems to be identified by the chronicler
(2 Chr. 4¹⁷). Sarthan is to be looked for, not in vicinity of Beth-shean, but
near Adam (Jos. 3¹⁶), *i.e.* probably the modern ed-Dāmieh, where the main
road has doubtless always crossed the Jordan. This is confirmed by 1 K. 7⁴⁶;
the bronze castings for the temple were made in the Jordan district, *at the
crossing* (ford) *of Adamah between Succoth and Sarthan* (read בגברת

---

* Rob., *BR².* iii. p. 306 f.; *SWP. Memoirs,* ii. p. 226.
† *SWP. Memoirs,* ii. p. 231; G. A. Smith, *Hist. Geogr.,* p. 581.   ‡ 6 Σαριρα.

אדמה[ה] for the meaningless כבדנה). The Succoth of 1 K. 7⁴⁶ is then not
'Ain es-Sâqût, about 9 m. from Beisân (Rob., *BR²*. iii. 309–312; and many), but
is the same place named in Gen. and Jos., east of the Jordan. With this Jud. 8¹ ⁵
admirably agrees; and we shall probably not err in ascribing זררח Jud. 7²²
to the author of S᷑ (J). As Abel-meholah is named with Şarthan in 1 K. 4¹²,
it also may come from J here.* The identification of Şarthan (צרח) with
Qarn Şarţabeh (Talm. סרטבא), the great landmark of the Jordan valley (Van
de Velde, Knob., Ke., al.), is not possible (Di.). — *Beth-shittah*, only here;
Shaţţa, 5] E. m. NW. of Beisân and about 6 m. E. of Zer'in (Rob., *BR².* ii.
p. 356) is much too near the supposed scene of the surprise. *Tabbath* also is
unknown. The narrative in v.²⁴, however, supposes that the places were in
the valley of the Jordan, toward the middle of its course.

23-25. The pursuit; death of the chiefs. — Gideon summons
other tribes to pursue the retreating foe. At his bidding the
Ephraimites pour down from their highlands and intercept the
Midianites in their flight down the Jordan valley. The two chiefs
are captured and slain. — Verse²³ is an editorial addition; v.²⁴· ²⁵
with 8¹⁻³ form the close of the narrative of E. — **23.** *The men of
Israel*] all the men capable of bearing arms. — *Naphtali, Asher,
and all Manasseh*] the men of these tribes, with Zebulun, had according to 6³⁵ been raised at the beginning of hostilities, only to be
summarily dismissed (7³·⁸). Now, before they could have reached
their homes, they are called out again. Even if we set 6³⁵ᵇ aside
as an exaggeration of the redactor, the difficulty in 7²³ is only in
part removed. Naphtali and Asher were too remote to be of any
use in such a pursuit. . *All Manasseh was called out and pursued
Midian* (cf. 3²ᶠ·), would not be exposed to this objection; but
cannot be part of the original text; for, first, it conflicts with 6³⁵ᵃ
7³·⁸; second, in 8¹, where Gideon is berated in such a menacing
tone by the Ephraimites, it is plain that he has not the whole tribe
of Manasseh at his back. The entire verse is therefore the
addition of a redactor. The form of the verse, with the ante-
position of the object, *And messengers he sent*, is exactly the same
as in 6³⁵. — **24.** Gideon sends messengers through the Highlands
of Ephraim, bidding the tribesmen hasten down into the Jordan
valley and cut off the retreat of the Midianites by holding against

---

* The text of 1 K. 4¹² is in disorder, "all Beth-shean which is beside Şarthan
below Jezreel" is obviously corrupt. No O.T. author could have felt it necessary
to describe in such a way the situation of Beth-shean.

them some of the streams which they must pass. — *Seize the water-courses against them, as far as Beth-barah*] cf. 3^{7f} 12^{M}. The watercourses (lit. *waters;* cf. *waters of Megiddo,* 5^{19}) are not the fords of the Jordan (3^{28} 12^{5}), but a stream emptying into the Jordan. The site of Beth-barah is unknown; in an attempt to fix the position of the stream we have to be guided by general considerations: first, it must have been large enough, when held by an enemy, effectively to stop the Midianites in their flight; second, it must be far enough south to give the Ephraimites time to get there before the Midianites. These conditions are best met by the Wady Fār'ah, a perennial stream, which in the spring is impassable at its mouth,* as are also the adjacent fords of the Jordan (Dāmieh). In the tongue of land between W. Fār'ah and the Jordan the Midianites would be in a *cul de sac,* where, in their disorder, destruction was inevitable. Finally, the road leading down this Wady from the highlands in a SE. direction would be the most advantageous line for the Ephraimites in their movement to intercept the foe. We may, therefore, with some confidence locate the scene of v.$^{24f.}$ near the mouth of the stream which comes from Wady Fār'ah.† — *As far as Beth-barah*] the site is unknown.‡ — *And the Jordan*] that is, hold the Jordan also against them. It may perhaps be suspected that the words have been added here and in v.^{b}, from 3^{28} 12^{5}.§ — **25.** The leaders are taken and slain. — *They killed Oreb at Oreb's Rock and Zeeb at Zeeb's Press*] the names of these places commemorated the fate of the chiefs. It has been thought that Is. 10^{26} (*the slaughter of Midian at Oreb's Rock*) follows a different tradition, in which Oreb's Rock, which in Jud. 7^{25} is only mentioned incidentally, was the scene of the principal encounter and the overthrow of Midian. ‖ But, in so far as the representation of Is. 10^{26} differs from that of Jud., it may be explained as the result of a very natural interpretation of the latter. The victory over Midian is

---

* *SWP. Memoirs,* ii. p. 385; "a narrow trench full of water . . . 5 yards to 10 yards across."

† This reasoning does not necessarily assume the historical accuracy of the narrative, but only adequate topographical knowledge on the part of the narrator.

‡ It can, of course, not be Maḥādet 'Abāreh, north of the mouth of Nahr Ġālūd (*SWP. Great Map,* sh. ix. Qk; *Memoirs,* ii. p. 79).   § Bu.

‖ Stud., p. 215; We.

alluded to also in Is. 9[4] Ps. 83[2-12]. It is worthy of notice that
Oreb and Zeeb are both animal names, Raven and Wolf.[*] —
And pursued Midian] on the text, see crit. note. This pursuit
comes too late after the capture and death of the chiefs; the
clause also interrupts the connexion between the account of the
death of Oreb and Zeeb and the bringing of their heads to
Gideon. The words are no doubt part of the attempt to harmonize 7[25]-8[3] with 8[4f.]. The redactor's representation is that the
main body of the Midianites escaped across the Jordan; the
Ephraimites, bearing their trophies, followed them over, and there
fell in with Gideon. — *On the other side of the Jordan*] harmonistic addition of the redactor.† Thé author of 7[24f.], on the
contrary, represented Gideon as following the Midianites in hot
pursuit down the valley, driving them into the arms of the
Ephraimites, who bring the heads of the chiefs to him as he
approaches the scene of the slaughter.

23. וַיִּזְעַק] v.[24]; וַיִּזְעַק 6[34. 35] cf. 4[10. 13]. — אִישׁ יִשְׂרָאֵל] see on v.[14]. — **24.** מַיִם]
running water, *stream*, Nu. 24[6] &c. — בֵּית בָּרָה] is often explained as equivalent
to בֵּית עֲבָרָה, ע being sloughed in the common speech (Cler., Reland, Ges.,
NV., al. mu.); but no such tendency appears in Heb. The premise of
Reland's conjecture, viz., that the place is identical with Βηθαβαρα (east of
the Jordan), in the Receptus, John 1[28], is untenable; and with it the chief
motive for the theory falls. 𝕲 Βαιθβηρα (Βαιθηρα A B al. is transcriptional
error) 𝕷𝕾 would rather suggest בָּאֵרָה; cf. Jerome, *OS*[2]. 106[19], quod interpretatur domus aquae, sive putei. — **25.** וְיֶקֶב זְאֵב] see on 6[11]; like גַּת it is
sometimes used for the whole; Dt. 15[14] &c. — וַיִּרְדְּפוּ אֶל מִדְיָן] the prep. is quite
anomalous; we should probably emend אֵת (cf. 𝕲𝕷𝕿). — רֹאשׁ עֹרֵב וּזְאֵב] two
genitives after one noun; see on 1[8]. The singular, רֹאשׁ, is in accordance with
Heb. idiom. — מֵעֵבֶר לַיַּרְדֵּן] *on the other side* (east) *of the J.*, where Gideon
was (𝕷𝕾, Ra., Ke., Be., Reuss.), Nu. 22[1] 34[15]; cf. מִצָּפוֹן ל 2[9], and note on 1[16]
(p. 34). Not, *from the other side of J.* (Cler., Stud., Ew. *GVI.* ii. p. 546,
cf. 541, Cass., al.). The view of Ges. (on Is. 10[26]), Cass., al., that Oreb's
Rock and Zeeb's Press were east of the Jordan, is mistaken.

VIII. 1-3. The Ephraimites quarrel with Gideon; their
anger is appeased. — The beginning strongly resembles 12[1-7].

* On animal names among Semites, cf. W. R. Smith, *Journ. of Philology*, ix.
p. 75 ff.; *Kinship and Marriage*, p. 190 ff., 218 ff.; Nöldeke, *ZDMG*, xl. 1886,
p. 156 ff.; J. Jacobs, "Are there Totem-Clans in the Old Testament," *Archæol.
Review*, iii. 1889, p. 145 ff.

† We., *Comp.*, p. 225; Sta., *GVI.* i. p. 187 n.; Bu., *Richt. u. Sam.*, p. 115; al.

Wellhausen regards the latter as a purely secondary development
of a motive borrowed from 8^{1-3}; * Kittel is of the opposite opinion,
viz., that 8^{1-3} is an imitation of 12^{1-7}.† The identity between the
two stories does not, however, extend beyond the beginning; the
sequel is as different as can be imagined, and in each is in entire
conformity with the situation.   That the Ephraimites, in the pride
of their pre-eminence as members of the leading tribe in Israel,
should resent being left out and so deprived of their share of
glory and of spoil, and should vehemently assail a leader who had
dared to succeed without their counsel and aid, seems so natural
a thing that we can without difficulty believe that it happened
more than once, or was the subject of more than one tale. —
1. *What trick is this thou hast played us, not to call us*] cf. 12^1.
The great tribe is jealous of its natural hegemony, and angry that
it should seem to be ignored; see above. — *They quarrelled with
him violently*] very likely with such threats as are uttered in 12^1.
—2. Gideon placates their anger by magnifying their achievement, and speaking of his own part as an insignificant one. The
skill with which his answer is turned reminds us strongly of 6^{31},
which our analysis would assign to the same author. — *What have
I done now to compare with you?*] now; after all. — *Is not the
gleaning of Ephraim better than the vintage of Abiezer*] an apt
and striking figure. The Ephraimites had indeed not been called
into action until after Gideon and his followers had gained the
first success over the enemy, but a far greater success had been
reserved for them in the slaughter of the invaders and the capture
of their chiefs. In contrast with the tribe of Ephraim, and in
congruity with the metaphor, Gideon does not name himself, but
his clan, Abiezer. — 3. The meaning of the figure. — *God has
given*] the name may perhaps be some indication of authorship;
but, as in many instances, the tradition is not consentaneous. —
What have I been able to do, to compare with you?] the pride of
the great tribe ought to be fully satisfied by the event; God has
thrown into their hands the chiefs of Midian. He himself had
only beaten up the game which they had killed. — *Their anger*

---

* *Comp.*, p. 229; cf. Doorn., p. 101.
† *Gdll.* i. 2. p. 72 n.; cf. p. 80 f.

against him was softened by this speech. · It is conjectured that
8³⁰ was the original sequel of 8³; see above, p. 176.*

1. [ויאמרו אליו איש אפרים] plur. with following collective subject. — מה הדבר
[הזה עשיה לנו] Ges.²⁶ p. 472; Paul, *Principien*, p. 114 f. — [הראת הראת] Baer;
the common edd. have הראות. The normal inf. is קרא; grammarians explain
the form in the text as due to the analogy of ריה (Sta. § 619 *k*; Kö., i. p. 611).
Possibly we should rather attribute יבלתי הראת to the analogy of the common
הקראת. — [כי הינה] *when* (𝕲𝕷𝕋𝕾); 2¹⁸ Hos. 11¹ &c. Be. construes as an
exclamation, *For thou wentest out!* — [בחזרה] 4³. — **2.** [ככם] v.³, an inexact but
not uncommon shifting of the point of comparison from the act to the person
(agent or object); Dt. 3²⁰ &c. A number of codd. and some of the oldest
edd. have כנב, *what have I done to you* (Ex. 12¹² 2 S. 18¹⁸). — [עללות] gleanings
of a vineyard (Mi. 7¹) or olive tree (Is. 17⁶); not of grain (ירקב). The pred.
adj. טוב is not infrequently uninflected; 1 S. 19⁴ 2 K. 5¹² &c., Davidson, *Syntax*,
§ 116, Rem. 3. — [מבציר] one of the rare cases in which a mute loses its
doubling in consequence of the reduction of the vowel; Ges.²⁶ § 20, 3 *b*. —
3. [אלהים] 𝕲𝕷 יהוה. — עשח [מה יכלתי עשח] inf. in direct regimen; · Gen. 37¹ Ex. 2⁵
18²³ Nu. 22¹⁸ &c.; cf. Jud. 11²⁶. — רוח [או רפהה רוחם], excited feeling, passion;
the specific definition is given by the context; cf. Job 15¹⁸ Eccl. 10⁴ (מרפא).
— [מעליו] cf. וירף ממנו Ex. 4²⁶, also Jud. 11³⁷.

4-27. The pursuit beyond the Jordan. — Gideon, with his
three hundred men, follows the Midianites across the Jordan.
The men of Succoth and Penuel refuse him food for his hungry
band; with threats of vengeance, he presses on (v.⁴⁻⁹). He surprises the camp and takes prisoners the two kings (v.¹⁰⁻¹²).
Returning in triumph, he inflicts condign punishment on Succoth
and Penuel (v.¹³⁻¹⁷), and slays the captive kings to avenge the
death of his brothers (v.¹⁸⁻²¹). He declines the offer of the kingdom (v.²²ᶠ). Of a part of the gold taken among the spoils he
makes an image (*ephod*) which he sets up at Ophrah (v.²⁴⁻²⁷).

The unity of this part of the story is obvious and unquestioned.
The only exception is v.²²ᶠ, in which the 'men of Israel' offer
Gideon the kingdom and he declines from theocratic motives.
These verses certainly do not belong to the narrative of J; see
comm. *in loc.* In the enumeration of the spoils (v.²⁶) some exaggeration by later editors or scribes may be suspected. On the relation of 8⁴ᶠᶠ to 6¹-8³, see above, p. 176 f.; and on the connexion
with ch. 9, see introduction to that chapter. — **4.** *Gideon came to*

---

* See, however, on 8²²ᶠ.

the Jordan] if our analysis be correct, this is a continuation of J's narrative. In 7^{22} he has told us that the Midianites fled to Ṣeredah, probably near the principal crossing of the Jordan between the vicinity of Shechem and the opposite region of Gilead. The Bedawin on their camels ($8^{21.26}$ cf. 6^5) easily outstripped the pursuit and made their escape across the river. The answer of the men of Succoth shows that they believed the raiders to be already far out of reach; the surprise of the camp shows that the Midianites imagined themselves to be so. — *Crossing over, he and the three hundred men*] the participial construction is an unusual one; the ordinary expression would be, *and crossed over.* Perhaps the word is a gloss; see note. — The three hundred men are evidently a constant feature in the different versions of the story; cf. 7^{6-8}. — *Exhausted and pursuing*] cf. 4^{21}. The ancient translators found the order of the words unnatural, and tried various shifts with them. — **5.** *Succoth*] evidently lay east of the Jordan, not very far from the ford; Jos. 13^{27} (cf. Ps. 60^6) locates it in the valley; Gen. 33^{17} (cf. $32^{30.31}$) brings it into connexion with Penuel, as in our passage; both are in the vicinity of the Jabbok (Nahr ez-Zerqā).[*] The sites have not been recovered. In the Jerusalem Talmud, Succoth is identified with Dar'ala, the modern Tell Deir 'Alla just north of the Zerqā; but it is very doubtful whether this is any more than an inference of Jewish scholars from the passages in the Old Testament which are cited above.[†] A place north of the Jabbok would be out of the line of Gideon's pursuit, if the other topographical notices of our story have been rightly interpreted. The connexion in Gen. also favours a site south of the Jabbok.[‡] — *Loaves of bread*] round flat cakes; 1 S. 10^3. — *To the men who are at my feet*] 4^{10}. — *Zebah and Zalmunna, the kings of Midian*] cf. Oreb and Zeeb, the chiefs of Midian, in ch. 7. The pronunciation of the names has very likely been perverted by malicious wit; see note. — **6.** The authorities of the town refuse Gideon's request. The translation, *princes of Succoth* (EV.), is not quite accurate, the

---

[*] On Succoth see Reland, *Palaestina,* p. 308; Neubauer, *Géog. du Talmud,* p. 248 f.; S. Merrill, *East of the Jordan,* p. 385 ff.

[†] See Merrill, "Identification of Succoth and Penuel," *Bibl. Sacra,* xxxiv. 1877, p. 742–754; on the other side, Paine, *ib.* xxxv. p. 481–498.   [‡] Köhl., Di., Del., al.

word means rather *officials;* here, the men who stood at the head of the council of elders; see on v.[14]. The disposition of the tribes east of the Jordan to pursue their separate interests, unconcerned by what befell their kinsmen across the river, is made a reproach to them in the Ode of Deborah; see on 5[17]. It is not improbable, moreover, that in Succoth and Penuel, as in Shechem (ch. 9), the native population predominated. It is hardly necessary to seek a motive for the refusal in the fear of reprisals by the Midianites.[*] They add to denial, derision. — *Are Zebah and Zalmunna already in thy power, that we should give thy soldiers bread?*] Gideon was on a bootless errand; the Midianites were already far away, and if he and his little company should come up with them, it would only be the worse for him. Why should they help him on in this wild expedition? — 7. He answers their jeer with a threat. When he returns victorious, he will requite their conduct as it deserves; cf. v.[15]. — *I will thresh your flesh with thorns of the desert and thistles*] cf. v.[16]. *With*, not of instrument, but of accompaniment, *together with*. He will throw them naked into a bed of thorns and trample them together, like grain on the threshing-floor.[†] This is the only natural interpretation of the words, but it does not seem to agree with v.[16], and the text is perhaps glossed; see note. Palestine has a great variety of thorny plants and shrubs, many of which are formidably armed. The meaning *threshing-sledges*, frequently attributed in modern dictionaries and commentaries to the word translated above, *thistles*, is a figment of bad etymology.

4. לְבַר] this use of the circumstantial ptcp. is anomalous (though cf. Nu. 16[27]).[‡] We expect וייעבר; and the text is either to be so emended (cf. 𝔊𝔏𝔖𝔗); or, more probably, עבר ('*ăbar*) was originally a marginal gloss, which, when transferred to the text, was forced into construction by pronouncing '*ōber*. — 5. סֻכּוֹ] *Jer. Shebiith*, ix. 2 (fol. 38[d]) identifies the places named in Jos. 13[27] in order from south to north: Beth-nimrah, בית נמרין (now Tell Nimrin); Succoth, דרעלה (later edd. תרעלה; modern Deir 'Alla); Zaphon,§ צפון ('Αμαθοΰς Fl. Jos., *antt.* xiii. 13, 3 § 356, cf. *OS²*. 219[75]; now Amateh, near the Jordan, north of Wady er-Rugeib). — וַיִּקַּח וְזִלְמֻנָּע] 𝔊 Ζεβεε καὶ Σαλμανα. 𝔐, as so often in similar cases, by an inept witticism makes

---

[*] Arias, Cler., Stud., Reuss, al.   [†] So 𝔗, rightly interpreted by Ki.
[‡] Cf. Ew. § 341 *b*, 3.   [§] Cf. Jud. 12[1].

the names mean *Victim* and *Protection refused*. What the former really was
can hardly be made out; [*] the latter is probably a compound of צלם, cf. צלמזבע
in an inscription from Teimâ.[†] With the second element, cf. יבם 1 Chr. 7²⁸,
המבע Gen. 36⁴⁰ (Edom). In all probability we have here a genuine Midianite
name. — **6.** [ויאמר שרי סכות] probably to be emended ויאמרו; the uninflected
predicate of the verbal sentence with a human subject is not in Hebrew used
with the same freedom as in Arabic; Ges.²⁶ § 145, 7; cf. Roorda, § 589. Compare 4¹⁰ 7⁸ 12⁶. — **7.** בתת יהוה . . . וירשתי] consec. pf. after temporal clause,
Dr³. § 123 β; Ges.²⁶ § 112, 5 *c*. — [את קוצי המדבר] *cum spinis* (𝕃, cf. 𝕊 כי,
𝕲 ἐν); so Drus., Cler., Stud. The preposition את is not instrumental, *I will
beat you with thorns* (Ki., Abarb., al. mu.). Others take את as *nota accusativi*
(Schn.); recent interpreters who adopt this view construe the verb with two
accusatives (Ew. § 234 *e*; Be., Ke., al.), *I will make the thorns thresh your
flesh*. None of these constructions is satisfactory. The first, which alone is
grammatically unimpeachable, is hardly the natural expression, and does not
seem to accord with v.¹⁶. It is possible that the words את קוצי המדבר ואת
הברקנים are a gloss borrowed from v.¹⁶, and that the original text in v.⁷ was
merely קוצים. — ודשתי את בשרכם is the most general word in the O.T. for thorn-
bushes. — [הברקנים] 𝕲ᴸ˟ Σ τρίβολοι ᾽A τραγάκανθαι 𝕃 *tribuli*, so also 𝕊 ₂,
Abulw., Ra., Ki., Abarb., and all older Christian interpreters. In the Egyptian dialect of Arabic *berqân* is the name of *Phaeopappus scoparius* Boiss.
= *Centaurea scop.* Sieber, a composite plant with thorny heads; see Ascherson
in Löw, *Aram. Pflanzennamen*, p. 429. This is entirely suitable in the context; a teasel or knapweed would be admirably suited to Gideon's purpose;
see on v.¹⁶.[‡] The meaning *threshing-sledges* was invented by J. D. Michaelis
(*Orient. Bibliothek*, vii. 1774, p. 17). The steps by which this result is obtained
are these: ברק ('lightning') might be applied to fire-stones; fire-stones might
be set in the bottom of the threshing-sledge; the whole implement might be
called from these stones, ברקן (or ברקני, Ges.): *ergo* ברקנים are threshing-
sledges.[§] Michaelis' theory was taken up by Gesenius in his *Lex.* (1810),[‖]
and has since maintained its place in commentaries and lexicons (Ges. *Thes.*,
MV., SS., Ew., Reuss, al.). It is rightly rejected by Stud., Be²., Ke., Wetzstein (*Zeitschr. f. Ethnologie*, v. 1873, p. 285), Löw (*Pflanzennamen*, p. 356).
Stud. rightly observed that את is entirely irreconcilable with this theory.

8. *Thence he went up to Penuel*] Succoth lay in the valley;
Penuel was farther from the Jordan, in the upland. From Gen. 32

---

[*] Note, however, the resemblance to Zeeb in the other version. If Zeeb originally stood in J's narrative also, it would have to be changed after 7²⁵.

[†] Nöldeke, *Berichte der Berliner Akademie*, 1884, p. 815; Baethgen, *Beiträge*,
p. 80 f. [‡] Older identifications, see Celsius, *Hierobotanicon*, ii. p. 192–195.

[§] Captives ground to death under threshing-sledges, Am. 1³ 2 S. 12³¹. For a
description of the modern Syrian threshing-sledge, see Post, *PEF. Qu. St.*, 1891,
p. 114. [‖] Cf. also Eichhorn, in his (3d) ed. of Simonis' *Lexicon* (1793).

it appears to have been on the Jabbok, at the point where the road from the north crossed the stream. It was evidently a position of importance, for one of the first acts of Jeroboam I. was to fortify Shechem and Penuel (1 K. 12²⁵). The name (Face of God) was perhaps originally given to some projecting rock in whose contour a face was seen ; compare the promontory Θεοῦ πρόσωπον on the coast near Tripolis.* It has not been identified ; Merrill would put it at Tulūl ed-Dahab. — He made the same request at Penuel as at Succoth, and got the same answer. — 9. *When I return successful, I will pull down this tower*] the stronghold of the town, which was itself probably unwalled ; cf. v.¹⁷ 9ᵍᶠ·⁸¹ᶠ·. Numerous remains of such towers (of course of later date) are found east of the Jordan.† — 10. *Zebah and Zalmunna were in Karkor*] the place is otherwise unknown ; Carcaria, one day's journey from Petra, with which Eusebius identifies it, is much too remote. On the topography in general see on v.¹¹. — *Their force was with them*] the clans which had taken part in the foray had not yet dispersed. The latter part of the verse is obviously inserted by the redactor to harmonize 8¹⁰ᵃ with 7²⁴ᶠ·. The fifteen thousand men whom the kings still had with them were the pitiful remnant of the host with which they invaded Palestine ; a hundred and twenty thousand fighting men had perished. The enormous figures remind us of ch. 19–21 (cf. *e.g.* 20²), and especially of Nu. 31, the destruction of Midian in the days of Moses. The original narrative may have given the numbers of the Midianite host which Gideon with his three hundred put to flight, but in the connexion it is not unnatural to suspect that the figures (15,000) have been raised. — 11. *Gideon went up by the road . . . , east of Nobah and Jogbehah*] the words omitted in the translation are generally interpreted, the road *of the dwellers in tents, i.e.*, of the Bedawin. So all the ancient versions ; cf. especially ℭ : The way to the camp of the Arabs who were encamped in tents in the desert east of Nobah. But the Hebrew text does not admit of any grammatical interpretation ; probably the name of a place originally stood here. *Jogbehah* is

---

* Strabo, xvi. p. 754 f.

† Porter, *Damascus*, ii. p. 195; Merrill, *East of the Jordan*, p. 15, 37, 405.

named in Nu. 32³⁶ among the cities built, or fortified, by Gad.*
It is now generally identified with Khirbet el-Gubeihāt, NW. of
'Ammān and about midway between that place and es-Salṭ.†
The site agrees sufficiently well with the scanty indicia of our
narrative. The general course of the flight from the fords of the
Jordan was then south-east, toward the great desert. *Nobah*
occurs in Nu. 32⁴², where we read that a clan Nobah (from the
context a branch of Machir) conquered Kenath and its dependencies, and gave the place its own name. Kenath is commonly
supposed to be el-Qanawāt in the Hauran ; ‡ but this cannot be
meant here. It has been suggested that the Nobah in our text
was the earlier seat of the clan, from which it migrated to the
north, to Kenath ; § but the identification of the latter with Qanawāt is rather to be given up. ∥ The Midianites, imagining that
they are safe from pursuit, allow themselves to be surprised.—
12. The two kings flee, but are pursued and taken. — *He threw
all the camp into a panic*] the panic of the Midianites seems to
come too late, after the flight and pursuit of the kings. Scharfenberg conjectured, *he devoted all the camp*, utterly destroyed it
(see on 1¹⁷). It is not necessary, however, to touch the text.
The capture of Zebah and Zalmunna is the point in which the
interest of the narration centres ; the rest in their fright fled in all
directions, leaving the kings to their fate ; cf. 2 S. 17², and with
the verb, Ez. 30⁹.¶

---

* Most of the other places in this list were in northern Moab ; several of them
occur also in the inscription of Mesha.

† See Burckhardt, *Syria*, p. 361 ; Conder, *SEP. Memoirs*, p. 111 f. The identification, Knobel on Nu. 32⁸⁵ ; Ewald, *G VI*. ii. p. 547 n. ; Dietrich, in Merx, *Archiv*,
i. 1867, p. 346-349 ; Be., Ke., Di., Bäd., al. G. A. Smith strangely supposes it to
have originated with Conder. In general, the author of this *Historical Geography*
is not very well informed about the history of geography.

‡ Descriptions of Qanawāt, Burckhardt, *Syria*, p. 83 ff. ; Merrill, *East of Jordan*,
p. 36-42 ; Bäd⁸. 207 f. Κάναθα, Fl. Jos., *b.j.* i. 19, 2 § 366 ; Ptol., v. 15, 23 ; Plin.,
n. h., v. 74. The identification is made by Euseb., *OS²*. 269₁₅, but is probably
mistaken ; we should not look for the Kenath of Nu. 32⁴² in the remote NE.
1 Chr. 2²³, when rightly translated, lends no support to the theory. Dt. 3¹⁴ Jos. 13³⁰.
which put the Havoth-jair in Bashan, are the result of a late and erroneous combination (Di., *NDJ.*, p. 201 ; Kue., *Th. T.* xi. p. 479 ff.) ; see below on 10⁴.

§ Di., *NDJ.*, p. 201 f. ; Sta., *G VI*. i. p. 149.

∥ Socin, Be.

¶ Stud.

8. פנואל] Merrill (*East of the Jordan*, p. 390–392) thinks that Penuel was at Tulûl ed-Dahab, conical hills, crowned by old ruins, which rise from the middle of the Jabbok valley to a height of 250 feet. The stream, with a sharp bend, winds between them. — With the name Penuel compare פן בעל in Carthaginian inscriptions to תנת פן בעל, in which Halévy and E. Meyer are very probably right in seeing, not a mystical epithet, "Tnt, face of Baal," but the name of a place; cf. promunturium quod Saturni vocatur, Plin., *n. h.*, iii. 19. — **10.** נקרקר] a similar name (Qarqaru) is found in inscriptions of Salmanassar and Sargon; apparently a place in the vicinity of Hamath (Schrader, *KAT*[2]. p. 180). In v.[11] 𝕿ⁿ puts the camp at 'Aro'er (see on 11[33]).[*] — בחמשת עשר אלף] with the irregular construction of the numeral cf. 2 S. 19[10] Jud. 20[25], Ges.[25] § 97, 2 n. — בני קדם] in a wider sense than in 6[3. 33], to include all the Bedawin. — הנפלים] *the slain*; 20[40] Jos. 8[25] Jer. 6[15] 8[12] &c. — שלף חרב] excludes non-combatants; the phrase 20[2. 15. 17. 35. 46] 2 S. 24[9] &c. The resemblances in this part of the verse to ch. 20 are to be noted. — **11.** השכוני באהלים] commonly rendered, *those who are lodged in tents*, i.e., the Bedawin, and explained, the road which they ordinarily took in crossing the country, perhaps a trail which avoided the larger towns. This interpretation is more ingenious than convincing. The construct state before a preposition is not infrequent (Philippi, *Status constructus*, p. 57; Ew. § 289 *b*; Ges.[25] § 130, 1); but the article before the construct is foreign to the whole genius of the Semitic languages, and is not rendered less objectionable by reference to other instances of the same error (Ps. 113[5. 6] 123[1]; cf. Philippi, p. 40 f.; Ol. on Ps. 113[5]). The pass. ptcp. is also a stumbling-block, not so much in itself (see Kö., i. p. 176 f.), as because the act. ptcp. of this verb is usual in this sense and construction. Finally, דרך with a gen. is elsewhere always the way to, or by, a place; not that used by such and such persons; † the road leading to the Bedawin camps, would be suitable here, but cannot be extracted from the text. — יונבה] 𝕮 רבּ‍א; by etymological combination. — והמחנה היה בטח] נכה is predicate, not adv. accus. of state (Be.). — **12.** החריד] so versions (exc. 𝕲[AL]). Scharfenberg conj. החרים; ‡ Schleusner הכרית. If an emendation is necessary, הבהיל (Ex. 23[28] Ps. 83[6]) would perhaps be preferable to either; cf. 𝕲[A] ἐξέτριψεν. Cf. however, Ez. 30[9] Zech. 2[4] 2 S. 17[2].

13–17. Gideon returns with his prisoners and punishes Succoth and Penuel. — 13.

The end of the verse is obscure. The words are now commonly understood to designate the point at which Gideon turned back, *from the pass of Heres;* § and the significance of this notice is supposed to be, that from this place

---

[*] Stud. suggested that ררר may be a harder pronunciation of ערער; cf. Aram. ארקא for ארעא.

† Nu. 21[1] is not an exception; *way of the spies* is inadmissible (Di. *ad loc*).

‡ Cf. Fl. Jos., διαφθείρω.   § 𝕲[A] al. 2, Be., Ke., al.

he returned to Succoth by a different road from that which he had taken in the pursuit, and so took the town by surprise.* In our ignorance of the topography, we may hesitate to pronounce decidedly against this explanation; but we cannot have much confidence in it. The text is not intact, and it is doubtful whether the slight emendation which this interpretation requires is sufficient to restore it. — 14. He caught a boy from Succoth and by questioning got from him a list of the principal men of the place. — *He wrote down for him the officials of Succoth and its elders*] in v.⁶ only the officials (*sarim*) are mentioned; in v.¹⁶ only the elders (*zĕqenim*). The latter are the heads of the families or septs which were settled in the town; all the functions of government, so far as they existed in such a state of society, were in the hands of the council of elders.† The word *sar*, on the other hand, designates an *officer, official,* especially one appointed by the government; cf. 9²⁰, the commandant of the city, &c. Here also it may perhaps mean military officers, the leaders of the men of Succoth in war; cf. the chiefs (*sarim*) of Midian, 7²⁵ 8³. — *Seventy-seven men*] one of those round numbers that are hardly meant to be taken arithmetically. In early times the number of elders in a city was naturally determined by the number of families that were able to establish their right to be represented in the council. — 15. With this description of the men who were to be held responsible for the affront he had received, Gideon came to Succoth. The place does not seem to have offered any resistance; it was probably not walled. — *Here are Zebah and Zalmunna, with whom you taunted me*] v.⁶. He had kept his prisoners alive in order to show them thus to the citizens of Succoth and Penuel. — *To thine exhausted men*] the adjective which Gideon himself uses in v.⁵ is effectively put in the mouth of the men of Succoth to aggravate their churlishness. — 16. He carries out his threat (v.⁷). — *He took the elders of the town and thorns of the desert and thistles, and threshed with them the men of Succoth*] for *threshed* 𝔐 has, *taught;* cf. 1 S. 14¹². None of the versions, however, seem to have read so, and the correspondence to v.⁷ is otherwise so close that we should expect the same verb which is used there.

---

* Ew.　　　　　　　　† See also 11⁵.

The form of torture intended is probably one to which there are
numerous references in Greek authors, and which has survived to
modern times under the name of *carding*. Thus Croesus is said
to have put to death a partisan of his brother: ἐπὶ κνάφου ἕλκων
διέφθειρε ; * and in Plato's Inferno the very worst offenders, such as
the tyrant Ardiæus, are tortured in this way ; † see note. — Budde
suspects that the words, *the elders of the town and*, are a gloss. —
17. Gideon carries out his threat by destroying the tower of
Penuel, and slays the inhabitants of the place. — It would be
hazardous to infer, from the fact that the chastisement of Succoth
precedes that of Penuel, that the author represented Gideon as
returning by a different road from that which he followed in the
pursuit ; it would be not unnatural for him to relate the fulfilment
of Gideon's threats in the order in which they were made (v.⁵⁻⁸),
without reflecting that on his way back he would come to Penuel
first.

13. הֶחָרֶס מַעֲלֵה] ⑥ᴬⱽᴸᴹᴼ s ἀπὸ ἀναβάσεων Ἀρες; ‡ so also 𝔖. Cf. Jerome
(*OS²*. 96₂), *adscensus Ares*, pro quo Aquila interpretatur *saltuum*, Symmachus
montium. The former renders הֶחָרֶס (cf. 1 S. 23¹⁹ 'Α εἰς τὸν δρυμόν), which
reminds us of the Moabite names קִיר חֶרֶשׂ, חַרְסָה. Σ represents הֶהָרִים;
O also is said to have had ὄρους; the word חֶרֶס was evidently a stumbling-
block, as in 1⁸⁵ (see Field *ad loc.*). מַעֲלֵה *pass* 1⁸⁶ Jos. 10¹⁰ 15⁷. ⑥ᴮᴺ ἀπὸ ἐπάνωθεν Ἀρες (τῆς παρατάξεως 2° in ᴮ is an accidental repetition), *i.e.* מַעֲלֵה; §
but this would require יֹרֵס. Others take הֶחָרֶס appellatively; so 𝕷 *ante solis
ortum ;* ∥ 𝕿, Ra., before the sun *set:* Ki. gives us the choice of these two
renderings. Neither is admissible; מַעֲלֵה is not the act of rising, but the place
where or by which one goes up, pass, steps, &c. (Schm.); the translation of
𝕿 confounds the word with Aram. סֵק, from a different root (cf. Dan. 6¹⁵).
If we interpret, *from the pass of Heres*, it will be necessary to emend מִמַּעֲלֵה ;
the composite preposition is consistent only with the interpretation of ⑥ᴮ ἀπὸ
ἐπάνωθεν; see Stud. — **14.** אֵלָיו וַיִּכְתֹּב] 2 S. 11¹⁴ &c.; cf. כָּתַב יִ Dt. 24¹ &c.
There is as little reason to depart from the usual meaning of the verb as there
is to infer from it that the Israelites of Gideon's time could all read and
write. — **15.** הֵיכֶם] v.⁵ הַיֶּכֶם. — **16.** סֻכּוֹת אַנְשֵׁי אֶת כָּרַב וַיִּלֶּד] the Hiph. of ידע
without i is anomalous. ¶ ⑥ has the same verbs as in v.⁷ (ἠλόησεν ᴮᴺ, κατέ-

---

* Hdt., i. 92; Plut., *de malign. Herod.*, p. 858.   † *Rep.*, x. p. 616 A.

‡ ⑥ᴹ ἐπί; cf. l *in ascensione Hares*.   § Cf. Stud., Ew.

∥ Similarly, RLbG., Abarb. (he turned back *at* sunrise), Vatabl., Tremell., Drus.,
Cler.

¶ In Nu. 16⁵ the spelling may intentionally leave the choice between Kal (⑥)
and Hiph.

Q

ἔαυεν ΑΜΟ g); * so also L *contrivit* (with the doublet, *et comminuit*). S renders *eštannad, tortured*. ₵ presents an unusual number of variants; ᵛᵉⁿ·² Ra., Ki. הבר, ᵐᵉᵃᶜʰ·,ᵐ נרר ('drag'), ᵃⁿᵗ· נריד (ᵛᵉⁿ·¹ נרד, typographical error); all seemingly rendering by the context. *He taught the men of Succoth a lesson* (Ew., *er witzigte*), would be well enough; but the unusual form in 𝔐 and the evidence of the versions make it most probable that the author wrote ויידש; a mutilated ש in the square alphabet might easily be read as ר. — On this form of torture cf. Hdt., i. 92; Plut., *de. malign. Herod.*, p. 858; Aristoph., *Acharn.* 319 f., with the Scholia; Plat., *Rep.* x. p. 616 A; Clem. Alex., *Strom.* v. p. 700 Potter; esp. Hesych. *s.v.* ἐπὶ κνάφων ἕλκων (Hdt., i. 92): τὸ γὰρ πρότερον οἱ γραφεῖς ἀκανθῶν σωρὸν συστρέψαντες τὰ ἱμάτια ἐπὶ τοῦ σωροῦ ἔκραττον· ὁ δὲ σωρὸς ἐλέγετο γράφος· ὁ οὖν Κροῖσος τὸν ἐχθρὸν περιέξανε ταῖς ἀκάνθαις καὶ οὕτως ἔφθειρεν.† In Jud. 8⁷·¹⁶ the LXX rendering of the verb is καταξαίνω. On *carding* see *New English Dict.*, s.v. *Card* and *Carder*.

18-21. Gideon puts Zebah and Zalmunna to death to avenge his brothers, whom they had killed in their foray. — 18.

Having executed his threat upon Succoth and Penuel, he turns on his prisoners. — *Where are the men whom you killed at Tabor?*] the menacing question shows that he knows what they have done, and challenges an avowal. They meet it, like admirable savages as they are, with a boast : They were just such men as you ; men of kingly figure. ‡ Because this answer does not formally correspond to the question, *where* are the men, many interpreters think it necessary to make the question correspond to the answer, and translate, *what kind of men were those that you slew?* § but this is against the usage of the particle, and much tamer than what the author wrote. — *Tabor*] is generally understood to be Mt. Tabor, on the northern side of the Great Plain, ‖ or a village of the name in the vicinity of the mountain.¶ But it is not clear what Gideon's brothers were doing up there, so far away from the seats of the clan ; the narrator does not intimate that they fell in a fight with the Midianites, but rather gives the impression that they were murdered at their homes. Moreover, the author of this

---

* Κατεξανεν is LXX, as a comparison of 𝔊ᴺ with B in the light of 𝔖 shows.

† See also Schleusner, *Thesaurus*, s.v. καταξαίνω.

‡ The spirit of this answer is quite lost when it is supposed that they were ignorant of Gideon's relation to their victims, as is done by Stud., al.

§ RS, EV., Be., al.

‖ See on 4⁶.

¶ Cf. 1 Chr. 6⁷⁷ (Heb. 6⁶²) Jos. 19²²; note also Aznoth-tabor, Chisloth-tabor.

chapter (J) seems not to lay the scene of the action in the Plain
of Jezreel, as the other version of the story does,* but in the
vicinity of Shechem.   For a conjecture, see critical note. — *They
were just like thee*] the nature of the resemblance is defined in
the next words; it was their princely stature and mien; cf. 1 S. 9²
16⁷·¹⁵ 1 K. 1⁶. The meaning is clear; on the text see note. —
19. *They were my own brothers!*] sons of the same mother as
well as the same father; Gen. 43²⁹ Dt. 13⁶ Cant. 8¹; cf. Gen. 20¹².
— *By Yahweh, if you had spared their lives, I would not have
killed you*] it is the personal wrong that whets his sword; brothers'
blood demands vengeance. — **20.** He calls on Jether, his oldest
son, upon whom, after himself, the blood feud devolved, to avenge
his uncle's death.   For the boy it is an honour; for the captive
kings an ignominy.   Jether is the same name as Jethro (Ex. 4¹⁸).
Besides Moses' Midianite father-in-law, it occurs as the name of
the Ishmaelite father of Amasa (1 K. 2⁵ cf. 2 Chr. 2¹⁷ 2 S. 17²⁵);
also of families of Judah (1 Chr. 2³² 4¹⁷) and Asher (1 Chr. 7³⁸),
and, with slight variation of form, of an Edomite clan (Gen. 36⁴⁰).
Commentators have felt some difficulty in explaining how this boy
came to be among the picked three hundred (7¹⁻⁸).   In reality 8⁴ᶠᶠ·
is not connected with ch. 7, but belongs to the older and simpler
version in which Gideon's followers were his clansmen of Abiezer
(6³⁴); Jether's presence in the expedition, therefore, need occasion
no surprise.   It is more than likely, moreover, that Gideon led his
prisoners home in triumph, and that they were put to death at
Ophrah, near the place where the murder had been committed.†
The boy had not the heart to draw his sword. — **21.** With true
Arab spirit the captives challenge Gideon to give the death-stroke
with his own hand. — *Slay us thyself, for a man has a man's
strength*] lit. *as the man*, so *is his strength*.   An immature boy is
not to be expected to do what requires a man's arm and a man's
heart.   Kimchi and others conceive the meaning to be that
Jether could not dispatch them outright, but would hack and
mangle them in his weak and clumsy efforts to kill. ‡ — Gideon
kills them and takes their spoil. — *The crescents which were on
the necks of their camels*] necklaces or collars (v.²⁶), the elements

---

of which were little golden crescents. They were worn by men (v.²⁶) and women (Is. 3¹⁸),* and, like all such ornaments, were originally amulets.† Riding camels are still often decorated with jingling strings of cowrie shells and metal crescents. In the O.T. camels appear only in the possession of the nomad neighbours of Israel and in the patriarchal story in Genesis.

18. איפה] *where*, Gen. 37¹⁶ 1 S. 19²² 2 S. 9⁴ (in all 10 times). So here 𝕲𝕿, Abarb., SS. Other renderings: τίνες 𝕲ᴹ, ποῖοι⁵ᴺ, *quales* 𝕷𝕾 ᵃ, Ki., Lth., EV., Cler., Schm., Be., Ke., Ges., MV., BDB., al. Stud., rightly feeling that it is hazardous to invent a new meaning for the particle for this one place, conj. אֵיכָה (cf. Doorn.); but איכה (τίνι τρόπῳ, see on 20³) is found only before verbs, and is not used in the sense of *qualis*. If the explanation given in the text be not thought sufficient, the most natural emendation would be מי אפוא Gen. 27³³ &c., *who, then, were* the *men*.—כמוך כמוהם] nominal sentence, lit., *the like of thee is the like of them;* 1 K. 22⁴ Gen. 18²⁵ 44¹⁸ Nu. 15¹⁵ Dt. 1¹⁷ Is. 24² Jos. 14¹¹, Roorda, § 488; cf. Ges.²⁶ § 118, 6.—אחד כתאר בני הפלך] most modern interpreters take אחד distributively, *each one resembled the children of a king;* AV., RV., with Lth., Cler., Schm. (*unusquisque sicut filii regis*), Be., Ke., al. mu. But אחד is nowhere used in this way,‡ and this interpretation did not suggest itself to any of the ancient translators or commentators. 𝕲ᴹ𝕷𝕿 render *unus ex eis;* 𝕲ᴮᴺᴬᴾⱽᴼ ᵇ Θ 𝕾 do not represent אהר at all. Ra. (alt.), Ki., Stud., connect it with the preceding as adverbial accusative, lit., *thy likeness was their likeness, all one;* but for this again there is no analogy. The text can hardly be sound; the simplest emendation is probably כי אחד.— תאר ' figure, stature, bodily presence.'—*At Tabor*] אלון הבור 1 S. 10³, not far from Bethel, § is as much too far to the south as Mt. Tabor to the north. It may perhaps be suspected that the true name of the place where Gideon's brothers were killed is preserved in 9³⁷ (טבור הארץ), and that it has been changed here to הבור in conformity with the representation of 6³³.—19. חי יהוה] a common form of oath; lit. *Yahweh is living;* Ges.²⁶ § 149.—לו החיתם . . . לא הרגתי] cf. 13²³. לו with pf. in hypothesis contrary to reality; Dr². § 139; Ges.²⁶ p. 482. Obs. the pf. in apodosis also; they are already as good as dead. החיה 'spare, let live,' Nu. 22³³ 2 S. 8² &c.—20. יהרו] = יהרג Ex. 4¹⁹.—21. כי כאיש גבורתו] in the sense in which we have translated the words (*quia juxta aetatem robur est hominis* 𝕷), כן גבורתו would be expected; but the ellipsis may be possible. 𝕲ᴰᴺ ὅτι ὡς ἀνδρὸς ἡ δύναμίς σου.—שהרנים] v.²⁶ Is. 3¹⁸ᵃ. The word is connected with Aram. Syr. סהרא ' moon,' and both name and thing appear to be of foreign origin.

---

* See Schroeder, *De vestitu mulierum*, p. 33–44; Hartmann, *Die Hebräerin*, ii. p. 265 ff. † Cf. Gen. 35⁴.

‡ The examples alleged, such as 1 K. 5² 2 K. 15²⁰, are essentially different; they all have the distributive ל. § See above on 4⁶, p. 113.

22, 23. Gideon declines the kingdom. — The Israelites offer to make Gideon and his descendants hereditary rulers; he refuses out of religious scruple. This does not agree with the representation of J in the preceding narrative, in which Gideon and his clansmen of Abiezer act for themselves and by themselves: *the men of Israel* appear on the scene quite unexpectedly; * we must imagine them convoked for the express purpose.† The refusal, v.^{23}, is at variance also with ch. 9, from which we see that Jerubbaal had, at least in the vicinity of Shechem, an authority which would in natural course devolve to his sons.‡ If v.$^{22. 23}$ belong to either of the two sources which we have tried to separate in ch. 6-9, it must be to E, in which the tribes of Manasseh and Ephraim, and perhaps others, take part in the campaign. For this origin of the verses we may also adduce 1 S. 8^7 10^{19} 12^{12} (E), in which the same condemnation of the kingdom, as conflicting with the sovereignty of Yahweh, is expressed in very similar terms. § A later writer (I)‖ would have no visible motive for introducing the offer and rejection of the kingdom in this place. If E is the author of the verses, they must have stood in his narrative after 8$^{1-3}$; the editor who combined 7^{23}-8^3 with 8$^{4-21}$ (Rje) would be constrained to transpose them to their present place. To this hypothesis it may be objected, that the author who represented the Ephraimites as meeting the victor in such a truculent mood (8$^{1-3}$) can hardly have conceived of their turning around and offering to make him king. If 8$^{1-3}$ are genuine, as I have tried to show, the only answer would be that 8$^{22. 23}$ belong to a secondary stratum in E (E$_2$), to which we might then perhaps ascribe 7^{23} also. This, again, would have the support of the corresponding passages in Samuel, which are commonly attributed to E$_2$. — **22.** *The men of Israel*] the body of freemen who formed the army; cf. 7^{14} 9^{55}. What tribes the author meant to represent as taking part in this assembly can hardly be determined; Manasseh and Ephraim pretty certainly, possibly also the others named in 7^{23}. — *Rule over us*] 9^2; cf. *reign* in Jotham's fable (9$^{8. 10. 12. 14}$).

* In 7^{14} in the mouth of the Midianite the phrase has a different connotation.
† Contrast 1 S. 11$^{12ff.}$.   ‡ We.
§ See Vatke, *Alttest. Theol.*, p. 263 f.; We., *Comp.*, p. 227; Co., *Einl².* p. 95 f.
‖ Kitt.

We should hardly attribute any significance to the fact that the latter word is not used here; [*] what they offer him and his descendants is in fact a kingdom, differing by the hereditary principle from the purely personal authority of the Judge (*shōphet*). —*Because thou hast delivered us*] cf. 10[18] 11[8.9]. To deliver his people in war is the very calling of a king; 1 S. 9[16] Is. 33[22] &c. — **23.** *I will not rule over you, nor shall my son rule over you; Yahweh shall rule over you*] cf. 1 S. 12[12.17.19] 8[7] 10[19] Hos. 13[xv.] 9[9] 10[9]. The condemnation of the kingdom as in principle irreconcilable with the sovereignty of Yahweh, the divine king, appears to date from the last age of the kingdom of Israel, those terrible years of despotism, revolution, and anarchy which intervened between the death of Jeroboam II. and the fall of Samaria, when history seemed to write large the words of Yahweh by a prophet of the time : Thou saidst give me a king and princes ; I give thee a king in my anger and take him away in my fury.[†] It first appears in Hosea and in the Ephraimite historians of his time or a little later (E₂).[‡]

On v.[22f.] see Wellhausen, *Comp.*, p. 226 f.; Stade, *GVI.* i. p. 190 f.; Kuenen, *HCO*. i. p. 348; Budde, *Richt. u. Sam.*, p. 115-117; Kittel, *GdH.* i. 2. p. 73 f. (cf. p. 5); Cornill, *Einl*[2]. p. 95 f.; Wildeboer, *Letterkunde*, p. 99. — We. and Sta. (cf. also Kue., Kitt.) surmise that in the original narrative the kingdom was not only offered, but accepted; a later editor corrected this in a theocratic spirit (v.[28]). — **23.** On the gods as kings in Semitic religions, see W. R. Smith, *Religion of the Semites*, p. 66 ff. The sovereignty of Yahweh was, of course, universally recognized in old Israel (cf. *e.g.* Jud. 5); the whole development of the religion presupposes this principle. But it is one thing to acknowledge Yahweh as the divine king, as Isaiah, for example, does,[§] and quite a different thing to conclude that he cannot endure the existence of a human king in Israel. This is by no means a necessary theological inference; it must have had a definite historical reason such as the experience of Israel in the 8th century afforded.

24-27. The origin of the idol at Ophrah. — At Gideon's request the warriors give him the rings which they have taken from the fallen Midianites. Of this gold he makes an idol

---

[*] Observe that *rule* is employed in v.[28] also, of Yahweh's sovereignty, and in 9[22] of Abimelech.   [†] Hos. 13[10f.]
[‡] Vatke, *Alttest. Theol.*, p. 478 n.; We., Sta., Co., Bu., Smend, *Alttest. Religionsgesch.*, p. 193 f.   [§] Is. 6[5]; see Smend, p. 205.

(*ephōd*) which he sets up at Ophrah. The Israelites worship it; and it becomes a cause of evil to Gideon and his family. — The making of the *ephōd* which stood in the holy place at Ophrah may very well have been narrated in J; it was a famous trophy of the great victory over Midian. The latter part of v.[27], which makes it a cause of apostasy to Israel and of ruin to the house of Gideon, expresses a very different feeling toward it; both the thought and the language betray a later writer (cf. 2[17], 2[3]). Verse[24-27a] are ascribed by Kuenen, Budde, and others to the older narrative, which spoke of the *ephōd* without a suspicion of disapproval.[*] The verses are, however, closely connected with v.[27], and in this connexion, as well as in the additions to v.[26], the hand of the editor must be recognized. — **24.** *Let me make a request of you*] the words connect very naturally with v.[22]; he declines the kingdom which in their gratitude for deliverance they offer him, but asks of them the golden ornaments they have stripped from the slain. If v.[22] are rightly ascribed to a different author from v.[24-27a],[†] the beginning of v.[24] must have been harmonized by the editor who combined them (Rje). In J the request could only be addressed to Gideon's followers, the Abiezrites. — *Every man give me the ring of his spoil*] ear-rings are probably meant; nose-rings appear in the O.T. only as women's adornments. — *They wore gold rings, for they were Ishmaelites*] *Ishmaelite* seems to be used here not of the race, but of the mode of life, Bedawin. In the genealogical systems, the Midianites belong to a different branch of the Abrahamidae from the Ishmaelites; see on 6[1]. We are to infer that such ornaments were not worn by the settled tribes.[‡] The half-verse is perhaps a gloss. — **25.** They willingly accede to his request; a mantle is spread on the ground, and the rings they had stripped from the slain are thrown into it. The *mantle* (*simlah*) was a wide outer garment or wrapper. It could readily be converted into a sack by bringing the corners together and tying them; cf. Ex. 12[34] Prov. 30[4]. — **26.** The weight of the

---

[*] Cf. Kitt. In v.[26] the list of spoils has been lengthened by other hands (Bu.). We. and Sta. consider the whole passage, v.[22-27], a later addition. See the authors cited above on v.[22], p. 230.　　　　[†] Kue., Co., Kitt.; cf. Bu.

[‡] The caravan-traders, whose connexions extended to the gold lands of Arabia, were far richer in such things than the peasants.

gold rings amounted to seventeen hundred shekels, not far from
seventy pounds. The figures are not excessively large, even if
they represent the spoil of Gideon's three hundred men ; a single
ring might often weigh half a shekel (cf. Gen. 24²²). — *Not
including the crescents, and the pendants, and the purple garments
worn by the kings of Midian*] cf. v.²¹. The half-verse is an editorial exaggeration such as we have noted in a number of other
places. This catalogue of things which were not used in making
the *ephōd* is quite superfluous, and only interrupts the narrative.*
—*Crescents and pendants*] coupled in the same way in Is. 3¹⁸,
the only other place where the latter word occurs. The translation *pendants* (? *ear*-drops) is suggested by the etymology ; just
what kind of jewelry is meant cannot be certainly known ; on the
crescents, see on v.²¹. — *The purple garments worn by the kings of
Midian*] the spoils of the kings naturally fell to the leader of the
expedition (v.²¹). Purple robes are the badge of royalty ; but
would J imagine the Bedawin chiefs riding to a foray in their
robes of state ? — *The necklaces that were on the necks of their
camels*] v.²¹. Budde sees in these words the only genuine part
of v.²⁶ᵇ, and regards v.²¹ᵇᵝ as a gloss, explaining in an unnecessary
way how Gideon got these crescents.† Wellhausen and Stade,
on the contrary, rightly hold v.²¹ to be genuine, and the whole of
v.²⁶ᵇ secondary ; observe the substitution of the general *necklaces*
for the rare and characteristic *crescents*. The author of v.²⁶ᵇ wished
to enumerate all that fell to Gideon in the distribution, as well as
what was given him at his request by the people, regardless of the
inappropriateness of the inventory in this place. — **27**. *Gideon
made it into an ephōd*] the *ephōd* was made of the gold rings of
the Midianites (v.²⁵ ²⁶ᵃ) ; ‡ v.²⁶ᵇ is obviously a gloss ; see above.
Ephōd is the specific name of a kind of idol ; cf. 17⁵ 18¹⁴ &c.
Hos. 3⁴. § This appears here from the material, and the quantity
of it employed, as well as from the verb, *place*. That it was so
understood by the editor is evident from his comment, *all Israel
went whoring after it*, his standing expression for heathenish or
idolatrous worship. The *ephōd* seems to have been peculiarly

---

* Especially the purple robes.   † *Richt. u. Sam.*, p. 116.
‡ The rings were amulets (Gen. 35⁴ ; cf. the Aram. קמיע) ; the gold was
already holy.   § Procop., μαντεῖον ἢ εἴδωλον.

an oracular idol; see more fully on 17⁵. — *And placed it in his
native city, Ophrah*] where it remained to later times. On the
verb see note. — *All Israel went astray after it*] 2¹⁷; it became
the object of an idolatrous cult, in which Israelites from all parts
of the land participated. — *And it became a snare to Gideon and
his family*] 2³; the cause of the ruin that overtook his house.
The clauses are an editorial addition, expressing the judgement of
a later time, and have possibly supplanted the original close of the
sentence. — **28.** Closing formulas of the editor; see on 3³⁰. —
And did not lift its head again] Zech. 1²¹; their power and spirit
were completely broken by their defeat. — **29.** *And Jerubbaal
ben Joash went and dwelt at his home*] the verse stands singularly out of place. That the making and setting up of the idol
at Ophrah is related before his return home, might perhaps be
explained by supposing that the writer wished to finish at once
telling what was done with the spoils of the Midianites; but v.²⁸
brings the story of Gideon to a formal close, v.²⁹ cannot stand
after it. Budde conjectures that v.²⁹ originally stood after 8⁵,
being the conclusion of the first of the two stories of the rout
of Midian; from this place it was necessarily removed when 8⁴ᶠᶠ·
was combined with 7³⁴–8³. If 8²²ᶠ· be from the same source, place
must be made for them between 8³ and 8²⁹.*

24. כאלה] cognate object. — ותנו] imv. corresponding to the preceding
impf. energ.; *and do you give.* — נזם] nose-ring is ordinarily על אף (נזם האף
פ, נאף), Gen. 24²² (Sam.) ⁴⁷ Is. 3²¹ Ez. 16¹² Prov. 11²². Cf. Jerome on
Ez. *l.c.* (*Opp.* ed. Vallarsi, v. 155); Hartmann, *Hebräerin*, iii. p. 205.—
25. נתון נתן] *certainly, we will give them;* emphasizing the willingness with
which they accede to his request; cf. 4⁹. — השמלה] the particular one taken
for the purpose, and made definite in the mind of the writer by that fact; cf.
on 7¹³, Ges.²⁶ § 126, 4; Davidson, *Syntax*, § 21 *e.* — **26.** The omission of the
unit of measure (*shekel*) is common; cf. 9⁴ 17²·³·⁴ &c. — השברנים] see on v.²¹.
— והנטיפות] the ancient versions took the word as the name of some kind of
necklace or collar.† Some Jewish interpreters connected it with נטף Ex. 30³⁴
(στακτή), and explain, capsules in which this sweet-smelling gum was worn
(older scholars quoted by Ki., RLbG., al.); so Schm., Buxtorf. Abulwalid
suggests that it may be equivalent to the Arab. *naṭafatᵘⁿ*, a small, clear pearl
(from its resemblance to a drop of water), or a bead of gold or silver (originally of spherical or elongated form) fastened to the lobe of the ear, ear-drop;

---

* For an alternative hypothesis, see note below.

† Only 𝕮 כלילא, *diadems, chaplets.*

cf. σταλάγμον. This interpretation is adopted by Schroeder, JDMich. (pearls). Ges. *Thes.*, Stud.; others simply, *ear-drops* (Be., Reuss, al.). See esp. Schroeder, *De vestitu mulierum*, p. 45-56. — בנדי הארגמן] the colour is a red purple, not violet: see Plin., *n. h.* ix. 133-135; Delitzsch, *PRE².* iv. p. 490 ff. The name is foreign; cf. Assyr. *argamannu*, Fr. Del., *Assyr. Hwb.*, p. 129.* The dye was extremely costly (Plin., *n. h.* ix. 124). — צבע] see on 6¹⁷; observe אשר immediately after. — 27. יאפ] on the etymology and meaning of this word, see note on 17⁵. — רצד] 6³⁷ Gen. 30³⁸ 1 S. 5² 2 S. 6¹⁷. — 28. כיס ן עידן] Bu. would emend בכל ימי גדעון, after 2¹⁸. — 29. *Jerubbaal*] if the verses came originally from E, we should probably have to assume that *Jerubbaal* had been substituted for *Gideon* by an editor. An alternative would be to suppose that the account of the making of the *ephod* comes from E₁ (instead of J, as in our analysis above); v.²⁹ would then be the conclusion of J's story, following immediately upon v.³¹. This hypothesis would also better explain the intimate connexion which now exists between v.²⁷ and v.³⁴⁻²⁷.

30-35.† Verses³³⁻³⁵ belong to the Deuteronomic framework of the book ; thought and expression correspond to those of D in 2¹²ff. 3⁷ (see below). What these verses contain in addition to the author's pragmatic formulas ; viz., that the Israelites adopted the worship of the Shechemite Baal-berith (v.³³ᵇ), and their ungrateful treatment of Jerubbaal's family (v.³⁵), is derived from ch. 9. These notices are inserted not as an introduction to ch. 9, ‡ but as a substitute for it. § Ch. 9, as will appear below, was not included by D in his Book of Judges. The story of Abimelech and the Shechemites did not naturally fall into his scheme of apostasy, oppression, and deliverance ; its moral was of a different kind. He therefore omitted it, only taking the worship of Baal-berith as an instance of the chronic lapse into heathenism, and summing up the rest in v.³⁵, as a proof of Israel's ingratitude to their defender, matching their forgetfulness of the divine deliverer.

Verses³⁰⁻³², on the contrary, form an introduction to the story of Abimelech ; some such preparation is presupposed in 9¹, where Abimelech first appears upon the scene. In their present form, however, these verses can hardly be attributed to the author of

---

* We should naturally expect the name of this colour to be of Phoenician origin, and to have come to the Assyrians from the West, rather than from the Assyrians to the Hebrews; and though we cannot at present prove this, it is the safer assumption. So also G. Hoffmann, *Z. A.* 1894, p. 337 f.

† On these verses see especially Budde, *Richt. u. Sam.*, p. 119-122.

‡ So most recent critics.   § Bu.

ch. 9 ; more than one phrase in them suggests rather a writer familiar with the Priestly narrative in Genesis.* There is no trace of a
Deuteronomic hand. In view of these facts, the hypothesis of
Budde is the most acceptable which has been proposed. It is
that the final editor (Rp) restored ch. 9, which Rd had omitted,
prefixing to it this introduction (v.³⁰⁻³²), the substance of which he
derived from the pre-deuteronomic source in which he found the
story of Abimelech. To this source probably belonged also the
notice of the burial of Jerubbaal; cf. 2⁹.—**30.** *Now Gideon had
seventy sons*] the number, 9²·⁵·¹⁸·²⁴·⁵⁶ ; cf. Abdon's seventy sons and
grandsons (12¹⁴), Jair's thirty sons (10⁴), &c.—*Who issued from
his loins*] lit. *thigh;* Gen. 46²⁶ Ex. 1⁵ cf. Gen. 35¹¹ (P)'.—*For he
had many wives*] the numerous hareem is an evidence of his
wealth and power; see below on 9².—**31.** *His concubine who
lived in Shechem*] 9¹·²·¹⁸. The woman was evidently a Canaanite,
and a free woman (see 9¹⁻⁵), notwithstanding Jotham's fling (9¹⁸).
The relation of Jerubbaal to her was probably like that of Samson
to his Philistine wife at Timnath, a *ṣadīqa* marriage ; see on 14⁵.†
—*He gave him the name Abimelech*] the name is not to be interpreted, 'My father (Jerubbaal) is king': as in all similar cases,
Melek is a divine title or name; cf. Ahimelech, Elimelech,
Nathanmelech; also Malchishua, &c. It is doubtful, however,
whether we should explain the name, 'Melek (the god-king) is
(my) father,' or 'Father of Melek'; the latter, impossible as it
sounds to our ears, is not without analogy in Semitic proper
names; see note. For the worshipper of Yahweh, he is the
King; for the Canaanites of Shechem, their Baal-berith.—
32. *At a good old age*] the phrase occurs only in Gen. 15¹⁵ (Rp)
25⁸ (P) 1 Chr. 29²⁸.—*And was buried in the tomb of Joash
his father*] cf. 2⁹ = Jos. 24³⁰.—*In Ophrah*] see crit. note.—
33. On v.³³⁻³⁵ see above, p. 234.—*As soon as Gideon died*] corresponding to the general theory of D (2¹⁹); the death of the
judge was always the signal for a lapse into heathenism ; cf. 2⁹ᶠ·¹¹⁻¹³,
3¹¹·¹³, 4¹.—*The Israelites again apostatized to heathenism*] lit.
returned and went whoring after the baals. Cf. v.²⁷ᵇ 2¹⁷; Ex. 34¹⁶ᶠ.

---

* Observe, *issuing from his loins* (v.³⁰); *a fine old age* (v.³²); see comm. on the vv.
† Bu., p. 121; cf. W. R. Smith, *Kinship and Marriage*, ch. 3; esp. p. 76.

Dt. 31[16]. The phrase is not that used by D in the Hexateuch
(*other gods*, 2[12. 19] &c.) ; it may have been chosen here with reference to the worship of Baal-berith, v.[b]. On the baals, see on
2[11. 13]. — *And made Baal-berith their god*] specification to the
general charge. Baal-berith, in 9[46] called El-berith, was the god
of Shechem, where he had a temple 9[4. 46].[*] The author of 8[33]
evidently assumes that the people of Shechem were Israelites,
and generalizes the local worship of Baal-berith into a defection
of Israel as a whole. Nothing is clearer, however, in ch. 9 than
that the population of Shechem was Canaanite ; the insurrection
fomented by Gaal is a rising of the native inhabitants against
the rule of the half-Israelite Abimelech ; see esp. v.[28]. — **34.** *Did
not remember Yahweh their god*] cf. 3[7]. — *Who rescued them from
the power of all their enemies on all sides*] cf. 1 S. 12[11] 10[18] ; with
the last phrase, Jud. 2[14] Dt. 12[10] 25[19] Jos. 23[1] 1 Chr. 22[9]. —
35. *And were not good to the family of Jerubbaal*] the substance
of Jotham's accusation (9[16-18]) ; as in the foregoing verses (v.[33. 34]),
what the Shechemites did is laid to the charge of all Israel. Deal
well with one, requite good with good, Gen. 21[23] Jos. 2[12] Jud. 1[24].
— *Jerubbaal Gideon*] the name Jerubbaal alone is used in ch. 9 ;
Gideon alone in ch. 8 (except v.[29]) ; on the margin between the
two, one name is glossed by the other. As the author draws
directly from 9[16], he may have written Jerubbaal here, though in
v.[28] he writes Gideon ; comp. on 7[1].

30. [וזרעון היו] cf. כי נשים רבות היו לו ; it is all in the past. — **31.** [ופילגשו]
19 *passim*, 20[4. 5. 6] ; in 9[18] Jotham says אמתו. Di. (on Gen. 25[6]) has observed
that in Gen. פילגשים is more than once introduced by R. — [גם היא] Gen. 4[22. 26]
19[38] 22[20]. — [וישם את שמו] cf. 2 K. 17[34] Neh. 9[7] Dan. 1[7] 5[12] (late; Bu.). —
[אביכיך] Gen. 20 21 26 ; cf. אחיכיך (1 S. 21 2 S. 8[17]),† and the Phoenician
names חבריך, and especially אחרבריך (חרבריך). In the last the grammatical
relation is unambiguous; the name is, Sister of Milk (Melek). Ahimelech
is accordingly, Brother of Melek, not, My brother is Melek, and Abimelech,
Father of Melek.‡ **32.** [בשיבה טובה] Gen. 15[15] 25[8] 1 Chr. 29[28]. — נקברה אבי
[הקזרי] grammatically incorrect. Doorn. would emend נקברה (6[24]) ; Kautzsch
(Ges.[25] p. 401) suggests that נקברה should stand either after ויקבר or at the
end of the verse. Another possibility is that אבי הקזרי is a gloss from 6[24], to

---

[*] See comm. on 9[4].

† Other compounds of *Melek*, see Baethgen, *Beiträge* p. 146.

‡ Nöldeke, *ZDMG.* xlii. 1888, p. 480 ; cf. Phoen. אמשתרת, Mother of Astarte.

which the preceding word was not brought into grammatical accord. —
33. ‏ירכעל נרעון‎] even as a gloss we should require ‏הוא נרעון‎; cf. 𝕲ᴮᴺ ᵃˡ. 𝕾.

IX. Abimelech and the men of Shechem.

— Abimelech, the half-Canaanite son of Jerubbaal, persuades the people of Shechem to have him for their ruler in preference to the other sons of his father. Abetted by them, he kills his brothers, — Jotham, the youngest, alone escaping the slaughter, — and is made king in Shechem (v.[1-6]). Jotham in a fable vents his contemptuous opinion of their new lord, upbraids them for their base ingratitude to Jerubbaal their defender, pronounces a curse upon them and their king, and flees (v.[7-21]). After three years the Shechemites fall out with Abimelech; an insurrection is fomented by one Gaal, a newcomer (v.[22-29]). Abimelech, apprised of the situation by the governor of the city, comes with his soldiers; Gaal goes out to fight with him; is beaten and driven back into the city, only to be cast out by the governor (v.[30-41]). In a second day's fighting, Abimelech takes the place by stratagem, puts the inhabitants to the sword, and destroys the city (v.[42-45]). The people of the neighbouring Tower of Shechem take refuge in the temple of El-berith; Abimelech burns it over their heads (v.[46-49]). While besieging Thebez, Abimelech is fatally hurt by a millstone which a woman threw from the wall, and dies by the sword of his armour-bearer. So Jotham's curse is fulfilled (v.[50-57]).

The character of the narrative as a whole displays a striking affinity to 8[4-21]; of the pragmatism which pervades large parts of ch. 6. 7 there is no trace.[*] We should be inclined, therefore, in conformity to our analysis of the preceding chapters, to ascribe it to J.[†] Budde, on the contrary, derives it from E, who, in retelling the old folk-story, introduced of his own invention the fable of Jotham (v.[7-21]).[‡]

The unity of the chapter has hitherto been almost unquestioned. It is, however, not unquestionable. There are clearly two accounts of the origin of hostilities between Abimelech and the Shechemites. In v.[22-25] an evil spirit sent by God stirs up the Shechemites;

---

* Stud., We., Co.   † Schrader-De Wette, *Einl*[6]. § 209.
‡ To E the chapter is attributed by Bruston also (Bu., p. 118 n.). On Jotham's fable, Kue., *HCO*[2]. i. p. 349. See further in crit. note below.

their armed bands rob all who pass through their territory: in
v.$^{26-29}$ a family of new-comers, headed by Gaal, incite a revolt by
appeals to race-pride and hatred. The sequel of the first of these
accounts is found in v.$^{42-45}$; Abimelech lays an ambush against
the city, takes and destroys it: that of the second is v.$^{30-41}$. We
obtain thus two complete narratives, and the confused repetitions
of the story as it now stands disappear. The fable of Jotham
(v.$^{7-21}$) is cognate to the first of these two narratives, and carries
with it its premises in v.$^{1-6}$; from this source v.$^{56f.}$ also is derived.
If our observation is correct, the version of the story in which
Gaal plays the leading part may be ascribed to J; the other to E.

No traces of D's hand are discoverable in the chapter. The
story of Gideon is concluded in the usual way in 8^{28}; the introduction to the story of Jephthah, 10$^{6ff.}$, follows. We must infer
from the absence of D's characteristic setting that the history of
Abimelech and the Shechemites was not included in the Deuteronomic Book of Judges, into whose pragmatism it could not easily
be coerced.* It was found, however, in the older Jehovistic book
which D worked over; the same sources run through it which we
have discovered in ch. 6–8; and that it lay before D appears from
8$^{33-35}$, which is his brief substitute for it. It must have been
restored by a still later editor, who wrote 8$^{30-32}$ to introduce it.†

An analysis of ch. 9 is attempted by Winckler (*Altorientalische Forschungen*,
p. 59 ff.), as follows: J 9$^{1-5. 21. 26-29. 41. 42. 43. 45-49}$; E 9$^{6 [7-20] 21 * 23-25. 30-33. 34-35}$
[v.$^{36-38}$ R?] $^{39. 40. 44. 45}$. To which of the two v.$^{50-54}$ belong is uncertain;
v.$^{22. 55-57}$ are added by D.

The story of Abimelech is one of the oldest in the Book of
Judges, and in various ways one of the most instructive. We
have learned from ch. 1 that the Israelites in no part of the land
completely dispossessed the native population; that, on the contrary, the latter, even where the new-comers were strongest, retained
many of the most important places. Ch. 9 gives us a glimpse of
the relations between the two peoples thus brought side by side.
The Canaanite town, Shechem, ‡ subject to Jerubbaal of Ophrah;

---

* See above, p. 234 f.

† See Bu., *Richt. u. Sam.*, p. 119-122; and above, Introduction, § 7.

‡ Predominantly Canaanite; Israelites were no doubt settled in the town; they
were not, however, ‘citizens of Shechem,’ but *gerim*.

his half-Canaanite son Abimelech, who naturally belongs to his mother's people (see on v.[1]) ; the successful appeal to blood, 'which is thicker than water,' by which he becomes king of Shechem, ruling also over the neighbouring Israelites ; the interloper Gaal and his kinsmen, who settle in Shechem and instigate insurrection against Abimelech by skilfully appealing to the pride of the Shechemite aristocracy, — all help us better than anything else in the book to realize the situation in this period.

Many scholars see in the story a kind of prelude to the history of the kingdom of Saul. Gideon, it is said, was in fact king in Ophrah, whatever we think of $8^{22f.}$; [*] that his sons would succeed him is a matter of course (9^2); Abimelech is formally created king (9^6), and reigns over Israelites (Joseph) as well as Canaanites ; a short-lived Manassite kingdom thus preceded the Benjamite kingdom of Saul. All this shows that Israel was feeling its way toward a stronger and more stable form of government.[†] There seems to me to be some exaggeration in this. It is a very uncertain, and in my opinion improbable, conjecture that $8^{22\ 23}$ supersede an older statement that Gideon was made king in consequence of his victory over Midian, as Saul after the relief of Jabesh Gilead. [‡] That Shechem had been subject or tributary to him, and had reason to expect that his sons would maintain their authority over the city, does not prove that he was in fact king in Manasseh and Ephraim ; that his authority descended not to one son, but to all of them jointly, implies quite the opposite. Abimelech is king of Shechem, a Canaanite town, in which, as among the Canaanites generally, the city-kingdom was the customary form of government. That he was also recognized as king by purely Israelite towns or clans is not intimated, and is not a necessary inference from the fact that he has the Israelites at his back in his effort to suppress the revolt of the Canaanite cities (9^{55}).

The moral of the story is brought out strongly, but naturally. Abimelech and the people of Shechem enjoy but a little while the

---

[*] The name *Abimelech* cannot be appealed to as evidence of this; see above, p. 235.

[†] See We., *Comp.*, p. 227; Kitt., *GdH.* 1. 2. p. 73 f.; especially Sta., *GVI.* i. p. 181 ff. (*Das manassitische Königthum*), esp. p. 190 f.

[‡] See above, comm. on 8^{22}.

fruits of their common crime ; then they fall out, and become
fatal to each other. Abimelech destroys Shechem, but loses his
life before Thebez, which had apparently conspired with Shechem
in the revolt. This righteous retribution is denounced beforehand
by Jotham, and the writer closes by pointing out how signally his
prophetic curse had been fulfilled. Studer remarks that we have
here a religious conception of history very similar to that of the
Greeks in the time of Herodotus and the contemporary tragic
poets, "who would have found in the fate of Gideon's house, if it
had belonged to their national cycle, fruitful material for their
magnificent compositions."

1–6. Abimelech is made king of Shechem. — Abimelech persuades the people of Shechem, his mother's town, to support him.
With money from their temple treasure he hires a band of bravos
and murders his brothers. He is formally made king of Shechem
and Beth-millo. — **1.** *Abimelech the son of Jerubbaal went to
Shechem*] after his father's death (8^{32}). *Jerubbaal* throughout
the chapter ; see on 6^{32} 7^1. — *To his mother's brethren*] the nearer
kinsmen ; cf. 14^3 16^{31}. — *The whole clan of his mother's family*]
the clan to which it belonged. *Shechem*, the modern Nâbulus,*
lay in a valley between Mt. Ebal on the north and Mt. Gerizim
on the south, in the heart of Mt. Ephraim. The neighbourhood
of the city is well-watered and exceedingly fruitful. The principal
road from Central Palestine across the Jordan to Gilead started
from Shechem (Gen. 32 33) ; the continuation of this road westward led down to the seaboard plain. The great north road from
Jerusalem through Bethel also passed through Shechem, continuing north by En-gannim (Genin) into the Great Plain, or
striking off NE. to Beth-shean. It had thus every advantage of
position, and was doubtless even in pre-Israelite times a pros-
perous and important place. It is mentioned more than once
in the patriarchal story (Gen. 12^6 33^{18} 34 35^4 $37^{12ff.}$). The treacherous attack on Shechem by Simeon and Levi (Gen. 34 49^{5-7})
must have been among the earliest attempts of Israelites to establish themselves west of the Jordan. It resulted, in the end, most
disastrously for the two tribes, which never recovered from the

---

* Flavia Neapolis ; Justin Martyr, *Apol.* i. c. 1 ; Schürer, *GjV.* i. p. 546.

vengeance which the Canaanites took upon them. At Shechem was the ancestral tomb of Joseph (Jos. 24³²); there according to Jos. 24¹·²⁵,* Joshua assembled Israel to receive his parting instructions and make the solemn covenant of religion ; cf. Dt. 11²⁹. In Shechem, also, the chief place of Ephraim, the assembled tribes made Jeroboam ben Nebat king (1 K. 12); one of the first acts of his reign was to fortify the place.† — **2.** He puts his kinsmen up to speak for him to the citizens. — *The freemen of Shechem*] v.³ 20⁵ 1 S. 23¹¹·¹² 2 S. 21¹²; llt., *the proprietors*, those to whom it belonged, the citizens ; then, perhaps, without distinction of citizen and metic, the inhabitants. — *Which is the better for you, that seventy men rule over you — all the sons of Jerubbaal — or that one man rule over you ?*] the authority of Jerubbaal, he intimates, would descend to his sons jointly, not to one designated successor. If this representation is true, it is evident that we cannot think of Jerubbaal as the founder of a kingdom, however short-lived ; for in that case the succession must have been his first care. Nor need we suppose that the people of Shechem recognized any right to rule in Jerubbaal or his sons ; they would succeed to his power, that is all. The evils of such a many-headed tyranny needed no argument ; the earliest political experience of men taught the lesson : οὐκ ἀγαθὸν πολυκοιρανίη· εἰς κοίρανος ἔστω, εἰς βασιλεύς. Wellhausen thinks that the monarchy is here regarded as an advance upon the patriarchal rule of the nobles, and infers that the story was not written till after the establishment of the kingdom in Israel. I do not think we need see in Abimelech's words deep reflections on the advantages of different forms of government, behind which must lie the experience of the monarchy. The present case was plain enough in itself. — *Remember, besides, that I am your own flesh and blood*] lit. *your bone and your flesh*; 2 S. 5¹ 19¹²·¹³; ‡ cf. Gen. 29¹⁴ 2²³. If, as has been suggested above (p. 235), Gideon's *concubine* who lived

---

* ﬡ: ⑥ *Shiloh.*

† On Nābulus, see Seetzen, *Reisen*, ii. p. 170 ff. ; Rob., *BR²*. ii. p. 275 ff. ; Rosen, *ZDMG*. xiv. 1860, p. 634 ff. ; Guérin, *Samarie*, i. p. 390-423 ; *SWP. Memoirs*, ii. p. 203-210 ; Bäd²., p. 218-223 ; G. A. Smith, *Hist. Geog.*, p. 119 f. — It has a singular interest from the fact that the last remnants of the Samaritans live there, and the rites of the old Israelite religion are still in some sort observed.

‡ In the last passage David makes the same appeal to the elders of Judah.

2

at Shechem (8^{31}) was a *ṣadîqa* wife, this appeal would have
double force ; for the children of such a marriage belonged to the
mother's tribe, not to the father's.* — 3. His mother's kinsmen
took up his cause, in which they doubtless discerned their own
interest, and easily persuaded the freemen. — *Their hearts inclined
to follow Abimelech, for they said, He is our brother*] he is one
of us. — 4. They furnish him money from the temple-treasure. —
Seventy shekels of silver from the temple of Baal-berith] the
temple, like those of other ancient peoples, had its treasure,
accumulated from gifts, payment of vows, penalties, and the like,
which was drawn upon by the authorities for public purposes,
or in times of emergency.† If there was any public treasure
besides, it was kept in the temple for security ; ‡ and the wealth
of private persons was often deposited there for safe-keeping. §
So it was, doubtless, in a small way, at Shechem. *Baal-berith ;*
cf. *El-berith* v.⁴⁶. The names are equivalent : *el* is the *numen
loci ; ba'al*, the god proprietor of the place. Baal-berith is
interpreted, *covenant Baal*, and explained either as the god who
presides over covenants, obligations, alliances, and the like ; ‖ or,
with a more particular reference, the god of the Canaanite league
at the head of which Shechem stood ; ¶ or who presided over
the treaty between the Canaanite and Israelite inhabitants of
Shechem.** It is wiser to confess that we know nothing about the
original significance of the name. With this money Abimelech
hired a band of bravos. — *Worthless and reckless men*] ready for
the commission of any crime. The seventy shekels curiously correspond to the seventy sons of Jerubbaal ; the price of their lives
was but a shekel each. — 5. With these followers he went to his
father's home in Ophrah and slaughtered his brothers. — *Seventy
men on one stone*] v.¹⁸. Like a hecatomb of cattle, cf. 1 S. 14³⁴.
This is not to be regarded as a wanton atrocity ; †† the very conformity to the precautions taken in slaughtering animals in the

---

* See on 14⁵.
† So at Jerusalem ; 1 K. 7⁵¹ 2 K. 20¹³, 1 K. 15¹⁸ 2 K. 18¹⁶ cf. 2 K. 12⁴ 9ff. 22⁴.
‡ So, *e.g.*, at Athens in the ὀπισθόδομος of the Parthenon ; at Rome in the temple
of Saturn on the Capitoline (Stud.).   § Cf. 2 Macc. 3¹⁰⁻¹².
‖ Cf. Ζεὺς ὅρκιος, *Deus fidius ;* Ges. *Thes.*, al. Other theories in Schm., *Quaest.*
3 (p. 914).   ¶ Ew., *G VI.* ii. p. 484.
** Ke. We might then perhaps think of the treaty, Gen. 34.   †† Stud.

open field * shows that the motive was to dispose of the blood, in which was the life of his victims, in such a way that they should give him no further trouble.† It is an instructive instance of the power of animistic superstitions. Compare the slaughter of the seventy sons of Ahab and the brothers of Ahaziah by Jehu, 2 K. 10[16. 12-14], and that of the princes of Judah by Athaliah, 2 K. 11[1-3]. Only Jotham, the youngest son, escaped ; cf. 2 K. 11[2].— 6. The Shechemites make Abimelech king.— *All Beth-millo*] here and in v.[20] named with Shechem, but distinguished from it, is supposed by many interpreters to be the same as the Tower of Shechem (v.[46-49]) ; ‡ but the identification is very doubtful, especially if we recognize two strands in the narrative. § — *By the massebah tree which is at Shechem*] the king was acclaimed at the sanctuary of Shechem, as Saul was at Gilgal (1 S. 11[15]). Under the holy tree at Shechem Jacob concealed the idols and amulets of his household (Gen. 35[4]) ; under it, too, Joshua set up the witness-stone, which had "heard all the words which Yahweh spoke " (Jos. 24[26], E). ‖ From the latter passage it appears that in the eighth century there was an old standing-stone (*massebah*) under the holy tree. The word *massebah*, which in later times was an offence, was mutilated by an editor or scribe ; see critical note.

1. Jos. 24 (E) assumes that at the end of Joshua's life Shechem was in the possession of the Israelites; Gen. 48[22] Jos. 24[32] give different accounts of the Israelite title to the place. That in the days of Abimelech it was still Canaanite appears beyond question from the following story. The difference in this point between Jos. 24 and Jud. 9 is an argument against ascribing the latter to E; see, however, Bu., p. 119 n. — On the use of מִשְׁפָּחָה see on 13[2]. בֵּית אָב is virtually a compound noun; cf. the plur. בֵּית אֲבוֹת Nu. 1[2] &c. (never בְּתֵי אָבוֹת); not, *the house of his mother's father*, but his mother's *father's-house*, family. — 2. דִּבֶּר בְּאָזְנֵי פּ] *speak in the hearing of*, before; for one's self (Gen. 50[4]) or in behalf of another (Gen. 44[18]); sometimes, address one in the presence of another (Gen. 23[10. 13. 16]). It does not appear that the phrase, which is a common one,¶ has any peculiar emphasis, *urge* the question (Kitt.). — הֲטוֹב בָּכֶם שִׁבְעִים אִישׁ ... אִם מְשֹׁל בָּכֶם אִישׁ אֶחָד] the alternative with אִם ... ה, 20[28] 2 S. 24[13] 1 K. 22[6. 15] &c.; cf. Jud. 2[22]. The subject of the inf. is here

* Cf. Dt. 12[16. 24].   † Somewhat similarly, Hitzig, *GVI.* i. p. 115.
‡ Serar., Schm., Stud., Be., Sta., al.
§ Winckler propounds as a novelty the old conjecture that Millo was the name of Abimelech's mother's family.   ‖ On holy trees, see on 4[11] 6[11].
¶ Cf. also, אָמַר בְּאָזְנֵי פ' 17[2]; הֵרַא Ex. 24[7].

separated from it by the complementary prep. and its object. In such cases
the subj. is to be regarded as a nominative; see Ges.[26] § 115, 2. — **4.** ריקים]
11[8] (Jephthah's band) 2 S. 6[20] 2 Chr. 13[7] (|| בני בליעל). Prop. ' empty ' (7[16]);
idle (Prov. 12[11] 28[19]); wanton (2 S. 6[20]). Others, *portionless* (𝕃 *inopes*),
like Jephthah himself (cf. Neh. 5[13]), men without a stake in society; or *good
for nothing*, like the empty ears of grain, Gen. 41[27], *homines nullius frugis*
(Stud.). Cf. ῥακά Matt. 5[22]; Kautzsch, *Aram. Gram.*, p. 10. — פחזים]
Zeph. 3[4] cf. Jer. 23[32] (פחוז) Gen. 49[4]. In Arab. the verb means ' act arro-
gantly, insolently, swagger '; in Aram. and Syr. it is used more particularly of
the impudent boldness of men heated by wine, or of reckless licentiousness.
The notion of perfidy which Abulw. finds in the Heb. word is not confirmed
by the usage. (𝔗 ren. l reschl. m. Aruch בהרין (cf. Ki.). — **6.** בית מליא] compare
the *Millo* (הסלוא, always with the article) in Jerusalem, 2 S. 5[9] 1 K. 9[15. 24] 11[27]
2 Chr. 32[5]; an important part of the defences of the city (𝕲 usually ἡ ἄκρα).
At a Beth-millo (query, in Jerusalem?) Joash was murdered (2 K. 12[21]).
Following 𝔗 בליהא (= Heb. סליה Is. 37[33], cf. Ra.) and the context in
1 K. 11[27], the word is commonly interpreted 'fill ' (of earth), earth-work
(Ges. *Thes.*), more specifically, an outwork covering the entrance to a city or
fortress (SS., cf. Sta., *GVI.* i. p. 343). These etymological explanations are
uncertain; the word is apparently Canaanite. We have no clue to the site;
the place must have been near Shechem. — עם אלון מצב] 𝔐 points מצב as
ptcp. Hoph. (Gen. 28[12], *a tree set up* (cf. Σ 𝕃), which is perilously near
nonsense. Context and construction require the designation of a particular
tree; in place of מצב we should have a genitive with the article. 𝕲[ALPV al. ş]*
πρὸς τῇ βαλάνῳ τῆς στάσεως pronounced מֻצָּב[ה] (Jos. 4[3] cf. 1 S. 13[23]); cf. 'A
ἐπὶ πεδίου στηλώματος 𝔗 עם מישר קמתא. In the light of Jos. 24[26] we need
have no hesitation in emending אֵלוֹן הַמֻּצָּב. That מֻצָּב is a noun of the same
meaning as מצבה (Stud., SS., al.) is a much more hazardous conjecture; the
article is indispensable, and the noun-type מֻצָּב inexplicable. In other places
the מצבה has been rendered harmless by substitution of מזבח (Gen. 33[20]); cf.
Gen. 31[49] (מצפה, cf. v.[48]) and 𝖲 a here *maṣpyâ*.

7–21. Jotham's apologue. — Jotham is apprised of the pro-
ceedings, and, from a safe position on Mt. Gerizim, shouts in the
ears of the assembly his fable of the trees who made them a king,
giving it a pointed application to the Shechemites and their new
lord. The application is not on all fours with the fable. The
proper lesson of the fable is, that the good and useful members
of the community have too much to do in their own station and
calling to leave it for the onerous responsibilities of the kingdom;
it is only the idle and worthless who can be persuaded to take the

---

* Also 𝕲[BN] with the doublet τῇ εὑρετῇ (הנמצא); cf. 𝔐.

office.   It is natural to see in the former part of the fable a reference to Jerubbaal, who declined the kingdom which the unworthy
Abimelech had just assumed ; * but if this contrast was in the
writer's mind, he does not bring it out more distinctly in the
sequel, which is exclusively occupied with Abimelech.   The most
striking incongruity is in the very point of the application.   In
v.¹⁸ the question is, whether the trees are acting in good faith
toward the box-thorn in making him king ; in v.¹⁶, whether in
making Abimelech king the Shechemites have acted in faith and
honour toward Jerubbaal and his house.†

From this discrepancy it has been inferred that the fable (v.⁸⁻¹⁵)
was not original with the author of v.⁷⁻²¹, but was borrowed by
him, perhaps from a collection of popular apologues, and put to
a use quite foreign to its native purport. ‡   It is somewhat hazardous, however, to draw this conclusion from the premises.   Faith
and honour are indeed used with a different reference in v.¹⁶ from
that which they implicitly have in v.¹⁵ ; the application is logically
defective.   But such looseness of connexion is not altogether
uncommon in the moral of apologues ; the parables of the New
Testament would furnish more than one example. §   While we
concede the possibility, therefore, that the author has here drawn
upon the stores of folk-wisdom, rather than on his own invention, this supposition is by no means necessary ; and it remains
the simpler and more natural hypothesis that the fable is of the
same conception with the rest of the speech.   If this be the
case, it is very doubtful whether we should see in the fable a
judgment upon the kingdom as a form of government, such
as a number of recent critics are disposed to find in it. ‖
The author had in mind a concrete instance, beyond which
he had no occasion to travel.   The attempt to determine the

* Ch. 8²³. So the older interpreters generally ; see comm. on v.¹⁸. The reason
for refusing the kingdom in 9⁸ᶠᶠ is totally different from that given in 8²³.

† This is true, even if, with Doorn., we regard v.¹⁶ᵇ⁻¹⁹ᵃ as a gloss ; for these
verses are at least a correct exposition of the author's meaning (Smend).

‡ See Reuss, *GAT.* § 104 ; Wildeboer, *Letterkunde d. O.V.*, p. 39-41 ; cf. Smend,
Alttest. Religionsgesch. p. 66 n.

§ Cf. *e.g.* the parable of the Unjust Steward, Lu. 16¹⁻⁹. Stud. refers to the confusion of figures in John 10¹ᶠ.

‖ So, in different ways, Reuss, Wildeboer, Bu., Smend, al.

age of the fable by its attitude to the kingdom is therefore very
precarious.[*]

Jotham's speech is hardly to be deemed historical; [†] it is the
way in which the author sets forth, at the appropriate moment,
the true nature of the new kingdom, and foretells what will come
of it (cf. v.[56]). It is noteworthy, however, that these words are
uttered, not, as in so many similar cases, by a nameless prophet,
or by an angel, but by the man from whose lips they come with
the most dramatic fitness. In this also we may perhaps see
evidence of the antiquity of the whole story. [‡] — With the apologue, cf. especially 2 K. 14[9].

7. *People told Jotham*] that the citizens of Shechem were
making Abimelech king. The author apparently represents
Jotham as addressing the multitudes assembled at the holy tree
to acclaim the king (v.[6]). The words lose much of their point if
we imagine that, after Abimelech had again left Shechem, Jotham
himself called the people of the town together on Mt. Gerizim
and delivered to them his speech. [§] — *He stood on the top of Mt.
Gerizim*] Mt. Gerizim is on the southern side of the valley in
which Shechem lies, Mt. Ebal on the northern; see above, on
v.[1]. [‖] From the summit of Gerizim, more than nine hundred feet
high, a man could hardly make himself heard by people in the
valley below; [¶] but the writer's language need not be pressed to
this absurdity. Modern travellers have remarked a projecting
crag on the side of the mountain, which forms a triangular platform overlooking the town and the whole valley, a natural pulpit
admirably suited to the requirements of the story.[**] — *Listen to
me, ye freemen of Shechem, and may God listen to you!*] may
God give ear to your prayers as you give ear to me.

8-15. The Fable. — 8. *Once upon a time the trees went about
to anoint a king over them*] they offer the kingdom first to the

---

[*] See, e.g., Reuss, Wildeboer.

[†] See, on the opposite side, Kitt., *GdH.* i. 2. p. 76.   [‡] We.   [§] Kitt.

[‖] On Gerizim see *Guérin, Samarie*, i. p. 424 ff.; *SWP. Memoirs*, ii. p. 148 f.
187-193.   [¶] Kue.

[**] Furrer, *Wanderungen durch Palästina*, 1865, p. 244 f°; *BL.* ii. p. 330; Bud[²],
p. 222.

olive, which in the zone in which it flourishes is the most valuable of trees to man ; olea . . . prima omnium arborum est (Columella).[*] In the fertile vale of Shechem (Nābulus) there are still extensive and beautiful groves of olive trees.[†] — **9.** The olive declines the proffered honour. — *Shall I stop my fatness, with which gods and men are honoured*] 𝔐 has, *which God and men honour in me ;* [‡] but this is probably an alteration from motives of reverence. [§] We expect something corresponding to v.[13], *my wine that rejoices gods and men;* and so the versions generally interpret, though the same motive which prompted the correction in 𝔐 is apparent in their renderings. [‖] As men anointed themselves on feast days, and as the head of a guest was anointed as a sign of honour, so oil was poured or smeared on the sacred stones which stood for the god, and in which, at least in older times, he was believed to dwell ; cf. Gen. 28[18] 35[14].[¶] And as oil is in Palestine an important article of food, taking the place of butter with us, it is offered to the gods with their bread.[**] — *And come to rule over the trees*] lit. *sway;* the characteristic movement of a tree (Is. 7[2]), represented as a gesture of authority ; his subjects must obey his beck and nod. — **10.** They next invite the fig to be their king, but he also declines. — **11.** *Shall I stop my sweetness and my prolific crop*] the fig tree bears at two or even three seasons of the year,[††] and its fruit, fresh or dried, is not only a delicious luxury but one of the food staples of the country. [‡‡] — **12.** Then they turn to the vine, only to meet the same refusal. — **13.** *Shall I stop my juice that gladdens gods and men*] exhilarates them. Wine was used in libations wherever the grape was known. Among the Greeks and Romans it was poured over the sacrificial flesh ; in Israel, at least

---

[*] *De re rustica*, v. 8; other ancient testimonies are collected by Celsius, *Hierobotanicon*, ii. p. 334 ff. On the olive in Palestine, see Anderlind, *ZDPV*. xi. 1888, p. 69-77; Thomson, *Land and Book*[2], iii. p. 33 ff.

[†] Van de Velde, *Narrative*. i. p. 386; Rosen, *ZDMG*. xiv. p. 638; Petermann, *Reisen*[2], p. 266.   [‡] So also most recensions of 𝔊 ; see crit. note.

[§] Geiger, *Urschrift*, p. 327.   [‖] Compare the translations of v.[13].

[¶] The custom prevailed very widely; see references in Di. on Gen. 28[18], and W. R. Smith, cited in the next note.

[**] See W. R. Smith, *Religion of the Semites*, p. 214 f. On the various uses of oil for food see *DB*. s.v.

[††] Pliny, *n. h.*, xvi. 113. 114; Shaw, *Travels*[2], 1757, p. 342; *DB*[2]. s.v.

[‡‡] Fig trees at Nābulus, see Rosen, *l.c.*; Anderlind, *l.c.* p. 80.

in later times, it was poured on the ground by the altar;＊ probably in the primitive practise it was poured out before or at the foot of the standing stone. The wine which the god thus partakes of with his worshippers has the same effect on him as on them.

The teaching of this part of the fable is that men whose character and ability fit them to rule are unwilling to sacrifice their usefulness and the honour they enjoy in a private station, for the sake of power. By the repetition of the offer and refusal, the author generalizes; no man of standing in the community would want to be king.† The general assertion may, however, be made for a particular application, and does not necessarily convey a judgement upon the kingdom in principle. Whether we find in it such a judgement will depend on our opinion about the origin of the fable; see above, p. 245. However that may be, the older interpreters were doubtless right in seeing in the fable in its present connexion a contrast between Gideon's refusal (8^{23}) and Abimelech's ready acceptance of regal name and power.‡ — 14. Their proffer of the kingdom being rejected by all the better sort, the trees come down to the common box-thorn, a plant of very opposite character from those which they had previously addressed; bearing no fruit, giving no shade, yielding no timber; a useless and noxious cumberer of the ground. — 15. Here at last they found one who was ready to be their king. — *If you are anointing me king over you in good faith*] if it be not jest and mockery, but serious earnest. — *Come, take refuge in my shadow*] put yourselves under my protection and confide in me. The irony of the fable has its climax in the seriousness of this pledge of protection: the image of the trees of forest and field seeking shelter in the shadow of the thorn-bush has in it the whole absurdity of the situation. Men wanted a king to defend them from their enemies (8^{22} 1 S. 9^{16}); of what use was a king who

---

＊ Ecclus. 50^{16}; Fl. Jos., *antt.* iii. 9, 4 § 234; see Di. on Nu. 15^7 28^7; W. R. Smith, *Religion of the Semites*, p. 213 f.

† The Midrash gives an allegorical interpretation: the olive represents Othniel; the fig, Deborah; the vine, Gideon. See *Yalqūṭ*, ii. § 65; Ra. *ad loc.* Jos. Kimchi explained the three trees of Gideon, his son, and grandson (8^{22}).

‡ See Cler. and Schm. on v.^{14}.

could not do that? — *But if not, fire shall go forth from the box-
thorn and devour the cedars of Lebanon*] it was doubtless not an
uncommon thing for a fire, starting among thorns, to spread to
field and orchard (Ex. 22⁶), or forest (Is. 9¹⁸), so that the lowly
thorn became the destruction of the stateliest trees. *The cedars
of Lebanon* represent the opposite extreme of creation from the
thorn; see 2 K. 14⁹, Jehoash's insulting answer to Amaziah of
Judah. Where there is no power to help, there may be infinite
possibilities of harm. Those who made the thorn king over them
put themselves in this dilemma: if they were true to him, they
enjoyed his protection, which was a mockery; if they were false
to him, he would be their ruin.*

8. הָלוֹךְ הָלְכוּ] the inf. abs. at the beginning of the sentence in cases like
this has very little emphasis; cf. Gen. 26²⁸ 43⁷. — מֵלוֹכָה] Qerē מָלְכָה; similarly
בִּיתֹנִי v.¹⁰·¹² Qerē חָדְלִי; cf. Ps. 26² 1 S. 28⁸, Ges.²⁶ § 48, 5; Kö., i. p. 163–166;
Praetorius, *ZATW.* iii. p. 55. — 9. הֶחֳדַלְתִּי] v.¹¹·¹³. The punctuation is entirely
anomalous, and has given rise to much discussion; see Stud., and Kö., i. p. 240–
242.† The most probable explanation is that the punctuation intends a Hoph.
with ה interrogative, assuming the elision of the ה preformative; *shall I be
compelled to give up,* &c. (Ol. § 89; Sta. § 175 a; Kö., i. p. 242). What the
author intended is another question. It seems at first sight simplest to take
the verb as Kal with ה interrogative (הֶחָדַלְתִּי); ‡ but חָדַל is never construed
with acc. (poetical instances where the object is an inf., such as Job 3¹⁷, are
not in point). I prefer, therefore, to regard it as Hiph. (הֶחְדַלְתִּי), 'cause to
leave off, stop.' § That the Hiph. does not elsewhere occur is of no great
weight. The absence of the interrogative particle is no objection; see the
following note. The idiomatic use of the perfect in these exclamatory questions is to be noted; cf. Gen. 18¹² 1 S. 25¹¹ (וְלָקַחְתִּי), Dr³. § 19. It seems to
be akin to the use of the perfect in hypotheses contrary to reality. ‖ The
interrogative particle is not usual in such cases. — דִּשְׁנִי], *pinguis oliva,* Verg.,
georg. ii. 424; Hor., *epod.* ii. 54 f.; cf. Rom. 11¹⁷. — אֵשֶׁר כִּי יְכַבְּדוּ אֱלֹהִים וַאֲנָשִׁים]
so 𝕲ᴬᴸᴹᴺᴼᴾⱽ ᔆ 𝔏. 𝕲ᴮ ἐν ᾗ δοξάσουσιν τὸν θεὸν ἄνδρες; 𝔏 *qua et dii utuntur
et homines;* 𝕿 *with which they honour Y., and in which men luxuriate;*

---

* Stud.
† Of the Jewish grammarians, De Balmis regards the form as Kal (fol. 91ᵇ end);
Abulwalid, as Hiph. (*Luma*, p. 325); Kimchi, as Hoph. (*Michlol,* fol. 63ᵇ f., ed.
Lyck).
‡ Stud., Be., Kö., al.; cf. Ges.²⁶ p. 167.
§ Ol., Sta.; cf. Ew. This reading is found in the margin of the first two Bom-
berg edd., and in an Erfurt cod. (JHMich.).
‖ There is a special reason for the impf. in Jud. 11³⁵.

5 *because by me God and men are honoured.*[*] How far these versions had a different text from 𝔐 is not clear. They have at least interpreted with a correct perception of what the context requires. For נ we must then emend כ (*with which*), and should prefer to pronounce the verb as Niph. (יְכֻבַּד), though the Pi. with indefinite subject is not impossible. — **10**. כרות] see on v.⁸. — **11**. מתק '] cf. the adj. מתוק 14¹⁴· ¹⁸. The primary sense seems to be, something which one sucks; cf. Syr. *mĕthaq* (Löw, *Pflanzennamen*, p. 333). — רגובתי] Ez. 36³⁰ Dt. 32¹⁸. — **13**. תירוש] *the juice of the grape, must,* Mi. 6¹⁵; frequently named with corn (דגן) and fresh oil (יצהר) as one of the chief products of agriculture, *e.g.* Jer. 31¹²; as such it is subject to the tithe (Dt. 12¹⁷), &c. The corresponding Syriac word ʿăṣîrā is defined in the native lexicons as 'must, fresh grape juice as it comes from the press'; see *PS.* 1635. In the O.T. תירוש is used not only of sweet must (עסיס), but of grape juice which has undergone fermentation (יין); cf. *e.g.* Hos. 4¹¹; so here. The etymology still maintained by Ges. *Thes.,* 633 f., Fleischer, al. (*quia inebriat, cerebrum occupat*) is at variance with both the form and meaning of the word. — **14**. האטד] *rhamnus,* 𝔊𝔏. So in Punic; Dioscorides, i. 119 (ed. Sprengel, i. p. 114), ῥάμνος· Ἀφροὶ ἀταδὶν (Boch., Cels., Löw, *Pflanzennamen,* p. 404); Arab., Syr. dial.; see Löw, p. 44. The common species in Palestine is *Lycium Europaeum* Linn., spread over the whole country (*DB².* i. p. 451).

16–20. The application. — 16. *And now*] to come to the moral. — *If you have acted in good faith and honour in making Abimelech king as you have done*] the words correspond to v.¹⁵ (*in good faith*), but are used with a different reference, as immediately appears. In v.¹⁶ the question is of their good faith to the new king; in v.¹⁶⁻²⁰ of good faith to Jerubbaal and his family. If it is thought too improbable a hypothesis that the author invented an apologue that does not in strict logic tally with the application he intended to make of it, the alternative is to suppose that he borrowed and adapted an older fable, the lesson of which was not quite the same that he wished to inculcate.† This explanation, however, creates other difficulties; for v.¹⁵ᵇ is obviously not a natural ending for an independent fable of the purport generally attributed to v.⁸⁻¹⁵; it is appropriate, and we might almost say intelligible, only as foreshadowing the ruin which Abimelech brought upon the Shechemites. Moreover, in the following narrative itself it is the unfaithfulness of the men of Shechem to

---

[*] Several older commentators whose exegetical tact was stronger than their grammar, translate 𝔐 in the same way; so Vatabl., Drus., Celsius, al.

† See above, p. 245.

Abimelech that is the cause of their undoing, however justly
this may be regarded as a retribution for their unfaithfulness to
Jerubbaal. The simplest and most natural explanation seems to
be that in pointing his moral the author's logic is not strictly
consequent. — *And if you have dealt well with Jerubbaal*] the
triple protasis in v.^{16} is separated from its apodosis (v.^{19b}) by a
parenthetic review of Jerubbaal's deserts and the sins of the
Shechemites (v.$^{17f.}$) ; v.^{19a} repeats the substance of v.^{16} to resume
the interrupted construction. In the nature of the case, v.$^{17f.}$ are
not organically related to the context, and could be omitted without leaving a gap. I see no sufficient reason, however, for regarding them as an interpolation ; they have a vigour and an individu-
ality of expression which are not usually found in glosses.* — *If
you have done to him as he deserved*] lit. *according to the desert
of his hands;* cf. Is. 3^{11}. — **17.** To give emphasis to the last
words, he reminds them of Jerubbaal's services, and of the way
in which they have been requited. — *In that my father fought for
you*] with deepening feeling, *my father*, instead of Jerubbaal as
before. — *And hazarded his life*] lit. *cast his life straight away*,
as a thing of which he recked not ; cf. 5^{18}.† — *And rescued you*]
it is to be noted that the writer thinks of the people of Shechem
as Israelites, at variance with v.$^{28f.}$. — **18.** *Whereas you have risen
against my father's house and have slain his sons*] this was their
return for the dangers he had incurred and the deliverance he had
wrought for them. The Shechemites had with full cognizance
furnished Abimelech the means to kill his brothers (v.^{24}), and
shared his guilt in the crime by which they jointly profited (cf. v^2).
— *Seventy men on one stone*] the words are here somewhat superfluous, and may be borrowed from v.^{5}. — *The son of his maidservant*] slave-concubine. In 8^{31} Abimelech's mother is Gideon's
concubine, apparently a free woman ; see comm. there. The
difference of representation probably existed in the sources. —
Because he is your brother] kinsman, fellow-countryman ; v.$^{2.3}$. —

---

* Doorn. thinks that v.$^{16b-19a}$ is all a gloss. Smend, who adopts this opinion,
recognizes that the verses are at least a correct exposition of the author's meaning
(*Alttest. Religionsgesch.*, p. 66 n.).

† The phrase, *cast behind one*, is commoner (1 K. 14^9 &c.). Cler. cites Lucan,
iv. 516: *Projeci vitam, comites,* &c.

19. *If, I say, you have acted in good faith*] resuming the protasis (v.[16]) after the digression, v.[17c]. — *Rejoice in Abimelech and may he rejoice in you*] I wish you all joy in one another in your new relation. The words have an ironical ring; much happiness may you have in this bramble-king of yours. — **20.** *But if not, fire shall go forth from Abimelech*] the figure of the fable, v.[15b]. — *And fire shall go forth from the freemen of Shechem, &c.*] here he goes beyond the fable; not only shall their unworthy king be fatal to them, but they to him. With this parting curse he left them; its fulfilment is declared in v.[56f], cf. v.[42-49. 50-54]. — **21.** Jotham made his escape to Beer, beyond the reach of Abimelech's vengeance. The site of *Beer* is unknown. S. Schmid and Studer are of the opinion that Beersheba, in the remote south, is meant. Others think that it is the same as Beeroth (Jos. 9[17] 2 S. 4[2]), now el-Bireh, three hours north of Jerusalem.* The name (Well) is too common to make this identification anything more than a possibility.

21. באר‎] Euseb. (*OS*[2]. 238₇₈) identifies Beer with a village of the name (Βηρα) 8 m. N. of Eleutheropolis; probably the modern Khirbet el-Bireh, W. of 'Ain Shems (Beth-shemesh); so Ke.† Maundrell (1697) and Reland (*Palaestina*, p. 617 f.) regarded el-Bireh north of Jerusalem as the Beer of our text. Eshtori Parchi (fol. 68[b]) identified this Bireh with Beeroth, and since Robinson (*BR*[2]. i. p. 452) this has been the prevailing opinion.‡ Many, as has been said above, believe Beer and Beeroth to be the same place, and put them both at el-Bireh. Beeroth belonged to the Gibeonite confederacy, and was doubtless at this time a Canaanite town (2 S. 21[1], cf. 4[2]).

22-25. The Shechemites and Abimelech fall out. — God sends a spirit of discord between Abimelech and the people of Shechem, in just retribution for their common crime. The Shechemites lie in wait in the mountains and rob passers by. — The verses form the introduction to one of the two accounts of Abimelech's attack on Shechem (v.[42-45]), and are parallel to v.[26-33]. This version may with considerable confidence be ascribed to E; observe *elohim*,

---

* On el-Bireh, see Rob., *BR*[2]. i. p. 451-454; Tobler, *Topographie von Jerusalem*, ii. p. 495-501; Guérin, *Judée*, iii. p. 7-13; *SWP. Memoirs*, iii. p. 8 f.; *DB*. s.v. "Beeroth."

† The distance is, however, considerably greater than Eusebius gives.

‡ Sandreczki and Ke. dissent, on the ground that el-Bireh is too remote from Gibeon.

v.^{23}, and compare the reflections of v.^{24} with Jotham's speech, v.$^{16-18}$, and v.^{57}. — **22.** *Abimelech ruled over Israel three years*] in the foregoing narrative we have heard only how Abimelech was made king of Shechem and Beth-millo (v.$^{6.18.20}$). In what follows it appears that he did not reside at Shechem, and he lost his life in trying to put down the revolt of Thebez. It is evident, therefore, that his power extended over other cities in Central Palestine ; that it included Israelites as well as Canaanites appears from v.^{55} ; but the statement that he ruled over Israel is not borne out by the rest of the chapter, and is strikingly at variance with v.$^{26-28}$, which speaks only of Shechem.* There is therefore good reason to suspect that this chronological note is not an original part of the story, but an editorial addition. — **23.** *God sent an evil spirit*] a mischief-making spirit ; compare the madness of Saul, 1 S. 16^{14} 18^{10} (the evil spirit of God) 19^{9}, and the delusion of Ahab's prophets, 1 K. 22$^{19-23}$. God is the author of the fatal mistakes and misdeeds of men, which they commit to their own undoing ; he sends a spirit of infatuation into them to impel them blindly to their ruin. This belief corresponds very closely to the Greek idea of ἄτη, even in the personification of this spirit (1 K. 22$^{21-23}$).† — *The men of Shechem were false to Abimelech*] cf. v.$^{15.16a}$. — **24.** God sent this spirit to foment mischief between them, in order that, in fitting retribution, these partners in crime might inflict upon each other the just punishment of their deed ; cf. v.^{57}, v.$^{4.18}$. Some disorder has been introduced into the text, apparently in the attempt to render it more explicit, or more emphatic ; see critical note. — **25.** *Put men in ambush on the hill tops to his damage, and robbed all who passed by them on the road*] the position of Shechem, on two of the main arteries of trade and travel through Mt. Ephraim, ‡ made this particularly serious ; cf. Hos. 6^9. In what way Abimelech was a sufferer by this above others, we are not told. He may himself have levied toll on those who passed through his district, in which case his revenues would fall off in the insecurity of the roads ; and doubtless those who were about his business, or who were bearing tribute to

---

* Cf. also v.^{22}.   † See Sta., *GVI.* i. p. 435 ; cf. above on 3^{10}, p. 87 f.
‡ See above, p. 240.

him (cf. 3[14]), would be especially welcome objects of plunder to the Shechemites. — *It was told to Abimelech*] the words have no connexion with the following story of Gaal's intrigue (v.[26-29]), but are parallel to v.[30-33], and would naturally be followed by the statement that Abimelech with his soldiers marched against Shechem. We probably have the continuation of this narrative in v.[42f.]; see there.

22. ויסר] pointed by ﬡﬡ as if derived from סור (like ויסר &c.), cf. הָסִירוּ Hos. 8[4]; in Is. 32[1] יָשֹׁרוּ as from שרר. The latter is preferable; see Kö., i. p. 328, 352; and note above on ויזר 6[38]. — 24. יבוא חמם . . . ורכם רמום על] אבימלך] the change of subject between the two inff. (*that the murder ... might come, and that he might put the guilt of their blood on Abimelech*) is intolerably harsh. ⑥ straightens out the construction by rendering τοῦ ἐπαγαγεῖν, but there is no reason to think that they read יהביא. Probably רשום was introduced by an ancient scribe who missed the government of רמם. The resulting awkwardness of structure reminds us of 3[2]. — חמם שבעים בני ירבעל] objective genitive, as usual with this noun; the crime committed against them, cf. Obad. 1[10] Hab. 2[8. 17] Gen. 16[5]. — 25. מארבים] ptcp. Pi., 2 Chr. 20[22f.]. — נזל] *rob*, c. acc. pers., cf. Dt. 28[29]; *carry off by force* (*rapere*) Jud. 21[23]. — עבר על] 1 K. 9[8] 2 K. 4[9].

26-41. Gaal incites the people of Shechem to revolt; they are defeated by Abimelech.

— Gaal, a new-comer in the place, persuades the Shechemites to throw off Abimelech's yoke, and puts himself at their head (v.[26-29]). He is disconcerted by Abimelech's sudden appearance before the town, but goes out to battle against him (v.[30-39]). The Shechemites are badly beaten, and driven within their walls; Gaal and his clansmen are thrust out (v.[40f.]). The narrative has the realism and the humour which belong to the best Hebrew folk-stories, and in many respects reminds us of the story of Samson. As the other strand in this chapter has in general the features of E, we may at least provisionally ascribe this part of the narrative to J.

26. *Gaal ben Ebed and his kinsmen*] *son of a slave* is evidently a perversion of the name, which was probably *Obed;* see crit. note. Whether these new-comers were Israelites or Canaanites is not clear; see on v.[28]. — *And moved into Shechem*] so the words should probably be translated. The expression is an unusual one, and hardly says what we should have expected in the context; but the Hebrew text is supported by all the versions. —

The citizens of Shechem put confidence in him] by what arts he insinuated himself into their confidence we may learn from the following verses, in which Gaal appears as a shrewd demagogue. —27. They celebrated the completion of the vintage, according to custom, by a feast at the temple of their god ; see note. Such an occasion could hardly fail to quicken local patriotism, and bring to the surface whatever latent dissatisfaction there was with the rule of their half-Israelite and evidently non-resident king.— *They ate and drank, and reviled Abimelech.* — 28. Gaal took advantage of this temper to instigate a revolt and offer himself as a leader. Unfortunately, v.²⁸ is obscure, and the text perhaps not intact. In the connexion the following points seem to be certain : 1. Gaal does not foment an insurrection of Israelite denizens against the rule of the Shechemite Abimelech, but of the native Shechemites against the half-Israelite Abimelech. 2. Of whatever race Gaal may have been, he identifies himself with the men of Shechem and speaks as one of them.* 3. He appeals to their national pride in *the people of Hamor father of Shechem*, the old blue blood of Canaan against this usurping half-breed. In this sense the verse is understood by Rashi, who gives, upon the whole, the most satisfactory interpretation of 𝕳 : "Who is Abimelech, that he should be ruler of Shechem, and who are the Shechemites, that they should be subject to Abimelech? Is not Abimelech the son of Jerubbaal, who was from the Abiezrite Ophrah ; † and is not Zebul merely his lieutenant? The master has no rightful authority in the city, and his lieutenant is of no account at all. If you are bent on getting yourselves masters, come and be subject to the men of Hamor, who was anciently the prince of the land ; why should we be subject to Abimelech?" The structure of the latter part of the verse is much simplified, however, if instead of the imperative, *Serve the men of Hamor*, we pronounce the verb as a perfect : *Were not the son of Jerubbaal and Zebul his lieutenant* (formerly) *subjects of the people of Hamor abi-Shechem ? Why, then, should we* (now) *be subject to him ?* In the first half of the verse the antithesis in the clauses,

---

* It is by no means clear that he was an Israelite, as We., Kue., al. think.

† *i.e.* an Israelitish stranger.

Who is Abimelech? and who is Shechem, that we should serve him? seems to many scholars to be unsatisfactory; they think that we should have a synonymous expression, as in 1 S. 25[10], "Who is David, and who the son of Jesse?" But in the light of the following, as I understand it, the antithesis is not only tolerable but effective. Is Abimelech king in his own right? Is Shechem naturally his empire, that we should·be subject to him? So far from it, he himself was formerly a subject of the old Hamorite nobility of Shechem. I see no necessity, therefore, for any radical change in the text; see critical note. — *Hamor abi-Shechem*] Gen. 33[19] 34; the old Canaanite aristocracy. — **29.** *Would that I had the direction of this people; I would get rid of Abimelech!*] like a consummate demagogue he first arouses the passions of his hearers, then adroitly puts himself forward as the man for the crisis. — *I would say to Abimelech, Enlarge your army and come out!*] I would defy him to maintain his authority over Shechem by arms. So ⦰: 𝔚 has, *he said to Abimelech.* In view of v.[30], the latter reading cannot be interpreted, he sent this challenge to Abimelech; we could only understand the words as a swaggering apostrophe in his speech to the Shechemites.*

26. נֶרֶד בֶּן עֶבֶד] ⦰[BN] * υἱὸς Ιωβηλ (ᴬⱽᴸᴹᴼ g ʇ Αβεδ). Ew., *GVI.* ii. p. 485, thought יבל (an old Canaanite name) the more probable reading; similarly Kue., Doorn., Sta., Kautzsch, Bu., Kitt.,† supposing that יבכר (Yahweh is Baal) was offensive to later scribes, and was intentionally altered to עבד. Ιωβηλ (for Ιωβηδ[68] by a common uncial error) is simply עובד; cf. 1 Chr. 11[47] (ᴮ) 1 Chr. 2[37] (ᴬ ᵃˡ·) 1 Chr. 26[7] (ᴬ ᵃˡ·) 2 Chr. 23[1] (ᴬ ᵃˡ·). So here codd. of ℵ (Ωβηδ[90] Ωβεδ[56] [Σ]ωβηδ[68] (dittogr.), and 𝕃 Obed. ‡ — The matter is of some importance, for if the name really were יבעל, we should be certain that Gaal was an Israelite, independently of the difficult v.[28]. — ויתברו בשכם] עבר כ׳, *pass through, traverse;* 1 S. 9[4] and very often. Dt. 29[11], which is cited by Be., al. in illustration of our verse, is not parallel; עבר בברית is probably to be explained from rites like those referred to in Jer. 34[18]. — **27.** הלולים] Lev. 19[24]; the fruit of trees in the fourth year of their bearing is קדש הלולים ליהוה.§ The word was evidently the name of a festive celebration, accompanied probably by noisy hilarity, and obligatory shouting in honour of the god. See Sprenger, *Leben Mohammad,* iii. p. 527; Lagarde, *Orientalia,* ii. p. 13-20;

* So Ki., Stud.; cf. Be.　　　　† Cf. also We., *TBS.* p. xii, f.
‡ So also Hollenberg, *TLZ.* 1891, col. 371.
§ On the reading הלולים and the rabbinical interpretation of this passage, see Geiger, *Urschrift,* p. 181 ff., Malbim on *Sifra* in loc. (הלולים § 67).

Mittheilungen, i. p. 227; We., *Prol³.* iii. p. 114, and esp. *Reste arab. Heidentumes,* p. 107-109. A similar feast at Shiloh, Jud. 21¹⁹ᵈᵗ. — **28**. On this verse see Oort, *Godgeleerde Bijdragen,* 1866, p. 991;⁰ Kuenen, *Th.T.* i. p. 703 f.; *GvI.* i. p. 299 f.; Wellhausen, *TBS.* p. xiii.; *Comp.,* Nachträge, p. 353 f. n.; Stade, *GVI.* i. p. 194 f.; W. R. Smith, *Th.T.* xx. 1886, p. 195-198; Kautzsch, *ZATW.* x. 1890, p. 299 f.; Kittel, *GdH.* i. 2. p. 77 f. — The versions agree substantially with 𝔐. 𝔊 has in the second clause καὶ τίς ἐστιν υἱὸς Συχεμ, which is adopted by Oort, Kue., Be., al.; also by We. (transposing *son of Jerubbaal* and *son of Shechem*).⁎ But, as W. R. Smith rightly urges, בן שכם does not mean *a Shechemite;* "the expression would not be idiomatic even if the Shechemites as a whole were called בני שכם instead of בעלי שכם." Sta. and Bu. therefore return in this particular to 𝔐. Farther עברו was read by 𝔊ᴸ עברו δοῦλοι αὐτοῦ,† beside which 𝔊ᴹ has the doublet κατεδουλώσατο τοὺς ἄνδρας Εμμωρ. The latter is adopted by We. (יעבידו), Oort,‡ W. R. Smith, Sta., Bu., al. We should then translate: Who is Abimelech and who Shechem, that we should be subject to him? By all means let the son of Jerubbaal and Zebul his lieutenant subject the people of Hamor father of Shechem. But why should we (Israelites) be subject to him? (WRS., Sta.). Kautzsch would emend יעבדו: Is he not the son of Jerubbaal, and Zebul his lieutenant? Well, let him (Zebul) serve him then, together with the Hamorites; § but why should we (Israelites) serve him? Attempts have also been made to relieve the difficulty by transposition: W. R. Smith thinks that v.²⁸ᵇ ought to follow immediately on v.²²; against which the objections of Sta. (*GVI.* i. p. 194 n.) seem conclusive. Bu. thinks that they should stand after v.²⁶. These critical operations seem to me all to start from false exegetical premises. It is assumed, originally on the ground of an erroneous explanation of 𝔊's Ιωβηλ = יעבל, that Gaal was an Israelite, and that he stirred up the Israelite part of the population to revolt against the rule of the Shechemite king, Abimelech. Thus W. R. Smith: "The whole verse is a Hebrew declaration of revolt against the king of Shechem (9⁶), who for three years has by the aid of his mercenaries tyrannized over Israel (v.²²). So too in v.²⁹ העם הזה is Israel, and Gaal closes with an open challenge to Abimelech to come forth (evidently from Shechem his capital) to meet the Israelites in the field." These assumptions conflict not only with the implications of the narrative, but with its plain words. Gaal gains the confidence of the בעלי שכם (v.²⁶), *i.e.* of the very people who made Abimelech king (v.⁶ ²⁰); it is at their vintage festival, at the temple of their god, that he makes his incendiary speech. W. R. Smith is constrained, therefore, to sever the verses from their context and remove them to a different place. If, however, we follow the guidance of the context, we shall see that Gaal instigates the native Shechemites, with

---

⁎ So also Oort, *Bible for Learners,* i. p. 395; Kitt.

† They are thereby constrained to take את as prep., σὺν τοῖς ἀνδράσιν Εμμωρ.

‡ Oort, Kue., al. formerly conjectured יעבדו, *Let the Hamorites serve them!*

§ אבי שכם is a gloss from Gen. 34⁶.

s

whose cause he identifies himself, to revolt against the half-Israelite Abimelech; * and shall have no occasion for a more radical change in the text than
to pronounce עָבְדוּ instead of עֲבָדָיו; cf. 1 S. 4⁹.† The antithesis in the last half-
verse is not between אנחנו and חמור אנשי; it is between אנחנו and בֶּן יְרֻבַּעַל וּ;
This son of Jerubbaal and his lieutenant Zebul were subjects of the Hamorites; why should we, freemen of Shechem, be subjects of his? — 29. מִי יִתֵּן]
Nu. 11²⁹ Jer. 8²³ Dt. 28⁶⁷ 2 S. 19¹ Is. 27⁴ Dt. 5²⁶ Job 23³ illustrate different
constructions of this phrase. See also SS. p. 449 f. — וְאָסִירָה] *that I might get
rid of Abimelech;* voluntative, Dr³. § 62. — וַיֹּאמֶר לַאֲבִימֶלֶךְ] 𝕲 καὶ ἐρῶ, וַיֹּאמֶר;
cf. 𝕾, whose ambiguous form is understood by 𝕲 as first person. Doorn.,
Reuss, Kitt., Kautzsch, emend accordingly. Cler. would give the vb. an
indefinite subject, *some one* told Abimelech; but in the context this is highly
improbable. — רַבֶּה] The origin of this anomalous ָ is not clear; Ol. § 247
suggests that it may be instead of the ֶ of the lengthened imv. (obs. the foll.
נָּא). This view is adopted by Kö. i. p. 534, but as there is no other instance
of this imv. in ל״ה, the explanation is doubtful. Some codd. and edd. have ֶ;
see HHMich.

30-34. Zebul warns Abimelech that treason is hatching. —

Zebul informs Abimelech of Gaal's intrigues, and suggests a plan
by which he and his followers may be drawn into an engagement
in the open field. — 30. *Zebul, the governor of the city*] an official
(*sar*) set over the place by Abimelech to represent him, not the
burgomaster of the town.‡ Wellhausen regards the words of
Gaal in v.²⁹, *Zebul, his lieutenant,* as mere abuse and insult;§
Zebul was not really an officer of Abimelech, but the head of the
Shechemites; he had so far sympathized with the movement
against Abimelech; Gaal, in order to supplant him, throws suspicion on his loyalty to the Shechemite cause; Zebul avenges himself by betraying Gaal to Abimelech.‖ This ingenious hypothesis

---

* See above, p. 255.

† Winckler conjectures עֲבָדוּ אוֹתוֹ, which he translates: If the Hamorites serve
him, &c.

‡ There were *sarim* at Succoth (8⁶), but we have no reason to believe that at the
head of the local government of Canaanite or Israelite cities there was a burgomaster or mayor.

§ *Comp.,* p. 353 f. n.; followed by Kautzsch, *Z.ATW.* x. p. 299.

‖ Only so, We. argues, can we comprehend Abimelech's course after Gaal had
been expelled (v.⁴¹). He did not allow himself to be deceived by Zebul's pretence
of loyalty; the latter was the real leader of the revolt, and perished in the fall of
the city. So also Kautzsch and Kitt. But if v.⁴²ᶠ is not the sequel of v.²⁶⁻⁴¹, but
another account of the fate of Shechem from a different source, this argument
ceases to have any cogency. See further, on v.⁴¹.

seems to me to conflict with the language of our verse, and with
the following narrative; see on v.[30ff. 41]. Zebul had no force at his
command in Shechem; it was not garrisoned like a conquered
city; it is difficult to see how a loyal official could have acted
differently in the circumstances, or what ground there is for imagining that he was implicated in the treason. Whether he was a
Canaanite or an Israelite does not appear. — **31**. *He sent messengers to Abimelech . . . saying*] the word omitted in translation
is anomalous and probably corrupt; the versions generally render,
secretly, or, *deceitfully, perfidiously*. It would be more to the purpose to have the name of the place where Abimelech made his
residence; cf. v.[41], *at Arumah;* see note. — *Gaal and his kinsmen are coming to Shechem, and are plotting to take the city from
thee*] the translation of the last words is based on the context;
they are rendered by the ancient versions, *invest, besiege the city
against thee,** which cannot be right. *Stir up the city to hostility†*
would suit the context, but is unsupported. — **32, 33**. Zebul
counsels Abimelech to come by night and conceal his forces in
the fields near the city. At sunrise he shall discover himself and
advance to the attack. Gaal and his followers will be drawn out
of the city to give battle in the open field, and Abimelech will
have them in his power. —*Thou shalt do to him as the occasion
serves*] 1 S. 10[7]. — **34**. Abimelech adopts Zebul's plan; and dis-
poses his men under cover in four divisions; cf. 7[16] and below, v.[43].

---

31. בְּתָרְמָה] 𝕲[APVLMO] s μετὰ δώρων (תרומה); 𝕭[N] ἐν κρυφῇ, 𝕷𝕿 *clam*,
𝕾 *per dolum;* all connecting it with תרמית, 'deceit, fraud,' חֶרְכָּה, *id.* So
Ra., Cler., Schm., Rosenm., Be., Cass., Kitt., Reuss. But, 1. הָרְכָּה is an
unexampled and really inconceivable type of noun (Jos. Kimchi). 2. If תרמה
were a synonym of מרמה, the text would not say that Zebul sent *secretly* to
Abimelech (בַחֵרי), but that he sent *deceitfully* or *fraudulently, i.e.* with intent
to deceive him (Stud.). Jos. Kimchi regarded it as the name of a place,
identical with ארומה v.[41] (see Ki., *comm. in loc.*); so RLbG., Abarb., Tremell.,
Piscator; cf. Reland, p. 585. Some modern scholars think that the same
name, probably Arumah, should be read in both places; so Stud., Doorn.
The construction with ב would then be explained, he sent messengers to A.,
who was at Arumah (Stud.). —[והנם צרים את העיר עליך] 𝕲[BN] περικάθηνται,
𝕬[PVLMO] πολιορκοῦσι, 𝕷 *oppugnat,* 𝕿 צירין, 𝕾 *obsident;* all taking 𝕸 correctly

---

* This is probably the intention of 𝕸.
† Lth., Cler., Schm., Stud., Ke., Kitt., al. mu.

as ptcp. of צור. The construction, however, is irregular; *besiege* is not צור
c. acc., but על צור. The forms of צור and צרר I. II. are much confused in the
punctuation (see SS. p. 621), but it is impossible to make צרים a *transitive*
derivative of צרר, nor, if we should emend צררים, would the only sense supported by usage, 'they treat the city in a hostile manner, attack it,' be satisfactory; 'make hostile, incite to hostility,' is wholly fictitious. Stade (SS.
p. 621ᵃ) conj. in this sense רִיָם כָּצָרִים (Hiph. of צרר II.), "falls nicht grössere
Verderbnis vorliegt." Possibly the author wrote צדים, 'lay snares for, plot to
take'; עָלֶיךָ would then be, to thy detriment. — 33. לָהֶם פשט] v.⁴⁴ 20³⁷ (אֵל)
Job 1¹⁷; of a body of men suddenly emerging from a covered position, and
rushing to storm a place or attack an enemy. — 34. ארבּעָה ראשׁים] see on 7¹⁶.

35-38. Abimelech's forces appear on all sides; Zebul taunts the braggart. — 35.

In the morning Gaal goes out to the gate of
the city.* As he stands there, Abimelech and his troops discover
themselves. — 36. Gaal descries them and exclaims to Zebul, *See,
there is a body of men coming down from the tops of the hills!*]
Zebul replies, *You see the shadow of the hills as men*] his fears
make him imagine enemies where there are none ; an insinuation
of cowardice which is succeeded by downright insult. — 37. The
enemy comes into clearer view; Gaal makes out the divisions
advancing from different directions. — *There is a body coming down
from near the Navel of the Land, and one division is advancing
from the way to the Diviner's Tree*] these localities are unknown :
the former would seem to be a sacred hill; the latter is a sacred
tree, whose name (*mě'ōněnîm*) indicates that it was, or had been,
the seat of a certain species of diviners; cf. the Moreh Tree,†
also in the vicinity of Shechem (Gen. 12⁶, cf. Jud. 7¹), and the
Maṣṣebah Tree, above v.⁶. The latter is not identical with the
Meonenim Tree of our verse ; apart from the difference of names,
the Maṣṣebah Tree was in all probability close to the town, which
the other, as our verse shows, was not. Whether the Meonenim
Tree here is the same as the Moreh Tree of Gen. 12⁶; is uncertain ;
the names are of somewhat similar, but not the same meaning,
and there is no reason why there may not have been three, or a
half dozen, well-known sacred trees in the vicinity of Shechem. —
38. Zebul's irony now turns to open taunt. — *What has become of*

---

* Not, *marched out* (Kitt.) ; he did not suspect the presence of the enemy.
† Perhaps an *oracle-tree*.

thy bragging] lit. *thy* (big) *mouth;* thy boastful words. — *When thou saidst, Who is Abimelech*] v.²⁸. — *Are not these the men for whom thou didst express such contempt? March out, now, and fight with them!*] Zebul, by reminding Gaal, doubtless in the presence of many bystanders in that public place, of his former boasts, goads him into fighting. He had indeed no choice ; if he declined the challenge, his prestige and influence in Shechem were gone.

39-41. The battle; defeat of the Shechemites. — **39.** Gaal put himself at the head of the citizens of Shechem and went forth to battle.* — **40.** The Shechemites seem to have made no stand against Abimelech, who chased them to the very gate of the city, with heavy losses. He did not, however, storm the place. — **41.** *Abimelech abode in Arumah*] if this name is to be restored in v.³¹ (see comm. there), he returned to his residence, satisfied with the chastisement he had inflicted upon the Shechemites for listening to the seductions of Gaal. *Arumah* is not otherwise known ; on the sole ground of the similarity of the names some scholars identify it with El-'Ormeh, two hours SE. of Shechem.† It has been conjectured that Arumah is the same as Rumah (2 K. 23³⁶), but this also is uncertain. ‡ — *And Zebul expelled Gaal and his kinsmen, so that they should not live in Shechem*] lit. *from living.* We can well imagine that in the smart of defeat the feelings of the Shechemites toward Gaal underwent a sudden revulsion, and that they were not unwilling to see him made a scapegoat ; perhaps also thinking that this would suffice to placate Abimelech. The verse manifestly brings the story to an end. Abimelech resides at Arumah ; Gaal and his clan are banished from Shechem. As the original close of the account of Gaal's insurrection (J) it is perfectly intelligible and appropriate. But it is just the opposite in its present position. After the withdrawal of Abimelech and the expulsion of Gaal, the fresh attack on Shechem, the discomfiture of its inhabitants by the same stratagem which had been

---

* Not, *spectante Sichimorum populo* **L**, Be.

† Van de Velde, *Narrative*, ii. p. 303, 307 ; Guérin, *Samarie*, ii. 2 f. ; *SWP. Memoirs*, ii. p. 387, 402. For the identification, Raumer, Mühlau, Tristram, al.

‡ The Ruma of Euseb. (*OS².* 288₁₀), in the vicinity of Diospolis, cannot be the place in our text. There was another Ruma in Galilee (Fl. Jos., *b.j.* iii. 7. 21 § 233). ⅋ has in our verse Ἀριμα.

employed the day before, and the destruction of the city, in which his authority had already been re-established, are inexplicable.

35. פתח שער העיר] v.⁴⁴ Jos. 8²⁹ 20⁴ and often; *the entrance of the gate.* The שער extends the whole depth of the wall, often many feet; פתח is the outer opening. — **36.** עם] *soldiery*, esp. foot soldiers; 4¹⁸. — **37.** טבור הארץ] 𝔊 ὀμφαλός, 𝕃 *umbilicus;* 𝕋𝕊 interpret *stronghold.* The meaning of the noun is hardly to be questioned (Mishna, Talm.); the sense in which it is applied here is uncertain. In Ez. 38¹², the only other place where it occurs in O.T., it is applied to Judaea as the centre of the earth. Comp. the ὀμφαλός at Delphi; *umbilicus Siciliae* (Cic. *contra Verr.* iv. 106, c. 48), *umbilicus Graeciae* (Liv., xxxv. 18; Stud.). So it is understood here by Ki., RJes.; an elevation in the middle of the district, at the intersection of several roads. We should have in any case to suppose that it had become a proper name;* but should hardly compare Mt. 'Αταβύριον in Rhodes (Stud.).† See above on 8¹⁸ (p. 228). — מעוננים אלון] Dt. 18¹⁰⁻¹⁴ Mi. 5¹¹; cf. מעונן, מעוננים, Is. 2⁶ Jer. 27⁹ 2 K. 21⁶; the verb, Lev. 19²⁶. See W. R. Smith, *Journal of Philology,* xiv. p. 118; We., *Reste arab. Heidentumes,* p. 148 n.; Sta., *GVI.* i. p. 505. What particular kind of divination these מעוננים practised is not clear. The root is probably עין (We., *l.c.*). — **38.** איה אפוא] *where, then,* Job 17¹⁵ Is. 19¹². On the enclitic אפוא, see BDB. *s.v.* — **40.** חללים] 16²⁴. — **41.** וישב] 𝔊ᴹᵐ καὶ ἐπέστρεψεν A. καὶ ἐκάθισεν ἐν Αρειμα = בארומה וישב. וישב אבימלך וישב. This is probably only a Greek doublet; but it suggests what may have been the original reading in 𝔐.

42–45. Capture and destruction of Shechem. — The next day, when the Shechemites came out of the city, Abimelech was in waiting for them. While two divisions attacked them in front, Abimelech himself, with the troops under his personal command, got between them and the city and cut off their retreat. After a day's fighting, Abimelech carried the place by assault, put the inhabitants to the sword, destroyed the city, and sowed the ruins with salt. This is not the continuation of the account in v.³⁴⁻⁴¹, which has its formal conclusion in v.⁴¹. We cannot imagine why, after their disastrous defeat of the day before (v.⁴⁰) and the expulsion of Gaal (v.⁴¹), the Shechemites took the field again (v.⁴²), especially as Abimelech had withdrawn, and there was no enemy

---

* *Navel of the land,* appellatively, for highest point (Ges.), is hardly possible in the plain prose of this story.

† The Greek name corresponds rather to Tabor.

in sight.[*] On the other hand, all becomes plain, if we see in v.[42] the original sequel of v.[29]: Abimelech learns that bands of Shechemites are infesting the neighbourhood, robbing and plundering on the highways, and takes measures to punish them. The next day, when they set out on such a predatory excursion, he is informed by his scouts, and lays an ambush for them. They, not suspecting the proximity of the enemy, fall into the snare and are cut to pieces. The city, weakened by the absence of a large part of its defenders, falls. Verses [42-45] are therefore to be ascribed to the same source with v.[29-25] (E). — **42.** *On the following day*] in the present connexion, the day after their defeat and the expulsion of Gaal ; in the original context (E), the day after Abimelech was apprised that they had begun their guerrilla warfare ; see above. — *The people went out into the country*] on an expedition like that described in v.[25]. — **43.** He concealed his forces in three divisions (7^{16} 9^{34}), in the neighbourhood of the city. When the Shechemites came out of the city, and had got to some distance from it, he rose from his ambush and attacked them. — **44.** More particular account of the execution of his stratagem. — *Abimelech and the body which was with him*] under his immediate command ; *cum cuneo suo* 𝔏. 𝔍, by mistake, *the bodies.* — *Made a dash and took their stand at the gate*] cutting off the retreat of those who had gone on the expedition, and preventing a sally from the town to relieve them. — *While the other two divisions rushed upon all who were in the fields and killed them*] the stratagem has some resemblance to that employed at the taking of Ai (Jos. 8).[†] — **45.** After a whole day's fighting, Abimelech took the city, put the inhabitants to the sword, pulled down the city, and sowed the site with salt. Sowing with salt seems to be a symbol of perpetual desolation ; nothing should henceforward thrive there ; cf. Dt. 29^{23} Jer. 17^6 Ps. 107^{34}. There is no other trace in the O.T. of such a custom.[‡] If Shechem was really destroyed at this time, it is not to be supposed that it long lay in ruins ; its position was too

---

[*] Fl. Jos. imagines that they went out to work in the vineyards (v.[27]) ; so Ra., Schm., Stud., Be., Ke., Reuss, al. mu. Of the older interpreters, Junius and Piscator controvert this opinion ; see Schm.   † In both accounts, J and E.

‡ See Thdt. *quaest.* 18 ; Bochart, *Hierozoicon,* ii. p. 223 f., ed. Rosenmüller. *Salt ground* is in Hebrew equivalent to desert.

advantageous, its vicinity too fertile for that. It was an important place in the early days of the kingdom (1 K. 12[1]), and was rebuilt and fortified by Jeroboam (1 K. 12[25]). A stratagem similar to that employed by Abimelech against Shechem is said to have been practised by Himilco against Agrigentum, and by Hannibal against Segesta.[*]

44. והראשים אשר זכו [] 𝕲[M] ἡ ἀρχὴ ἡ μετ' αὐτοῦ, 𝔏 *cum cuneo suo*, as the sense requires; † 𝕲[AVL] ἀρχαί. 𝔅𝔑 οἱ ἀρχηγοί, an attempt to get around the text which is repeated by Ki., RLbG. Other ingenious exegetical conjectures, the common feature of which is that the interpreter supplies what, if he were right, the writer must have said expressly, may be seen in Abarb., Schm., Cler., Be., al. Emend, הראש (JDMich., Reuss, Kautzsch, al.); האנשים (Stud.) would remove the difficulty, but is on critical grounds not so probable. — 45. ויזרעה מלח [פלח] cf. ארץ מלחה סלחה, Jer. 17[4] Job 39[6] Ps. 107[34].

46–49. Destruction of the Tower of Shechem.

— The people of the Tower of Shechem, hearing of the fate of the city, take refuge in the temple of El-berith. Abimelech burns their asylum over their heads, and they perish in the flames. — The verses are apparently a continuation of the preceding narrative of the destruction of Shechem.— **46.** *When the inhabitants of the Tower of Shechem heard it*] what Abimelech had done to the city. The Tower of Shechem (Migdal-Shechem) was not a citadel within the city, like that at Thebez (v.[51]), in which the people took refuge when the city was captured, but an unwalled town in the neighbourhood of Shechem, though not immediately adjacent to it. It owed its name to a tower which stood there, ‡ and was the site of the temple of El-berith. Its inhabitants were Shechemites, who had joined in the insurrection against Abimelech, and now, with good reason, feared his vengeance. As in v.[6.20] the people of Beth-millo join with those of Shechem in making Abimelech king, it has often been thought that the same place is meant here ; § but there is no obvious ground for this, while the difference of names is decidedly against it. The situation of the Tower of Shechem is not known ; from v.[49] it may perhaps be inferred that

---

[*] Frontinus, *Strategem.*, iii. 10, 4, 5 (Cass.); see also Polyaenus, v. 10, 4.

† So also Fl. Jos., *antt.* v. 7, 4 § 247.   ‡ Cf. the tower of Penuel, 8ª.[17].

§ So, after Serarius and other older scholars, Stud., Be., Ke., Reuss, al. *Millo* also is supposed to be the name of some kind of fortification; see on v.[6].

it was, like Shechem itself, in the valley, or on the lower slopes of one of its sides. — *They went into the . . . of the temple of El-berith*] the meaning of the word passed over in the translation is entirely unknown. Some of the ancient versions render, *stronghold*,* and many modern scholars think that they find etymological support for the interpretation, *tower, citadel*. In 1 S. 13⁶, however, the only other passage in which the word occurs, it clearly denotes a hiding-place, not a fort. Others think, therefore, of an artificial cave, or underground chamber; but this also is based on a somewhat remote etymology, and does not altogether suit the requirements of v.⁴⁹. — For *El-berith* some Greek texts have *Baal-berith*, as in v.⁴. It is not certain that the same temple is meant. The temple of El-berith at the Tower of Shechem was apparently not immediately adjacent to the city; on the other hand, it is not very probable that there were two temples in the same vicinity dedicated to the same divinity.† The difference of the names signifies little. In early times, they were substantially equivalent, the *el* (*numen*) which was worshipped at a place was naturally its *ba'al* (the divinity of the place). It is also possible that *El* is here a later substitution for *Baal*. ‡ — **47.** Abimelech learns that the people of the Tower of Shechem are all gathered in one place. — **48.** He leads his men to a hill hard by, to get wood to set their asylum on fire. — *Mt. Zalmon*] the situation of this hill is not known. § To identify it, on the strength of the name, with the southern peak of Gerizim, on which stands the tomb of a Moslem saint, Sheikh Selmān el-Farsi, is an absurdity. — With his axe, Abimelech cut branches of trees, put them upon his shoulder, and bade his men with all speed follow his example. — **49.** Every man with his load of brush on his shoulder, they return with Abimelech, pile the wood against the place in which the

---

* **θ, L** (v.⁴⁹); so Lth., EV., al. mu.

† Temples, that is, houses for the god, can hardly have been very numerous in those days. At most places of worship there was probably only an altar under the open sky, with its accessories, the sacred stones and posts, which required no housing. The temple, in Canaan as in Greece, originally existed only where there was an idol to keep in it. See E. Meyer, *Gesch. d. Alterthums*, ii. p. 429 f.

‡ Cf. Eljada, the son of David, for Baaljada; cf. above, p. 195.

§ Mt. Salmon, Ps. 68¹⁴, is more probably east of the Jordan; see Wetzstein, quoted by Guthe, *ZDPV.* xii. 1870, p. 230 f.

Shechemites had taken refuge, and set it on fire. About a thousand men and women perish in the flames.

46 צריח [אל צריח בית אל נריח v.⁴⁹ bis, plur. צרחיב ı S. 13⁶¹. The ancient versions apparently render from the context, *stronghold* (⑤ ὀχύρωμα * ℒ *praesidium*). Many modern lexx. and comm. interpret, *tower*, *citadel* (Ki., RLbG., Cler., Simon., Ges., MV., al.), following Abulwalid, who compares Arab. صرح,† a large, high building, standing apart (*TA.*). De Dieu referred to the Eth. in the sense of *upper story* or *room;* JDMich. in that of *temple*, thinking of an open court in the interior of the temple, while Stud. understands the *vabs* itself. Both these explanations are far-fetched; neither really gives us what is wanted here (cf. v.⁴⁹), and neither is conceivable in ı S. 13⁶, where the צרחים are places of concealment (named with caves, holes, cliffs, pits), as all the versions rightly understand. ‡ Ra. refers to older Jewish interpreters who take the word in the sense, *underground chambers* (*voûtes*); he himself explains it in both places as a *stockade* (*palissades*). Modern scholars have compared the Arab. ضريح 'grave, narrow excavation for the body at the bottom of the grave.' § The word occurs also in the Nabataean inscriptions from Teimā, צריחא, where it appears to be a grave or sepulchral chamber excavated in the rock (Doughty, *Documents épigraphiques*, 8₃, ₄ = Euting, *Nabatäische Inschriften*, 15₃,₄; cf. Nöldeke, *ib.* p. 55). ‖ From this it has been inferred that the Heb. צרח meant an excavation in the earth or rock, perhaps made as a place of refuge. But although this would suit the context in Samuel well enough, it is hardly possible in our passage (cf. v.⁴⁹), and the whole etymological construction is very dubious. — בית אל נרית [⑤ᴬᴹ Βααλ διαθήκης, ᴾ Βααλ Βεριθ, ᴸ Ηλ διαθήκης, ℒ *fanum dei sui Berith*. — **48.** הר

---

* Another, ἄκρα; Θ ⑤ᴮᴺ συνέλευσις.

† Synonym of قصم. Cf. *Qorān*, 28⁸⁸ 40⁸⁸ (tower reaching to heaven) 27⁴⁴. So in Sabaean, צרח, צרחת (*CIS.* Pt. iv. 1₄; Halévy 353₉, in Hommel, *Südarabische Chrestomathie*, p. 96), and Eth., in which the word means a conspicuous building (temple, palace), also the upper story or chamber of a house (like Heb. עריה, *e.g.* Jud. 3²⁰⁻²¹). In none of these languages does the signification 'citadel, tower for defence' seem to be demonstrable. (Of a watch-tower, in Arab. Polyglott, 2 K. 18⁸).

‡ ⑤ βόθροι ℒ *antra* ℭ *caverns in the rock* ⑤ *chasms*. In Jud. 9⁴⁶ also an anonymous translator renders ἄντρον.

§ In distinction from an excavation at the side (*laḥd*); see Ibn Hishām, p. 1019. Illustrations of these two modes of burial, from Cyprus, see Perrot et Chipiez, *La Grèce primitive*, p. 649.

‖ The צריחא is distinguished from the נוחא, *niches*. See also G. Hoffmann, *ZA.* 1894, p. 329 ff. S. Rau (*De aedibus Hebraeorum*, 1764, p. 4, c. JDMich., *Supplementa*, p. 2151) conjectured that for צויחה Ps. 68⁷, which OLS render *grave*, צריחה should be read; cf. also SS. p. 622.

חלֹצין] 𝕲ABLN Ερμων M Αερμων (Hermon); an old error; Euseb. *OS*[2]. 295₇₃ Σελμων. — הקרדמות] Jer. 46[22] Ps. 74[5]. The plur. is difficult. There is no evidence or probability that the plur. was used of a single axe (Be.; originally *bipennis*, Stud.), and the explanation of Schm., al., that Abimelech took a number of axes to distribute to his followers, is an ingenious but improbable exegetical makeshift. We expect קרדמו 1 S. 13[20]; cf. 𝕲APVLMO 𝕃. — שׂוכה סעיף] שׂכה v.[49], MH. סכה (Aram., Syr.). It is generally rendered *branch* (𝕲BN 𝕃), but in view of סעיף it should perhaps be taken as collective, *brush*; cf. 𝕲A al. φορτίον, Fl. Jos., φάκελλοι.* Probably עצים is not *trees*, but *fire-wood* (𝕲[96]). — מה ראיתם עשׂיתי] object clause without conjunction, Ges.[26] § 157 a; Roorda, § 523. In English also it is possible to say, What you saw I did, &c.; cf. the brachylogy, 7[17]. — מהרו עשׂו] *do quickly*. In this verbal apposition, the first verb is of secondary (adverbial) importance in the sentence. — **49**. שׂכה] 𝕸 pronounces שֹׂכֹה, *his branch*. Ki. explains this as contracted for שׂוכָהו, or as made from a corresponding masc. שׂוך.† If the suffix were indispensable in this distributive phrase, as Be. contends, it would be necessary either to accept the latter explanation, or to emend שׂוכתו; cf., however, Ex. 12[3] Job 42[11]. Doorn. pronounces שׂוכָה, *a branch*. — ויצית עליהם את הצריח באשׁ] הצית is construed, like its English equivalent, in two ways: set something on fire (באשׁ), or set fire to (ב, rarely עַל) something. The suff. in עליהם cannot refer to שׂוכה, but to the people.

50-55. Abimelech attacks Thebez. — While assaulting its citadel he is mortally hurt, and dies by the hand of his armour-bearer. His followers disperse. — **50**. *Abimelech went to Thebez*] from the connexion we should infer that the attack upon Thebez followed immediately the destruction of the Tower of Shechem; and probably, further, that Thebez had previously been subject to him, and had joined in the revolt set on foot by Shechem. Thebez, which is mentioned only here and in the reference to this story 2 S. 11[21], is put by Eusebius thirteen miles from Neapolis on the road to Scythopolis.‡ Robinson identified it with the modern Ṭūbās, a large village in a very beautiful situation. § — **51**. *There was a castle within the city*] lit. *a tower of stronghold;* cf. the figurative use of the phrase, Ps. 61[3] Prov. 18[10]. — *All the men and women, all the inhabitants of the town*] Heb. *and all the inhabitants* (freemen); ‖ commonly explained as an explicative use of

---

* Cf. Cler., Stud.　　　† A masc. is found in MH.　　　‡ *OS*[2]. 262₄₄.

§ *BR*[2]. ii. p. 317, iii. p. 305. On the place see also Guérin, *Samarie*, i. 357-359; *SWP. Memoirs*, ii. p. 229. The place had been identified long before Robinson, by Eshtori Parchi (fol. 66ᵇ end).　　　‖ See above, on 9[2].

the particle (*even*) ; see note. — *And went up on the roof of the tower*] no doubt it had a flat earthen roof, with a parapet, from which they could defend it. — **52.** Abimelech led the attack on the tower. — *He came close up to the door to burn it*] it was too strong to be forced. Cf. v.⁴⁹. — **53.** *A certain woman threw an upper millstone*] the upper, movable stone of a hand mill, a foot or upwards in diameter and perhaps two inches thick, made of the hardest kind of stone.* It was a woman's implement and a woman's weapon, but its weight made it a formidable missile when hurled from the height of the tower. — *Smashed his skull*] so Pyrrhus of Epirus is said to have been killed at Argos. He had forced his way into the city, and, in the street fighting which followed, his head was broken by a tile thrown by a woman from the roof of a house.† — **54.** To perish by the hand of a woman was an ignominy worse than death ; in all haste he calls on a man to despatch him. — *His attendant armour-bearer*] all warriors of distinction had such a squire ; cf. 7¹¹ 1 S. 14⁶ᶠ· 16²¹ 31⁴⁻⁶. — *Lest men say of me, A woman killed him*] the older commentators compare the words of the tortured Hercules in the *Trachiniae* of Sophocles, l. 1062 f. :

γυνὴ δέ, θῆλυς φῦσα κοὐκ ἀνδρὸς φύσιν,
μόνη με δὴ καθεῖλε φασγάνου δίχα,

and the imitation of the passage in Seneca's *Hercules Oetaeus* (l. 1180 ff.), in which the resemblance to our verse is closer : dirus o nobis pudor | o turpe fatum. femina herculeae necis | auctor feretur, morior Alcides quibus. ‡ — *His squire ran him through*] compare the death of Saul, 1 S. 31⁴. — **55.** *The men of Israel saw that Abimelech was dead*] the soldiers who fought under Abimelech against Thebez, and therefore presumably against Shechem, were Israelites. The point, as Wellhausen has noted, § is of prime importance for the understanding of the story. It confirms the interpretation we have adopted above, that the revolt of Shechem was a Canaanite movement. They had raised

---

* Descriptions of these mills, Thomson, *Land and Book*², I. p. 107 f.; Wilkinson, *Ancient Egypt*, i. p. 358 f. (ed. Birch); cf. Hoheisel and Goetz in Ugolini, *Thesaurus*, xxix. The upper stone of such a mill in the Museum of Andover Seminary weighs about 27 pounds.   † Paus., i. 13. 7; Plut, *Pyrrhus*, 34.

‡ Cf. also Judith, 16⁸⁻⁹ (8-11).   § *Comp.*, p. 353.

Abimelech to power because he was one of themselves; they tried to throw off his yoke when they found that he was, after all, his father's son. Whether the Israelites who formed Abimelech's army were his subjects (v.²²), or whether they took his side in the conflict against the Shechemites, because he was an Israelite, and Jerubbaal's son, the too brief story does not tell us.

51. נגדל עז] עז in this sense is prob. originally derived from عَان = עו (*med. ū*), 'take refuge' (cf. בעזו 6²⁸ مَعَان); but it has become confused with עז from עזז, عزّ; see SS. p. 497 *a*; JDMich., *Supplementa*, p. 53 ff. — וכל בעלי העיר] cf. 10¹⁰ 20³⁶. The examples of this *waw explicativum* (Ew. § 340 *b*; Ges.²⁶ § 154 n. *b*), at least in the older writers in the O.T., are most of them, for one reason or another, dubious. In the present instance it is possible that the conjunction was inserted by a scribe who understood בעלי העיר as 𝔊^{A al.} 𝔏 did, οἱ ἡγούμενοι τῆς πόλεως, instead of *citizens*. The author may have written, "All the men and women, — all the citizens of the town" (comprehensive apposition). A more radical conjecture would be that the last words, which are lacking in 𝔊ᴰ, are an addition by a later hand; it is likely, however, that the omission in 𝔊ᴮ is accidental; cf. ᴺ. — **53.** אשה אחת] see note on 13². — פלח רכב] 2 S. 11²¹, the upper stone, also called simply רכב, 'the rider,' Dt. 24⁶; opp. פלח תחתית Job 41¹⁶. The mill is רחים; the two stones are perh. called פרים because the mill is *cleft* between them. — ותרץ] a wholly anomalous form; Ew., Bö., Kö., regard the punctuation as an attempt to discriminate from ירץ (from רוץ), comparing וירק Ex. 16²) (רבם); but, if this were really the motive, we should expect more frequent instances of such discrimination. Moreover, the device in this case would be peculiarly ill-chosen, since *i* is properly the vowel of Hiph. רץ; it has in fact misled Ki., who derives the form from רוץ. — גלגלת] *skull*, 2 K. 9³⁵ 1 Chr. 10¹⁰ (prob. textual error); elsewhere only in reckoning *per capita* (P and Chr.). — **54.** מהרה] adverbial accus.; on the position of the word see SS. s.v. — ודקר] 1 S. 31⁴ = 1 Chr. 10⁴ Nu. 25⁸ &c. (MII.); the specific word for 'run through, transfix.'

56, 57. The moral of the history. — The destruction of Shechem and the death of Abimelech was a divine retribution for their crime against Jerubbaal's house, the fulfilment of Jotham's curse (v.²⁰). There is no trace of the characteristic pragmatism of D; the verses may with probability be ascribed to E.[*]

56. *God requited the crime of Abimelech, which he committed against his father in killing his seventy brothers*] lit. *made it come*

---

[*] Budde.

back on Abimelech, the complement, *upon his head* (1 S. 25⁵⁷), is expressed only in the following sentence, but psychologically belongs to both. —**57**. *And all the wickedness of the Shechemites God requited upon their heads, and the curse of Jotham the son of Jerubbaal came true to them*] was fulfilled; with the verb cf. 1 S. 9⁶ Dt. 13² Is. 5¹⁹ &c.

X. 1-5. The Minor Judges: Tola and Jair.*—Tola (v.¹ᶠ·) and

Jair (v.³⁻⁵), with Ibzan, Elon, and Abdon (12⁸⁻¹⁵), form a group of five judges (with whom Shamgar, 3³¹, is often reckoned as the sixth), of whose exploits nothing is related. These judges are introduced in standing formulas entirely different from those which form the setting of the stories of [Othniel], Ehud, Deborah and Barak, Gideon, Jephthah, and Samson, and exhibit no trace of D's distinctive pragmatism. The character of the scheme of the Minor Judges is best exemplified by the notice of Elon (12¹¹⁻¹²),† which contains absolutely nothing else: "And there judged Israel after him, Elon the Zebulonite; and he judged Israel ten years. And Elon the Zebulonite died, and was buried in Aijalon in the land of Zebulun." The notices of Tola and Jair differ from this pattern only in the opening words, "There arose after him." Besides the name and origin of the judge, the years of his rule, and the place of his burial, we have in the case of three of them (Jair, Ibzan, and Abdon) the number of their sons, sons and daughters, sons and grandsons; evidence that they were persons of rank and consequence. The names of Tola, Jair, and Elon occur elsewhere in the genealogical systems. Tola is a son of Issachar (Gen. 46¹³ Nu. 26²³), that is, a clan (Nu. *l.c.*), and, as may be inferred from 1 Chr. 7¹ᶠ, the leading clan, of that tribe; Puah, here his father, appears in the lists as his brother, that is, another clan of Issachar. Elon is a son (clan) of Zebulun (Gen. 46¹⁴ Nu. 26²⁶); and the name of his burial place, though differently pronounced by 𝕳, is doubtless the same, the chief seat of

* On the so-called "Minor Judges" see Nöldeke, *Untersuchungen zur Kritik des A. T.*, 1869, p. 181-184; Wellhausen, *Prolegomena*³, p. 238, *Comp.*, p. 217 l. 356; Stade, *GVI.* i. p. 69; Budde, *Richt. u. Sam.*, p. 96-98; Cornill, *Einl.*², p. 99 l.; Kittel, *GdH.* i. 2. p. 9-14. See also Introduction, §7.

† As that of the other judges by Othniel; above, p. 84, and Introduction, §4.

the clan. Jair is a son of Manasseh (Nu. 32^{41} Dt. 3^{14} 1 K. 4^{13}) ;
in another place (1 Chr. 2^{21-23}), a great grandson of Judah on his
father's side, and of Machir ben Manasseh on his mother's. The
identity of the Jair named in all these places with the judge in
our text is proved by the constant association with the Havoth-
jair (villages of Jair) in Gilead ; see on v.⁴. The names of Ibzan
and Abdon do not occur elsewhere, but the mention of their
numerous posterity has naturally the same significance as in the
case of Jair ; they are extensive clans with numerous branches and
alliances. Their prosperity and dignity are symbolized by the
fact that their sons and grandsons rode upon asses. In the case
of all five of these Minor Judges, therefore, we probably have, not
the names of individuals, but of clans.* The chronological
scheme of the Minor Judges also differs from that of the others.
Elsewhere we find uniformly, first, the duration of the oppression ;
second, the duration of the period of security under the judge ;
there is an interregnum between each judge and the next. In
the case of the Minor Judges, on the contrary, we have only the
number of years each judged Israel, and there is no intimation of
an interval between them ; the formula, *And after him*, implies,
rather, that the writer meant to represent their rule as consecutive.
The first of these ways of reckoning corresponds to D's whole
construction of the history as a rhythmical succession of apostasy,
with consequent oppression and deliverance, and the chronological data appear imbedded in his formulas; the second does not
accord with this theory. Moreover, the seventy years assigned to
the Minor Judges appear to be independent of the systematic chronology of the book, and to disturb its symmetry. It has been
inferred from this that the Minor Judges were introduced into the
book by a hand later than the Deuteronomic author (D).† The
question is one of considerable difficulty ; it can be advan-
tageously discussed only in connexion with the problems of the
chronology and composition of the book in general ; see Introduction, §§ 4, 6, 7.

---

* This does not exclude the possibility that individuals may have borne these
names (cf. above on $3^{l.m.}$, p. 91) ; but for the author of the notices in the Book of
Judges the individual is clearly lost in the clan.

† So We., Sta., Bu., Co. Against this inference see Kue., *HCO²*. p. 342; Kitt.

Of the source from which these notices are derived we can affirm nothing.

1. Tola. — *There arose after Abimelech to deliver Israel*] according to Budde's not improbable hypothesis, the same hand (the last editor) restored ch. 9, which D had omitted,[*] and introduced the Minor Judges. — *To deliver Israel* was the mission of the judge ; see on 2^{16} 3^{10}. From what foes, or by what deeds, he delivered Israel, is not narrated. — *Tola the son of Puah*] both are names of clans of Issachar ; see above, p. 270. — *Son of Dodo*] the name Dodo (var., Dodai) occurs twice in the list of David's heroes, 2 S. 23^9 1 Chr. 11^{12} 27^4 and 2 S. 23^{24}. It has lately been found in the form Dudu on the Amarna tablets.[†] The versions, with the exception of 𝔗, take the word as appellative, *son of his* (Abimelech's) *uncle* (father's brother). — *A man of Issachar*] on the text see note. — *He resided at Shamir in Mt. Ephraim*] there was also a Shamir in the Highlands of Judah (Jos. 15^{48}). The Shamir of our text, the seat of a clan of Issachar, probably lay in the north-eastern part of the Highlands of Ephraim, not far from the plain of Jezreel. See on 5^{15} (p. 151). The branches of Issachar which established themselves south of that valley, had their settlements among those of the great tribe of Joseph, and, like Benjamin on the south, seem frequently to be included when it is spoken of.[‡] Shamir has not been identified. Schwarz suggested Sānūr, a ruined stronghold on a detached rocky hill about midway between Nābulus and Genīn ;[§] but this seems to be too far south and west for a settlement of Issachar, and there is no other argument for the identification than the very dubious one of similarity of sound. — **2.** *He judged Israel twenty-three years*]

---

[*] See above, p. 235.

[†] In the inscription of Mesha king of Moab (l. 12), הודה seems to be the name of a divinity. The Dūdu of the Amarna letters (Winckler, *Thontafelfund von El Amarna*, No. 38, l. 1, &c.) is apparently a Canaanite official at the Egyptian court. See also Sayce, *Higher Criticism*, p. 215.

[‡] This may account, on the other hand, for the fact that Issachar is not named in places where we should expect it, as in ch. 4 and 6–8.

[§] *Das heilige Land*, 1852, p. 119. On Sānūr see Rob., *BR²*. ii. p. 312 f. ; Guérin, *Samarie*, i. p. 344-350 ; *SWP. Memoirs*, ii. p. 157 f. ; Bäd⁶., p. 228. Raumer, Van de Velde, Guérin, al., would identify Sānūr with the Bethulia of Judith ; see *DB²*. i. p. 420 f.

the same formula is used of each of the Minor Judges, also of Jephthah (12⁷) and Samson (15²⁰), but not of any of the other heroes of the book. On the chronology, see Introduction, § 7.— *He died and was buried in Shamir*] from this notice, which, *mutatis mutandis*, is repeated in the case of the other Minor Judges, we are probably to infer that the tomb of the eponymous ancestor of the clan was in later times shown at Shamir.* Cf. 2⁹.

1. תולע בן פואה] the latter name is written in the same way 1 Chr. 7¹; in Gen. 46¹³ Nu. 26²³, פֻּוָה. See *Ochla we-Ochla*, No. 201, and Norzi on Gen. *l.c.* As appellative, תולע is the 'crimson worm, cochineal' (*Coccus ilicis*); פואה, a plant from which a red dye was obtained (*Rubia tinctorum*, Linn.; Löw, *Pflanzennamen*, p. 251); † the coincidence is noteworthy. On animal names see on 7²ᵇ.— בן דודו] 𝕲 υἱὸς πατραδέλφου αὐτοῦ (πατρὸς ἀδελφοῦ ᴾⱽᴺ ᴵ⁵); similarly 𝔖. 𝔏, *patrui Abimelech*. Ki. notes that some codd. of 𝔗 had בר דוד (*n. pr.*; so Ra.); others, בר אח אבוהי, *i.e.* Abimelech's uncle. 𝕲ᴹ has καὶ ἀνέστησεν ὁ θεὸς (cf. 2¹⁶·¹⁸) . . . τὸν θωλα υἱὸν φουα υἱὸν καριε [καρηε] πατραδέλφου αὐτοῦ, καὶ αὐτὸς κατῴκει κ.τ.λ. Hollenberg (*ZATW.* i. p. 104 f.) infers that in 𝔐 and the versions a name, קָרֵחַ (2 K. 25²³ Jer. 40⁸), has fallen out, and that the original text read: 'Tola the son of Puah, the son of *Ḳareaḥ*, his (Abimelech's) uncle, a man of Issachar.' The conjecture is attractive, but hardly sound: the suff. in דודו naturally refers to Puah, not to Abimelech; and to explain how a brother of the Manassite Jerubbaal could be of Issachar, we should have to travel quite outside the text.‡ The recension of 𝕲 which furnishes this name omits the words, *a man of Issachar*, which the scheme requires. Perhaps καριε is only a corruption and displacement of Issachar.§ —איש ישׂשכר] the definite, *the* man of Issachar, is out of place; I should emend, איש מישׂשכר (cf. 𝔏𝕮𝔖); cf. 1 S. 9¹ and see note on 7¹⁴.

3. **Jair.**—*Jair the Gileadite*] see on Havoth-jair, v.⁴ᵇ.— *He judged Israel, &c.*] see on v.².— 4. *He had thirty sons*] cf. Ibzan's thirty sons and thirty daughters (12⁹); Abdon's forty sons and thirty grandsons (12¹⁴). More explicitly than in the latter cases, Jair's sons are connected with as many branches or settlements of the clan. — *Riding on thirty saddle asses*] as Abdon's descendants rode on seventy saddle asses (12¹⁴); cf. also 5¹⁰. The

---

* See Sta., *GVI.* i. p. 449 ff.
† Ἐρυθρά, *Onom. vaticana, OS².* 199₂₆; *rubrum*, Jerome, *ib.* 6₇₁.
‡ Cler. Half-brother; wife's brother; sister's husband (Hollenb.). See against Hollenberg, Be². *ad loc.*
§ This explanation is, however, by no means free from difficulty.

T

ass was highly esteemed as a riding beast, and was used by men and women of rank (Jud. 1[14] 1 S. 25[20] 2 S. 17[23] 19[33] Zech. 9[9] &c.), as it has always been in the East.[*] It may be suspected that in the verse before us the words have been interpolated from 12[14] (Abdon's sons and grandsons); the conflation being facilitated, if not occasioned, by the similarity between the Hebrew word *asses* and *towns*. See critical note. — *And they had thirty towns; these are still called Havoth-jair, and are in the land of Gilead*] *havvoth* may have originally denoted, like the Arabic *hiwā'*, with which it is commonly connected,[†] a group of Bedawin tents; but with the transition to pastoral life it would naturally be applied to more permanent settlements. In the O.T. it is used only of these Havoth-jair. It has been thought that the name Hivvite is of the same origin.[‡] The conflicting statements about the number and situation of the Havoth-jair have been a source of considerable perplexity to commentators; see a full discussion of the difficulties in Studer. The original account of the conquest of this district is in Nu. 32[39.41f.], a passage which belongs to the oldest stratum of Hebrew historiography and is akin to Jud. 1.[§] In connexion with the conquest of Gilead by Machir, Jair took the *havvoth* of the Amorites in Gilead (cf. v.[39]), whence they are called Havoth-jair; while Nobah took Kenath with its dependencies and gave it his own name, Nobah.[∥] These fragmentary old notices are now incorporated in the younger history of the Mosaic conquest of the lands east of the Jordan : the conquest of this region by Machir (Manasseh), however, falls apparently in the period of the Judges, *i.e.* after the main body of Israel had established themselves west of the Jordan.[¶] In entire accord with Nu. 32[41] is Jud. 10[4], according to which the Havoth-jair, thirty in number, were in the land of Gilead (cf. also 1 Chr. 2[22]). Other passages, which put them in Bashan, are the result of later misunderstanding; so Dt. 3[14] cf. v.[4] (sixty fortified cities), and

---

[*] See Bochart, *Hierozoicon*, l. p. 151 ff., ed. Rosenm. In the modern East, see *DB*[2]. i. p. 267 f.　　† It is not a Hebrew word.　　‡ See note on 3[5], p. 83 f.

§ See Bu., *Richt. u. Sam.*, p. 60, 87, who makes these verses a sequel to Jos. 17[14-18], and ascribes them to J in the original context of Jud. 1.

∥ See above on 8[11].

¶ Originally only Gad and Reuben stopped east of the Jordan.

Jos. 13³⁰, both of which belong to the latest redaction of the history.* In 1 K. 4¹³ the mention of the Havoth-jair is interpolated from Nu. 32⁴¹.† The account in 1 Chr. 2²³, finally, which makes Jair, who had twenty-three cities in the land of Gilead which were subsequently lost to Geshur and Aram, of mixed Judaean (Hezron) and Manassite (Machir) descent, must reflect post-exilic relations. — *The land of Gilead*] see on 11¹. — 5. *Jair died, and was buried at Camon*] cf. v.². Camon was doubtless east of the Jordan; ‡ not improbably Kamūn, which is named by Polybius in connexion with Pella.§ The site has not been recovered. Eusebius erroneously identified it with Kammōna, in the Great Plain six miles northwest of Legio, now Tell Qaimūn. ||

4. עירים] עִיר is generally a riding ass, Gen. 49¹¹ Jud. 10⁴ 12¹⁴ Zech. 9⁹; a beast of burden, Is. 30⁶·²⁴. In Arabic, specifically the *wild* ass; see Hommel, *Namen der Säugethiere*, p. 121–123. — עירים²] the substitution of this form for the regular plur. of עִיר, עֲיָרִים, is generally explained as an intentional play on the word, to connect it more closely with עֲיָרִים 'asses' (Ki., Schm., Stud., al. mu.).¶ Perhaps it originated in an accidental repetition of the preceding. — חַוֹּת] 𝔊ᴮ ἐπαύλεις. The word is connected by Abulw. with Arab. *ḥayy*, 'tents of a clan, clan, kindred' (see above, p. 83 f.); similarly Cler. (on Nu. 32⁴¹), comparing Arab. *ḥiwā'*, 'group of tents, camp.' This is better than Ges. (*Thes.* p. 451), direct derivation from חַוָה = חָיָה, 'place where men live, habitation,' comparing German names like Aschersleben, &c.

X. 6–16. The moral of the history repeated and enforced. Preface to a new period of oppression.

— The religious pragmatism of the history, with its recurring cycle of apostasy, subjugation, and deliverance, is set forth with all explicitness in the Introduction, 2¹¹–3⁶. In the framework of the book, in which the stories of the judges are set, the leading motives of this ouverture are generally repeated in a sentence or two of set phrases, but in one or two cases they are more fully developed (3⁷⁻¹⁰ 6¹⁻¹⁰), while in the passage before us they are expanded to almost as great

* Di., *NDJ.* p. 201; Kue., *Th. T.* xi. p. 479 ff.   † Klosterm. It is lacking in 𝔊.
‡ Fl. Jos.   § Polyb., v. 70, 12; Reland, *Palaestina*, p. 679.
|| *OS²*. 272₆₅. On Tell Qaimūn see Rob., *BR²*. iii. p. 114 f.; Guérin, *Samarie*, ii. p. 241 ff.; *SWP. Memoirs*, ii. p. 48, 69 f. Eli Smith (1844) and Robinson suggested that Tell Qaimūn — Kammōna — Kuamōn (Judith 7⁴) is the Jokneam of the O.T. (Jos. 12²² &c.), and this identification is in all probability right.
¶ Cf. 𝔊 πώλους, πόλεις.

length as in $2^{11\text{f.}}$. We have learned that $2^{11\text{f.}}$ is not entirely the work of the author of our Book of Judges (D), but contains the substance of an older introduction, conceived in a similar spirit, which we saw reason to attribute to an elohistic source (E).[*] The same phenomena meet us again in 10^{6-16}: with the characteristic phrases of D is intermingled another strain, which toward the end predominates; and the affinity of this element with E is here even more evident than in the former case. Why this extended introduction should stand thus in the middle of the book is not apparent. It may have its explanation in a different order of the pre-Deuteronomic Book of Judges. Stade surmises that in E it immediately followed the story of Ehud (3^{15-30}), and that its sequel has not been preserved.[†] Budde conjectures that it was E's introduction to the account of the Philistine oppression.[‡] As it does not appear that E contained a story of Samson, it would then be supposed, further, that in its original connexion it was followed by the history of the Philistine aggressions in the time of Samuel and Saul.

On 10^{6-16} see Stade, *ZATW*. I. p. 341–343, *GVI*. i. p. 70; Budde, *Richt. u. Sam.*, p. 128 f.; Kuenen, *HCO²*. i. p. 340 f.; Kittel, *GdH*. i. 2. p. 8. — Stade urges the resemblance of the non-Deuteronomic elements in the passage to Jos. 24 (E₂). To that source he ascribes v.$^{6b. 8}$ (except *the Israelites* 1⁰ and the 18 years) 10^{9}. $^{13f. 0\,14f.}$; even v.$^{11f.}$ appears to have an elohistic basis.[§] Budde's analysis is very similar. Kue. and Kitt., on the contrary, discover no traces of E. The former ascribes the passage as a whole to D: the latter attributes v.$^{6f.\,8b.\,10a\,(?)}$ ‖ to Ri. (redactor of the older Book of Stories of the Judges), the rest to R^d (redactor of the present Book of Judges); the suggestions of E in the latter are due to a peculiar predilection of the last redactor for the style of E.

6. The verse begins with the standing formulas of D; cf. 2^{11-13} 3^7 &c., 1 S. 7^4 12^{10}. The catalogue of foreign religions, which includes those of all the neighbouring nations (cf. 2^{13} Dt. 6^{14} $13^{7f.}$), Syria, Phoenicia, Moabites, Ammonites, Philistines, is not improb-

---

[*] See above, p. 63 f., 68 ff.

[†] *ZATW*. i. p. 342. That it was not originally the introduction to the story of Jephthah, he infers from 11^4, and from the fact that the theological pragmatism of 10^{6-16} is entirely foreign to that story.

[‡] *Richt. u. Sam.*, p. 128. Cf. v.^{7}, and observe Judah and Benjamin in v.^{9}.

[§] Cf. altogether Jos. 24^{19-23}.   ‖ V.^{16a} belongs to Ri.'s source.

ably a secondary amplification. — *Forsook Yahweh*] v.[10. 13] 2[12. 13] Jos. 24[20] (E). — **7.** Cf. 2[14. 20] 3[8] 4[2] 1 S. 12[9]. — *The Philistines and the Ammonites*] the author of these words intended 10[6ff.] to stand as an introduction not only to the Ammonite oppression (10[17]–12[7]), but to the Philistine supremacy. Of the latter, however, there is no further mention in the following context; it is the Ammonites who, after crushing Israel east of the Jordan, invade Judah, Benjamin, and Ephraim. The Philistine domination begins with 13[1] (Samson), and continues to the time of Samuel (1 S. 7, E). In their present connexion, the words, *into the power of the Philistines*, are manifestly out of place. They may have been inserted by the latest editor for the purpose of extending the scope of the introduction to include ch. 13-16. The alternative is to suppose, with Budde, that in E 10[6-16] originally prefaced the account of the Philistine oppression.[*] This is perhaps the more probable hypothesis. — On the Ammonites cf. 3[13], and see on 11[4]. — **8.** *And they broke and crushed the Israelites in that year eighteen years*] from what follows the subject appears to be the Ammonites only. The impossible collocation, *in that year eighteen years*, must be attributed to editorial interpolation or composition. The eighteen years probably belong to D's chronology (cf. 6[1] 13[1]) ; *in that year* is more suitable to the verbs at the beginning of the verse, which suggest a signal catastrophe rather than long-continued subjugation and oppression, and may, as Kittel thinks, be from the source from which ch. 11[4ff.] is derived.[†] D's text may then have run : And he sold them into the power of the Ammonites eighteen years. — The rest of the verse, with v.[9a] appears to be an expansion of *the Israelites*, v.[8a] ; the oppression was universal, both east and west of the Jordan. — *The land of the Amorites, which is in Gilead*] cf. 11[19ff.] ; the relation to the latter passage is additional evidence of the late date of v.[8b]. — **9.** The Ammonites even crossed the Jordan and invaded Judah, Benjamin, and Ephraim ; see on v.[8b]. Judah is mentioned only in 15[9-11] 18[12]. — *Israel was in great straits*] 2[15] 1 S. 30[6]. — **10.** Cf. 3[9. 15] 4[3] 6[6.7]. — *We have sinned against thee*] v.[15] 1 S. 12[10] 7[6] Nu. 14[40] 21[7] Dt. 1[41]. The formula of confession is peculiarly frequent in E (E[2]). — *Forsaken Yahweh*] v.[6. 13] 2[12ff.].

---

[*] See above, p. 276.   [†] Cf. *that year*, with. *after a year* (מימים) 11[4].

8. כשנה ההיא] naturally, the year in which Yahweh gave Israel into their power. The year of the death of Jair (Ra., RJes. 1⁹) is far-fetched. The difficulty which these words make in connexion with the following *eighteen years* has constrained the interpreters to various ungrammatical shifts. ﬗ endeavours to soften the collision by carrying the second number over to the next half-verse; cf. Schm., Ke., al. ﬡᴹ 𝕷 omit the troublesome words.* — איכר בגילד] the Gileadite Amorites. In the writer's view the Israelite settlements east of the Jordan were on territory conquered from the Amorites, not taken from Moab and Ammon. The same theory is expounded at length in 11¹⁵⁻²⁷; see there. Gilead here, as often, is the whole region of Israelite occupation east of the Jordan. — 10. זבנו אלהינו וגי] read יהוה אלהינו. So 7 codd. (De Rossi) ﬡᴬᴺ 𝕿𝕷ᵛ; † sporadic correction attesting the sound feeling that the name is indispensable.

11–16. Yahweh reproaches the Israelites with their apostasy.

— They have learned neither wisdom nor gratitude by their past experience. He will deliver them no more ; they may appeal to the gods they have chosen. They confess their sin and put away the foreign gods. Yahweh cannot bear their distress. — Compare 2¹ᵇ⁻⁴ (the angel at Bochim), 6⁸⁻¹⁰ (prophet), 1 S. 7²ᵇ 10¹⁷⁻¹⁹ 12⁶ᶠᶠ· Jos. 24²⁰⁻²³. Verses ¹³· ¹⁶ have the distinctive marks of E's style ; in the preceding verses the text of E appears to have been altered and expanded by R, to whom the catalogue of oppressors, in its present form, must be attributed. — 11, 12. The Hebrew text presents an anacoluthon which can hardly be imitated in English : Nonne ab Ægyptiis et ab Amoritis et ab Ammonitis et a Philistaeis — et Sidonii et Amalec et Maon oppresserunt vos, et clamastis ad me, et liberavi vos e potestate eorum? The construction is changed in the middle, and v.¹¹ thus left without its predicate (liberavi vos). ‡ Such an anacoluthon is, however, awkward in this simple sentence, and the disorder is perhaps due to transcriptional error. The versions render : § Did not the Egyptians and the Amorites . . . oppress you, and you cried unto me, and I delivered you from their power? See note. The catalogue of the seven nations, the counterpart of the seven

---

* It is perhaps not without significance that in 11²⁶ (the 300 years) these 18 years seem not to be reckoned.

† *Dominum*, which seems to have no Latin attestation, was introduced by the Clementine editors; see Vercellone.

‡ See De Wette, *Stud. u. Krit.* 1831, p. 305; Stud.; Ges.²⁶ § 167, 2.

§ Except ﬡBN.

varieties of heathenism in v.⁶,* corresponds to 2¹ᵇ (he sold them
into the power of their enemies on all sides), as v.⁶ᵃᵇ to 2¹³. The
text of E, as is frequently the case with such lists, has been amplified by a later editor; originally it must have contained the names
of the peoples whose oppressions had been related in E's Book
of Judges, and probably in the order of his narrative. If it had
been preserved intact, it would have given us a valuable criterion
for the reconstruction of his work. The editor, on the contrary,
has accumulated the names of neighbouring nations without any
discoverable principle of selection or order. We read in it the
names of some which nowhere else appear as oppressors, while
we miss others, notably Moab and Midian, which we should certainly expect to find. — *The Amorites*] this is referred by the commentators to Sihon king of Heshbon (Nu. 21²¹ᶠᶠ·); † but how the
invasion and conquest of the Amorites by Israel, which is there
narrated, can be converted into an oppression of Israel by the
Amorites, ‡ and put in conjunction with the tyranny of the
Egyptians, they do not explain. The name is omitted by 𝔖. —
The Ammonites] the only Ammonite oppression recorded in the
book is that in the following chapter, from which they were delivered by Jephthah; we should not expect to find it referred to in
this introduction as a thing of the past. In 3¹³ the Ammonites
are named as allies of Moab under Eglon, but since Moab itself
is not named in our catalogue the supposition that the writer was
here thinking of Eglon's time is excluded. The omission of
Moab was felt by the versions to be unaccountable, and the name
is introduced by 𝔊 after the Ammonites, § by 𝔖 instead of the
Amorites. — *The Philistines*] in immediate connexion with the
Ammonites, as in v.⁷. The period of Philistine supremacy began
near the end of the time of the judges (Samson), and lasted till
the days of David. The commentators are compelled to refer here
to Shamgar (3³¹); see there. — **12.** *The Sidonians*] Phoenicians;
see on 3⁸ (p. 79, 81). There is no record in the O.T. of an
invasion or subjugation of Israel by the Phoenicians. ‖ That by
Phoenicians the author meant the northern Canaanites (Jabin,
ch. 4), or that the Phoenicians may have held a kind of hegemony

* Rashi.   † So, e.g., Be., Ke.   ‡ Note the verb.   § Except 𝕺ᴺ.
‖ In Am. 1⁹ they are slave-dealers, not captors; cf. 2 Macc. 8¹¹·³⁴.

among the northern Canaanites, in virtue of which they supported
them in their wars with Israel,* are hypotheses which admit of no
refutation, because they have no foundation.   More probably the
introduction of the Sidonians here is due to the mention of them
in v.⁶⁰; cf. 1 K. 11³³. — *Amalek*] the Amalekites are named in 3¹³
as allies of Eglon, in 6³·³³ as joining Midian in its annual raids.†
Others refer to Ex. 17⁸ᶠ. — *Maon*] the Maonites first appear in
Chronicles as enemies of Jehoshaphat of Judah (2 Chr. 20¹), and
of Uzziah (2 Chr. 26⁷); they are mentioned also in the time of
Hezekiah (1 Chr. 4⁴¹).   Their seats were south of the Dead Sea;
in all probability the name is preserved in Maʿān,‡ on the old
caravan road from Damascus to Arabia, four hours east of Petra.
The occurrence of the name in this list of early oppressors of
Israel is hard to explain.   Of the ancient versions 𝕿 alone agrees
with 𝕳; some recensions of 𝕲 have Midian; others, with 𝕴,
Canaan; 𝕾 has Ammon here.   That Midian should be omitted
from the list altogether after the story of Gideon (ch. 6–8) is
quite as strange as that Maon should be included, and very many
critics adopt the emendation suggested by 𝕲, *Midian*.§   The
emendation is so self-evident that it is suspicious.   It is possible,
after all, that the editor, who, as the whole catalogue proves, was
little concerned about historical accuracy, may have written the
name of an Arab people of his own times, the Minaeans.‖   The
omission of Midian is not more strange than that of Moab.   See
note. — *And you cried unto me, and I delivered you from their
power*] cf. 1 S. 12¹⁰ and the places cited above on v.⁷⁰. — **13.**   In
spite of all this they have forgotten him (v.¹⁰ 2¹²·¹³) and served
other gods (Dt. 7⁴ 11¹⁶ Jos. 24²·¹⁶ 1 S. 8⁸). — *Therefore I will not
deliver you any more*] cf. 2²¹. — **14.**   Let them cry to the gods
they have chosen; they may deliver them in their time of distress; cf. Jer. 2²⁸ Dt. 32³⁷ᶜ 2 K. 3¹³. — **15.** *We have sinned*] see

---

* Be., referring to Jud. 18⁷·²⁸.

† The mention of Amalek in both places appears to be due to the redaction.

‡ Le Strange, *Palestine under the Moslems*, p. 39, 508 f.; Burckhardt, *Syria*,
p. 436 f.; Doughty, *Arabia Deserta*, i. p. 32 ff. — In 1 K. 11¹⁸ Then., Sta., al. would
read *Maon* for *Midian*; an unnecessary change, see above, p. 179.

§ So Be., Doorn.; cf. Stud.

‖ See Glaser, *Skizze der Gesch. u. Geogr. Arabiens*, ii. p. 450–452; Sayce, *Higher
Criticism*, p. 39–46.

on v.[10]. Verses[15. 16] seem to be entirely derived from E. — *Do thou unto us all that seems good to thee; only rescue us this day*] punish us thyself in any way that thou seest fit, but save us now from our enemies; cf. 2 S. 24[14]: "Let me fall by the hand of Yahweh, for his compassion is great; but by the hand of man let me not fall"; 2 Macc. 10[4]. With the phrase, *whatever is good in thy sight*, cf. 1 S. 3[18] 2 S. 15[26], and in different applications, Jud. 19[24] 1 S. 1[23] 11[10] 14[40] 2 S. 10[12]. — **16.** *So they put away the foreign gods from among them*] Jos. 24[20. 23] 1 S. 7[3] Gen. 35[2. 4] cf. Dt. 31[16]. *Foreign gods* is the phrase of E, for which the Deuteronomic expression is, *other gods*. — *He could bear the misery of Israel no longer*] his pity for his people (Hos. 11[8]) and his indignation against their enemies overcome him; he can no longer stand aloof and see the heathen oppress Israel. On the Hebrew phrase see note. — **17, 18.** In the original connexion of E, v.[16] must have been immediately followed by the raising up of the deliverer (cf. 11[1f.]). Verses[17f.] are an editorial introduction to the story of Jephthah, the material of which is all drawn from ch. 11, as 8[33-35] is derived from ch. 9.[*] — **17.** The Ammonites gathered for war and encamped in Gilead; the Israelites were assembled at Mizpah; cf. 7[1] 1 S. 4[1] 29[1] &c. The two armies confronted one another, but the Israelites had no leader. This representation does not agree with 11[29], from which it appears that Jephthah had to raise the clans himself; the latter verse is, however, probably from the hand of an editor; cf. also 11[4]. — **18.** *The people, the chiefs of Gilead*] the words are explained as a restrictive apposition,[†] but the technical name does not render the expression any less awkward. Perhaps the original text has been glossed. — They anxiously inquire where they shall find a champion and leader. The man who leads them to victory shall be made chief of all Gilead; cf. 11[8. 9. 11].

11. הלא ממצרים וג'] to explain the anacoluthon it is supposed that the author began intending to say, הלא ממצרים . . . הושעתי אתכם (Ges.[26] § 167, 2). But neither הושיע nor הציל, 'deliver, rescue' from an enemy or oppressor, is in Judges construed thus with מן; they always take מיד (הושיע 2[16. 18] 6[14] (מכף) 8[22] 10[12] 13[5]; הציל 6[9] 8[34] 9[17]). There is no discernible reason why the author

---

[*] Mizpah (v.[17]) is derived from 11[11] in its present form; hence 10[17f.] is later than the great interpolation, 11[12ff.]   [†] Be., al.

should not have written, הלא הושעתי אהכם מיד מדרים וג׳, or הלא מיד מצרים הושעתי וג׳, אהכם ומיד וג׳. 𝔐 with its supposed anacoluthon is thus suspicious on grammatical grounds. 𝕲ᴬᴾⱽᴸᴹᴼ s ι * 𝕷𝕾 make the nouns in v.¹¹ as well as in v.¹² subjects of the vb. נשח, and the text should probably be emended accordingly. — 12. ובנכין] Μαδιαμ 𝕲ᴬᴰᴸᴹ ι, Χανααν ᴾⱽᴼ ᵃᴸ. s Σ, Canaan 𝕷 (thinking doubtless of 4² &c.). כנון is a not impossible corruption of כנע in old Hebr. or transitional alphabets. — 14. רוע ץ רפל [ויוסיפו לנם Jos. 10⁶ 2 S. 10¹¹ Jer. 11¹⁵ Ez. 34²²; in a different idiom, Jud. 7², see note there. — 16. וקצר נפטי] lit. *his soul was shortened;* his patience was exhausted. We speak of a short temper, impatient and hasty. In Hebrew the phrase is used for complete discouragement, when endurance itself is exhausted, Ex. 6⁹ Nu. 21⁴ Job 21¹; but also of a man who is tired out by importunity, Jud. 16¹⁶. The application of these words to God was a stumbling-block to some of the Jewish interpreters; but cf. Mi. 2⁷ Zech. 11⁸. — כמל] rare in old prose, Gen. 41⁵¹ (E) Nu. 23²¹ Dt. 26⁷.

XI. 1-XII. 7.—Jephthah delivers Gilead from the Ammonites.

Jephthah the Gileadite has been driven from his home to the adjacent Syrian district of Tob, where, with a band of wild fellows, he leads the life of a freebooter (11¹⁻³). When the Ammonites make war on Gilead, the elders persuade him to come and take command against the enemy, promising to make him the head chief of all Gilead. He returns with them, and is made chief by the people (v.⁴⁻¹¹). He sends messengers to the king of Ammon, contesting his claim to the lands between the Jabbok and the Arnon: Israel conquered this territory from the Amorites and has held it undisputed for three hundred years. The Ammonites refusing to recognize Israel's title, hostilities commence (v.¹²⁻²⁸). Jephthah vows that if Yahweh gives him victory, he will sacrifice the first who comes out of his house to meet him on his return (v.³⁰ᶠ.). He subdues the Ammonites, taking from them twenty cities (v.³²ᶠ.). Returning in triumph to Mizpah, his only daughter comes out to meet him, heading the chorus of women. The father's heart is rent, but he can not take back his word; after a respite of two months, he performs his vow. The fate of Jephthah's daughter is commemorated by the women of Israel in an annual four days' festival (v.³⁴⁻⁴⁰).

The Ephraimites are jealous because they were not called out for the war, and cross the Jordan to avenge the slight, but are

---

* 𝕲ᴰᴺ Σ agree with 𝔐.

beaten by Jephthah. In their flight many are cut off by the Gileadites at the fords of the Jordan, being betrayed by their pronunciation (12¹⁻⁶). After judging Israel for six years, Jephthah dies and is buried in Gilead (v.⁷).

The long diplomatic communication, defending Israel's title to Gilead (11¹²⁻²⁸), is manifestly foreign to the original story.* The historical argument is derived chiefly, and in part verbally, from Nu. 20, 21 (see comm. below) ; and, though purporting to be an answer to the claim of the Ammonites (v.¹³), in reality deals exclusively with Israel's relation to the *Moabites* (v.¹⁷. ¹⁸).† Even in the appeal to the king (v.²⁴), the name of Chemosh, the national god of Moab, stands, instead of Milcom, the god of Ammon ; and the conduct of the present king is contrasted with that of Balak king of Moab, who waged no war with Israel. The cities named in v.²⁶ are well known Moabite cities.‡ There is general agreement among critics that 11¹²⁻²⁸ is a late interpolation, the motive of which is to establish the title of Israel to its possessions between the Arnon and the Jabbok.§ The insertion of this long speech has done some injury to the margins of the original narrative. Verses ³⁰. ³¹ are violently severed from v.¹¹ᵃ, of which they are the original sequel ; v.¹¹ᵇ seems to belong after v.³¹ ; v.²⁹ is further a very awkward redactional doublet to v.³², necessitated by the intrusion of v.¹²⁻²⁸ before v.³⁰ᶠ. See comm. on the verses. At the beginning of ch. 11, the editor seems to have endeavoured with indifferent success to make out something more definite about the hero's origin, taking the hint from v.⁷. Chapter 12¹⁻⁶ is regarded by Wellhausen as a later appendix to the story. The difficulties in the connexion of these verses with ch. 11 are, however, exaggerated ; the story does not bear the marks of a late fabrication ; and there seems to be no sufficient reason why it may not be from the same hand with 11⁴⁻¹¹. ³⁰⁻⁴⁰. See more fully below, and cf. on 8¹⁻³.

---

* See Stud.; Nöldeke, *Untersuchungen*, p. 195 n.; We., *Comp.*, p. 228; Bu., *Richt. u. Sam.*, p. 125; al.

† Even in v.¹⁵, where alone they are named, the Ammonites come only in the second place.

‡ Nu. 21²⁴⁻²⁶ treats the whole kingdom of Sihon, from the Jabbok to the Arnon, as having been originally Moabite.

§ The occasion of the interpolation may have been the intrusion of the Ammonites into the old territory of Israel at the beginning of the 6th century, cf. Jer. 49¹.

Wellhausen and Stade find in the story of Jephthah no historical elements at all.   Jephthah himself is a shadowy figure, whose
origin and end are equally obscure ; of his great victory over the
Ammonites, we are told nothing definite.   The whole point lies in
the sacrifice of his daughter, which serves to explain the Gileadite
women's festival.*   Stade infers from 11[1] that Jephthah was the
heros eponymus of a despised Gileadite clan, or one not of full
blood.   Goldziher treats Jephthah and his offering as mythical.†
The objections ·to the historical character of the hero and of the
main features of the story do not seem to be sufficiently well
founded.   That the circumstances of his victories over the Ammonites were not remembered, or are not more fully narrated
here, does not prove that nothing of the sort happened ; the
mythical features which may be recognized in the annual celebration of the women of Gilead may have attached themselves
to an historical event such as is here related. ‡

1-3. **Jephthah's antecedents.** — The bastard son of Gilead,
he is driven from home by his brothers, and with a band of free
companions lives the life of a marauder in the district of Tob.
The facts in this introduction are drawn from the story, which
must have begun by telling who Jephthah was, and probably how
he came to be in Tob (cf. v.⁸).   The genealogical notice which
makes him a son of Gilead (v.¹ᵇ) is clearly not original ; with it
naturally falls the story of his expulsion by the legitimate sons of
Gilead (v.²).   From v.⁷ we should rather infer that he had been
banished by the authorities, the elders of Gilead.   A not unnatural
misunderstanding of the latter verse may have given rise to v.¹ᵇ·².§

1. *Jephthah the Gileadite was a great warrior*] 6¹²·1 S. 9¹. —
He was the son of a harlot] cf. Abimelech, 8³¹ 9¹⁸.   The trait may
very well belong to the original story. ‖   The following words, on
the contrary, *and Gilead begot Jephthah*, appear to be a misinterpretation of the patrial adjective, the Gileadite, in the sense and
form of the later genealogical systems ; Gilead is the name of a

---

* We., *Comp.*, p. 228 f. ; Sta., *GVI.* i. p. 68.
† *Der Mythos bei den Hebräern*, p. 113 ff. = *Mythology among the Hebrews*, 1877,
p. 96 ff., 104.   ‡ Cf. Kue., Bu., Kitt.   § Cf. Bu., p. 125 f.
‖ Bu., *l.c.* p. 125, is of the opinion that this also is secondary.

region or of its population (5^{17}), not of a man. Having made this
beginning, the editor understands Jephthah's words to the elders of
Gilead in v.[7], *You have hated me and driven me out of my father's
house*, and *his brethren* (clansmen) v.[3], literally, and combining it
with v.[1b] (Jephthah a bastard), interprets the whole situation in
v.[2]: the legitimate sons drove out their illegitimate half-brother.*
— **2.** Besides Jephthah, Gilead had sons by his lawful wife. When
they grew up, they drove Jephthah away. — *Thou shalt have no
inheritance in our father's house, for thou art the son of another
woman*] if v.[1b. 2] were an integral part of the old story, and therefore
to be interpreted historically, we might, with Stade, regard Jephthah as the name of a Gileadite clan which did not stand on an
equal footing with the others of its kin.   But as the name nowhere
occurs in this character,† and nothing in the subsequent story
suggests anything of the kind, the solution adopted above seems
preferable. — **3.** *Jephthah fled from his brethren*] cf. v.[7]; expelled
from his father's house. — *The district of Tob*] v.[5]. The men of
Tob appear in 2 S. $10^{6.8}$ among the Syrian allies of the Ammonites
in their war with David, in immediate connexion with Maachah;
the same district is perhaps meant in 1 Macc. 5^{13} 2 Macc. 12^{17}.
We have no other clue to the situation of Tob; it was apparently
not very remote from Gilead, probably to the NE. — *There collected to Jephthah worthless fellows, and went out* (on forays) *with
him*] lit. *were raked together*. The outlawed man naturally took
to the life of a freebooter on the outskirts of the settled land.
So David did when compelled to flee from Saul (1 S. $22^{1f.}$ 23^{1-5} 25
$27^{7ff.}$ &c.). His companions were of the same class; wild and
reckless fellows, 9^4. Such a life was not esteemed dishonourable. ‡

1. יפתח] probably a decurtate theophoric name; cf. פתחיה, יפתחאל.—אשה
זונה] 16^1 Jos. 2^1 and often, cf. אשה פילגש 19^1; see note on 4^4. As in the case
of Rahab, early Jewish interpreters try to soften the word; see below on v.[2].
— ויגרשו] the Hiph. is common in P and Chr., also Dt. 4^{25} 28^{41} (Di., *Gen.*, p. 106;
Dr., *Introd.*, p. 127; Giesebrecht, *ZATW.* i. p. 235 f.); older writers use

* So substantially, Bu.

† Cf. Jos. 15^{43}, a town in the Lowlands of Judah; Jiphthah-el in Zebulun,
Jos. 19^{14}.

‡ Cf. of the Greeks, Thuc., i. 5; Germans, Caes., *b.g.* vi. 23, Latrocinia nullam
habent infamiam, quae extra fines cujusque civitatis fiunt. The sentiments of the
Arabs on this subject are well known.

the Kal both in the sense 'beget' and 'bear.' The clause attaches very
awkwardly to the preceding: ⅏ makes a better connexion, ἢ ἐγένησεν τῷ
Γαλααδ (^{BN}), or καὶ ἔτεκεν τῷ Γ. (^{APVLMO}); but we should hardly take this
for the original reading (Gies.). — רֵאשִׁית הַנְּחָלִים] Nu. 18^{20} (ב) Jos. 19^9 (ב-יר)
Nu. 32^{19} (רֵא). — אִשָּׁה אַחֶרֶת] 1 Chr. 2^{26}. The word does not mean _peregrina_
(JHMich., cl. Dt. 29^{27} Jer. 22^{26}), still less, _of another tribe_ (rabbinical interpretation in Ki.); nor does it necessarily connote inferiority. — 3. אֶרֶץ טוֹב]
in 2 S. 10$^{6-8}$ the versions take אִישׁ טוֹב as a proper name; cf. Klosterm. (king
of Maachah).* In _Jer. Shebiith,_ vi. 1, fol. 36^c the region of Tob to which Jephthah fled is said to have been סוסיתא; Neubauer (_Glog. du Talmud,_ p. 239)
identifies this with the Hippos of Josephus (_vita,_ 65 § 349), in the Decapolis.†
S. Merrill adopts this combination; but it rests, so far as the Talmud is
concerned, on a very insecure basis. (See also Mühlau in Ri. _HWB.,_ s.v.)

4-11. When war breaks out with the Ammonites, the sheikhs
of Gilead go after Jephthah, and beg him to take command in
the war. He expresses his surprise that in their straits they should
seek the aid of the man whom they have driven into exile. They
promise that he shall·retain his power and be head of all the
inhabitants of Gilead. Upon these terms he returns with them
and is proclaimed commander and chief. — **4.** This verse seems
superfluous beside v.^{5a}, and is omitted by some Greek manuscripts; Studer questions its genuineness. Of the two, however,
it is perhaps more likely that v.^{5a} was inserted by the editor. —
After a time] perhaps we should interpret, after a _year;_ cf. _that
year,_ 10^8. They overran the Israelites unresisted the first year,
but the next season, when they again invaded the country, the
elders summoned Jephthah. — _The Ammonites_] a people closely
akin to the Moabites, to whom they seem to have stood in a
relation somewhat similar to that of Edom to Israel. They lay
to the northeast of Moab, and east of the Israelite settlements,
on the border of the desert. Their principal city was Rabbah of
the Ammonites ('Ammān), on the upper Jabbok. In the fertile
region adjacent to this city they probably early settled down to
agriculture, but the great body of the tribe seems to have always
remained at least semi-nomadic. That they periodically harried
their Israelite neighbours and lifted their cattle, is only what the

---

* In the parallel 1 Chr. 19^{16} the name is omitted.

† On the site of Hippos see Schumacher, _ZDPV._ ix. 1886, p. 324 f. 349 f.;
Clermont-Ganneau, _PEF. Qu. St.,_ 1887, p. 36-38.

Bedawin along the margin of the Syrian desert have always done. Not seldom their invasions had a more serious character. An Ammonite attack on Jabesh-gilead was the occasion which made Saul king (1 S. 11[16.]) ; David waged an embittered war against them (2 S. 10–12). — **5.** See above on v.[4]. — *The elders of Gilead*] v.[8. 9. 10. 11] cf. 8[16] ; the heads of the families and clans ; with a modern word, the sheikhs. *Gilead* is often used for the whole territory occupied by Israel east of the Jordan, as Canaan for their possessions on the west of the river. This territory, whose natural boundaries are the Yarmūk on the north and Wady Mōǵib (Arnon) on the south, is divided by the Zerqā (Jabbok) into two parts, the northern of which is now called Ǵebel 'Aǵlūn, the southern, the Belqa. It is the latter which is the scene of our story.[*] — **6.** *Come with us and be our commander*] an extraordinary authority, a kind of dictatorship, is meant ; see note. — **7.** Jephthah expresses his surprise that, after the way they had treated him, they should come to him for help in their straits. — *Are not you the men that hated me, and expelled me from my father's house ?*] not only from the house, but from the family ; making him a tribeless man, without rights or protection. In such a state of society, expulsion from the clan is far more than banishment ; it makes a man an outcast and an outlaw. The justice or injustice of his banishment is not mooted ;[†] they have, in any case, no reason to expect help from him. — **8.** *Therefore we have now returned to thee*] the particle refers, not to the last words of Jephthah (because we are in straits), but to his first question : Because we did banish thee, we have now sought thee out to bring thee back. — *So go with us and fight with the Ammonites, and thou shalt be our chief, even of all the inhabitants of Gilead*] 10[18]. Such a sentence may also be conceived as conditional : If thou wilt go . . . thou shalt be, &c. ; but it is a mistake to regard this as a form of the Hebrew conditional sentence. — **9.** He repeats their proposition, that there may be no misunderstanding. — *If you take me back to fight with the Ammon-*

---

[*] On Gilead, see Burckhardt, *Syria*, p. 347–372 ; Tristram, *Land of Israel*, ch. 22, 23 ; Merrill, *East of the Jordan*, 1881 ; Conder, *Heth and Moab*, 1883 ; *SEP. Memoirs*, I. 1889 ; G. A. Smith, *Hist. Geogr.*, p. 517–590 ; *DB².* s.v.

[†] Cler.

ites, and Yahweh gives them over before me, I shall be your chief]
it is unnecessary to give the words an interrogatory inflection. —
10. *Yahweh shall be a witness between us*] shall hear and take
note of the words which have passed between us ; cf. Gen. 31⁴⁹,
Yahweh shall keep watch between us, when we are out of each
other's sight. — *That we will do just as thou sayest*] lit. *if we do
not do;* the usual form of affirmative oath or asseveration. —
11. Jephthah goes with them, and the people acclaim him chief
and dictator ; cf. 9⁶. So Saul is acclaimed king by all the people
at Gilgal (1 S. 11¹⁵) ; Rehoboam goes to Shechem to be made
king by all Israel (1 K. 12¹) ; Jeroboam is made king there by
the northern tribes (1 K. 12²⁰) ; cf. also 1 K. 1⁹ᶠ· (Adonijah),
v.ˣˣᶠ· (Solomon). It has been generally inferred from v.¹¹ᵇ, in connexion with 10¹⁷, that Jephthah was acclaimed at Mizpah. This is
in itself highly probable ; the Gileadites would naturally assemble
for the purpose at their principal holy-place (cf. 9⁶ 1 S. 11¹⁵
1 K. 1⁹·³³ 12¹ &c.). But 10¹⁷ is part of the editor's introduction,
and 11¹¹ᵇ is misplaced ; it originally stood in close connexion with
v.ˣᵛ·, from which it has been separated by the interpolation of v.¹²⁻²⁹,
and closer examination shows that its proper place is after v.ˣ¹,
not before v.³⁰ ; see below. — *Jephthah uttered all his words before
Yahweh at Mizpah*] at the holy place, before the stele, altar, or
idol, in which the deity was believed to dwell, or which symbolized
his presence ; cf. 1 S. 1⁹ (𝕲) ¹⁵·¹⁹ 7⁶ 10¹⁹·²⁵ 11¹⁵ 15³³ 2 S. 5³ 21⁹ 6²·¹⁴
2 K. 19¹⁴. In the present context the words can only mean, he
repeated before Yahweh what he had said to the elders of Gilead
when they came to solicit his aid (v.⁹).[*] The only object in such
a repetition would be to bind them by a religious sanction to keep
their promise ; but in that case he must have made them solemnly
repeat their pledge (v.⁸·¹⁰), his words would not hold them ; and,
furthermore, the promise of the elders had already been fulfilled
by the people (v.¹¹ᵃ). On the other hand, the statement is pertinent, if indeed it is not indispensable, in the account of Jephthah's vow, v.ˣᵛ· cf. v.³³·³⁶ ; see further on v.³¹. — *Mizpah* is not
Mizpah in Benjamin (Jos. 18²⁶ Jud. 20 21 1 S. 7 10¹⁷ Neh. 3⁷

---

[*] Stud. It is hardly permissible to stretch the words to cover all that had passed
between him and the elders (Ra.).

&c.),* but Mizpah in Gilead (v.³⁴ cf. v.²⁹ Hos. 5¹). The site has not been recovered; in our story we might think of Gébel Osha', an hour north of es-Salṭ, from whose summit the view takes in a large part of Palestine.†

4. The verse is lacking in 𝕲ᴮᴺ: it is found in all other recensions of 𝕲 and in all the other versions. ‡ The omission may be due to homœoteleuton; or, less likely, to the same feeling of the redundancy of the verse which has led Jerome to condense in translation. — ימים] after a time; 14⁸ 15¹ Jos. 23¹ ימים רבים, after a long time; or, after a year; see below v.⁴⁰. — On the Ammonites see Stade, GVI. i. p. 120; Ri. HWB., DB²., s.v. — 5. זקני גלעד] cf. Nu. 22⁴ (Midian) 22⁷ (Moab) 1 S. 4⁸ (Israel) &c. Elders of a city, Jud. 8¹⁶ 1 S. 11³; cf. זקני העיר freq. in Dt. — 6. קצין] v.¹¹; synonym of ראש Mi. 3¹·⁹; joined with שבט and כשל Prov. 6⁷; commander of troops Jos. 10²⁴; dictator Is. 3⁶·⁷; cf. also Is. 1¹⁰ 22⁸ Da. 11¹⁸. — 8. לכן] there is no occasion for departing from the ordinary meaning of the particle. In Jer. 5², sometimes adduced for the sense 'nevertheless, notwithstanding,' the St. Petersburg codex reads לאכן; the other exx. cited in Noldius do not support the meaning alleged. — והלכה] perf. in an urgent entreaty; Drᵈ. § 119 δ; followed by two other consec. perff. — 9. The protasis with a ptcp., 9¹⁶ cf. 6³⁶ and note there; Friedrich, Conditionalsätze, p. 16. The apodosis begins, not with ונתן (Drᵈ. § 137 α): 'if you are going to bring me back . . . Yahweh will deliver them up,' but with אנכי אהיה. — 11. Mizpah. From Jos. 13²⁶, רמת המצפה Ramath-mizpeh, it is frequently inferred that Mizpah of Gilead is the same with Ramoth-gilead (1 K. 4¹³), which was the seat of an ancient sanctuary (Jos. 20⁸ Dt. 4⁴³), and a strong place of great importance in the Syrian wars (1 K. 22³ᶠ. 2 K. 8²⁸ 9¹ᶠ.). According to Euseb. (OS². 287₉₁), Ramoth was a village 15 m. W. of Philadelphia ('Ammān), perhaps the modern es-Salṭ. But Ramah and Mizpah (Mizpeh) are both common names, and the Ramoth of the Kings must have been much further north. § The form [ה]מצפה] Jos. 11⁸ 13²⁶, cstr. Jud. 11²⁹ ᵇⁱˢ 1 S. 22³. What may be the reason of this variation in pronunciation is not clear. The fem. cstr. does not occur, but we have the locative המצפתה.

12–28. The title of Israel in Gilead. — Jephthah demands the reason of the Ammonite invasion; the king replies that he makes war to recover the territory between the Jabbok and the Arnon, which Israel, when it came up from Egypt, took from Ammon, and concludes with a demand for its surrender (v.¹²ᶠ.).

---

* Reland. Grove, al., transport the Mizpah of Jud. 20, 21 to Gilead; see there.
† See Burckhardt, Syria, p. 353 f.; Bäd⁸., p. 180. ‡ 𝕲ᴸ ᵃˡ. omit v.⁴.
§ We should naturally look for the Mizpah of Gen. 31⁴⁹ on the Aramaean frontier, in northern Gilead.

Jephthah denies the claim of the Ammonites to this region : Israel took no land from Moab or Ammon ; on the contrary, it scrupulously respected the rights of Edom and Moab ; when denied a passage through those countries, it made a long circuit to the east, avoiding them altogether, and never crossed the Arnon, the border of Moab (v.[14-18]). But when Sihon, the Amorite king of Heshbon, refused them transit, they invaded and conquered his kingdom, which extended from the Jabbok to the Arnon, and from the eastern desert to the Jordan. What Chemosh has given to his people they possess by right ; Israel has the same title to the lands which Yahweh has given them by conquest (v.[19-24]). The claim now set up is a new one : Balak, who was king of Moab when Israel occupied this region, did not assert his title to it by going to war with them ; for three hundred years Israel has dwelt unmolested in Heshbon and the other cities which Ammon now claims. The wrong is wholly on the side of the invader. Yahweh shall decide between them (v.[25-28]). The representations of Jephthah's ambassadors are unheeded, the spirit of Yahweh (battle fury) comes upon him, and he passes over to fight with the Ammonites (v.[29]). — On the interpolation, see above, p. 283.

12. Jephthah demands of the king what right the Ammonites have to invade the territory of Israel. — *What have I to do with thee*] 2 K. 3[13] &c. ; what is there between us to justify this war ? The question is asked only to give occasion to the following historical disquisition. *I* is really Israel, as in v.[27], not Jephthah. — 13. The king answers that Israel had taken possession of lands belonging to Ammon. — *From the Arnon to the Jabbok, and to the Jordan*] the territory in dispute was bounded by the Arnon on the south and the Jabbok on the north, and extended westward to the Jordan. The eastern limit was the Syrian desert (v.[22]). The Arnon, now Wady Mōǵib, flows from the east into the Dead Sea, about midway between its northern and southern ends. The valley of the Mōǵib is a deep ravine with precipitous walls.* — *The Jabbok*, now Nahr ez-Zerqā (Blue River), is the principal

---

* See Burckhardt, *Syria*, p. 372-375 ; Seetzen, *Reisen*, ii. p. 347 ; Tristram, *Land of Moab*, p. 140-143.

eastern affluent of the Jordan, into which it falls about two-fifths
of the way from the Dead Sea to the Sea of Galilee.   It also flows
through a deep ravine, which divides the high lands into two
regions of very different character, the Belqā and Gebel 'Aglūn.
The sources of the stream are near 'Ammān (Rabbah of the Ammonites), whence it flows, first in an easterly, then in a north-
westerly course, then almost due west till it emerges from the
mountains. — *So now restore them peaceably*] the plural pronoun
(fem.) must be understood of the cities in this region ; cf. v.²⁶.*
— **14, 15.** Jephthah's answer is a general denial : Israel did not
take territory from either Moab or Ammon ; cf. Dt. 2⁹·¹⁹. Thus
far, the controversy has been with Ammon only ; now Moab is
introduced by the side of Ammon ; what follows has reference
exclusively to Israel's relations to *Moab*, and the argument has no
bearing at all on the point which is supposed to be in dispute ;
see above, p. 283.   As a matter of fact, the cities north of the
Arnon were Moabite, as we know both from the Moabite inscription of King Mesha and from the prophets (Is. 15 16 Jer. 48
&c.).†   The only Ammonite city named in the O.T. is Rabbah
(Philadelphia, 'Ammān).   The Ammonites profited by the disas-
ters of Israel, and occupied a considerable part of the old territory
of Gad (Jer. 49¹ Ez. 25¹⁶· ; cf. 1 Macc. 5⁶ᶠᶠ·). — **16.** *Israel went in
the desert as far as the Red Sea, and came to Kadesh*] the first
words are generally thought to refer to the crossing of the Red
Sea (Ex. 13¹⁸ 14), but apart from the strangeness both of the
expression itself and of the juxtaposition with the following, the
mention of the fact has no relevancy in this connexion.   It is
rather, perhaps, a not altogether distinct reminiscence of Nu.
14²⁵ᵇ (E), connected with 20¹⁴ᶠᶠ· (E). — *Kadesh*] now generally.
identified with 'Ain Qudeis. ‡ — **17.** *Israel sent messengers to the
king of Edom*] from Kadesh.   The verse is plainly dependent,
even in expression, upon Nu. 20¹⁴⁻²¹ (E).   In Dt. 1 2⁴⁻⁸ no mention
is made of these negotiations with Edom. — *He* (Israel) *sent to
the king of Moab also, but he would not consent*] no account of

---

* Be. (cf. Nu. 21²⁶) ; not, the *lands of Moab* and Ammon (Stud.).

† Cf. also Jud. 3¹²ᶠᶠ· ; above, p. 90 f.

‡ Rowlands, in Williams, *Holy City³* i. p. 467 f.; Trumbull *Kadesh Barnea*,
p. 237 ff.

this embassy is now found in the Pentateuch, and as there is no
apparent reason why an editor should have omitted it, if it existed
in his sources, it may fairly be doubted whether the author of our
passage had any authority for the statement. He might naturally
reason that, if Israel proposed to pass around the southern end of
the Dead Sea, the consent of Moab was as necessary as that of
Edom.—*So Israel remained at Kadesh*] Nu. 20[1] Dt. 1[46].—**18.** The
Israelites made a long circuit around Edom and Moab, going
south along the western frontier of Edom to the head of the Gulf
of 'Aqabah (Red Sea), and then through the desert to the east of
Edom and Moab (Nu. 20[22] 21[4]) ; * cf. the somewhat different representation in Dt. 2.— *They came up on the east of the land of Moab,
and encamped beyond the Arnon*] Nu. 21[11. 13]. — *They did not enter
the territory of Moab ; for the Arnon is the boundary of Moab*]
Nu. 21[13] 22[36]. It is not necessary to suppose that the author
means the eastern boundary ; † he may have represented the
Israelites as keeping beyond the limit of settlement on the east of
Moab till they crossed the wadies which ran into the Arnon from
the east, and then turning westward along the northern side of the
Arnon ; this is apparently the representation of Nu. 21[13].

12. מה לי ויךָ] cf. further 2 S. 16[10] 19[22] Jos. 22[24] 2 K. 9[18] &c. The idiom
occurs not only in Hellenistic Greek, but in the classics; see Valckenaer on
Hdt., v. 33, Eurip., *Hippol.* 224, cited by Stud.; Ges. *Thes.*, p. 769. So also
in Syr. and Arab. (concomitant object; Caspari, § 402).—**13.** אהרן] not the
lands (ארצות, cf. v.[16]) which belonged jointly to Moab and Ammon (Stud.), but
the cities. ‡ 𝔊[VMO] 𝔏 *cam.*—**16.** ויבא . . . וילך . . . נכליהם] ויךָ apodosis to the
temporal protasis (Dr[3]. § 127 β); not to be included in the protasis (Kitt.), making the apodosis begin with וישיח.—עד ים סוף] possibly the words have been
misplaced. In v.[18] (וילך במדבר) they would be much more pertinent.—וירא
אבה] 19[10]; synon. of לא שמע v.[5], cf. Is. 1[19] אם האבו ושמעתם. The verb is found
almost exclusively with the negation (the exceptions are Is. *l.c.*, and Job 39[9]
in a rhetorical question equivalent to negation); 'refuse assent or consent;
decline, refuse.' The meanings ' be desirous, be willing ' frequently attributed
to the verb are fictitious. — **18.** במזרח שמש] 20[48] Dt. 4[47] Is. 41[25] &c. (prevail-

---

* The description of the route in Nu. 21 is made up of heterogeneous elements.
† In which case the name Arnon must be applied (as it very well may have
been) to the long southeastern branch of the Mōgib, the Seil es-Sa'ideh, the head
of which is near Katrāneh on the Ḥaġġ road. See *DB[2]*. i. p. 247 n.
‡ Stud. gathers from the word that the king of the Ammonites had accused
Israel of occupying territory which belonged to Moab, as well as that of Ammon.

ing in later books); כזרח הישבר Nu. 21[11] Jos. 1[18] 13[6] 2 K. 10[28] &c. The
omission of the article is probably explained by the fact that the phrase is a
unit in sense, like *sunrise*, *sunset*, &c., and construed like words designating
direction (צפון, &c.), which do not admit the article. The next step is to drop
the genitive, Am. 8[12] &c. — בעבר ארנון] Nu. 21[13] כעבר, on the other side of the
Arnon; that is, from Moab. Not *south* of the Arnon (Di. on Nu. *l.c.*), or *east*
of its upper course, but *north* of it, having crossed its head wadies in the
desert, east of the Moabite settlements, Nu. *l.c.*; cf. Dt. 2[24].

19. Israel asks of Sihon permission to cross his country, through
which they must needs pass to reach the Jordan and invade
Canaan. — *King of the Amorites*] of the new Amorite kingdom
which had been established north of the Arnon, in lands wrested
from Moab (Nu. 21[26-30]).* — *Heshbon*] one of the chief cities of
Moab (Is. 15[4] Jer. 48[2] &c.) ; for a time in the possession of Israel
(cf. v.[26]). Its ruins, which still bear the old name, Ḥesbān, lie
about sixteen miles east of the mouth of the Jordan.† — *Let me
pass through thy country*] Nu. 21[22] Dt. 2[27]. — *To my place*] cf. Nu.
10[29]. — **20**. *But Sihon refused Israel passage through his territory*]
so the text is to be emended on the authority of 𝕲[A 𝔞l.] ; 𝔐 has,
Sihon did not trust Israel to pass, but the use and construction of
the verb *trust* are anomalous ; see note. — *Sihon collected all his
forces and encamped at Jahaz*] Nu. 21[23] Dt. 2[32]. *Jahaz* is a
Moabite city, named in conjunction with Heshbon and Elealeh.‡
It was shown in Eusebius' time between Medeba and Debus. § —
21. Yahweh gave the Amorites into the power of the Israelites,
who conquered them and occupied all their territory ; Nu. 21[24]
Dt. 2[33-37]. — **22**. The boundaries of this territory more exactly
defined ; it was precisely the district now claimed by Ammon
(v.[13]) ; cf. Nu. 21[24-26] Dt. 2[36f.]. In both the latter passages it is
carefully explained that Israel took no territory from the Am-

---

* Whether this representation is historical or not, is a question into which we
need not enter here; see E. Meyer, *ZATW.* i. p. 128 ff.; Sta., *GVI.* i. p. 117 f.;
on the other side, Di., *NDJ.* p. 133; Kitt., *GdH.* i. 1. p. 207 ff.

† On Heshbon see Reland, *Palaestina*, p. 719 f.; Le Strange, p. 456; Burckhardt,
Syria, 365; Tristram, *Land of Israel*[3], p. 528 f.; *SEP. Memoirs*, i. p. 104 ff.; *DB*[2].
i. p. 1348.   ‡ See Mesha's inscription, l. 19. Is. 15[4] Jer. 48[21, 34].

§ *OS*[2]. 264[94]. Δηβοὑς is probably Dibon. Reland (*Palaestina*, p. 825) conj.
Ἐσβοὑς (*OS*[2]. 253[77]), Heshbon, which appears intrinsically more probable. The
scene of the battle seems to have been not far from Heshbon. Jahaz has not been
identified; for a long list of guesses, see *DB*[2]. s.v.

monites, and in both the Jabbok is the boundary between their conquests and the possessions of Ammon. This seems to mean that the upper course of the Jabbok, whose general direction is north,* formed the eastern frontier of the Israelite territory in this quarter, along which they bordered on Ammon. In Jud. 11¹³ ²², however, the Jabbok is clearly the northern boundary of the region in dispute, which extends eastward to the desert (v.²²), leaving no place at all for Ammon.

23, 24. The divine right of conquest. — *So now, Yahweh, the god of Israel, dispossessed the Amorites before his people Israel, and wilt thou possess them*] their (*sc.* the Amorites') territory. Question of indignant surprise ; cf. on v.⁶. — **24.** *Shouldst thou not possess the territory of those whom Chemosh thy god dispossesses,† and we possess the territory of all whom Yahweh our god dispossesses ?*] the translation is as literal as possible, preserving, at some sacrifice of English idiom, the recurring verb. The conquests of a people are the conquests of its god, who bestows upon them the territory of the conquered ; they hold it by a divine right which should be respected by others who hold their own territories by the like title. — *Chemosh* is the national god of Moab (1 K. 11³³ cf. 11⁷ 2 K. 23¹³), and Moab is the people of Chemosh (Nu. 21²⁹ Jer. 48⁴⁶), just as Yahweh is the god of Israel, and Israel the people of Yahweh. So in the inscription of Mesha, king of Moab, we read that the king of Israel oppressed Moab a long time, "because Chemosh was angry with his land" (l. 5f.) ; he erects a sanctuary to Chemosh in gratitude for deliverance (l. 3).‡ The reality and power of the national god of Moab were no more doubted by the old Israelites than those of Yahweh himself. A conspicuous illustration of this is 2 K. 3²⁷, where a signal disaster of the Israelite arms before the capital of Moab is attributed to the fury of Chemosh, excited by the sacrifice of the king's son. § The national god of the Ammonites, on the contrary, was Milcom

---

* First N.E., to Qal'at ez-Zerqâ, then N.W. to its junction with Wady Gerash, where it finally turns to the west ; see also on v.¹³.

† On the text, see note.

‡ Cf. also l. 8 f., 12 f., 14, 19, 17 f.

§ See Baudissin, *Studien zur semit. Religionsgeschichte,* i. p. 55 ff. ; Smend, *Alttest. Religionsgesch.,* p. 111 f. On Chemosh, see Baethgen, *Beiträge,* p. 13-15.

(1 K. 11⁸ cf. 11¹ 2 K. 23¹³; also Jer. 49¹·³).* From the fact that Chemosh is named here instead of Milcom, older commentators inferred that Chemosh was worshipped by the Ammonites as well as by Moab.† In itself there is no difficulty in admitting this; we know that both Chemosh and Milcom were worshipped in Israel for centuries; but it is inconceivable that the conquests of Ammon should be attributed to the national god of the sister people, as it would be that the conquests of Israel should be ascribed to any god but Yahweh. Others are inclined to assume that Milcom may also have been called Chemosh; ‡ or that Chemosh is a slip of the pen on the part of the author; § or a scribe's blunder. ‖ But the whole preceding and following context has to do with Moab only, and the name of Chemosh is not an accident to be explained by itself; the error runs through the whole learned argument.

20. ולא האמין סיחון את ישראל עבר] pro tuto non habebat Sihhon, Israëlem transire, Ges. *Thes.*; cf. Ew. § 336 *b*. The construction is anomalous (Job 15²², רא יאמין יוב בני חשך, is not parallel), and the comparison of the accus. with inf. is misleading. 𝕲^AVI.MO 𝕾 𝕮 has καὶ οὐκ ἠθέλησε Σηων τὸν Ισραηλ διελθεῖν, which probably represents ויבאן אריכ נהן את ישראל; ‖ וינבאן סיחון וני; cf. Nu. 20²¹ יעבר בנבלי; ¶ יאמן was corrupted to יאבן, which necessitated the introduction of the negative, giving the text of 𝔐, followed by 𝕲^AN 𝕮𝕾. — ויחנו בירצה] in Is. 15⁴ Jer. 48³⁴, Mesha, l. 19, the name is יהץ. The locative *a*, Nu. 21²³ Dt. 2³², seems to be mistaken for fem. ending, as in Jer. 48²¹ Jos. 13¹⁹ 1 Chr. 6⁵⁸; Sta. § 342 *d*.** — **24.** את אשר יוריתך כמוש וני] the double accusative would compel us to take the verb in a different sense (*cause thee to possess*, 2 Chr. 20¹¹), thus destroying the symmetry of the sentence. The final ו has arisen by dittography from the following.

25, 26. The right of adverse possession. — The king of Moab at the time of the conquest did not try to recover this territory; for three hundred years Israel has been in unchallenged possession of it. — **25.** *Now, art thou any better than Balak son of Zippor, king of Moab? Did he have any contention with Israel, or did he ever go to war with them?*] the story of E (Nu. 22ᶠᶠ·), on which the author is probably here as in the foregoing dependent,

---

* Mispronounced in 𝔐.   † Cler., Schm.; against this explanation, Stud.
‡ Be.   § Baethgen.   ‖ Sayce.   ¶ Cf. also Nu. 21²³; ולא נ־י, Dt. 2³⁰ לא אבה נ־י.
** Hitz. (*Jes.*, p. 187 f.) and Kneucker (*BL* s. v.) think that there were two cities, Jahaz and Jahazah.

gives the answer : Balak did not contest with Israel the possession
of the lands north of the Arnon.   Is the present king of Ammon,
then, a greater man than Balak, that he would vindicate his claim
to this territory?   The question is not whether he has a better
claim than Balak, from one of whose recent predecessors the
country had been taken by the Amorites,* but whether he thinks
himself superior to Balak, able to do what Balak did not dare,
namely, to try to take this territory from Israel ; cf. 1 S. 9² Am. 6²
Nah. 3⁸. — 26. Why had they not recovered these cities in the
three hundred years during which Israel had inhabited them
unmolested? — *In Heshbon and its dependencies*] Nu. 21²⁵; the
towns and villages which belonged to it (1²⁷ &c.). — *Aroer*] is not
named in Nu. 21 ; Dt. 2³⁶ 3¹² Jos. 12² 2 K. 10³³ locate it on the
banks of the Arnon, the southernmost city of Israel east of the
Jordan ; cf. Mesha, l. 26, Jer. 48¹⁹.   Eusebius gives a good
description of its situation.†   The ruins, still bearing the name
'Arā'ir, lie on the edge of the precipitous north bank of Wady
Mōǵib, where the Roman road crosses the gorge. ‡ — *And in all
the towns which are adjacent to the Arnon*] along its northern
side ; the southern border of Israel.   Instead of these places in
the extreme south, ⅏ has: in Heshbon and its dependencies, *and
in Jaazer and its dependencies, and in all the cities along the
Jordan.*§   Jaazer (Nu. 21³² 2 S. 24⁵ &c.) was eight or ten miles
west of Philadelphia ('Ammān), ‖ and is described as a frontier
town of Ammon (Nu. 21²⁴ ⅏).   The reading of ⅏ in our verse is
obviously original ; Aroer and the Arnon in 𝕳 were suggested by
v.¹⁸ (cf. Nu. 21¹³ff.), and represent the tendency of late editors
and scribes to enlarge the borders of Israel at the expense of all
its neighbours. — *For three hundred years*] the addition of the
numbers given in the preceding chapters for the duration of the
several " oppressions " and the rule of the successive judges gives
the sum of three hundred and nineteen years, or, if the eighteen
years of the Ammonite oppression (10⁸) be omitted, three hun-

---

dred and one years.* The coincidence is so close as to suggest that the computation was made upon the basis of the present chronology of the book. If this be the case, the figures must have been inserted by the last editor, or a still later hand.† The connexion of v.²⁶ with the preceding would be much more intimate if the number were omitted: Did Balak make any opposition when Israel settled in Heshbon . . . Why didst thou (Moab) not reclaim them at that time. — **27.** Israel has in no way offended against Ammon; the latter is altogether in the wrong in the present invasion. — *I have committed no fault*] the *I* is Israel, not Jephthah; see above on v.¹². — *Let Yahweh, who is arbiter to-day, decide between Israelites and Ammonites*] the order of the words seems to favour this construction, ‡ rather than that which connects *to-day* with the principal verb, *Let Yahweh the judge decide to-day.* § Compare in general, 1 S. 24¹¹ᶠ·¹⁵ Gen. 31⁵³ 16⁵. ∥

25. רָטִיב טיב אַתָּה] the words are regarded by many as standing in the same relation to each other as the following הָרִיב רָב אם נִלֹחֹם נִיחֹם, the first טוב being inf. absol., the second, participle.¶ So Schm.; Roorda, § 565; Ew. § 312 a; SS. There is no similar case (Roorda); and we should perhaps have to suppose that the bold and unusual construction was suggested by the analogy of the following clauses. Others take both words as adjectives, the reiteration being emphatic, *art thou so much better* (Ges.²⁵ § 133, 1 n.; Green, § 296, 3 a). The analogy of the following clauses may be recognized also in this explanation. It is not to be assumed that the writer was conscious of the grammatical difference which we make between adj., ptcp., and inf. abs.; for him טוב was טוב. — 𝕲ᴮᴺ μὴ ἐν ἀγαθῷ ἀγαθώτερος σὺ ὑπὲρ Βαλακ (= 𝕸): 𝕲ᴬᴾⱽᴸᴹᴼ ς τ Θ μὴ κρείσσων εἰ σὺ κ.τ.ἑ. It is possible that the repetition of טוב is due to a scribe, rather than to the author. — הָרִיב רָב] ריב is a controversy about rights; cf. 12². — אם נִלֹחֹם נִלֹחֹם] the inf. abs. formed from the perf. stem, Sta. § 626 c; used

<hr/>

* Cushan-rishathaim (3⁸), 8; Othniel (3¹¹), 40; Eglon (3¹⁴), 18; Ehud (3³⁰), 80; Jabin (4³), 20; Deborah (5³¹), 40; Midianites (6¹), 7; Gideon (8²⁸), 40; Abimelech (9²²), 3; Tola (10²), 23; Jair (10³), 22 = 301; Ammonites (10⁴), 18; total, 319. The years of Joshua and the survivors of the generation of the conquest (2⁷) are not taken into the account.

† The alternative is to suppose that 300 is a round number, the coincidence of which with the sum of the years in the present chronology is purely accidental, — a very improbable hypothesis.   ‡ 𝕰, Stud., Be.

§ 𝕸 (accents) 𝕾, Schm., Ke., Kitt., al.; cf. Cler.

∥ On Yahweh as judge, see Smend, *Alttest. Religionsgeschichte*, p. 99 ff., esp. p. 103 f.   ¶ Cf. 16²⁵.

with the perf. on account of the assonance; Bö. § 985, 1; 988, 2 *b*. —
26. ערעור '] elsewhere ערער (Mesha, l. 26, Nu. 2³⁶ and uniformly in the Pentateuch), or ערוער (*e.g.* Jos. 13²⁵); see Frensdorff, *Massoret. Wörterb.*, p. 314;
Norzi, *ad loc.* The name seems to be an internal plural. On the etymology,
see Lagarde, *Semitica*, i. p. 30. — עד ידי ארנון ר'] more commonly ידי ר', Ex. 2⁶
Nu. 13²⁹ Jer. 46⁶ Dan. 10⁴ (streams, cf. Dt. 2³⁷), Jos. 15⁴⁶ Ez. 48¹ (אי, cities);
adjacent to. Not, *on both sides of the Arnon* (Kitt.), which contradicts the whole
theory of the author, and is without support in usage; cf. Nu. 34⁸. — 𝕲ᴬᴹ ε ἐν
Εσεβων . . . καὶ ἐν Ιαζηρ καὶ ἐν ταῖς θυγατράσιν αὐτῆς καὶ ἐν πάσαις ταῖς
πόλεσιν ταῖς παρὰ τὴν Ἰορδάνην. Other recensions have ἐν Αροηρ or ἐν γῇ
Αροηρ (ᴮ); ᴸ omits the clause altogether. *Juxta Jordanem* also 𝕷. — ובדין
הצדתם לא] 𝕲ᴮᴺ διὰ τί οὐκ ἐρρύσω αὐτούς.* The sing. *thou* has been used
throughout, and is intrinsically preferable here; we should therefore probably
pronounce הצרתכ (Stud.); the masc. suffix for the fem. is not infrequent;
here, if necessary, it might be explained as *ad sensum* for the people of the
cities. — בעת ההיא] *at that time;* 3²⁰ 4¹ 12⁶ 14⁴ 21¹⁴·²⁴, and frequently. There
is no instance in the O.T. in which the phrase approaches the sense, *during
all that time.* This gives considerable support to the hypothesis advanced
above on other grounds, that *three hundred years* is an interpolation. —
27. וישבט יהוה השפט היום] the accents indicate that היום is to be taken with the
principal verb (against Be.).

28, 29. The king of Ammon pays no heed to Jephthah's representations. The spirit of Yahweh comes upon the champion,
and he leads against the foe. In v.²⁹ the redactor endeavours to
recover the thread of the narrative, which is broken by the long
interpolation, v.¹²⁻²⁸. — **29.** *The spirit of Yahweh*] see on 3¹⁰, and
cf. 14⁶·¹⁹ 1 S. 11⁶. — *He went over to Gilead and Manasseh, and
went over to Mizpeh of Gilead;* † *and from Mizpeh of Gilead he
went over to the Ammonites*] it is not possible to form any satisfactory notion of these movements or of their object. In v.¹¹
Jephthah was already in Gilead, and probably at Mizpah, where
he apparently still is in v.³⁴·; his setting out against the Ammonites is related in due course in v.³². In itself it is conceivable
enough that these journeys to and fro in Gilead and Manasseh
were for the purpose of raising the tribes for the war, ‡ though we
should expect some indication of the fact (cf. 6³⁵ 7²⁴ &c.); but
this cannot be the intention of the author of the chapter, according to whom the Israelites were already assembled (v.¹¹ᵃ cf. 10¹⁷).

---

* The other recensions of 𝕺 have ἐρρύσαντο (ᴹ ἐξείλαρτο).
† On the form *Mizpeh* see on v.¹¹, p. 289.   ‡ Be.

In short, v.² is a somewhat unskilful attempt to fasten the new cloth, v.¹⁹⁻²⁹, into the old garment.

30, 31. Jephthah's vow. — These verses should stand immediately after v.¹¹ᵃ; having been acclaimed chieftain by the people, Jephthah vows that if Yahweh will give him victory over the Ammonites, he will offer him a human sacrifice, v.³⁰·³¹; these fateful words were uttered *before Yahweh* at Mizpah, v.¹¹ᵇ cf. v.³⁵·³⁶. He then puts himself at the head of the people and marches against the Ammonites, v.³². The order has been deranged by the introduction of v.¹²⁻²⁹, and perhaps still further by the accidental consequences of the interpolation; see above on v.¹¹. — **30.** *Jephthah made a vow to Yahweh*] cf. Gen. 28²⁰⁻²² 1 S. 1¹¹ 2 S. 15⁷ᶠ. — **31.** *Whoever it may be that comes out of the door of my house to meet me, when I return successful from the Ammonites shall be Yahweh's, and I will offer him up as a burnt offering*] the original sequel of this verse is v.¹¹ᵇ: *And Jephthah spoke all his words before Yahweh at Mizpah.* — Quemlibet in hoc loco cogitaverit Jephte secundum cogitationem humanam, non videtur unicam filiam cogitasse; alioquin non diceret, cum illam cerneret occurrisse, Heu me, filia mea, impedisti me; in offendiculum facta es in oculis meis. . . . Sed quem potuit cogitare primitus occurrentem, qui filios alios non habebat? An conjugem cogitaverit?* — That a human victim is intended is, in fact, as plain as words can make it; the language is inapplicable to an animal, and a vow to offer the first sheep or goat that he comes across — not to mention the possibility of an unclean animal — is trivial to absurdity. It is not, therefore, a rash vow to sacrifice *whatever* first meets him,† for which he is punished,‡ but a deliberate one. See further on v.³⁹, and note at the end of the chapter.

32, 33. The war; defeat and subjugation of the Ammonites. — *Jephthah went over to the Ammonites to fight with them*] he took the aggressive, and, as appears both from the language here and from the next verse, invaded their territory. § — **33.** *He beat them from Aroer till you come to Minnith, twenty cities, and as*

---

* Aug., *quaest.* 49.
† Fl. Jos., *antt.* v. 7, 10 § 263, ὑποσχόμενος . . . πᾶν ὃ τι καὶ πρῶτον αὐτῷ συντυχοι ἱερουργήσειν.   ‡ Thdt.   § Fl. Jos.

far as Abel-keramim] the direction and extent of this victorious
advance cannot now be made out. *Aroer* cannot be the city of
this name on the Arnon (v.²⁶),* but "Aroer which is in front of
Rabbah" (Rabbah of Ammon), Jos. 13²⁵;† that is, as is generally understood, east of that city. *Minnith* is connected by
Eusebius with a village called in his day Maanith, four miles
from Heshbon on the road to Philadelphia;‡ for Abel-keramim
(Vineyard-meadow) he suggests a village Abel six miles from
Philadelphia, in what direction is not indicated.§ The situation
of Maanith does not suit the requirement of our text; we should
look for Minnith in Ammonite territory beyond Aroer, not in the
immediate vicinity of Heshbon. The other identifications proposed are not verifiable. — *Twenty towns*] summary account of
Jephthah's conquests; cf. Jos. 10⁴⁰ᶠ. But for these words, which
stand moreover in a somewhat suspicious place, we should take
the verse as a description of the battle. — *The Ammonites were
subjugated*] see on 3³⁰; cf. 8²⁸ 1 S. 7¹³.

29. עבר [ויעבר את הגלעד with acc. 'go over, pass, *to* a place,' 18¹⁸ cf. 12¹
Am. 5⁶ 6² Is. 23⁶ &c. (SS.). 'Pass *through*, traverse,' a region is עבר ב׳, 1 S. 9⁴
and often. — [עבר בני עמון] an anomalous expression. Like other verbs of
motion, when the goal is personal, עבר is construed with אל (ל׳), v.³² 12⁹ &c.
See Ges.²⁵ § 118, 2. The instances where the acc. is found (poet. and late;
cf. 1 S. 13²¹), only make it more probable that in our verse we have the language
of a comparatively late redactor. — 31. [היוצא אשר יצא] the cognate subject
appears to emphasize the indefiniteness (universality) of the promise, *Whoever it may be.* — [אשר יצא לקראתי is used only of persons; כדלתי ביתי would not
be said of domestic animals. — [והיה ליהוה והעליתיהו עלה] the last words explain
the first, which by themselves might be understood in the sense of 1 S. 1¹¹.
Moses Kimchi interpreted the second clause as an alternative, Shall be consecrated to Yahweh (if unfit for sacrifice), *or* (if suitable) I will offer it as a
burnt offering. See below, note on v.⁴⁰. — 33. The Ammonite Aroer is
named only here and in Jos. 13²⁵, ער ערוער אשר על פני רבה. The phrase על פני
in topographical notices generally means 'east of' (see on 16³). In 2 S. 24⁵
Aroer on the Arnon is meant; see We., *TBS.* p. 217, 221; Dr., *TBS.* p. 285 f.;
Di., *NDJ.* p. 514; so also Nu. 32³⁴ (against *DB².* i. p. 248). Nu. 21²⁴ ⑥,
they took all his [Sihon's] country, ἀπὸ Ἀροηρ ἕως Ἀρνων, is probably, like

---

* Stud.
† In this verse (P) it is allotted to Gad, which gets "half the country of the
Ammonites, as far as Aroer," &c. It was therefore an Ammonite town.
‡ *OS².* 280₄₄; cf. Fl. Jos. *l.c.*, Μανίθη. § Κώμη ἀμπελόφορος Ἀβελ, *OS².* 225₄.

מיר in 𝔐, an error for מיבק.—כְּיִית] in Ez. 27[17], *wheat of Minnith*, the text is corrupt; see Co. Buckingham's Menjah, 6 or 7 m. NE. of Hesbān on the road to 'Ammān, with which Kneucker (*BL.* s.v.) and others would identify Minnith, seems not to exist; see Tristram, *Land of Moab*, p. 155; *SEP. Memoirs*, and *Map*. Minyeh (Conder, *Heth and Moab*, p. 252) is much too far south.—אבל כרמים] Euseb. notes two other Abels, one 12 m. E. of Gadara (modern Abil), the other between Damascus and Paneas. Tristram (*Land of Moab*, p. 154 f.), supposing the battle to have been fought at the Moabite Aroer, on the Arnon, would recognize our Abel-keramim in the Kurm Dhibān, a mile or two east of Dhibān.

34-40. Jephthah's return; his meeting with his daughter; the fulfilment of his vow. — Jephthah returns in triumph. Among the women who celebrate the victory with choral dances his only daughter comes joyfully to meet him. The father is in despair, but he must keep his fatal vow. The maiden receives her doom in a heroic spirit; she is ready to die, since Yahweh has avenged her father of his foes; she only asks two months' respite to mourn her maidenhood. When they are over she returns, and Jephthah fulfils his vow. In her memory the women keep a four-days' festival every year. — **34.** *Jephthah came to his home at Mizpah*] from Mizpah he set out to the war, v.[11b. 32]. That he had a home there, we learn first from this verse; from v.[3-11a] we should not have suspected it. The two representations are not necessarily irreconcilable. — *There was his daughter, coming out to meet him*] the author depicts the scene with great vividness; cf. 4[22] 5[28f.]. — *With tambourines and choral dances*] as the women met David, 1 S. 18[6f.] (cf. 21[11] 29[5]), or as Miriam celebrated the overthrow of Egypt at the Red Sea, Ex. 15[20f.]. — *She was absolutely an only child; besides this one he had neither son nor daughter*] expressions are accumulated to emphasize the total bereavement which thus confronted him. — **35.** *He rent his garments*] a gesture of violent grief or mourning, Gen. 37[29] 2 S. 13[19. 31] Job 1[20] and often. — *Oh, my daughter, thou hast ruined me*] lit. *felled me*, as by a deadly blow; 2 S. 22[40] cf. Jud. 5[27]. — *Thou art become the author of my calamity*] with tragic emphasis, *Thou!* The translation of the English version, *Thou art one of them that trouble me*, is, at least for the modern reader, both feeble and misleading; the verb is one of the strongest in the language; cf. Gen. 34[30] Jos. 6[18] 7[25] 1 S. 14[29] 1 K. 18[17. 18]. — *Inas-*

*much as I have spoken a solemn word to Yahweh, and cannot go
back*] lit. *have opened my mouth wide*, uttered a great and dread-
ful vow; cf. Job 35[16] Ps. 66[13]. With the last words compare
Am. 1[3] &c. — **36**. She feels her doom in her father's passionate,
though vague words, and answers with tragic heroism, So let it
be! Since it appears in v.[37] that she is fully aware of her fate,
although it has not been named, Budde conceives that, by
accident or design, part of the dialogue has been omitted between
v.[35] and v.[36]; the daughter must have asked the meaning of her
father's enigmatic speech, v.[35], and he must have given the explicit
answer.[*]   To me it seems, on the contrary, much more in accord
with the native art of the story-teller that he lets the situation and
a woman's quick presentiment suffice, without this prosaic explanation. — *My father*] all the pathos of the situation is in the
word. With a woman's tenderness and a woman's courage, she
strengthens him for what is before them both: Thou hast uttered
thy vow to Yahweh; do to me what thou hast vowed. Lit. *as it
hath proceeded from thy mouth;* Nu. 30[3]. The spoken word is
conceived as a real thing; cf. Is. 55[10f]. — *Since Yahweh hath
wrought for thee vengeance of thine enemies*] for such a victory
she is content to die. — **37**. She asks only a brief respite. — *Spare
me two months*] cf. 1 S. 11[3]. — *That I may go down upon the
mountains and weep because of my maidenhood*] mourn that my
young life is cut off in its flower. — **38**. Jephthah grants her
request, and sends her away for two months, which she spends
with her companions in mourning, among the mountains. —
39. When the time was up, she returned to her father. — *And he
did to her what he had vowed to do*] v.[31b]. The reserve of the
writer, who draws the veil over the last act of the tragedy, has
been abused by the rationalistic interpreters who choose to
imagine that he did something altogether different from what
he had vowed; see note below. — *She not having known a man*]
circumstantial clause; she died a virgin, Gen. 24[16] &c. To connect and translate, *He did to her what he had vowed, and she did
not know a man*, that is, remained unmarried for the rest of her
life,[†] is ungrammatical;[‡] if the writer had meant this he must

---

[*] *Richt. u. Sam.*, p. 126.   [†] DKi., Cler., Kö., al. mu.   [‡] Be., Bu.

have written the last clause differently. On the history of interpretation see note below, p. 304 f. — **40.** It became the custom for the Israelite women to observe annually a four days' mourning for Jephthah's daughter. — *To lament*] this interpretation, which is that of the ancient versions,* suits the construction and context better than, *commemorate, celebrate*, which most modern commentators adopt.

34. וְהִנֵּה] cf. 1 S. 9¹⁴ Ex. 4¹⁴ Gen. 24¹⁵. ⁴⁵ &c. הִנֵּה of unexpected coincidence; see on 4²². — תֹף] בְּתֻפִּים וּבִמְחֹלוֹת is a tambourine, used as an accompaniment of women's choral dances, Ex. 15²⁰ 1 S. 18⁶ (cf. Ps. 68²⁶ 150⁴), and on other festal occasions, Is. 5¹² 24⁸ &c. See Niebuhr, *Reisebeschreibung*, i. p. 180 f.; Lane, *Modern Egyptians⁵*, p. 366; *DB*. s.v. "Timbrel." On the dances see Spencer, *De legibus ritualibus*, l. iv. c. 4; Leyrer, *PRE²*. xv. p. 206-208; *DB²*. i. p. 703-705; Wetzstein, *Zeitschr. f. Ethnologie*, 1873, p. 285 ff.; cf. Delitzsch, *Hoheslied*, p. 170 ff. — וְרַק הִיא יְחִידָה] *ac tantum illa unigenita fuit.* Cf. Job 1¹⁶, וָאִמָּלְטָה רַק אֲנִי לְבַדִּי.—אֵין לוֹ סֵמֶנּוּ בֵּן וָבַת] the masc. suff. is perhaps to be explained as attraction to the following בֵּן, and is more probably from the hand of a scribe than of the author. ⑹ᴬᵛᴸᴹᴼ πλὴν αὐτῆς. The Massora notes six passages in which מֶמֶנּוּ is read where מֶמֶנָּה would be expected (סְבִירִין); see Norzi *ad loc.*, and Frensdorff, *Massoret. Wörterb.*, p. 255. — **35.** הַכְרֵעַ הִכְרַעְתִּנִי] Hiph. is here causative to Kal in the sense, 'sink down, collapse' (the knees giving way) under a blow or wound, 5²⁷ 2 K. 9²⁴; hence, *strike down*, prostrate, lay low, not *bring low, i.e.* humble (EV.). The identity of the consonants with those of the following עָכַר, in which we may recognize an intentional paronomasia, has led to considerable confusion in the versions. — הָיִיתָ בְּעֹכְרָי] not, *one of those who*, but, *as, in the character of, one who brings disaster on me;* cf. Ps. 118⁷ 54⁶ Ex. 18⁴, Ges.²⁶ p. 366; Roorda, ii. p. 204 f. It may be questioned whether the punctuation, which makes the ptcp. plural, is correct; cf. Ex. 18⁴ with Ps. 118⁷. — בְּעֹכְרָי] Ez. 2⁸ Nu. 16⁹⁰ Dt. 11⁶ Gen. 4¹¹. — **37.** הֶרְפֵּה מִן סֵל] Dt. 9¹⁴, הִרְפֵּה לְ 2 K. 4²⁷ 1 S. 11³. — רֵעִיתִי] corrected by the Qerē to רֵעוֹתַי as in v.³⁸. The Kethīb would be pronounced רֵעִיי, cf. רֵעְיָתִי Cant. 1⁹ &c. (°רעיה); Sta. § 192 b. — **38.** שְׁנֵי חֳרָשִׁים] cf. שֶׁנֶה חֳרָשִׁים v.³⁰. — **39.** וְהִיא לֹא יָדְעָה אִישׁ] the pronoun shows that this is not the consequence of the preceding: *He did to her as he had vowed, and* (consequently) *she did not know a man,†* for which we should have simply וְלֹא יָדְעָה אִישׁ, but an additional circumstance. — וַתְּהִי חֹק וְגו'] should be joined to the following verse. The false division may be due to an interpretation such as that appended in some copies of ⑹. — **40.** מִיָּמִים יָמִימָה] *from year to year;* 21¹⁹ 1 S. 1³ 2¹⁹ Ex. 13¹⁰, cf. above on 11⁴. — לְהַנּוֹת] ⑹ θρηνεῖν; similarly all the ancient versions Ra., al. D. Kimchi, in conformity with his theory of solitary confinement, interpreted, *to talk with, and console her;* similarly

---

* So also Lth., AV., al.　　　　† Cler., al.; recently, Kö.

RLbG., Abarb., Drus., Cler., al.　Tanch. explained, after Arab., *celebrate*, *praise* (see note above on 5[11]); so Stud., Be., Ke., Cass., Oettli, RV., al. mu. The construction with ל is not favourable to this, and there is also a phonetic difficulty in the equation.　It is better to abide by the exegetical tradition, supported by the construction and the indications of the context, than to follow the guidance of a very dubious etymology.

Jephthah's vow. — On the history of interpretation see especially Reinke, *Beiträge zur Erklärung des Alten Testamentes*, i. p. 419 ff.; Köhler, *Bibl. Geschichte*, ii. 1. p. 100 f.; the older literature also in Pfeiffer, *Dubia vexata*, cent. ii. *locus* 60; *Exercitationes biblicae, exerc.* 7; Dresde, *Votum Jephtae*, 1767; ° cf. a Lapide *ad loc.* — The older Jewish and Christian interpreters, without exception, understood the words in their plain and natural sense; Jephthah fulfilled his vow by offering his daughter as a burnt-offering.　See for the former, Fl. Jos., *antt.* v. 7, 10 § 263-266; *Taanith*, 4[a]; ℭ *in loc.*; *Beresh. rab.* § 60, and parallels; *Yalqut*, ii. § 68; Ra.　So of the Fathers, Orig., Chrysost., Greg. Naz., Thdt., Procop., Ambros., August., Hieron., Epiph., Ephrem Syr., al.; ° followed by Beda, Hugo Victor, Th. Aquinas, and the scholastic exegesis generally; see a Lap., *ad loc.*　The notion that she was not offered in sacrifice, but shut up in a house by herself, where she lived and died unmarried, appears first, so far as I am aware, in the Kimchis (end of 12th cent. A.D.).　D. Kimchi's explanation was adopted by RLbG., Abarb., Sol. ben Melech; a Lyra, Arias, Vatabl., Jun., Drus., Cler., de Dieu, al. mu., many of whom suppose that she was dedicated to the service of the sanctuary in menial offices, and prohibited to marry; see esp. Cler.　The sound exegetical sense of Luther rejected these rationalistic subterfuges; in the marginal note on 11[30] he writes:　Man will, er habe sie nicht geopfert, aber der Text steht klar da (Be.).　The literal interpretation is maintained by the Jesuit commentator Serarius, as well as by Seb. Schmid, Pfeiffer, al.; while L. Cappel modified it by the hypothesis that the necessary implication of the vow was, that if the first living thing which met him on his return was not sacrificable, it should be put to death as חרם, and that this was the fate of his daughter.†　The interpretation which resolves the sacrifice into a " spiritual burnt offering " has found expositors in modern times in Hengstenberg, Reinke, Auberlen, Cass., Köhler, König (*Hauptprobleme*, p. 74 f.), al.; see Be. *ad loc.*　On the other side are Vatke, Stud., Ew., Hitz., Oehler, Diestel, H. Schultz, Reuss, Nöld., Kue., We., Sta., Baudissin, Kitt., WRSmith, al. — A parallel from classical legend is the story of Idomeneus told by Servius on *Aeneid.* xi. 264: ‡ Idomeneus rex Cretensium fuit; qui, cum tempestate laboraret, vovit se sacrificaturum Neptuno de re, quae ei primo occurrisset, si reversus fuisset; sed casu cum ei filius primus occurrisset, quem cum, ut alii

---

* The texts of the Fathers are collected and commented on by Reinke, *op. cit.*
† *De voto Jephtae*, 1683; reprinted in *Crit. sacri*, on Jud. 11[30].
‡ Repeated with slight variations on *Aen.*, iii. 121.

dicunt, inmolasset, ut alii, immolare voluisset, ob crudelitatem regno a civibus
pulsus est. The story of Iphigeneia suggests itself to every one.* The annual
lamentation of the women of Gilead for Jephthah's daughter appears to
belong to a class of ceremonies, the original significance of which, often
disguised by the myth, is mourning for the death of a god,† and in many of
which evidence of primitive connexion with human sacrifices survives. In
the last respect the parallel with Iphigeneia is instructive; for Iphigeneia was
originally a name of Artemis Tauropolos, at whose festival at Brauron, and
afterwards at Athens, a human sacrifice was enacted, even to the point of
causing the blood to spirt from the victim's throat under the sacrificial knife.‡
At Laodicea on the Phoenician coast, the annual sacrifice of a stag was
regarded as a substitute for the more ancient sacrifice of a maiden.§ The
native goddess to whom the offering was made is identified by Pausanias
(iii. 16, 8), doubtless on this account, with the Brauronian Artemis. There
seems no good reason why we should not include the mourning for Jephthah's
daughter in this class. As in the case of Iphigeneia, the original significance
of the myth has been entirely lost in its translation into heroic legend. The
presence of this primitive mythical element in the story of Jephthah's daughter
does not strictly exclude the possibility that Jephthah himself and his victory
over the Ammonites, and even the sacrifice of his daughter, may be historical.
The latter, indeed, would give the simplest explanation of the way in which
the myth was translated into legend.

**XII. 1-7. Jephthah is assailed by the Ephraimites; he
defeats them in battle and cuts off their retreat.** — The
Ephraimites cross the Jordan, threatening dire vengeance upon
Jephthah because they were not called to join in the war against
the Ammonites (v.¹). Jephthah replies that the Gileadites in
their contest with Ammon had sought the aid of Ephraim in
vain; seeing that there was no help to be got from them, they had
hazarded unsupported an invasion of Ammon; why should the
Ephraimites now attack them? (v.²·³). He assembles his tribesmen and defeats Ephraim. The fugitives are intercepted in their
flight at the fords of the Jordan, and, being betrayed by a peculiarity of their speech, are slaughtered on the spot (v.⁴·⁶). Jephthah,

---

* Especially in that form of the legend in which Artemis demands Iphigeneia
as a victim in fulfilment of her father's vow, made in the year of her birth, to sacrifice the fairest thing that the year should bring forth (Eurip., *Iphig. Taur.* 18 ff.).

† Or for the abduction of the deity (Kore).

‡ Eurip., *Iphig. Taur.* 1449 ff., esp. 1458–1461; see Robert-Preller, *Griechische
Mythologie⁴*, p. 312 f.; Stoll, in Roscher, ii. p. 304 f.

§ Porphyry, *de abstin.*, ii. 56; see W. R. Smith, *Religion of the Semites*, p. 447 f.

after judging Israel six years, dies and is buried somewhere in
Gilead.

Wellhausen regards 12^{1-6} as secondary:* it comes too late,
since in 11^{34} Jephthah is already at home, and according to 11^{39} at
least two months have elapsed; the answer, 12^2, affirming that the
help of Ephraim had been sought and refused, does not accord
with ch. 11; the whole conduct of the Ephraimites, who had no
business on that side of the Jordan, and were not, as in 8^{1-3},
inflated by victory, is here without motive. The story is a mere
copy of 8^{1-3}, "originating with some one who did not comprehend
Gideon's conciliatory course, and wanted to give the arrogant
tribe a slap." That Jephthah had returned and dismissed his
forces is assumed by 12^4 also. The two months (11^{39}) make no
real difficulty: even if the Ephraimite invasion fell in that period,
the writer would finish the story of Jephthah's vow before relating
it. The resemblance to 8^{1-3} is obvious; but it is not evident that
12^{1-6} is a mere copy of 8^{1-3}, with a variation animated by dislike of
Ephraim.† The genuineness and historical character of the
verses are rightly defended by Kuenen, Budde, Cornill, and
Kittel. The *shibboleth* scene is too original to be attributed to a
"tendency" fiction, especially as it has nothing to do with the
supposed tendency. The exaggerated number of the slain is of
itself no reason for rejecting the whole story.

1. — *The Ephraimites were called out and crossed to Zaphon*]
Zaphon lay in the Jordan valley, on the eastern bank of the river,
near Succoth (Jos. 13^{27}); according to a passage in the Jerusalem
Talmud, it was the later 'Amathō, Amathūs, the modern Amateh,
a little north of the Zerqā (Jabbok), at the mouth of Wady er-
Rugeib; see on 8^5. ‡ Others, *passed northward*,§ which is unintelligible. — *Without calling us to go with thee*] 8^1. — *We will burn
thy house over thee*] 1 K. 16^{18} cf. Jud. 9^{49} 14^{15} 15^6. — **2.** *I and my
people were engaged in a contest, and the Ammonites oppressed us*

---

* *Comp.*, p. 229; so also Sta., *GVI.* i. p. 68.

† Kitt., *GdH.* i. 2. p. 72 n., on the contrary, thinks 8^{1-3} an imitation of 12^{1-6}; see
above, p. 216.

‡ So Stud., Ew., Ke., Cass., al. On Amathūs see Euseb., *OS².* 219_{71}; Reland,
Palaestina, p. 308, 559 f.; Burckhardt, *Syria*, p. 346.

§ So the ancient versions; older commentators; Be., al. mu.

sorely] so ⑤ ; in 狍 the second verb has been accidentally dropped ; see crit. note. — *I called upon you, but you did not deliver me from them*] Jephthah speaks, not in his own name, but in that of his people, Gilead, to which the pronouns refer; cf. 11[12, 27]. No such request is narrated in ch. 11, but the narrative there certainly does not exclude it. An unsuccessful attempt to get help from their stronger neighbours across the Jordan may very well be supposed to have preceded the mission of the elders of Gilead to recall Jephthah, with which the story of Jephthah begins. There was no occasion for mentioning such an attempt in that connexion. — **3.** *And when I saw that thou wouldst not deliver, I took my life in my hand*] 1 S. 19[5] 28[21]; cf. Jud. 9[17]. — **4.** *So Jephthah collected all the men of Gilead*] they had returned to their homes after the defeat of the Ammonites ; the threatening move of Ephraim, therefore, did not follow at once upon Jephthah's victory. It is otherwise in 8[1], where the whole situation is different. — *And the men of Gilead beat Ephraim*] the rest of the verse is wholly unintelligible. The current interpretation is fairly represented by RV.: " Because they (the Ephraimites) said, Ye are fugitives of Ephraim, ye Gileadites, in the midst of Ephraim, and in the midst of Manasseh." * They were not a tribe, but a crew of runagate Ephraimites ; they had no tribal lands of their own, but lived by sufferance in the territories of Ephraim and Manasseh. This insult so exasperated the Gileadites that they followed up their victory with signal vindictiveness.† Neither the language nor the facts, however, allow this interpretation. The word rendered *fugitive* does not mean *runagate*, but *survivor*, one who escapes from a disastrous battle or the like peril, as in v.[5]; nor had the extraction or the situation of Jephthah's countrymen any resemblance to that with which they are supposed to be taunted. The origin of the corruption was the accidental repetition of a clause from v.[5]. ‡

1. ויעבר צפונה] acc. of place to which, after עבר; cf. 11[29]. Cf. צפון Gen. 46[16], צפיון Nu. 26[15], son (clan) of Gad. ⑤[APVLMO] ß ç take צפונה as a proper name (Σεφεινα, &c.). ⑤[BN] 'ΑΣΘ εἰς βορρᾶν. — 2. איש ריב הייתי] party to a controversy, quarrel; whether the one assailed (Jer. 15[10]) or the assailant (Is. 41[11]

* So, virtually, 𝕃, al. mu.

† So, *e.g.*, Ew., *GVI.* ii. p. 455; Be., Ke., Cass., Oettli; cf. Ki.   ‡ We.

Job 31[35]).— וכני קטון מאר] might perhaps be explained as concomitant object. 𝕲ᴬᴾⱽᴸᴹᴺᴼ ς e καὶ οἱ υἱοὶ Αμμων ἐταπείνουν με σφόδρα = בני קטון קטוני מאר; the verb might easily be omitted by a scribe after קטון. So Semler, Doorn., Bu. — וקע זק] וָאֶזְעַק אֶרְכֶם c. acc., 'call one,' Neh. 9[28]; the construction is however so unusual that it is probably better, with 𝕲 (except ᴮ), to read אליכם; or to pronounce וָאַזְעֵק (Hiph.), *I tried to call you out.* — 3. ואשיבה] Ven¹., Norzi, Baer; cf. JHMich. The form ואיבה in the received text (Ven².) is probably a mere blunder.—4. כי אמרו פליטי אפרים אתם וני] in ς the second half-verse is asterisked, as a hexaplar addition to the LXX,[*] and the entire half-verse is lacking in 𝕲[58 64 75]. The other codd. of the same recension (ᴹ, codd.[54 59 82 108 128 134]) omit from כי אמרו to the end of the verse. The words כי אמרו פליטי אפרים were copied out of place from v.[5]; ארם was necessarily added to complete the structure of the clause. The origin of the rest of v.[4b] is not so obvious: the asyndeton בתוך אפרים בתוך כנסה suggests that the latter is a correction of the unintelligible, *in the midst of Ephraim.*

5. The Gileadites seize the fords of the Jordan to cut off the flight of the routed foe; 3[28] 7[24]. — *And when the fugitives of Ephraim would say, Let me cross*] those who escaped from the field of battle tried singly to slip across the fords, but found them occupied by the enemy. To their challenge, *Art thou an Ephraimite?* they answered, *No;* but fell unsuspectingly into the trap which the Gileadites set for them. — **6.** *Then say s h i b-bóleth, and he said sibbóleth*] the meaning of the word ('ear of grain,' Gen. 41[5ff.] &c.; or, perhaps more probably, 'flood' in a stream, Ps. 69[3] Is. 27[12] †) is of no moment; any other word beginning with *sh* would have served as well.‡ So in the Sicilian Vespers, March 31, 1282, the French were made to betray themselves by their pronunciation of *ceci e ciceri;* those who pronounced *c* as in French (*sesi e siseri*) were hewed down on the spot.§ When the revolt against the French in Flanders broke out, May 25, 1302, the gates were seized, and no one allowed to pass who could not utter the — to a French tongue unpronounceable — *scilt ende friend?* ‖ — *And did not pronounce it exactly right*] lit. *fix.* He did not succeed in getting it right. Others explain, *did not take heed,* pay attention, comparing the idiom, 'fix

---

[*] In the only copy of ς which is known, the asterisk is wrongly placed *before* Ephraim 1°; the necessary correction is made by Roerdam and Lagarde. Probably it originally stood after the Ephraim 2°; cf. cod.⁵⁴ &c.　　† Ra., Ki., al.

‡ Ki. supposes that they actually used other words; this is but a typical instance.　　§ Be.　　‖ Cass.

the mind' on something. — Those whose tongues thus bewrayed them were cut down at the fords. — *There fell of Ephraim at that time forty-two thousand men*] cf. 3³⁰. In the battle and the flight; the numbers are doubtless much exaggerated, cf. 8¹⁰.

6. The LXX understood שבלת to be a password or countersign (σύνθημα, see Schleusner, *s.v.*); this interpretation is most fully expressed in 𝔊ᴹ, καὶ ἔλεγον αὐτοῖς Εἴπατε δὴ σύνθημα καὶ λέγοντες σύνθημα οὐ κατηύθυναν τοῦ λαλῆσαι οὕτως, κ.τ.λ.; see Thdt., who is guided by the Syriac to the correct explanation. 𝔊ᴮ 'A, al. translate στάχυς. The Greek had no way of reproducing the distinction of sounds represented by שׁ and ס, the former of which appeared to Roman (and doubtless to Greek) ears peculiarly barbarous; see Jerome, *de nominibus hebr.* (iii. 15, ed. Vallarsi; *OS²*. 10₆). What the peculiarity of the Ephraimites' pronunciation was, we can of course not know; [*] still less should we make this verse the basis of extensive inferences about Hebrew dialects. — ולא יכין ידבר כן] is referred by many recent comm. to the idiom הכין לב ל 2 Chr. 12¹⁴ 19³ 30¹⁹ Ezra 7¹⁰, with ellipsis of לב (Stud., Ges. *Thes.*, al.), but the phrase itself does not seem to be old, and the alleged examples of the ellipsis (1 S. 23²² 1 Chr. 28² 2 Chr. 29³⁶) may be better explained in other ways. The impf., which must be taken as frequentative, is singular in the series of narrative tenses. Perhaps we should emend ולא יָכֹל; in that case we should render כן *thus*, *i.e.* as the Gileadites pronounced it to them. — שחט] of human beings, 1 K. 18⁴⁰ 2 K. 10⁷·¹⁴ Jer. 41⁷ &c.; often of human sacrifices, Ez. 23³⁹ Is. 57⁵.

7. *And Jephthah judged Israel six years, and he died and was buried*] the formula is the same with which the notice of each of the Minor Judges is brought to a close; 10²·⁵ 12¹⁰·¹²·¹³, cf. also 15²⁰. Considerable weight has been laid upon this fact in some theories of the chronological system and composition of the book; see Introduction, § 4, 7.† In the notice of Jephthah's burial place there is evidently some corruption of the text. 𝔐 reads, *in the cities of Gilead* (in *one of* the cities of Gilead, ‡ is quite impossible); 𝔊 and 𝔏 render, *in his city, Gilead*, or, *in his city in Gilead*; 𝔖, *in a city of Gilead*. Studer conj., *in Mizpah of Gilead* (11²⁹), Jephthah's city (11³⁴).

7. וייקבר בערי גלעד] 𝔊 ἐν τῇ πόλει αὐτοῦ Γαλααδ (ᴮ ἐν πόλει αὐτοῦ ἐν Γαλααδ) 𝔏 *in civitate sua Galaad.* Cf. 8ᴴ בעירו בעפרה. Gilead, however, is not a city, but a country. Stud. conj. כמצפה גלעד 11²⁹; this may perh. find

---

[*] See J. Marquart, *ZATW.* viii. 1888. p. 151-155.

[†] See Nöld., *Untersuchungen*, p. 190 ff., who reckons his 6 years with the Minor Judges; Kue., *HCO².* i. § 18, n. 7; Bu., *Richt. u. Sam.*, p. 135; Kitt., *GdH.* i. 2. p. 12 f.   [‡] Ki., Drus., EV., al. mu.

some support in 𝕲ᴹ ἐν τῇ πόλει αὐτοῦ ἐν Σεφε (al. Σεφ) Γαλααδ * (representing a Hebrew text in which the כ of כסם was already lost, not mutilation in Greek of Μασσηφα). Perhaps the original text had only בעירו *in his city;* the name נירי might easily be derived from רגירי (cf. v.¹⁶), or כסם from 11²⁹; cf. also 1 S. 28². A literal translation of 𝔐, *in the cities of Gilead,* has given rise to the Midrash that Jephthah died by inches, by the sloughing off of his limbs (as in elephantiasis, Arab. *ǵuḏ̣ām*), which were buried where they fell; *Bereshith rab.,* § 60.

8–15. The Minor Judges; Ibzan, Elon, Abdon. — See introduction to 10¹⁻⁵.

8–10. Ibzan. — 8. *And there judged Israel after him*] cf. 10², "There arose after him and judged Israel." Through this verse the following series of Minor Judges is annexed to the story of Jephthah, as in 10¹ the former series to that of Abimelech. This is doubtless the work of the late editor who inserted the Minor Judges in the book ; see Introduction, § 6. — *Ibzan of Bethlehem*] probably not Bethlehem in Judah,† but Bethlehem in Zebulun (Jos. 19¹⁵), now Beit Laḥm, about seven miles WNW. of Nazareth, and a somewhat less distance west of Ṣaffūrieh.‡ The other judges of this group, as well as all those whose stories are told in the preceding chapters, belong to Israel ; apart from the story of Othniel, Judah first appears incidentally in the story of Samson. The name Ibzan occurs nowhere else. — 9. *He had thirty sons, and he sent out thirty daughters*] married them into other families. — *And brought in from outside thirty daughters* (as wives) *for his sons*] this is most naturally interpreted, as in the case of Jair (10¹⁻⁵), of a clan with numerous branches and offshoots and many connexions with other clans. — *He judged Israel for seven years*] 10²; cf. 12⁷ 15²⁰.

11, 12. Elon. — The standing form in which the notices of the Minor Judges are cast appears here in its simplest terms ; it contains nothing besides the name of the judge, his origin, burial place, and the length of his rule. See above, p. 270. — *Elon the*

---

* Fl. Jos., v. 7, 12 § 270, θάπτεται ἐν τῇ αὐτοῦ πατρίδι Σεβεη (Lat. *Sebethi*).

† Jewish tradition ; *Baba bathra,* 91ᵃ ; *Yalqūṭ* on Jud. 3 (ii. § 42) ; Ra. (Ibzan is the same as Boaz).

‡ Seetzen, *Reisen,* ii. p. 139; Rob., *BR².* iii. p. 113; Guérin, *Galilée,* i. p. 393 f.; *SWP. Memoirs,* i. p. 270.

Zebulonite died, and was buried at Elon, in the land of Zebulun]
Elon is a son of Zebulun, Gen. 46[14], *i.e.* a Zebulonite clan, Nu. 26[26].
The distinction made in $\mathfrak{M}$ between the name of the hero and
that of his burial place (seat of the clan) is artificial; cf. $\mathfrak{G}$.[*]
The place is otherwise unknown.

13-15. Abdon. — The last of the Minor Judges is Abdon ben
Hillel, of Pirathon in Ephraim.   Pirathon was the home of one
of David's heroes, Benaiah the Pirathonite; 2 S. 23[30] 1 Chr. 11[31]
27[14]; the name occurs also 1 Macc. 9[50], Fl. Jos. xiii. 1, 3 § 15, in
a list of places fortified by Bacchides.   It is generally identified
with Fer'atā, six miles WSW. of Nābulus (Shechem),[†] which
Conder and others take for Ophrah; see on 6[11]. — According to
v.[15], Pirathon was *in the land of Ephraim, in the hill-country of
the Amalekites*.   This is frequently combined with 5[14] (Ephraim,
whose root is in Amalek), and the presence of the name in this
part of Mt. Ephraim explained by supposing, either that the
region was an older seat of the Amalekites, from which they had
been expelled by the growing power of the Canaanites, or that in
the early part of the period of the judges Amalekites from the
south had intruded into this part of the highlands, and occupied
it long enough to fasten their name upon it, but had been driven
out again before the time of Saul.[‡]   Text and context in 5[14] are,
however, much too obscure to shed any light upon this verse.
The name Abdon is found in the genealogical tables of the
Chronicles, in Benjamin, 1 Chr. 8[23], 8[30] = 9[36].[§]   If Pirathon be
Fer'atā, this coincidence must be regarded as accidental.[‖]   But
Fer'atā seems to be too far north for the Pharathon of 1 Macc. and
Josephus; and perhaps we should rather be guided by Chr. to
look for Pirathon in Benjamin.   Ewald conjectured that for
Bedan, 1 S. 12[11], *Abdon* should be restored;[¶] but the more
probable correction is *Barak*.[**] — **14.** *He had forty sons and*

---

* See Nöldeke, *Untersuchungen*, p. 184.

† Eshtori Parchi, fol. 67[a]; Rob., *BR*[2]. iii. p. 134; Guérin, *Samarie*, ii. p. 179 f.

‡ See Ew., *GVI*. i. p. 359; Nöldeke, *Amalekiter*, p. 12; *BL.* i. p. 112. Nöld.
inclines to the latter hypothesis.

§ It is also the name of a town in Asher, Jos. 21[30] 1 Chr. 6[74]; read so also in
Jos. 19[28].   ‖ Nöld.   ¶ *GVI*. ii. p. 514; Nöld., *Untersuchungen*, p. 134.

** $\mathfrak{G}\mathfrak{S}$, Then., We., Dr., Klost., al.

thirty grandsons, who rode on seventy saddle asses] an evidence of wealth and rank; cf. 5¹⁰ 10⁴ 2 S. 16² 13²⁹; see on 10⁴. The numerous posterity is to be interpreted as in the case of Ibzan and Jair; cf. also 8²⁰.

8. אִבְצָן] compare אֶבֶץ, a town in Issachar, Jos. 19²⁰; the tradition of the name is however insecure; see 𝕲. — 10. אֵילוֹן] so also in v.¹²; with both ˙ and ו (same consonants as in בְּאֵילוֹן). So MSS. and edd., and so 𝕲 already read ('Αιλωμ, &c.).* Baer emends twice אֵילֹן on the authority of *Massora finalis* אַ²¹; but on this Massora see Frensdorff, *Massoretisches Wörterbuch*, 265, n. 6. — 12. אֵילוֹן] cf. אַיָּלוֹן and אֵילוֹן side by side, Jos. 19⁴². ⁴³ (in Dan; see on Jud. 1³⁵). In the present case there is good reason to believe that the names of the judge and of the town were originally pronounced, as they are written, alike; prob. Ēlōn, Gen. 46¹⁴ (Nöld., *Untersuchungen*, 184).

XIII.-XVI. The adventures of Samson.

LITERATURE.† — A. v. Doorninck, " De Simsonsagen. Kritische studiën over Richteren 14-16," *Th. T.* xxviii. 1894, p. 14-32.

1. *Samson's birth*, ch. 13. — The Messenger of Yahweh appears to the wife of Manoah and promises her a son. During her pregnancy she shall observe a strict regimen, for her son shall be a devotee from birth (13¹⁻⁷). At Manoah's prayer, the Messenger reappears and repeats his injunctions (v.⁸⁻¹⁴). He ascends to heaven in the flames of the sacrifice (v.¹⁵⁻²³). The child is born, grows up, and begins to be possessed by the spirit of Yahweh (v.²⁴⁻²⁵).

2. *Samson's marriage to the Timnathite, and what came of it;* ch. 14, 15. — Samson resolves to marry the daughter of a Philistine of Timnath (14¹⁻⁴). On one of his visits to Timnath he encounters a lion in the way, and kills him with his bare hands. Some time after, passing that way, he finds the carcass occupied by a swarm of bees, and takes the honey (v.⁵⁻⁹). At his wedding he propounds a riddle suggested by this adventure (v.¹⁰⁻¹⁴); by the aid of his wife the answer is discovered (v.¹⁵⁻¹⁸). In a rage he pays the forfeit, and rushes away without consummating the marriage (v.¹⁹⁻²⁰). When his anger has cooled off he returns, to find

---

* Cf. 1 *Ahialon*.

† For the older literature, see Reuss, *GAT.* § 106. On the mythical interpretation see below, note at the end of ch. 16.

that his bride has been given to another (15^{1-3}). He avenges himself by letting loose foxes with fire brands tied to their tails among the grain fields of Timnath. The Philistines burn the woman and her father as the authors of the mischief ($v.^{4-6}$). Samson retaliates, and takes refuge in a rocky fastness of Judah. The men of Judah deliver him bound to the Philistines, but he breaks the ropes and, with an ass's jaw-bone, slays a thousand Philistines ($v.^{7-17}$). The spring in Lehi ($v.^{18-20}$).

3. *Samson carries off the gates of Gaza;* 16^{1-3}. — Samson visits a harlot at Gaza. The Philistines lie in wait for him, but in the middle of the night he arises, pulls up the posts of one of the city gates, and, putting gate, posts, and bar on his head, carries them off to a hill near Hebron.

4. *Samson and Delilah;* 16^{4-31}. — Samson loves a woman of Sorek, named Delilah. She is bribed by the Philistines to find out the secret of his marvellous strength ($v.^{4f.}$). Thrice he deceives her; but at last, weary of her importunity, he tells her the truth ($v.^{6-17}$). The Philistines secure and blind him, and put him to grinding at a hand-mill in prison ($v.^{16-22}$). At a great feast of Dagon he is brought into the temple to gratify the multitude. With a return of his old strength, he overthrows the principal pillars which support the roof, and brings the whole temple down in ruins, perishing with the Philistines ($v.^{23-31}$).

The adventures of Samson differ markedly from the exploits of the judges in the preceding chapters of the book. Ehud, Deborah and Barak, Gideon, and Jephthah were leaders, who, at the head of their tribesmen, "turned to flight the armies of the aliens," and delivered their countrymen. Samson is a solitary hero, endowed with prodigious strength, who in his own quarrel, single-handed, makes havoc among the Philistines, but in no way appears as the champion or deliverer of Israel. It is easy to see why he should have been a favourite figure of Israelite folk-story, the drastic humour of which is strongly impressed upon the narrative of his adventures; but not so easy to see what place he has in the religious pragmatism of the Deuteronomic Book of Judges, or, indeed, in what sense he can be called a judge at all. Even the external connexion with the book is of the slightest character;

the familiar formulas with which the histories of the judges are introduced and concluded are here at their lowest terms (13^1 15^{20} 16^{31b}). In the narrative itself no trace of D's hand is detected.[*]

The three principal stories, ch. 13, 14 f., 16, are connected by more than one link, and probably belonged to a cycle of folk-tales long before they assumed a literary form. Ch. 14 presupposes ch. 13, and the catastrophe in ch. 16 turns upon the loss of his sacred locks; cf. esp. 16^{17} with 13^5. The stories of the cycle need not all be of equal age; it is not improbable, for instance, that the tale of his birth in ch. 13 is of later origin than the rest;[†] but, as we have them, they are in substance and form so similar that we must attribute them to the same writer.[‡] In ch. 13 and 14 a later hand has made some additions and alterations, by which, in ch. 14 particularly, the narrative is somewhat confused, nor is the text in other parts quite intact;[§] but there is no evidence that the redactor had more than one original source. In $15^{17. 19f.}$, where this might be suspected, the doublet may with greater probability be referred to the folk-story itself.[‖]

Böhme demonstrated that the language and style of ch. 13 have a strong resemblance to J in the Hexateuch;[¶] and to this source the whole group of stories of Samson is with considerable probability ascribed by Budde.[**] The reasons for thinking that this is the case lie not so much in particular expressions, as in the tone and spirit of the whole narration.[††] Whether from J or not, the chapters undoubtedly belong to the oldest stratum of the book. The tales themselves, which are, of course, much older than the

---

[*] From the position of the closing formula, 15^{20}, Budde and Cornill surmise that D omitted ch. 16, which was afterwards restored by another hand, just as was done in the case of Abimelech, ch. 9. See above, p. 234 f.

[†] Bu., *Richt. u. Sam.*, p. 131; cf. We., *Prol².*, p. 256 = *History of Israel*, 1885, p. 245; Doorn., *Th. T.* 1894, p. 17.   [‡] We., Kue., Bu.

[§] On the text, see Doorn.; Sta., *ZATW.* iv. 1884, p. 250 ff.; Bu.; Doorn., *Th T.* 1894, p. 14 ff.

[‖] So also Bu. On the attempts to analyze the story see Bu., p. 132 f.

[¶] *ZATW.* v. 1885, p. 261 ff.

[**] *Richt. u. Sam.*, p. 132 f. Against this opinion see Kue., *HCO².* i. p. 355 f.; Kitt., *Stud. u. Krit.*, 1892, p. 57 f.; *GdH.* i. 2, p. 16 f.; see above on 6^{11a}, p. 183 n. and Introduction, § 6.

[††] Bruston thinks that in ch. 13 the narrative of the first Jehovist has been worked into that of the second Elohist, to whom all the rest of 13-16 belong. (Bu., p. 134 n.)

book, are almost the only specimens of their kind that have been
preserved; and they give us a glimpse of a side of old Israelite
life and character which is rarely represented in the Old Testament. The scrapes into which Samson's weakness for women
brought him, the way in which he turned the tables on those who
thought they had got the best of him, the hard knocks he dealt
the uncircumcised, and the practical jokes he played on them,
must have made these stories great favourites with a story-loving
race, such as all the Semites are; and the rude humour which
plays through them all, no less than the entire absence of moral,
proves them genuine tales of the people. What basis of fact the
stories may have, is not easy to tell. The name of the hero and
various traits of the story seem to invite a mythical explanation,
and many attempts have been made to resolve the whole into a
solar myth. Other parts of the story, however, are refractory, and
can only be translated as myth by the most ingenious arbitrariness.
On this question see note at the end of ch. 16.

XIII. Samson's birth. — 1. The usual introduction by the
Deuteronomic author; see on 3¹². — **2.** *There was a certain man
of Zorah, of the clan of the Danites, whose name was Manoah*]
from Zorah and Eshtaol, which is almost always named with it,
came the Danites who, migrating to the north, established themselves at the sources of the Jordan (Laish-Dan), 18². ⁸. ¹¹. In Jos.
19⁴¹ it is assigned to Dan (on its border), but in 15³³ to Judah;
it was fortified by Rehoboam (2 Chr. 11¹⁰). It is the modern
village of Ṣur'ah, on the northern side of Wady eṣ-Ṣurār, opposite
'Ain Shems (Beth-shemesh) on the southern; see on 1³³.* — *The
clan of the Danites*] 18¹¹. ¹², cf. 17⁷, the clan of Judah. On the
original settlements of Dan, see on 1³⁴. ³⁵; and on the history of
the tribe, and the relation between the story of Samson and that
of the migration of the Danites (ch. 18), see on 18¹. *Manoah*,
only in this and the following chapter. The more picturesque
details with which Josephus embellishes his story are supplied by

---

* Euseb. (*OS²*. 293₂₉) locates it ten miles from Eleutheropolis on the road to
Nicopolis. It was recognized by Eshtori Parchi (fol. 69ᵃ); Rob., *BR².* iii. p. 153,
cf. ii. p. 12, 17; Guérin, *Judée,* ii. p. 15-17; *SWP. Memoirs,* iii. p. 158; Bädᵈ., p. 163;
see map of the territory of Dan, *DB²*. i. p. 701, and cf. above, p. 53 f.

his imagination.* — *His wife was barren and had not borne children*] cf. Gen. 11[30]. So the mother of Samuel (1 S. 1[?]), and of John the Baptist (Luke 1[7]); in the patriarchal story, Sarah, Rebekah, Rachel. The child of a long unfruitful marriage is in a peculiar sense the gift of God, and his birth portends some greater purpose of God for him.

2. *Zorah* was resettled by the *Golah* after the return from the exile, Neh. 11[29]; the Manoahites of Zorah (observe the preservation of the name) traced their origin, in part through Shobal, in part through Salma, to Calebite clans; 1 Chr. 2[52-54].† — [ויהי איש אחד] 1 S. 1[1] 2 S. 18[10] Jud. 9[53]; see We., *TBS.* p. 26, 34; Dr., *TBS.* p. 1; and especially Roorda, § 480 n., who rightly discriminates the case before us from others with which it is frequently confounded. — [משפחת הדני] 18[2. 11. 19] (by the side of שבט 18[1. 19]; see there); cf. משפחת בית לוי 17[7] (in Jos. 7[17] כי יהודה is error for שבט), Zech. 12[18]. משפחה is properly the clan, a number of which make the tribe; it is itself composed of a number of families (בית אב), 1 S. 10[21] Jos. 7[14].

3–7. The Messenger of Yahweh announces Samson's birth.

— The Messenger of Yahweh appears to Manoah's wife and announces the birth of a son. During pregnancy she shall abstain from wine and things unclean; for the child is to be a devotee from the womb, no razor shall ever touch his head. He shall be the first to deliver Israel from the Philistines (v.[3-5]). She relates the occurrence and the words of the Messenger to her husband (v.[6f.]). — The whole scene strikingly resembles in conception and expression the visit of the Messenger of Yahweh to Gideon (6[11f.]), and is naturally attributed to the same author.‡ The story has been slightly retouched in places by a later hand, but not so much changed as ch. 14.§

3. *The Messenger of Yahweh*] see on 2[1] 6[11]. — *Behold, thou art barren and hast not borne*] v.[?]. The following words, *and thou shalt conceive and bear a son*, by their awkward anticipation of v.[5a], and by the different grammatical structure, betray themselves as an interpolation. || — **4.** *Be careful, and do not drink wine and*

---

* *Antt.* v. 8, 1-3 § 275 ff.
† We., *Comp.*, p. 231; cf. also Be. *ad loc.* We. remarks the occurrence of Manahath ben Shobal in the Edomite lists also, Gen. 36[23].
‡ Stud., Böhme, Bu., al.
§ On the text see Böhme, *ZATW.* v. 1885, p. 261 ff.; cf. Bu., *Richt. u. Sam.*, p. 130. || Be., Böhme.

intoxicating drink] Heb. *shekar:* Sicera [*shekar*] Hebraeo ser-
mone omnis potio nuncupatur, quae inebriare potest ; sive illa quae
frumento conficitur ; sive pomorum succo ; aut quum favi deco-
quuntur in dulcem et barbaram potionem, aut palmarum fructus
exprimuntur in liquorem, coctisque frugibus, aqua pinguior cola-
tur.* When named with wine, as it often is, it includes all other
varieties of intoxicating drink ; v.[7. 14] 1 S. 1[15] Luke 1[15] ; cf. the laws
Lev. 10[9] (priests), Nu. 6[3] (Nazirites). See *DB²*. i. p. 812. — *And
not to eat anything unclean*] v.[7. 14]. The flesh of tabooed animal
kinds, carrion, and the like, is probably meant. The consecrated
child must be kept *in utero* from defilement. The rules for the
Nazirite, Nu. 6[1ff], contain no special prescription on this head,
which was covered by the general law (Dt. 14 Lev. 11). The
Jewish doctors, observing this, make *unclean* here equivalent to
prohibited to the Nazirite; that is, the other products of the vine,
Nu. 6[3f].† — Böhme thinks that these words (and the corresponding clauses in v.[7. 14]) are the addition of a later hand, which exaggerates the strictness of the regimen. As this is, however, not
suggested by the law in Nu. 6, nor by any other example, their
genuineness may with good reason be maintained. — **5.** *Thou art
with child, and wilt bear a son*] Gen. 16[11] (J) cf. Is. 7[14]. The
present is taken by many as an immediate future, *thou art about
to conceive,* ‡ but this is unnecessary, and, in view of Gen. 16[11],
less probable. — *A razor shall not be used on his head*] 16[17]
1 S. 1[11] Nu. 6[3] (different expressions). — *For the boy shall be a
devotee from the womb*] v.[7] 16[17] cf. 1 S. 1[11]. — *He will be the first
to deliver*] begin to deliver ; the verb is used as in 10[18] : Who is
the man who will be first to fight with the Ammonites. The words
have been taken to imply that Samson should only *begin,* but not
complete, the work of deliverance, § and Wellhausen would recognize an allusion to Saul ; ‖ but it is doubtful whether the writer
put so much reflexion into the word *begin;* cf. 13[25] 16[22]. — **6.** *A
man of God came to me*] v.[8] 1 S. 2[27] 9[6. 7. 8] &c. The Messenger
appeared as a man ; his words showed that he was an inspired
man ; in later phrase, a prophet. — *His appearance was like that*

---

* Jerome, *ep. ad Nepotianum,* c. 11 (*Opp.* ed. Vallarsi, i. 264). It includes, therefore, beer, cider, mead, date wine, &c.   † Ra., al.   ‡ So ⦿A al. ℔, EV., and many.
§ Ki. 2º, Schm., Drus., Rosenm., al.   ‖ *Comp.,* p. 231.

of the Messenger of God, very awful] inspiring awe and reverence, not terror; see Gen. 28[17] Ex. 34[10] &c. — **7.** She repeats to Manoah the words of the Messenger. — *From the womb to the day of his death*] this is implied, though not expressed, in v.[5].

3. והרית וילדת בן] 𝕲[BN] only καὶ συλλήμψῃ υἱόν. This is a fragment of a different translation from v.[5. 7] (ἐν γαστρὶ ἔχεις); the probable inference is that the LXX did not originally contain the words. — **4.** יכבר] see the passages from the Talm. and Midrash cited by Ki. *Lex.* s.v.; also Levy, *NHWb.* s.v. — טמא] of prohibited animal kinds, Dt. 14[8. 10. 19] Lev. 11[4. 5. 7] &c., of carrion (ונבלה, טרפה), Lev. 22[8] cf. Ex. 22[30]. — **5.** כי הנך הרה וילדת בן] v.[7] Gen. 16[11]. The pronunciation seems to be a compromise between ptcp. and perf., and is perhaps meant to hint to the reader that the ptcp. (which would be more usual after הנה) is to be understood in a future sense (perf. consec.); cf. 𝕲. So Ki., Kö. i. p. 404–406. The author prob. intended a perf. — ומרה לא יערה על ראשו] 16[17] 1 S. 1[11]; cf. Nu. 6[5] תער לא יעבר על ראשו. The etymology of מירה (masc., n. b.!), which occurs only in the stories of Samson and Samuel, is obscure. — נזיר אלהים יהיה] v.[7] 16[17]; *a religious devotee*. In ordinary cases the obligation of the *nazir* was assumed only for a certain period, which was terminated by a sacrifice of his hair at the sanctuary, Nu. 6[18]. In the light of similar practices in other religions, we may with great probability infer that this sacrifice was the original content of the vow. From the moment that it was assumed, the locks were consecrated and inviolable.[*] They were not merely the outward sign of the wearer's devotion, but, being themselves sacred, they consecrated him, and thus brought him under certain incidental prohibitions (taboos). That he must with peculiar pains guard against pollution by contact with death, is intelligible without further explanation. The Hebrew *nazir* had also to abstain from wine and intoxicating drinks, and from every product of the vine (cf. Jud. 13[14] Am. 2[11f.] Nu. 6[3f.]); compare the abstinence imposed on priests during their service, Ez. 44[21] Lev. 10[9]. In the case of Samson and Samuel the obligation was imposed for life by the mother's consecration of the unborn child, but this is signalized as something extraordinary, rather than the oldest form of the Nazirate (Ew., al.).[†] Such abstinences have nothing to do with morality. The commentators who have to prove Samson a blameless judge are much embarrassed by the Philistine women. Ki. (on v.[6]) imagines that he must have converted them. — נזיר

---

[*] Cf. Ez. 44[20]. On similar consecration of the hair see Spencer, *De legg. ritual.,* iii. *diss.* i. c. 6; Goldziher, "Le sacrifice de la chevelure chez les Arabes," *RHR.* xiv. 1886, p. 49–52, cf. x. p. 351 ff.

[†] On the Nazirate and similar vows see W. R. Smith, *Religion of the Semites,* p. 306 ff. (esp. 314 f.), 463 f.; cf. *Kinship and Marriage,* p. 152 ff.; Wellhausen, *Reste arabischen Heidentumes,* p. 118, 166 f.; Stade, *GVI.* i. p. 479, 388 f.; Smend, *Alttest. Religionsgesch.,* p. 152 ff.; Nowack, *Hebr. Archäologie,* ii. p. 133 ff. For the older literature see *DB[1]*. s.v.

אלהים] would be best represented by a compound word — if we had one — like Gottgeweihter. — מן הבטן [מן] from the womb on, *i.e.* from his birth; v.[7] *to the day of his death.* — יומת [והוא יחל להושיע ונ] cf. 2 K. 10[22] Jud. 13[25] 16[19. 22]. — 6. [איש האלהים] the particular one who came; idiomatic use of the article, Ges.[25] § 126, 4; see above on 7[18] 8[25]. — [כלאך האלהים] v.[9]; but כלאך יהוה v.[3. 13. 15. 16. 17. 20. 21]; cf. 6[20]. In v.[6] we might find a motive for the variation (cf. 2 S. 14[20]); but this explanation would not extend to v.[9]. More probably the substitution is accidental, due to the influence of the adjacent איש האלהים.

8-23. The second visit of the Messenger.

The Messenger returns at Manoah's request; the woman calls her husband, and to him the Messenger repeats his former prescriptions (v.[8-14]). Manoah invites him to stay and eat with them, but he declines, nor will he disclose his name (v.[15-18]). Manoah offers a kid upon the rock; as the flame rises, the Messenger ascends in it to the sky (v.[19-21]). Manoah fears death, for they have seen a god, but his wife reassures him; if Yahweh had meant to destroy them, he would not have accepted their sacrifice nor shown them such a portent (v.[22f.]). — 8. Manoah prays that the Messenger may come again and show them what they shall do about the boy that is to be born, how they shall treat him. — *Manoah besought Yahweh*] the somewhat unusual verb occurs in the Hexateuch only in J. — 9. *And God hearkened to the words of Manoah*] God twice (as in v.[6]), instead of Yahweh as constantly in what follows; perhaps occasioned in all cases by the preceding, *man of God.* There is no reason to suspect that the variation has any critical significance; see note on v.[6]. — 10. The woman calls her husband. — *The man who came to me the other day has appeared to me*] lit. *on the day* (on which he came). The Hebrew phrase is unusual; the versions generally render, *on that day;* see note. — 11. Manoah follows her to the field, and accosts the stranger, asking whether it was he who before spoke to his wife. — 12. *Now, if what thou sayest comes true, how shall the boy be brought up, and what shall he do*] what is the rule or regimen prescribed for him, and what shall his calling be; or, perhaps, his mode of life? — 13, 14. The Messenger does not answer Manoah's question further than to repeat his injunctions; the mother shall do exactly as she has been told; she shall not eat any product of the vine, drink wine or intoxicating drink, or eat anything unclean.

Böhme leaves to the author only the words, *wine and intoxicating drink she shall not drink;* the rest he regards as editorial amplification. In regard to the last clause (tabooed foods), see above on v.⁴. The other products of the vine are explicitly forbidden, Nu. 6³ᵗ⁻; they are not mentioned above in v.⁴ or v.⁷. The extension of the prohibition to everything that comes from the vine is no evidence of later date; the taboo doubtless from the beginning included the vine itself, as did that observed by the Rechabites,* or that imposed upon the Roman Flamen Dialis, who was not allowed even to walk under a trellised vine.† Nor is it conclusive against the genuineness of the words that they do not occur in v.⁴·⁷. It is not the author's manner to repeat himself with such notarial exactness; cf. the last clause of v.⁷ with v.⁴. — **15.** *Let me press thee to stay, and prepare before thee a kid*] pregnant expression, prepare and set before thee. Compare Gen. 18⁵ᶠᶠ·, and especially the story of Gideon, 6¹⁷ᶠᶠ·—**16.** *If thou press me, I will not eat of thy meat; and if thou wilt make a burnt offering, offer it to Yahweh*] the Messenger keeps up the character of a man of God (v.⁶). In the story of Gideon the Messenger lets him bring the food, and then converts it into an offering. In the patriarchal story, Gen. 18, Yahweh eats the meal which Abraham prepares. Compared with this, the behaviour of the Messenger of Yahweh in the stories of Gideon and Manoah seems to represent a more advanced stage of theological reflexion. We must, however, bear in mind that in Israel, as elsewhere, the intercourse of God with men was believed to have been more intimate and natural in the remote past; and need not, therefore, infer that Gen. 18 is older than Jud. 6 13. — *For Manoah did not know that he was the Messenger of Yahweh*] cf. Mark 9⁶ᵗ·. This cannot be the reason for the Messenger's reply, ‡ but for Manoah's invitation v.¹⁵ᵇ. § The words would then naturally stand before v.¹⁶ᵃ, ‖ and Böhme accordingly transposes v.¹⁶ᵃ and v.¹⁶ᵇ: Let us detain thee and prepare before thee a kid; for Manoah did not know, &c. And the Messenger of Yahweh said to Manoah, &c. The words are, how-

---

* Jer. 35⁶ᶠ·.
† Plut., *Quaest. Rom.*, 112; Aulus Gellius, x. 15, 13. For the explanation of this prohibition see W. R. Smith, *Religion of the Semites*, p. 465 f.; Frazer, *Golden Bough*, i. p. 183 ff. ‡ Schm. § Kl. ‖ Cf. Cler., Stud.

ever, even more apposite as an explanation of Manoah's request
to know the name of his visitor, v.[17] : *What is thy name, that when
thy word comes true we may honour thee* ; *for Manoah did not
know that he was the Messenger of Yahweh. And the Messenger
of Yahweh replied, &c.* In any case the clause is misplaced, and
this dislocation suggests that it is a comment, perhaps originally a
marginal gloss, rather than part of the original narrative.* —
17. *What is thy name, that when thy word comes true we may
honour thee*] cf. v.[12] and 1 S. 9[6] : The man is held in honour; everything that he says surely comes true. Manoah would know the
name of the man of God (as he supposes him to be), that he may
in the event render his due of grateful honour. — 18. *Why doest
thou inquire about my name, seeing it is ineffable*] cf. Gen. 32[29].
The name is incomprehensible; beyond your capacity to hear
and understand; cf. Ps. 139[6], Knowledge is beyond my capacity;
it is high above my reach. Not that the name itself is mysterious
or miraculous. Böhme regards the last clause as a gloss; but in a
gloss we should doubtless have a more commonplace phraseology.

8. ויחר פנוח אל יהוה] in the Hexateuch this verb occurs only in J (Gen.
25[21] &c.); cf. 2 S. 21[14] 24[25].—כי ארוני] see note on 6[18].—וייראנו] *advise
us;* give us a *tora* to go by.—הילד] ptcp. Pual; generally explained as
rejection of מ preformative (Ges.[26] § 52 end); more properly an alternative
form of the ptcp. without *m*; cf. Arab. *qatūl* and *maqtūl* (Ol. § 250 *e*; Sta.
§ 617 *b*; Lagarde, *Bildung der Nomina*, p. 63 f.). See in general, Kö. i.
p. 433 f. The indication of *ū* by ו to avoid ambiguity; cf. Jud. 18[29] Job 5[7].
— 9. והיא יושבת בשדה ובנוח אישה אין עמה] two circumstantial clauses, *she being
in the field, and her husband not with her.* — 10. ותהבר האשה ותרץ] the first
verb is a modifier of the second; the collocation may also be asyndetic; cf. 9[48]
&c.—בים] if the text is sound, we may compare the idiomatic uses of כים
and כהיום, We., *TBS.* p. 36 n. — 12. עתה יבא דבריך] cf. 1 S. 9[6]. For רבריך
(plur.) very many codd. and edd. of 𝔐 (De Rossi) with 𝕲𝕷𝕾 have the
sing. דבריך; in v.[17] this correction is made in the margin of 𝔐. The discord
in number between the verb and its subject is not impossible in Hebrew,
see Ges.[25] § 145, 7; but it is more probable that the plural is to be attributed to a scribe; see further on v.[17]. On the massoretic authority for the
plur. see Norzi. — 14. נפן היין] only Nu. 6[4]. — 15. נעצרה נא אותך] the word

---

* Stud. ingeniously justifies the position of the clause by assuming an intentional ambiguity in Manoah's invitation : We will set before thee a kid, or, we will
offer in thy presence a kid ; and finds a reference to this alternative sense in the
disjunctive reply of the Messenger.

Y

generally implies forcible restraint, and here elegantly expresses the urgency of the invitation to stay. — [ועשה לפניך ונ'] ךושה, dress and cook an animal, 6[19] 1 S. 25[18] Gen. 18[7.8] &c. Possibly, as Stud. thinks, there is an intentional ambiguity in the phrase here, as in כנוה 6[18], the writer meaning to hint at the sacrificial sense. — 16. [לא אכל בלחמך] Prov. 9[5]. More usual would be partitive מ:. — The comment of Thdt. on the response of the Messenger is: Τροφῆς, φησίν, οὐ δέομαι· θυσίαν οὐ δέχομαι. τοῦτο μὲν γὰρ θεοῦ, ἐκείνο δὲ τῆς ἀνθρωπίνης φύσεως ἴδιον. ἐγὼ δὲ οὔτε ὡς ἄνθρωπος χρῄζω τροφῆς, οὔτε τὴν θείαν ἁρπάζω τιμήν. — 17. [מי שמך] as the question is really about a person, who he is, the personal interrogative מי is used ad sensum; elsewhere כה שמך Gen. 32[29], מה שמו Ex. 3[13], grammatically regular; see Ew. § 325 a. — [ורנריך] Qerē (with 𝕾𝕷𝕾) רנרך sing., which many codd. and edd. have in the text; see De Rossi. The same correction is made in 1 K. 8[26] 18[36] 22[13] Jer. 15[16] Ps. 119[17.161] Ezra 10[13]; Ochla we-Ochla, No. 131. — 18. [והוא פלאי] regularly formed adj. from פלא; pronounce pil'i: the margin directs that it be read with suppression of א, pēli. Cf. the fem. פלאיה Ps. 139[6], unnecessarily altered by the Qerē. פלא is what surpasses human power or comprehension, and therefore excites wonder and admiration, Is. 29[14] 9[5] 25[1] Ex. 15[11] Pss.; see note on נפלאת 6[13]. 𝕾 renders here, והוא כפריש, which is of importance for the interpretation of שם המפרש in the Talmud, &c.

19. *Manoah took the kid and the cereal oblation, and offered it up on the rock to Yahweh*] the *cereal oblation* (*minḥah*) is probably added here and in v.[23] by a later hand, for the sake of liturgical correctness.[*] Cf. Gideon's cakes (*maṣṣoth*), 6[19-21]. — *The rock*] 6[20] (different word),[21]. The article probably indicates that it was a rock customarily used for the purpose, a natural monolithic altar; in v.[20] it is twice called *the altar*; see there. — The rest of the verse presents serious difficulties. The words, *while Manoah and his wife were looking on*, which recur in v.[20] and are beyond doubt original there, have probably been introduced in v.[19] by an accident of transcription.[†] The two words which remain defy every attempt to construe them grammatically. By a very slight emendation we obtain, *he offered it up on the rock to Yahweh, who worketh wonderfully*;[‡] cf. Ex. 15[11] Ps. 77[14]. The words would then refer, not to the portent which is described in v.[20], but to the predicted birth of a son. Such a special ascription to the "wonder-working Yahweh," by which the sacrifice bore the title of the occasion, would be in entire accord with ancient religion. The words have none of the marks of a gloss; the expression is far too

---

* Böhme.   † Ba.   ‡ 𝕾𝔄 al. 𝕷

characteristic and too difficult. * — 20. *As the flame ascended from the altar to the sky*] the scene so closely resembles that in the story of Gideon (6[21]) that there was a strong temptation to supplement the one narrative from the other,† as is done in all detail by Josephus here. ‡ Kimchi, for example, represents the fire as coming out of the rock and devouring the offering.§ Some modern critics have suspected that something of this purport originally stood in the place of the corrupt v.[19b]. ‖ But the stories, similar as they are, are nowhere exactly alike ; they are variations of the same theme, such as popular story-tellers delight in, not a pedantic repetition of it. In ch. 6 Gideon brings out food to his visitor, who bids him lay it on the rock, and then himself converts it into a burnt offering : here the Messenger declines the offered food, but suggests a sacrifice, which Manoah accordingly prepares and offers on the rock (the technical word implies not merely the placing of the victim on the rock, but the burning it) ; there is really no room in the story for a parallel to the bringing of the fire out of the rock in ch. 6. We have no reason, therefore, to think that the text is here abridged. — *The altar*] twice in the verse. Studer finds in the substitution of *the altar* for *the rock* (v.[19]) confirmation of the suspicion which, on other grounds, he entertains of the whole verse ; Böhme supposes that the altar was introduced by a later hand in the interest of liturgical correctness, and would restore in both instances, *the rock*. The possibility that the text has been thus altered is to be admitted (cf. 1 S. 14[34 35]) ; but the necessity of Böhme's emendation is not obvious. The kid was offered as a burnt offering on *the rock*, which therefore, whether usually or on this occasion only, served as an altar.¶ Why the author may not in the sequel have spoken of it under the latter name, I do not see. Indeed, one might perhaps discover in the very identification evidence of a primitive time. —*The Messenger of Yahweh ascended in the flame of the altar*] cf. the colourless interpolation in 6[21], end. —21. *And the Messenger of Yahweh*

---

* Against Be., Böhme.

† We have seen reason to think that 6[21b] is an interpolation of this kind from 13[20].

‡ *Antt.* v. 8, 3 § 283 f. It is to be noted that Josephus does not narrate Gideon's sacrifice at all.   § So also Schm., al.   ‖ Stud., Be.   ¶ Be.

did not appear again to Manoah and his wife] not, *was no longer
visible to them.* — *Then Manoah knew*] when he saw him ascend
in the altar flame ; cf. 6²¹, Gideon saw that he was the Messenger
of Yahweh when he brought the fire out of the rock. Böhme
regards the first sentence of this verse as an editorial addition ;
v.²¹ᵇ should follow immediately upon v.²⁰ᵇ . There is, however, no
manifest motive for the interpolation, while the author may have
thought it worth while to say that the Messenger, who had visited
them twice, did not return again. Probably, if we had been
writing the story, we should have put this sentence after v.²¹ ; but
the author preferred to finish what he had to say about the Messenger at this point. The old Hebrew writers did not always have
the same notions about good style that are entertained by modern
critics. — **22.** Manoah is greatly alarmed. — *We shall surely die,
for we have seen a god*] 6²² ; see comm. there. The word, *a god*,
conveys too much to us, but we have no other to translate it by.
The Hebrew *elohim* is used for any superhuman being ; cf. 1 S.
28¹¹, where the witch of Endor at the sight of Samuel's ghost
exclaims, " I see a god (*elohim*) rising from the earth." — **23.** His
wife reassures him. — *If it had been Yahweh's pleasure to kill us,
he would not have taken a burnt offering from us*] the words *and
a meal offering* are, as in v.¹⁹, probably of later insertion. By what
signs the acceptance of a sacrifice was recognized, we do not
know. — *And would not have showed us all these things, and
would not now have announced to us such a thing*] the first clause
refers to the appearance of the Messenger and his wonderful
departure ; the second to the promise of a son and the injunctions
connected with it. The order may be explained by the fact that
the most striking sight, the ascent of the Messenger in flame,
connected itself with the sacrifice. Böhme attributes both clauses
to editorial expansion. This appears to me possible as regards
the first (he would not have showed us all these things) ; but I
see no reason to doubt the genuineness of the last clause.

19. קל הצור [קל הצור] 6²¹; cf. הפליא 6²⁰ and note there. — וַיַּפְלִא לַעֲשׂות [לעשות] cannot by
any ingenuity be construed.* The conj. והוא מפליא לעשות (Maur.) gives us,
as Stud. rightly observes, a second circumstantial clause, which will not fit into

---

* Ewald's, *und es regt sich wunderbar,* is wholly inadmissible.

the context. 𝔊ᴬᴾⱽᴸᴹᴺᴼ ε s τῷ κυρίῳ τῷ θαυμαστὰ ποιοῦντι, 𝔏 *Domino mira-bilia facienti*, followed by 𝔏 *Domino, qui facit mirabilia*. The Greek translators therefore read, ליהוה הַמַפְלִיא לַעֲשׂות, which gives a satisfactory struc-ture and sense. 𝔊ᴮ (alone) καὶ ἀνήνεγκεν... τῷ κυρίῳ, καὶ διεχώρισεν ποιῆσαι, which represents the text of 𝔐, and agrees literally with 𝔗, which here and else-where renders הפליא by פרש, Pael and Aphel. We may with some plausibility conj. that διεχώρισεν is the translation of Aquila. 𝔐 is an attempt to construe the words with the following clause, after the words ומנוח ואשׁתּו ראים were accidentally transferred to this place from the next verse. With the construc-tion הפליא לעשׂות cf. Is. 29¹⁴ יכן הנני יסף להפליא את העם הזה הפלא ופלא, 2 Chr. 26¹⁵, כי הפליא להגזר, Joel 2²⁶ (God) עָשָׂה עמכם להפליא. It is a "direct causative Hiphil" (König's term), and may take an accusative (עֵצָה Is. 28²⁹, הסֵר Ps. 31²³, כֶּרֶה Dt. 28⁵⁹ &c.), or a gerund in definition. — 20. המזבח עֹלה] 𝔖 interpreting as Fl. Jos. and many others, *from the rock.*—21. ויֹּאסף ונ'] the interpreta-tion, *was no more seen by them*, i.e. disappeared from their sight (Ki. 2°), is against the usage of this idiomatic phrase, which expresses not continuity, but repetition; cf. Ex. 10²⁸·²⁹ 1 S. 15³⁵; Gen. 8¹² Jud. 8²⁸ 2 K. 6²³ &c.— להראה] 1 S. 3²¹; cf. הַרְאֵה Prov. 16¹⁶, ראֵה Gen. 48¹¹,* &c. See Kö., i. p. 534 f.— 23. לֹא לִקַח... חָפֵץ לו] cf. 8¹⁹ and note there.—ני הרֵאנו ונ'] 𝔊 † καὶ οὐκ ἂν ἐφώτισεν ἡμᾶς, cf. v.⁸ καὶ φωτισάτω ἡμᾶς (𝔐 ויֹּירֵנו); ‡ presumably reading הירֵנו and translating (as in the other places cited) by pseudo-etymological connection with אור. The reading is tempting; we might conjecture that the corruption which made הראנו of it led to the further amplification of the verse by the addition of what now seemed lacking, a mention of the words spoken to them. — כָּעֵת] *now, just now.* καθὼς [ὁ] καιρὸς 𝔊ᴬᴮᴸ: lacking in 𝔊ᴵⱽᴹᴺᴼ 𝔏; sub ast. s. The word is difficult, because it seems to oppose the hearing, as recent, to the seeing and the sacrifice. We might conj. כִּי כֹּה (cf. 21²²), but should then have to regard this as the original beginning of the apodosis of לו, and all that intervenes from לֹא לִקַח as an editorial interpolation.

24, 25. Samson's birth and childhood. — *She gave him the name Samson*] no etymology or explanation of the name is suggested, nor is there any hint of its significance elsewhere in the story. It is derived from *shemesh*, 'sun,' and if we remember that Beth-shemesh, just across the valley from Manoah's home, was sacred to the sun-god, such a name will hardly appear unnatural among these Danites. On the form of the name see note, and on the mythical interpretation, see note at the end of ch. 16. —25. *The spirit of Yahweh first stirred him up at Mahaneh Dan* (Dan's Camp) *between Zorah and Eshtaol*] as the text now stands, we

---

* Perhaps in the two last examples we should pronounce as inf. abs. (Sta.).
† Except 𝔅𝔑.
‡ Cf. also 4 Reg. 12³ 17²⁷·³³.

must suppose that there he first had one of those fits of demonic rage which were so terrible to his enemies. The occasion and results of this outbreak are not related. The verse cannot be the introduction to ch. 14; we should rather have to regard it as originally the introduction to a lost story of Samson's first exploit. The topographical notices, however, excite suspicion. The home, or at least the family burial-place, of Manoah was between Zorah and Eshtaol (16[31]); *Dan's Camp*, on the other hand, was at Kirjath-jearim in Judah, on the western side of that town (18[12]). The latter statement, which there is no reason to question, is indirectly confirmed by the name itself: whatever its origin, 'Camp of Dan' is a much more natural name for a place in Judah than for one in the midst of the Danite settlements about Zorah. This consideration weighs against the hypothesis, for which there is no support, that there were two Camps of Dan, one at Kirjath-jearim, and one between Zorah and Eshtaol.[*] It is possible that neither of the conflicting topographical notices in our verse is original, and that the author wrote simply, *The boy grew up, and Yahweh blessed him; and the spirit of Yahweh began to stir him up*, disquiet him. Upon this, ch. 14 might very well follow; cf. 14[4]. — On Zorah see above, on v.[2]; on Eshtaol, see on 16[31].

24. שִׁמְשׁוֹן] Fl. Jos., ἰσχυρὸν δ' ἀποσημαίνει τὸ ὄνομα, deriving it from שֶׁמֶן (see on 3[29]); similarly E. Meier.[†] Others explain it as an intensive formation from שׁמם (שַׁמְשׁוֹן for שַׁמְמוֹן), 'devastator,' or (giving a fictitious "primary" sense to the root) 'mighty'; so Be¹., Diestel, Ke., Köhler, al. Ew. (*GVI,* ii. p. 559) thought it possible to connect the name with שׁמשׁ 'serve,' 'the servant' *sc.* of God, *i.e.* the Nazirite. These are all efforts of misdirected ingenuity to evade the palpable derivation from שֶׁמֶשׁ 'sun'; ‡ cf. שִׁמְשַׁי Ezra 4[8ff.], ירחו Jericho, from ירח 'moon,' and the Palmyrene n. pr. ירחי (Baethgen, *Beiträge,* p. 162), &c. — עָם כַּל ¹] [וַתָּחֶל רוּחַ יהוה לְפַעֲמוֹ Niph., Gen. 41[8] Dan. 2[3] Ps. 77[5] Hithp. Dan. 2[1]; cf. פָּעַם. The sense in all these passages is, 'disquiet, perturb'; the primary meaning is uncertain.

XIV., XV. Samson's marriage and its consequences. § — The

story is of one fabric throughout, and is probably derived from J, but a good many additions and changes have been made by later editors or scribes, which disturb the simple and natural progress of the narrative. One of the most misleading of these alterations is that which lets Manoah and his wife accompany Samson to Timnath ($14^{5, 6b}$), with the insertion of the words, *to marry her*, in v.^{5a} ; the journeyings to and fro thus become an insoluble puzzle. Confusion has also been introduced by (or *in*) the dates in v.$^{14b, 15a}$, and toward the close of ch. 14 an accidental corruption of the text has made the sequel unintelligible.*

XIV. 1-4. Samson announces his purpose to marry a Philistine woman of Timnath. — *Samson went down to Timnath*] from his father's home at Zorah (13^2). Timnath † is in Jos. 19^{43} allotted to Dan; in Jos. 15^{10} it is set down as a frontier town of Judah. According to Jud. 1^{34}, the Danites had been thrust back from this region by the Amorites. In the Philistine invasion, Timnath fell into their possession. ‡ Early in the history of the kingdom, no doubt, it was incorporated in Judah ; but, according to 2 Chr. 28^{18}, was reconquered by the Philistines in the time of Ahaz (736–728 B.C.). It still bears the name Tibneh, and lies about an hour west of 'Ain Shems (Beth-shemesh, Har-heres, 1^{35}), and somewhat farther southwest of Ṣur'ah (Zorah). § — **2.** On his return he asks his father to get her for his wife. The negotiations for a bride were the business of the bridegroom's father ; cf. Gen. $34^{4ff.}$ — **3.** His parents object to his marrying a Philistine ; he should take a wife of his own people. Samson, however, persists. — *His father and his mother*] the last words are probably an addition to the original text (conformation to v.^{2}) ; the verb in Heb. is in the singular ; observe also *my people*, and the sing. in Samson's reply, *Get* (thou) *her for me ;* it is naturally the father who answers. — Are there no women among his own kinsmen or of his own race, that he must needs go take a Philistine wife? Cf. Gen. $24^{3f.}$ $26^{34f.}$ $28^{1f. 8f.}$. — *The uncircumcised Philistines*] *uncircumcised* is an opprobrious word which is applied almost exclusively to the Philistines

---

* See Stade, *ZATW.* iv. 1884, p. 250 ff.; Budde, *Richt. u. Sam.*, p. 130 f.; Doorninck, "De Simsonsagen," *Th. T.* xxviii. 1894, p. 14-32.

† Not to be confounded with Timnath-heres, 2^9.   ‡ See above, p. 80 f.

§ Rob., *BR².* ii. p. 17; Guérin, *Judée,* ii. p. 30 f.; *SWP. Memoirs,* ii. p. 417.

among the neighbours of Israel; cf. 15¹⁸ 1 S. 14⁶ 17²⁶·³⁶ 31⁴ 2 S. 1²⁰;
see Jer. 9²⁵·²⁶. Circumcision seems to have been generally practised by the other peoples of Palestine.[*] On the Philistines, see
on 3³. — *For she suits me*] v.⁷; lit. *is right in my eyes.* — **4.** In
this seeming perversity there was a divine purpose of which his
parents were not aware; cf. Gen. 24⁵⁰. — *For he* (Yahweh) *was
seeking an opportunity of the Philistines*] an opportunity for
Samson to do them a mischief; cf. 2 K. 5⁷, which suggests that
the rare word may have the by-sense, 'opportunity, occasion for a
fight.' — The second half-verse is superfluous here, and is very
probably an editorial addition derived from 15¹¹; [†] observe the
generalization, *over Israel* (cf. 13¹). Doorninck regards the whole
verse as a gloss, introduced by some one who felt the need of
some such explanation of the marriage of an inspired man and
judge of Israel with a heathen woman. The words seem to me,
however, to be perfectly natural in the context, and not to involve
any such reflexion. The refusal of Samson's father to get the
woman for him as a wife in the usual way, explains how he came
to contract an exogamous marriage. This was the origin of a
succession of complications, in each of which Samson has an
injury to requite, so that the mischief which he does the Philistines is always legitimate retaliation (cf. esp. 15³); he always has
a just *occasion*. And it is in entire accord with the religious
character of the folk-story that this is ascribed to the purpose of
Yahweh.

1. בְּתִמְנָתָה] v.²; cf. כרמי הבנה v.⁵, Jos. 19⁴³. The name of the place was
doubtless תמנה, with the Canaanite fem. ending which we find in numerous
names of places.[‡] In Hebrew it appeared to be construct, and there was
therefore a special tendency to replace it by the accus. תִמְנָתָה. — **3.** ויאמר לי
ואבי ואמו] observe the sg. verb (cf. v.⁶ᵃ). The constr. is possible; but the
discord in number is more prob. due to the interpolation of אבי. — . . . . מבנות
וּבְכֹל] *among;* cf. בבנות v.¹·²; a good illustration of the way in which ב comes
to its so-called partitive sense (13¹⁶), and of the difference between it and מן
partitive, ב representing the part in the unity of the whole, מן as separated
from it. — אחיך] 16³¹ 9¹·³·¹⁸, *thy kinsmen.* — וכל כבי] ἐν παντὶ τῷ λαῷ σου
𝕲ᴸᴹ 𝕾; conformation to preceding. — **4.** תאנה] the vb. (Pi.) Ex. 21¹³ (Pu.)

---

[*] The Shechemites, Gen. 34, are an exception.
[†] Bo., supposing, further, that the father's refusal has been omitted by the editor.
The latter also seems to me probable; see on v.⁵.   [‡] Sta., p. 183.

Ps. 91¹⁰ Prov. 12²¹† (Hithp.) 2 K. 5⁷ (c. c. ל pers.)⸒ The primary sense is prob. ‘its time, the right time, came,’ &c. (cf. Arab.). Hence האנה ‘opportunity, occasion.’ The pronunciation of the noun is anomalous; cf. תרבה 9⁸¹; see Ol. § 213 a; Sta. § 262. The same word appears to have been read by the Greek translators in Prov. 18¹ (προφάσεις ζητεῖ); see Cappel, *Crit. sacr.*, ii. p. 604 f., ed. Vogel and Scharfenberg.

It is not explicitly said that Manoah adhered to his position and declined to abet his son in his perverse course, but it is distinctly enough implied in v.⁴ᵃ, and to be inferred with certainty from v.⁵⁻⁷, where Samson takes the business into his own hands, as well as from the nature of the marriage which he contracts. It is evident there that he has no intention of taking his bride to his father's home, as he proposes in v.¹·³; it is understood that she is to remain in her father's house.* That is, Manoah having refused to receive this Philistine daughter-in-law, Samson makes a ṣadîqa marriage in Timnath, with which, as a matter of course, his parents have nothing whatever to do.

This state of the case is partly obscured in the text before us through the insertion by a later hand of the words, *and his father and mother*, in v.⁵ᵃ, with the corresponding addition of v.⁶ᵇ, and of *his father* in v.¹⁰ᵃ, by which it is made to appear that Manoah yielded and undertook the customary negotiations for an ordinary marriage. The motive of this change was doubtless the difficulty which men in subsequent times found in conceiving that the hero, in open disregard of parental authority, contracted such a marriage among the Philistines. But, as is fortunately often the case, the editor did not carry through his alterations with sufficient thoroughness, and the resulting inconsistency and confusion betrays his hand. Thus v.⁷ is left untouched, while *his father*, as the subject of v.¹⁰ᵃ, manifestly comes too late. And, apart from this, the fact that the comrades of the bridegroom (v.¹¹) are not Samson's kinsmen and friends from Zorah, but Philistine youths, is incontrovertible evidence that the marriage was not sanctioned by his family.†

The removal of these interpolations leaves a text which is free from all difficulty, a plain and straightforward narrative. Manoah having refused his aid and consent, Samson goes by himself to

---

* This is not merely a consequence of the quarrel; see esp. v.¹⁰ 15¹.
† This restoration of the text follows Doorn. and Sta.

Timnath to arrange for his marriage (v.⁵). **As he is approaching
the town, a lion encounters him ; the fury comes on, and he kills
it with his bare hands (v.⁶).** He goes on, and has a satisfactory
interview with the woman (v.⁷). After some time spent in Timnath he returns to Zorah ; * on his way he finds the honey in the
carcase of the lion and takes some to his father and mother,
without telling them where he got it (v.⁹·). He goes down again
to Timnath for his wedding, and makes a feast according to custom, taking thirty young Philistines as comrades (v.¹⁰·). During
the festivities he propounds his riddle, with a wager that they
cannot answer it before the seven days of the feast are over
(v.¹²⁻¹⁴ᵃ). They are unable to solve it, and appeal with threats to
his bride to beguile him of his secret (v.¹⁴ᵇ·¹⁵) ; she finally exhausts
his patience, and he tells her (v.¹⁶ᶜ·). On the last day, before he
enters the bride chamber, they triumphantly declare the answer
and claim the forfeit (v.¹⁸). In a rage, he rushes off, kills thirty
Ashkelonites, and pays the wager ; † then, without seeing his wife
again, he returns to his father's house. To repair this disgrace,
she is married out of hand to his best man (v.¹⁹·²⁰).

The story is admirably told ; and the text, with the exception
of the intentional changes which have been discussed, in excellent
preservation.

6. *Samson went down to Timnath*] the chief reasons for omitting the words, *and his father and his mother*, have already been
given ; observe also that when the lion comes roaring to meet
him, his parents are not with him (v.⁵ᵇ), and that in v.⁷ there is
no further mention of his father, precisely at the point where we
should expect it if he had accompanied his son. — *And he came
to the vineyards*] ꘫ, *they came*, ‡ necessitated by the introduction
of *his father and his mother* in the preceding sentence. — *A full
grown young lion came roaring towards him*] to explain the
singular pronoun the commentators are constrained to suppose
that Samson, in his eagerness, had outstripped his slower parents,§
or that he had taken a by-path through the vineyards, while they

---

* The words, *to marry her*, are a particularly ill-placed gloss.
† This also is probably a later addition ; see on v.¹⁹.
‡ Cf. ⊕ᴸ, and see crit. note.   § Ki.

followed the main road and heard nothing of his adventure.[*]
— **6.** *The spirit of Yahweh rushed upon him*] with overmastering
power; an access of divine rage in which he was irresistible;
cf. v.[19] 15[14], 1 S. 10[6, 10] 11[6] 18[10] (Saul) 16[13] (David); with other
verbs Jud. 3[10] 6[34] 13[25]. On the spirit of Yahweh see on 3[10]; it is
here conceived of as a physical force.[†] — *He tore it asunder as
a man tears a kid*] the verb occurs in Lev. 1[17], in an old ritual,
of the tearing of a fowl. *The tearing of a kid* may perhaps also
be a reference to some ceremonial act; the point of comparison
is not so much the ease with which it was done, as the way in
which it was done; he tore the lion limb from limb with his bare
hands.[‡] Compare the similar stories of David (1 S. 17[34-36]) and
Benaiah (2 S. 23[20]). So the Greek athlete Polydamas is said to
have killed a large and powerful lion in Olympus, without any
weapon, imitating thus the famous exploit of Hercules.[§] In many
representations of the combat of Hercules with the Nemean lion,
the hero is strangling the beast with his bare hands.[‖] — *He did not
tell his father and mother*] the words are an interpolation derived
from v.[16] (cf. v.[9]), and fit into the story very ill.[¶] — **7.** *He went
down and spoke to the woman, and she suited Samson*] lit. *was
right in his eyes* (v.[3]). It was Samson who went down and spoke
to the woman, not his father,[**] who appears very much belated
on this errand in v.[10]; see comm. there. Bertheau explains:
After the parents had arranged the marriage (v.[5f.]), and, with
Samson, had returned to Zorah, he used to go down and talk
to the maiden, and on more intimate acquaintance she pleased
him well (v.[7]).[††] This is perhaps as good an illustration as could
be given of the absurdities into which the interpolations lead the

---

[*] Schm., Stud., Be., al. mu.; cf. v.[8].

[†] Doorn. (*Th. T.* 1894, p. 16 f.) regards this clause, together with v.[19a] and 15[14ba],
as foreign to the original text.

[‡] As a matter of fact, to dismember a living animal in this way, even a kid, is
not very easy; for which reason Cler. supposes that a boiled kid is meant.

[§] Pausanias, vi. 5, 5.

[‖] See Baumeister, *Denkmäler des klass. Alterthums*, i. p. 655; Furtwängler in
Roscher's *Lexikon*, 2195 ff.

[¶] See above, p. 329.

[**] 𝔊 harmonizes: *they went down and spoke to the woman.* Speak *for* the woman
would be רכר ב (1 S. 25[39]).

[††] All just like a properly conducted German courtship!

interpreter. — 8. *And he went back after a while*] from Timnath
to his father's house at Zorah. So the context imperatively
requires. In v.[7] he visits Timnath and arranges the preliminaries
of his marriage ; having done so, in the interval before his wedding,
he returns to his home ; by the way he finds the honey in the
carcase of the lion he had slain as he went down to Timnath ;
goes along eating it on his way to his parents' home (v.[9.]). The
order of events is plain and natural. This order is completely
deranged by the addition in our text of the words, *to marry her*.
We have to suppose that after his visit to Timnath (v.[7]), Samson
went home, leaving his parents at Timnath, where they are (v.[9])
when after a while he himself returns thither (v.[8]). But in v.[10]
his father *comes down*, and we have therefore to assume that, after
Samson's return to Timnath, Manoah went to Zorah and returned
again. This succession of purposeless journeyings to and fro is
not intimated in any way in the narrative itself ; it is simply a
complicated and improbable hypothesis necessitated by the words,
to marry her, in v.[8] ; and the clumsiness of the hypothesis is the
strongest evidence that these words do not belong to the original
story,* — *And he turned aside to see the remains of the lion*] which
lay off the pathway, in the vineyards (v.[5]). — *There was a swarm
of bees in the carcase, and honey*] we are to imagine the body
dried up, the skin and shrivelled flesh adhering to the ribs, the
belly hollow.† In a hot and dry climate this change would not
take a great while ; ‡ a longer time would be necessary for bees to
take possession of the mummied carcase, and deposit honey.
The story, however, does not represent Samson's discovery as an
every-day occurrence ; it is part of a wonderful history, and to be
judged not by the prosaic probabilities of fact, but by the verisimilitude of the marvellous. Bochart adduces from Herodotus
the story of the bees that made a hive of the scull of Onesilus,
which the people of Amathus had fastened up over the city gate.§
It is not unlikely that the story of the bees in the carcase of the
lion is further to be connected with the wide-spread belief of the
ancients in the spontaneous generation of these insects in decaying

---

* Doorn., Sta.   † Not merely the osseous skeleton ; S, Cler., al.

‡ Oedmann, *Sammlungen aus d. Naturkunde*, u. s. w., vi. p. 135 f.

§ Hdt., v. 114 ; Bochart, *Hierozoicon*, iii. p. 358, ed. Rosenm.

bodies of animals, familiar to us through Vergil.[a] —**9.** *He scraped it out into his palms, and went along eating it. And he came to his father and his mother*] at his home ; see on v.[5]. — *He did not tell them*] v.[16b].

5. וירד כפשן] omit ואביו ואמו for the reasons set forth above.[†] — וינאו] read ויבא with 𝕲[BN] καὶ ἦλθεν. 𝕲[ALM] καὶ ἐξέκλινεν εἰς ἀμπελῶνα ‡ (= ויסר v.[5]) is perhaps an early attempt to explain how his parents, who according to v.[5] accompanied him to Timnath, knew nothing of his adventure. 𝕲[IVO] ἐξέκλιναν. — נביר אריה] cf. Ez. 19[1.6]. The כפיר is a full-grown young lion, in the wantonness of his superabounding strength. See Bochart, *Hierozoicon*, ii. p. 3 ff.; Tristram, *Natural Hist. of the Bible*[b], p. 115 ff. — שאן לקראתו] the specific word for the roaring of the lion. The construction is pregnant; cf. 1 S. 16[4] 21[2] Jud. 15[14] 19[8]. — **6.** וישסעהו כשסע הגדי] Lev. 1[17] ובשק אתו בכנפיו לא יבדיל; trop. 1 S. 24[8] (נברים). The procedure directed in Lev. 1[17] is described as a rending of the victim by hand, without actual severance of the parts; see Ra. *ad loc.*; *Sifra, Wayyikra*, Parasha 7 (§ 9) with the comm.; *Zebachim*, 65[a.b] 66[a]. — ויא הגיד ונ'] interpolation; see above. § — **8.** וישב מימים לקחתה] Bochart, following RLbG., interprets, *after a year* (11[40]), cf. Selden, *Uxor Hebr.*, ii. c. 8; but this is here in the highest degree improbable. — כפלה] from נפל, as πτῶμα from πίπτειν, *cadaver* a cadendo (Ges. *Thes.*) — אריה] on the anomalous form see Ol. § 216 *d.*; ‖ cf. אריה (ארי) v.[5]. — **9.** וירדהו אל כפיו] רדה, in this sense not elsewhere in O.T., is freq. in MH.; *scrape, e.g.* the thin sheets of bread from the sides of the oven (תנור), or honeycomb from the sides of the hive (כוורה); Levy, *NHWb.* iv. p. 427 f. For the latter, cf. *M. Shebiith*, x. 7; *Baba bathra*, 66[a]; *Baba mezia*, 64[a] (see Ra. on the last passage); cf. also the *nom. instrum.* מרדה, *Taanith*, 25[a], &c. This specific sense is abundantly established. That it does not occur again in O.T. is not strange; it is precisely these household words of the old Hebrew which are not found in it unless by fortunate exception.[¶] There is no reason to suspect the text (SS.). The etymologizing interpretations, 'break, break out' (Mich. *Suppl.*, Ges. *Thes.*, al.), "sich bemächtigen des Honigs" (Be. al.), are worthless. — אל כפיו] in pregnant constr., 'into his hands'; naturally, with a stick or something of the kind. The considerable variations of 𝕲 are apparently derived from a Hebrew copy in which כפיו had become corrupted to פיו. — וילך הלך ואכל] with two inff. abss., Jos. 6[9.13] 1 S. 6[12] 2 S. 3[16] 2 K. 2[11] &c. — וילך 2°] prob. through the influence of the preceding verbs; ויבא would be more natural.

---

[a] *Georg.*, iv. 299 ff. Many other authors are quoted by Bochart, iii. 353 f., among them Philo, *de sacrificantibus, Opp.* ed. Mangey, ii. p. 255. Other lit. is cited by Rosenm. in his notes on Bochart, and Stud. Merx, "Der Honig im Cadaver des Löwen," *Prot. Kirchenzeitung*, 1887, 17. col. 389-392, I have not seen.

[†] Doorn., Sta.   [‡] 𝕲[M] ἀμπελῶνας.   [§] Doorn., Sta.

[‖] For other explanations see the authors cited by Buhl, Ges. *HWb*[12], s.v.

[¶] Abulw., Ki. *Lex.*, al. refer to this sense Jer. 5[31]; so Buhl.

10-18. The wedding; Samson's riddle. — **10.** *He went down to the woman and made a feast there]* • 𝔐 and the versions : *His father went down to the woman* (*!*), *and Samson made a feast.* This introduction of the father here has a peculiarly absurd effect; especially after the other gloss, *to marry her* (v.⁹); see on v.⁵ and v.⁸. — *For so bridegrooms used to do*] on such occasions. The note is manifestly added because the custom of the narrator's time was different. The difference lies not in the length of the festivities,† but in the fact that it was given by the bridegroom at the home of the bride's parents, instead of his own, which was altogether exceptional. On wedding customs see note on v.²⁰. — **11.** *And he took thirty comrades, and they were with him*] these comrades were Philistines (v.¹⁸), and took the place of the kinsmen and friends of the bridegroom, who in an ordinary marriage would have attended him to the bride's home, and thence conducted the couple in festive procession to his house. So the story originally ran, as we see especially from v.¹⁵ᵇ, where it is clear that they were invited guests, not special constables. Through misunderstanding, or possibly to remove offence, this has been so changed that the Philistines themselves select these comrades; and a motive for this unusual course is discovered in their apprehension that Samson might be up to some mischief. Thus has arisen the present text, which runs in 𝔐: *And when they saw him, they took thirty comrades;* saw what a dangerous-looking fellow he was. Many Greek manuscripts, representing a slightly different pronunciation of the Hebrew word, *since they feared him;* see crit. note. — **12.** As everywhere in the world, the wedding festivities were enlivened by various pleasantries and plays of wit. ‡ Samson gives out a riddle, with a wager that the guests cannot answer it before the week is out. — *If you can tell me what it is, during the seven days of the feast,* § *and find it out, I will give you, &c.*] the words, *and find it out* (yourselves), which are lacking in several recensions of 𝔊, are a gloss taken from v¹⁸, as the inappropriate position of the words in 𝔐 also

---

* Or, *And Samson went down* (Sta., Doorn.).
· † Stud.
‡ On riddles at feasts, see Bochart, *Hierozoicon*, lii. p. 382 f., ed. Rosenm.
§ The seven days, cf. Gen. 29²⁷ Tob. 11¹⁰; Wellhausen, *GgN.* 1893, p. 442.

shows.* The author of the gloss desired an express proviso against such unfair means as the Philistines took to learn the secret. — *Thirty fine linen wrappers and thirty gala dresses*] one for each of the comrades. The linen wrappers (Is. 3^{23} Prov. 31^{24}) were not undergarments,† but rectangular pieces of fine, thin, and therefore costly, linen stuff, which might be worn as an outer garment over the other dress, or as a night-wrapper upon the naked body ; ‡ see note. — *Gala dresses*] apparel which was worn on festival or ceremonial occasions, instead of the every-day raiment (v.^{12, 19} Gen. 45^{22} 2 K. 5^5). — 13. If they are unable to guess the riddle, they shall pay the same wager. They accept the conditions : *Propound thy riddle, and let us hear it !* — 14. *Out of the eater came something to eat, and out of the strong came something sweet*] the adjectives in the second member are descriptive epithets, respectively, of the substantives in the first, which they replace in poetic parallelism. It is unnecessary, therefore, to try to make out a perfect antithesis between the adjectives independently ; § there is in reality but one antithesis, not two. — *They could not tell the riddle*] it was, in truth, a very bad riddle, and quite insoluble without a knowledge of the accidental circumstance which suggested it. The following dates are evidently not in order. According to 𝔐, they could not make out the riddle for *three* days, and on the *seventh* day appealed to Samson's bride to learn the answer for them. ‖ 𝔊 ¶ and 𝔖 have in v.^{15}, the *fourth* day, instead of the seventh, which agrees better with v.^{14}.** It does not appear, however, why they should give up in the middle of the week. It is more probable that the error lies in the other number, and that in v.^{14} we should restore, *for six days*.†† The story would then run naturally : They cudgel their brains in vain for six days ; on the seventh and last day, in despair of the solution, they try Samson's wife. Their vehemence in v.^{15} is better motived if the time is rapidly drawing to a close than if they addressed themselves to her several days sooner. A

---

* Sta., Doorn. † Lth., Cler., Schroeder, Ges., MV., SS., al.
‡ Talmud, Abulw., Tanch., Ki., al. § Bochart, al.
‖ Ra., Ki., a Lyra, Vatabl., al. understand the seventh day of the week (Sabbath), which was the fourth day of the feast. ¶ 𝔊^L agrees with 𝔐. ** So Be.
†† The Hebrew words for *three* and *six* differ only in one consonant.

new difficulty meets us, however, in v.[17], where we read that the woman wept upon him the whole seven days that they had the feast ; and on the seventh day, tired of her incessant badgering, he gave in, and told her the answer. If the companions first appealed to her on the *seventh* day (v.[15] 劉), or even on the *fourth* day (𝔊𝔖), her weeping seems to begin prematurely on the first day.* Some commentators explain that she had teased him for the first six days merely out of her own curiosity, and that on the seventh her importunity was redoubled by the threats of her countrymen.† If this had been the meaning of the writer, the order of the narrative or the construction of v.[16a] would in all probability have been different ; as it is, nothing of the kind is intimated in the text. The dates in v.[14.15] are therefore, even after their internal contradiction is removed by the emendation *six*, irreconcilable with those in v.[17]; one or the other must be interpolated. The words in v.[17] do not read like a gloss, and the removal of them leaves a rather awkward sentence ; the omission of the numbers in v.[14] and v.[15], on the contrary, makes no break, and Stade rightly rejects them. According to the original story, then, the Philistines gave up the riddle right away, thinking it an easier and surer way to win the wager, to learn the answer from Samson himself through their countrywoman. For six days he is obdurate to her persuasions and tears, but at last can bear it no longer and discloses the secret. The interpolation in v.[14.15] may have been due to the feeling that the Philistines would not give up so easily. — **15.** The Philistines set Samson's bride to discover his secret. — *Beguile thy husband*] 16[5]. — *And make him tell us the riddle*] make him betray himself through thee to us. — *Lest we burn thee, &c.*] 15[6], cf. 12[1] 1 K. 16[15]. — *Did you invite us hither to impoverish us ?*] see crit. note.

10. The original text read : ‏ויהי‎ ‏וירד שמשן אל האשה ויעש שם משתה ת׳‎. — **11.** ‏ויהי‎ ‏וראו׳‏כ אות׳‎] *when they saw him*, sc. the Timnathite wedding guests (*cum ergo cives loci illius vidissent eum*, 𝕷); the subject is, however, not at hand in the context. With 劉 agree 𝔊[B] 𝕷𝔖𝕿, while 𝔊[APVMNO] 𝔯 𝔰 have ἐν τῷ φοβεῖσθαι αὐτοὺς (sub obel. 𝔰) αὐτὸν = ‏בְּיִרְאָם‎; ‡ cf. Fl. Jos., διὰ δέος τῆς ἰσχύος τοῦ νεανίσκου. The editor who introduced these words probably wrote ‏בראותם‎;

---

* Rashi's explanation is, that she wept the remainder of seven days, viz., from the fourth on.　　　　† Schm., Ke., Be.　　　　‡ Cf. also 𝔊[L].

כיראהם,* which is hardly a natural expression in this connexion, is meant to be more explicit. — ויקח] the text is to be emended, not by supplying the subject פלשתים (Doorn².), but by reading ויקח, *He* (Samson) *took*, &c. — 12. שלשים סדינים] the כי was a fine stuff, of domestic manufacture (Prov. 31²⁴), an article of luxury (Is. 3²³). The Talmud mentions various uses to which it was put; as a curtain (*M. Yoma*, iii. 4, *Jer. Sota*, fol. 24ᶜ), wrapper (*Menach.*, 37ᵇ), shroud (*Jer. Kilaim*, ix. fol. 32ᵇ). *M. Kilaim*, xxiv. 13, enumerates three varieties; see Levy, *NHWb.* iii. p. 480. All these uses suppose that it was a sheet of considerable size. So it is interpreted by Abulw., Tanch., Ki., Saad. on Is. 3²⁹, JDMich., al. See Schroeder, *De vestitu mulierum*, p. 339-361; Hartmann, *Hebräerin*, ii. p. 346 f. — 14, 15. The original text and the first form of the gloss seem to have been: ולא יכלו להגיד החידה (שבעת ימים : ויהי ביום) עד ויאמרו לאשת שמשון ואיך (היבכיני) .— פתי את אישך] *beguile*, 2 S. 3²⁶ 1 K. 22³⁰·³¹·³² &c. — הלירשנו] inf. Kal (Ki., Kö. i. p. 412). The usual inf. is רשת. Perhaps the inf. ירש was used for distinction in the sense 'reduce to poverty,' cf. Niph. נורש 'be reduced to poverty.' Contamination of signification through confusion with רש 'poor' may be suspected. Some copies have הלירישנו (JDMich., cf. Ki. *Comm.*, and *Lex.* s.v.); others, to exclude this, הלירשנו (see Norzi).† — הלא] the alternative, *or not*, is אם לא, not הלא, and would, even if correctly expressed, be out of place here. Read הֲלֹם *hither*,‡ which is found in some Hebr. manuscripts and is supported by 𝕿. See Bruns, in Eichhorn's *Repertorium*, xiii. p. 70; De Rossi, Baer.

16. She teases him day by day to tell her the riddle. — *Samson's wife annoyed him by weeping*] was burdensome to him; Nu. 11¹³ cf. Gen. 45¹⁵. — *Thou only hatest me, and dost not love me at all*] his professions of love are belied by his conduct, which proves the opposite. Co-ordination of affirmative and negative for emphasis. He replies to her reproaches that he has not even told his own parents; that he does not disclose the riddle to her is therefore no proof of lack of love or confidence. — **17.** She gave him no rest from her tears and importunities all the seven days that they kept the feast (v.¹²), until on the last day he gave in, and told her. § — *Because she besieged him*] 16¹⁶; pressed him harder and harder. She at once communicated the secret to her countrymen. — **18.** The Timnathites waited till the last moment, to heighten their triumph and his discomfiture. — *On the seventh day, before he went into the bride-chamber*] at night. So Stade

---

* Be. would read כִּירְאָם, cf. 2 S. 3¹¹.
† Baer has ־ in his text, ־ in the apparatus.
‡ Stud., Sta., al.   § See on v.¹⁴.

with much probability conjectures ; cf. 15¹.* The text, generally interpreted, *before the sun set,*† is unintelligible. See on v.¹ᵃ and crit. note. He sees how he has been duped. — *If you had not plowed with my heifer, you would not have found out my riddle*] used illegitimate means. The rhyme of the original cannot well be imitated in English. —**19**. In a fury, which is not merely anger at the deception that has been practised on him, but an access of the possession to which he is subject (13⁵ 14⁶), he rushes away from the feast and his bride. — *To Ashkelon*] the city of Ashkelon was on the seacoast between Gaza and Ashdod; ‡ a two days' journey from Timnath across the whole breadth of Philistia. So remote a place, and a large fortified city besides, hardly agrees with the general impression we receive from the context, that Samson rushed off from the feast in a rage, surprised some neighbouring Philistine village and slew the inhabitants, returned to Timnath with the spoil, paid his wager, and was away to his father's home before the fit was over. Now, there is a Khirbet 'Asqalūn little more than an hour south of Timnath,§ and if the half-verse were genuine, we should be strongly inclined to think that in the original story this, and not Askelon on the coast, was the scene of Samson's exploit. We need not, in such a narrative, nicely weigh the probabilities of his finding among the spoil precisely the articles he had wagered. ‖ Stade has given good reason, however, for regarding the entire half-verse as an addition to the narrative, made by an editor who thought it unworthy of Samson to run away without paying the wager which he had lost, even though the Philistines had won unfairly. In the original story, v.¹⁹ᵇ followed immediately upon v.¹⁸ ; Samson, in a passion, returned to his father's house. That v.¹⁹ᵃ is secondary is evident from the fact that the slaughter of the Philistines at Ashkelon has no consequences in the story, in which everything else is so closely knit in the nexus of cause and effect.¶ These considerations,

---

* *ZATW.* iv. 1884. p. 253 f.; the conjecture is accepted by Bu., Kautzsch, Doorn². † 𝕲𝕷𝕰. ‡ See *DB².* s.v. § *SWP. Memoirs,* iii. p. 107.

‖ The explanation which would evade this difficulty by supposing that Samson made the raid on Ashkelon to reimburse himself for the expense he had been at in *buying* all these clothes (Be.) is more ingenious than plausible.

¶ *ZATW.* iv. 1884. p. 255 f.; cf. Doorn. *Th. T.,* 1894, p. 15 f.

especially the last, seem to me decisive. — *He was angry, and went up to his father's house*] angry at the way in which he had been treated by his companions, and especially at the perfidy of his wife, which he resents by deserting her. Stade infers from v.[18], *before he entered the bride-chamber*, that the marriage had not been consummated.* They held back, as has been said, to the last moment, and just as he was on the point of entering the chamber, they give their answer: *What is sweeter than honey, and what is fiercer than a lion?* Instantly seeing through the plot and upbraiding them for it, he rushes out of the house, and away to Zorah. In thus mocking her he inflicted on her the keenest disgrace, and made her and her family a laughing-stock. To repair this disgrace, her father at once gave her into the arms of the παράνυμφος, and the interrupted wedding was completed. — **20.** *To his comrade who had been his best man*] to the one of the thirty "comrades" who had borne the part of the φίλος τοῦ νυμφίου (John 3[29]).

16. [רק שנאתני] *all you do is hate me;* see notes on 3[2] 11[24]. — [וירך אניר] exclamatory question of surprise and reproach, cf. 9[9] 11[23]. — **17.** [הציק] usually with ל pers.; lit. 'make it strait for some one,' reduce him to straits, extremities. Of invasion and siege, Dt. 28[53. 55. 57] Is. 29[2. 7] Jer. 19[9]. With acc., Job 32[18] (of inner constraint). — **18.** [בטרם ינא החרסה] 𝕲𝕷𝔈 *before the sun set,*† followed by substantially all the comm. The form הרסה is explained as locative accus.; the significance of the case is supposed to be forgotten (cf. הבנתה v.[9]). But הרס 'sun' is a rare word (Job 9[7] Is. 19[18], see on Jud. 1[35]), which we should not expect to find in old prose instead of שמש, and the assumption that the locative is used as a nominative is no less improbable. The case of הבנתה v.[8] is entirely different (see there), and the instances in late poetry where the ending â is due to the striving after more sonorous forms, or blundering archaism, do not make the occurrence of the form here any easier to explain. Stade's emendation, החרדה (15[1]), is one of those comparatively rare conjectures which are self-evident when once they have been hit upon. — [לולא חרשתם בעגלתי] 𝕲 εἰ μὴ κατεδαμάσατε τὴν δάμαλίν μου,‡ probably for the sake of the paronomasia. § — **20.** [לשרעהו אשר רעה לו] the verb (only here) is apparently denominative from רע. — On marriage and wedding customs see WRSmith, *Kinship and Marriage in Early Arabia,* 1885; Wellhausen, *Die*

---

* Does Fl. Jos. intimate this by his τὸν δὲ γάμον ἐκείνου παραιτεῖται? (Cler. on 15[1]).   † 𝕲[B] (alone) *before the sun rose;* cf. 8[18].

‡ 𝕲[B] Θ ἠροτριάσατε ἐν τῇ δαμάλει μου.

§ Hardly intended in an obscene sense like חרש MH. (RLbG 20).

Ehe bei den Arabern, GgN. 1893, p. 431–481; Stubbe, *Die Ehe im Alten Testament,* 1886; ° Nowack, *Hebr. Archäologie,* i. p. 155 ff. Marriage customs in the modern East, Russell, *Aleppo²,* 1794, i. p. 281 ff.; Lane, *Modern Egypt-ians⁵,* p. 155 ff.; Wetzstein, *Zeitschrift für Ethnologie,* v. 1873, p. 287–294. The marriage of Samson is the only instance in the O.T. in which the bride remains in her father's house, and the husband lives with her or visits her there; but such unions were probably not uncommon in early Israel.

XV. 1–8. Samson burns the Philistines' grain fields. —

When Samson's anger cools, he goes down to Timnath to visit his wife, but finds that she has been given to another. To revenge himself, he turns loose three hundred foxes with firebrands tied to their tails, and sets fire to the grain in the fields. Enraged at their loss, the Philistines burn the woman and her father, who had been the occasion of the mischief. Samson retaliates, and takes refuge in a rocky fastness in Judah. — 1. *After a while, in the time of wheat harvest*] the season is noted, to prepare for the story of the destruc-tion of the grain fields, v.⁴⁵. — *Samson went to visit his wife with a kid*] as a present to her, a kind of morning gift. This is another indication of the nature of the marriage ; it is not impossible that such a gift was expected at every visit of the husband.* A kid seems to have been a customary present in such circumstances ; cf. Gen. 38¹⁷. ²⁰. ²³ (Judah and Tamar). When he proposes to enter the inner part of the house to see his wife, her father interposes. —2. *I thought you must certainly hate her, so I gave her to thy comrade*] the best man at the wedding, 14²⁰. — He has a younger and fairer daughter whom he offers him in her stead, but Samson declines. — 3. *Samson said to them*] cf. v.⁷. It is not necessary to suppose that in either case the words were spoken in their hearing ; the threat was addressed to them. — *I am without fault toward the Philistines, if I do them an injury*] he cannot be blamed for retaliating upon them for the wrong that he has suf-fered ; they have given him just occasion (14⁴). — 4. The ingen-ious form which his revenge takes is one of those strokes of rude wit in which folk-stories delight. — *Three hundred foxes*] many

---

* In old Arabia such a gift would be called *sadāq,* the present a man makes to his female friend (*sadiqa*) ; see W. R. Smith, *Kinship and Marriage,* p. 76; Wellhausen, "Die Ehe bei den Arabern," *Nachrichten der kgl. Gesellschaft der Wissensch. zu Göttingen,* 1893, p. 431–481, esp. p. 465 ff.

interpreters, reflecting that the solitary habits of the fox would make it very difficult to catch such a number, and that Samson's great strength would be of no avail in such an undertaking, suppose that the author meant *jackals*, which roam in packs, and could easily, it is said, be caught by the hundred.* That the Hebrew name may have included jackals as well as foxes is quite possible ; the Arabs are said in some places to confound the jackal with the fox,† and in the modern Egyptian dialect the classical name of the fox is given exclusively to the jackal. ‡ The decision of the question is of importance only to those who take the story as a veracious account of an actual occurrence. They should consider, however, whether the author would thank them for their attempts to make Samson's wonderful performance easy. — Having caught his foxes, Samson turned them tail to tail, and put a torch, that is, a stick of wood wrapped with some absorbent material and saturated with oil,§ between each pair of tails. — 5. He set the torches on fire, and turned the foxes loose into the Philistines' standing grain. — *And burned both the shocks and the standing grain*] Ex. 22⁶. — The following words, *and the vineyards* [and] *olive orchards*, are probably an addition by a later hand, exaggerating the mischief. — A remarkable parallel to this story is found in a Roman ceremony described by Ovid, in which, at the Cerealia in April, foxes with lighted torches tied to their tails were turned loose in the Circus. ‖ Older scholars, who noted the resemblance, explained it by supposing that the Romans had borrowed the custom from the Phoenicians, among whom it kept

---

* Bochart, Cler., Rosenmüller, Ke., Cass., Tristram (*DB*². i. 1086 f.), RV.ᵐᵍ·, al. mu. In Ps. 63¹¹ *jackals* seem to be meant.

† Niebuhr, *Beschreibung von Arabien*, p. 166. The jackal is not found in the desert; Doughty, *Arabia Deserta*, ii. p. 145.

‡ See Lane, *Arab.-Engl. Lexicon*, p. 338ᵃ. Hommel, *Säugethiere*, p. 310 f., seems to be mistaken in his very positive assertion.

§ See 7¹⁶.

‖ *Fasti*, iv. 681 ff. Ovid gives a rationalistic explanation, according to which the custom commemorated the burning of the grain-fields at Carseoli by a boy who, for sport, had tied a wisp of burning hay to a fox's tail. See Preller, *Römische Mythologie*, ii. p. 43 f., where the cognate ceremonies of the Robigalia are also discussed; cf. also Suidas, *s.v.* Νεύρια (Bochart, p. 202 f.). Analogous customs among the Arabs, see Wellhausen, *Reste arab. Heidentumes*, p. 157 f.; Goldziher, *Muhammedanische Studien*, i. p. 34 f.

alive the memory of Samson's foxes.[*]　Some modern writers
give to both the same mythical interpretation.[†] — 6. The fire
spread far and wide through the fields of the Philistines. They
seek for the perpetrator of this enormous mischief, and, having
found out, revenge themselves on those who were the cause of it.
— *They went up*] from other parts of the land ; it was not the work
of the neighbours in Timnath alone. — *And burnt her and her
father's house with fire*] savage retaliation for what they had suffered by fire. The reading of 𝕲𝕾, *and her father's house*, is to be
preferred to 𝔜, *her father;* cf. 14[13]. — 7. *Samson said to them*]
see on v.[3]. — *If this is the way you do, I will surely be avenged of
you, and after that I will leave off*] let you alone. On the construction, see note. — 8. *He smote them, hip and thigh, with a
great slaughter*] lit. *leg on* (*over, over and above*) *thigh;* apparently a proverbial expression for complete overthrow, the exact
meaning of which we do not understand. — *He went down and
stayed in the fissure of the cliff Etam*] cf. Is. 2[11] 57[5]. The rock
or cliff of Etam was in Judah (v.[9ff.]), [‡] probably near the town of
the same name which appears in the list of places fortified by
Rehoboam between Bethlehem and Tekoa (2 Chr. 11[6]) ; see also
the list of towns in Judah which in 𝕲 is appended to Jos. 15[59].[§]
About half an hour south of Bethlehem, near the village of Artās,
is an 'Ain 'Atān, [||] which is doubtless the Etam of Chronicles and
Josephus, and with which the Etam of our story is identified by
Stanley and others.[¶] Schick locates the scene of Jud. 14 in the
vicinity of 'Artūf, and makes an ingenious attempt to identify Lehi
(Khirbet eṣ-Ṣiyyagh), and the cliff Etam ('Arāq Isma'in).[**] The
situation is entirely suitable, lying much nearer Timnath and Zorah

---

[*] Serarius, Bochart. The obvious objections to this hypothesis are urged by
Cler.

[†] See esp. Steinthal, *Zeitschr. für Völkerpsychologie*, ii. p. 134. See note at the
end of ch. 16.

[‡] In 1 Chr. 4[3] we find a Judahite clan, Etam.

[§] According to Fl. Jos., Solomon's gardens were there (*antt.* viii. 7, 3 § 186;
two *schoeni* from Jerusalem).

[||] Rob., *BR*[2]. i. 477; Guérin, *Judée*, iii. p. 117 f., 303; Bäd[3]., p. 134 f.; esp.
Schick, *ZDPV.* i. p. 152 f. See also Neubauer, *Géogr. du Talmud*, p. 132.

[¶] Stanley, *Jewish Church*, i. p. 371; Kneucker, *BL.* s.v.; Guérin, *l.c.*; Birch,
PEF. Qu. St. 1881, p. 323 f.; Be[2].; Grove-Wilson, *DB*[2]. s.v.; al.

[**] *ZDPV.* x. 1887, p. 131 ff., esp. 143 ff., 152 ff. (map, after p. 194).

than 'Ain 'Atān; the rock is an almost vertical cliff, with a large cave, very difficult and even dangerous of access.

3. (נקיתי הפעם מפלשתים) נהה בן פלי:, Nu. 32[22] cf. 2 S. 3[28] (כפם), be free, quit of all claims, so that they have no right to redress or satisfaction. — הפעם] 6[59] 16[18, 28]; in the Hexateuch only in J. — **4.** ויבן] Hiph.; see Norzi *ad loc.*, and the grammarians there cited. The rule laid down for these forms in *e* is that Kal has ַ (*e.g.* ויבן), Hiph. ַ as here; Hayyug ed. Nutt, p. 62, l. 30 ff.; Ki., *Michlol*, fol. 116ᵃ, ed. Lyck. — Two foxes or jackals tied tail to tail in this fashion would certainly not run far in the same direction; "they would most assuredly pull counter to each other, and ultimately fight most fiercely" (Col. H. Smith in Kitto's *Cyclopaedia*, art. "Shual"). Houghton (*DB*[1] s.v. "Fox")* would relieve the difficulty by supposing that they were tied together by a cord two or three yards long; but this is against the plain sense of the text. — **5.** [ויד כרם זית] in the Talmud (*Berach.*, 35ᵃ) זית is construed as a genitive, *olive plantation;* so Ki. 2°, RLbG., Ke., RV. This is without warrant in usage; if the words are genuine they must be emended, ויד זית, or at least, וזית; cf. 𝕿. — **6.** [התמני] patrial adj. from a fem. noun (תמנה), formed like יזרי 1 Chr. 2[54] from צרעה; see Ol. § 218 *c*; *Mufaṣṣal,* § 295; Wright, *Arab. Gram.*, i. § 251. Compare קעילתי 16[2] from קעילה. — ואת אניה] many codd. of 𝕸 (De Rossi), with 𝕲𝕾,† read ואת בית אניה, which is probably the original text (Lilienthal, 1770). — **7.** [כי אם נתתי] כי אם after an oath, 2 K. 5[20] Jer. 51[14], 2 S. 15[21] Ruth 3[12] (Kethib); without preceding particle of swearing, 1 S. 21[5]. — The variations of 𝕲 seem to have no critical value. — **8.** [שוק על ירך] 𝕿 interprets, *horse and foot* (so Ra., Ki. 1°, Tanch., RLbG.), without support in usage, or probability. Ki. 2° explains that in their headlong flight they fell, *leg over thigh*, as we say, 'heels over head.' Castell and Cler. conjectured that it was a wrestler's term (cf. ὑποσκελίζειν, *supplantare*), he tripped them up. Other guesses may be seen in Schm. and Rosenm.‡ The Arab. idioms sometimes adduced in illustration (see Lane, *Arab.-Engl. Lex.*, p. 1471) are not parallel. — [סלע] is rendered *hole, cave*, or the like by 𝕲𝕷, Ra., and most modern scholars. In Is. 17[6] 27[10] סעיפים are twigs or branches of trees, cf. סעפה Ez. 31[6, 8] and the vb. denom. סעף Is. 10[33]. Abulw., Tanch., Ki., regard the application of the word to rocks as tropical in the sense of extremities, hence, *peaks, crags*.§ So Cler., Vatabl., Drus., CBMich., in Velthusen and Kuinoel, *Commentt. theol.*, v. p. 470. Cf., however, the Arab. šu'beh, cleft in a mountain, and forked branch of a tree; JDMich., *Supplementa*, No. 1763; BSZ. *s.v.* — [וירד] cf. וילכדו v.[13]. It is hazardous to urge these verbs in endeavouring to fix the site of Etam; cf. 11[37] and esp. 2 S. 5[17]. — [עיטם] another Etam is mentioned in 1 Chr. 4[32] among the villages of Simeon, in conjunction with 'Ain-rimmon (Um er-rumāmim, three or four

---

* Cf. *DB*[2]. p. 1087ᵃ.   † Not 𝕲𝕯𝕹.
‡ The expression greatly puzzled Aug.; see *quaest.* 55.
§ Cf. Aquila, Is. 57[5], and 𝕷 *ibid.*

JUDGES

hours N. of Beersheba), and here Van de Velde, Ke., Mühlau, al. would seek
Samson's refuge (Ri. *HWB*[1]., MV., *s.v.*). This is, however, far remote from
the scene of all his other adventures; it was not in Judah; and, finally, in the
original of the list, Jos. 19[7], the name is not עיטם but עין. Conder formerly
proposed Beit 'Atâb (*SWP. Memoirs*, iii. p. 22 f.; *Tent Work*, i. p. 275–277),
against which see Schick, *ZDPV.* x. p. 144 f.; Wilson, *DB*[1]. i. 1004. For
Conder's opinions see also *PEF. Qu. St.*, 1876, p. 176, 1883, p. 182.

**9–13. The Philistines seek Samson; the men of Judah take
him to give him up. — 9.** The Philistines invade Judah to make
Samson prisoner and revenge themselves upon him. — *Made a
raid upon Lehi*] 2 S. 5[18.22]. — *Lehi*, only in this chapter (v.[9. 14. 17. 19])
and 2 S. 23[11].[*]   From the following verses it appears that it was
nearer the Philistine border than Etam.   The site is unknown ;
Schick would identify it with Khirbet eṣ-Ṣiyyagh, which he supposes to represent Siagōn, the Greek equivalent of the Hebrew
Lehi, 'jawbone.'[†] — **10.** They announce their purpose to take
Samson, and to do to him as he has done to them ; cf. v.[11] 1[7]. —
11. To deliver themselves from the invaders, the men of Judah
resolve to capture Samson and deliver him to the Philistines.   In
Judah the Danite Samson was a stranger, who had no claim to the
protection of the tribe.   The conduct of Judah appears to us
pusillanimous, but there is no sign that the author of the chapter,
who was probably himself a Judaean, took such a view of it.   He
probably thought only of the opportunity which was thus given
Samson to make havoc among the uncircumcised. — *Three thousand men*] a flattering estimate of Samson's prowess. — They
upbraid him for having given this provocation to their Philistine
masters ; What did he mean by doing such a thing?   He replies
that it was only fair retaliation (cf. v.[10]). — **12.** They explain
what they have come to do.   He stipulates that they shall not
themselves do him any harm. — **13.** They pledge themselves not
to put him to death ; they will only bind him and deliver him to
the Philistines.   On this assurance he surrenders himself to them.
They bind him with two new ropes (16[11f.]), and bring him from
his refuge.

---

[*] On 2 S. 23[11] see note.

[†] Cf. Fl. Jos., *antt.* v. 8, 8 § 300, χωρίον ὁ Σιαγὼν καλεῖται.   See above, p. 342 ;
and cf. *ZDPV.* x. p. 154 f. n. ; so also Conder, *PEF. Qu. St.* 1883, p. 182.

14-17. Samson breaks his bonds, and kills a thousand Philistines with an ass's jawbone. — 14. His captors bring him to Lehi, where the Philistines are waiting for him. As they come to meet him with premature shouts of triumph, the spirit of Yahweh comes mightily upon him ($14^{6.19}$; see on 3^{10}). — *The ropes which were on his arms became like flax that has caught fire*] 16^9; they disappeared in a flash. — *His bonds melted off his hands.* — **15.** He snatches the first weapon that came to hand. — *A green jawbone of an ass*] heavy and tough; an old weathered bone would be too light and brittle to serve such a purpose.* — *And killed a thousand men*] compare the slaughter of the Philistines by Shamgar (3^{31}), and by Shammah (2 S. 23^{11}). It is noteworthy that the latter was also at Lehi.† — **16.** Samson celebrates his victory in a couplet, punning on the name of his singular weapon in a way which we cannot imitate :

> *With the jawbone of an ass I have piled them in heaps;*
> *With the jawbone of an ass I have killed a thousand men.*

𝔐 pronounces the verbs in the first line as nouns, *a heap, two heaps, i.e.* heaps upon heaps; cf. Ex. 8^{14} (8^{10}). Many recent scholars, following an etymological conjecture of Doorninck's, translate, *I have flayed them clean;* ‡ see note. — **17.** *When he had finished saying this, he threw the jawbone away, and so the place got the name Ramath-lehi*] the author interprets this name, by a false etymology, " the throwing of the jawbone "; in reality, Ramah, as in Ramoth-gilead and many other names of places, means ' height' ; § see below, p. 346.

9. In 2 S. 23^{11} for רְהָיָה 𝔐 Θηρία 𝔊, read, with 𝔊$^{L\,al.}$ *ἐπὶ σιαγόνα*, and Fl. Jos., לְחְיָה; Bochart, Kennicott, Ew., Then., Bö., We., Ke., Kamph., Dr., al. mu. — 12. הִשָּׁבְעוּ לִי פֶּן הִפְגְּעוּן] cf. 21^7 (יברחי with inf.), Is. 54^9 (מן with inf.).

---

* See Bochart, *Hierozoicon*, i. p. 171 ff., ed. Rosenm., with the writers cited by Rosenm., p. 171, n. According to Moslem tradition the first blood in the cause of Islam was drawn with the same weapon. A party of Meccan idolaters having come upon the believers at prayer in a retired place, words led to blows, and Sa'd Ibn Abi Waqqās broke the head of one of the heathen with the jawbone (*laḥy* = Heb. *leḥi*) of a camel (Ṭabari, i. p. 1169; Ibn Hishām, p. 166).

† Note also the similarity of the names; see above on 3^{31}, p. 106.

‡ Or, *shaved them;* Doorn., Matthes, Bu., Kautzsch, Buhl.

§ So 𝔐 correctly pronounces it.

—**14.** ‏רוא בא ער יחי‎] circumstantial clause preceding the principal sentence; cf. 18³ 19¹¹ 1 S. 9¹¹, with pf. Gen. 44⁴ Jud. 3²⁴ 18²², Dr³. § 169; Davidson, *Syntax*, p. 188–190. — ‏וסיחים הריני יקראי‎] continuation of the circumstantial clause; with the pregnant constr. cf. 14⁶ 19³, ‏הריע‎, hurrah in triumph, Jer. 50¹⁵. — **15.** ‏יהי‎] Dt. 18³; here the under jaw. — ‏טריה‎] Is. 1⁶ of a recent wound; cf. Arab. *ṭariy*, ‘fresh, moist, juicy.’ * 𝕲 ἐρριμμένην, 𝕷, follow the common Aram. sense of ‏טרי‎. — **16.** ‏נרחי החטור הטור חטרתים‎] 𝕳 took the last two words as nouns (‏חמר‎ paronomastic by-form of ‏חמר‎ Ex. 8¹⁰; cf. 1 S. 16²³), the sg. and dual being joined as in 5³⁰. 𝕲 rightly read them as inf. abs. and finite verb. It is most natural to connect this verb with ‏חמר‎ ‘heap,’ Ex. 8¹⁰ (J); ‏חמר חמרתים‎, *I heaped them all up*; cf. 𝔖𝔗. 𝕲 translates, ἐξαλείφων ἐξήλειψα αὐτούς (𝕷 *delevi*). Doorn. would combine this with Arab. *ḥamara*, ‘pare, skin, shave’; † ‘as a razor takes the hair off the face, so Samson had cleared the Philistines off the earth’; Buhl (BSZ. *s.v.*), better, *Ich habe sie gründlich geschunden*. There is, however, no trace of this meaning or anything like it in Hebrew. — ‏רמת יחי‎] *Height of Lehi*; cf. ‏רמת נגב‎, ‏רמת נירע‎, ‏רמת‎. ‡ So 𝕳 pronounces (‏רמת‎); 𝕲 and 𝕷 also connect with ‏רום‎. The author etymologizes, “the throwing of the jawbone” (‏רמה‎).

18, 19. Origin of the spring En ha-Qôrē at Lehi. — 18.

After his hot work he was very thirsty, and finding no water cried to Yahweh. — *Thou hast given thy servant this great victory*] cf. 1 S. 19⁵ 2 S. 23¹⁰,¹² — *And now shall I die of thirst, and fall into the hands of the uncircumcised?*] exclamatory question. — **19.** *And God clave the Mortar which is in Lehi*] Heb. *Maktesh;* probably a round and somewhat deep basin, called from its form “the Mortar,” perhaps with a cleft in one of its sides from which the water flowed. There was a Maktesh in Jerusalem also (Zeph. 1¹¹), doubtless so called from its configuration. He drank of the water thus miraculously given, and his strength revived. The name of the spring perpetuated the memory of his cry and God's answer. — *En ha-qôrē*] interpreted by the author, Spring of the Caller, *i.e.* the man who called to God in his need. In reality, ‘the caller’ (*qôrē*) is the Hebrew name of the partridge (1 S. 26²⁰ Jer. 17¹¹), and the original significance of the name was doubtless, Partridge Spring. § — *Which is at Lehi to this day*] a witness to the fact; cf. 1 S. 6¹⁸: the great stone on which they set down the ark is a witness to this day, in the field of Joshua the Beth-

---

* So 𝕷 here. See Bochart, i. p. 171, ed. Rosenm.

† JDMich. had long before combined 𝕲𝕷 with the Arabic word.

‡ 𝕲 Ραμαθ, Ρεμμαθ. § Stud., We., Reuss.

shemite.* The words are wrongly divided in 𝕸, the Spring of the Caller which is in Lehi, unto this day. — **20.** *He judged Israel twenty years, in the days of the Philistines*] see on 12¹, and Introduction, § 7.

19. נקב] cleave a rock, to bring forth water, Is. 48²¹ (referring to Ex. 17⁶ or Nu. 20¹¹). —אהריב] elsewhere in the context יהוה.—הבכהש] Zeph. 1¹¹ Prov. 27²², MH. (more freq. fem. מכתש, Levy, *MHWb.* iii. p. 117; see Jerome on Zeph. 1¹¹, *Opp.* ed. Vallarsi, vi. 686); the vb. Prov. *l.c.*, MH. freq. Of an excavation in the earth shaped like a mortar, *Tos. Nidda*, viii. 6 (p. 650, ed. Zuckerm.); as the proper name of a place, in an inscription published by de Vogüé, see SS. p. 347.† Very many interpreters, ancient and modern, understand by יחי here, not the place so called (v.⁹ cf. v.¹⁷), but the ass's jawbone (v.¹⁶). הבכהש is then explained of a hollow in the bone, probably the socket of a large tooth; cf. ὅλμος 'mortar,' ὁλμίσκος (Poll., ii. 93) 'socket of a tooth,' *mortariolum*. So numerous Fathers, some of the Rabbis who discuss the question in *Beresh. rabba*, § 98; Ra., Bochart, Grot. Others interpret, *molar tooth*; so 𝕮reuchl. m. ven.1 (בכה) Σ 𝕷.‡ Accordingly Bochart, Grotius, and others suppose that after having once thrown the jaw away he picked it up again and drank from it. But that this is not the author's meaning is clear from the fact that he says that the spring was to be seen at Lehi *to this day*. See esp. Clericus, who refutes Bochart at length, and quotes on his side Ussher, Arias Mont., Castell, Schm., al. *Lehi* was probably so called from some real or fancied resemblance to the jaw of an animal; comp. the peninsula Ὄνου γνάθος in Laconia, just within Malea, Strabo, viii. 5, 2, p. 363 (Steinthal, We.). § What the point of resemblance was it is idle for us to imagine. In the hillside or at its base was a round depression, called from its shape Maktesh, Mortar, and in this was En ha-qōrē, the Partridge Spring. In these verses we have, therefore, a very good example of the variety of aetiological legend which grows out of the explanation of names of places by popular etymology. ‖ Ramath-lehi is the place where Samson threw away the jawbone; Maktesh, a hollow which God made to reach water to quench Samson's thirst; while En ha-qōrē is the spring which burst forth in response to his call. We may safely go a step further, and apply the same explanation to the whole story of the slaughter of the Philistines; בלהי in Hebrew may be understood either *at Lehi* or *with a jawbone*. The story has

---

* We., Dr.

† *Maktesh* a rock in the place called Lehi, 𝕮ven. 2 al. (see Ki.), RLbG., cf. Fl. Jos.

‡ 𝕮ven. 2. ant. al. בכה; see Ki., *Comm.* and *Lex.* Ki. explains כבה as socket of the tooth; but see *Aruch*, s.v. בכה²; and Bochart, i. p. 176.

§ Beer-lahai-roi (Gen. 16¹⁴) is probably a name of the same kind; יהי ראי, wild goat's jawbone, We. *Prol*⁸. p. 339. We. refers also to Wakidi, p. 298, n. 2, Yaqūt iv. p. 353off.: Arab names of places; *Lahy*, or *Lahyu*, *gamal*, camel's jaw.

‖ See Bernheim, *Lehrbuch der hist. Methode*²., p. 263 f.

no mythical features. — Samson's fountain was shown in Jerome's time and later in the vicinity of Eleutheropolis; see Rob., *BR².* ii. 64 f.; Guérin, *Judée,* ii. p. 318 f. Modern attempts to identify Lehi have thus far led to nothing. Van de Velde's Tell el-Lekiyeh, 4 m. N. of Beersheba, is far too remote (see on v.[8]); Guérin's Khirbet 'Ain el-Lehi, NW. of Bethlehem (*Judée,* ii. p. 396 ff.), is unverified, and is also too far away; on Khirbet es-Siyyagh see above, p. 344. Conder finds an 'Ayūn Qāra, NW. of Zorah (*Tent Work,* i. p. 277); the name does not appear in the *Name Lists* of the Survey. See *DB².* i. p. 939; Ri. *HWB¹.* p. 898.

XVI. 1–3. Samson carries off the gates of Gaza. — Samson
visits Gaza and lodges with a harlot. The Philistines learn of his presence, and lay their plans to kill him in the morning. He rises in the middle of the night, pulls up the gate-posts, and carries off the city-gates to a hill near Hebron. — The story is of the same character with the rest of the cycle, and doubtless of the same origin. In v.[2] a later hand appears to have exaggerated the precautions taken by the Philistines, from which some confusion results.

1. *Gaza*] the most southern city of Palestine on the coast and on the land route to Egypt through the desert. Its position made it, from the earliest times, a place of great commercial and military importance ; its name is found in the Egyptian lists from the time of Thothmes III.,[*] long before the Philistine invasion, as well as in the Amarna tablets ; and it is still a thriving city of 16,000 inhabitants.[†] — *A harlot*] Jos. 2[1] Gen. 38[15] &c. — 2. *It was told the Gazaites, Samson is come hither*] the first verb has accidentally dropped out of 𝔐. The rest of the verse is hard to understand. If the Philistines were lying in wait for him *at the gate of the city*, it is not easy to conceive how Samson could pull up and carry off the gates unmolested ; if the author imagined that the guards were asleep,[‡] he could hardly have failed to give us some intimation, — and what sound sleepers they must have been ! Studer would omit the words *all night* in v.[2],[§] and suppose that they lay in wait

---

[*] Müller, *Asien u. Europa,* p. 159.

[†] On Gaza see Reland, *Palaestina,* p. 787-800; Neubauer, *Géog. du Talmud,* p. 67 f.; Le Strange, *Palestine under the Moslems,* p. 441 f.; Stark, *Gaza und die philist. Küste,* 1852; Rob., *BR².* ii. p. 36-43; Guérin, *Judée,* ii. p. 178-211; *SWP. Memoirs,* iii. 234 f., 248 ff.; Gatt, *ZDPV.* vii. p. 1-14, viii. p. 69-79; G. A. Smith, *Hist. Geog.,* p. 181-189; Bäd³., p. 157 ff.   [‡] Cler., al.   [§] So also Doorn.

for him at the gates *all day*, but when the gates were closed at night, feeling sure that he could not escape, withdrew until morning. But if this had been the author's meaning, he would have written *all day*, or, *until the gates were closed*, or, *until sunset* (when every one would understand that the gates were shut, cf. Jos. 2⁵). I suspect that the whole of v.⁴ᵇ is a later addition, intended to make Samson's escape the more wonderful by exaggerating the precautions which the Philistines took to prevent it. A less radical, but at the same time less probable, conjecture would be that the author wrote, *They surrounded the house, and lay in wait for him all night long;* supposing that in the darkness Samson slipped through their lines. — *They kept quiet all night, saying, When morning dawns we will kill him*] they had no reason to think that he would try to leave the place by night, or that he could get out, after the gates were closed, even if he attempted it ; so they did nothing, confident that in the morning they would be able to find and kill him. The half-verse seems to me to exclude v.⁴ᵇ, with its contradictory representation that they lay in wait for him all night at the gate. — **3.** In the middle of the night he arose, and made his way through the deserted streets to the city gate. — *And laid hold of the doors of the city gate and the two gate-posts, and pulled them up, together with the bar*] the two leaves of the gate were not hinged to the gate-posts, but turned on pins moving in sockets in the sill and lintel. The bar was let into the two posts, and secured by some kind of a lock.* Samson pulled the posts out of the ground, and carried off in one piece the doors and the whole framework. — *And put them on his shoulders, and carried them up to the top of the hill that faces Hebron*] the distance from Gaza to Hebron cannot be far from forty miles. A late Latin tradition, of which the inhabitants of the city are said to know nothing,† fixes the place where Samson deposited the gates of Gaza at El-Munṭār, ‡ a hill SE. of Gaza, and only a quarter of an hour outside the walls, § and this site is adopted, against the plain text, by some recent commentators, who are

---

* See *DB*². i. p. 1129.   † Rob., *BR*². ii. p. 39 n.

‡ Sandys (1611), Quaresmius (1616-25) ; see Rob. *l.c.* So also Bertrand, Guérin.

§ On El-Munṭār see Rob., *BR*². ii. p. 39; Guérin, *Judée*, ii. p. 188 L; *SWP. Memoirs*, iii. p. 237; Bäd³., p. 159; Gatt, *ZDPV*. vii. p. 1 L

inclined to reduce as much as possible the wonderful character of Samson's feats.* It is possible, as Bertheau suggests, that some natural formation on a hill near Hebron may have been called the "Gates of Gaza," and that the story thus had an origin similar to those in the preceding chapter (Lehi); but it is clear that the narrator was not aware of any such local connexion in this case, and the hypothesis is neither necessary nor probable.

1. וילך שמשון עזה] 𝕲ᴬˢᴸᴹ s ε καὶ ἐπορεύθη Σ. ἐκεῖθεν (sub obel.*) εἰς Γάζαν. This connects the story with the close of the preceding (15¹⁹); from the scene of his exploit at Lehi he went to Gaza. No one would be likely to make such a connexion across 15²¹, while after that verse the somewhat awkward particle would easily be dropped. The ἐκεῖθεν (משם) is therefore probably original. — 2. לעזתים] patrial adjective from fem. n. pr. preserving the fem. ending t; contrast התמני 15⁶. The verb is lacking: 𝕲 ἀνηγγέλη, ἀπηγγέλη = ויגד. The other versions supplied the verb in translation. — ויתחרשו] Hithpa.'; Hiph. is usual. Like החשה (18⁹) and דמם (1 S. 14⁹), החריש means 'keep still' in both senses of the Engl. words, silent, and motionless, inactive; in the latter sense 2 S. 19¹¹ Ex. 14¹⁴. — לאמר עד אור הבקר והרגנהו] 𝕲ᴬᴾˢᴸᴹᴼ ἕως φωτὸς πρωὶ μείνωμεν (sub obel. * s) καὶ ἀποκτείνωμεν αὐτόν. μείνωμεν is probably inserted to smooth the construction in Greek. In 𝔐 the principal verb is left to be understood from the preceding; with the aposiopesis cf. esp. 1 S. 1²². The question may be raised whether the cons. pf. והרגנהו is to be taken as belonging to the clause of עד (till the morning dawns and we kill him), or as the apodosis of that clause (wait till the morning dawns, and *then* we will kill him). Cf. Jos. 1¹⁵ 6¹⁰ Gen. 29⁸ 1 S. 1²² 2 S. 10⁶; Dr³., p. 135 Obs., thinks that in these instances the general structure of the sentence favours the former alternative, and that if the latter were true we might expect rather ואחר with impf. (Jos. 2¹⁶).† It must be borne in mind, however, that the consec. pf. in these cases is not *grammatically* subordinate, but co-ordinate. The structure is precisely the same in Jud. 6¹ᴵᴷ 1 S. 10⁸ 14²⁴ Gen. 27⁴⁶, where the pf. psychologically belongs to the time clause, as in Ex. 33²²ᶠ· Jos. 6¹⁰, where it psychologically belongs to the main sentence. The Hebrew only *says:* Expectabis donec veniam ad te et ostendam tibi quid facias (1 S. 10⁸); et protegam dextera mea donec transeam et tollam manum meam et videbis posteriora mea (Ex. 33²²ᶠ·). This indifference of construction represents a certain looseness of conception; the question which our more logical apparatus of particles and tenses compels us in translating to answer in one way or the other can hardly have occurred to the writer and his readers at all. Only in cases where some emphasis was thrown on the temporal relation of the following verb do we find it introduced by אז or אחר. — 3. וישאו בדלתות ונ׳] this verb is pronounced by 𝔐 as *primae gutturalis* also 1 K. 6¹⁰ Eccl. 7¹ᵘ·; elsewhere

---

always א־פ; so 12⁶ 16²¹ 20⁴; Kö., i. p. 393. — וַיִּסָּעֵם] 16¹⁴; pull up, out of the ground, Is. 33²). Transitive only in these places. — יְרִחַ כָּם] the bar of the gate, freq. named with the doors, 1 S. 23⁷ Dt. 3⁶ 2 Chr. 8⁵; sometimes of metal, 1 K. 4¹³; oftener, no doubt, of wood, Am. 1⁵ Nah. 3¹⁴. — אֲשֶׁר עַל פְּנֵי הֶבְרוֹן] in front of; in topographical use frequently equivalent to *east* (cf. שְׂמֹאל left-hand = north; יָמִין right-hand = south; אַחֲרֵי west, Jud. 18¹²), 1 K. 11⁷ 2 K. 23¹³ Zech. 14⁴; Dt. 32⁴⁹ 34¹; 1 S. 15⁷ Jos. 13⁸; 1 K. 6³ 7⁶ Ez. 42⁸; expressly, Nu. 21¹¹ (south, Jos. 18¹⁴; west, Jos. 15⁸). Elsewhere, *overlooking*, Nu. 21²¹ 23²⁸ Gen. 18¹⁶ 19²⁸. In no sense could a hill 250 feet above the sea-level, and less than a mile from Gaza, be said to be עַל פְּנֵי חֶבְרוֹן; El-Muntār is, moreover, not on the road to Hebron, or in the direction of that city.

4-22. Samson and Delilah.

— Samson again falls in love with a Philistine woman, in the valley of Sorek. She is bribed by the rulers to discover the secret of his perilous might. Three times he deceives her, but at last, tired of her incessant importunity, reveals the truth. While he sleeps in her lap, his locks are shaved off; when he awakes his strength has left him. His enemies bind him and put out his eyes; he is led off to Gaza, and set to grind at the mill in prison. — **4.** *Afterwards*] loose connexion; 2 S. 2¹ 8¹ &c. — *The valley of Sorek*] Jerome notes a village, Cafarsorec, in the region of Eleutheropolis, near Saraa (Zorah), Samson's home.* The English survey found ruins of Sūrik, three-quarters of an hour west of Ṣur'ah (Zorah), on the north side of Wady Ṣurār.† The valley of Sorek was probably this great Wady, whose fertility is remarked by modern travellers.‡ Sorek is in Hebrew the specific name of a choice variety of grape (Is. 5² Jer. 2¹¹ Gen. 49¹¹), from which the valley may well have received its name; cf. the valley of Eshcol (grape cluster) near Hebron (Nu. 13²³). — *Whose name was Delilah*] the current etymological interpretations of the name, *languishing, love-lorn,* or *delicate,*§ are ludicrously inapt. — **5.** *The tyrants of the Philistines*] see on 3³. — *Beguile him*] 14¹⁵. — *And find out by what means his strength is great, and by what means we may be able to cope with*

---

* OS². 153₆; cf. 295₇₈. Saraa is ten miles north of Eleutheropolis, OS². 293₂₉ 151₁₀.   † SWP. Memoirs, iii. p. 53.

‡ Guérin, *Judée,* ii. p. 31 f.; SWP. Memoirs, iii. p. 3; cf. G. A. Smith, *Hist. Geog.,* p. 218-222.

§ Ges., MV., Be., al. For older *jeux d'esprit* of the same kind see *Sota,* 9ᵇ. Mythological explanations, Steinthal, *Z.l'Psych.,* ii. p. 140 f.; Wietzke, *Der biblische Simson,* p. 44 f.; see note below, at the end of ch. 16.

him, that we may secure him to torment him] not, *wherein his
great strength lies,** which destroys the correspondence between
the two clauses, and is grammatically inexact.† They imagine
that this strength depends upon some secret means which he
employs, some charm or amulet. ‡ *And we will each give thee
eleven hundred shekels of silver*] probably each of the *five* Philistine rulers (3³). The number *eleven hundred* is a somewhat
singular one (cf. 17²); Reuss suggests that it may mean, over a
thousand. The intrinsic value of the shekel is about sixty cents;
the sum offered is meant to seem enormous.

6–9. The first trial; the seven bowstrings. — 6. Delilah
sets about the task, and asks Samson what makes him so strong,
and with what he could be bound to torment him. — **7.** *If they
should bind me with seven green bowstrings which have not been
dried, my strength would fail, and I should be like any other
man*] seven, the charmed number. *Bowstrings*, cords made from
the intestines of animals are probably meant. They were to be
green, in which state they were less likely to fray or break than
when they had been dried, while at the same time the knots would
set much more firmly. — **8.** The Philistine princes furnish her
with such cords, which she would not have at hand in the house,
and she binds him with them. We may imagine that this was
done as if in sport, or while he slept, as in v.¹⁴·¹⁹. — **9.** *And she
had the liers in wait ready in the inner room*] to seize Samson if
the experiment succeeded. As it is presumed in the following
trials that Samson was not aware of the presence of these men, we
have to suppose that they did not rush out of their concealment
at Delilah's signal, but waited to see whether the cords held or
not. — *The Philistines are upon thee, Samson! And he snapped
the bowstrings as a strand of tow snaps when it comes near the
fire*] lit. *scents the fire;* without actual contact; cf. Job 14⁹, the
dried-up tree revives at the scent of water. Compare also 15¹⁴.
— *So the secret of his strength was not disclosed.*

10–12. The second trial; the new ropes. — 10. *Thou hast
cheated me and told me falsehoods*] v.¹³·¹⁵. — **11.** *If they should*

---

bind me fast with new ropes, with which no work has been done]
which have never been strained or chafed; cf. 15¹³. For the rest,
cf. v.⁷. — 12. Cf. v.⁸. — *He snapped them off his arms like a thread*]
v.⁹ 15¹⁴; *thread*, in contrast to rope. Observe how the expression
is varied in the three places.

4. צִרִים] Baer, or שִׁירָה Ven²., Norzi, Mich.; not שׁוּרָה Ven¹., Jablonski, Van
der Hooght.—5. נדול [נָכֶה כּחַ נדוֹל is predicate, the attributive adjective
would have the article; so in the following instances, v.⁶·¹⁵.—וּבְּכֶה נוּכַר לוֹ]
Gen. 32²⁶ 1 S. 17⁹ Nu. 13³⁰ cf. Jer. 20⁷ 38²² Obad.⁷; *be a match for him,
able to overcome him.*—וְנֶתֶן לוֹ] the only instance of Kal impf. 1 pl. of this
vb. with *a.*—7. יְתָרִים לַחִים [יֶתֶר Ps. 11² cf. מֵיתָר Ps. 21¹³; Arab. *watar,*
'string of a bow, chord of a lute'; Syr. *ithar,* id. (made from the intestines of
sheep, &c., Karmes. in PS. 1652). 𝕲ᴬᴮᴾˢᴸᴺᴼ ⌐ ̣ *ἐν ἑπτὰ νευραῖς ὑγραῖς,*
similarly 𝕃, Abulw., Ra., JDMich., Stud., Be. 𝕲ᴹ *κλήμασιν ὑγροῖς* (or *κλημα-
τίσιν ὑγραῖς*), cf. Fl. Jos. *κλήμασιν ἑπτὰ . . . ἀμπέλου,*⁎ *withes.* So Ki.,
Vatabl., Cler., AV., RV., al.—אֲשֶׁר לֹא חֹרְבוּ] Pual, causative passive; *have not
been dried.* For their proper use it was indispensable that they be thoroughly
dried, so as not to stretch; for the present purpose green gut was more
flexible to tie, the knots less liable to slip, and the cord itself less likely to
split.—וְהִלְּ־] v.¹¹·¹³ (𝕲) Is. 57¹³.—הָאדם] human kind; the genus in contrast to the exceptional individual; hence sometimes equivalent to *the rest of
mankind, other men;* Jer. 32²⁰ Ps. 73⁶.—8. וַיִּקְחוּ] Hiph.—9. הָארֵב] collective; cf. אֹרֵב 9²⁰.—רֶנֶּעְרָה] Is. 1³¹⁽ MH.—הָרִיחַ] Hiph. of sense-perception;
cf. האֵזין &c.—10. הֵתֵל [הֵתֵל, Gen. 31⁷ Ex. 8²⁵.

13, 14. The third trial; weaving his locks in the loom. —

She again upbraids him for the deception he has practised on her;
he tells her that if his hair were woven into the web his strength
would leave him. — In 𝔐 there is a lacuna between v.¹³ and v.¹⁴,
as may be clearly seen in RV.: "And he said unto her, If thou
weavest the seven locks of my head with the web. ¹⁴ And she
fastened it with the pin, and said," &c. The end of what Samson
said and the beginning of what Delilah did are lacking; cf. v.⁷⁻⁹·
¹¹ᶠ·¹⁷⁻¹⁹. The Greek versions enable us to restore the original text.
The difficulties which remain are due to our imperfect acquaintance
with the structure of the loom and the process of weaving. In
particular, an error about the nature and use of the *pin* early led
to misinterpretation, and that to glosses in both 𝔐 and the versions. It was not a nail or peg, driven into the wall (𝕲) or the

---

⁎ *Viligenea vincula,* Florus, iii. 20, 4, cited by Schleusner.

ground (𝕃), or stuck in the cloth-beam of the loom to keep it
from unrolling,* but a pointed piece of wood corresponding to
the σπάθη of the Greek weaver, which was used to "beat up" the
woof in the chain, in order to make its threads lie close together
and form a firm texture.† We restore and translate, accordingly:
**13. . . . *If thou weave the seven braids of my head along with the
web, and beat up with the pin, my strength will fail and I shall be
like any other man.* 14. *So while he was asleep Delilah took the
seven braids of his head, and wove them into the web, and beat up
with the pin,* &c.** ‡ We are to imagine the simplest kind of an
upright loom,§ in which an unfinished piece of stuff was standing.
While Samson sleeps on the ground with his head close to the
loom, ‖ Delilah weaves his long hair into the warp with her fingers,
and beats it up tight and hard. He was thus most securely
fastened, in a prostrate position, to the frame of the loom, the
posts of which were firmly planted in the earth. — *And she said,
The Philistines are upon thee, Samson! And he awoke from his
sleep, and pulled up the loom and the web*] as he sprang up, he
pulled the posts of the loom out of the ground by the hair of his
head, which was fast in the web. The same misunderstanding
which has given rise to glosses in 𝕲 and 𝕃 in the first half-verse
has here led to the insertion in 𝔐 of the words, *the pin,* before
the loom, which betrays that it is a gloss by its ungrammatical
construction.

13. את שבע מחלפות ראשי] the braids in which his long unruly locks were
plaited to keep them out of the way; cf. v.¹⁹. Stud. remarks that πλόκαμοι
is frequently employed of consecrated locks, *e.g.* Aesch., *Choeph.* 6; Eurip.,
Bacch. 494; cf. also Pollux, ii. § 30. See Spencer, *De legibus rit.,* iii. diss. i.
c. 6, § 1. — Of the words which have accidentally fallen out of 𝔐 we have
two Greek versions. One of these is represented by ᴮ: ¶ *ἐὰν ὑφάνῃς τὰς*

---

* Ki., AV., al.

† Braun, *De vestitu sacerdotum,* 1698, p. 253. Stud. feels constrained by היתה
הארג v.¹⁴ to interpret יתד, not of the σπάθη which was used in the upright loom, but
of the "lay" (κτείς, *pecten*) of a horizontal loom; similarly Ke., Cass. But this is
on all accounts impossible.   ‡ See crit. note.

§ Such looms are described by Robinson, *BR².* i. p. 169; Palmer, *Desert of the
Exodus,* 1871, i. p. 125; see also Nowack, *Hebr. Archäologie,* i. p. 240 f.

‖ Different representations of how she got Samson there, *PAOS.,* Oct. 1889,
p. 178; Doorn²., p. 28.

¶ So, with slight variations, 𝔑.

ἑπτὰ σειρὰς * τῆς κεφαλῆς μου σὺν τῷ διάσματι | καὶ ἐγκρούσῃς τῷ πασσάλῳ
εἰς τὸν τοῖχον, καὶ ἔσομαι ὡς εἰς τῶν ἀνθρώπων ἀσθενής. καὶ ἐγένετο ἐν τῷ
κοιμᾶσθαι αὐτὸν καὶ ἔλαβεν Δαλειδα τὰς ἑπτὰ σειρὰς τῆς κεφαλῆς αὐτοῦ καὶ
ὕφανεν ἐν τῷ διάσματι | καὶ ἔπηξεν τῷ πασσάλῳ εἰς τὸν τοῖχον, καὶ εἶπεν κ.τ.ἑ.
The other is found in its most complete form in ᴹ and **s**: † ἐὰν διάσῃ τοὺς
ἑπτὰ βοστρύχους τῆς κεφαλῆς μου ἐν ἐκτάσει διάσματος, καὶ ἐγκρούσῃς τῷ
πασσάλῳ εἰς τὸν τοῖχον καὶ ἐπυφάνῃς ὡς ἐπὶ πῆχυν, καὶ ἀσθενήσω καὶ ἔσομαι
ὡς εἰς τῶν ἀνθρώπων. καὶ ἐκοίμισεν αὐτὸν Δαλιδα, καὶ ἐδιάσατο τοὺς ἑπτὰ
βοστρύχους τῆς κεφαλῆς αὐτοῦ μετὰ τῆς ἐκτάσεως, καὶ κατέκρουσεν ἐν τῷ
πασσάλῳ εἰς τὸν τοῖχον, καὶ ὕφανε, κ.τ.ἑ. The translation given in the text
follows the former of these two versions, which represents in Hebrew: אם
האריגני את שבע מחלפות ראשי עם המסכת | ותתקע ביתד וחליתי והייתי כאחר האדם : ויהי
בשכבו ותקח דלילה את שבע מחלפות ראשו ותארג במסכת ונר. The words were dropped
by a scribe who skipped from ביתד in v.[13] to the same word in v.[14]. Similarly
Houbigant, Be., Doorn.; Moore, *PAOS*. Oct. 1889, p. 176-180, where the
technical terms are explained, and *The Book of Judges in Hebrew*, in the
Sacred Books of the O.T., edited by P. Haupt. — [היתד הארג] no grammatical
explanation of the article in היתד is possible; the word is a gloss, probably
originally written in the margin by one who understood *the pin* in v.[13b. 14a] as
is done by **⑥** and **Ⱡ**, and missed here an explicit mention of the pulling out
of the pin.

**15-22. Samson discloses his secret, and is shorn of his
strength. — 15.** *How canst thou say, I love thee, when thou dost
not confide in me?*] cf. 1 K. 9[3]. Lit. *seeing that thy heart* (the
inner man with its secret thoughts) *is not with me;* cf. v.[17], "he
told her all his heart," *i.e.* all his mind, all that he knew about
the source of his strength. Not, *thy affection is not given to me,*
which is in itself a feeble tautology and does not accord with v.[17f].
— *Thrice already thou hast cheated me*] v.[10. 13]. — **16.** Cf. 14[17].
She beset him continually with her reproaches and importunities,
and urged him till his patience was utterly exhausted (10[16]) ; as
we might say with an imitation of the Hebrew phrase, he was tired
to death of it. — **17.** *He told her all his mind*] v.[15. 18] ; all that he
knew. — A razor had never been used on his head, for he had
been a religious devotee from infancy (13[5]) ; if he were shaved,
his strength would leave him, and he would become as weak as
other men ; cf. v.[7. 11. 13] (⑥). — **18.** Delilah saw that at last he had
told her the truth, and summoned the Philistine rulers, assuring
them that they would not be cheated again. They came, bringing

---

* See Pollux, *l.s.c.*   † Most other manuscripts present a mixed text.

the money they had promised (v.[5]). — **19.** She put him to sleep
on her lap (cf. v.[14] 𝔊), and calling a man who was in readiness,
had him shave off the seven braids of Samson's hair.   According
to 𝔐, she shaved it off herself; but then it is not apparent why
the man is mentioned at all ; it is not satisfactory to suppose that
he merely handed her the razor.[*]   Either the verb must be taken
causatively,[†] which is scarcely warranted by usage or construction,
or the text must be emended to read, *he* shaved, &c. — *And she
began to torment him, and his strength departed from him*] from
the words, *I will shake myself free*, v.[20], we are probably to understand that she bound him ; cf. v.[6].[‡]   𝔊 renders, *he began to be
brought low*,[§] which reading is preferred by Doorninck ; but the
passive is in itself less forcible, and the active is supported by v.[6].
How she tormented him is not related ; Jerome interprets, *coepit
abigere eum, et a se repellere.*   Perhaps the words refer merely to
her alarming cry, *the Philistines are upon thee.* — **20.** *He awoke
from his sleep, and thought, I shall get off as I have done time
and time again*] escape, go free ;[‖] not, *go out as at other times.*[¶]
— *I will shake myself free*] from the bonds with which Delilah had
secured him ;[**] or from the Philistines.[††]   Others interpret, *I will
shake myself awake.*[‡‡] — *For he did not know that Yahweh had
departed from him*] see 1 S. 18[12] 28[15] ; it would be the same thing
to say, *the spirit of Yahweh* (1 S. 16[14]).   If we would understand
the author's meaning, we cannot conceive his words too con-
cretely ; cf. v.[19b], *his strength departed from him.* — **21.** *The Philistines seized him and bored out his eyes*] 1 S. 11[2] Nu. 16[14].   The
Assyrian monuments represent the blinding of captives with a
sharp instrument ;[§§] cf. 2 K. 25[7]. — They took their prisoner down
to Gaza, their chief city.   Jewish teachers saw a retributive justice
in this : in Gaza he first went whoring ; therefore in Gaza he was
a prisoner.[‖‖] — *And made him fast with bronze shackles*] 2 S. 3[34]
2 K. 25[7]. — *And he was employed in grinding in the prison*] turn-

---

[*] Ki. 2[o].   [†] Ki. 1[o].

[‡] We might almost be tempted to conjecture that the words, *she bound him*, have
been accidentally omitted.   [§] Except B.   [‖] So, rightly, Ki., Reuss, Kittel.

[¶] EV., with most comm.; Schm. interprets, *go out to fight* with the Philistines.
[**] a Lyra, Be.   [††] Schm.   [‡‡] Ki.
[§§] Botta, *Monument de Ninive*, pl. 118; reproduced, *DB*[1]. s.v. "Punishments."
[‖‖] *Sota.* 9[b]; see the whole passage.

ing the handmill. This was hard and menial labour (Is. 47²) ;
in the household generally done by slave women. Among the
Greeks and Romans, being put to work at the mill was a not
uncommon and much-dreaded punishment of slaves, to which
there are many references in the comic poets.* Freemen were
also punished in this way for slight offences.† — The older commentators compare the story of Nisus of Megara, whose daughter,
Scylla, plucked out while he slept the purple hair in the middle
of his head on which his life depended. ‡ — 22. *His hair began
to grow as soon as it was shaved off*] this verse looks forward to
v.²⁹ᵃ, where Samson does the mightiest feat of all. The story
makes his strength inseparable from his sacred locks : when he is
shorn of them it leaves him ; when it is restored to him they must
have grown again.

19. הדיקה לו] the usual construction of this verb; cf. 14¹⁷ (accus.). —
כל הימים] *perpetually, constantly ;* Gen. 43⁹ 1 S. 18²⁹ 23¹⁴ Jos. 4²⁴, freq. in Dt.
and Jer. — ויהאלצתו] Pi. The vb. is common in Syr.; 'straiten, press, distress'; synonym of 'a'iq (= Heb. הציק). — למות] *to the point of death.* —
17. אם גלחתי ונ׳] on the form of the cond. sent. see Dr⁴., p. 177 f.; cf. v.⁷·¹¹·¹³
(imperf. in protasis). — 18. כי הגיד לה] Qerē ל׳, with all the versions and many
codd. and edd. of 𝔐 (De Rossi). The Kethib is mechanical repetition of
the preceding כי הגיד לה. — ותקרא אליה] the perf. consec. is impossible (against
Be.); read ותקרא, which a number of codd. have; Stud., Ke. — 19. ותהישנהו] Pi.¹
ותקרא—] על ברכיה 𝔊ᴬᴾˢᴸᴹᴼ s t ἀvὰ μέσον, i.e. בין, which Doorn. adopts. —
לאיש] idiomatic determination, the man called for the purpose; see on 8²⁶.
— 𝔊 s t τὸν κουρέα (ᴮ alone ἀνδρα), 𝔏𝔖 *tonsorem ;* the context suggested the
more specific term. The Hebrew text lacks here something of its usual definiteness. — ותגלח] we should probably emend ותגלח. — לענותו] 𝔊ᴬᴾˢᴸᴹᴺᴼ
s t καὶ ἤρξατο ταπεινοῦσθαι, prob. pronouncing the inf. as Pual, לענות, or
poss. לענות (𝔐 Ex. 10³); adopted by Doorn., Kautzsch. — 20. אצא כפעם
בפעם] 20³⁰·³¹ Nu. 24¹ 1 S. 3¹⁰ 20²⁵; cf. שנה בשנה, חדש בחדש, יום ביום, &c. On
עפם see on 15⁸. — ואנער] connected in the same tense with אצא, since not two
consecutive acts are meant, but two simultaneous moments in one act. With
the vb. cf. Hithpa. Is. 52². ההתנערי מעפר קומי שבי ירושלם. Ni. is elsewhere
(Ps. 109²³ Job 38¹³) § passive to Pi. (Ex. 14²⁷ Ps. 136¹⁶). Perhaps, in the

---

* See Marquardt, *Privatleben der Römer*, 1879, p. 179, 405; Plaut., *Bacch.* 781;
Terent., *Phorm.* i. 2, 20; *Andr.* i. 2, 28; &c.

† *Cod. Theodos.* ix. 40, 3. 5. 6; Socrates, *hist. eccles.*, v. 18.

‡ Apollod., *Bibliotheca*, iii. 15, 8 § 2; Ovid, *Metam.* viii. 8 ff. 77 ff.; cf. the similar
story of Pterelaos and his golden hair, Apollod., ii. 4, 7 § 4; ii. 4, 5 § 5 f.

§ In the latter it is perhaps a gloss ; see Siegfried.

absence of a complement, it should be taken here in the sense, 'arouse myself to activity, exert myself' (𝕿, Ki., Cass.); cf. MH. נִעֵר (Levy, *NHWb*. iii. p. 414). — וֹהוּא לֹא יָדַע] *for he did not realize;* circumst. clause. — בֵּנחֻשׁתַּיִם] the dual, as we speak of a pair of handcuffs. — וַיְהִי טֹחֵן] lit. *he became a grinder,* it was his permanent occupation. — בְּבֵית הָאֲסִירִים] here and in v.[25] Qerē הָאֲסוּרִים, prob. intended, not as plur. of אָסִיר, which would be trivial and at variance with the principle of the correction in Gen. 39[20], but of אָסוּר (15[14]); cf. בֵּית הָאֵסוּר Jer. 37[15], 'house of bonds,' not, 'of the bound.' In any case the correction is unnecessary. — לְצַמֵּחַ] Pi. only of growth of hair, 2 S. 10[5] Ez. 16[7]; Kal, Lev. 13[37].

23–25. The Philistines celebrate their triumph at Gaza. —

23. The rulers of the five Philistine cantons (3[3]) assemble at Gaza to offer a great sacrifice to their god, Dagon. *Dagon* was worshipped by all the Philistines ;[*] we hardly know enough about their religion, however, to affirm that he was their national god, in the sense in which Chemosh, for example, was the god of Moab. Of the character and worship of Dagon we know only what is to be gathered from the passage before us and from 1 S. 5. According to Philo Byblius, who gives him a place in his Phoenician theogony, he was a god of agriculture, Ζεὺς ἀρότριος ; but this is probably only an etymological interpretation of the name. Another etymology derives the name from the Hebrew *dag,* 'fish.' Since David Kimchi (died about 1235 A.D.), it has been the common opinion that the idol of Dagon spoken of in 1 S. 5[4] had the form of a man from the waist up, while below the waist it was in the likeness of a fish ; but this theory is probably no more than an ingenious attempt to explain the corrupt text of 1 S. 5[4] by the aid of etymology ; see crit. note. — *And for festivities*] lit. *for rejoicing.* Their rejoicing before the god was the demonstrative expression of their gratitude (cf. Dt. 12[12. 18] 16[11] 27[7] Lev. 23[40] Neh. 8[10-12]). It is going quite beyond the evidence, however, to infer from this celebration, as some scholars are inclined to do, that the worship of Dagon had always a joyous and festive character. — *Our god has given Samson, our enemy, into our power*] just as the Israelites would have said under like circumstances ; cf. 11[21] Dt. 3[3], Mesha's inscription, l. 14 f., 19, 32, &c. — **24.** *When the people*

---

[*] There was a temple of Dagon at Ashdod; 1 S. 5[1ff.] 1 Macc. 10[84] 11[4]. Places bearing the name Beth-dagon represent other seats of his worship; see note.

saw him, they set up a shout in honour of their god] the verb is
the same which enters into the composition of Hallelujah, 'raise
the obligatory shout or song in honour of Jah'; see on 9⁷. —
For they said, &c.] these are not the words of the *hallel* shout,
which was probably a standing formula consisting of the names
and honorific epithets of the god, but an improvised hymn setting
forth the reason and meaning of their praises. The hymn is
formed upon a single rhyme, five times repeated, a thing very
common in Arabic, but of which there are not many examples in
the Old Testament :

> *nathan elōhênū beyadênū*
> *eth ōyebênū,*
> *we-eth macharib arsênū,*
> *wa-asher hirbah eth chalalênū ;* •

lit. *Our god has given into our hands our enemy, and the devastator
of our country, and the man who multiplied our slain;* the reference is obviously to 15⁴ᶠᶠ·¹⁴ᶠᶠ·. — **25.** *And when they were in high
spirits*] 18²⁰ 19⁶; the phrase is often used of exhilaration from the
effects of wine, 1 S. 25³⁶ 2 S. 13²⁸. They order Samson to be
brought from the prison to amuse them. — *He made sport before
them*] perhaps, as Milton imagines, by harmless exhibitions of his
strength. When he had thus amused them for a while, they
let him stand between the columns to rest. For surmises about
the construction of the temple, see on v.²⁶.

23. There was a Beth-dagon in the Judaean Lowland (Jos. 15⁴¹), and
another on the boundary of Asher, probably in the coast plain south of Carmel
(Jos. 19²⁷). An inscription of Sennacherib mentions a Bît-daganna in the
vicinity of Joppa (*Prism Inscr.* ii. 60); Eusebius locates a village named
Kefar-dagon between Diospolis and Jamnia, now Daḡūn (*PEF. Qu. St.*,
1874, p. 279). A Beit Degan exists also SE. of Nābulus (Rob., *BR²*. ii.
p. 232, 280). It is possible that some echo of the description which classic
authors give of Derceto, worshipped on the same coast, may have reached
Kimchi's ears; not a few more modern scholars have identified Dagon with
Derceto. Kimchi's representation of Dagon as half man, half fish, is not
derived from Jewish tradition; neither the ancient versions, Jerome, nor the
Talmud, know anything of such a figure. Rashi describes the image as a fish;
RLbG. as a man; Abarb. as fish from the waist up, but with hands and feet
like a man. The combination of Dagon with the man-fish Ὠδάκων of Berossus

---

• Pronounce *ch* as in Scotch ' loch.'

has no better foundation than the accidental and incomplete resemblance of the names. What the figures of men-fish from Assyrian sources, such, *e.g.* as are reproduced by Schrader in Riehm's *HWB.* s.v. (with the legend, "The fish-god Dagon"!), represent, is unknown. It is certain that they have nothing to do with the Babylonian god, Dagan, whose name is usually conjoined with those of Anu and "Ninib." Whether Dagan is connected in any way with the Philistine Dagon is not clear. See further, art. "Dagon" in *New Bible Dictionary* (A. & C. Black), where the literature will be found. — ולשבחה] fem. *nomen verbi*, Ki. — **24.** ויהללו את אלהיהם] besides the authors cited above (p. 256 f.), see Holzinger, *ZATW.* ix. p. 104. In the sense, 'extol,' the verb is employed also of men, *e.g.* Gen. 12¹⁶ Cant. 6⁹ Prov. 27² &c.; this is probably secondary. — חילו] plur. written defectively (Ki.); cf. 9⁴⁰. — **25.** כיטוב] the consonant text would be read כי טב (perf., 1 S. 16¹⁶·²³, Bö. § 1133, 1); the margin substitutes כטוב (inf.), construction as in 2 S. 13²⁸, כטוב לב אמנון בין, Esth. 1¹⁰; Dr., *TBS.* p. 234; Stud. The editors seem to have ignored the perfect. Kö., i. p. 445, recognizes only pl. טבו, and p. 447 seems to deny the inf. altogether. This is one of eight cases in which the text has two words, for which the margin reads one; *Ochla we-Ochla*, No. 100, Mass. on 2 Chr. 34⁶. — וייצחק] jussive; cf. ויצחק just below and note there. — האסירים] see note on v.²¹. — ויצחק] צחק Ez. 23³²; with these two exceptions only in Pentateuch; cf. צחק just above and v.²⁷. See König, *Einl. in das A. T.*, p. 151; Wright, *Comparative Grammar*, p. 60. — ויכבירו אותו בין הכבורים] play on the word. The doubling of the *m* in עמוד is inorganic, and merely preserves the preceding *ă*; cf. Arab. 'amūd.

26–30. Samson pulls down the house upon their heads. —

26. Samson asked the attendant who held his hand, to guide him in his blindness, to place him so that he could rest himself by leaning against the columns. The attendant was hardly a lad (EV.); we naturally think of a servant attached to the prison. — *Let me touch the columns on which the house is supported, that I may lean against them*] the two middle columns, v.²⁹. — **27.** *Now the building was full of the men and women, and all the tyrants of the Philistines were there; and on the roof were about three thousand men and women, looking on at Samson's playing*] the text seems to require us to imagine that the exhibition of Samson took place in the open court of the temple of Dagon. *The house* may then be supposed to have been a hall of columns, open toward the court, or the prostyle of the temple itself. Spectators of rank crowd the house; multitudes of others throng upon the roof, from which they overlook the court. When Samson has sufficiently amused them, he is placed near the columns in front of the house, or is led into the interior, perhaps in order that the magnates gathered in it may have a nearer view of him. He grasps the two middle columns, and by dislodging them brings down the whole edifice in ruins. No little ingenuity has been expended in the effort to conceive a method of architectural construction by which this might be made to seem possible.* There is some reason in the text itself to suspect that the three thousand men and women on the roof are an addition to the original narrative, exaggerating the catastrophe. If that be the case, the author may have represented the Philistine aristocracy assembled in the banqueting hall of the temple,† the roof of which can very well be imagined to have been supported on a pair of central pillars. Such a construction was suggested by J. B. Wideburg: ‡ potuerunt . . . quatuor trabes primariae, quibus reliquae minores insertae binis columnis in medio erectis imponi, quo facto, subtractisque deinceps columnis, necesse fuit trabes quoque impositas labi, quarum lapsum mox totius aedificii ruina consequi debuit.

26. נער] 'servant'; 19¹¹ 1 S. 9³ and often. — הניח [הניחה אותי] הנית with acc. is prop. 'put down, leave' in a place; sometimes implying previous removal thither, 'bring and leave'; Gen. 2¹⁵ Ez. 37¹⁴ Is. 14¹; so here (Cler., Reuss). *Suffer me that I may feel* (EV., with 𝔏𝔖, al. mu.) would be הניחה לי, and would be naturally construed with the inf. or with the cohort. 1 sing. (למשש or ואמשש. Others, *let me go*, release my hand; so 𝔗, Ke., Cass., Kittel; cf. Schm. *Let me rest* (𝔊ᴬᴾᴮᴸᴹ ↄ ε, Be.) would also be הנ׳ לי. — [והיכשני] Qerē והמישני as from מוש, § by the not infrequent confusion of עין with ין; cf. ימישו Ps. 115⁷. The sense requires והמישני (משש); see Kö., i. p. 360. The Qerē may intend to hint at a double sense, *let me remove the columns* (Mi. 2³); cf. Ki. — 27. והבית כלא האנשים והנשים] the article may perhaps be explained, those whom the occasion brought together; but this does not seem quite natural. Graver objection lies against the article in הראים below, which hardly admits of a grammatical explanation. ‖ These difficulties appear to have been created by the intrusion of the intermediate clauses, the removal of which leaves a complete and faultless sentence: והבית מלא האנשים והנשים הראים

---

* See Schm., Cler., Stud., Cass.; Sir Christopher Wren, *Parentalia*, p. 359 (quoted in Rosenmüller, *Das alte und neue Morgenland*, iii. p. 56 f.); Faber, *Archäologie*, p. 444; Stark, *Gaza*, p. 332-334.

† So Fl. Jos., *antt.* v. 8, 12 § 314-316. Such a room was found at much smaller sanctuaries; see 1 S. 9²².

‡ *Mathesis biblica*, Jena, 1730; quoted by Rosenm., *Scholia, ad loc.*; cf. also Wren, cited above, note *.   § The common vb. in Syr.

‖ If this stood alone, it would be properly regarded as dittography; cf. 𝔊ᴬᴾᴮᴸᴹᴼ.

בַּיְתָה שִׁמְשׁוֹן. In this text a scribe or editor may have missed a mention of the סְרָנִים (who were present, v.⁸), and introduced them somewhat awkwardly.* The three thousand men and women on the roof,† of whom nothing whatever is said in the sequel (v.⁸), may be a still later exaggeration of the ruin Samson wrought; compare the further exaggeration in Thdt. (*quaest.* 22), three thousand men and many times more women. This restoration, which is suggested and commended on purely grammatical grounds, would relieve the chief difficulty in imagining the scene described in v.²⁵⁻³⁰.

28. Samson prays for one moment of his old strength. — *O Lord Yahweh, remember me, and give me strength but this once, O God, that I may avenge myself on the Philistines for one of my two eyes*] lit. *a vengeance of one of my two eyes.* So the Hebrew text must be translated : the greatest evil he could inflict on them would be but partial retribution for the loss of his sight. ‡ The ancient versions render, *in one act of vengeance for my two eyes;* § others translate, *at once.* ‖ There is a grim humour in the words as we read them in 𝔐, which is altogether in character and may very well be original; see crit. note. — **29.** *Samson grasped the two middle columns on which the house was supported, and braced himself against them, one with his right hand, the other with his left*] the last words belong to both verbs; primarily to the first. Others, through a misapprehension of the context, interpret, " the ... columns on which the house was supported and on which it rested," which is mere tautology. — **30.** *Let me die myself with the Philistines*] lit. *let my soul die.* The soul is not in the Old Testament, as it is in our thought, the immortal in man. It is the breath-like something (*nefesh*, cf. ψυχή) which goes out and vanishes when he dies. There is nowhere a suggestion that the soul survives the man whose life it was; the inhabitants of the nether-world (*sheol*) are not *souls* but shades (*refaim*, εἴδωλα). — *He thrust with all his might*] we are probably to imagine that, standing between the two columns, he pushed them apart by extending his arms.¶ Others render, *bowed*, supposing that he put his arms around the columns and, bearing forward, carried

---

* Observe also שַׁבָּה for שָׁם, of which there is no other instance in Jud.

† 𝔊ᴮ ὡς ἑπτακόσιοι; cod. 237 conflate, ὡς τρισχίλιοι ἑπτακόσιοι.

‡ *Jer. Sota,* i. 8, fol. 17ʰ; Ra., Ki., Schm., Böttch., Stud., Ges. *Thes.*, p. 911, Be., Ke. § 𝔊ᴸ, Cler., Reuss, Kittel, al.

‖ AV., RV., after older scholars, Cass.   ¶ Be.

them with him; others still, *he lifted,*[*] or *pulled,*[†] *with all his might;* but none of these seems to accord as well with the meaning of the verb, and with v.[29], as the interpretation adopted above. — *The house fell on the rulers and all the people that were in it*] nothing is said about the fate of the multitude on the roof; see on v.[27]. — So in his death he killed more of the Philistines than he had in his life; it was the climax of his achievement. Clericus quotes Tacitus's account of the collapse of the wooden amphitheatre at Fidenae, in the reign of Tiberius, in which fifty thousand persons are said to have been buried in the ruins.[‡]

28. אך הפעם הזה] Gen. 18[32] Jud. 6[39] cf. 15[3] 16[18]. פעם is elsewhere uniformly fem. (2 S. 23[8] is corrected in the margin); הזה may be a later insertion. — ואנקמה נקם־אחת משתי עיני] with the construction cf. Lev. 26[25] Ps. 79[10] Jer. 50[29] 51[11]. ⅁ ἐκδικήσω ἐκδίκησιν μίαν (BN ἀνταπόδοσιν μίαν), L *pro amissione duorum luminum unam ultionem recipiam;* but if we should adopt this interpretation and emend, נקם אחד or נקמה אחת, we should involve ourselves in difficulty with the preposition in משתי, for which in this sense we should expect על (Stud.). Doorn. omits the numeral. § — משתי (ה) is regular (Ki.); the *ι* is affected by the preceding reduced vowel; cf. Kö. ii. p. 208. — **29.** וילפת] Niph. Ru. 3[8] Job 6[18] '. The exegetical tradition, 'lay hold of, embrace,' is probably founded on the context. In Arab. *lafata* means 'twist, wring,' *e.g.* a man's neck; *'alfatu* is a man with a powerful grasp, who hoists, or wrings, him who grapples with him (Lane). The verb here may have the sense, 'seize with a firm grasp.' — ויסמך עליהם] the subject is Samson (⅁A al. L S Schm., Cler., Ke., Cass., Be., SS., al. mu.), *he braced himself against the columns,* for the supreme effort. The construction which makes בית subject is defended by De Wette, *Stud. u. Krit.,* iv. 1831, p. 306; Stud.

31. Samson's kinsmen recover his body and bury him in the ancestral tomb. — *His kinsmen and all his family*] lit. *brethren and father's house;* see on 9[1]. — *Between Zorah and Eshtaol*] on *Zorah* see on 13[2]; *Eshtaol,* usually named with Zorah (Jos. 15[33] 19[41] Jud. 13[25] 18[2. 11]), according to Eusebius ten miles north of Eleutheropolis, ‖ is identified with the small modern village Eshū'a, thirteen English miles N. of Beit Gibrin, and near Ṣur'ah (Zorah).¶ Here Samson's burial place was shown in later times, in the family tomb of the Manoahites; cf. 8[32] 12[7] 10[1-5] 12[8-15]. — *He had judged Israel twenty years*] see on the chronology, Introduction, § 7.

Mythical interpretations of the story of Samson. — The similarity, in several particulars, between the story of Samson and that of Herakles was early noticed; see Euseb., *chron. canon.*, ed. Schoene, ii. p. 54 (some compare his deeds with those of Herakles); Philastr., *de haeres.*, c. 8; Georg. Syncellus, *chronogr.*, ed. Dindorf, i. p. 309 (κατὰ τούτους τοὺς χρόνους Σαμψὼν ἦν, ὁ παρ᾽ Ἕλλησι βοώμενος Ἡρακλῆς).* Many modern writers have made the same comparison, and inferred that Samson is the Hebrew counterpart of the Phoenician Melqart, the Greek Herakles; and that the story of his deeds was either originally a cognate myth, or has taken up numerous mythical elements. See G. L. Bauer, *Hebräische Mythologie*, 1802, ii. p. 86 ff.; ° G. Kaiser, *Comm. in priora Geneseos capita*, 1829, p. 186 ff.; Brockhausen, "Simson als Baal-Herakles," *Annalen d. Theol.*, 1833; ° Vatke, *Alttest. Theologie*, 1835, p. 369 f.; E. Meier, *Poet. National-Literatur d. Hebr.*, 1856, p. 103 ff.; Roskoff, *Die Simsonsage und der Heraclesmythus*, 1860; Steinthal, "Die Sage von Simson," *Zeitschr. für Völkerpsychologie*, ii. 1862, p. 129–178; Engl. translation, "The Legend of Samson," in Goldziher's *Mythology among the Hebrews*, transl. by R. Martineau, 1877, p. 392–446; Seinecke, *Gesch. des Volkes Israel*, i. 1876, p. 253–257; M. Schultze, *Handbuch d. ebräischen Mythologie*, 1876, p. 121, 147, 187, &c.; E. Wietzke, *Der biblische Simson der aegypt. Horus-Ra*, 1888; "The Samson Saga and the Myth of Herakles," *Westminster Review*, cxxi. 1884, Apr., p. 305–328; G. A. Wilken, *De Simsonsage*, 1888; ° R. Sonntag, *Der Richter Simson: ein historisch-mythischer Versuch*, 1890.° — The older writers contented themselves with drawing out the parallels to the Herakles myth: † each begins his career of adventure by strangling a lion; each perishes at last through the machinations of a woman; ‡ each chooses his own death. Samson's fox-catching is compared with the capture of the Erymanthian boar, the Cretan bull, the hind of Artemis; the spring which is opened at Lehi to quench his thirst, with the warm baths which Sicilian nymphs open to refresh the weary Herakles; § the carrying off of the gates of Gaza reminds some of the setting up of the Pillars of Hercules, ‖ others of Herakles's descent to the nether-world.¶ Meier and Ewald even discover that Samson has exactly twelve labours, like Herakles (in late systems). Steinthal not only identifies Samson with Melqart-Herakles, but attempts to explain the whole story as a solar myth, by a thorough-going application of the method which Max Müller and his school introduced in Aryan mythology. He is followed in the main by Goldziher, Seinecke, and Jul. Braun (*Naturgesch. der Sage*, 1864, i. p. 272,

---

* The author goes on to recite some of the deeds of Herakles; adding that some put Herakles rather earlier, others say that he lived longer than Samson.

† See Serarius (1609), quoted by Rosenmüller, *Scholia*, p. 357 f.

‡ The attempt has even been made to connect the names Delilah and Deianira (Nork, E. Meier).

§ Diod. Sic., iv. 23.

‖ E. Meier.

¶ Steinthal. On these comparisons see esp. Roskoff, p. 100 ff.

442 °).* Wietzke identifies Samson with the "Egyptian Herakles," Horus-Ra. The Philistine women all represent Sheol-"Tafenet"; the Philistines, with whom he is in perpetual strife, are the children of Set-Typhon. The tale of Samson follows the Sun-god through the year; Spring (ch. 14), Summer (15¹⁻⁴), Autumn and Winter (15⁸ᵇ⁻¹⁹); ch. 16 is his descent to the world below; he breaks the gates of Hades (16¹⁻³); bound by Delilah, he loses his eyes and his strength, but his might returns and he triumphs as a god over his foes (16⁴⁻³⁰). — The name שמשון is derived from שמש, 'sun' (see above, p. 326); Steinthal and others compare it with דגון from דג, 'fish,' but the formation is too frequent to allow us to attach any significance to this coincidence, even were the latter etymology more certain than it is. That שמשון is equivalent to שמש is not probable, nor is the explanation which would make it a diminutive acceptable; it might mean "sun-worshipper,"† a name which would not be strange in the vicinity of Beth-shemesh (above, p. 325).‡ A legend whose hero bore such a name would attract and absorb elements of an originally mythical character, such as the foxes in the corn-fields perhaps represent; § but if this be true, all consciousness of the origin and significance of the tale had been lost, and the mythical traits commingle freely with those which belong to folk-story. This explanation is at least as natural as the alternative, that an original solar myth has been transformed into heroic legend, with the admixture of a large non-mythical element. The historical character of the adventures of Samson may be given up without denying the possibility, or even probability, that the legend, which is very old, has its roots in the earth, not in the sky. ‖

XVII.-XXI. Two Additional Stories of the Times of the Judges.¶

XVII., XVIII. The migration of the Danites.

The first of the two supplementary stories relates the origin of the image in the famous sanctuary of Dan. — A man named Micah, whose home was somewhere in the Highlands of Ephraim, is the proprietor of a shrine, with an image and oracle, and has a Levite

---

* Against Steinthal, see Wellhausen-Bleek, *Einl⁴*, 1876, p. 196; Flöckner, "Ueber die Hypothese Steinthals, dass Simson ein Sonnenheros sei," *Theol. Quartalschrift*, 1886, 1887; ° Baethgen, *Beiträge*, p. 162 ff.   † See Nöldeke, *ZDMG*. xlii. p. 480.

‡ To connect Delilah (דלילה) with "Night" (לילה), as Wietzke and Kittel do, is mere punning.   § See above, p. 341 f.

‖ See Hitz., *GVI*. i. p. 123; Roskoff; G. Baur in Riehm, *HWB*. s.v.; Kittel, *GdH*. i. 2. p. 81 f.; Baethgen, *Beiträge*, p. 162.

¶ See Introduction, § 5. Auberlen, "Die drei Anhänge des Buchs der Richter," *Stud. u. Krit.*, 1860, p. 536-568.

as his priest (17^{1-13}).   The Danites, who have hitherto been unable
to get any permanent possession in Canaan, send from their seats
in the southwest a party to explore the land.   Passing through
the Highlands of Ephraim, the scouts halt at Micah's house and
consult his oracle (18^{1-6}).   Receiving a favourable response, they
go on, and find Laish, at the sources of the Jordan, inviting attack
by its isolated situation and the unguarded security of its people
(v.$^{7-10}$).   On their representations, a considerable part of the tribe,
numbering six hundred fighting men, migrates to the north, carrying off as they go Micah's image and his priest (v.$^{11-26}$).   They
capture Laish, put its inhabitants to the sword, and settle there,
giving it the name of their own tribe, Dan (v.$^{27-29}$).   They set up
Micah's image in the holy place, where it remained to later times,
ministered to by a priesthood which was reputed to be descended
from Moses (v.$^{30f.}$).

The narrative is not all from one hand.   The inventory of
Micah's idols, *ephōd, teraphim, pesel, massekah*, in various permu-
tations, is confusing.*   The origin of the last two is related in
17^{3-4}; that of the other two is apparently independent (v.^{5}).
Micah's priest is a wandering Levite from Bethlehem, whom he
hires to make his home with him (v.$^{8-11a}$) ; while in v.^{7} he is a
young Levite who was living in the neighbourhood (cf. 18^{15}).†   In
the account of the sending out of the Danite spies (18^2) there is
a manifest plethora, as there is also in v.^{5} and in v.$^{6-10}$; in the
verses which describe the robbery of Micah's sanctuary (v.$^{13-21}$)
we find not only redundancy but conflicting representations, and
the confusion resulting from the attempt to combine them has
been increased by various glosses.   Finally, the two statements
concerning the duration of the cultus at Dan (v.$^{30.\ 31}$) cannot both
come from the same source.

Oort, ‡ Wellhausen, § and Kuenen ‖ explain these phenomena
as the result of somewhat extensive interpolations, the disorder
occasioned by these being aggravated, as is often the case, by

---

* Gramberg and Reuss think that all these names are used for a single image.
Others suppose that there were two, or three.   † Compare also v.^{10a} with v.^{11b}.

‡ "De heiligdommen van Jehovah te Dan en te Bethel vóor Jerobeam I.,"
Th. T. i. 1867 (p. 285-306), p. 288 f.   § *Comp.*, p. 232 f.; cf. p. 356 f.

‖ *HCO²*. i. p. 358-360.

corruption of the text and secondary glosses. The motive of the interpolations was to throw contempt upon the sanctuary at Dan; its famous image of Yahweh was made of stolen silver, to which a curse clung ($17^{2\cdot4}$). Vatke * and Bertheau † recognized two narratives united by a redactor, and attempted to separate them; Budde ‡ offers a continuous analysis of ch. 17, 18. The two narratives originally resembled each other very closely, and considerable uncertainty must exist in the details of the analysis, but the composite character of the chapters appears to me sufficiently established.

Vatke's analysis is based upon the erroneous assumption that only one Levite is mentioned in the chapters. The Danites carried off Micah's son, Jonathan, who was of the tribe of Manasseh (18^{30} cf. 17^1). In the other narrative the Levite is also carried off, but disappears in the sequel. Bertheau ascribes to one account, $18^{13.\ 15.\ 17\ *}$ (the priest was standing at the gate) v.$^{18b-20.\ 22a.\ 27b-29}$; to the other, $18^{14.\ 16.\ 17\ *.\ 18a.\ 21-23.\ 26b.\ 27a}$. In the former the priest is persuaded to accompany the Danites, and himself bears off the *sacra*; in the other, he is carried off by force. The inconsistency of this analysis is shown by Kue. (*l.c.*). Budde reconstructs the two accounts as follows: I. $17^{1.\ 4.\ 8-11a.\ 12aa.\ 13}$ $18^{1b.\ 2*.\ 3*.\ 4b*.\ 5.\ 6a.\ 8*.\ 9*.\ 10*.\ 11*.\ 12.\ 13*.\ 15*.\ 17*.\ 18*.\ 19-20.\ 31}$. II. $17^{2a.\ 5b\beta.\ 4a.\ 5b.\ 5ba.\ 4b.\ 7.\ 12b.\ 11b.\ 12a\beta}$ $18^{1b.\ 2*.\ 3*.\ 4a.\ 6b.\ 7*.\ 8*.\ 9*.\ 10*.\ 11*.\ 13*.\ 14.\ 17*.\ 14*.\ 18*.\ \ldots\ 30}$. Similarly Kittel (*GdH.* i. 2. p. 19; cf. also Kittel's analysis in Kautzsch, *Das Alte Test.*): I. $17^{1.\ 5}\ldots^{8-11a.\ 12aa.\ 13}$ $18^{1b.\ 2aa.\ 2b.\ 3b-7*.\ 8-10aa.\ 10b-14*.\ 15*.\ 16*.\ 17*.\ 18a*.\ 18b-29\ (31?)}$. II. $17^{2-4.\ 6f.\ 11b.\ 12a\beta.\ b}$ $18^{1a\ (2a\beta?).\ 3a.\ 7*.\ 10a\beta}$, parts of v.$^{14-18.\ 20\ (30?)}$. — In nearly all the places where the text is redundant and confused it is possible to disengage two strands of narrative; but to which of the two sources they should be attributed, there are in many instances no criteria to determine; every attempt at a reconstruction in detail must at best be one of several possibilities. The first of the two narratives ran somewhat as follows: A man of Mt. Ephraim, Micah by name, had a shrine (בית אלהים) containing an *ephod* and *teraphim*, and consecrated one of his sons as priest ($17^{1.\ 5}$). Afterwards, a wandering Levite from Bethlehem in Judah, in search of employment, came that way, and was hired by Micah, who installed him in the place of his son, rejoicing that he had now a regular priest (v.$^{8-10.\ 11a.\ 12b.\ 13}$). The Danites, who have as yet made no permanent settlement, send out an exploring party ($18^{1.\ 2a*}$). They come to Micah's house, and pass the night there (v.^{2b}). (They fall in with his priest, and inquire,) ' What business hast thou here? ' (v.^{3b*}). He replies that Micah has hired him as his priest (v.^{4b}). They bid him consult the oracle for them (v.^{5}), and receive from him a favourable response (v.^{6}). They come to Laish, and find its people secure

* *Alttest. Theol.*, 1835. p. 268.　　　　† *Richt.*, p. 241 f.
‡ *Richt. u. Sam.*, p. 138-144.

and confident (v.[7*]). Returning, they urge their clansmen to go against the
place, which will be an easy conquest and a most desirable possession (v.[9*, 9*]
[10*]). Accordingly, six hundred fighting men of the clan, with their families,
set out on the expedition (v.[11*, 12, 13]). The spies apprise them that in the
village are an *ephōd* and *teraphim* (v.[14]). The armed band halts at the gate
(v.[16]), while the five spies go to Micah's house to take the *ephōd* and *teraphim* (v.[18a]).* The priest, who is standing at the door, demands what they
are doing (v.[17b*, 18b]); they bid him hold his peace and come with them, and
be the tribe's priest (v.[19]). Without more ado, he takes the images and
accompanies them; they join the main body, and march away. Micah raises
the villagers and pursues them, but is driven back by rude threats (v.[20-26]).
The Danites take Laish, and set up Micah's images in their sanctuary (v.[27-28,
30*]). The second account is not so completely preserved, especially toward
the end. It begins by relating the circumstances under which Micah's images
(*pesel* and *massēkah*) were made, of silver which had been stolen from his
mother (17[2-4]). For his priest he had a young Judaean Levite who was living
in the neighbourhood (v.[7]), whom he treated as one of his own sons (v.[11b, 12a]).
The sending out of the Danite exploring expedition must have been related
substantially as in the other account (18[1f*]). As they come into the vicinity
of Micah's house, they recognize the voice of the young Levite, and turning
aside thither inquire of him what he is doing there (v.[3*]). He replies: So
and so Micah has done to me (v.[4a]). They find Laish dwelling in security,
after the manner of the Phoenicians (v.[7*]). They report to their kinsmen at
home, and bid them make no delay to occupy the land (v.[8-10*]). They
accordingly emigrate from their former seats (v.[11*]). On their way they
come to Micah's home, and turn aside thither to the house of the young
Levite, and salute him (v.[15]). In what follows it is only clear that they got
possession of Micah's *pesel* and *massēkah*, and carried them off; it is probable
that the young Levite accompanied them voluntarily. To this source v.[31]
seems to belong. Traces of it are also perhaps to be recognized in the
account of the taking of Laish. Budde attributes the first of the two narratives, as restored by him, to E. *Teraphim*, which are not often mentioned in
the O.T. (Hos. 3[4] with *ephōd*, 1 S. 15[23] 19[13, 16] 2 K. 23[24] &c.), are found in
the Hexateuch only in E, Gen. 31[19, 34f], which also affords a striking parallel
to Micah's pursuit, Jud. 18[21ff]; cf. Gen. 31[23] with Jud. 18[22]; 31[30] with 18[24].
The comparatively rare רגל, 'spy out,' is found in Gen. 42 Nu. 21[32] (E); the
story of Rahab and the taking of Jericho, in which the word occurs, is also
prob. from E. Cf. also אלהים Jud. 18[5, 10]. It would then be natural to ascribe
the other version of the story to J, but for this Budde has no positive grounds,
while Jos. 19[47] (𝕲) might argue against it.† Kitt., whose analysis agrees
substantially with Budde's (see above, p. 367), doubts whether the second
version ever existed by itself; the obvious tendency to put all the actors in

---

* Or, perhaps, the body of the emigrants halted at the gate while the armed men
went to Micah's house.   † *Richt. u. Sam.*, p. 144 f.

an odious light suggests that it may be wholly the work of an editor. This
hypothesis, which is virtually that of Oort and Wellhausen (above, p. 366 f.),
hardly does justice to the facts which point to composition rather than interpolation. The evidence which Budde has adduced is perhaps not conclusive.
So far as the general impression which the narrative makes may be trusted, I
should be strongly inclined to ascribe the first version to the same hand from
which we have the stories of Samson, the first version of the history of Gideon,
and other parts of the Book of Judges which Budde, I think rightly, attributes
to J.

The note, " In those days there was no king in Israel, every
man did as he pleased " (17⁶ 18¹ᵃ cf. 19¹ 21²⁵), is probably the comment of an editor, who felt it necessary to explain how such law-
less doings went unrestrained and unpunished. That the writer of
these words must have lived before the exile is perhaps too posi-
tively affirmed by Kuenen. Chapter 18³⁰·³¹ throws some light on
the age of the stories. Verse⁸¹ tells us that the image which
Micah had made stood in Dan as long as the house of God was at
Shiloh. Unfortunately, we do not know when this temple was
destroyed. In the historical books there is no mention of it after
the time of Eli; in the next generation the priests of his house
were at Nob, and it is commonly believed that Shiloh was destroyed during the Philistine wars. But Jeremiah (7¹²·¹⁴) points
to Shiloh as a conspicuous example of a holy place which Yahweh
had destroyed for the wickedness of Israel, in a manner which
hardly suggests that he is drawing his lesson from such ancient
history, and others therefore think of the Assyrian wars. According to v.³⁰, the priesthood of the line of Jonathan presided at Dan
down to the deportation, by which is probably meant the deporta-
tion of the inhabitants of that region by Tiglath-pileser in 734 B.C.
(2 K. 15²⁹).* There seems to be no decisive reason why v.³⁰·³¹·
should not be ascribed to the sources from which the two versions
of the story are derived,† though this has been doubted,‡ and in
the nature of the case cannot be proved.

The first version of the story, at least, seems to be very old; it
speaks of Micah's *ephōd* with as little prejudice as the older narrative in ch. 8 of Gideon's. The origin of the image in the

* See on this captivity, Schrader, *KAT*², p. 254-257 = *COT*. i. p. 246 ff.; Tiele,
Babylonisch-assyr. Gesch., p. 220 f., 232 ff. † Be., Bu., Kitt.
‡ We., *Comp.*, p. 232, cf. 357; Kue., *HCO*², i. p. 359 f.

famous sanctuary at Dan is an interesting matter of history; the way in which the Danites got possession of it makes a very good story. The author's sympathies, so far as he shows them, are on the side of the spoilers; he makes them not only rob Micah, but mock him.

In the second version, especially in 17[1-4], many scholars think that the whole motive is to cast reproach upon the sanctuary at Dan;[*] its venerated image was made of silver which a son had stolen from his own mother; when the money was recovered and dedicated to Yahweh, the greater part of it was kept back by fraud; the idol itself was stolen from its owner by the Danites. It is by no means clear, however, that the author had anything of the sort in mind. If such had been his prime motive, he would surely have begun by telling the story of the theft; but this is not done, nor is there any trace of contempt or even condemnation in the following narrative. Chapter 17[1-4] merely explains how so costly and splendid an idol came to be in the possession of a private person; it was an *ex voto* for the recovery of the money. If this interpretation be correct, there is no necessity for regarding the second version as much younger than the first.

The historical value of these chapters is hardly inferior to that of any in the book. The picture of the social and religious state of the times which they contain is full of life, and bears every mark of truthfulness. The tribe, or clan, of the Danites, unable permanently to establish itself in the south (1[34] cf. Jos. 19[47] 𝔐 and 𝔊), sends its spies to seek a new location. They find an isolated and unguarded Phoenician town in the far north, and six hundred fighting men, apparently the greater part of the tribe, migrate .thither, sack the town, and occupy it. In this narrative, apart from its own importance for the history of this tribe, we have doubtless a type of many similar enterprises in the period of conquest; cf. esp. Jos. 17[14-18]. Images of Yahweh, sometimes of considerable cost and splendour, are found in the possession not only of a judge, like Gideon (8[27]), but of private persons, who may even have a shrine or small temple (*beth-elohim*) for them. Where there was such an image, a priest was needed. If no better

---

[*] Oort We., Kue., Kitt.

was at hand, a man might consecrate one of his sons; but a Levite
was preferred (17¹³), that is, a member of the hereditary guild who
possessed the traditional religious lore and, especially, technical
skill in consulting and interpreting the oracle. The Levites were
not all of one tribe; it is to be noted that the Levites in ch. 17 f.
and in ch. 19 are all in some way connected with Bethlehem of
Judah, and the young Levite whom Micah installs as priest in the
second version of our story is expressly said to have been "of the
clan of Judah." The famous sanctuary at Dan contained an
image which the Danites had carried off from Mt. Ephraim in
their migration. Its priesthood, to the end, claimed descent from
Moses, as was perhaps the case with the priests of other northern
sanctuaries.

The period in which the action of these chapters falls is not
determined by their position in the book. In the Book of Judges
proper they were evidently not included at all. The later editor
who, to our good fortune, preserved them could hardly have introduced them into the body of the book, with its strongly marked
plan and purpose; and the migration of Danites from Zorah and
Eshtaol might seem to find its fittest place immediately after the
story of Samson, the scene of which is the Danite settlements in
and around those towns. But we cannot safely draw from the story
of Samson, in which Danites are settled at Zorah and Eshtaol, the
converse inference that the migration of ch. 18 occurred after the
time of Samson, i.e. after the beginning of the Philistine aggressions, and therefore toward the end of the period of the judges;
for the narrative does not imply that all the Danites joined in the
expedition to Laish, wholly abandoning their old seats, and it is
on other grounds improbable that this was the case.* There is
no intimation either in the story of Samson or in ch. 18 of such a
pressure from the side of the Philistines as might force the Danites
out of their settlements; 18¹ agrees perfectly with 1³⁴, and we shall
do better, therefore, to explain their failure to establish themselves
there by the stubborn resistance of the native population of the
Lowland, the Amorites (1³⁴, cf. Jos. 19⁴⁷ᶠ.). The removal of a con-

---

* Danites in the south are presupposed by the allotment in Joshua. Note also
the tomb of Samson (16³¹), and the survival of the name Manoah in this region
after the exile (see above, p. 316).

siderable part of the tribe may have left room enough for those who remained behind. Chapter 5[17] shows that in the time of Deborah the tribe was already in its northern seats. The migration related in ch. 18 may therefore, with considerable probability, be assigned to a time not very long after the Israelite invasion of Canaan. Chapter 18[30] would fix it in the next generation after the invasion, if we could be confident that no links in the genealogy are omitted.[*]

XVII. 1-6. Micah's idols. — A man of Mt. Ephraim, Micah by name, confesses that he has in his possession the silver which has been stolen from his mother, and restores it. Of part of it she has an idol made, which is in Micah's house. Micah has a shrine, makes an *ephōd* and *teraphīm*, and consecrates one of his sons as priest. — 1. *There was a man of the Highlands of Ephraim, whose name was Micáyehu*] on the Highlands of Ephraim, see on 3[7]. The name and residence of the man seems to have been the same in both narratives. *Micáyehu*, v.[4]; elsewhere in the chapters the common shorter form of the name, *Micah* (v.[5, 8, 9] &c.) ; cf. Micayehu ben Imlah, 1 K. 22[8], and Micah the Morasthite, Mic. 1[1]. — 2-4. Micah, dreading his mother's curse, confesses the theft, and makes restitution ; she dedicates the silver to Yahweh, and has two hundred shekels of it made into an idol, which is in Micah's house. The verses belong to the second account. The text is not in order ; the money passes back and forth in an unaccountable way : in v.[3a] he returns it to his mother ; in v.[3b] she declares her purpose to give it back to him ; in v.[4a] he again returns it to her. Budde conjectures that the last words of v.[3], *and now I will return it to thee*, and the beginning of v.[4], have been accidentally displaced from their original position after v.[2a]; v.[3a] is then a restoration of v.[4a], not exactly in the right place. For another hypothesis, see below. — 2. *The eleven hundred shekels of silver*] compare the eleven hundred shekels which the Philistine rulers promise Delilah (16[5]).[†] — *Which were taken from thee*] by

---

[*] In this period it is put by Fl. Jos., *antt.* v. 3. 1 § 175-178, and the Jewish chronologists generally : see *Seder Olam, c.* 12, ed. Meyer, p. 33 (in the days of Cushan-rishathaim) ; Ra., Ki., Ke., Auberlen, al. mu.

[†] Some Jewish scholars inferred from this coincidence that Micah's mother was Delilah, an opinion which Ra. rejects as incompatible with the chronology.

theft, as appears from the following ; the neutral expression, *taken*, is perhaps employed with intention.* —*And thou cursedst, and further saidst in my hearing*] cursed the unknown thief. What she said is not found in the text ; interpreters supply from the context, *didst utter* the curse *in my hearing*,† but it is doubtful whether the Hebrew will admit this, and the force of the particle (*also, even, further*) is lost. Budde surmises that the words of the curse itself have been suppressed, through a scruple which has in other instances led to alterations in the text ; see, *e.g.*, 1 S. 25²⁵. ‡ In view of the derangement which unquestionably exists in these verses, the conjecture may be hazarded, that the words which are missing here have been preserved in v.⁴ᵇ, and that we should reconstruct : And thou cursedst, and also saidst to me, ‘ I sacredly consecrate the silver to Yahweh . . . to make an idol,’ — the silver is in my possession, I took it ; and now I will return it to thee. § And his mother said, Blessed is my son of Yahweh. So he returned the silver to his mother, and she took two hundred shekels, &c. (v.⁴). — Upon this hypothesis, he was moved to make restoration, not merely by fear of his mother's curse, but by the fact that the silver itself was thus rendered sacrosanct, or put under a taboo, ‖ so that to keep or use it would be a sacrilege which Yahweh was sure to avenge.¶   The transposition of v.³ᵇ may have been made by a scribe who, misunderstanding the connexion, thought that the consecration (v.³ᵇ) should stand closer to the execution of the vow (v.⁴). — *And his mother said, Blessed of Yahweh is my son*] the curse cannot be unsaid, but may be neutralized by a blessing ; therefore, after restitution or expiation made, the offending party seeks the blessing of the injured, to avert further evil (2 S. 21³ Ex. 12³²). Curses and blessings, we must remember, are not, in the conception of men in this stage of culture, mere wishes, but real potencies of good and evil. The word has a magical power. A blessing once uttered, even if obtained by fraud, cannot be revoked (Gen. 27, esp. v.³³⁻³⁷) ; a

---

* But cf. 18²⁴.   † See, *e.g.*, Cler.

‡ On this verse see We., *TBS.*; Dr., *TBS.* ad loc.

§ That this is the necessary order is seen by Tanchum, who, assuming a hysteron proteron, rearranges in precisely this way.

‖ See W. R. Smith, *Religion of the Semites*, p. 434.   ¶ So Ziegler, 1791.

curse, once launched, pursues its object like an Erinys.[*] The
curse, therefore, inspires religious terror; and a parent's curse is
the most terrible of all. The working of such beliefs upon the
guilty conscience can be readily imagined. In such a case as
this, the curse involved not only the criminal, but all who, being
cognizant of the wrong, made themselves accessory to it by con-
cealing their knowledge (Lev. 5^1 Prov. 29^{24}); it was therefore an
effective means of extorting testimony. In a more advanced
stage of religion, it is Yahweh who executes the curse in righteous-
ness, and it is harmless to the innocent.[†] Here, if our restoration
of the verses is right, the fear which the curse inspires is reinforced
by the perils of the taboo; see above, p. 373. — **3.** *So he returned
the eleven hundred shekels of silver to his mother*] these words
stand in their proper place in v.^{4a}, following the promise to restore
them, v.$^{3b\beta}$; see above, p. 373. — *I sacredly consecrate the silver
to Yahweh*] in the present order of the context, this dedication
must be regarded, not as her original intention (*I had consecrated
it*), but as a purpose formed upon the recovery of the money, to
avert the consequences of the curse, which, contrary to her expectation, had lighted on the head of her own son; for their probable
original position and significance, see above on v.^{2}. — *From my
hand to my son*] the words are variously interpreted: ut de manu
mea suscipiat filius meus, et faciat sculptile;[‡] or, for the benefit
of my son, *i.e.* to expiate his guilt;[§] or, to furnish and adorn his
shrine.[‖] As it is not the son, but the mother, who has the image
made, the second of these explanations is the most satisfactory in
the present context. If the original order of the verses was as
has been conjectured above, the son would be named merely as
the beneficiary. But 𝕲 has, *from my hand alone;*[¶] no one else
can fulfil the vow of consecration, and, by having an image made,
lift the taboo from the rest of the silver. This is almost certainly
the original reading; and it strongly confirms the conjectural

---

[*] Cf. the ordeal, Nu. 5^{11-28}; Zech. 5^{1ff}.

[†] Cf. Dt. 27^{14-26} 1 K. 8^{31}, and see, in general, Selden, *De synedriis, l.* ii. *c.* 11; *Opp.* i. 1448 ff.; Ew., *Alterthümer,* p. 20 f. = *Antiquities,* p. 19 f.; Stade, *GVI.* i. p. 491 f.; W. R. Smith, *Religion of the Semites,* p. 434; Smend, *Alttest. Religions-gesch.* p. 109, 114. A striking modern instance is to be found in Besant, *Life of E. H. Palmer,* p. 328 f.   [‡] 𝕴; so substantially Ra., Ki., Stud.

[§] Schm.   [‖] Be.   [¶] Except 𝕭𝕹.

restoration which is proposed above. — *To make an idol*] lit. *a
graven image and a molten image;* Heb. *pesel* and *massekah.
Pesel* is properly a carving, sculpture, carved figure in wood or
stone ; in the O.T. always the image of a god.[*]   As such images
were the oldest, and probably always the most common, *pesel* is
also used generically for ' idol,' including such as were cast in
metal (Is. 30[22] 40[19] 44[10] Jer. 10[14] ; cf. Jud. 17[4]).   The proper name
of the latter was *massekah,* or *nesek* (Is. 41[29]) ; they were, as the
name imports, cast in a mould, and generally, it seems, of gold or
silver.   The name is applied particularly to the little golden bulls
(images of Yahweh) which were worshipped in the Northern
Kingdom (2 K. 17[16] cf. 1 K. 12[28]), and to the similar image which
Aaron made at Horeb (Ex. 32[4.8] Dt. 9[12.16] Neh. 9[18]).   *Pesel* and
massekah are coupled in Dt. 27[15] to comprehend every kind of
idol (cf. also Nah. 1[14] Is. 48[5]), and similarly in the parallelism of
prophetic discourse (*e.g.* Jer. 10[14] = 51[17] Hab. 2[19] Is. 42[17]).   In the
passage before us the conjunction of the two terms cannot be
explained in this way, and creates serious difficulty.   The natural
interpretation of the words in the context is, that two idols of
different kinds are meant, one carved in wood or stone, the other
cast in silver ; and this appears to be confirmed by v.[4b], and by
the subsequent narrative, in which the two names constantly recur
side by side as if they stood for two distinct things.   On the other
hand, the idol is an image of Yahweh (v.[3]), and we see no motive
for making, besides the costly silver idol, a cheaper wooden one [†]
to stand in the same shrine.   Further, both *pesel* and *massekah*
are made by the silversmith : he made a *pesel* and a *massekah,*
and *it* stood in Micah's house (v.[4]).   Observe also the singular
verb, which can refer to but one image.   Finally, in 18[30] we read
only of the *pesel* which the Danites set up ; but it is surely in the
highest degree improbable that they carried off both a wooden
and a silver idol, and set up in their own sanctuary only the less
valuable of the two.   We are warranted, therefore, in seriously
questioning the text, and a closer scrutiny of the composite text
of 18[14. 17. 18. 20] confirms our suspicion.   Only in the first of these
verses is the order natural, *ephod, teraphim, pesel, massekah;* in

---

[*] See on 3[19], p. 94 f., 97   [†] Cf. Is. 40[20].

v.[17.18], on the contrary, we find *pesel, ephōd, teraphim, massekah,* suggesting that the last name was added in the process of composition or subsequently; and to support this inference, in v.[20] *massekah* does not occur at all,* while in v.[30f], as already noticed, *pesel* stands alone. It is reasonably certain, therefore, that the author of this second narrative wrote throughout only *pesel,* and that an editor or scribe, observing that the idol (*pesel*) was of silver, added the more exact term *massekah.*† This hypothesis relieves the difficulties which have so much exercised interpreters. — *And now I will return it to thee*] the words of Micah, which should immediately follow v.[2a], *the silver is in my possession; I took it.* — 4. *So he returned the silver to his mother*] in the original context this clause was preceded by v.[2b], *Blessed by Yahweh is my son;* cf. v.[2a]. The interpreters who follow the present order of the text are not able to give any reasonable explanation of the words. ‡ — *His mother took two hundred shekels of silver and gave them to the silversmith*] what became of the other nine hundred is not said. Kimchi explains that the two hundred shekels were the wages of the artist, the remainder of the silver was made into the image; a Lyra and others, that the rest of the money was used for furnishing and adorning the shrine; § Auberlen, that the woman through avarice broke her vow, and gave to Yahweh only a small part of the consecrated treasure; ‖ Kuenen, adopting this explanation, finds here additional evidence of the author's desire to cast contempt on the worship at Dan.¶ All these interpretations are far-fetched, and they are really superfluous. The intention of the dedication (v.[3]) was not to devote the whole of the treasure to the making of an image, but to compel the thief to restore it by putting the whole under a taboo until she herself had made, from this silver, an image of Yahweh. If the author had understood that the woman vowed to make the whole weight of metal into an image, he would have given his own explanation of the discrepancy. *The silversmith* appears in the Old Testament chiefly as

---

* It is added in 𝔊, however.
† Possibly also he was thinking of the molten image at Dan; 1 K. 12[28] 2 K. 17[16].
‡ See Auberlen, *Stud. u. Krit.,* 1860, p. 548; Be., Ke., al.
§ Stud., Be. ‖ So also Oort, Cass., al.
¶ See above, p. 360 f, 370.

a maker of idols (Is. 40¹⁹ 41⁷ 46⁶ Jer. 10⁹·¹⁴).* — *And he made it into an idol*] Heb. *pesel* and *massekah*; see on v.³. — *And it was in Micah's house*] the singular verb shows that the writer was speaking of one idol, not of two.

1. וישמו פיכיהו] ' Who is like Yahweh '; the two other names in the book which are compounded with Yahweh are Joash, the father of Gideon (ch. 6), and Jotham, his son (ch. 9). Names thus formed become common in the next age, that of Saul and David. See v. Bohlen, *Genesis*, p. civ.°; Nestle, *Die Israelitischen Eigennamen*, p. 68 ff.; König, *Hauptprobleme*, u. s. w., p. 26 f. On names compounded with יהוה, see also M. Jastrow, Jr., *JBL.* xiii. 1894, p. 101 ff. — **2.** אשר לקח לך] the interest of the possessor in the loss of the money is uppermost in the writer's mind, rather than the fact that the money is taken away (מאתך); *qui surrepti tibi fuerant* (Cler.). So 𝕲ᴬᴾᴮᴸᴹ ς τοὺς ληφθέντας σοι, 𝕋𝕾. The common ~ ירח (take to one's self) has misled other interpreters; 𝕲ᴰᴺ Σ, 𝕃, *quos separaveras tibi*. Similarly Ew., whose interpretation (*GVI.* ii. p. 491) is a masterpiece of contorted exegesis. — ואתי אליתי] the old endings of the 2 sg. fem. The pron. in this form seven times (Frensdorff, *Massoret. Wörterbuch*, p. 230; cf. Norzi); in the verb it is more frequent; see Bö. ii. p. 132; Kö. i. p. 151. אלה Kal, 1 K. 8⁸¹ † Hos. 4² 10⁴. — וגם אסרה באזני]‡ *and didst utter it* (the curse) *in my hearing*, would be at least, וגם דברה באזני; in Gen. 4⁸ Ex. 19²⁵, where אמר stands in a similar way, what was said being omitted, the text is at fault. We have therefore either to infer that the words spoken have been intentionally dropped (Bu.), or, as I have suggested above, that they have been transposed to v.⁸; see below at the end of v.⁸. — ברוך בני ליהוה] *blessed of Yahweh;* by Yahweh. ל with passive, Ges.²⁶ § 121, 3; Ew. § 295 c; cf. 1 S. 15¹⁸ Ru. 2²⁰ Gen. 14¹⁹. — **3.** הקדש הקדשתי] *I sacredly dedicate;* perf. of resolve, fixed purpose, psychologically presented as an accomplished fact; Dr³. § 13; Ges.²⁶ § 106, 3. — מידי רבני] so 𝕲ᴰᴺ𝕃𝕋; 𝕾 ᴮ, *from the hands of my son*. 𝕲ᴬᴾᴮᴸᴹᴼ ς ε κατὰ μόνας, i.e. רבדי, which is probably the true reading; see above, p. 374. The corruption may have arisen by the correction of a misread רבדי, or through simple misunderstanding. — פסל] plur. פסילים, see on 3¹⁹; on the verb *ib.*; an idol, Ex. 20⁴ Dt. 5⁸ (decalogue); likeness of men or animals, *ib.*, Dt. 4¹⁶·²³·²⁵; work of the hands of an artisan (חרש), Dt. 27¹⁵ Is. 40¹⁹·²⁰; of wood, Is. 40²⁰ 44¹⁵ 45²⁰ cf. Dt. 7⁵ (שרף); stone (Babylonian), Is. 21⁹ (שבר); metal, Jer. 10¹⁴ (work of the צורף) Is. 40¹⁹ 44¹⁰ (נסך). — מסכה] Ex. 34¹⁷ (J's decalogue), אלהי מסכה לא תעשה לך, Lev. 19⁴; bull image (of Yahweh), Ex. 32⁴·⁸ Dt. 9¹²·¹⁶ Neh. 9¹⁸, 2 K. 17¹⁶ (of gold; cf. also Is. 30²²) Hos. 13² (silver); images of Canaanite gods, Nu. 33⁵² (צלמי מסכתם), cf. 1 K. 14⁹. מסכה is apparently a loan-word. To cast, found, metal is in Hebrew not יסך (Is. 40¹⁹ 44¹⁰ʰ), but יצק (1 K. 7 &c.), while in Phoenician (as in Syr.) נסך is used; see Bloch,

---

* Eight times; the exceptions are Prov. 25⁴ Neh. 3⁸·³², See also Acts 19²⁴ᶠᶠ.
† For אלה ª read ואלה (Klosterm.). ‡ See on 9², p. 243.

Phoenicisches Glossar, p. 45, cf. s.v. פסל *ib.* p. 42. The Israelites first became acquainted with this kind of images, as with the art of the founder altogether, in Canaan.[*] This may account for the fact that the oldest prohibition of idols (Ex. 34[17]) names only the מסכה; it was a new and conspicuously foreign thing. Some scholars who, with sound exegetical discernment, have felt that the narrative admits but one idol, have endeavoured to reconcile the text with this interpretation by the hypothesis that *pesel* means the wooden core of the image, *massekah* a silver covering with which it was overlaid; *pesel* and *massekah* are the composite name of such an idol. That this was not the understanding of the author (or editor) is manifest from 18[17. 18], where the two words, which on this theory should be inseparable, are separated from each other by two other nouns. There is no warrant elsewhere in the O.T. for this opinion, against which the etymological meaning of *massekah* is in itself conclusive; plating a wooden image with gold or silver is not casting. Others understand by *pesel* the image, by *massekah* the metal base or pedestal on which it stood; so Schm., Hengstenb., Ke., al. This is wholly at variance with the usage of the latter word. — The restoration of v.[2-3] proposed in the text would read as follows: ויאמר לאמו אלף וכאה הכסף אשר לקח לך ואת אליה ונס אמרה באזני 'הקדש הקדשתי את הכסף ליהוה מידי לבני לעשות פסל' הנה הכסף אתי אני להחזיר תרה אשיבנו לך. ותאמר אמו 'ברוך בני ליהוה.' וישב את הכסף לאמו ותקח אמו מאתים כסף והתנהו לצורף וגו'.

5. Micah has a shrine and oracle; he installs his son as priest. —Verse[5] is not the continuation of v.[4], but its counterpart in the other version of the story; the *ephōd* and *teraphīm* which he makes for his shrine correspond to the *pesel* and *massekah* which Micah's mother has made, and which are in his house; see above, p. 366 f. — *The man Micah had a shrine*] † the words must originally have followed v.[1]; the form of the sentence suggests that *the man Micah* has been repeated here by the editor, to recover connexion with v.[1] after the introduction of v.[2-4]. *Shrine;* lit. *god-house,* a small temple which sheltered the idol or other object of worship, as the house of God at Shiloh (18[31]) held the ark. There was need of such a house only where there was an image or an oracle; ‡ the older and commoner representatives of the deity, the sacred post (*asherah*) or stone pillar (*massebah*), stood beside the altar on the high place under the open sky, or beneath the

---

[*] Solomon's founders were Phoenicians; 1 K. 7[1ff.].

† H. Pierson, *Dactylicndienst*, 1866, p. 65,[o] interprets the words of a *beth-el* or sacred stone; see Oort, *Th. T.* i. 1867, p. 286 f.

‡ Stade, *GVI.* i. p. 465; Nowack, *Hebr. Archäologie*, ii. p. 16 f.; cf., for Greece, E. Meyer, *GdA.* ii. p. 429 f.

sacred tree.* The temple in our text belonged to a rich private
citizen of Mt. Ephraim, who was its proprietor, as Gideon was of
that at Ophrah in which he set up his *ephod*.† — *And made an
ephod and teraphim*] Gideon's *ephod*, made of seventeen hundred
shekels of gold and ' set up ' in the sanctuary at Ophrah, an object
of worship (8^{27}), was clearly an idol of some kind. ‡ Micah's
ephod is constantly associated with *teraphim*, which were certainly
idols; when the Danites carry off his *ephod* and *teraphim*, he cries
after them, You have taken the gods (or, god) which I made
(18^{24}).§ In 1 S. 21^9 we read that Goliath's sword was preserved
at Nob as a trophy, wrapped in a mantle *behind the ephod*, which
we must imagine, therefore, as standing free from the wall. In
the history of Saul and David the *ephod* is employed in consulting
the oracle of Yahweh (1 S. 14^{18} ⑤ cf. v.^{3}; 23$^{6.9}$ 30^7). ‖ In all
these passages the *ephod* may be an idol; but it must be admitted
that, with the exception of Jud. 8^{27}, none of them imperatively
requires this interpretation. All that can with certainty be gathered from them is that it was a portable object which was employed
or manipulated by the priest in consulting the oracle. In the
Priest's Law-book, the *ephod* is a part of the ceremonial dress of
the High Priest, to which the oracle-pouch containing the Urim
and Thummim is attached;¶ but, while it is probable that the
oracle of the High Priest is a survival of the ancient priestly oracle
by the *ephod*, it is impossible to explain the references to the
ephod in Judges and Samuel by the descriptions in P. See further
in crit. note. — The *teraphim* were idols (Gen. 31^{19} cf. v.^{30}, *my
gods;* 35$^{2.4}$); we find them not only in the possession of the
Aramaean Laban, in the patriarchal story, but in the house of

---

* The *lishkah*, 1 S. 9^{22}, was a hall for sacrificial feasts, not a temple.

† It was a common thing in the ancient world for a family or clan to be the
proprietary custodians of a holy place; see E. Meyer, *Gd.A.* ii. p. 431; Wellhausen,
Reste arab. Heidentumes, p. 128 f.; cf. Ibn Hishām, p. 303.

‡ It would be more exact to say, an *agalma;* in using the word *idol* here and
below, I do not wish to be understood to assume that it was iconic.

§ We cannot argue here from the material used; the two hundred shekels of
silver (v.^{4}) belong to a different strand of the narrative.

‖ It is perhaps not without significance that in all these cases the oracle is consulted, not at a holy place, but by a commander in the field, or by David in the
Philistine country. David's *ephod* came from Nob (1 S. 23^6).

¶ See Nowack, *Hebr. Archäologie*, ii. p. 118 ff.

David (1 S. 19[13-16]); from the last passage it appears that they
were sometimes of considerable size. In Hos. 3[4] *teraphim* are
named in close connexion with the *ephod*, as in the chapters
before us, and, like the *ephod*, were employed in divination
(2 K. 23[24] Ez. 21[21] • Zech. 10[2]). It has been inferred from
Gen. 31 1 S. 19 Jud. 17[5], that the *teraphim* were household
gods; † and recently the theory has been advanced that they
were the images of the ancestors of the family, so that the consultation of the *teraphim* was a species of Manes oracle. ‡ Of this
there is no evidence; even that the *teraphim* were specifically
household gods is scarcely borne out by the usage (cf. esp.
Ez. 21[21]). See crit. note. — Having a shrine, Micah now needed
a priest, to take charge of the house and to consult and interpret
the oracle (18[30]). — *He installed one of his sons, and he became
his priest*] lit. *filled the hand of one of his sons*, the technical
term for the investiture of a priest (v.[12] 1 K. 13[33] Lev. 8[33] &c.).
The original meaning of the phrase is not certainly known. §
Some scholars take it to mean that Micah placed in his son's
hands the parts of his first sacrifice (cf. Ex. 29[22-25] Lev. 8[25-28]
2 Chr. 13[9]); ‖ others think that it signifies that Micah gave him
his wages or an earnest of them in hand, to bind the bargain; ¶
others still interpret, he bestowed on him the office of priest. **
With the installation of Micah's son compare 1 S. 7[1]: when the
ark was brought to Kirjath-jearim, to the house of Abinadab, he
consecrated Eleazar his son to keep the ark.

5. אפוד] that the *ephod* in Jud. 8[27] was an idol is not entirely a new theory.
𝔖 has in this place ‏ܦܣܝܠܐ‎ (*sic;* 𝔖[AO], Ephr., BB.), which may be a scribal

---

• Heb. 21[26].

† See, *e.g.*, a Lapide, who compares the Roman Lares and Penates; Schm.,
Pfeiffer, Ew., Oehler, al.

‡ Stade, *GVI.* i. p. 467; much more confidently, Schwally, *Leben nach dem
Tode*, p. 35 ff.; cf. Nowack, *Hebr. Archäologie*, ii. p. 23.

§ See Nowack, *Hebr. Archäologie*, ii. p. 120 f.

‖ So, most recently, Baudissin, *Gesch. d. alttest. Priesterthums*, p. 183 f.; similarly Di.

¶ Vatke, *Alttest. Theol.*, p. 273 f.; We., *Prol*[3]. p. 130. This would do very well in
v.[12] cf. 18[4b], but is hardly natural in the case of Micah's son (v.[5]); nor have we any
explanation of the fact that the phrase is used only of priests.

** Ges.; Halévy, *REJ.* xxi. 1890, p. 209; *BSZ.*, al.; see crit. note.

error, but is understood by Ephrem (i. p. 320) and all subsequent interpreters as an image (see esp. Bar Baḥlūl, *s.v.*). Procopius Gaz. explains ἐφούδ, 8¹⁷, by μαντεῖον ἤ εἴδωλον. Jerome controverts the opinion of some in his time who thought that Micah's *ephōd* was made of silver (*ep. 29, ad Marcellam*).* Of an idol the word is understood in Jud. 8²⁷ 17 by JDMich., *Supplementa*, p. 109 (1792); Eichhorn, Ges., De Wette, Gramberg, Vatke, Stud., Reuss, Kue.,† We., Sta., WRSmith, Kautzsch, Bu., Smend, Kitt., Nowack, al. mu.; cf. also Ew., *Alterthümer*, p. 298 n.; IISchultz, *Alttest. Theol*⁴. p. 135; FWSchultz, *PRE*². s.v., al. ‡ To carry the *ephod* before Yahweh is the prerogative of the priesthood (1 S. 2²⁸); § according to 1 S. 22¹⁸ all the priests at Nob exercised this right; ‖ cf. also 1 S. 14⁶ 14¹⁸ 𝔊. In 1 S. 2¹⁸ the boy Samuel ministered before Yahweh, *girt with a linen ephōd* (אפור בד), and David appeared in the same dress in the procession which brought the ark to Jerusalem (2 S. 6¹⁴ cf. v.²⁰ and 1 Chr. 15²⁷). What connexion there is between this linen *ephōd* and the gorgeous *ephōd* of the High Priest in P is again not clear. Older commentators, almost without exception,¶ and many modern scholars think that the *ephōd* is in all places, including Jud. 8²⁷ 17 18, a piece of the priest's dress: so Di. (*Exod. u. Lev.*, p. 299); Ri. *HWB.* s.v.; Be., Ke., Cass., Köhl., König (*Hauptprobleme*, p. 59 ff. = *Religious History of Israel*, p. 107 ff.); Robertson (*Early Religion of Israel*, p. 229 ff.); al. mu. — From the etymology of the word little is to be learned. JDMich. inferred from Is. 30²², אָמְרָה כָּסַח וְהָבַךָ, compared with the parallel clause, that Gideon's אפור was a wooden image covered with metal, and his opinion has obtained general acceptance among those who think that the *ephōd* was an idol; but this is extremely doubtful. The verb אפר in Heb. (Ex. 29⁶ Lev. 8⁷) is denominative; as is also אֲפֻדָה Ex. 28⁸ 39⁵. Lagarde, with great probability, connects the word with the root יפד, which appears in Arab. *wafada*, ' come as an envoy ' to a ruler, or great man, &c.; ** and in Syr. ܐܦܘܕ, a long robe (used in 𝔖 to translate אפור; in 𝔖 often for λόγιον). See Lagarde, *Bildung der Nomina*, p. 178; *Mittheilungen*, iv. p. 17. This etymology does not, however, help us much toward explaining the meaning of the word אפור in the O.T.; that חשׁכ האפור is the garment of approach to God (Lag.) is more ingenious than plausible. — הרפים] the etymology is obscure.†† Some older

* See also a Lap. on 8²⁷.

† *Hibbert Lect.*, p. 82; against his earlier opinion, *Godsdienst v. Israël*, i. p. 99–102 = *Religion of Israel*, i. p. 96–100.

‡ That the *ephōd* was in the form of a bull (De Wette, Vatke) is a groundless conjecture which is properly rejected on all hands.

§ The verb נשׂא does not mean ' wear ' (a garment).

‖ 𝔐 has אִישׁ נֹשֵׂא אפור בָּד, but the last word is not found in 𝔊.

¶ See esp. Jerome, *ep. 29*.

** The pilgrims to Mecca are envoys of God.

†† See esp. Roediger, in Ges. *Thes.*, p. 1519 f., where a full, but by no means exhaustive, conspectus of opinions is given.

writers derived the word from רפה or רפא; * and recently Neubauer, Sayce,†
and Schwally have queried whether it should not be connected with רפאים.‡
A less remote etymology connects תרפים with MH. הירף, תרפות, &c. (also
Aram.), ' foulness, obscenity '; spec. *pudendum*. See *Tanchuma, Wayyāṣe*,
near the end: רבה נקראו הרפים ימי שהן כביה הורף; § cf. *Jer. Abodah zarah*,
ii. 3, fol. 41ᵇ; *Zohar* (Buxt., 2664). So Tanchum on Jud. 17⁵; Gusset,
Lex. s.v. If this is its origin, we should have to explain the word as an
opprobrious perversion or substitution, like נבל, שקוץ, נדידים, and others.‖
𝔊 renders most frequently, εἴδωλα; 'Α μορφώματα. Observe 𝔊, 1 Reg. 19¹³
κενοτάφια. The diverse opinions of the Jewish commentators concerning the
nature and form of the *teraphim* are collected by Buxtorf, *Lex. Talmud.*,
2660 ff.; cf. Beyer, *Additamenta*, p. 194 ff. The most remarkable is, that it
was a mummied human head; *Jer. Targ.*, Gen. 31¹⁹; *Pirqe de R. Eliezer* (8th
cent. A.D.), c. 36; see Buxtorf, *l.c.* With this compare the description of this
kind of divination among the Harranians, Chwolsohn, *Ssabier*, ii. p. 19 ff.,
388 f.; and Chwolsohn's notes, p. 150 ff. As *teraphim* first appear in the
O.T. in the possession of the Aramaean Laban, it is very probable that these
stories about the Harranians are the source of the Jewish descriptions of the
teraphim head cited above. — On the Teraphim see Spencer, *De legibus ritualibus, l.* iii. *diss.* 7, who argues with considerable force that the Urim and
Thummim were of the same nature with the Teraphim, and took their place;
Selden, *De Dis Syris, synt.* i. *c.* 2, with Beyer's *Additamenta;* Pfeiffer, *Exercitationes biblicae, exerc.* iv.; cf. also Jerome, *ep.* 29, *De Ephod et Theraphim.*

6. *In those days there was no king in Israel; every man did as
he pleased*] 21²⁵ cf. 18¹ 19¹; a note by the editor, who thought it
necessary to explain how such doings were possible. It has been
argued that such a comment would be natural only for one who
lived in a flourishing period of the monarchy, and that the editing
of ch. 17, 18, must therefore have taken place before the fall of
the kingdom of Judah.¶ This is perhaps not strictly cogent; an
editor who lived in the Babylonian exile might have made the
same remark. But, as there are no traces in the chapters of the
exilic point of view, it is probable that the verses cited were
written before that time. — **7.** The verse belongs to the second
version of the story, in which it followed v.⁴: the young Judaean

* The former in *Zohar*; see Beyer, *Additamenta* to Selden, *De Dis Syris*, p. 188
(1672); Pfeiffer, *Exercitationes biblicae*, iv. § 2 f.; Hoffmann, *PRE¹*. i. p. 59.

† *Z.A.* ii. p. 95.

‡ Schwally, *Leben nach dem Tode*, p. 36 n.; cf. Nowack, *Hebr. Archäologie*, ii.
p. 23. § Levy, *NHWb.* iv. p. 674; Kohut, *Aruch completum*, viii. p. 285.

‖ Tanchum surmises that it was formed by metathesis from פרה.

¶ So, *e.g.*, Kue., Bu.

Levite, who is living in Micah's neighbourhood, is as one of his own sons (v.¹¹ᵇ), and is installed by him as his priest (v.¹ᵃ). Verse ᵃ⁻¹¹ᵃ is the counterpart of this in the other narrative: the Levite man wanders forth from Bethlehem to find a place for himself; he comes to Micah's home, and is hired by him to be his father and priest in the room of his son. The words, *from Bethlehem of Judah*, in v.⁷, which occasion an awkward redundancy, were probably introduced by the editor from what went before v.⁸ in the first narrative. — *There was a young man* (from Bethlehem of Judah) *of the clan of Judah, and he was a Levite*] how a Levite could be *of the clan of Judah* has greatly perplexed interpreters. Theodoret discusses the difficulty at length, and offers two explanations:* 1. The words are an epexegesis of those which immediately precede: Bethlehem of Judah, that is, belonging to the clan of Judah;† but, taken in this way, they are entirely superfluous. 2. The Levite's mother was of the tribe of Judah;‡ but that would not make him a member of that tribe, still less could he be of both his father's and his mother's tribes, as this theory really assumes. A like objection lies against the opinion of many modern scholars, that he is said to be of the clan of Judah because his parents' home was at Bethlehem.§ Kuenen would reject the words as a gloss;∥ but the last thing a scribe would think of would be to represent a Levite as a member of another tribe.¶ The true explanation probably is that *Levite* here designates his calling, not his race. He was a regularly trained priest, who possessed the traditional religious lore, and especially the art of using and interpreting the oracle. The calling was doubtless, like all others, ordinarily, though not exclusively, hereditary; and in later times all Levites were supposed to be descended from an eponymous ancestor, Levi. This genealogical fiction was made

---

* *Quaest.* 25.   † So Ki., RLbG., Schm., Cler., JHMich.

‡ So also Ra.; Ki. rightly replies that there is no instance in which a man is said to be of his mother's tribe.   § Stud., Ke., Be., Cass.

∥ Oort, *Th. T.* i. p. 289; *Godsdienst van Israël,* i. p. 258; *Th. T.* vi. p. 651; *HCO²,* i. p. 358, 360; *Th. T.* xxiv. p. 11. So, earlier, JDMich., Dathe, al. The words are lacking in 𝔊ᴮᴺ ₛ.

¶ Smend. Studer's hypothesis, suggested by the Talmud, that the gloss is inspired by the same motive which in 18³⁰ changed Moses to Manasseh, is too fine-drawn.

the easier by the fact that there was an old tribe, Levi, of the same stock with Judah and Simeon, which had been broken up, and whose scattered members may in considerable numbers have followed the calling of priests, which their relation to Moses naturally opened to them.* But in early times it was not the pedigree, but the art, that was the essential thing; and there was no more difficulty in the statement that this Levite was of Judaean blood than in the fact that Samuel, who was of Ephraimite descent, was brought up as a priest at Shiloh. — *And he was residing there*] 19[1. 16]; as the Hebrew word implies, living as a client among a tribe of which he was not a member. *There*, is not at Bethlehem, as commentators have felt constrained by v.[8] to interpret, but in the neighbourhood of Micah's home in the Highlands of Ephraim; cf. 18[1a].†

7. והוא לוי] לוי has the usual form of a gentile adjective, and it has been conjectured that the name of the tribe Levi is merely the gentile adj. from לאה (Leah), the name of the stock of which Reuben, Simeon, Levi, and Judah are branches; ‡ and this explanation, though not entirely free from difficulty, is certainly possible. The tribe of Levi was associated with Simeon in the treacherous attack on Shechem (Gen. 34[25-31]), which was repudiated by Israel (Gen. 34[31]); the two tribes never recovered from the vengeance which the Canaanites took upon them, but were completely broken; their scattered members attached themselves as clients to other tribes (Gen. 49[5-7]). § On the tribe of Levi see Nowack, *Hebr. Archäologie*, ii. p. 87 ff., and the literature cited there, p. 87. — Still more obscure is the origin of the name לוי in the sense of priest (Ex. 4[14] &c.). If a Hebrew etymology is to be sought for it, the primary meaning would be, one who is attached to, or associates himself with, a person or thing; cf. Nu. 18[2. 4] Is. 14[1] 56[3]; see Lagarde, *Orientalia*, ii. p. 20 f.; *Mittheilungen*, i. p. 229; Baudissin, *Priesterthum*, p. 50, 74 n. We should then most naturally explain לוי as one who is attached to God, or to the holy place; but this is purely conjectural. In the inscriptions from Southern Arabia, לוא occurs in the sense of ' priest,' לואת, ' priestess ' (Hommel, *Südarabische Chrestomathie*, p. 127). We might be tempted to combine this

---

* This combination is, of course, purely conjectural; the relation between the old tribe Levi and the Levite priests is involved in the densest obscurity. See We., *Prol*[3]., p. 146 f.

† Ch. 17[5] comes from a different source. There is no reason to question the genuineness of the words נר גר שם in v.[7], as Smend is inclined to do.

‡ We., Sta., WRSmith, Nöld. Leah is perhaps " the wild cow tribe "; Nöld., al. For another hypothesis, see Jastrow, *JBL*. xi. p. 121.

§ Levi appears to have been more completely destroyed than Simeon; cf. Jud. 1[a. 17].

with the Arab. *lawiya*, a portion of food set aside for an honoured guest (cf.
1 S. 9²³), which We. had noted (*Reste arab. Heidentumes*, p. 114 n.); the
lawiya would be originally the priest's portion. — ורו כס יר] the verb גור is
used of one who resides among men of another clan, tribe, or people, where,
as he is without the protection of his own kin, he must depend for protection
on some individual or family of the community, whose client he becomes; see
Nowack, *Hebr. Archäologie*, i. p. 336 ff.; W. R. Smith, *Religion of the Semites*,
p. 75 ff. The sentence does not allow us to interpret the words, he resided
there, as referring to his former residence at Bethlehem; *there* can only be, in
the vicinity of Micah's home.

8. From the first narrative; see above on v.⁷. It must have
been preceded by a sentence or two, introducing this Levite;
perhaps simply, "Now there was a Levite from Bethlehem of
Judah." This was omitted by the editor, as a doublet to v.⁷;
only the last words, *from Bethlehem of Judah*, were inserted by
him from this source in v.⁷ and v.⁸, in both of which they are out
of place. It is noteworthy that the Levites of ch. 17, 18, and of
19–21 all come from Judah, and two of them, at least, from
Bethlehem. It is a not improbable surmise that the fragments of
the broken tribe of Levi attached themselves to Judah, as Simeon
did. A close connexion with Judah is indicated also by the names
of Levite families such as Libni, Hebroni, Qorḥi; Korah (Qorah)
was originally a clan of Judah.* — *And the man went from the
city* (from Bethlehem of Judah) *to live where he should find a
place*] not necessarily seeking employment as a priest. In the
course of his wanderings, he came to the part of the Highlands
of Ephraim in which Micah lived. The words, *as he journeyed*
(EV).,† lit. *in making*, or, *to make his journey*, represent an
unusual phrase in Hebrew, and may perhaps better be translated,
to accomplish the object of his journey; see crit. note. — **9.** Micah
learns who and what the stranger is. — **10.** He hires him as his
priest. — *Stay with me and be my father and priest*] 18¹⁹; *father*
is a title of respect given to prophets (2 K. 6²¹ &c.) and priests, as
also to the king's chief minister or vizier (Gen. 45⁸). The connecting notion is probably that of a revered adviser, counsellor;
the use of the word *father* in our text does not necessarily imply

---

* We., *Israelitische u. jüdische Geschichte*, p. 151 n.

† So most interpreters; he had no intention of staying there; Ki., Schm., Cler., al.

that this Levite was a man of mature years, in contrast to the
'youth' of v.[7].* — *I will give thee ten shekels of silver a year, and
a complete suit of apparel, and thy living*] the man lived in Micah's
house (18[15]). The offer was evidently regarded as an advantageous one for the Levite. — **11.** *The Levite agreed to stay with the
man*] these words should follow immediately upon Micah's offer,
v.[10a]; the last words of v.[10], *and the Levite went*, which now interpose, have either arisen by transcriptional accident or are a fragment of the other source.† — *And the youth was to him as one of
his sons*] this half-verse belongs to the second narrative (v.[2-4,7]);
the young Judaean Levite, who resided there, and was perhaps a
client of Micah, becomes like a son to him. — **12.** *And Micah
installed the Levite, and the youth became his priest*] v.[5]. I am
inclined to ascribe the whole of this half-verse to the second
narrator, continuing v.[11b]; though the first clause would fit equally
well in the other version, after v.[11a]. The second half-verse: *And
he was in Micah's house*, belongs to the first account (after v.[11a]);
the young Levite of the other has a house of his own (18[15]). The
union of the two sources has led to a multiplication of explicit
subjects. — **13.** Micah is greatly elated by his good fortune. —
*Now I know that Yahweh will prosper me, because I have got the
Levite as priest*] the close of the first narrative. Micah's son,
who had temporarily filled the place, was, after all, only a layman
in such things; he confides more in the knowledge and skill of
the trained priest, and is assured that under the guidance of such
an interpreter of the mind of Yahweh he will prosper in everything.

8. עשה דרך [לעשׂות דרכו does not, I believe, occur in the O.T., natural as
the phrase 'make a journey' appears to us; דרך is often 'errand, mission,
object of a journey'; cf. 18[4,6]. — **10.** לימים] *annually:* 2 S. 14[26]. — [ערך בגדים
Ex. 40[23]; the pieces of raiment laid out in order. — ומחיתך] 6[4]; *victus.* — וילך
הלוי] cannot stand thus before ויואל הלוי. ‡ Possibly a scribe wrote by mistake,
וילך הלוי לשבת וג׳, which was afterwards corrected by himself, or a later hand,
by the insertion of the correct ויואל הלוי. The alternative is to suppose that
the former words are a stray fragment of the other version of the story; but it
is not easy to see where they could be brought in.

---

* Joseph was a father to the Pharaoh (Gen. 45[8]), though but a young man.
† Corruption of the text is recognized by Stud., Be., al.
‡ Note the attempt of 𝕲[M] to relieve this difficulty by transposition.

XVIII. 1-7. The Danites send out an exploring party, who halt at Micah's village and consult his oracle. — *In those days, &c.*] see on 17[6]; editorial comment on the irregularities related in the preceding verses. Jerome erroneously joined the words to the following: *In diebus illis non erat rex in Israel, et tribus Dan quaerebat possessionem sibi*, &c., and was naturally followed in the division of the chapters which was introduced in the Latin Bible in the 13th century, and from it into the printed Hebrew Bible.[*] — *And in those days the tribe of the Danites was seeking for itself a territory to settle*] *and* is inserted by the editor to regain his connexion after the introduction of v.[1a]. *Territory:* properly estate, hereditary possession in land. The following sentence, as it stands, must be translated: For there had not fallen to it, up to that time, among the tribes of Israel [anything] as a possession. The verb has no subject, the construction is harsh, the phraseology suggests a later hand, and possibly the whole clause is a correct gloss to the preceding. See crit. note.

1. יבקש הדני] cf. Dt. 10[8] 29[7]. In the genealogical system, Dan and Naphtali form a subordinate group (Bilhah) of the Rachel tribes, and are thus connected, though not on an equal footing, with Joseph and Benjamin. The Danites first attempted to establish themselves on the SW. of Joseph, but were prevented by the native Amorite population from gaining or maintaining a hold in the maritime plain, and were pushed back into the hills in the angle between Ephraim and Judah (Jud. 1[34]). As narrated in the chapter before us, and more briefly in Jos. 19[47] (cf. 𝕲), the greater part of the tribe migrated to the extreme north, where they settled at the sources of the Jordan. Notwithstanding the census, Nu. 1[39] 26[43], which gives Dan over 60,000 fighting men, the tribe was apparently always a small one. But one son (clan) of Dan is named in the genealogies (חשים Gen. 46[23], שוחם Nu. 26[42]). In Jud. Dan itself is called a clan (משפחה, v.[2. 11. 19] cf. 13[2]), perhaps more accurately than a tribe (שבט); † the six hundred fighting men who migrated seem to have been the major part of the tribe. In the Song of Deborah Dan is reproached for standing aloof from the national cause (5[17]). The reputation of the Danites for boldness, doubtless displayed in forays and attacks on caravans rather than in war, is celebrated in Gen. 49[16-18] Dt. 33[22]. In the later history of Israel Dan plays no part. It appears in the rolls, 1 Chr. 12[35] 27[22], but is missing in the genealogies, 1 Chr. 2-12, and in the N.T. Apocalypse, 7[5-7]. — כי לא נפלה לו

---

* See "The Vulgate Chapters and Numbered Verses in the Hebrew Bible," *JBL.* xii. 1893, p. 73-78.

† See R. Jesaia on v.[19].

... נבחלה] cf. Ez. 47[14] Nu. 34[2] 26[53]; transitively Ez. 47[22] 45[1] esp. Jos. 13[4] 23[4].[*] The subject or object in all these cases is the land of Canaan or its inhabitants; Stud. would supply here הארץ.

2. The redundancies of the verse are due to the union of two closely parallel accounts. One of these seems to have told the story somewhat as follows: The Danites sent five men of their clan from Zorah and Eshtaol, to spy out the land. And they came to the Highlands of Ephraim and halted there for the night. The other may be reconstructed: They sent able men, representing the whole tribe, and said to them, Go explore the land. — *Of their clan*] v.[11] cf. 13[2] with the note there, 17[7]. The word may, however, be pronounced as a plural, *of their several clans;* see critical note. The parallel in the second source is, *of their various branches* (lit. *extremities*), out of all parts of the tribe; cf. 1 K. 12[31] 13[33] 2 K. 17[32]. — *Men of ability*] the word is sometimes used of personal qualities, courage, prowess, skill, virtue, sometimes of property; cf. 1 S. 9[1] 14[32] &c.; see crit. note. — *Zorah and Eshtaol*] the seats of the Danites in the story of Samson; see on 13[2] 16[31], and above, p. 372. — *To spy out the land*] v.[14. 17], the verb, Gen. 42[9. 11. 14. 16] Nu. 21[32] Jos. 6[22ff] 7[2] &c. — *And to explore it*] see the next clause; the two verbs are similarly coupled in 2 S. 10[3]. — *And they came to the Highlands of Ephraim, to Micah's home, and halted there for the night*] this has a complete parallel in the following verse. — **3.** *As they were in the neighbourhood of Micah's home, they recognized the voice of the young Levite, and turned aside thither*] the young Levite belongs to the second version of the story in ch. 17; see above, p. 367 f. In what way they recognized his voice (1 S. 26[17]) we are not told; most interpreters think of some peculiarities of dialect such as betrayed the Ephraimites (12[6]), which showed that he was a southerner and not a native of Mt. Ephraim.[†] Others imagine that they heard him reciting prayers or hymns, from which they knew that he was a Levite;[‡] we should then have to understand their question, *What art thou doing in this place?* to be merely the expression of their surprise that a Levite was practising his calling at a place

---

[*] For other examples see Drus., *in loc.*
[†] a Lyra, Drus., JHMich., Stud., al.　　　　　[‡] Abarb., Be.

where there was no public temple or frequented holy place. The most natural explanation of the words is, that the Danites had formerly known the young man; and it is by no means impossible that the author of this version of the story meant to be so understood. He does not tell us where the young Judaean Levite's former home was; [*] and may have imagined him as living near the Danite settlements (cf. 15⁹ᶠᶠ).[†] — *Who brought thee hither, and what art thou doing here, and what is thy business here?*] the multiplication of questions, of which the last two are almost exactly parallel, is best explained as the result of the union of two sources. The first two clauses must be taken together, and may with some probability be ascribed to the second of the two accounts. [‡] — **4.** Gives the priest's answer from both sources. — *Thus and so Micah has done to me*] as has been related above (17¹¹ᵇ·¹²ᵃ). — *He hired me and I became his priest*] 17¹⁰·¹¹ᵃ. — **5, 6.** They bid the priest consult the oracle for them, to know whether their expedition will be successful. The consultation of the oracle may have had a place in both narratives; v.⁵·⁶, however, seem to be homogeneous, and to belong to the first version of the story (the *priest*, v.⁶ᵃ).[§] — *Inquire of God*] 1¹, cf. 1 S. 23²·⁴·⁹⁻¹² 30⁷ᶠ· 14¹⁸ᶠ· 1 K. 22⁵ᶠᶠ· &c. Upon such a question the will of God was probably ascertained by the use of the lot in some form; see especially 1 S. 14⁴⁰ᶠᶠ ⑮.[‖] — **6.** The response is favourable; the expedition is under the eye of Yahweh; he sees and takes cognizance of it. There is no ground for regarding the phrase as an example of oracular ambiguity.[¶] — **7.** The party proceeds on its way, and finds in Laish a place whose broad and fertile fields excite their cupidity, while its isolated situation and the unsuspecting security of its inhabitants promise to make it an easy conquest. — *Laish*] or *Leshem* (Jos. 19⁴⁷), under the later name, Dan (v.²⁹), often mentioned in the O.T. as the most northern

---

[*] See on 17⁷.

[†] *From Bethlehem of Judah,* 17⁷, is derived from the parallel narrative, and may possibly have supplanted a conflicting statement about the young Levite's home.

[‡] Assuming that the first half-verse is correctly interpreted above.

[§] Bu. ascribes v.⁵·⁶ᵃ to the first source; v.⁶ᵇ to the other.

[‖] Urim and Thummim: We., *TBS.*, p. 93 f.; Dr., *TBS.*, p. 89; see also above on 17⁵.

[¶] Schm., *JHMich.*: against this view, Stud.

settlement of Israel,* was not far from the Lebanon and the sources of the Jordan.† According to Eusebius it was four miles distant from Paneas (Bāniās) on the road to Tyre.‡ The name is preserved in the modern Tell el-Qāḍi,§ a large mound at less than an hour's distance from Bāniās, at the foot of which are two great springs which feed the most copious of the sources of the Jordan.‖ Several ancient writers confuse Dan with the neighbouring Paneas,¶ and this identification has recently found a defender in G. A. Smith.** — In the following clauses the union of the two narratives has occasioned not only repetition but grammatical discord. One of the accounts seems to have read : They found the people who were in it undisturbed and secure ; the other : They found the *city* dwelling in security, after the manner of the Phoenicians (an unwarlike trading folk). The continuation of the former is probably : *And they were remote from the Phoenicians, and had nothing to do with any one else*] many Greek manuscripts read here,†† nothing to do with *Syria*, which is preferred by Budde. Laish lay in the valley belonging to Beth-rehob (v.²⁸), which was in David's time a petty Aramaean kingdom (2 S. 10⁶) ; the Aramaeans of Maachah (*ib.*, 1 Chr. 19⁶) were probably also neighbours, cf. Abel (meadow of) Beth-maachah.‡‡ The reading Syria (*aram*) is therefore not intrinsically improbable ; but the Hebrew text gives a perfectly good sense, and the external attestation of *aram* is too slight to weigh against it. The intervening clauses are unintelligible. The translation in RV., " For there was none in the land, possessing authority, that might put them to shame in anything," §§ cannot be extorted from the

* " From Dan to Beersheba " (20¹) is a standing phrase for the whole length of Palestine. † Fl. Jos., *antt.* v. 3, 1 § 178, cf. viii. 8, 4 § 226.

‡ *O.S².* 275₃₁ 249₂₃, cf. Jerome, *ib.* 136₁₁.

§ The Arabic *Qāḍi*, like the Hebrew *Dan*, means *judge*.

‖ See Thomson, *Bibl. Sacra*, 1846, p. 196 ff.; Rob., *BR².*, ii. p. 439, iii. p. 390-393; Guérin, *Galilée*, ii. p. 338 ff.; *SWP. Memoirs*, i. p. 139 ff.; Bäd⁸., p. 265 f. See also Le Strange, *Palestine under the Moslems*, p. 418 f.

¶ So, *e.g.* Thdt.; see Reland, *Palaestina*, p. 918 f.; Thomson, *l.c.*

** *Hist. Geogr.*, p. 473, 480 f. Smith argues that Paneas was a place of much greater strength than Tell el-Qāḍi, commanding the entrance to the valley; and that without the possession of Paneas it would be impossible to hold Tell el-Qāḍi.

†† But not in the corresponding passage, v.²⁸; see crit. note.

‡‡ 2 S. 20¹⁴·¹⁵·¹⁸. §§ Similarly Ki., Schm., Cler., Cass., al. mu.

Hebrew text with a rack, and is nonsense when done. Bertheau
would emend, in conformity with v.[10], *there is no lack of anything
in the land,*[*] and strike out the two following words, which he
renders, *possessing wealth*, as a gloss. For a different conjecture,
see crit. note.

2. מִמִּשְׁפַּחְתֵּנוּ] **FALSE** sing.; better perhaps מִמִּשְׁפְּחֹתֵנוּ, plur. 𝕲. — מְקוֹמֶהֶם]
elsewhere, in a similar use, only in the phrase, מְקוֹם הָעָם; † see the passages
cited in the text, and cf. Ez. 33[2] Gen. 47[2]. — בְּנֵי חַיִל] 2 S. 2[7] 13[28] Dt. 3[18];
1 S. 18[17] 2 S. 17[10] &c.; אִישׁ חַיִל Jud. 3[29], plur. 20[44.46]; וּבְנֵי חַיִל 6[12] 11[1]. — לִרְגֵּל]
אֶת הָאָרֶץ] see also Dt. 1[24] Jos. 2[1] 1 S. 26[4] 2 S. 15[10]; Bu. (*Richt. u. Sam.*, p. 145)
notes that the word is found most frequently in E, to which source he is disposed to attribute this version of our story. — 3. הִנֵּה עַם בֵּית מִיכָה] on the
construction see on 15[14]. — 4. זֶה וָזֶה] 2 S. 11[25] 1 K. 14[5]; cf. כָּזֹאת וְכָזֹאת
2 S. 15[16]. זֹה is not here fem. (apocopation of זֹאת as in MII.); ‡ were the
two genders put side by side, the feminine would not stand first; it is probably
only a case of dissimilation (Ew. § 105 *b*). — 5. הֲיַצְלִיחַ דַּרְכֵּנוּ] 𝔐 pronounces
transitively (Hiph.), but if דֶּרֶךְ is subject, we require the Kal, הֲתִצְלַח (Jer. 12[1]);
we must either pronounce thus (that we may know whether our expedition
will succeed; so 𝕲[BN.ALSM] §) or emend, הַיִצְלִיחַ (whether he will give success
to our expedition; 𝕲[PVO al.], § cf. Gen. 24[42]). The former alternative is the
more probable (SS.). — 6. וַיֵּלְכוּ לִשְׁלוֹם] Ex. 4[18] 1 S. 1[17] 20[12] 2 K. 5[19] &c. —
וְנֹכַח יהוה] cf. Prov. 5[21] Ez. 14[7]. — 7. לְלַיְשָׁה] locative of לַיִשׁ v.[14. 27. 29]. In Jos. 19[47]
the name twice occurs in the form לֶשֶׁם 𝔐; We. (*De gentibus et fam. jud.*,
p. 37) would pronounce *lesham*, לֶשֶׁב, after the analogy of מֵישַׁב from יָשַׁב.
Another לַיִשׁ or לֵיׁשָׁה in Benjamin, Is. 10[30]; cf. Palṭi ben Laish, 1 S. 25[44]. —
וַיֹּשֶׁבֶת לָבֶטַח] the ptcp. cannot agree with עַם (cf. יֹשֶׁבֶת וּבֹטֵחַ immediately below); ‖
neither can it agree with the suff. in בְּקִרְבָּהּ (videruntque populum, qui in medio
ejus, habitantis juxta morem Zidoniorum secure, quietum et confidentem;
Schm.), JHMich., Be., Roorda, § 458; and even if we could accept this
explanation of the construction, the tautology would remain (Stud.). The
fem. יֹשֶׁבֶת refers to the *city*; and in its original context was probably preceded by some such words as, וַיִּרְאוּ אֶת הָעִיר, or, אֶת לַיִשׁ; cf. Jer. 33[16] Is. 47[8]
Zeph. 2[15]. Cler. would emend יֹשֵׁב to restore the concord. With the phrase
יֹשֶׁבֶת לָבֶטַח cf. Is. 47[8] Zeph. 2[15]; living confidently, without apprehension;
here of false security, fearing no foe, taking no precautions, as in 8[11]. —
כְּמִשְׁפַּט צִידֹנִים] not הַצִּדֹנִים; in Phoenician fashion. — שֹׁקֵט וּבֹטֵחַ] v.[27]; for the

---

[*] So also Bu.; Ra. endeavours to extract this sense from 𝔐.

† Not, *of the lowest of the people*, but *of all sorts of people;* see Ki. on 1 K. 12[31].

‡ So, *e.g.*, Be., Driver in *BDB.*, Buhl, and most.

§ These codd. represent, not a different reading, but a different construction of
the Greek verb.

‖ Ki. cites Ex. 5[16] Jer. 8[5] as instances in which עַם is construed as fem., but in
both the text is clearly at fault.

former verb see 3[11]. —[ואין מכלים דבר בארץ] *there was no one to put them to shame* (or, insult them) *in anything*, is wholly irrelevant. The versions give no help. The conjecture, ואין כנא כדבר בארץ, *there is no one to restrain* (us) *from anything in the land*, involves the least change in the consonant text, but is entirely unsupported.* — עצר] these words are even more difficult than those which precede; עצר ' is taken by most to mean *authority* (lit. 'restraint, coercion'), cf. the vb. 1 S. 9[17] 2 Chr. 14[10]; so Abulw., Ki., al. mu.; by others it is rendered, *wealth, treasure* (𝕲𝕷), in support of which the

Arab. غَضِرَ, a man became rich, came to have the comforts of life in abundance, is cited (Ges. *Thes.*, Stud., Be., al.). It is more probable, however, that the verb led the ancient translators to guess that עצר was equivalent to אוצר.† The text appears to be incurably corrupt; the words are hardly a gloss (Be., Bu.). —[ודבר אין להם עם ארם] 𝕸 𝕲[BN] 𝕷𝕾: 𝕲[APSLMO] s ε καὶ λόγος οὐκ ἦν αὐτοῖς μετὰ Συρίας (ארם); so also in the long addition which these manuscripts have in v.[9], but in v.[28] they also read μετὰ ἀνθρώπου. In both the old Hebrew alphabet and the square character ד is so often mistaken for ר, and *vice versa*, that such variations have little authority. The words have been differently understood: they had no *alliance* (Ra., Ki., Schm., Stud.), or, they had no *controversy, quarrel* (Cler.).

8-10. The report of the exploring party. —The spies return, and urge their tribesmen to set out at once against Laish, whose wide and fertile lands they praise in glowing language, while from its isolated location and the false security of its people they augur an easy conquest. —The narrative is redundant and confused, and the text not wholly in order. In v.[9] 𝕲 has a long addition, which, in part at least, may be genuine. —**8**. *And their clansmen said to them, What do you . . . ?*] the verb seems to be lacking; if the text is sound, we might restore, *report;* what word do you bring back?‡ One of the Greek versions puts the words into the mouth of the spies: The five men came to their clansmen, to Zorah and Eshtaol, and said to their clansmen, Why are you sitting idle?§ Budde emends accordingly, and his reconstruction is commended by the fact that it also disposes satisfactorily of the first words of v.[9b], which in 𝕸 form an abrupt and awkward exclamation. In the other recensions of 𝕲 we read: Up! let us march against them; for we entered and went about in the land as far as Laish, and we saw the people that inhabit it in security,

---

* See *The Book of Judges in Hebrew*, in loc.; and Scharfenberg, *Animadversiones*, ii. p. 79 f. † Cler. ‡ Cf. Ra., Ki., al. mu. But see crit. note. § 𝕲[BN].

&c. We may be inclined to see at least in the words, *we entered and went about in the land as far as Laish*, a part of the original text; in 𝔐 the place to which they propose to lead their clansmen is not named at all. A satisfactory reconstruction of the sources is hardly possible.* — **9.** *Up, and let us go against them*] cf. 1[1.4]. — *We have seen the land, and it is very fertile*] the words would seem to imply that the party had Laish in view when they set out; this would also explain the suffix, *against them*, just before, which leads Budde to suspect the text. — *And you are sitting idle!*] when you have such an opportunity. The exclamation is some-what harsh; *Why* are you sitting idle? would be better.† — *Do not delay to go to occupy the land*] this seems to have been followed in the original context by the words, *for God has given it into your power*, v.[10a.β]. — **10.** *The region is of wide extent*] the territory which will fall into your hands by the capture of the city; cf. Gen. 31[n] Is. 22[18] Neh. 7[4]. Compare particularly the account of the raid of the Simeonites, 1 Chr. 4[ff.].

8. [ויאמרו להם אחיהם מה אתם] the context of 𝔐 requires us to supply some-thing like כִּשְׁיָבִים רָנָר (Ra.); cf. 2 S. 24[18] Nu. 13[30].‡ 𝔊 τί ὑμεῖς κάθησθε; Bu. conjectures that κάθησθε represents מַחֲשִׁים v.[b]. Against this it is proper to say that κάθημαι never translates החשה or חריש; מחשים is variously rendered by 𝔊 in v.[9] ἡσυχάζετε, σιωπᾶτε, ἀμελεῖτε. We might explain κάθησθε by cor-ruption of ארב בשביכ (haplography), falsely corrected כיבב. 𝔊[BN] καὶ εἶπον τοῖς ἀδελφοῖς αὐτῶν. On the text see further, *The Book of Judges in Hebrew*. — [קומה] read וּמה, with codd. and old edd. (Houbigant). — **10.** [רחבת ידים] stretching wide to right and left.

11-13. The Danites set out on their migration. — Six hundred

armed men, with their women and children, their flocks, and all their movable property (v.[21]), migrate from Zorah and Eshtaol. They encamp in the vicinity of Kirjath-jearim, whence they pass to the Highlands of Ephraim. The verses belong chiefly, if not entirely, to the first version of the story. § — **11.** *Six hundred men girt with weapons of war*] in fighting order. — **12.** *They encamped at Kirjath-jearim in Judah*] Eusebius puts Kirjath-

---

* For an attempt, see Bu., *Richt. u. Sam.*, p. 141.   † Budde; see above on v.[8].
‡ Cf., however, Ru. 3[16], בְּרֵי אֵשֶׁת־; Davidson, *Syntax*, p. 7.
§ Only in the words, *thence . . . from Zorah and Eshtaol*, is there an appearance of duplication.

jearim nine or ten miles from Jerusalem on the road to Diospolis
(Lydda, Ludd); [*] it is identified by Robinson with Qaryet el-
'Ineb, better known as Abū Ghōsh; [†] but this is by no means
certain. [‡] Kirjath-jearim was one of the cities of the Gibeonite
confederacy, Jos. 9[17]. From 1 S. 6[21] 7[1f.] it appears that in the time
of Samuel it was inhabited, at least chiefly, by Judahites. *In
Judah*, in the verse before us, is merely topographical, and does
not certainly warrant the inference that the Judaean occupation
goes back to as remote a time as that in which the action of this
chapter falls. — *On this account the people gave the place the name
Mahaneh Dan* (Dan's Camp), *which it bears to the present day:
It lies west of Kirjath-jearim*] lit. *behind* it; see note on 16[3]. [§]
Whether this explanation of the origin of the name is historical
may be questioned. The persistence of such a name would suggest a permanent encampment rather than a transient halting place
in the migration of the tribe; see also on 13[25]. [‖] Kirjath-jearim
was but two or three hours distant from Zorah and Eshtaol, and a
close connexion between the places is assumed in the genealogies
in 1 Chr. 2[50. 52-54], which may perhaps be interpreted as indicating
that Zorah and Eshtaol were in post-exilic times colonized from
Kirjath-jearim (observe also the Manoahites, v.[52. 54]) ; the population was then Calebite. — **13.** Thence they moved on to the Highlands of Ephraim, and came to Micah's home.

14–21. The Danites take possession of Micah's idols. — The
members of the exploring party inform their clansmen that there
is an idol and oracle in the village, and they at once resolve to
carry them off. — The account of the way in which they got
possession of the images is badly confused by interpolations and
glosses, and baffles emendation or analysis. It seems that in the
first narrative the six hundred armed men halted at the entrance
of the village, while the five spies, who knew, from their former
visit, where the sacred things were, went to get them. They were

---

[*] *OS*[2]. 271[40] cf. 234[94].
[†] *BR*[2]. ii. p. 11 f.; Tobler, *Topographie*, ii. p. 742 ff.; Guérin, *Judée*, i. p. 62 ff.
[‡] Ibid[a]., p. 19. Henderson and Conder propose Khirbet 'Erma; see *SWP.
Memoirs*, iii. p. 43–52; G. A. Smith, *Hist. Geogr.*, p. 225 f.
[§] The last sentence is a note or gloss of later date.
[‖] See Schick, *ZDPV*. x. p. 137; Guthe, *ib.* n. Cf. Thuc., iv. 42, 2.

challenged by the priest, who demanded what they were about.
They bade him hold his peace and come with them to be the
tribe's priest. He took the *ephōd* and *teraphim*, and went with
them. The second account related how, when they were in the
neighbourhood of Micah's home, they turned aside thither and
came to the house of the young Levite and saluted him (v.[15]).*
What followed is not preserved, or is not certainly recognizable in
the present context; the author must have narrated how they
went to the house of Micah and carried off the idol (*pesel* and
massekah).† Probably in this version also the Levite was persuaded to accompany them; it is hardly to be supposed that the
author would have said so much about him in ch. 17 unless he
played a part in the subsequent story. — **14.** From the first
account. — The word *Laish*, which is wanting in many copies
of ᵱ, is obviously a gloss. — *Do you know that there are in these
houses an ephōd and teraphim ?*] Micah evidently lived in a small
open village. The words, *and a graven image and a molten image*
(*pesel* and *massekah*), are added by the editor; see above, p. 366.
— *And now make up your minds what you will do*] cf. 1 S. 25[11].
No more than the hint was needed. — **15.** *And they turned aside
thither, and came to the house of the young Levite* (*to Micah's
house*) *and gave him a friendly greeting*] the words in parenthesis
are a harmonistic note. The verse comes from the second narrative (the young Levite). — **16.** *And the six hundred men with all
their armour on were standing at the entrance of the gate, who
were of the Danites*] the main body halted without the village.
The last words are superfluous, and may be a gloss meant to pre-
clude the misunderstanding that they were the defenders of the
place. That the six hundred men were standing at the gate, is
repeated in v.[17bβ]; we are also twice told how the spies went to
Micah's house and took the idols (v.[17a. 18a]). Some critics therefore regard the whole of v.[16] as a doublet to v.[17bβ], introduced by

---

* For other attempts to separate the threads of the narrative, see Be., Bu.; cf.
above, p. 367 f.

† Wellhausen (in Bleek, *Einl*[4]. p. 198 f.) formerly surmised that while the spies
engaged the young Levite in conversation, the rest of the party stole the gods; but
this opinion, still maintained by Bu. (*Richt. u. Sam.*, p. 143), We. has given up
(*Comp.*, p. 356 f.).

an unskillful editor or scribe.* If this opinion is sound, we should include v.¹⁷ᵃ in the same judgment. — **17. And the five men who went to spy out the land went up**] the superfluous explicitness with which these men are described, as in the corresponding case of the " six hundred men girt with their weapons of war," is more in the manner of an editor or scribe than of the author of the narra-tive, who, when he is allowed, tells a straight story in a clear and vigorous style ; see above on v.¹⁴. — **Came thither, took the pesel and the ephōd and the teraphim and the massekah**] the asyndeton, which in English would make no great difficulty, is very unusual in old Hebrew, and in such a connexion almost unparalleled. This grammatical difficulty is an additional reason for thinking that v.¹⁷ᵃ is not from the hand of the author of the narrative ; see above. — **And the priest was standing at the entrance of the gate**] of the village (cf. v.¹⁶). From v.¹⁸⁻¹⁹, however, it is clear that the meeting with the priest took place at the sanctuary, not at the gate. If the clause belonged to the original story, we should have to suppose that the author wrote, *at the door of the house*, or simply, *at the door*, and that the mistake arose from confusion with the armed men at the entrance of the village. But it is equally possible that the whole clause is a gloss. — **And the six hundred men girt with weapons of war**] the predicate has to be supplied from the preceding, *were standing at the entrance of the gate;* but this can hardly be the author's construction. It is possible, though hardly probable, that the words were originally the subject of the verbs in v.¹⁸.† — **18. And these went to Micah's house, and took the ephōd and the teraphim**] *these* seems to refer to the five men who had visited the place before, in distinction from the six hundred armed men who halted at the entrance of the village. 𝔏 has, *the graven image of the ephōd:* the graven image (*pesel*) is probably a gloss ; the words, *and the molten image* (*massekah*), at the end are also added to complete the inventory. — **The priest said to them, What are you doing ?**] the priest was at Micah's house, in or near which was his shrine (17⁵), not at the gate of the village (v.¹⁷). — **19. From** this point on

---

* We. (Bleck⁴, p. 199; cf. *Comp.*, p. 356) ; Bu.
† Be. thinks them a gloss from v.¹¹, ¹⁶.

the narrative runs smoothly and without evidence of duplication.
Verse [19a]. continue v.[19b] and belong to the first narrative. — *Keep
quiet! Clap thy hand on thy mouth and go with us*] the gesture
of one who forces himself to keep silence, or suppresses an exclamation of surprise, &c., Job 29⁹ 40⁴. — *Father and priest*] 17¹⁰.
— *Is it to your advantage to be priest to a single household, or to
be priest to a tribe and a clan in Israel*] the order of the last
words, *tribe and clan*, is singular. — **20**. The priest was elated
(16²³ 19⁶·⁹) by the brilliant prospect, and taking the *ephod* and
teraphim put himself in the midst of the Danites. 𝔐 adds, *and
the graven image;* 𝔊, *the graven image and the molten image;* see
above on v.[14. 18]. — **21**. The Danites turned and went off, putting
their children, cattle, and other wealth in front, while the armed
men marched behind to protect the column from pursuit.

11. חגור כלי מלחמה] cf. v.[16. 17]; the complement of the ptcp. is the second
accus. after a *verbum induendi*, which is retained in the passive; Ges.²⁵ § 121,
2 n. — **12.** על כן קראו] men gave it the name which it still bears. — **14.** לרגל
את הארץ ליש] *Laish*, which is asterisked in 𝔊ˢ ᵇ, and wanting in 𝔊ᴾⱽᴹᴼ, is
obviously a gloss. Bu., however, retains *Laish*, and cancels לרגל את הארץ. —
נבתים האלה] cf. v.²²; Micah's home was a cluster of houses, a small hamlet.
— **15.** אל בית הנער הלוי בית מיכה] the last words, identifying the house of the
Levite with that of Micah, are apparently a gloss derived from 17¹²ᵇ, in the
other version of the story. — ויבאו באות איש וג'] we should expect האיש; cf. v.¹⁷.
— פתח השער] v.¹⁷ 9⁴⁰ 2 S. 10⁸ 11²³ &c.; שער is never used of the entrance of a
dwelling-house. — **17.** באו שמה לקחו את פסל] the asyndeton is without parallel in simple narrative; the examples from impassioned speech which are
adduced by Stud., Be., al. are not in point. We formerly proposed to make
the verbs imperative, and connect them with the end of v.¹¹: Now know what
you must do; Go thither, take the idol, &c.* This reconstruction is adopted
by Bu. (*Richt. u. Sam.*, p. 141); more likely the clauses were inserted by a
late hand from v.¹⁸. — In v.[17. 18] the Greek versions represent substantially the
text of 𝔐; in 𝔊ᴸ v.[17b. 18a] are omitted by homoeoteleuton (χωνευτόν-χωνευ-
τόν), and the omission in 𝔊ᴮ (against ᴺ) is probably due to the same cause
(εἰσῆλθον – εἰσῆλθον); the words καὶ ὁ ἱερεὺς ἑστώς are then a subsequent
correction. — **18.** פסל האפור] *ephod-image*, is explained by Ki. as an idol
clothed with an *ephod*. It is either a gloss or a transcriptional error; cf. 𝔊.
— **19.** הכבב היתך כהן וג'] with the construction cf. Gen. 2¹⁴. — או היתך וג'] the
second member of the disjunctive question is regularly introduced by אם, *e.g.*
9², see note there; או is unusual, cf. Eccl. 2¹⁹, Ges.²⁵ § 150, 2, n. 2 *b*. —

* Bleek⁴, p. 198 f.; retracted, *Comp.*, p. 232, 356 f. — Be. (p. 249) is mistaken in
saying that some codd. of 𝔊 take the verbs as imperatives.

21. ‏[הַכְּבוּדָה‎] *wealth*, cf. ‏כבוד‎ Gen. 31¹ Is. 10³ &c.; not specifically *valuables* (ℒ). Others, connecting the word with the primary sense of ‏כבד‎, interpret, ‘the *heavy* baggage,’ *impedimenta ;* Ra., Stud., al., cf. 𝔊ᴮ.

22–26. The pursuit. — Micah and his neighbours pursue and overtake the Danites, but are rudely repulsed and return empty-handed. — Compare in general Laban's pursuit of Jacob, Gen. 31²⁴ᶠᶠ : from the similarity of the two narratives, Budde surmises that they are derived from the same source (E). — **22.** When they had already gone some distance, Micah, who had hastily summoned his neighbours, overtook them. — **23.** They called to the Danites to halt. — *They turned their heads*] lit. *their faces ;* cf. 1 K. 8¹⁴ 2 Chr. 29⁶. Without arresting their march, they shout back, What has brought you out ? — **24.** *You take my gods that I made, and the priest, and go off, and what have I left ? What a question to ask me, What is the matter with thee !*] Micah's feelings, his despair at his loss, and his amazement at the impudence of the robbers, are admirably brought out. *My gods,* or *my god ;* cf. Gen. 31³⁰, ³². — **25.** Observe the grim humour of the reply. — *Don't let thy voice be heard in our company ; some fierce fellows might fall upon thee, and so thou cast away thine own life and that of thy household*] *fierce fellows ;* lit. *men of acrid temper ;* cf. 2 S. 17⁸, where David and his old comrades are said to be as savage as a she-bear robbed of her whelps. It is suicidal folly to provoke such men. — **26.** Paying no more attention to the few peasants whom Micah had collected, the Danites continue their march. He also recognizes the disparity of force, and sadly turns back.

27–31. The conquest of Laish. — The Danites find the place undefended, as their spies had reported ; they capture and burn it, and build a city of their own on the site, which they name Dan. They put the idol which they took from Micah in the holy place and install the priest. — Some slight redundancies in v.²⁷⁻²⁹ may be attributed to the hand of the editor ; v.³⁰, ³¹ probably come from the two chief sources of the story. — **27.** *They took what Micah had made*] his whole apparatus ; perhaps the name of the object (*ephod* and *teraphim*) has been omitted in order to make the statement more general. — *They came to Laish, &c.*] see v.¹.

— *Put the inhabitants to the sword and burned the city*] cf. 1⁸ and
1⁵.—**28.** Cf. v.⁷, and v.⁹ ⓖ.— *It is in the valley which belongs to
Beth-rehob*] this note on the situation of Laish-Dan may be by a
later hand. *Beth-rehob* is otherwise unknown. It cannot be the
place named in 1⁸¹ among the cities which Asher was unable to
conquer (see also Jos. 19²⁸·³⁰).ᵃ More probably it is the Rehob of
Nu. 13²¹ (P), the northern limit of the exploration of Moses' spies.
In the verse just cited the name of Rehob stands by the side
of the Gateway of Hamath,† but there is no grammatical connexion between the two, and it is not impossible that the latter is
a gloss to Rehob. Beth-rehob is mentioned also in 1 S. 14⁴⁷ ⓖ,
in the list of Saul's conquests, in connexion with Zobah.‡ It was
in the 10th century B.C. an Aramaean state (2 S. 10⁶·⁸).§ Robinson
would put Beth-rehob at Gebel Ḥūnin, where there are ruins of a
fortress, in a commanding position.‖ Others have thought of
Qal'at Buṣra, about an hour north of Dan. If we were disposed
to add one more to these guesses, we might with greater probability conjecture that Beth-rehob was the ancient name of Paneas.
—**29.** *They called the city Dan, after the name of their ancestor
Dan, who was born to Israel*] Gen. 30⁶ᵉ; the last words, unnecessarily emphasizing the genealogical relation, may be a gloss. —
Whereas Laish was the name of the city originally] cf. 1¹⁰·¹¹·²³,
and for the expression, Gen. 28¹⁹ (R); the notice is superfluous
here, after v.²⁷ᶠ, and may be an editorial note. This is the only
case in the O.T. in which a city bears the name of a tribe; probably the population of the city substantially made up the tribe. —
30, 31.¶ The two verses are plainly parallel; each tells how the
Danites set up Micah's idol in their new sanctuary, and how long
the cultus thus established lasted. Verse³⁰ probably belongs to
the first version of the story in ch. 17, v.³¹ to the second. The
author of the former must have given at the outset some account
of the priest from Bethlehem who is now abruptly introduced in
17⁸ as *the man*, and it is not a violent supposition that Jonathan's
name and pedigree originally stood there. The editor who united
this with the other version, in which the young Levite lived in

---

* Cler.   † See on 3⁸.   ‡ See ⓖᴸ ⁸² ᵃˡ·; Klostermann.
§ See above, p. 390.   ‖ *BR²·* iii. p. 370-372.
¶ On these verses see C. H. Graf, *De templo Silonensi*, 1855.

Micah's neighbourhood, omitted the antecedents of 17³ and inserted the pedigree in 18¹⁰, where probably only the name Jonathan originally stood. The hand of an editor may perhaps also be recognized in the last words of v.³⁰, *till the depopulation of the land;* the author of the narrative probably lived before 734 or 722 B.C.* — **30.** *The Danites set up for themselves the idol*] v.³¹ᵃ. If our hypothesis about the source of the verse be correct, *idol* (*pesel*) may have been substituted by an editor for an original *ephod.* — *Jonathan the son of Gershom the son of Moses and his descendants were priests to the tribe of Dan*] Gershom, the eldest son of Moses, Ex. 2²² 18³. In 𝕴 an *n* is inserted above the line, to indicate that this priest of an idolatrous cult was rather a son of the idolatrous king Manasseh (2 K. 21) † than of Moses; see critical note. That the priests of Dan claimed a Mosaic lineage is a fact of very great interest. ‡ It was not the only Mosaic priest-hood in Israel, as is clear from Dt. 33⁸, and from the patronymic Mushi among the Levites (Nu. 3³³ 1 Chr. 6¹⁹ (6⁴) &c.). — *Down to the time of the depopulation of the land*] probably the deporta-tion of the people of Northern Galilee by Tiglath-pileser in 734 (2 K. 15²⁹) is meant.§ If the clause is from the hand of an editor, however, it is possible that it refers to a still later time. — **31.** *As long as the house of God was at Shiloh*] on Shiloh see below on 21¹⁹. *The house of God:* cf. 1 S. 1⁷·²⁴ 3¹⁵; the passages in Samuel make it quite clear that a temple, not a tent, is meant. ‖ How long this temple stood is not known.¶ Bertheau thinks that there must be some closer connexion between the cessation of this cul-tus at Dan and that at Shiloh, and finds it in the religious changes introduced by Jeroboam I. His new temple at Bethel, with its image of Yahweh in the form of a bull, so overshadowed the older

---

* On other hypotheses see critical note.

† Not of the tribe of Manasseh (Ew.).

‡ It is natural to connect this with the fact that Abel and Dan were proverbially places in which the old customs of Israel were most tenaciously preserved (2 S. 20¹⁸ 𝕲; see We., Dr., Klost.).

§ Cler., Nöld., Köhler, Stud., Be., al. mu. Older scholars referred the words to the Philistine wars (cf. 1 S. 4²¹ᶠ), so that the terminus would coincide with that in v.³¹; so the Jewish author of the *Quaestiones hebr. in libros Paralipom.*, printed in the works of Jerome, Ki., Grot., Hengstenb., Ke., al. Houbigant conjectures הארן, till the carrying away of the *ark;* so Bleek, Cass., Riehm (*Einl.,* i. p. 396); cf. König, *Einl.,* p. 257. ‖ See Graf, *De templo Silonensi.* ¶ See above, p. 369.

sanctuary at Shiloh, which had lost its holy ark, that it fell into decay; the splendid image which he set up at Dan (1 K. 12²⁹) took the place of the old idol stolen from Micah. We cannot see, however, why, if the author meant, *to the time of Jeroboam ben Nebat*, he should have expressed himself so obliquely. Jeroboam's image of the bull at Dan need not have supplanted the older idol.[*]

22. הכה הרחיקו] asyndetic circumstantial clause; v.⁸ 15¹⁴. Notice the use of the causative stem, interpose a distance; cf. הקריב, get near; Wright, *Arab. Gram.*, i. p. 36; Ges.²⁶ p. 145. — וידביקו] 20⁴⁵ 1 S. 31² 2 S. 1⁶ Gen. 31²³. — **25.** ואספתה נפשך] cf. Ps. 26⁹ 1 S. 15⁶ and the use of Niph. Jud. 2¹⁰ &c. — **29.** אשר ילד] cf. ל4⁸ Job 5⁷ Ruth 4¹⁷. The form is regarded by Bö. (§ 906 *c*), Barth, Buhl, al., as passive Kal. — **30, 31.** Kue. (*HCO².* i. p. 359 f.) thinks that the two verses are by different hands, but neither of them the original close of the story, of which at most only fragmentary remains may be preserved in v.⁸¹. We. formerly (following Stud.) regarded v.³¹ as genuine, v.³⁰ as an interpolation (Bleek⁴, p. 199); † this opinion he subsequently modified: the two verses prob. do not belong together, but there is no reason to think that v.³¹ is older than v.³⁰ (*Comp.*, p. 357). Bu. ascribes v.³¹ to the first narrative, v.³⁰ to the second: Jonathan ben Gershom is not the priest whom the Danites carried off, for in that case his name would have been given at his first appearance (17ᴬ); he must therefore belong to the other version of the story, according to which the young Levite did not accompany the Danites; Jonathan is the priest whom they got in his place, — whence and how, we are not told, — when they set up their sanctuary. But, as has been said above, it is not likely that the author of the second account would have said so much about this young Levite in the beginning of the story, if he played no part in the sequel (see p. 395); nor is it probable that, if Jonathan was not Micah's priest at all, but was procured by the Danites from elsewhere, the author would have failed to say something more about him. — **30.** יהונתן כן נרשׂם בן כנשׂה] many codd. and old edd. have מנשׁה; see De Rossi *ad loc.* and *Appendix*, vol. iv. p. 227. ‡ 𝕲ᴺ has Moses, which also stands, by the side of Manasseh, in the conflate text of 𝕲ᴹ, Thdt., 𝖘, Bar Hebr.; 𝕲ᴬᴮᴸᴼ have Manasseh; 𝕃 *Moysi*; 𝕾 Manasseh, but Ephr. Syr. (i. p. 327) Moses. The נ *suspensum* is explained in *Jer. Berachoth*, x. 2 (fol. 12ᵈ): עון הלוי אם וכה בן ; more fully *Bab. Baba bathra*, fol. 109ᵇ: כיהה ואם לאו בן מנשה ; more fully *Bab. Baba bathra*, fol. 109ᵇ: Gershom, it

---

[*] According to Klostermann (*Samuelis u. Könige*, p. 348 f.), the opinion that Jeroboam put one of his new idols at Dan rests only on a corruption of the text in 1 K. 12²⁸·³⁰; the verses originally spoke only of the *ephōd* at Dan. See also Farrar, "Was there a Golden Calf at Dan?" *Expositor*, Oct. 1893, p. 254–265.

† Similarly Ew. (*GVI.* ii. p. 492); Schrader, al. See esp. Stud., p. 384–387.

‡ On letters above the line (Ps. 80¹⁴ Job 33:13, 15), see *Ochla w-Ochla*, No. 160; Buxtorf, *Tiberias*, c. 16; Geiger, *Urschrift*, p. 258 f.; Harris, *JQR.* i. p. 137.

is admitted, was the son of Moses, but because he (Jonathan) acted like
Manasseh the text connects him with Manasseh; a similar explanation may
be given of 17⁷, which connects him with Judah, Manasseh's tribe.* This
interpretation is repeated by the Jewish commentators; *e.g.* Ra.: for the
sake of Moses' fair fame *n* is inserted to change the name; and it is written
above the line to show that it is not really Manasseh but Moses; see also Ki.
on 17⁷, Rashbam on *Baba bathra*, l.c., Norzi *ad loc.*, al. Glosses to the same
effect are found in a number of codd. of 𝕸; Kennicott, *Dissert. generalis*,
ed. Bruns, p. 41, 497, 522. Tanchum offers a different hypothesis: the name
is written thus to hold the balance between discrepant traditions. It was left
for Protestant theologians (Schm., Cler., Hottinger, al.) to be more scrupu-
lous than the Jews, and defend the reading Manasseh.† In the genealogical
system Gershon or Gershom ‡ is the first-born son of Levi; in P the Gershonites are one of the three branches of the tribe of Levi, though altogether overshadowed by the Kohathites to whom Aaron belonged. In the allotment of
Levitical cities (Jos. 21²⁷⁻³³ 1 Chr. 6⁷¹⁻⁷⁶) the Gershonites have all the northern
cities (in East Manasseh, Issachar, Asher, Naphtali). The interpretation of
these facts, in the light of our verse, seems to be that the priests at Dan and
other northern sanctuaries like Kedesh, and Golan beyond Jordan, formed a
group (Gershonites) which traced its lineage to Moses. The importance of
these priesthoods declined as the northern sanctuaries were more and more
eclipsed by those of the central, and eventually the southern tribes (Kohath,
Jos. 21²⁰⁻²⁶ ⁹ᶠᶠ). Gershonite Levites were, in the genealogical apprehension,
descendants of a Gershon ben Levi, who takes the place of the Gershom ben
Mosheh of our text; cf. Eleazar ben Aharon and Eliezer ben Mosheh. § —
31. לספּה את להם וישׂימו] שׂים of setting up idols, 1 K. 12²⁹ 2 K. 21⁷ Jer. 7³⁰ 32³⁴
(Stud.).

XIX.-XXI. The tribe of Benjamin is nearly exterminated by the other Israelites. ‖

The second of the supplementary narratives gives the story of
the war with Benjamin, its cause and consequences. — The concubine of a Levite residing in the Highlands of Ephraim deserts him
and returns to her father's home in Bethlehem of Judah (19¹ᶠ).
He follows her to bring her back. After tarrying for several days,

---

* See also *Shir ha-Shirim rab.* on 2⁶. It is at least a curious coincidence that
in Josephus the first High Priest of the Samaritan temple on Mt. Gerizim is named
Manasseh (*antt.* xi. 8, 2 ff.).

† See, further, Blau, *Masoret. Untersuchungen*, p. 48,° and *JQR*. Jan. 1895, p. 333.

‡ On the orthography see Frensdorff, *Massoret. Wörterbuch*, p. 277.

§ There was also a branch of the Merarite Levites which bore the name מושׁי,
i.e., *Mosaites*.   ‖ See Auberlen, *Stud. u. Krit.*, 1860, p. 549 ff.

they set out on their return late in the afternoon, and are constrained to halt for the night at Gibeah, where they find entertainment in the house of an old man who is not a native of the place
(v.⁴⁻²¹). The men of the town set upon them as the Sodomites
upon Lot's guests; the Levite surrenders his concubine to them,
and in the morning finds her dead on the threshold (v.²²⁻²⁷). He
proceeds to his home, cuts the woman's body in pieces, and sends
messengers through the land, calling on Israel to avenge the outrage (v.²⁸⁻³⁰). — The Israelites assemble, four hundred thousand
strong, hear the cause, and resolve to punish the men of Gibeah
as they deserve (20¹⁻¹¹). They demand of the Benjamites the
surrender of the guilty men; but the Benjamites refuse and prepare for war (v.¹²⁻¹⁷). After consulting the oracle, the Israelites
join battle, but are worsted (v.¹⁸⁻²¹). The second day they have
no better success (v.²²⁻²⁸); but on the third day, by a stratagem,
capture Gibeah and cut the Benjamite army to pieces; a remnant
of six hundred men escapes to the wilderness (v.²⁹⁻⁴⁷). The towns
of Benjamin are burned, and all their inhabitants, men, women,
and children, put to the sword (v.⁴⁸). — From the slaughter the
Israelites return to Bethel, in great distress that a tribe is lacking
in Israel. For though six hundred men survive the battle, all the
Israelites have sworn not to give their daughters in marriage to
men of Benjamin (21¹⁻⁷). They send an expedition against
Jabesh in Gilead, which alone of all the cities of Israel failed
to send its contingent to the great levy, with orders to slay all its
people, only saving alive the virgin girls. In this way they procure
wives for four hundred of the Benjamites (v.⁸⁻¹⁴). Two hundred
being still lacking, they counsel the Benjamites to conceal themselves in the vicinity of Shiloh at the time of the annual feast of
Yahweh, and when the maidens of the place come out to dance
in the vineyards to carry them off by force; promising to appease
the girls' fathers and brothers. This plan being successfully carried out, the Israelites disperse to their homes (v.¹⁵⁻²³).

The narrative of the war with Benjamin is altogether different
from any of the other stories in the book.[*] The numbers are
exaggerated to absurdity: the levy of Israel is four hundred

---

[*] See We., *Comp.*, p. 233 ff.

thousand men ; the Benjamites muster twenty-six thousand.[*]   In
the first two days' fighting the Israelite loss is forty thousand men,
while the Benjamites do not lose a man ; on the third day the
tables are turned, and the Benjamites are almost annihilated, with
an apparent loss of only thirty men on the other side.   The spontaneous and united action of all Israel is even more surprising
than the prodigious numbers.   It is perfectly clear from the
stories of the judges that there was in this period no union of any
kind among the Israelite tribes.   Leaders like Ehud, Gideon, and
Jephthah have at their back only their immediate clansmen, or
at most a group of neighbouring tribes ; and their success sometimes excites the fierce jealousy of others ($8^{1ff.}$ $12^{1ff.}$).   Even in
the great struggle with the Canaanites under Sisera, in which all
that Israel had gained in Central Palestine was imperilled, Deborah was unable to unite all the tribes in the common cause ; not
only Judah and Simeon, who are not even named, but Reuben,
Gad, Dan, and Asher stood aloof.   But in ch. 20 21 all the twelve
tribes are gathered together as one man, " from Dan to Beersheba,
and the land of Gilead," and, without a leader, consult and act as
if by a common instinct.   This singular unity, it is to be observed
further, is not political, but religious ; it is not as a nation or a
people that Israel acts, but as a general assembly of the church ;
the only officers who are named are the " elders of the congregation."   This is in glaring contrast to the pictures of the religion of
old Israel which the Book of Judges gives us ; the conception of
Israel as a church instead of a people or a nation is characteristic
of the post-exilic stratum in the Hexateuch and of the Book of
Chronicles.[†]   The language of Jud. 20, also, puts it in the same
company.   These evidences of very late date are, in the main,
confined to ch. 20 21^{1-14} ; ch. 19 and the end of ch. 21, on the
contrary, are of the same general character as the other stories
in the book ; ch. 19 has an obvious affinity with ch. 17 18 ; $21^{19ff.}$
has eminently the note of antiquity.

---

[*] In the Song of Deborah the fighting strength of the tribes is put down at forty
thousand. The only numbers in the Book of Judges which are comparable to
those in ch. 20 are those given for the losses of Midian (8^{10}).

[†] Such a conception could only arise at a time when the national life of Israel
was a thing of the remote past.

The most probable explanation of these facts is, that a contemporary of the Chronicler took the old story in hand, and put in place of the original account of the way in which the other Israelites punished the outrage at Gibeah his own representation of the way such a thing should be done by the congregation. In this composition, which is of the nature of Midrash, the author probably followed the order of the older narrative and in considerable part preserved its language. Traces of the later hand may perhaps be recognized in ch. 19 also. It is possible that the older text was itself composite; in 19$^{1-13}$ the story is redundant and confused, and more than one attempt has been made to solve the difficulties by analysis, but without conspicuous success.[*] The oldest form of the story may perhaps be derived from J.

The historical character of ch. 20 21$^{1-14}$ will scarcely be seriously maintained; in the whole description of the war there is hardly a semblance of reality. But the old story must also have related how the report of the crime at Gibeah excited the horror and indignation of the Israelites, and how, when Benjamin refused to surrender the guilty parties, they not only vowed to interdict the connubium with that tribe, but visited them with savage retribution which even threatened the existence of the tribe (see esp. 21$^{16ff.}$). That this narrative has an historical basis, I see no reason to deny. It is, of course, incredible that the tribe of Benjamin was almost exterminated only a generation or two before the time of Saul; but the events related in these chapters probably fall in a much earlier period, and the catastrophe, serious as it evidently was, cannot have had anything like the proportions given to it by the later writer in ch. 20. Nor does it appear to me at all probable that the whole story is a fiction inspired by Jewish hatred of Saul and all the places which were associated with his memory.[†]

In Hos. 9^9 the prophet declares that Israel in his day has sounded the depths of depravity, "as it did in the days of Gibeah"; in 10^9 we read, "From the days of Gibeah thou hast sinned, O Israel." The older commentators generally understood

---

[*] See below, p. 407.
[†] Güdemann, Graetz, We., Kue.; see below, p. 408.

these verses to refer to Jud. 19–21.* 𝔗, however, interprets 10⁹ of the choice of Saul as king,† and this interpretation has recently been revived by Wellhausen and others.‡ The outrage at Gibeah, Jud. 19, is not to be laid at the door of Israel, which so promptly and severely punished the perpetrators; and the crime, atrocious as it was, did not make an epoch in Israel's career of wickedness. On the other hand, Hosea regards the making of other kings beside Yahweh as apostasy, just as truly as the worship of other gods beside him.§ The context of Hos. 10⁹ is very difficult, and v.⁹ᵇ, which we should expect to throw light on the meaning of v.⁹ᵃ, is itself hopelessly obscure. Wellhausen's argument, however, does not seem to me convincing. The crime of the Benjamites of Gibeah, in the ancient way of thinking, brought guilt upon all Israel; it defiled Yahweh's land and people. That Israel expiated it in the blood of the offenders did not undo the deed, which might well serve the prophet as a type of abominable depravity, the first plunge into that depth to which all Israel had now sunk. On the other hand, if Hosea had meant, "From the days when Saul of Gibeah was made king at Gilgal" (1 S. 11¹⁵), he would hardly have expressed himself in the enigmatical phrase, "From the days of Gibeah."‖ It does not necessarily follow that Hosea had read Jud. 19–21 even in its original form; though if the oldest version of the story comes from J, it is not impossible that he may have done so.

On the critical problems in ch. 19–21 see Wellhausen, *Comp.*, p. 233–238; *Prol³.*, p. 243–245; Güdemann, *Monatsschrift für Gesch. u. Wissensch. d. Judenthums*, 1869, p. 357 ff.; º Graetz, *Gesch. d. Juden*, i. p. 351–355; Kuenen, *HCO².* i. p. 360 ff.; Böhme, *ZATW.* v. p. 30–36; Budde, *Richt. u. Sam.*, p. 146 ff.; Kittel, *GdH.* i. 2. p. 21 f. — Wellhausen regards the story as of the same character and age throughout: the greater vividness and appearance of reality in ch. 19, which Stud. had observed, are due entirely to the author's art; the chapters are full of reminiscences of passages in the older literature; it may

* So Jerome, Cyrill. Alex., Ra., Ki., Abarb.; Drus., Grot., Eichh., Rosenm., Nowack, Reuss, al. plur. Some of the older interpreters go back to ch. 17 18, to show how all Israel had sinned in tolerating idolatry, and explain in this way their defeat in the first two days' battle.

† Jerome (on Hos. 9⁹) offers this as an alternative; see also Ra. on Hos. 9⁹.

‡ We., *Comp.*, p. 237; *Kleine Propheten*, in loc.; Sta., *GVI.* i. p. 580; Smend, *Alttest. Religionsgesch.*, p. 194; cf. also Kue., *HCO².* i. p. 361 f.　　§ We., *l.c.*

‖ Against We., see also Bu., *Richt. u. Sam.*, p. 147; Kitt., *GdH.* i. 2. p. 21 n.

well be doubted whether the narrative has any basis of historic fact; that the author is animated by hatred of the Benjamite kingdom is manifest. Most other scholars recognize that an older story underlies the work of the post-exilic author or is combined with it. Bertheau thinks that two strands are to be found in ch. 19, and in ch. 20 21 offers the following analysis: A, 20[1. 2b-10. 14. (16). 19. 24-28. 29-36a. 47] 21[5-14]; B, 20[2a. 11-13. 15-17. 30-23. 36b-44. 45. 46. 48] 21[1-4. 15-23]. But the formal criteria upon which Be. mainly relies, such as the use of בני ישראל in A, איש ישראל in B, are insufficient, and his results by no means satisfactory. Budde finds in 19[4-15] clear evidence of double narration, which cannot be explained as mere redundancy or by assuming interpolations. Compare, e.g. the parallel clauses (different number) in v.[9b], v.[10a] with v.[11a], v.[11b. 12] with v.[13], the change of number in v.[16], the multiplication of terms for the close of day in v.[8. 9. 11]. To separate the two strands seems impossible; Be.'s attempt is rejected. From v.[16] on the narrative runs smoothly and straightforward. Both sources are old; throughout there is the closest affinity not only to Gen. 19, but to other old portions of the Pentateuch and Samuel;[*] one of them is probably J. In ch. 20 the surest criterion is the place where the Israelites assemble: in the older source Mizpah, in the later Bethel. Bu. accordingly analyzes the chapter as follows: A (Mizpah), 20[1&a. b. 3b-10. 3a. 14. 18. 29. 30b-39. 40-42a], part of the very confused conclusion; B (Bethel), 20[1&β. 2. 11-13. 15. 17. 20-29. 30-33a. 34a. 35-39a], part of the closing verses. Verse [39] is introduced in A in conformity with B; v.[33b. 34b] in like manner are intruded in B after A; v.[16. 18] are glosses derived from 3[16] and 1[1. 2]; so are also v.[7b] and v.[28] to הבה. In ch. 21 Bu. ascribes to A, 21[1 (?). 15. 17a. 18. 19 *. 20b-22. 23]; to B, v.[2-5. 9. 10. . . . 12 *. 13. 14a. 24]; v.[16. 17b. 19 *. 20a] are editorial interpolations in A; v.[6-8. 11. 12 *] in B.[†] In ch. 20 21 B is certainly post-exilic and entirely unhistorical; the union of A and B may be the work of the editor who added ch. 17–21 to the Deuteronomic Book of Judges; in any case the fusion of A and B must have taken place at a very late time. Kuenen's explanation is, that a Judaean story, which originated in the days of the kingdom, was thoroughly worked over in, or more probably after, the exile, in the spirit of Judaism. The chapters give plain evidence, not of the fusion of two sources, but of successive amplification and correction: 20[27b. 28a] are inserted to remove a perplexity which v.[26. 27a] might create; 20[36b-46] is an expansion (after Jos. 8) of v.[29-36a]; 21[5-14] an attempt to remove, at least in part, the offence of v.[15-23]. — The hypothesis proposed in the text (above, p. 405), that an author of the age and school of the Chronicler substituted for the middle of the original story a Midrash of his own, appears on the whole the most acceptable. It is simpler than to suppose, with Bu., that this Midrash existed separately and was united with the older story by a still later redactor. If I am not mistaken, the Midrash of the Book of Kings, upon which the Chronicler drew so largely, presents an analogous case. I should freely admit, however, that the analogy of the Book

---

[*] See Bu., p. 149 f., where a number of these parallels are collected.

[†] In ch. 21 Böhme, *Z.l TW.* v. p. 30-36, distinguishes three sources.

of Chronicles itself may be urged in support of Budde's theory. But Budde's analysis, like' Be.'s, seems to me in many particulars unsatisfactory; and the extreme difficulty of the analysis, in a case where we should expect it to be peculiarly easy, is itself a reason for doubting the correctness of the assumption that two sources have been united by an editor. — The towns which are pilloried in this story are Gibeah, Saul's home, and Jabesh in Gilead, by the relief of which Saul became king, and whose grateful inhabitants held so loyally to him; while the Levite, who is so outrageously treated, comes from Bethlehem, David's birthplace. The coincidence is certainly striking. Güdemann inferred that the motive of the whole story was Judaean animosity against Saul : * the places and people that were most intimately associated with his history were held up to infamy; the inhabitants of Gibeah were guilty of an unspeakable crime; his tribe of Benjamin upheld them; the people of Jabesh were the only men in Israel who took no part in the holy war. Similarly Graetz (*Gesch. d. Juden*, i. p. 351-354); see also We. (*Comp.*, p. 237); Kue. (*HCO*. i. 363 f.). Graetz concludes, further, that the story, with which ch. 17 18 are closely connected, originated in the time of Solomon; and, unquestionably, such an animus would be more easily explained in the early years of the Judaean kingdom than after the exile, when We. supposes that the chapters were written. The analysis leads us to make a distinction, however, which these critics do not observe. The crime at Gibeah is narrated in the old story; Jabesh in Gilead appears only in the post-exilic supplement. It is by no means impossible that the history of Saul may have furnished the association which led the later writer to fix on Jabesh as the place which, at least by neutrality, showed its sympathy with Benjamin; but the connexion is entirely secondary, and the coincidence on which Güdemann's theory rests is not original.

XIX. 1-9. The Levite and his concubine. — She leaves him ; he follows her to her father's house and stays there some days, repeatedly postponing his departure. — **1.** *In those days*] editorial ; loosely dating the following story in the period of the Danite migration, which is further defined as before the establishment of the monarchy. — *And there was no king in Israel*] that is, *when there was no king*, 17⁸ 18¹ 21²⁵.† — *There was a Levite residing in the remote parts of Mt. Ephraim*] cf. 17¹. Probably the northern part of the Central Highlands is meant ; it is noteworthy that neither here nor in ch. 17 18 is a town named. — *Resided:* see on 17⁷. — *A concubine from Bethlehem in Judah*] it has been observed above that all the Levites mentioned in ch. 17 18, 19-21 are in some way connected with Judah, and two of them with

* In the article cited above, p. 406.   † See above, p. 369.

Bethlehem.* — 2. *His concubine committed fornication against him*] so 𝕸. The text is suspicious; the older Greek version reads, *was angry with him;* see critical note. — *She went from him to her father's house, to Bethlehem of Judah, and was there some time, four months*] the last words are in loose apposition, and may perhaps be a gloss (cf. 20⁴⁷). — 3. The man followed her to her home. — *To speak affectionately to her, to bring her back*] cf. Gen. 34³ and especially Hos. 2¹⁴. On the text see critical note. — *He had with him his servant and a pair of asses*] v.¹⁰·¹⁹; to carry the necessary provisions for the journey, and for the woman to ride. — *And she brought him into her father's house*] if the text be sound we must imagine that he first apprised the woman of his coming, and that she met him and took him home. But the oldest Greek version has simply, *he went to her father's home,* and it is not improbable that here, as in the first half-verse, 𝕸 has been altered in consequence of the feeling that, as the man was the injured party, it should be the woman who tried to win him back. — *When the girl's father saw him, he came gladly to meet him*] 𝕷 renders well, *occurrit ei lactus.* The separation was a disgrace which the restoration of the man's favour removed.

1. אשה פילגש] see on 4⁴, p. 114. — 2. [ותזנה עליו פילגשו] there is no exact parallel to the construction; זנה is elsewhere construed with על, אחרי, מתחת, once with תחת; observe also ותזנה, instead of the normal ותזן. Of the versions 𝕲^BN 𝕷 represent ותזנח, which they interpret, with Jewish commentators, *she deserted him;* see Ra., RLbG., Abarb., cf. Ki.; 𝕿 ורחקת, *she despised him, spurned him.*† 𝕲^APVLMO [ε καὶ ὠργίσθη αὐτῷ, following which Dathe conj. ותרגז (cf. Neh. 2¹⁹); Bö. proposed ותזנה; Schleusner, Stud., Ew., We., al. prefer ותזנה, which, however, is regularly transitive. Another hypothesis is that the original text, represented by 𝕲^A al., was ותאנף עליו,‡ which was corrupted to ותנאף (she committed adultery), and that the reflection that she was not a wedded wife led to the substitution of ותזנה (she committed whoredom). The Jewish interpreters found the text very difficult: How could a concubine, who was neither wife nor slave, commit adultery against her lover? If she

---

* Page 371. It may be added that the only other places in the pre-exilic historical books in which Levites are mentioned are 1 S. 6¹⁵ 2 S. 15²⁴ 1 K. 8⁴ 12³¹; all of which seem to be secondary or Deuteronomic. See now Nowack, *Hebr. Archäologie,* ii. p. 91 n.

† Cf. Fl. Jos., *antt.* v. 2, 8 § 136 f., where the grounds of the separation are explained at length in this sense.

‡ Usually אנף ב. An example of the confusion of the two verbs is found in *Chullin,* 63ª; see Levy, *NHWb.* i. p. 112ᵇ; Jastrow, *Dictionary,* p. 86.

did so, how could the Levite (lawfully) go after her and take her back? (RLbG.). See *Gittin*, 6ᵇ, and *Tosaphoth* in loc. — 3. לדבר על לבה] Gen. 34³ 50²¹ 2 S. 19⁸ Hos. 2¹⁶ Is. 40² Ruth 2¹³. — להשיבו] Qerē, with all the versions, להשיבה, undoubtedly restoring the original reading; the Kethib probably intended יהשיבו, *that she might win him back*, reflecting that he was the offended party. Maurer and Ke. refer the suff. of the Kethib to לבה, *to restore it* (sc., *her heart*). — נער חברים] 2 S. 16¹ cf. 2 K. 5¹⁷ Is. 21⁷·⁹. — ויביאהו בית אביה] 𝕲ᴬᴾⱽᴸᴹᴼ ﹩ ε καὶ ἐπορεύθη = ויבא, which agrees much better with the following. The same motive which occasioned the Kethib יהשיבו in v.⁸ seems to have led to the corresponding change of subject in 𝕴 here. — וישמח לקראתו] cf. 14⁵ 15¹⁴.

4. *His father-in-law, the girl's father, detained him*] concubinage with a free woman is a species of marriage, and brings the man into the same kind of relation to the woman's family as ordinary marriage; cf. v.⁵ 15⁶ 8³¹; see also comm. on 1¹⁶. Perhaps the synonymous phrases, *his father-in-law*, and *the girl's father*, come from different sources; cf. also v.⁵·⁹. In v.⁴⁻⁹ the Levite is several times on the point of setting out, but is over and over again persuaded to postpone his departure. The lingering of the narrative, the multiplication of identical or equivalent phrases, the alternation of singular and plural verbs, and especially the doublets in v.⁹·ᵃ give ground for the surmise that two versions of the story have been united; but the attempts to analyze the verses have not been successful. The solution which appears to me most plausible is, that in the first account the Levite remains three days with his father-in-law; on the fourth day, as he is preparing to depart, his host persuades him to fortify himself for the journey by a meal; they linger over the table till afternoon, when, declining an urgent invitation to spend another night, the Levite with his companions sets out on his return (v.⁴·ᵃ ᵃᵃᵝ·ᵇ·⁹ᵃ). In the other version they feast together on the day of the Levite's arrival (v.⁶ᵃ); the girl's father invites his guest to pass the night there; in the morning he urges him to stay another night; on the third day detains him for a feast, as in the other account, and reluctantly allows him to depart, late in the day (v.⁴·⁷·ᵃᵃᵃ·⁹ᵃ).† — 5. *On the fourth day they rose in the morning*

---

* In v.⁹, however, textual criticism has a word to say.

† Be. ascribes to the first source v.⁴·⁵·⁶·⁹ (as far as לינו); to the other v.⁷·⁸ and the rest of v.⁹. This analysis is criticized by Kue., Bu.

and prepared to go] 𐤒 *and he stood up to go.* If the words belong to the original narrative, the verb should probably be put in the plural, as in the translation above. — *Stay thy stomach*] lit. *heart,* v.[8] Gen. 18[5].* — *A bit of bread*] Gen. 18[5] 1 K. 17[11]; it is becoming in the host to depreciate the meal which he offers to his guests. — **6.** *So the two men sat, and ate and drank*] the woman, of course, did not eat with them; compare again Gen. 18. The verse is perhaps the original sequel of v.[3]. — *And the girl's father said to the man, Consent now, and spend the night*] for the verb see on 1[xr],† cf. 17[11]. — *And enjoy thyself*] 16[x]; here, as often, of the hilarity of the table. — **7.** *When the man arose to go*] we are probably to understand that he accepted the invitation of v.[6]; the next morning, when he was making ready to go, his host insisted on his staying another day. — *His father-in-law urged him, and he passed the night there again*] urged him, Gen. 19[3] 33[11]. — **8.** *He arose on the morning of the fifth day*] the fusion of the two narratives seems to have added one to the number of days. — *And tarry till the day decline*] an invitation to tarry till afternoon before beginning a long journey is in itself strange, and appears still more strange beside v.[9], where the advanced hour of the day is urged as a reason why they should not set out till the following morning. Perhaps the author wrote, *so they tarried* (a change of but one letter in Hebrew). On the variations of the Greek translators see note. — **9.** The repetitions in this verse are rendered the more striking by the abrupt changes of number. The invitation to stay over night is given twice, and in both cases the lateness of the hour is urged as a reason for doing so. The language in both instances is extraordinary, and there are other reasons for thinking that the Hebrew text is not intact. It seems necessary to adopt the emendation suggested by 𝕲[L al.]: *See, the day has declined toward evening; spend the night here to-day also, and enjoy thyself,* which gives a perfectly good sense and construction. See critical note. — *And you shall arise early in the morning for your journey, and thou shalt go to thy home*] lit. *thy tent.* The last clause may come from the parallel narrative; in view of the unusual expression it is, however, more probably a gloss.

---

* The metaphor is frequent in Latin. Comp. also the gloss, Is. 3[1b].   † P. 47.

5. סְתָר־נָא לְבִּכְךָ v.⁸ [סְתָר לְךָ]. The punctuation is anomalous; in v.⁸ ָ must be ŏ, and in v.⁵ (with conjunct. accent) can hardly be meant otherwise, though Ki. and Norzi take it as â; see Kö., i. p. 261 f., cf. 95 f. The verb, however, has elsewhere a in impf. and imv., and סְעָד is therefore probably to be treated as a case of false analogy to forms like יִרְדְּ־נָא from verbs imperf. o. — [לחב ר פֿ] second accusative, support some one with something, after the analogy of 'satisfy one with something' (סבע) &c.; cf. סמך Gen. 27³⁷ Ps. 51¹⁴, Ges.²⁶ § 117, 5 b β. — **7.** [וַיֶּאֱסָר בו] Gen. 19³·⁹ (literal sense), 33¹¹ 2 K. 2¹⁷ 5¹⁶; see also SS. p. 600ᵃ. — [וישב וילן] returned and spent the night, that is, spent the night again; 1 S. 1¹⁹ &c. — **8.** [והתמהמהו עד נטות היום] for the verb see 3³⁰. 'A ῥωθρεύθητι, Σ διάτριψον. 𝕲¹⁵·¹⁸·⁶⁴·⁸⁵ ᵐᵍ στραγεύθητι [sic] 'loiter'; hence, by a frequent uncial error, 𝕲ᴬᴾⱽᴸᴼ στρατεύθητι; for which στράτευσον ⁽ᴮ⁾ is a grammatical correction. For στραγ[γ]εύεσθαι = התמהמה see Hexapla on Gen. 19¹⁶ Hab. 2³·* A different reading is represented by 𝕲ᴹ ⁽³⁹·⁷⁵·⁸⁸⁾ ℵ διεπλάτα αὐτόν, or ⁽⁵²·⁷⁷·cf·¹⁶·¹³¹⁾ διεπλάτυνε αὐτόν; the verbs πλατάω and πλατύνω appear elsewhere as variant renderings of פתה, read as Piel or as Hiph. The translators therefore probably read here ויפתהו.† This has a genuine look. The imv. of 𝔜 must, for the reasons set forth in the text, be corrected to the impf., and perhaps the original text may be restored ויפתהו ויתמהמה ונ׳, and he coaxed him, and he lingered till the day was declining. — [עד נטות היום] cf. 2 K. 20¹¹, the declining of the shadow on a dial; see also below the equivalent expressions in v.⁹. — **9.** [רפה היום לערוב] the words might be literally translated, the day has grown feeble to setting; but there is no proper parallel to the use of either verb.‡ The poetical expression is noted by We. as an evidence of late date. — [הנה חנות היום] these words are still more difficult; even if we let the inf. after רנה pass,§ it is the camping, settling down, of the day, is an unexampled metaphor, especially in plain narrative prose. 𝕲ᴸ has: ἰδού κέκλικεν ἡ ἡμέρα εἰς ἑσπέραν· κατάλυσον δὴ ὧδε ἔτι σήμερον, καὶ μείνατε ὧδε, καὶ ἀγαθυνθήσεται ἡ καρδία σου.‖ Omitting the doublet, καὶ μείνατε ὧδε,¶ this represents: הנה נטה היום לערב לין הנה עיר היום וייטב לבבך; cf. also 𝕾.

10-21. The journey to Gibeah. — Refusing to delay longer, the Levite sets out on his journey. He passes by Jerusalem, where he is unwilling to lodge, and when overtaken by nightfall, he stops at Gibeah. The men of the town leave him sitting in the

---

* The active στραγγεύω in the sense of the middle is alleged by Schol. Arist. Lys. 17; Etym. magn., p. 330 (Liddell and Scott; see also Schleusner, s.v.).

† Scharfenberg's conj. that they read ההרו or הקערו is in no way probable.

‡ For the latter, we may, under stress, compare Is. 24¹¹.

§ The explanation of Ew. § 299 a, is not satisfactory; the exx. in Dr³. p. 176 n. are scarcely parallel.

‖ Similarly, with variations which may be disregarded here, 𝕲ᴬᴹ s.

¶ In s sub ast., in M omitted.

marketplace, but he finds entertainment in the house of a stranger.
— Through v.[10-15] the repetitions and redundancies continue ; cf.
v.[10:11. 11b. 12:13]. — **10.** He declines to spend another night ; and sets
out, some three hours before sunset. — *Arrived at a point opposite
Jebus, that is, Jerusalem*] from Bethlehem to Jerusalem is a walk
of about an hour and a quarter ; [*] the Eastern traveller would
probably be rather longer on the way.   Following the main road
from Bethlehem to Nābulus (Shechem), they would pass to the
west of Jerusalem.   Jerusalem is called here, with reference to its
non-Israelite population (v.[12]), *Jebus ;* the same name in 1 Chr. 11[tf.]
is an intentional archaism.   The common opinion, that Jebus was
the native name of the city which in later times was called Jerusalem,[†] rests on these passages and Jos. 15[8] 18[16. 28]. [‡]   It has no real
ground in the O.T. ; against the usage of P and Chr. we may
safely put Jud. 1[7. 21] Jos. 15[63] 2 S. 5[6].   The question has been set
at rest by the Amarna tablets,[§] in which the name *Urusalim*
repeatedly occurs, while there is no trace of a name corresponding
to Jebus.   Probably Jebus is merely a learned derivative from the
name of the Jebusites, in whose hands Jerusalem remained down
to the time of David.[||] — *He had with him a pair of saddled
asses*] v.[3]. — *And his concubine was with him*] some Greek manuscripts, for completeness, add, *and his servant* (v.[3]). — **11.** As
they were near Jerusalem the day was already far spent, and the
servant proposed to his master that they should seek shelter in
the Jebusite town for the night. — **12.** His master will not consent to spend the night in a foreign city, whose inhabitants are
not Israelites ; they will keep on to Gibeah.   By this contrast the
author makes the conduct of the Gibeathites appear doubly base.
— **13.** *And he said to his servant*] apparently parallel to v.[11b. 12].
— *In Gibeah or in Ramah*] the order in which the places are
named seems to indicate that Ramah was the more remote from
Jerusalem.   It is the modern er-Rām, two hours north of that

---

[*] Bäd[s]., p. 121.

[†] See, *e.g.*, Thdt., *quaest.* 2 ; Hitz., *GVI.* i. p. 102 ; Grill, *ZATW.* iv. p. 138 ; cf.
Di., *NDJ.* p. 485 ; al. mu.

[‡] Observe the use of *Jebusite* for inhabitants of Jerusalem.

[§] About 1400 B.C., before the Israelite invasion ; see *ZA.* vi. p.

[||] See on 1[8].

city.* —14. *The sun went down on them*] the day was well advanced when they set out from Bethlehem (v.⁹) ; it had far declined when they passed Jerusalem ; the sun set as they were by Gibeah (v.¹¹). The sudden nightfall, which in Palestine follows sunset almost without twilight, compelled them to seek shelter at once. — *Gibeah which belongs to Benjamin*] 20⁴; elsewhere called Gibeah of Benjamin (1 S. 13² ¹⁵ 14¹⁶), or of the Benjamites (2 S. 23²⁹), is probably the same which, as the home of Saul (1 S. 10²⁶), is called Gibeah of Saul (1 S. 11⁴ Is. 10²⁹ &c.), and distinct from Geba (Is. *l.c.*, 1 S. 14⁵). The latter is undoubtedly the modern Geba', opposite Makhmās (Michmash) ; Gibeah cannot be so certainly identified. The similarity of the two names has led to much confusion in our texts, which greatly complicates the question.† From the present passage it appears that Gibeah was on or near the road from Jerusalem north by Ramah. Robinson,‡ following a suggestion of Gross,§ locates it at Tell (or Tuleil) el-Fūl, about half way between Jerusalem and er-Rām, and a quarter of a mile east of the main road, ‖ and this site has been accepted by many scholars.¶ Tell el-Fūl suits the requirements of our story sufficiently well, though if we were guided by it alone we should probably prefer a site nearer to Ramah, such as Khirbet Rās eṭ-Ṭawil, a mile further north.** —15. *They turned off there*] 18¹ ¹⁵ ; the village lay on one side of the road. — *He came and sat down in the public square of the town*] just within the gate ; Gen. 19² Dt. 13¹⁶ Neh. 8¹ 2 Chr. 32⁶. — *No one took them into his house to spend the night*] v.¹⁸ ; contrast Gen. 24²¹⁻³¹ 19¹⁻³. — 16. While they were waiting in the public place, an old man came in from his work in the field. — *Now the man was from Mt. Ephraim, and was residing in Gibeah ; but the inhabitants of the place were Benjamites*] shelter was at last offered them, not by a native of Gibeah, but by a stranger in the place (cf.

---

* Rob., *BR*², i. p. 576. It was identified by Eshtori Parchi, fol. 68ᵇ.

† See, *e.g.*, 20¹⁰. Gibeah is only the feminine form of Geba ; in meaning (' hill ') they are identical.

‡ *BR*². i. p. 577-579.

§ *Stud. u. Krit.*, 1843. p. 1082 ; Valentiner, *ZDMG.* xii. p. 161 ff. ; *Bibl. Sacra*, 1844. p. 598.   ‖ *Bäd*⁸., p. 214.

¶ Guérin (*Samarie*, i. p. 188-197), Tristram, Mühlau, Socin, Di., al.

** See Wilson, *DB*², s.v. " Gibeah."

Gen. 19$^{1\text{ff.}}$). It is not improbable, however, that this trait, perhaps suggested by Gen. 19, was introduced by a later hand to exaggerate the inhospitality of the Gibeathites; the one honest man in the city was a stranger.* That the inhabitants of the place were Benjamites is much more like an editor's note than part of the old narrative; the author's contemporaries can hardly have required such information.† — **17, 18.** The old man sees the traveller in the square and inquires of his journey. The Levite answers that they are on their way from Bethlehem, where he has been visiting, to his home in the more distant part of the Highlands of Ephraim. The words which follow in the Hebrew text are full of difficulty: *and to(?) the house of Yahweh I am going.* By the house of Yahweh we must understand Shiloh,‡ or perhaps rather Bethel (20$^{18.\,\text{26f.}}$). Everywhere else in the story, however, and even in the immediately preceding context, we are given to understand that the Levite is returning to his own home, which is not at Shiloh or Bethel, but at some nameless (that is, to the writer unknown) place in the interior of Mt. Ephraim. This difficulty would remain in full force even if we could interpret with Schmid, *near the house of Yahweh I live;* § but the language does not admit this rendering. ⑥, without variation, gives, *and I am going* (returning) *to my home,* which is in entire harmony with the context, and can hardly have arisen by correction of our Hebrew text; the latter may possibly have its origin in the erroneous resolution of an abbreviation. — **19.** They ask only a shelter; they are abundantly provided for all their needs beside. — *We have chopped straw and provender for our asses, and bread and wine for myself and thy maidservant and the boy with thy servants*] cf. Gen. 24$^{25.\,32}$. — *There is no lack of anything*] 18^{10}. — **20.** The old man hospitably takes upon himself all their entertainment. — *All that thou needest shall be my charge; only do not spend the night in the square*] cf. Gen. 19$^{2f.}$. — **21.** Cf. Gen. 24^{32} 18^{4}. ‖

---

* Bu. We. adduces these clauses as evidence of the late origin of the story.

† Cf. the topographical glosses, 21^{19}.

‡ Ra., Ki., Abarb., Drus., Cler., Rosenm., Be., al.

§ So also Cocceius, Stud., Cass., Ke., al.

‖ Compare the example of Arab hospitality, Doughty, *Arabia Deserta,* ii. p. 136.

[הַהִיא רַד כָּאר] 10. [עִר נֹבֵחַ] 20⁴⁸ Ez. 47¹ᵐ; cf. עִר נגר, Neh. 3¹ᴸ·²⁶.—11. 𝕲ᴮᴺ προσέβηκει; APVLMO κεκλικυῖα. The context requires a perfect; we must emend יָרד. The view of Kö., i. p. 399, that the shortened form belonged to the living language is most improbable.—12. עִיר נכרי] *oppidum gentis alienae* (𝕷 𝕲ᴬ ᵃˡ. 𝕿), not, εἰς πόλιν ἀλλοτρίαν, 𝕲ᴮᴺ 𝕾.—אשר לא מבני ישראל הֵנָּה] the fem. plur. pronoun can only be referred to the notion of plurality inherent in the indefinite עִיר (*any city ... which are not of the Israelites*); so Ki.; see Roorda, § 414, cf. Jer. 4²⁹. Others translate according to the context, *quae non est de filiis Israel* (𝕲ᴬ ᵃˡ. 𝕷𝕾 𝕿ʳᵒᵘᶜʰ.), or take הנה as an adverb, ἐν ᾗ οὐκ ἔστιν ἀπὸ υἱῶν Ισραηλ ὧδε (𝕲ᴮᴺ). Some codd. of 𝕸 (De Rossi) have הֵכָה, which is doubtless merely a scribal correction, but a sound one: *any town of strangers, who are not of the Bene Israel.* So 𝕿ᵛᵉⁿ. ˡ. ². ᵃⁿᵗ ᵃˡ. —ועברנו עד גבעה] that the adversative after a negative sentence (we will not do so, but so) should be expressed by simple consec. perf., instead of by כי or כי אם is striking; the examples of adversative ו after a negative cited by Ew. § 354 *a*, are not exactly similar; cf., however, Gen. 17⁵. The words read very much like a gloss suggested by the following (v.¹⁴ᵇ).—13. [לֶךְ ונקרבה] imv.; so, instead of the normal orthography לֵךְ, Nu. 23¹⁸ 2 Chr. 25¹⁷; see Massora on 2 Chr. *l.c.*—באחד הבקמות] some good codd. have באחת (De Rossi); on the gender of בקום see the lexicons.—14. [אֵצֶל] *beside;* with names of places Dt. 11³⁰ 1 K. 1⁹ 4¹². — *Gibeah which belongs to Benjamin.* The most important argument for Tell el-Fûl is derived by Robinson from Fl. Jos., *b.j.* v. 2. 1 § 51, where he locates Γαβαθ Σαουλ on the road from Gophna (Gifnā) to Jerusalem, 30 stadia from the latter, and apparently near the junction of the road from Emmaus (Nicopolis, Amwās), which comes into the north road just above Tell el-Fûl. Cf. also Jerome, *ep.* 108, 8 (*Opp.* ed. Vallarsi, i. 690). See further *BD²*. s.v. "Gibeah-of-Benjamin."—15. [ואין איש מְאַסֵף אותם] v.¹⁸; lit. *gather in.* The word, esp. the intensive stem, suggests the polite urgency which a host would display, as in Gen. 19⁸.—16. [מֵן מעשהו] *his occupation;* cf. 1 S. 25². [מֵן הַשָּׂדֶה] the open country, in distinction from the enclosed town.—17. [וּיִשָּׂא עֵינָיו] 2 S. 12⁴ Jer. 14⁸.—18. [ואת בית יהוה אני הלך] this is explained by Noldius (p. 126), Ew. (p. 691), Be., al., as limit of motion; but את before this accusative is anomalous, and is not explained by the inversion (Be.), else we should have it more frequently. The interpretation of Schmid makes את prep., and takes הלך in the sense of *versari* (like התהלך), *I walk* (live) *near* (at) *the house of Yahweh;* equivalent to saying, I am a Levite. Schm. connects the words closely with the following. But why should any one take such a roundabout and obscure way of saying, *I am a Levite,* or *I minister at the house of Yahweh?* 𝕲 καὶ εἰς τὸν οἶκόν μου ἐγὼ πορεύομαι (ἀποτρέχω) = ואל ביתי אני הלך. In 𝕸 בית יהוה may have been produced by a scribe who mistook ביתי for an abbreviation of בית יהוה.—19. [הֵבֶן] Arab. *tibn*, is the broken straw from the threshing-floor which takes the place of hay; Jer. 23²⁸ Gen. 24²⁵·³² 1 K. 5⁸.—[מספיא] always with ו, Gen. 24³² 42²⁷ 43²⁴; * in all these

---

* The verb occurs only in the Talmud.

places *grain* is obviously meant. — עֲבֻר] a number of Heb. codd. (De Rossi) have עֲבוּר, which some of them point as sing. As sing. it is rendered by 𝕷𝕿𝕾; 𝕾 takes it as plur. — **20.** רַק] the first רַק is in effect equivalent to *entirely*; the second to *only*. — אַךְ הָרֶק] in pause for אַךְ הָרָק 2 S. 17¹⁶; Ges.²⁵ § 29, 4 *c*, n. — **21.** וַיָּבֶן] Qerè וַיָּבֶל like וַיֵּבֶךְ from בכה &c. (Ki., *Mikhlol*, 128ᵇ, ed. Lyck). The reading וַיָּבֶן in some codd. and edd. (among them Jablonski; see JHMich.) is to be ascribed, as Norzi shows, to the accidental dislocation of a sentence in Ki.'s comm. *ad loc.*, by which the note on אֵ֣שׁ רֵ֣ישׁ, "first radical with *pathah*," was made to refer to וַיָּבֶן, cf. Bomberg's first ed. of the comm. (1518). The verb is regarded by Ki. and most moderns as denominative from בְּלִיל Is. 30²⁴ Job 6⁵ 24⁶'¹, *he prepared mixed food for the asses*; cf. *Jer. Rosh ha-shanah*, i. 2, fol. 56ᵈ. The verb properly means 'stir, mix by stirring'; in P esp., mix the מִנְחָה (סֹלֶת, בָּצֵק, הַלּוֹת) with oil. See further, *BSZ.*, s.v.

22–28. The Levite's concubine is ravished and maltreated so that she dies.

— Verses ²²⁻²⁴ have a striking resemblance to Gen. 19⁴⁻⁸; it is not improbable that the similarity of the situation has led to more or less extensive conformation of the narrative in Judges to the story of Lot; see below. Wellhausen argues from the resemblance that the story is a late imitation of Gen. 19. — **22.** As they are enjoying themselves at supper, the men of Gibeah surround the house, and demand that the Levite be given up to them to gratify their unnatural lust. — *Vile scoundrels*] 𝕷 and the modern versions, *sons of Belial*. The phrase is an opprobrious term for base and wicked men (1 S. 2¹² 2 S. 16⁷ 1 K. 21¹⁰·¹³ &c.); the etymology and proper sense of the word are obscure; see crit. note. — *Pounding on the door*] cf. Gen. 19⁹, and for the verb Cant. 5². — *Bring out the man who has come to thy house, that we may know him carnally*] cf. Gen. 19⁵ Rom. 1²⁴⁻²⁷. In 20⁵ the Levite speaks of the intention of the Gibeathites to kill him. Doorninck is of the opinion that our verse has been conformed to Gen. 19⁵; the author of the story wrote, Bring out the *woman* . . . that we may know *her*.* But the Levite might very well represent their purpose as an attempt upon his life; while if Doorninck's restoration be accepted, there is nothing in ch. 19 to intimate that the man was in any way molested or threatened, and 20⁵ is left without any foundation. —

---

* P. 131; so also Bu. In the same way the story is softened by Fl. Jos., *antt.* v. 2, 8 § 143 ff. Verse ²⁴ must then be regarded as an interpolation from Gen. 19⁸ (Be. Bu.); see below.

23, 24. The owner of the house remonstrates with them. He has received the strangers under his roof and protection ; to violate this right is itself an infamous crime. — **23.** *Nay my brethren, do not do a wrong* (Gen. 19[7]), *since this man has come into my house* (Gen. 19[3b]) ; *do not commit this wanton deed*] the last word (v.[24] 20[6] ; EV. *folly*) is frequently used of offences against the laws governing the relations of the sexes (Gen. 34[7] 2 S. 13[12] Dt. 22[21]) ; it does not occur in the story of Lot, Gen. 19. — **24.** He offers to expose to them his own daughter and the Levite's concubine. Bertheau thinks that the whole verse has been interpolated from Gen. 19[8], with which it is almost verbally identical : there is no allusion to this offer in the sequel ; the connexion and movement of the narrative would be better if v.[25] immediately followed v.[23] ; some grammatical irregularities are also pointed out.[*] Such an addition, bringing the story into still closer agreement with Gen. 19, would be entirely natural ; the resemblance between the two verses is too mechanical to be the result of mere reminiscence. — **25.** They refuse to listen to him ; cf. Gen. 19[9]. — *So the man seized his concubine and put her forth to them out of doors*] the Levite gives up the woman to save himself.[†] To us this seems quite as bad as the conduct of the mob in the street ; but nothing indicates that the author felt that it merited condemnation or contempt. And not only the proffer of Lot (Gen. 19[8]), but the favourite episode of the patriarchal story, in which a wife is surrendered by her husband out of fear of harm to himself,[‡] shows that the ancient Hebrews were far from possessing the chivalrous feeling which we find among the old Arabs. § — *They let her go at the approach of dawn*] the first signs of day (Jos. 6[15] 1 S. 9[26]) ; compare the expressions in the next verse. — **26.** *As the morning appeared*] Ex. 14[27] Ps. 46[6]. — *She came, and lay prostrate at the door of the man's house where her master was, till daylight*] mas-

---

[*] So also Bu. Doorn. (p. 131) proposes to emend by omitting all mention of the concubine.

[†] Fl. Jos., writing for Roman readers, narrates that the men of Gibeah took her by force.

[‡] Told twice of Abraham and once of Isaac ; Gen. 12[10ff.] 20 26. This story is the more offensive to us on account of its religious flavour.

§ This repulsive feature of the narrative in Jud. is no reason, therefore, for ascribing it to a late date (We., *Comp.*, p. 235, cf. p. 357).

ter (v.[27]) ; not the usual expression for husband, cf., however, Gen. 18[12]. — **27.** In the morning the Levite opened the door and went out to pursue his journey. — *There was the woman, his concubine, lying at the house door, with her hands on the sill*] overtaken by death in the last effort to gain a place of safety. — **28.** The verse contrasts rudely with the pathos of v.[27b]. The man's speech makes the impression of indescribable brutality, but the author had no such intention. — *Get up; let us go*] Josephus puts the best face on the matter ; the Levite supposed that she was only fast asleep. — Finding that she was dead, he put the body upon the ass and went to his home.

22. אנשי בני בלייל] explained as substitution of a genitive (annexation) for apposition (Philippi, *Status Constructus*, p. 63; Ges.[25] § 130, 5); better, suspended annexation (Dr., *TBS.* p. 166); cf. אשה בערת אוב, בהירת בת ציון, &c. In the present instance the text may be a conflation of the readings אנשי בלייל and בני בלייל; or we may restore אנשים בני בלייל 20[18] Dt. 13[14] 1 K. 21[10]. בני בלייל is variously rendered in 𝕲, oftenest, as here, υἱοὶ παρανόμων; [*] 'A here and usually, υἱοὶ ἀποστασίας, O here Βελιαλ.[†] As a proper name in the form Βελιαρ the word occurs in *Orac. sibyll.*, iii. 63, 73 (in a passage of Jewish origin), ii. 167; frequently in the *Testamenta XII. Patr.*; in the *Ascensio Jesaiae*, &c.; see Baudissin, *PRE*[2]. s.v. The oldest etymology of the word is found in *Sanhedrin*, 111[b], בני בלייל בנים שפרקו עול שמים מצואריהב, 'men who have thrown off the yoke of Heaven from their necks' (בלי + עול).[‡] So also Jerome in a gloss in his translation of Jud. 19[22]: *filii Belial, id est, absque jugo*. Modern lexicographers derive it from יעל (only in Hiph. הועיל, cf. Is. 44[10] Jer. 7[8]), in the sense of 'good-for-nothing, worthless' (Cocceius, Ges., MV., and most); or from בלה (Ki., כל יכלה ובל יצליח, ne'er-do-well; similarly, Hupfeld), in the sense, 'low, base' (Fürst, cf. JDMich.). These etymologies are extremely dubious; the word is without analogy in the language. — ויסבו את הבית] Niph., Gen. 19[4] Jos. 7[9] *l. c.*, נסב; made themselves a ring around the house. — מתרפקים] the precise force of the reflexive is not clear; perhaps *certatim pulsantes* (Ges. *Thes.*). — **23.** אל נא אחי אל תרעו נא] Gen. 19[8]; אל אחי אל תרעו. — **24.** ופילגשהו] the correct form פילגשו v.[2.5]; cf. יצרו Gen. 1[12] and often (P); for other instances of this monstrous form see Bö. § 872 *B.*; Sta. § 345 *c.* — אותם (twice), ירדם] masc. suff. referring to the two women! This accumulation of grammatical blunders in a single sentence strengthens the suspicion that the verse is a late addition. — וענו אותם] *force, ravish*, Gen. 34[2]

---

[*] In 1 S. υἱοὶ λοιμοί; other translations are ἀνυπότακτος, ἀνυπότατος (Σ), ἄφρων, υἱὸς ἀφροσύνης, ἀπαίδευτος (Η).

[†] For the Latin renderings see Vercellone on Dt. 13[18] (i. p. 520).

[‡] So Ra. on Dt. 13[14]. This agrees with the renderings of 'A and Σ (above, n. [*]).

2 S. 13¹². ¹⁴ Dt. 22²⁴. ⁵ᵗ. — [רָבָר הַנְבָלָה הֹזֹאת cf. רִבֶר הַתֹּעֵבָה הֹזֹאת Jer. 44⁴. — 25. ונ׳] Norzi, Baer; many edd. have וַיֵּצֵא (Ven.¹·², Buxt., Plant., Jabl., Opit., Van der Hooght., Mich.), agst. the Massora; see Norzi *ad loc.*; Massora on Nu. 17²⁸ and on Dt. 4²⁷; Frensdorff, *Massoret. Wörterbuch,* p. 89. — [וַיִּתְעַלְּרוּ בָה] maltreated her, made cruel sport, cf. 1 S. 31⁴, Jer. 38¹⁹; the primary sense seems to be 'play a trick upon one,' Nu. 22²⁹ Ex. 10² 1 S. 6⁶. — [בַּעֲלוֹת הִשָּׁחַר Qerē בַּעֲלוֹת, which a number of codd. have received into the text (De Rossi). The Massora (*Ochla we-Ochla,* No. 149; *Massora finalis,* sub ב¹⁰; cf. Norzi *ad loc.*) enumerates six other instances in which ב with inf. is corrected to כ; the printed edd. exhibit numerous variations. The Qerē conforms the text to Jos. 6¹⁵ 1 S. 9²⁶; in Jon. 4⁷ the Massora preserves בַּעֲלוֹת הִשָּׁחַר. — In this use כ signifies, 'simultaneously with' the action of the inf. verb; ב, 'in (at) the time of, in the course of, on the occasion of,' that action. Obviously there are many cases in which either might be used, with a scarcely perceptible difference of conception. See further, Cappell, *Critica sacra* (ed. Vogel), i. p. 238 f.; Buxtorf, *Anticritica,* p. 483; Elias Levita, *Massoreth ha-Massoreth* (ed. Ginsburg), p. 188. — **26.** [רִפְנוֹת הַבֹּקֶר] the corresponding phrase, רִפְנוֹת עֶרֶב, Gen. 24⁶³ Dt. 23¹³; cf. also מְנֹה הַיּוֹם Jer. 6⁴ Ps. 90⁹; as the morning (evening) turns its face toward us, approaches; ל 'toward.' — [וְנֹפֵל, fall and lie; cf. v. ⁷ וַיִּפֹּל, and see p. 101. — [פֶּתַח בֵּית רָאֵיהָ this adv. accusative (instead of the usual ב) is almost confined to the nouns פֶּתַח and בַּיִת; it is not improbable that the difficulty of articulating the labial combinations בִּפְתַח, בְּבֵית, may explain the preference for the accus.; so Ges.²⁶ § 118, 2 *b.* — [אֲדֹנֶיהָ] pl. of superiority, Ges.²⁶ p. 386. — **28.** [וְאֵין עֹנֶה *no one answered;* much more forcible than 𝕲's, *she did not answer, for she was dead.*

29, 30. The Levite publishes through all Israel the infamous crime of the Gibeathites. — 29. *When he reached home, he took the knife, and laid hold of his concubine, and cut her up, limb by limb, into twelve pieces*] the words employed are the proper terms for cutting up the carcase of an animal (1 S. 11⁷ 1 K. 18²³·³³); in the ritual, for the cutting up of the victim for sacrifice (Lev. 1⁶·¹² 8²⁰ &c.).* — *And sent her through all the territory of Israel*] just so Saul cut up a yoke of oxen at Gibeah, and sent the pieces by messengers *through all the territory of Israel* (1 S. 11⁷), to raise the Israelites for the relief of Jabesh Gilead. In Saul's case, the significance of the act is explained: so it shall be done to the cattle

---

* If the twelve pieces are meant to correspond to the twelve tribes of Israel (Ra.), we should be inclined to regard the words as a later addition to the story: there is no trace in the Book of Judges of the system of twelve tribes. Perhaps, however, they are merely the twelve joints of the limbs, the head and trunk not being included.

of every man who does not join Saul for the war; here the object
can only be to excite the horror and indignation of all beholders.
It has been suspected that the verse before us is modelled after
1 S. 11⁷.* — **30.** The Hebrew tenses at the beginning of this
verse can only be taken as frequentative : † *And it would come to
pass that every one that saw it would say, Such a thing has not
happened, &c.* The oldest Greek version, however, had a different
introduction to the verse : *And he charged the men whom he sent
out, saying, Thus shall ye say to all the men of Israel, Did ever a
thing like this happen, from the day when the Israelites came up
from Egypt to this day? Take counsel about it and speak out.*
The last clause is much more natural in the mouth of the Levite
or his messengers than of those to whom his message came, ‡ and
the text represented by ⑹ is on every ground to be preferred;
see critical note.

29. רבאכלה] Gen. 22⁶⋅¹⁰, Prov. 30¹⁴ parallel to חרב. — וינתחה לעצמיה] *limb
by limb;* cf. *Chullin,* 28ᵇ (top), (בההה) רבנחה אבר אבר; the verb 20⁶. —
30. והיה כל הראה ואמר] Rosenm., Ke., al. supply ראמר : the Levite imagines
the effect on the beholders, saying to himself, *Every one that sees it will say,
Such a thing was never seen.* But this is quite unwarranted, and does not
touch the difficulty at the end of the verse. ⑹ᴬᴾᴹᴼ *t* (sub obelo ⑹¹²¹ s) §
have, as a doublet : καὶ ἐνετείλατο τοῖς ἀνδράσιν οἶς ἐξαπέστειλεν λέγων Τάδε
ἐρεῖτε πρὸς πάντα ἄνδρα Ἰσραήλ 'Εἰ γέγονε κατὰ τὸ ῥῆμα τοῦτο κ.τ.ἑ. See
further, *The Book of Judges in Hebrew.* — שימו לכם עליה וְדִבְּרוּ] the commentators supply לב, *put your mind upon it* (cf. Is. 41²⁰); Sta. proposes
לְבֶבֶם, which would be easier. Probably, however, for עצו (Is. 8¹⁰), ‖ we
should with ⑹ read עֵצָה (θέσθε . . . βουλήν), to which there seems to be no
objection, though the phrase שימו עצה does not elsewhere occur; cf. 20⁷,
הבו . . . עצה.

XX. In the history of the war with Benjamin two elements of
very diverse character are discovered. One of these is evidently
the continuation of the story in ch. 19, the other is akin to P and
the Chronicles.¶ Bertheau and Budde think that the two were

---

* We.   † Dr². § 121. Obs. 1.

‡ Cf. 20⁷. It is possible that the clause has been brought up here from 20⁵; but
the phraseology is rather unfavourable to this conjecture.

§ This text seems to be supported by Fl. Jos. also (*antt.* v. 2, 8 § 149).

‖ With these exceptions, only Чᵉʳ. Ҁᵉᵃᵗʰ. Talm. (*Kiddushin,* 80ᵇ).

¶ See above, p. 405.

united by a redactor, who harmonized them as well as he could by introducing into each the distinctive features of the other, a procedure which greatly increases the difficulty of analyzing the chapter.* Kuenen, on the other hand, regards the later element in the chapter as merely an expansion and exaggeration of the old story by a writer of the age and spirit of the Chronicler. The difference between these two theories is not as great as appears at first sight ; for Budde also would doubtless acknowledge that the second narrative is based upon the first, which it follows closely ; the question resolves itself into this : did the later version ever exist separately? I have given above (p. 407 f.) the considerations which incline me to think, with Kuenen, that it did not ; but freely admit that these reasons are not decisive.

XX. 1-10. The Israelites assemble, hear the Levite's story, and resolve to punish the perpetrators of the outrage. — The verses are in the main from the older narrative ; v.$^{1a\beta\cdot 3}$ are clearly by a later hand, and in the following verses some expressions suggest that the original has been here and there retouched ; whether any part of v.$^{9\cdot 10}$ is derived from the older source is doubtful. — **1.** *And all the Israelites went out*] for war ; see on 2^{15} (p. 73). The last words of the verse, *to Yahweh to Mizpah*, come from the same source, but can hardly have been the immediate continuation of the first clause ; we should expect some such connexion as, *and came together*, which has been supplanted by the fuller description of the assembling of the congregation which the later writer has given in v.$^{1\beta}$. Mizpah in Benjamin was an ancient holy place (1 S. 7$^{5ff\cdot}$ 10$^{17ff\cdot}$).† With the neighbouring Geba, it was fortified by Asa to defend the northern frontier of his kingdom (1 K. 15^{22} cf. Jer. 41^{9}). After the destruction of Jerusalem in 586 B.C., Mizpah was chosen as the residence of the native governor, Gedaliah, whom Nebuchadnezzar appointed (Jer. 40^{14} 41 2 K. 25^{23ff}) ; and had this attempt at reorganization succeeded, would no doubt, under Jeremiah's influence, have become a religious centre for the Jews who were left in the land. When the

* For the attempts to separate the two sources, see above, p. 407 f.

† In the younger of the two histories of Samuel and the foundation of the kingdom. Grove's hypothesis (*DB*[1]. s.v.), that the rendezvous of the Israelites in Jud. 20 was Mizpah in Gilead (11^{11}), requires no refutation.

temple was desecrated by Antiochus Epiphanes (168 B.C.), the
God-fearing Jews assembled at Mizpah, not only because it was
over against Jerusalem, but because it was an ancient sanctuary
(1 Macc. 3[48].).* Robinson conjectured that Mizpah stood upon
the modern Nebi Samwil, about two hours NW. of Jerusalem, and
the highest point in its vicinity ; † and this site, which agrees with
all the data in our possession, has been accepted by the majority
of recent scholars. ‡ Nebi Samwil is only about two miles from
Tell el-Fūl (Gibeah). — *And the congregation assembled as one
man*] every word betrays the post-exilic author ; the *congregation*,
the religious assembly, takes the place of the *people ;* § the verb
has the same associations ; the collocation of the two words
belongs specifically to the phraseology of P in his descriptions
of the Mosaic age (Lev. 8[4] Nu. 17[7] Jos. 18[1] 22[12] &c.). ‖ The
instinctive unanimity of this assembly is in striking contrast to the
lack of unity among the Israelite tribes which appears in all the old
stories of the judges ; see above, p. 404. — *From Dan to Beersheba*] 1 S. 3[20] 2 S. 3[10] 17[11] 24[2. 15] 1 K. 4[25'] ; cf. *from Beersheba to
Dan* (Chr.). The northern and southern limits of the kingdom
of David and Solomon. — *And the land of Gilead*] all Israel east
of the Jordan ; see on 5[17] 11[5]. Jabesh in Gilead was the only city
in all Israel whose inhabitants did not appear in the great congregation (21[8]). — **2.** *The principal men of all the people*] lit. *the
corners ;* tropically, *the chief supports ;* or, with a figure drawn
from the corner towers of a city wall, *the prominent men ;* ¶ the
same metaphor, 1 S. 14[38] Is. 19[13] Zech. 10[4] (Zeph. 3[6]). — *Took
their stand*] 1 S. 10[19]. — *All the tribes of Israel, in the assembly
of the people of God*] the first words are in all probability a gloss
to the preceding, *all the people ;* the alternative is to insert the
conjunction, *and all the tribes.*** — *The assembly of the people of
God* (cf. Mi. 2[5] Jer. 26[17] Ps. 107[32]) ; the people assembled in its
religious capacity, 1 S. 17[47] 1 K. 8[14. 55. 65] 12[3] and often in P. —

---

* Reminiscence of Jud. and Sam. is manifest in this passage ; see esp. v.[44. 46].

† *HK*[2]. i. p. 460. On Nebi Samwil see Tobler, *Topographie v. Jerusalem*, ii.
p. 874 ff. ; Guérin, *Judée*, i. p. 363-384 ; *SWP. Memoirs*, iii. p. 12 f. ; Bd[2]., p. 119.

‡ Van de Velde, Di., Be., Ke., Tristr., GASmith. In defence of the theory see
esp. Birch, *PEF. Qu. St.*, 1881, p. 91-93 ; 1882. p. 260-262. Others have proposed
Tell el-Fūl (above, p. 414), or Scopus (Stanley, Grove, al.).

§ Cf. *the assembly*, 21[5. 8].   ‖ See further in crit. note.   ¶ Ki.   ** ⑥▲ al. **L.**

Four hundred thousand footmen who drew sword] the words are
perhaps a gloss from v.[17], introduced by the same hand which
above added all the tribes of Israel to the principal men. With
the numbers compare 1 S. 11[8] 2 S. 24[9] and the standing six hundred thousand of P in the history of the Exodus.[*] It may help
us to comprehend the prodigious exaggeration of these figures to
remember that the total strength of the German army which in
1870 besieged Paris — a city having a population of a million and
three-quarters — was about two hundred and forty thousand men.
The regular troops under the command of Titus at the siege of
Jerusalem in the year 70 A.D. consisted of only five legions. —
3. *The Benjamites heard that the Israelites had gone up to Mizpah*] Mizpah, the point of rendezvous, is as nearly as possible the
centre of the territory of Benjamin ; the distance from Gibeah in
a direct line is not above three miles. The half-verse anticipates ;
the negotiations with Benjamin begin in v.[12]. Budde conjectures
that v.[3a] originally stood immediately before v.[14]. — *And the Israelites said, Say, how did this crime happen*] from the message (19[30])
they know only that a horrible deed has been committed ; they
now call on any who are cognizant of the facts to disclose them.
— The Levite tells his story ; cf. 19[22-30]. — **4.** *The Levite, the
husband of the murdered woman, responded*] the Hebrew, *man*,
is as applicable to concubinage as to matrimony ; cf. 19[4.5], the
woman's father, his father-in-law. — *To Gibeah which belongs to
Benjamin, I came, &c.*] 19[14]. Gibeah is the guilty village ; its
name stands with emphasis at the beginning of the answer. —
5. *The freemen of Gibeah attacked me*] lit. *arose against me.* —
*Me they meant to kill, and my concubine they ravished so that she
died*] see on 19[22] ; their purpose might very well be described as
an attempt on his life, especially since his concubine actually died.
under their maltreatment ; there is no necessary contradiction
between the two verses.[†] — **6.** See 19[29]. — *All the country of the
possession of Israel*] a parallel is scarcely to be found in old
prose (cf. 19[29]) ; [‡] *the possession* may be a gloss by the later
hand. — *Because they have committed abomination and wantonness in Israel*] cf. 19[23.24]. Here also the later writer seems to

---

[*] Cf. also Jud. S[10].   [†] See Ki. on 19[28].   [‡] We.

have added the word *abomination*, which is frequent in Ezekiel
for incest and similar crimes; cf. also Lev. 18[17] 19[29] 20[14]. —
7. *Here you all are, Israelites; give your word and counsel
here*] cf. 19[30] 2 S. 16[20]. — **8.** The people resolve to punish the
perpetrators of the outrage. — *We will not go, each to his tent;
and we will not return, each to his house*] the two sentences are
exactly equivalent; the latter is probably an otiose amplification
by the later writer. On the other hand, the conclusion, 'until we
have punished the men of Gibeah,' which we should expect here,
is lacking.

1. וַחִקָּהֵל הָעֵדָה] Lev. 8[4] Nu. 17[7] &c.; esp. Jos. 18[1] 22[12]. עֵדָה 21[10. 13. 16];
1 K. 8[5] (not in 𝕲[B]) 12[20] (in a context which has been considerably retouched),
Hos. 7[12] (unintelligible and doubtless corrupt); see Giesebrecht, *ZATW.* i.
1881, p. 243 f. In Jud. 14[8] we have the word used of a swarm of bees.
These are the only instances in pre-exilic contexts. הִקְהִיל, נִקְהֵל, occur in
Jer., Dt. and later; further see 1 K. 8[1. 2] 12[21]. — עַד . . . לְמֵן [לְמֵן] of place,
Zech. 14[10]; of time, Jud. 19[30]; other phrases, לְמֵאִישׁ וְעַד אִשָּׁה לְמַעַן וְעַד זָקֵן,
לְמִגָּדוֹל וְעַד זָקֵן &c.; [הַמִּצְפָּה] on the forms מִצְפֶּה and מִצְפָּה see on 11[11], p. 289. —
2. [פִּנּוֹת כָּל הָעָם] the metaphor is probably the same as in the Arab. *rukn*,
'corner, main stay, noble' (Lane, p. 1149[a]); Ges., *Jesaia*, i. p. 624; cf.
Ephes. 2[20] 1 Pet. 2[6] (Is. 28[16]). — [בִּקְהַל עַם הָאֱלֹהִים] cf. 21[5. 8]; on the usage of
קָהָל see Holzinger, *ZATW.* ix. p. 105 f. — [שֹׁלֵף חֶרֶב] v.[15. 17. 25. 35. 46] cf. 8[10]
1 Chr. 21[6] &c.; We., *Comp.*, p. 236. — **3.** [דִּבְרוּ אֵיכָה נִהְיְתָה הָרָעָה הַזֹּאת] is not
in Hebrew an indirect question (Dr. in *BDB.* p. 32[b]). אֵיכָה Dt. 1[12] 7[17]
Jer. 8[8] &c. נִהְיְתָה 19[30]. — **4.** [הָאִישׁ הַלֵּוִי] 19[1]; see on 4[4], p. 114. — הָאִשָּׁה
הַנִּרְצָחָה We. (Bleek[4], p. 202, *Comp.*, p. 236) notes this expression as "völlig
unhebräisch"; Bu. suspects that the words are a gloss; cf. however הָאִשָּׁה
הַנֶּחְצָבָה 1 S. 1[26], Ez. 16[42]. — **5.** [בְּכָלִי הַנְּבָעָה] cf. כַּלֵּי שֶׁכֶם 9[2] and comm. there.
p. 241. — [אוֹתִי דִּמּוּ לַהֲרֹג] the verb Is. 10[7] (‖ חָשַׁב) Is. 14[24] (‖ יָעַץ), Nu. 33[56],
'conceive a plan in imagination.' — [דָּמוּ] 19[24]. — **6.** 𝕲[b] בְּכָל שְׂדֵה נַחֲלַת יִשְׂרָאֵל
παντὶ ὁρίῳ κληρονομίας κ.τ.λ. is probably only free translation under the influence of 19[29]; cf. 𝕷𝕿. שָׂדֶה, 'territory, land' (*ager*), see on 5[4]. נַחֲלַת יִשְׂרָאֵל
is Palestine, cf. Ez. 35[16] Is. 58[14] Dt. 4[21] &c. — [וּזִמָּה] Ez. 16[27. 43. 58] 22[9. 11] 23
passim; cf. Jer. 13[27] Job 31[11] cf. v.[9] Hos. 6[9] cf. v.[10]. The word is a late
gloss which was not in the copy from which the oldest Greek translation was
made (> 𝕲[APVLMO]; 𝕲[S] sub ast. ζεμμα, cf. ɴ; 𝕭 ζέμα).* The reading ζεμμα,
a mere transliteration of זִמָּה, is doubtless from Θ (cf. Hexapla Lev. 18[17]
Ez. 16[27] 22[9]); ζέμα is perhaps the attempt of a scribe to make Greek of it
(Scharfenberg). — **7.** [הִנֵּה כֻלְּכֶם בְּנֵי יִשְׂרָאֵל] בְּנֵי יִשְׂרָאֵל is not predicate, *you are
all Israelites*, which is meaningless, but vocative. הִנֵּה כֻלְּכֶם is a complete

---

* 𝕲[N] has a double translation of נְבָלָה.

proposition; cf. הנני in response to a call, Gen. 22[1] 1 S. 3[4] 22[12]; ℒ *adestis omnes filii Israel;* so Lth., Schm. — רבו . . . קצה] 2 S. 16[20]; רבו, only in imv. — הלם] *hither,* 18[3], to this case, not, ' on the spot, at this time ' (Be., SS.). — 8. ראו נרך איש יאהלו] the plural לאהליו is much more common in this phrase; in the two other instances in which the sing. is found (2 S. 18[17] 2 K. 14[12]) it is corrected to the plur. by the Qerē.

9, 10. The Israelites adopt a plan.

— They will detail one-tenth of the force to collect provisions for the rest ; then they will requite the crime of the Gibeathites as it deserves. — In this form the verses can hardly be ascribed to the original narrator ; what part of them, if any, is derived from his story, it is scarcely possible to decide. The difficulty is increased by the faultiness of the text. — 9. Before the last words of v.[9], *against it by lot,* the verb is lacking : 𝕲 has, *We will go up against it, &c.,* which may represent the original text.* In the sequel nothing is said of casting lots ; most commentators suppose that one man in ten was drafted by lot to serve in the commissariat, the remainder being thus virtually chosen for active service ; † but this is not altogether natural. If the missing verb is rightly supplied by 𝕲, we should be inclined to connect the words, *we will go up against it by lot,* with v.[18], in which they inquire of the oracle what tribe shall first go up ; and as v.[18] unquestionably belongs to the secondary, if not to a tertiary, stratum in the chapter, v.[9b] would fall with it. — 10. *And we will take ten men from a hundred, of all the tribes of Israel, and a hundred from a thousand, and a thousand from a myriad, to procure provisions for the people*] we are to imagine three hundred and sixty thousand men sitting down within an hour's march of Gibeah, while forty thousand foragers scour the country for provisions. ‡ These absurdities would be lessened if, with Budde, we could ascribe v.[10] to a different source from v.[2b, 17], and regard the last clauses, *a hundred from a thousand, &c.,* as editorial exaggeration ; but this appears very haz-

---

* It may, however, merely be supplied from the context ; 𝕷𝕾𝕰 have filled the lacuna differently. Bu. conjectures, *We will cast lots over it* (cf. 𝕾), which suits the following verse better, but requires a greater change in the text ; see further in crit. note.　　　　　　　　　† Ki., Stud., al.

‡ Like P in the narratives of the Exodus, the author seems to have no difficulty in conceiving all these thousands as concentrated at a single point ; in his imagination they do not occupy space.

ardous ; it is really only for the vast " congregation " of v.[1][17] that
such an organization of the commissariat is necessary. — In v.[10b]
the text is again faulty, as may be seen with sufficient clearness in
AV., " that they may do, when they come to Gibeah of Benjamin,
according to all the folly that they have wrought in Israel," though
the difficulty of the Hebrew text is here in good part glossed over.
When they come is generally explained, when the foraging parties
return ;[*] others interpret, that the people, when they come to
Gibeah, may do as the folly they have wrought in Israel deserves.[†]
On either interpretation, the position and construction of the
words are in the highest degree unnatural, if not grammatically
impossible. The omission of them leaves an unimpeachable sentence and sense : *to do to Gibeah of Benjamin as all the wantonness which it has wrought in Israel deserves.* See crit. note. —
11. *All the Israelite forces gathered together to the city like one
man, as confederates*] so the Hebrew text must be translated.
The verse presents considerable difficulty, both in itself and in its
relation to the narrative in which it stands. *The city* must be
Gibeah, but this is not easy to reconcile either with the preceding,
where the Israelites are already assembled at Mizpah in the immediate neighbourhood, and v.[14] where the Benjamites concentrate at
Gibeah, or with v.[18a], in which Bethel appears to be the head-
quarters of the united Israelites (see on v.[18]). The verse is doubtless one of the later additions to the narrative. The last words,
as confederates, are generally thought to refer to the unanimity
with which they acted, *eadem mente, unoque consilio.* [‡]

9. נפלה עליה] 𝕲 ἀναβησόμεθα ἐπ' αὐτὴν ἐν κλήρῳ as if reading נפלה עליה
בגורל; in this collocation of words the verb might easily be dropped; Ki.,
RJes., al. mu., supply נעלה to complete the sense. 𝕿 נתחני עלה בקרבא, *we will
be told off against it by lot,* evidently connecting it with v.[10]; 𝕾 *we will cast
lots upon it,* in which way Cler. would complete the sense (נפיל עליה בגורל).[§]
Bu. would emend ונפילה בגורל and make the words the beginning of v.[10]; the
phrase הפיל בגורל does not, however, occur in O.T. (always הפיל גורל), and is
dubious Hebrew. On the whole, therefore, it seems safest to follow 𝕲,
though it must be allowed that its ἀναβησόμεθα may be only an easy conjec-

* Abarb., Schm., JHMich., Stud.   † Ke.
‡ 𝕃; so probably 𝕿𝕾; Ra., Ki., Schm.
§ Cf. also Be., Ke., who assume an aposiopesis, *against it by lot!* treat it like a
heathen city; cf. Nu. 33[51], 30[?] &c.

ture. — **10.** לקחת צדה לעם לעשות לבאם לנבע ונ׳] that the text is corrupt is evident at a glance. First of all, for לנבע we must read לגבעה; they had nothing
to do with Geba. Further, in the logic of speech, the three infinitives should
have the same subject, viz., the foragers. If the author had meant to say, as
the interpreters suppose: We will take ten men out of every hundred . . . to
procure provisions for the army, that, when they return, we (or the army) may
do to Gibeah as they deserve, — he would have expressed himself very differently. 𝕲ᴬᴵᴾᵛᴮᴸᴼ ᵦ λαβεῖν ἐπισιτισμὸν τῷ λαῷ ἐπιτελέσαι τοῖς εἰσπορευομένοις
τῇ Γαβαα κ.τ.ἑ.,* i.e. יבאים לגבעה, the ptcp. probably taken after the analogy
of Gen. 23¹⁰ (πάντων τῶν εἰσπορευομένων εἰς τὴν πόλιν), for all the inhabitants
of the city. 𝕲ᴹ transposes the ptcp., τῷ λαῷ τοῖς εἰσπορευομένοις ἐπιτελέσαι
τὴν Γαβαα, to get provisions for the people, namely, for those who are going
in to requite Gibeah, &c. Neither יבאו 𝕸 nor יבאם 𝕲 can be tolerated
between לעשות and לגבעה. The general context gives no security for a more
positive conjecture; the most plausible explanation is that the word came in
as a gloss to לעם, perh. meant as inf., *that they may go* to do to Gibeah, &c. —
11. חברים] כאיש אחד חברים in the sense of associated, allied tribes, Ez. 37¹⁶;
perhaps we may compare the Ḫabiri of the Amarna tablets. 𝕲† has for
חברים ἐρχόμενοι (ἐρχόμενος), which is probably a corruption of ἐχόμενοι, for
חברים; cf. Ex. 26⁸ Ez. 1⁹. The versions all seem to support 𝕸.

**12–17. The Israelites demand the surrender of the guilty
men; the Benjamites refuse, and prepare for war.** — The
account of the negotiations seems to belong entirely to the later
embellishment of the narrative; v.¹⁴ alone is probably original. —
12. *The tribes of Israel sent men through all the tribe of Benjamin*] 𝕸, all the *tribes* of Benjamin; cf. 1 S. 9²¹. — *What wickedness is this, &c.*] compare the procedure prescribed in Dt. 13¹²⁰,
also Jos. 22¹¹ᶠ. — **13.** They demand that the offending Gibeathites
be given up. — *That we may put them to death, and extirpate
the evil from Israel*] a peculiarly Deuteronomic conception and
phrase; ‡ elsewhere only in Dt. By the death of the criminal the
community expiates the crime, and averts from itself the consequences which the unexpiated guilt of one of its members would
bring upon the whole clan, tribe, or people; cf. the familiar examples of Achan (Jos. 7), and of Saul and the Gibeonites (2 S. 21).
— *The Benjamites refused to listen to the words of their brethren
the Israelites*] the fraternal spirit in which this war is carried on

---

* 𝕲ᴼ εἰς τὴν Γαβαα.   † Except ᴮ.

‡ Driver, *O. T. Lit.*, p. 93, *Deut.*, p. lxxx.; Holzinger, *Einl. in den Hexateuch*,
p. 285.

is touching ; cf. v.[22, 23]. — **14.** *The Benjamites assembled from the towns to Gibeah, to go out to battle with the Israelites*] the verse is an indispensable part of the story, and probably comes from the original source, in which it would naturally follow v.[3a]. If v.[3b-8] (or [3b-10]) are in substance from the same source, v.[3a] must have been displaced ; it should follow those verses and precede v.[14a]. — **15.** The Benjamites mustered, from their towns, twenty-six thousand warriors, exclusive of the inhabitants of Gibeah, who raised[*] seven hundred men. There is a discrepancy of eleven hundred between this total and the sum of the figures given in v.[44-47], while the summary in v.[35] does not agree with either. In v.[15] 𝔊 has *twenty-five thousand*, which more nearly tallies with v.[44-47], but may, for that reason, be suspected of being a correction.[†] — *Not including the inhabitants of Gibeah ; they mustered seven hundred young warriors*] "seven hundred young warriors" is also the number of the left-handed slingers in v.[16]. This identity of number and phrase is suspicious. — **16.** *Out of all this force there were seven hundred left-handed young warriors ; every one of this number could sling a stone at a hair and not miss*] see above on v.[15b]. Budde thinks v.[16] a gloss derived from 3[15], [‡] but neither the contents of the verse nor the tradition of the text warrant so summary a dismissal of the difficulty ; v.[16b], which is not suggested by anything in the context or any parallel in the O.T., has a strong presumption in its favour ; v.[16a] may have originated in an accidental repetition of the words *seven hundred young warriors* from v.[15b], which were then worked into the context in v.[16a] as well as the case permitted. I conjecture, therefore, that the author wrote : [15b] Not including the inhabitants of Gibeah, who mustered seven hundred young warriors. [16b] All this force

---

[*] Bu.

[†] Cf. Fl. Jos., *antt.* v. 2, 10 § 156 (25,600). According to 𝔐 the total strength of the Benjamites, including the men of Gibeah, was 26,700 (v.[15]). In the third day's battle there fell 18,000 + 5000 + 2000 = 25,000, while 600 escaped from the slaughter (v.[44-47]). There remain thus 1100 to be accounted for. Ki. and others have supposed that this number of Benjamites were killed in the first two days' fighting, in which their losses are not recorded (v.[21. 25]) ; but it is hard to imagine that the author, who enters so minutely into these statistics, should have left the losses in the first two days to be learned by this kind of calculation. See below on v.[44ff].

[‡] *Richt. u. Sam.*, p. 152.

(*i.e.* all the Benjamites, cf. v.[17b]) could sling a stone at a hair line and not miss.* The skill of the Benjamites as archers and slingers is celebrated also in 1 Chr. 12[2ff].† Their fabulous marksmanship may possibly be noted here in order to help explain the heavy losses of the Israelites in the first two engagements.‡ — **17.** *And the Israelites, excluding Benjamin, mustered four hundred thousand fighting men*] the author's conception of the solidarity of Israel is such that he thinks it necessary formally to except Benjamin from the general levy raised against that tribe !

12. בני שבטי בנימן] cf. 1 S. 9[21] שבט כשמחות שבטי בנימן. In both cases the error seems to have been occasioned by a שבט in the preceding context. All the versions here render a singular. The explanation of We., Sta., Dr., al. (in Samuel), Be., al. here, that the archaic form of the constr. sg., שבטי, is intended, is less probable. The Jewish comm. assume that שבטי is here equivalent to כמשחות; see esp. Ki., who cites the converse use of משחה for שבט, 13[2] 17[7] Jos. 7[17]. — **13.** האנשים בני בליעל] cf. 19[22] and note there. — ונעברה ירה מישראל] read הרעה; the indispensable article has been lost by haplography. Cf. the Deuteronomic ובערת הרע מישראל, Dt. 17[12] 22[22]. — ולא אבו בנימן] Qerē inserts בני before בנימן; the correction belongs to the class technically called קרי ולא כתיב, in which a word not found in the consonant text is inserted; there are, according to the Massora, ten instances in the O.T.; see *Ochla we-Ochla*, No. 97. The correction here is no doubt right (Stud., cf. ⑥), though לא אבו בנימן presents no grammatical difficulty. — **15.** ויתפקרו בני בנימן] cf. v.[15. 17], ויתפקדו, 21[9]; התפקדו Nu. 1[47] 2[33] 26[62] 1 K. 20[27]. The forms are anomalous and have been variously explained: (*a*) as Hithpael (Ki., Ges., Ew., Ol., Kö., al.); or (*b*) as *t* reflexive of Kal, corresponding to Aram. Ithpe'el, Arab. Ifta'ala (Nöld., Kautzsch, Sta.). The correctness of the tradition may be questioned; the latter is the more acceptable explanation of the forms. See on the one side Kö., i. p. 198 f.; on the other, Ges.[26] p. 150. — עשרים ושבעה אלף איש] ⑥[APVLMNO] ϛ *ε* εἴκοσι καὶ τέντε χιλιάδες (⑧ al. τέντε καὶ εἴκοσι): ⑧ εἴκοσι τρεῖς χιλιάδες is apparently quite isolated. § Fl. Jos. gives the total 25,600, prob. by simple addition of v.[15. 17]. — לבד מ־] v.[17] S[21]. — הפברו] with the construction Stud. compares Dt. 3[5] 1 K. 5[30]; see also 2 Chr. 9[14]. — **16.** מכל העם הזה שבע מאות איש בחור] in ⑥[S] ϛ these words are asterisked; they are wanting in ⑥[AL al.]; cf. also ⑧. ‖ It appears therefore that the pre-hexaplar Greek version, as well as 𝔏𝔖, recognized only the seven hundred Gibeathites; ℭ alone agrees with 𝔐. It is

---

* This emendation is supported by the versions; see crit. note.
† Some of them of Saul's clan; v.[2. 3].
‡ This may, however, be ascribing to the author too much reflection.
§ Perhaps ⑧ represents an erroneous שלשה for ששה of 𝔐.
‖ See *The Book of Judges in Hebrew*.

possible that the words in v.¹⁴ were lost by homoeoteleuton in the Hebrew manuscript from which 𝔊 was translated; but more probable that the corruption is in 𝔐. — אשר יד ימינו] see on 3¹⁵. The words seem to have been borrowed from the description of the Benjamite Ehud (3¹⁵), perhaps by some one who took the word in the sense, ἀμφοτεροδέξιος (𝔊𝕃); it is scarcely likely that he meant to represent the whole corps as left-handed. — [כי זה הרע cf. v.¹⁷ᵇ, כי זה איש בלחכה. The sing. זה is explained by the sing. antecedents and the sing. predicate.[*] הרע I S. 17⁴⁰ 25²⁰. — נאבן] ב instrumenti. — [רקשערה Norzi, Baer; cf. Ki., Michlol, 147ᵃ, ed. Lyck. Locative of שער Is. 7²⁰; Ges.[26] p. 244. The common text, השערה, is fem. (nomen unitatis) of שער or שער. — ולא יחטא] make a miss; the verb might also be pronounced as Kal.

18–28. The first two battles; the Israelites are defeated with heavy losses.

— After inquiring of the oracle at Bethel what tribe shall first deliver the attack, the Israelites march upon Gibeah and take position before it (v.¹⁸⁻²⁰). The Benjamites sally from the town and attack them with such fury that twenty-two thousand Israelites are left on the field, while the assailants sustain no loss (v.²¹). Undaunted by their repulse, the Israelites offer battle the next day on the same ground (v.²²). They go up to Bethel and weep before Yahweh till evening; they consult the oracle to learn whether they shall renew the fight, and receive an affirmative response (v.²³). In the second day's engagement, the Benjamites inflict on them a loss of eighteen thousand men (v.²⁴ᶠ). The Israelites withdraw to Bethel, and weep, fast, and offer sacrifices to Yahweh; they inquire of Phinehas the priest whether they shall continue the war, or desist; Yahweh bids them fight again, and promises them success the next day (v.²⁶⁻²⁸). — Verse ¹⁹ probably belongs to the original narrative; all the rest is secondary; v.²³, which is absurd after v.²², seems to be a later interpolation borrowed from v.²⁶⁻²⁸, and v.²⁴ may have been inserted by the same hand to restore the connexion. This way of making war, in which the operations are immediately directed by Yahweh through his oracle, and the fighting interspersed with religious exercises, is altogether different from the wars of the judges in the former part of the book. It is not history, it is not legend, but the theocratic ideal of a scribe who had never handled a more dangerous weapon than an imaginative pen.

---

[*] Cf. Lev. 11⁴ Dt. 14⁷, Driver, Deuteronomy, p. 161.

18. *They arose and went up to Bethel*] see on 1²³ (p. 40, 42)
and 20²⁷. As the narrative now runs, the Israelites assemble at
Mizpah (v.¹), then collect at Gibeah itself (v.¹¹), where they are
confronted by the Benjamites (v.¹⁴). Now they turn about and
march away to Bethel, three or four hours distant to the north, to
consult the oracle. The later writer was much more concerned
that the "congregation" should act in accordance with correct
theocratic principles than that the verisimilitude of the story
should be preserved. — *And the Israelites inquired of God, Who
of us shall first go up to battle against the Benjamites ? And
Yahweh answered, Judah first*] substance and phrase are obviously borrowed from 1¹ᶠ.* In the following verses nothing is to
be discovered of such a precedence of Judah. Bertheau suspects
that the verse is an interpolation in the later narrative ;† but it is
quite as likely that both the borrowing and the resulting inconsistency should be attributed to the author of that narrative himself. —
19. Perhaps part of the original story. — From Mizpah, where they
assembled (v.¹), the Israelites marched against Gibeah to punish
its inhabitants as they had resolved (v.⁸ with its original sequel).
Verse ¹⁹ was probably followed by v.²⁹. — **20.** The Israelites move
out for battle and form their lines in the vicinity of Gibeah. Cf.
v.²·³⁰ Gen. 14⁸.‡ — **21.** The Benjamites march out against them
from Gibeah, and slaughter twenty-two thousand men. Lit. *destroyed of Israel twenty-two thousand men to the earth ;* left them
slain on the field ; cf. v.²⁵, the verb also v.³⁵·⁴² 2 S. 11¹ Dan. 8²⁴.
— **22.** *The people, the Israelites, took courage, and again arrayed
their battle on the same ground*] it is possible that the old story
also told of a repulse of the Israelites in their first assault, and
that this is the basis of the verse before us ; the first words are
not altogether in the manner of the post-exilic writer, and the
contradiction between v.²² and v.²³ would thus be explained. If
this is not the case, v.²³ must be an interpolation by a still later
hand, derived from v.²⁶⁻²⁸. — **23.** The Israelites go up (to Bethel,
v.¹⁸·²⁶) and weep before Yahweh until evening (v.²⁶ 21² cf. Jos. 7⁶
Joel 2¹²·¹⁷) ; they inquire of Yahweh whether they shall again

---

* The words of 1¹ are perhaps incorrectly understood ; see crit. note.
† So also Bu.
‡ The parallels to Gen. 14 in these verses are to be especially noted.

engage in battle with their brethren of Benjamin, and are bidden
to do so (v.⁷ᶠ). On the origin of this verse see above on v.ᵃ.
The day of humiliation before Yahweh cannot possibly follow the
formation for battle on the second day (v.ᵃ), nor can we construe
v.ᵃ as a parenthesis in the pluperfect.* — **24, 25.** On the second
day the Israelites again advanced against the Benjamites; the latter, as before, marched out to meet them, and inflicted upon them
a loss of eighteen thousand warriors; cf. v.²¹.† — **26.** The Israelites withdraw to Bethel. — *And wept, and sat there before Yahweh,
and fasted that day until evening, and offered burnt offerings and
peace offerings before Yahweh*] cf. v.ᵃ 21².⁴. They made the most
strenuous efforts to propitiate Yahweh; cf. Dt. 1⁴⁵ Ezra 10¹ Joel 2¹⁷
(weeping), 1 S. 7⁶ Joel 1¹⁴ 2¹⁵ (fasting). *Burnt offerings and
peace offerings* are frequently named together (21⁴ 1 S. 10⁸ 11¹⁵
13⁹ 2 S. 6¹⁷ 24²⁵ &c.). The former were wholly consumed by fire
upon the altar (6²⁶ 11³¹ 13¹⁶ᵃ); while in the latter, after the fat
was burned and the priest had received his perquisites, the rest
of the flesh furnished a feast for those who brought the offering.
The translation *peace offering* is conventional; ‡ the original significance of the term is unknown. Others render 'thank-offer-
ings,'§ or σωτήρια. ‖ — **27, 28.** They consult the oracle again; cf.
v.¹⁸·ᵃ. Verse ²⁷ᵇ and ²⁸ᵃ, which interrupt the connexion, are no
doubt late glosses,¶ meant to explain why the sacrifices were
offered and the oracle consulted at Bethel instead of Shiloh, where
the ark is commonly supposed to have remained from the days of
Joshua (Jos. 18¹⁰) to those of Eli. The same reflection led many
interpreters to take the words *beth el* in this chapter appellatively,
the house of God, that is, Shiloh.** There is no other mention of
the ark in the Book of Judges. The phrase *ark of the covenant
of God*, in 𝔐 1 S. 4⁴ 2 S. 15²⁴ 1 Chr. 16⁶; cf. the more frequent,
ark of the covenant of Yahweh. Neither is found in old and

---

* 𝕷, Vatabl., AV., RV., al. Stud. conj. that the verses are accidentally transposed.

† On the question whether the oracle (v.ᵃ) was deceptive or false, see Stud.; cf.
also Ki., Schm., Cler., Ke.

‡ 𝕭 in Reg., Ἀλθ, 𝕷, AV., al. mu.　　　　　　　　　§ Fl. Jos.

‖ Philo. See Nowack, *Hebr. Archäologie*, ii. p. 211 ff.　　　¶ Be.

** So 𝕷 in v.¹⁸: *venerunt in domum Dei, hoc est, in Silo;* Ra. (on 19¹⁸), Ki. (on
20²⁶), RLG. 1⁰, Vatabl., Drus., Cler., AV., al. mu.

sound texts.* — **28.** *And Phinehas, the son of Eleazar, the son of Aaron stood before him in those days*] the mention of Phinehas would fix the time of the action in the first generation after the occupation of Western Palestine,† to which period it is assigned by Josephus and the Jewish chronology ; ‡ but this is probably no more than the guess of a very late editor or scribe. § It is possible that v.^{28aa} is an older gloss than v.^{27b} : in any case we must render, in accordance with the usage elsewhere (Dt. 10^8), ‖ Phinehas . . . stood before *him*, that is Yahweh (v.^{27a}), rather than, before *it* (the ark, v.^{27b}).

The question why Yahweh allowed the Israelites, whose conduct in the whole affair was beyond reproach, to be so severely punished in the first two battles, was early raised by the interpreters. The answer most frequently given is, that it was because they had tolerated the idolatry of Micah and the Danites (ch. 17 18).¶

18. ‏בית אל‎] two words; Ven.$^{1.2}$, Buxt., Jablonski, Opit., Van der Hooght, JHMich., Mant., al. plur. Baer ‏בית־אל‎, in conformity to the general rule laid down in his *Liber Genesis*, p. 76. See on the other side, Norzi on Gen. 12^8 and *h. l.* The Jewish interpretation here (𝕃, *in domum Dei, hoc est in Silo* : see on v.^{27}) shows that the name was read as two words; and Norzi here remarks that wherever ‏בית אל‎ has appellative sense it is written *divisim*. — ‏וייראו בית אלהים‎] see on 1^1; cf. 18^6 20$^{13.26}$. — ‏יהודה בתחיה‎] so 𝕃𝔖𝔗 also read. The ellipsis of the significant verb is not frequent in Hebrew; the text would be construed, *Judas sit in principio* (cf. 𝕃, Schm.). 𝕲 repeats ἀναβήσεται, which also stands in 1^2. In the present passage the words can only mean, Who shall be first in the attack; not, who shall first attack, as in 1^1; but it is doubtful whether the Hebrew will bear this sense; see on 1^1 (p. 13). — **20.** ‏איש ישראל‎] v.$^{11.17.20 \text{ bis } 22}$; alternating with ‏בני ישראל‎ v.$^{1.3.7.14.19}$ &c. ‏איש ישראל‎ appears chiefly in the secondary stratum; but the use is not constant enough to serve as a criterion for the analysis, as Be. would use it. — **21.** ‏ארצה . . . וישחיתו‎] ‏ארצה‎ must be taken with the verb. 𝕲^M adds στω-

---

* See We., *TBS.* p. 55; Seyring, *ZATW.* xi. 1891, p. 114-125; Couard, *ib.* xii. 1892, p. 60 ff., 68.   † See Ex. 6^{25} Nu. 25$^{7ff.}$ Jos. 22^{13} 24^{33}; cf. Jud. 18^{30}.

‡ *Seder Olam*, c. 12. According to the Jewish interpreters Phinehas consulted the oracle for the Israelites in Jud. 1^1; see comm. there.

§ " In the whole period of the judges we read nothing of the ark, or of the High Priest " (Stud.).

‖ 1 K. 3^{15} is not parallel, not to raise the question of the text there (cf. 𝕲).

¶ *Sanhedrin*, 103^b; *Pirqe de-R. Eliezer* (*Yalqût*, § 86) ; Ra., Ki., Abarb. Substantially the same explanation is given by Cyrill. Alex. on Hos. 9^9. The more general answer, it was a punishment for their sins, is given by Orig., Thdt., Isidor. Pelus., Procop. Gaz.; see also a Lyra, Schm. (*qu.* 4), a Lap.

μέτων ρομφαίαν, as in v.²⁶. — 22. ויתחזק הָעָם איש ישראל] the last words are redundant; cf. v.²⁶. With the verb cf. 1 S. 4⁹. — 23. The difficulty in the position of this verse is felt by Jerome, who translates: *ita tamen ut prius ascenderent et flerent coram Domino*. Others evade the difficulty by a vague translation of v.²², they prepared to fight again (Schm., al.),* but the language of v.²³ᵇ is as explicit as possible: they formed their line of battle again on the same ground on which they had formed on the first day. — ויעלו בני ישראל] Bu. adds בית אל, cf. v.²⁶; this emendation would be necessary if v.²³ were an integral part of the later narrative. — נגש] לגשת למלחמה of hostile approach, 2 S. 10¹³ Jer. 46³; cf. הרב v.²⁴ Ex. 14²⁰. — 26. כל בני ישראל וכל הֶעָם] cf. v.²³, explained as the explicative use of the conjunction, *even* all the people; but the redundancy is not removed by the name; see on 9⁵¹, p. 269. — ויעלו עֹלות ושלמים] 21⁴ (the only other instance in Jud.). On the שלמים see Fl. Jos., *antt.* iii. 9, 2 § 228 f. (θυσίαι χαριστήριοι); Philo, *de victimis*, p. 243, 245 f. (σωτήριον, περὶ σωτηρίου); Sifra, *Wayyiqra*, Par. 13, § 16; † Di. on Lev. 3¹; see comm. on Lev. *l.c.* — 27. ארון ברית האלהים] 𝕲ᴬᴸ⁻ᴹ s κυρίου; so also 𝕮𝕾; cf. 1 S. 4⁴. ᴮᴾⱽᴺ κυρίου τοῦ θεοῦ, 𝕷 *arca foederis Dei*. — 28. נֶצָב לפניו] not, *stood before it* (EV.), but *before him;* in priestly service, Dt. 10⁸ 18⁷ Ez. 44¹⁵ &c.

29-44. The third battle; rout and slaughter of the Benjamites.

The description of the battle is badly confused: in v.³⁵ the battle is over, the Benjamites have been defeated and twenty-five thousand one hundred of them slain; in v.³⁵ᵇ we are back again at the beginning of the fight; the stratagem and the discomfiture of the Benjamites is narrated again, with all detail; on the field and in the flight twenty-five thousand are killed (v.⁴⁴⁻⁴⁶). The second account is clearly the older; we may perhaps ascribe to it: v. ²⁹. ³⁵ᵇ. ³⁷ᵃ. ³⁸. ³⁹ ᵃ. ⁴⁰⁻⁴²ᵃ. ⁴⁴ᵃ. ⁴⁷.‡ The rest is later amplification and embellishment. The stratagem has a striking resemblance to that employed by Joshua against Ai (Jos. 8¹⁴ᶠᶠ, cf. especially Jud. 20³⁷ᶠ. with Jos. 8¹⁹ᶠᶠ.), but the phraseology is throughout different, nor does our narrative bear the stamp of a copy.§ Doublets in the legendary history are not necessarily evidence of literary dependence. There is no reason why such a ruse, in which there is nothing very original, may not have been told, or, for that matter, practised, more than once.

---

* Cf. Cler.   † Cf. Malbim's comm. *in loc.*

‡ Traces of retouching may be discovered here and there in these verses, *e.g.* in v.⁴⁷. In v.⁴⁴ᵃ, the original numbers may have been smaller; but this cannot be confidently affirmed. We must not judge even the older narrative by our standards of historical probability.   § We.

29. Israel put men in ambush against Gibeah around the town ; cf. 9[22. 34. 43] &c. The verse seems to come from the old story, which probably proceeded to tell how the Benjamites went out to battle against the Israelites (as in v.[21. 25. 31]), on which v.[29] would naturally follow. The next verses (v.[30-36a]) are in the main by the later author. — **30.** The Israelites advanced against the Benjamites on the third day, and formed their line of battle as they had done on previous occasions. — **31.** The Benjamites marched out to meet the enemy, and began to make a slaughter among them as on the former days. The verse is in substance derived from v.[39b]. — *They were drawn off from the city*] the words stand parenthetically in the sentence, in whose syntax they are not included ; the form of the verb is also anomalous. The clause is doubtless a gloss borrowed from Jos. 8[16]; cf. below, v.[32].* — *On the roads, one of which goes up to Bethel and one to Gibeah, in the field*] these roads are mentioned also in v.[32. 45]. The description here is not intelligible : there was a road from Gibeah to Bethel, on which the author may very well have represented the first encounter between the Benjamites, who marched out of Gibeah, and the Israelites, who were advancing from Bethel, as taking place ; but what shall we make of the second road, leading to Gibeah ? A number of interpreters have felt constrained to regard the Gibeah here meant as a different place from that elsewhere named in these chapters, *Gibeah in the field.*† Others have conjectured that Geba should be read ; others, Gibeon. But it is doubtful whether we have a right to expect of the author a clear conception of the topography ; cf. the laboured effort to tell us where Shiloh was, 21[19].‡ — **32.** The Benjamites thought that the enemy was routed as in the former battles ; but the Israelites were only feigning flight to draw the defenders away from the town. In substance derived from v.[39b. 36b]; in phraseology patterned after Jos. 8[5. 6]. — **33.** *All the men of Israel arose from their place and formed line of battle at Baal-tamar*] Bertheau understands that they abandoned their first line and fell back in feigned disorder to Baal-tamar, where they re-formed. This agrees well enough

---

* Be.   † Pisc., Tremell., AV., RV., Stud., Cass., Grove, al.
‡ Cf. also Dt. 1[1b] 11[30] &c.

with the requirements of the stratagem, but does violence to the author's language : *arose from their place* cannot mean, *made a stand and reformed their lines.** Nor do we escape from the difficulty if, with Studer, we treat the verb as pluperfect; the Israelites *had abandoned* their first position, &c. It might be suspected that the half-verse came from the older narrative, in which it would have a passable sense and connexion after v.[29], but the construction is so negligent, not to say ungrammatical, that this conjecture is hardly to be entertained. *Baal-tamar* is otherwise unknown. According to Eusebius, there was in his days a Beth-thamar in the vicinity of Gibeah.[†] The name of the place was given it by its sacred palm tree, which some scholars have proposed to identify with Deborah's palm (4[5]) ;[‡] but the latter, ' between Ramah and Bethel,' is too remote. [§] — *And the ambush of Israel rushed forth from its place, west of Gibeah*] so the text is to be emended with the oldest versions ; cf. Jos. 8[4. 9. 19].[‖] 𝕴, which has been translated in a variety of ways, is unintelligible and plainly corrupt. *Meadows of Gibeah* (AV.) follows 𝔗 ; *Maareh-geba* (RV.)[¶] is merely a transcription of the Hebrew words. The verb *rushed forth* is an Aramaism ; the word used for *west* is found only in comparatively late writers.[**] — **34.** The men who had been put in ambush, ten thousand young warriors out of all Israel, gained a point opposite Gibeah. 𝔗 and some manuscripts of 𝕴 read *south of Gibeah ;*[††] but this is either an accident, or an attempt to give more definiteness to the somewhat vague expression in the text. — The Benjamites, who were now hotly engaged with the main body of the Israelites, did not perceive the disaster which was imminent ; cf. v.[41] Jos. 8[14]. — **35.** *Yahweh defeated Benjamin*] 2 Chr. 13[15] 14[12]. — The Israelites slaughtered twenty-five thousand one hundred Benjamites, all warriors. [‡‡] The statement of the total loss properly concludes the account of the battle, as in v.[21. 25. 46], cf. 3[29] Jos. 8[25] &c. On

---

* *Their place* might mean the place where they had been encamped (v.[19]), or where they had been concealed (Jos. 8[19]).   † *OS*[2]. 238[75].   ‡ See above, p. 113 f.

§ 𝔗 understands by Baal-tamar, Jericho, *the city of palms* (1[16] 3[13]).

‖ Be.; see crit. note.   ¶ With 𝔊𝔅N.

** We cannot, therefore, accept Bu.'s opinion, that v.[33b] is derived from the older narrative.   †† So Houbigant.   ‡‡ With the phraseology cf. v.[21. 25].

the numbers, see above on v.[15].—**36ª.** *And the Benjamites saw that they were beaten*] the few hundred survivors. The words make a ludicrous impression after v.[36].

29. אָרְבִים] the plur. Jos. 8[4] Jer. 51[12]; cf. מָאֹרְבִים Jud. 9[35] 2 Chr. 20[22]. The collective sing. אורב is more usual.— אֶל־הגבעה] cf. Jos. 8[2]. לְעִיר.—**30.** כפעם בפעם v.[31] 16[20] (p. 357).—**31.** הָנְתְּקוּ מִן הִעִיר] Hophal; the unassimilated נ suggests Aramaic influence (Kautzsch, *Gram. d. Biblisch-Aramäischen*, § 42); the asyndetic perf. is hardly susceptible of a grammatical explanation,—that of Roorda (§ 524) will not pass. If the words were on other accounts to be deemed genuine, it would be best to emend, וַיִּנָּתְקוּ Jos. 8[16] (cf. Sta. § 126 *c*); but they are obviously premature.— וַיֵּחֵלּוּ] חלל Hiph.; cf. below v.[39].— הַחֵלִים] v.[39], a proleptic figure; smite slain men, smite them dead.— נְגוּתָה נִגְּתָה] Gibeah in the field is not the intention of the accents, which rightly take בשדה as in construction parallel to בַּמְסִלּוֹת, *on the roads . . . in the open field.*—**32.** כְּבָרִאשֹׁנָה] Jos. 8[4. 6] (כָּאשֶׁר), cf. v.[39] below.*— וַנִתַּקְנֻהוּ] Kal; on ק see Ges.[26] § 20, 2 *b*; Kö., i. p. 309 f.—**33.** וְכֹל אִישׁ יִשְׂרָאֵל קָמוּ מִמְּקוֹמוֹ] the coll. subject is construed first with a plural and then with a singular, which is certainly not elegant. Be.'s translation, *they arose, each from his place,* is not admissible.— יָגִיחַ] the vb. in O.T. only of the bursting forth of water (Ez. 32[2] Job 38[8] 40[23]; נֹחִי Mi. 4[10] is very questionable); cf. the n. pr. גיחון 1 K. 1[33]. In 𝔗𝔗, on the other hand, the Aphel of this verb is a very common word for, 'attack, make war upon,' oftenest in phrase אגח קרבא, but also without קרבא, *e.g.* Dt. 20[10] Jos. 23[8] Jud. *h. l.*, &c.— מִמַּעֲרֵה גָבַע] 𝕲[AFVSLMO] ς ε ἀπὸ δυσμῶν τῆς Γαβαα, *i.e.* מִמַּעֲרַב גִּבְעָה; so also 𝕷 *ab occidentali urbis parte*.† 𝕲[B] Μαραανγαβε, [N codd.] Μααρα [τῆς] Γαβαα. 𝕾 saw in the first word מְעָרָה, 'cave,' rendering, *from the cave which is in Gibeah;* 𝕿 מַחְשֵׁךְ נבריא, probably connecting with the root ערה, 'bare, treeless stretch of country' (not the most eligible place for an ambush ! ‡), cf. Ra.; Ki., comparing Is. 19[7] (עָרוֹת), § Ps. 37[35], thinks the word may signify a place covered with verdure.—**34.** מִנֶּגֶד לַגִּבְעָה] numerous codd. of 𝔐 (Kenn., De Rossi) נֶגֶב, which is found in the margin of the Bomberg Bibles of 1518, 𝕿; so Houbigant would emend. For נֶגֶד ל cf. Dt. 28[66] and, in another sense, Prov. 14[7].— כִּי נֹגַעַת עֲלֵיהֶם הָרָעָה] v.[41]; the dependence of v.[34] on v.[41] is apparent in the unusual complementary preposition; cf. Jer. 51[9] 1 K. 6[27] (אֶל).

36ᵇ–44. Another account of the battle.

— The verses contain, not the sequel to the description of the battle in v.[31-36a], but a complete parallel to it. ‖ As far as v.[42a] this narrative appears to be intact, and bears every mark of being derived from a much

---

* On ל before prepositions see *BDB.*, s. v., Note.
† נֶגֶב in prose only in Chr. (Stud.).   ‡ Be.
§ According to the Jewish interpretation.
‖ See the ingenious artificial connexion in 𝕷.

older and better source than v.[31-36]. In what follows v.[42] we may probably ascribe to the same source, v.[44a. 47]; the rest appears to be entirely the work of a later hand. — **36b**. *The men of Israel gave ground to Benjamin, for they relied on the ambush which they had laid against Gibeah*] v.[29], which belongs to this source, must have been followed by an account of the beginning of the engagement, which has been superseded by v.[31ff.] or buried in those verses.* — **37**. *And the ambush made haste and rushed upon Gibeah; and the ambush moved out, and smote all the city without quarter*] the repetition, together with a change in the grammatical construction, make it probable that the second half-verse is a gloss. — **38**. *The time had been agreed upon by the men of Israel with the party in ambush,†*] *for them to send up the signal smoke from the city*, **39**. *and that the men of Israel should turn about in the battle*] that upon this signal the Israelites, who were retreating in feigned discomfiture, should turn upon their pursuers; cf. the description of the execution of this stratagem in v.[40. 41]. This is the only construction which makes v.[39a] tolerable in the context. Its verb is generally translated as an historical tense, *And the men of Israel turned about*, which leaves v.[38] without any proper conclusion; anticipates v.[41], where this movement is narrated in due order; and thus constrains the interpreters to take the verb *turn* in v.[39] in the opposite sense from that which it has in v.[41],‡ or to treat v.[39b. 40] as a parenthesis in the pluperfect, *Now Benjamin had begun to kill, &c.*; § — in a word, throws the whole context into confusion. — The Benjamites began killing the Israelites, and slew some thirty men. — *For they thought, They are completely beaten before us, as in the former battle*] cf. v.[31. 32a]. Budde thinks that v.[39] is an interpolation derived from v.[31]. ‖ It seems to me, on the contrary, that v.[39a], at least, is indispensable here, and that v.[31] is copied from it; but the phraseology has either been retouched by the author of the additions, or conformed to v.[31] by a scribe. The last words, *as in the former battle*, are probably not original. — **40**. The fire signal

---

* See above on v.[36].

† It is unnecessary to depart from the usual meaning of מועד and render, *the agreement* (Be., al.). ‡ Ki., al. mu.

§ RV.[mg], al. ‖ makes v.[39] a parenthesis. ‖ *Richt. u. Sam.*, p. 152.

began to rise from the city, and when the Benjamites looked behind them, the *holocaust of the city* was rising to heaven; cf. Jos. 8[20], and for the phrase, Dt. 13[17]. — **41.** According to the preconcerted plan (v.[34. 38a]), the Israelites turned upon their foes, who were thrown into a panic, for they saw the disaster which had overtaken them; cf. v.[34b]. — **42.** They turned to retreat in the direction of the wilderness, hard pushed by the Israelites. Lit. *the fighting clung to them.* The wilderness lay to the east of Gibeah, the steep uncultivated hill-sides and ravines in which the Highlands of Ephraim break down to the Jordan valley; see below on v.[47]. — The rest of the verse is obscure, and has given rise to a great variety of diverse explanations. A literal translation is: "And those who were (or came) from the cities were destroying him (Benjamin) in the midst of it (or him)." The last pronoun seems to refer to *the way* (to the wilderness) in the first clause: the people of the towns along the line of their flight fell upon them and slaughtered the fugitives on the way.[*] This interpretation, which is the only one that the words appear to admit, labours under great difficulties when we try to harmonize it with the representation of the rest of the chapter. The towns between Gibeah and the wilderness were all, in the times respecting which we have more definite information, Benjamite; but even if we assume that at this early time they were inhabited by Ephraimites, it is to be supposed that the men of these towns were in the Israelite army.[†] The half-verse, with v.[43], is undoubtedly an addition by the later writer; and in all probability he meant to say that the division which had taken Gibeah now issued from the town and intercepted the retreating Benjamites,[‡] who were thus caught between two bodies of the enemy, just as the men of Ai were in Jos. 8[22], which passage seems to have suggested our verses. If this conjecture be correct, v.[42b] originally ran: And those from the city were slaughtering them (the Benjamites) in the midst, *i.e.* between them and the main body of the Israelites. The plural, *the cities,* may have arisen by accident, or

---

[*] So substantially Cler., Be., Cass. (with different explanations of the pronoun; on which point cf. also Ra., Ki.). For a very ingenious but impossible explanation of this and the following verse, see Stud.　　　　　[†] Schm.

[‡] So **L**, cf. **T**.

through the propensity of scribes to exaggeration.* — 43. From the same hand as v.⁴²ᵇ. The text is corrupt, probably in consequence of successive glosses. — *They encircled Benjamin*] cf. Ps. 22¹⁷. The oldest Greek translators read, *they cut Benjamin to pieces*, and this is probably the original text; see crit. note. — There follow two clauses whose grammatical structure stamps them as glosses. The verb in the first occurs nowhere else in the O.T. or later Hebrew, and the whole clause is not improbably a corrupt variant of the following words; see crit. note. — The last clause of the verse, *as far as a point opposite Gibeah on the east*, must be connected with the first verb (*they cut Benjamin to pieces*), and marks the limit of the pursuit and slaughter; but the text cannot be sound. The Israelites certainly did not desist from the pursuit in the immediate vicinity of Gibeah, that is, at the very start. In view of the frequent confusion of the two names, it may be conjectured that the author wrote *Geba*; and if Rimmon (v.⁴⁵·⁴⁷) be rightly identified with Rammōn, the emendation receives considerable support from the topography.† Geba (Geba') lies in the line of flight from Gibeah (Tell el-Fūl) toward Rammōn, and the great Wady es-Suweinit, with its difficult passage between Geba' and Makhmās, would naturally check the pursuit. — 44. The loss of Benjamin was eighteen thousand men, all valiant men. The last clause betrays its late date by its grammatical form; but v.⁴⁴ᵃ seems to be derived from the old story. Its phraseology is different from that of the later writer in v.²¹·²⁵·³⁵, and the number of the slain is not the same. Verse ⁴⁵, which adds to the number first five thousand and then two thousand, thus bringing the total up to twenty-five thousand, as in v.³⁵, has the appearance of a harmonistic artifice, and is much more naturally explained if the eighteen thousand of v.⁴⁴ belonged to the original data.

36. נסע אל הָאָרֵב] Jer. 7⁴ Ps. 4⁶ 31⁷; more frequently construed with ב. — 37. וַיָּחִישׁוּ] 'direct causative Hiphil,' Kö., i., p. 507. Cf. Kal Is. 8¹·³; Hiph. Is. 5¹⁹ (28¹⁶ is doubtful). — וַיִּמְשֹׁךְ אל] 9³³·⁴⁴ (קר). — וַיַּמְשֵׁךְ הארב] 4⁶ (p. 118). — לפי חרב] *without quarter*; see on 1²⁵. — 38. הרב] some codd. (De Rossi) הרב; so 𝔊ᴬᴾˢᴸᴼ 𝔖 (μάχαιρα, cf. also 𝔱); probably τῆς μάχης (ᴮᴺ) has the same origin: ᴠᴹ omit the word, as do 𝔏𝔖. הֶרֶב would be imv. Hiph. of רבה;

to construe this with the following inf. it would be necessary to strike out the
suffix of רְלֹוּרם (Stud.); הרב להרבות, lit. *multiply to send up* (cf. 1 S. 1¹² &c.),
might perhaps be understood, *send up a great deal of smoke;* so ᘓ, Ra.,
Vatab., Schm., Cler., JHMich., Ke. 2°, Stud. 1°. — Cassel defends the text by
the analogy of הַרְבֵּה כָּנָסִי Ps. 51⁴ (Qerē הֶרֶב), but the construction there is
different. Apart from the grammatical difficulty, the introduction of this imv.
in the midst of the narration is highly unnatural. Hitzig on Ps. 51⁴ gives to
הרב here the (Arabic) sense 'flight'; so Ew., *GVI.* ii. p. 498 n. But *Flight!* is
as unsuitable as *Sword!* It is probable that הרב is an accidental mutilated
repetition of דאבב; * הרב a correction meant to make at least the word intelligible. — כמשאת העיר] Bu. emends, קרב; but if the verse is construed as I
propose, this is not necessary. — **39.** וירדף איש ישראל] the finite verb continues the infinitive construction in v.³⁸; cf. (with change of subject, as here)
Gen. 18²⁶ Ex. 33¹⁶ 2 S. 13²⁸, Dr⁴. § 118. These examples show that we should
emend יְרֹדֵף, consec. perf. The imperf. consec. is due to misinterpretation
under the influence of v.⁴¹ᵃ. This compelled the interpreters to take הפן here
in the sense, *turned their backs;* in v.⁴¹ in the sense, *turned their faces, confronted* (Ki., al. mu.). — להבות חיליב] the חיליב prob. came from v.³¹; in old
prose we should have simply להבות בישראל. — ונניף] inf. abs. Niph. before a
perf.; see on 11²⁵, p. 297 f. — כבלחצה הראשנה] Ges.⁵ § 118, 6 b. — **40.** כשאת]
v.³⁸ Jer. 6¹; cf. כשאה Is. 30²⁷, and MII. כשאה, כשאת, Levy, *NHWb.* iii. p. 266,
'fire signal, torch'; the construction and use of which is described in *M. Rosh
ha-shanah*, 22ᵇ. ᘓˢᴸᴹ ᵃˡ. well πυρσός; † cf. Hdt. vii. 182. — כליל עשן] explan-
atory apposition to הכשאת. — כליל העיר] Dt. 13¹⁷ (the city which seduces to
apostasy is to be burned כליל ליהוה); cf. 1 S. 7⁹ Ps. 51²¹, and כליל in Phoenician (*CIS.* i. 165a 4, 7. 9. 11 167ᵇ). ‡ — **41.** הפן] turned on their pursuers, Jos. 8²⁰.
— ויבהל] *were in consternation, dismay;* Ex. 15¹⁶ 1 S. 28²¹ 2 S. 4¹ Jer. 51³².
— **42.** ואשר מהעיר משחיתים אותו בתוכו] Jerome, with sound exegetical tact,
gives what the context requires: *sed et hi qui urbem succenderant, occurre-
runt eis.* ᘓᴹ οἱ ἐν τῇ πόλει (ἀπὸ τῆς πόλεως). ᘓ also understands the
division which had been placed in ambush; so Ra., Ki. No explanation of
the text is possible; we must emend: ואשר מהעיר משחיתים אותו בתוך. For the
last word compare Jos. 8²²; עריב may have arisen by dittography. — **43.** כתרו]
in Ps. 22¹⁸ the verb is parallel to סבב; § for the figure cf. also 1 S. 23²⁶, כתירים
(א), where Klosterm. would read כקדים. In the sense *surround* the word is
understood here by Ra., Ki., and most. Abulw., Tanch., give it the meaning,
gave no respite, as in Job 36², and in Aram. and Syr., but their interpretation is not acceptable. ‖ ᘓ κατέκοπτον, κατέκοψαν, ἔκοψαν, read כתתו or כתתהו,
from which ᵿ could easily arise. The last clause of the verse, which could
hardly be connected with כתרו, supports the reading of ᘓ. — **43.** הדריפהו מנוחה]

---

* Be., Bu.   † ᘓᴬ by transcriptional error πυργος.

‡ See, however, Bloch, *Phoen. Glossar*, p. 35.

§ Hiph. Hab. 1⁴ is questionable.

‖ See the long explanation of Abulw., *Lex.* 336.

the causative stem of ררף is found nowhere else either in the O.T., MH. or
Aram., nor is it easy to imagine what force it could have; * the difficulty is
increased by the noun, on which see below. — הֲרִיכָהוּ] in O.T. הררין is usually
'cause one to tread a path, guide him in a way'; in the sense 'trample'
(grapes, Am. 9¹⁸ Jud. 9²⁷; olives, Mi. 6¹⁵; trop., enemies, Is. 63³) we find
only Kal. In Jer. 51³³ the Hiph. is prob. like Aphel in Targums, 'let (cattle)
tread, thresh'; Job 28⁸, generally rendered *tread*, is perhaps *reach, attain*, as
in the Talmud (*Abodah zarah*, 15ᵇ = *K'ethubim*, 60ᵇ), Syr., Arab. In the last
sense the verb is taken here by Ra., Ges. *Thes.*, MV.; *they overtook them.*
The asyndetic perfects show that neither הרדיפהו nor הרדיכרו is part of the
original text. It is not a remote conjecture that the former is merely a
corruption of the latter (obs. the close resemblance of the letters, and the
spelling of both). — כְּנוּחָה] 'resting place' (Nu. 10³³), peaceful, unmolested
abode (Dt. 12⁹ &c.) seems quite out of place in this context, whether we
interpret *at, to,* or *from* (their) resting place; and the construction is as hard,
or rather as impossible, in the one case as in the other. If the word is
correctly transmitted, it must be a proper noun; it would then be better
to take it, not as accus. of limit (to Menuah, Lth., Merc., Stud.), but as
terminus a quo (כְנוחה), with 𝕲ᴴᴺ ᵃˡ. ἀπὸ Νουα. In 1 Chr. 8² נוּחָה † appears
as a son of Benjamin (Benj. clan), and it is thus *possible* that כְּנֻחָה may be
sound. Others would take כנוחה adverbially, *quietly*, or *easily;* so 𝕾, Tremell.,
Pisc., Winer, al., without warrant in usage.‡ In view of the state in which
the middle of the verse is, it is impossible to have any confidence in the text.
— On the confusion of וּכְבֶה and עֶבֶ), see v.³³ and above, p. 414. — **44.** את כל
אֵלֶה אַנְשֵׁי חַיִל] so also in v.⁴⁶. The use of את before a nominative belongs to
the later language, in which it is employed to give prominence to a noun,
without regard to its syntax; Ges.²⁶ p. 351 f.

45-48. A remnant of the Benjamite warriors escape; their towns are burned and the inhabitants slaughtered.

— Verses ⁴⁵, ⁴⁶
seem to be harmonistic additions, to bring the eighteen thousand
of v.⁴⁴ up to the round twenty-five thousand of the later writer;
v.⁴⁷ is from the old story, which may have gone on to narrate the
destruction of the Benjamite towns and massacre of their popula-
·tion. Something of this sort seems to be presupposed in 21¹ᵃᶠᶠ.,
but v.⁴⁸ in its present form is undoubtedly late. — **45.** The Benjamites turned and fled to the wilderness, to the rock Rimmon.
The beginning of the verse is verbally identical with that of v.⁴⁷.
— *And they made a gleaning of them on the roads, five thousand
men*] with the figure cf. 8². — *And they pursued them closely as*

---

* *Call to one another to pursue* (Ra., Ki.), will not do.
† 𝕲ᴮ l姫. ‡ See against this theory, Stud.

far as Gidom(?), and killed two thousand of them] of Gidom
nothing else is known; one recension of 𝔊 has Gibeah (or
Geba).* — **46.** The whole number of Benjamites who fell on
that day was twenty-five thousand fighting men: 18,000 (v.^{44})
+ 5000 + 2000 (v.^{45}) = 25,000; cf. v.^{35}, and see on v.^{15}. — *On
that day; all these were valiant warriors*] the words *on that day*
stand in a very awkward place, and, with the following clause,
may be a scribe's gloss.† — **47.** From the older narrative. — *They
turned and fled to the wilderness, to the rock of Rimmon, six
hundred men*] all who escaped from the signal disaster that had
overtaken the tribe. In its original connexion the verse probably
followed closely upon v.^{42a}, perhaps only v.^{44a}, or the substance of
it, intervening. *Rimmon* was in the time of Eusebius a village
fifteen Roman miles from Jerusalem, in a northerly direction.‡
It was discovered by Robinson in Rammōn,§ somewhat over
three miles east of Beitin (Bethel), and a less distance (forty
minutes) south of eṭ-Ṭaiyibeh, on a high and rocky hill. This
would lie in a corner of the territory of Benjamin, in the wilderness of Beth-aven (Jos. 18^{12}). ‖ — **48.** The Israelites returned from
the pursuit and destroyed the Benjamite towns with all that was in
them. — *To the Benjamites*] those who had not taken the field,
senes impuberes mulieres atque imbelles.¶ They massacred them
all. — *Man and beast and everything that was there*] as in the
case of a city devoted to destruction (the *ḥerem*), Dt. 2^{34} 3^6
Jos. 6$^{17ff.}$ Dt. 13$^{15f.}$. — *All the towns that there were, they committed
to the flames*] 1^8; see note there (p. 21).

45. וַיַּגְדִּילֻהוּ] cf. Jer. 6^9; the use of the trope in simple narration is striking.
— גִדְעֹם] 𝔊^N Γαβαα Γαβα (^{236}); APVSLM ε Γαλααδ. 𝔖 *Gibeon*, which is not
in the direction of this retreat. — **48.** מְתֹם עַד־עִיר] so the Massora (on Ps. 38^4);
cf. Norzi. In Dt. 2^{34} 3^6 Job 24^{12}, however, we find עִיר מְתִם, *town of men,*
male population, as many codd. and some old edd. read here (De Rossi).
This is doubtless the writer's meaning; ** תֹם, *entire*, gives no sense.†† The
phrase is borrowed from Dt.; the conj. כְּמֵאָה (Buhl) is unnecessary.

---

* The word may perhaps be read as an infinitive, *till they cut them off;* cf. 21^6.
† A literal translation of the verse is: *And all who fell of Benjamin were twenty-
five thousand men drawing sword, on that day; all these were men of valour.*
‡ *OS^2.* 287$_{59}$.   § *BR^2.* i. p. 440; iii. p. 290.
‖ See Rob., *l.c.*; Guérin, *Samarie,* i. p. 215; *SWP. Memoirs,* ii. p. 292 f.; Bäd^3.,
p. 121.   ¶ JHMich.   ** Stud.; cf. JHMich.   †† Cf. 𝔖 Dt. 2^{34} 3^6; cf. 𝔗 ram. ib.

XXI. 1-14. To provide the surviving Benjamites with wives, Jabesh in Gilead is destroyed. — As soon as the Israelites have leisure from their bloody work to contemplate its results, they are greatly afflicted by the prospect that Benjamin will disappear altogether from among the tribes of Israel (v.⁷·⁶). All the women of the tribe have been slaughtered, and the rest of the Israelites have sworn a great oath not to give their daughters in marriage to Benjamites (v.¹·⁷); the six hundred survivors must therefore die childless and the tribe become extinct. In this perplexity they hit upon a plan which promises to accomplish a double purpose. Of all Israel, Jabesh in Gilead alone had not sent its contingent to the war. Twelve thousand men are therefore sent thither, with orders to exterminate the whole population of Jabesh, sparing only the virgin girls. In this way four hundred of the Benjamites are furnished with wives (v.⁹·¹⁴, cf. v.³).

The story shows in every trait the hand of the post-exilic author, and is plainly patterned after Nu. 31, in a tertiary stratum of P. The numerous repetitions may be due in part to the bungling of the author, in part to glosses by still later hands.* — **1.** *Now the Israelites had sworn at Mizpah, No one of us will give his daughter in marriage to Benjamin*] v.⁷·¹⁸ cf. ²². This oath, upon which the story of the rape of the Shilonites as well as the expedition to Jabesh of Gilead turns, had a place in the older narrative, and not impossibly v.¹ is derived from this source.† — **2.** *The people came to Bethel*] whither in the later form of the story the Israelites resort to humble themselves before God and consult the oracle (20¹⁸·²³·²⁶). — *And sat there until evening before God, and lifted up their voice and wept immoderately*] lit. *a great weeping*, 2 S. 13³⁶ Is. 38³, cf. Jud. 20²³·²⁶, also 2³ Nu. 25⁶ Joel 1¹³ᶠ. — **3.** They complain of Yahweh's mysterious providence — *Why, O Yahweh, God of Israel, has this happened in Israel, that one tribe is missing to-day from Israel*] cf. v.¹⁵ in the older story, from which v.⁶ also is derived. — **4.** On the following day they built an altar and offered sacrifices. The building of an altar at Bethel, an ancient

---

* Böhme (*ZATW.* v. p. 30-36) would distinguish three sources: A v.⁶⁻¹⁴, B v.¹⁻⁵, C v.¹⁵⁻²³. Of these B is an amplification of A; C a contradictory representation, which none the less is later than A and dependent upon it. Budde regards v.⁶⁻⁸·¹¹·¹²ᵇ as editorial glosses in the younger narrative; see above, p. 407. † Bu.

holy place, is singular ; all the more since in 20[36] they have already offered sacrifices there. The verse, as well as v.[4], is perhaps a gloss, introduced by a scribe or editor whose mind was filled with reminiscences of the old literature ; cf., *e.g.*, 2 S. 24[25]. — **5.** They inquire who from among all the tribes had failed to respond to the summons ; for they had sworn that any who did not appear at the rendezvous at Mizpah should be put to death. The first half-verse anticipates v.[8a] ; v.[4. 5] interrupt the natural connexion of v.[6] with v.[3] ; the style of v.[5] is unusually awkward and incorrect. It is not unlikely that both verses were inserted by an editor. — *Who is there that did not come up in the assembly*] 20[2] ; cf. 21[8]. — *For the great curse had been pronounced upon every one who did not go up*] cf. 1 S. 14[24. 28. 29]. Not, *they had made a great oath concerning him that came not up, &c.,*[*] which would be quite differently expressed in Hebrew. — *Namely, that he should unfailingly be put to death*] cf. 1 S. 14[39. 44]. — **6.** They were sorry for Benjamin ; v.[15], on which v.[6] as well as v.[3] is dependent. — *Their brother*] 20[23. 28]. — *And they said, One tribe is cut off from Israel*] cf. v.[3. 15]. The figure is taken from a tree which is mutilated by lopping off one of its branches ; cf. Is. 10[33] 14[12]. — **7.** *What shall we do for them, for the survivors, for wives ?*] *for the survivors* has probably been introduced, for greater explicitness, from v.[16]. — *Seeing that we have sworn by Yahweh not to give them any of our daughters in marriage*] v.[1. 18], cf. v.[20b]. — **8.** They inquire who, of all the tribes of Israel, had not come up to the gathering of the clans at Mizpah ; cf. v.[5]. — *Now not a man had come to the camp from Jabesh in Gilead, to the assembly*] the last words (v.[5] 20[2]) may have been added by a scribe to whom *camp* did not sound sufficiently ecclesiastical. The entire half-verse is, strictly speaking, superfluous beside v.[9], but such circumstantiality is the delight of late writers. — **9.** A muster of the tribes disclosed the fact that there was no one present from Jabesh. — *Jabesh in Gilead*] the only historical mention of the place in the O.T. is in the history of Saul (1 S. 11 31[11-13] 2 S. 2[5f.] 21[12f.]). From these passages we learn only that it was within a day's journey of Beth-shean. The notices in Josephus do not fix the site more exactly.† Eusebius tells us that in

---

* AV., RV., al.   † *Antt.* v. 2, 11 § 164; vi. 5, 1 § 71; 14, 8 § 375.

his time it was a village on high ground, six miles from Pella on
the way to Gerasa.* The name survives in Wady Yābis,† which
opens into the Jordan valley about ten miles SSE. of Beisān, and
nearly opposite Ibzīq (Bezek), where Saul mustered the tribesmen
for the relief of Jabesh (1 S. 11⁸).‡ Robinson suggested the ruins,
ed-Deir, on the south side of the Wady about three hours from
the Jordan,§ and has been followed by most recent writers.
Merrill proposes Miryamin, on the road from Pella (Ṭabaqāt
Faḥl) to Gerash, an hour and forty minutes from the former
place. |

10-14. The expedition against Jabesh. — 10. The congregation (20¹) sends thither twelve thousand men, with orders to massacre the whole population of the city, men, women, and children.¶
— **11.** More explicit instructions. — *Every male, and every woman
that has lain with a male, shall ye exterminate*] Nu. 31¹⁷; the unusual phrases prove that the author took Nu. 31 as his pattern;**
see note. It is evidence of the bungling character of his imitation,
that the writer omits the very necessary injunction to preserve
alive the virgins (v.¹² Nu. 31¹⁸).†† — **12.** They found among the
inhabitants of Jabesh, *four hundred virgin girls, who had not
known a man carnally* (Nu. 31³⁵ ‡‡), and brought them to the
camp. — *To Shiloh, which is in the land of Canaan*] just so in
Jos. 21² 22⁹; in the latter passage, as here, perhaps in contrast to
Israelite territory east of the Jordan. It is none the less remarkable that the writer should deem it necessary to define in this way
the situation of the famous sanctuary; see v.¹⁹, where we find a
minute topographical note. It is hard to say whether this explicitness is merely the archaeological style of a late author,§§ or an
indication that he wrote for readers in foreign lands, perhaps him-

---

* *O.S²*. 268₈₁.

† It is not improbable that the name Jabesh also ('dry') belonged originally to
the Wady, and was afterwards given to the town on its banks.   ‡ See on 1⁵, p. 16.

§ *BR²*. iii. p. 319 f. On the site see also Tristram, *Land of Israel*, p. 556.

| Amer. Palest. Explor. Soc., Fourth Statement (1877), p. 80-82.

¶ Cf. Nu. 31⁴ᶠ.   ** See above, p. 445.

†† It is found, however, in most copies of 𝔊.

‡‡ Thirty-two thousand Midianite maidens! How they were able to recognize
the virgins, see *Jebamoth*, 60ᵇ; Pfeiffer, *Dubia vexata*, p. 358 f.   §§ We.

self lived in exile.* Why the expedition against Jabesh finds the main army at Shiloh instead of Bethel (v.²), we do not learn ; most likely the writer is already shifting the scene to prepare for the story of the seizure of the maidens of Shiloh (v.¹⁹ᶠ·), though that story is in reality quite incompatible with the presence of the Israelite encampment at Shiloh. — 13. The congregation sends friendly overtures to the surviving Benjamites in their fastness at Rimmon. — 14. The latter return, and are presented with the women who were saved alive from the sack of Jabesh. — *And they did not suffice for them so*] there were still two hundred lacking. Thus the way is prepared for the introduction of the old story of the rape of the Shilonite maidens as supplementary to the capture of maidens at Jabesh.

2. וַיַּכּוּ כְּנֵי נְדִיד] absolute object qualified by an adjective; Ges.⁂ § 117, 2 n. *a*; A. Müller, *Gram.*, § 410. — 3. יהוה אלהי ישראל] see on 4⁶, p. 115. — 4. [נְרוֹת וּשְׁלֵיט] see on 20²⁶. — 5. [הַשְּׁבוּעָה הַגְּדוֹלָה] *they had made a great oath* (AV.) would be in Hebrew: כִּי שְׁבוּעָה גְדוֹלָה הָיְתָה דָם. For שׁבוּעה equivalent to אָלָה 'curse,' see Neh. 10³⁰ Nu. 5²¹. — [מוֹת יוּמַת] frequent formula for the death penalty in the laws, *e.g.* Ex. 19¹² 21¹², ¹⁵; in P, Ex. 31¹⁴, ¹⁵ Nu. 15³⁵ 35¹⁶ &c., Lev. 20² 24¹⁶, ¹⁷. — 8. [מִי אחד] *what single one.* — 10. [כִּבְנֵי הֶחָיִל] cf. Dt. 3¹⁸ 2 S. 2⁷ 13²⁸ &c. — [וְהֻרַגְתֶּם וְרֶטַח] Dt. 2³⁴ 3⁶ Jos. 8²⁵. — 11. [אִשָּׁה יֹדַעַת מִשְׁכַּב זָכָר] *mulier experta concubitum maris*, v.¹²; the phrase is found only in Nu. 31¹⁷, ¹⁸, ³⁵; cf. Lev. 18²² 20¹³ Ez. 23¹⁷.† — [הַחֲרִימוּ] see on 1¹⁷, p. 35, 36. — 12. [שִׁלֹה cf. בְּשִׁלֹה v.¹⁹, שִׁלוֹ v.²¹ᵇⁱˢ; besides these variations we find שִׁילֹה Gen. 49¹⁰·. See Norzi on Gen. 49¹⁰ Jud. 21¹⁹; Frensdorff, *Massoret. Wörterbuch*, p. 322 f. (n. 4). — 14. [וַיֵּלְכוּ כַאֲשֶׁר רָב כֵּן] מְצָא 'suffice,' Nu. 11²², Jos. 17¹⁶ Zech. 10¹⁰ (Niph.). We might also render here: They (the Israelites) did not find enough for them.

15–25. The rape of the Shilonites. — The Israelites are at a loss to know how to provide wives for the remaining Benjamites. They advise them to conceal themselves in the vineyards around Shiloh at the time of the annual feast of Yahweh, and surprise and carry off the girls who come out to take part in the dances ; and promise to pacify the kinsmen of the maidens, if they are minded to avenge the rape. The plan is carried out ; the Benjamites seize a wife apiece, go back to their own district, and rebuild their

---

* Stud.

† In Nu. 31¹⁷ Jud. 21¹² in the still more circumstantial form, *puellae virgines quae virum non cognoverant in concubitu maris.*

towns. The Israelites return to their homes. — The story comes from the older source, but has been somewhat extensively glossed by the later writer; v.[16], the topographical notes in v.[19], v.[21] (at least in part), are of this origin. The text has suffered considerably in v.[17a] and v.[22]. — **15.** *The people was sorry for Benjamin, because Yahweh had brought a catastrophe upon the tribes of Israel*] v.[3.6]; with the last clause (lit. *made a breach in*), cf. 2 S. 6[8] 5[20] Ex. 19[22.24]. The destruction of a tribe was not an issue to be contemplated with indifference. If the extinction of a family or a clan was a matter of serious concern, to prevent which every precaution was taken, much more that of a tribe. And for the same reason: it involved the cessation of the cults which were its bond of union, and that might well be fraught with malign consequences. The feeling and action of the Israelites here are entirely in the spirit of a primitive time, and by no means indicate that the story was invented at a late period.* — **16.** The first half-verse, at least, is the work of the younger author, who thus attaches the old story of the rape of the Shilonite maidens to his account of the destruction of Jabesh.† — *The elders of the congregation*] Lev. 4[15]. — *What shall we do for those that are left, for wives?*] the two hundred who did not get wives of the girls brought from Jabesh. — *For women had been exterminated from Benjamin*] cf. 20[48]. Budde thinks that this half of the verse also is by the later hand. It seems to me to have its proper place in the original narrative between v.[16] and v.[17c]. The cause of the Israelites' regret in this version also was the apprehension that the survivors would have no posterity, and the tribe thus die out; it must therefore have contained a statement substantially equivalent to v.[16b]. On the other hand, in the younger context the statement is, to say the least, superfluous after 20[48] 21[7.8.14]. — **17.** The first clause is generally explained: The survivors of Benjamin must remain in possession of the hereditary lands of the tribe; the

---

* This natural motive is no longer understood by the author of v.[3], to whom the cause of grief appears to be that one tribe is lacking of the sacred number twelve.

† It would be possible to regard the verse, with the exception of the words, *the elders of the congregation*, as part of the original narrative; *those that were left* would then be the survivors of the battle. But this is superfluous before v.[17], and the language is not favourable to the supposition.

2 G

victors renounce their right to divide the conquered territory among themselves.* But this, although in itself a sufficiently good sense, is wide of the text, and not in accord with the context, in which the question is, not what shall be done with the lands of the Benjamites, but how they shall be supplied with wives.† The text is palpably corrupt; from the structure of v.¹⁷ᵇ· ¹⁸ᵃ, the premises in v.¹⁵· ¹⁶ᵇ, and the sequel v.¹⁹, we may conjecture that the verse originally contained a question: *How shall a remnant be saved for Benjamin, and not a tribe be wiped out of Israel?* ‡ This would connect well with v.¹⁵, and with v.¹⁶ᵃ, *Seeing that we cannot give them wives of our daughters. — Wiped out*] made to disappear utterly; 2 K. 21¹³ Gen. 6⁷ 7²³ &c. — **18.** *Seeing that we cannot give them wives of our daughters*] circumstantial, closely connected with the preceding. — *For the Israelites had sworn, Cursed is he who gives a wife to Benjamin*] v.¹. This interdict of the connubium with Benjamin is the point on which the story in ch. 21 turns, equally in the original and the secondary version. It was natural enough that fathers who heard the tale of the Gibeathites' brutality should refuse to give their daughters to men of their tribe. If v.¹ is derived from the older source, we should probably regard v.¹⁸ᵇ as an editorial repetition, made the more necessary that, in consequence of the insertion of v.²⁻¹⁴, v.¹ was now somewhat remote.

19–22. A way discovered to evade their oath. — 19. They cannot recall their oath and dare not break it, but there is a way in which it may be evaded; the Benjamites must take their wives by force. — *The feast of Yahweh is held at Shiloh annually*] this feast, with its dances among the vineyards, was doubtless, like that at Shechem (9²⁷), a local vintage festival. Budde takes these words as addressed to the Benjamites, and supposes that they were immediately followed by v.²⁰ᵇ. This is probably the original intention of the author. — *Shiloh* is the modern Seilūn, whose situation is mi-

---

* So Ki., Lth., AV., RV.

† That, in order to maintain their possession of the lands, they had to have wives and children (Ra., al.), is true enough, but too remote a reflexion here.

‡ So the verse is understood by the authors of one recension of ⬤; see crit. note.

nutely described in the following topographical gloss.* — *Which is
north of Bethel, east of the road which leads from Bethel to Shechem,
and south of Lebonah*] *Lebonah* is the modern el-Lubban, about an
hour NW. of Seilūn.† On Bethel (Beitin) see on 1²¹; on Shechem,
see on 9¹. Shiloh early lost its importance as a religious centre; ‡
it lay somewhat off the main road, and after the exile may have been
so little known as to make such glosses necessary; see also above,
on v.¹². —20. They bid the Benjamites lie in wait in the vineyards. In the original form of the story v.²⁰ᵇ probably followed
v.¹⁹ᵃ, which was addressed to the Benjamites; the insertion of
v.²⁰ᵃ was necessitated by the introduction of the glosses in v.¹⁹ᵇ;
see on v.¹⁹ᵃ. — 21. *When the girls of Shiloh come out to dance in
the choruses*] such dances in celebration of victory (11³⁴ Ex. 15²⁰
1 S. 18⁶), or at religious festivities (Ex. 32¹⁹; cf. also Cant. 6¹³). §
— *Then come out of the vineyards, and seize you each his woman
of the daughters of Shiloh, and be off to the land of Benjamin*]
compare the rape of the Sabine maidens by the Romans. ‖ The
borders of the Benjamite territory may have been two hours away.
— 22. The Israelites promise their friendly intervention, if the
kinsmen of the maidens threaten vengeance. — The offer of their
good offices would be entirely in keeping with the character of
the original narrative; but the verse abounds in grammatical
faults which cannot all be laid at the door of the scribes, and it is,
on the whole, more probable that it is an addition by the later
writer. The text is unusually corrupt. — *If their fathers or brothers come to complain to us, we will say, Grant them to them*] the
stolen maidens to their captors. 𝔐 has, *Grant us them;* that is
apparently, as a favour to us, allow the Benjamites to keep their
captives.¶ The next clause is literally, *For we did not take each*

* Rob., *BR².* ii. p. 269-271; Guérin, *Samarie,* ii. p. 21-27; *SWP. Memoirs,* ii.
p. 367-369; Bäd⁸., p. 217. It was correctly identified by Brocardus, Eshtori Parchi,
fol. 68ᵃ; as earlier by Moslem geographers; Le Strange, *Palestine under the Moslems,* p. 477. 527.

† Rob., *BR².* ii. p. 271 f.; Guérin, *Samarie,* ii. p. 164 f.; Bäd⁸., p. 217. It was
recognized by Eshtori Parchi and Maundrell.   ‡ See on 18²¹; also p. 369.

§ See above, on 11⁴⁴, p. 301, 303.

‖ Livy, i. 9 f.; Plut., *Romulus,* 14 f. This also was occasioned by a refusal of the
connubium.

¶ The second pronoun (*them*) is then of the wrong gender, but so, on any interpretation, is the pronoun *their* twice in the preceding clause.

his woman in the war, which is interpreted, We did not reserve
for each of them his wife, but killed all the women of the tribe ; [*]
or, We did not procure for each of them a wife in the war against
Jabesh in Gilead, in which only four hundred were obtained.[†]
The latter is much the more probable explanation of the words, if
not the only one which they admit. [‡]　A better reading is found
in many Greek manuscripts : Be indulgent to them ; for *they did
not get* each his wife in the war ; that is of the women whom we
took by the attack on Jabesh. 鶏, *we did not take*, may be a
correction prompted by the reflection that the war on Jabesh was
not made by Benjamin, but by the speakers. Other recensions of
𝕲 have, *Be indulgent to them, that they took each his wife by
war*,[§] *i.e.* carried off the maidens of Shiloh, *vi et armis ;* see crit.
note. [‖] — The rest of the verse is also extremely difficult. A
literal translation is : *For ye did not give them ; now ye will incur
guilt* (or, the penalty), from which no suitable sense can be
extorted. The renderings, *else would ye now be guilty*,[¶] or, *that
ye should be guilty*,[**] are grammatically unsatisfactory. Studer
conjectured, *For had you given them to them, you would be guilty*,
sc. of breaking your oath (v.[1. 7. 18]) ; but as your daughters were
taken by force you have done no wrong, and will do none if you
leave them in the possession of their captors. This gives a good
sense, and requires the slightest change in the text ; though it is
not altogether free from objection ; see crit. note. —**23.** The Benjamites follow the counsel, and carry off as many of the dancers
as there were of themselves ; with them they return to their own
territory, rebuild their towns, and dwell in them. — **24.** The Israelites now at last return to their homes. — The verse is by the later
author, as both conception and expression show beyond question.

---

[*] AV., after Ki. (cf. *Michlol Yophi*).　　　　　[†] RV., with 𝕰, Ra.

[‡] It would be possible to interpret : Grant us them as a favour ; for we did not in
the war (with Benjamin) take each his woman (of the virgins of the tribe, whom we
might have kept for ourselves, Nu. 31[18. 35]). Had we done so, we might now have
given the surviving men wives of these captives ; as it is we must beg them of you.
In conceding them you need not fear the oath ; for *you* did not give them, &c. But
this requires us to supply too many things which must have been expressed, if this
had been the author's meaning.　　　　　[§] Cf. 2 K. 14[7].

[‖] If the words be supposed to belong to the old narrative, this emendation, which
is adopted by Bu., is necessary. Be. regards this clause as a gloss.

[¶] RV., after Ew. § 337 c ; Be., al.　　　　　[**] Ra., Ki., AV. al.

We are to imagine the "congregation" religiously remaining together until the last Benjamite is married; then returning by tribes and clans to their respective territories, and finally dispersing to their individual possessions. — **25**. *In those days there was no king in Israel; every man did as he pleased*] 17⁶ 18¹ 19¹; final comment on the whole history, which may have originally stood after v.²³.

15. כי עשה יהוה פרץ] 2 S. 6⁸, David was angry, עַל אשר פרץ יהוה פרץ בעֻזָּה. We must not, therefore, understand by פרץ here, 'a gap.' — **16.** הנותרים] *the remainder*; Jos. 17². ⁶ 21³⁴ &c.; in the sense (indicated by the context), those who remained alive, Lev. 10¹⁶. — כי נשמרה כבנימן אשה] cf. Gen. 34³¹ 2 S. 21⁶ Am. 2⁹, freq. in Dt. — **17.** ויאמרו ירֻשַּׁת פליטה לבנימן] cannot be translated, *there must be an inheritance for them that are escaped of Benjamin* (EV.), which would require at least, ירֻשָּׁה לִפְלֵיטַת בניסן. Bu. conjectures, נִשְׁאֲרָה פליטה; but the context and the structure of the following clauses seem to require something like, אֵיךְ תִּשָּׁאֵר, or אֵיךְ הֻשְׁתָה; cf. 𝔊ᴹᴼ πῶς ἔσται κλῆρος διασωζόμενος τῷ Βενιαμιν ... καὶ οὐ μὴ ἐξαλειφθῇ φυλή, κ.τ.ἑ. — **18.** ואנחנו לא נוכל ונ'] circumstantial; *seeing that we cannot;* no other explanation of the emphatic pronoun is natural. — אָרוּר] with ptcp., a construction which is very common in Dt.; cf. Jer. 48¹⁰. — **19.** חַג יהוה] Ex. 10⁹ (J?) Hos. 9⁵ Lev. 23³⁹; Am. 5²¹ 8¹⁰ &c. — מיָמִים יסִיסָה] *annually*, 11⁴⁰; see note there. — **20.** ויצו] the correction of the Qerē, ויצו, is necessary. — **21.** וחלו במחלות] Kal in this sense only here; cf. חֻלָל (Polel) v.²³. — וחטפתם] Ps. 10⁹ᵇⁱ (MH., Aram., Syr., Arab.).* — **22.** אבותם או אחיהם] masc. suffixes, referring to the captured women. This negligence is not uncommon. — לריב אלינו] Jer. 12¹ Job 33¹³; for having allowed this thing to be done, or for letting it pass unpunished. — חָנֵּינוּ אותם] חנן with two accus., Gen. 33⁵ Ps. 119²⁹. 𝔐 is supported only by 𝔊ᴮ † and 𝔗. ‡ 𝔊ᴾⱽᴼ have ἐλεήσατε αὐτούς, ὅτι οὐκ ἔλαβεν ἀνὴρ γυναῖκα αὐτοῦ ἐν τῷ πολέμῳ, *i.e.* חָנּוּ אותם כי לא לקחו איש אשתו בסלחמה; the same text is represented also in a somewhat different translation by א, and by 𝔰 𝔱, 𝔖, and is very probably the original reading. § 𝔊ᴸᴹ omit the negative, חנו אותם כי לרחו איש אשתו ונ', kindly forgive them that they each took his wife in war, *i.e.* by forcible means. This seems to me, not the original text (Bu.), but an erroneous interpretation. ‖ — כי לא אתם נתתם להם כעת תאשמו] 𝔐 is here supported by all the versions. It is impossible, however, to construe or explain the last clause. Stud.'s conjecture, לי (or לא) for לא, is highly probable; the two particles are not infrequently confounded in 𝔐 and the versions; cf. 2 S. 19⁷ 2 S. 13¹⁸ Gen. 23¹¹

---

* On the gender of ויצו see Ges.²⁶ p. 451.   † Alone, against א.

‡ Ed. ven.¹, reuchl., cod. Br. Mus.; the current text is corrupt.

§ Stud.; or perhaps, הֵן אוהב, *grant them* (the maidens) to them.

‖ Against a reading sustained by 𝔊ᴸᴹ, 𝔰 weighs heavily; the concurrence of א is also noteworthy.

1 S. 20¹⁵ ᵇⁱˢ. See Hitzig, *Begriff der Kritik*, p. 141; We., *TBS.*, Dr., *TBS.*
on *ll. cc.** If this emendation be adopted, we should also read כִּי עָתָּה, the usual
introduction of the apodosis after יו (*e.g.* Nu. 22²⁹), instead of כָּעַה: For had
you given them to them, you would now be guilty.† The only objection to
this is the tense of the verb in the apodosis (usually the perf.); but, *you would
be guilty*, may perhaps stand for, *you would have incurred guilt.* — וְאִשֵּׁי]
Norzi: Baer הָאִשֵּׁמוֹ. On the dagesh see Kö., i. p. 64. — 23. וַיִּרְאוּ נָשִׁים] in
the sense of 'take a wife, marry' (יִרַח אִשָּׁה, so Stud.), נשׂא is late (We.);
here, however, the meaning is rather *tollere* (Bu.). — כֵּן הַמְחֹלֲלִיּ] Polel ptcp.;
cf. Kal above, v.²¹. — 24. וַיִּתְהַלְּכוּ כֵּסַב] Hithpa. seems to be used with the
force, 'go in different directions.' — מִשָּׁם] 1° from Shiloh; 2° from the central
point of each clan.

---

* See also Cappell, *Critica sacra*, i. p. 264 ff., 311 (ed. Vogel).
† I have proposed the same emendation in 13²³.

INDEX

I. MATTERS.

II. HEBREW WORDS AND FORMS.

III. GRAMMATICAL OBSERVATIONS.

IV. PASSAGES INCIDENTALLY DISCUSSED.

ABBREVIATIONS.*

AV.,	Authorized English Version, 1611.	DB., DB².,	Dictionary of the Bible, edited by W. Smith, 1st ed. 1863, 3 vols.; vol. i. 2d ed. 1893.
Ba.,	Johannes Bachmann.		
Bäd⁸.,	Bädeker (Socin-Benzinger), Palästina und Syrien, 3d ed. 1891.	De.,	Franz Delitzsch.
		Di.,	August Dillmann.
BB.,	Bar Bahlūl.	Doorn.,	A. van Doorninck.
BDB.,	Hebrew and English Lexicon of the Old Testament, &c.; edited by F. Brown, S. R. Driver, and C. A. Briggs, 1891 ff.	Dr.,	S. R. Driver; Dr²., Hebrew Tenses, 3d ed. 1892.
		EV.,	English Versions (AV. and RV.).
Be.,	Ernst Bertheau.	Ew.,	Heinrich Ewald.
Bi.,	Gustav Bickell.	Ff.,	Church Fathers.
Bl.,	Friedrich Bleek.	Fl. Jos.,	Flavius Josephus, ed. Niese, 1887–1895.
BL.,	Bibel-Lexikon, ed. by D. Schenkel, 5 vols., 1869–1875.		
		GAT.,	E. Reuss, Geschichte des Alten Testaments, 1881; 2d ed. 1890.
BSZ.,	Gesenius' Handwörterbuch über das Alte Testament; 12 ed. by Buhl, with the assistance of Socin and Zimmern, 1895.	Ges.²⁵,	Gesenius' Hebräische Grammatik, 25th ed., by E. Kautzsch, 1889.
		Ges. Thes.,	Gesenius, Thesaurus linguae Hebraeae et Chaldaeae V. T., 1829–1858.
Bö.,	Fried. Bötticher, Ausführliches Lehrbuch der hebräischen Sprache, 2 vols., 1866, 1868.	GdH,	K. Kittel, Geschichte der Hebräer, i. 1, 2, 1888, 1892.
Bu.,	Karl Budde.		
Cass.,	Paulus Cassel.	GjV.,	E. Schürer, Geschichte des jüdischen Volkes im Zeitalter Jesu Christi, 2 vols., 1886–1890.
CIL.,	Corpus Inscriptionum Latinarum.		
CIS.,	Corpus Inscriptionum Semiticarum.	GVI.,	Geschichte des Volkes Israel (Ewald, 2d and 3d ed., 1864–1868, 8 vols.; Hitzig, 1869; Stade, 1887 f., 2 vols.).
Co.,	C. H. Cornill.		
COT.,	E. Schrader, The Cuneiform Inscriptions and the Old Testament, 1888.		

---

* See Preface, p. viii. Abbreviations which are in common use, such as the names of classic authors and Church Fathers and the titles of their works, are not included.

ThLZ., Theologische Literatur-
zeitung.

ThT. Theologisch Tijdschrift.

Tr.-Jun., Tremellius-Junius.

Vat., Vatablus (the annotations
printed by Robert Ste-
phens and included in
Critici Sacri under the
name of Vatablus).

We., Julius Wellhausen; We.,
Comp., Die Composition
des Hexateuchs und der

historischen Bücher,
1889.

ZATW., Zeitschrift für die alttestamentliche Wissenschaft.

ZDMG., Zeitschrift der Deutschen
Morgenländischen Ge-
sellschaft.

ZDPV., Zeitschrift des Deutschen
Palästina-Vereins.

ZWTh., Zeitschrift für wissenschaft-
liche Theologie.

SIGNATURES FOR THE HEBREW TEXT AND VERSIONS OF THE OLD TESTAMENT.

𝔐 Hebrew consonant text. 𝔐ⁱᵘᵈ·
𝔐ˢᵃᵐ· Jewish and Samaritan recensions of the Pentateuch.

𝔐 Massoretic text, with vowels and
accents.

𝔊 Greek versions: 𝔊ᴬᴮ &c., see § 8.
'A Aquila; Σ Symmachus; Θ Theodotion.

𝔩 Old Latin (pre-Hieronymian); k
Coptic-Sahidic ; ℓ Ethiopic ;

𝔰 Hexaplar Syriac; made from
the Greek (see § 8).

𝔏 Latin version of St. Jerome.

𝔖 Syriac version (Peshitto): 𝔖ᴬᴴ
&c., see § 8.

𝔞 Arabic version, made from the
Syriac.

𝔗 Targum: 𝔗ᵒⁿ· ¹ &c., see § 8.
𝔗ᵉʳ· Jerusalem Targums.

The International Theological Library

Edited by Professor CHARLES A. BRIGGS, D.D., and
Professor STEWART D. F. SALMOND, D.D.

EDITORS' PREFACE

THEOLOGY has made great and rapid advances in recent years.
New lines of investigation have been opened up, fresh light
has been cast upon many subjects of the deepest interest, and
the historical method has been applied with important results.
This has prepared the way for a Library of Theological Science,
and has created the demand for it. It has also made it at once
opportune and practicable now to secure the services of special-
ists in the different departments of Theology, and to associate
them in an enterprise which will furnish a record of Theological inquiry up to date.

This Library is designed to cover the whole field of Christian Theology. Each volume is to be complete in itself, while,
at the same time, it will form part of a carefully planned
whole. One of the Editors is to prepare a volume of Theological Encyclopædia which will give the history and literature
of each department, as well as of Theology as a whole.

The Library is intended to form a series of Text-Books for
Students of Theology.

The Authors, therefore, aim at conciseness and compactness
of statement. At the same time, they have in view that large
and increasing class of students, in other departments of
inquiry, who desire to have a systematic and thorough exposition of Theological Science. Technical matters will therefore be thrown into the form of notes, and the text will be
made as readable and attractive as possible.

The Library is international and interconfessional. It will
be conducted in a catholic spirit, and in the interests of Theology as a science.

Its aim will be to give full and impartial statements both of